SCOTLAN]

Classificat.___ ___ ___ _____ g

MW01101025

This year Scotland has introduced a new Classification and Grading of Accommodation Scheme. It offers a guarantee of the range of facilities and their quality. More details of the scheme are to be found on pages vi and vii towards the front of this book.

Since printing "Scotland: Where to Stay—Self Catering 1987" it has been brought to our attention that a small amount of the classification and grading information highlighted in entries throughout this book requires to be amended. We have, therefore, taken the opportunity to list the amendments on the next page and hope that you will find the scheme helpful in planning your 1987 self catering holiday in Scotland.

SELF CATERING—WHERE TO STAY

Page No.	Location	Name of Establishment	Incorrect Class & Grade shown	Correct Classification & Grading
13	Appin	Mrs Mathieson Appin House	Up to Commended 👑👑👑👑	Commended 👑👑👑
31	Badachro	Glencairn Holidays Ltd	Omitted	Up to Commended 👑👑👑👑
31	Badachro	Mrs M. C. MacKenzie, London	Omitted	Awaiting Inspection
36	Balmacara	Balmacara Holiday Homes	Omitted	Awaiting Inspection
42	by Beauly	Miss C. M. Henderson Teandalloch Farm	Omitted	Commended 👑👑👑👑
51	Boat of Garten	Miss K. M. Grant West Cullachie	Omitted	Approved 👑👑👑
91	Dervaig	Mr J. G. King Glen Houses	Omitted	👑👑👑
110	Easter Deans	Mrs J. P. Campbell Glenrath Farm	Omitted	Commended 👑👑👑👑👑
118	by Elgin	North East Farm Chalets	Omitted	Commended 👑👑👑
123	Findochty	Mr A. Scott, Turiff	Omitted	Commended 👑👑👑
133	Fraserburgh	Mrs M. Greig, 131 Charlotte Street	Omitted	Commended 👑👑

CORRECTIONS/AMENDMENTS

SCOTLAND
WHERE TO STAY

SELF-CATERING

INSIDE BACK FLAP: KEY TO SYMBOLS AND PAGE MARKER

Published by the Scottish Tourist Board   P.O. Box 705, Edinburgh EH4 3EU

Cover: Highly Commended Self-Catering property near St Andrews.

ABOUT THIS BOOK

This is the 15th annual edition of the Scottish Tourist Board's official guide to self catering holidays in cottages, flats, chalets and houses. Holiday caravan parks have a separate section. The entries, which have been completely revised for 1987, cover the whole of Scotland, and are in alphabetical order by place-name. Each place-name in the body of the text has a map reference and a grid reference. Where the word *by* appears in the place-name, this means the property or caravan is situated several miles from the main town or village. It is recommended that you confirm the exact location at the time of enquiring.

SELF CATERING HOLIDAYS

More and more people every year are enjoying the freedom of a self catering holiday in Scotland. There are cottages, chalets, holiday flats, houses and caravans available all over the country to suit your particular needs.

They're ideal for families. Quite often they're built in woodland or on the shores of a loch, and there's always something of interest nearby. The children can tramp in and around without upsetting anyone. You can feel free to eat when you want to; to come and go just as you please; to laze around 'at home' and do nothing much; or to get out and about and visit the castles and houses, the hills, the glens or the beaches that are near you. You can find out about many of these places on page xi, and in the Scottish Tourist Board publications listed on page 351.

If you feel energetic, you can go pony trekking or sailing, go fishing or play golf. Many of these facilities are nearby—look for the symbols indicating they are available locally.

MAKING A BOOKING

While there is far more self catering accommodation in Scotland than ever before, there is also an ever-increasing demand for it. The most popular times, as is the case with all types of holidays in Scotland (except winter sports!), are late July and August. If it is necessary for a holiday to be taken in these months, early booking is absolutely essential.

When you accept offered accommodation, on the telephone, or in writing, you are entering into a legally binding contract with the proprietor of the establishment. This means that if you cancel a reservation or fail to take up the accommodation (regardless of the reaons) the proprietor will be entitled to compensation if it cannot be relet for all or a good part of the booked period. If a deposit has been paid it is likely to be forfeited and an additional payment may be required.

DISABLED VISITORS

Many places listed in this book welcome disabled visitors. Those which have been inspected under the Scottish Tourist Board's Classification and Grading Scheme have their access facilities shown thus:

  ♿   Access for wheelchair users without assistance

  ♿ A Access for wheelchair users with assistance

  ♿ P Access for ambulant disabled

It is always advisable to telephone the establishment in advance for further information.

Details of the criteria used for these symbols are shown on page 337. Further details from STB.

The undernoted organisations are also able to provide further information and advice:—

Scottish Council on Disability
Information Dept
Princes House
5 Shandwick Place
EDINBURGH EH2 4RG
Tel: 031-229 8632

Holiday Care Service
2 Old Bank Chambers
Station Road
HORLEY
Surrey RH6 9HW
Tel: Horley (02934) 74535

Holiday Caravan Parks in the section starting on page 307, have their own scheme for checking the facilities for disabled visitors— look for the D symbol. However the suitability of these places does vary considerably and it is advisable to check with an establishment before booking.

ABOUT THIS BOOK

COME IN SPRING AND AUTUMN

If you don't have to come in the peak holiday months, it is still advisable to make your booking as early as you can. More and more people are realising that the best time for a holiday in Scotland is spring — April, May and June — and autumn. In those months, whatever form of transport is used, getting around is easier, the weather is more reliable and the colour of the countryside is at its best.

And, of course, there is more choice of accommodation — but make your arrangements in good time.

FACILITIES

Before booking, please make sure the facilities you require are available: these facilities are indicated by symbols (e.g. ♣, ♠, ♠ etc) along with each entry, and a key to these symbols will be found on the back flap.

These facilities are shown whether or not the accommodation meets the minimum standards; and it should be stressed that even when an entry does not have the 'minimum standards' symbol, this does not mean it will not prove to be eminently satisfactory. These standards are very comprehensive.

The facilities mentioned are not necessarily contained in each unit: particularly in the case of static caravans, where the facilities may be nearby on the site. It should be understood that where a variety of accommodation is offered, the facilities listed against the entry do not necessarily apply to each property, e.g. where a number of caravans are on offer, some may have running water and mains drainage, some may not. So please check that what you want is available.

RESERVATIONS

Enquiries and applications for reservations should be made direct to the address given (if making a written enquiry, please enclose a stamped addressed envelope for a reply), and not to the Scottish Tourist Board.

Your travel agent will always be delighted to help you and to take care of your travel arrangements.

LATE BOOKING SERVICES

If you have difficulty in finding self catering accommodation after the start of the season, there are several late booking services to help you. Some of these are organised by local tourist offices (see pages xix-xxv for addresses).

Most of the commercial agencies listed on pages 334 to 336 of this guide also offer late booking services for their properties.

COMPLAINTS

Any complaints or criticisms about individual establishments should, where possible, be taken up immediately with the management. In most cases the problems can be dealt with satisfactorily, thus avoiding any prolonged unhappiness during your stay.

If this procedure fails to remedy the grievance to your satisfaction, and particularly where serious complaints are concerned, please write to the local Tourist Organisation (see page xix).

VALUE ADDED TAX (VAT)

Please note that VAT is calculated by establishments for this publication at a rate of 15%. Any subsequent changes in this rate will affect the price you will be charged.

PRICES

Unless stated otherwise, minimum let is one week, and prices, which are supplied by the owners, and/or operators, are to be used only as guidelines. To make this booklet available for 1987, the information was collected from proprietors in the summer of 1986 and changes may have occurred since the guide went to press. Prices are shown in pounds and include VAT as applicable.

The information given in this publication is as supplied to the Scottish Tourist Board and to the best of the Board's knowledge was correct at the time of going to press. The Scottish Tourist Board can accept no responsibility for any errors or omissions.

September 1986

FRANÇAIS

OÙ SE LOGER EN ECOSSE

Bienvenue en Ecosse!

Voici le guide touristique officiel des hôtels et pensions de famille en Ecosse, publié par l'Office écossais du tourisme. Revu chaque année, ce guide est reconnu depuis trente ans comme le plus complet en son genre. Des hôtels, pensions de famille et résidences universitaires de toutes les régions de l'Ecosse y sont classés selon l'ordre alphabétique des localités. Sauf indication contraire, l'indicatif téléphonique est celui de la localité.

Au moment de mettre sous presse, il ne nous est pas possible de donner des prix définitifs; il est vivement conseillé aux visiteurs de demander confirmation des prix lorsqu'ils effectuent la réservation.

Nous avons signalé à l'attention des gourmets les hôtels qui offrent les spécialités de la cuisine écossaise (recettes écossaises traditionnelles à base de produits écossais de haute qualité).

NB. L'Office écossais du tourisme (Scottish Tourist Board) décline toute responsabilité en cas d'erruers ou d'omissions.

AVERTISSEMENT: CHIENS ETC.

Il est rappelé aux visiteurs étrangers que l'introduction d'animaux domestiques en Grande-Bretagne est soumise à une réglementation très stricte, qui prévoit une longue période de quarantaine. Etant donné le danger de propagation du virus rabique, des peines très sévères sont prévues pour toute infraction aux réglements.

SUR LES ROUTES D'ECOSSE

Veillez à attacher votre ceinture de sécurité, si votre voiture en est munie. Le port de la ceinture est obligatoire en Grande Bretagne.

La légende des symboles se trouve au volet de la couverture, qui fait aussi office de signet.

Logez a l'enseigne de l'hospitalité Ecossaise voir page 330.

DEUTSCH

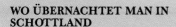

WO ÜBERNACHTET MAN IN SCHOTTLAND

Willkommen in Schottland!

Dieses Buch ist der offizielle Führer des Schottischen Touristenbüros für Ferienübernachtungen in Privatpensionen in Schottland. Seit dreißig Jahren wird dieses Buch als das umfassendste seiner Art anerkannt. Es wird jedes Jahr auf den neuesten Stand gebracht. Hotels, Gasthäuser und Unterbringung in den Universitäten in allen Teilen Schottlands sind hier nach Ortsnamen in alphabetischer Reihenfolge aufgeführt. Die jeweilige Vorwahlnummer ist unter dem Ortsnamen zu finden, außer, wenn sie extra angegeben ist.

Zu Beginn der Drucklegung dieses Buches ist es noch nicht möglich, feste Preise anzugeben, und Besuchern wird daher geraten, sich nach den Tarifen zu erkundigen, wenn sie Buchungen vornehmen.

Das Schottische Touristenbüro (Scottish Tourist Board) kann keine Verantwortung für eventuelle Fehler oder Auslassung von Preisen und Einrichtungen übernehmen.

Als weitere Hilfe haben wir die Privatpensionen gekennzeichnet, die echte schottische Küche—Taste of Scotland— anbieten. Das bedeutet, daß hier traditionell schottische Rezepte verwandt werden unter Benutzung schottischer Produkte von hoher Qualität.

HUNDE

Das Mitbringen von Tieren jeder Art aus dem Ausland ist wegen Tollwutgefahr strengstens untersagt. Die Übertretung dieses Gesetzes wird mit hohen Strafen belegt.

AUTOFAHREN IN SCHOTTLAND

Schnallen Sie sich immer an! Es wird nun zur Pflicht. (Vorausgesetzt, Ihr Auto ist mit Sicherheitsgurt ausgestattet.)

Die Zeichenerklärungen befinden sich im eingeklebten Faltblatt am Ende des Buches.

Übernachten sie dort, wo sie das Zeichen für echt Schottische Gastlichkeit Sehen Seihe Seite 332.

CLASSIFICATION AND GRADING OF ACCOMMODATION IN SCOTLAND

STAY WHERE YOU SEE THE SIGN OF A REAL SCOTTISH WELCOME

We've made sure there's a comfortable welcome waiting at hundreds of places to stay in Scotland.

Now there's no need to puzzle over which hotel, guest house, B & B or self-catering accommodation best suits you.

We've introduced a new easy to understand classification and grading scheme so you can find at a glance *exactly* what you're looking for.

WHAT DOES CLASSIFICATION MEAN?

The *classifications*, from 'Listed' to five crowns, are awarded according to the *range* of facilities available. In hotels, guest houses and B & Bs, a 'Listed' classification guarantees, for example, that your bed conforms to a minimum size, that hot and cold water is available at all reasonable times, that breakfast is provided and that there is adequate heating according to the season.

In self-catering accommodation, one crown means that you have a minimum size of unit, at least one twin or double bedroom, dining and cooking facilities suitable for the number of occupants, and a refridgerator.

Naturally, more crowns mean more facilities. A five crown establishment will provide many extras for your holiday comfort. To name just two, in five crown hotels *all* rooms have 'en suite' bathrooms, and five crown self-catering units provide the labour-saving fittings of home, including a dishwasher.

All classifications have been checked by our fully-trained team of independent officers.

CLASSIFICATION AND GRADING OF ACCOMMODATION IN SCOTLAND

WHAT ABOUT GRADING?

While classification is all about facilities, *grading* is solely concerned with their *quality*. The grades awarded— 'Approved', 'Commended' or 'Highly Commended'—are based upon an independent assessment of a wide variety of items, ranging from the appearance of the buildings and tidiness of the gardens, to the quality of the furnishings, fittings and floor coverings. Cleanliness is an absolute requirement—and, of course, our officers know the value of a warm and welcoming smile.

Like classification, grading is carried out by the Scottish Tourist Board's expert team.
You can find excellent quality in all kinds of places to stay in Scotland, irrespective of the range of facilities offered: for example, a 'Listed' B & B, with the minimum of facilities, but offering excellent quality, would be awarded a 'Highly Commended' grade while a five crown self-catering property would be graded as 'Approved' if the quality of its extensive facilities was assessed as average.

SO HOW DOES THE NEW SCHEME HELP YOU PLAN YOUR HOLIDAY?

Quite simply, it offers a guarantee of both the range of facilities and their quality. Many of the establishments listed in this brochure have been inspected and this is highlighted in their entries. When you choose accommodation that has been classified, or classified and graded, you have the reassurance that what is being offered has been independently checked.

Equally, if you're on a touring holiday, and booking accommodation as you go, the new scheme can help you. All places to stay which have been inspected bear a distinctive blue oval sign by their entrance showing the classification and grade awarded. And if you call in at a Tourist Information Centre you can ask for a list of local establishments that have joined the scheme, which will include those which are shown in this brochure as *awaiting inspection* at time of going to press. Whatever kind of accommodation you're looking for, you can be sure the new classification and grading scheme will help you find it.

Please note that where self-catering establishments offer a number of units of differing classifications and grades, their entry in this brochure is shown as 'Up to' the highest award held. You should ascertain the specific classification and grade of an individual unit at time of booking.

Please also note that establishments are visited annually and therefore classifications and grades may therefore change from year to year.

Camping and Caravan parks have their own grading scheme. Details of this are on page 322.

YOUR HOLIDAY IN SCOTLAND

USEFUL INFORMATION ABOUT SCOTLAND

TRAVEL

Bookings for rail, sea and air travel to Scotland and within Scotland should be made through your travel agent, or directly to British Rail, airlines and ferry companies. The Scottish Tourist Board will be glad to give you information but cannot make your bookings for you.

Seats may be booked in advance on the main long-distance coaches, aircraft and for berths and cabins in the steamers to the islands. Sleeping berths on trains should always be booked well in advance. It is necessary to book seats for 'extended' coach tours and also for day coach outings operated from most holiday and touring centres.

Car hire bookings should also be made in advance wherever possible, especially for July and August. Taxis are readily available in Edinburgh, Glasgow, and other major centres at controlled charges. Taxis are generally available in most communities, but in smaller, less populous areas charges may vary considerably.

DRIVING

The 'Rules of the Road' are the same in Scotland as in the rest of the U.K. While there is limited motorway mileage in Scotland, the roads are uniformly good. In the remoter areas there is a considerable mileage of one-way roads, with frequent passing-places. Please, *never* use these passing-places as lay-bys—or for overnight parking of caravans. Slow-moving traffic (and motorists towing caravans), are asked to pull in to passing places, where appropriate, to let faster traffic through.

When touring in the far north and west particularly, remember that petrol stations are comparatively few, and distances between them may be considerable. Some petrol stations close on Sundays. Fill your tank in good time, and keep it as full as possible.

Remember, it is now law that the driver and front passenger must wear seat belts.

SCOTLAND'S WEATHER

Did you know that in June, places in the north of Scotland have an average of 18-20 hours of daylight each day, and that resorts on the east coast are particularly noted for their hours of sunshine?

June has those marvellous long evenings when it's light till very late, and the palm trees which grow on the west coast must say something about how warm it is.

Yes, we do have to admit, it does sometimes rain in Scotland; but rainfall is surprisingly low despite the age-old myths. The rainfall in the Edinburgh area, for example, is almost exactly the same as that around London—and Rome for that matter. And don't forget, even if you do get caught in a shower, that Scotland is well-endowed with a whole host of indoor attractions to keep you entertained till long after the sun has come out again.

PUBLIC HOLIDAYS

The Bank Holidays which are also general holidays in England do not apply in Scotland. Most Bank Holidays apply to banks and to some professional and commercial offices only, although Christmas Day and New Year's Day are usually taken as holidays by everyone. Scottish banks are closed in 1987 on 1 and 2 January, 17 April, 4 and 25 May, 3 August, 25 and 28 December. In place of the general holidays, Scottish cities and towns normally have a Spring Holiday and an Autumn Holiday. The dates of these holidays vary from place to place, but they are almost invariably on a Monday.

MONEY

Currency, coinage and postal rates in Scotland are the same as in the rest of the U.K. Scotland differs from England in that Scottish banks issue their own notes. These are acceptable in England, at face value, as are Bank of England notes in Scotland. Main banks are open during the following hours:

Monday, Tuesday, Wednesday: 0930-1230; 1330-1530

Thursday: 0930-1230; 1330-1530; 1630-1800

Friday: 0930-1530

Some city centre banks are open daily 0930-1530 and on Saturdays.

In rural areas, banks post their hours clearly outside and travelling banks call regularly.

SHOPPING

The normal shopping hours in Scotland are 0900-1730, although bakeries, dairies and newsagents open earlier. Many shops have an early closing day (1300) each week, but the actual day varies from place to place and in cities from district to district.

Many city centre shops also stay open late on one evening each week.

EATING

Lunch in restaurants and hotels outside the main centres is usually served between 1230 and 1400. Dinner usually starts at 1900 or 1930 and may not be served much after 2100. Where you know you may arrive late it is advisable to make arrangements for a meal in advance. An alternative to dinner is High Tea, usually served between 1630 and 1830.

A TASTE OF SCOTLAND

When eating out, don't forget to sample a 'Taste of Scotland'. Look out for the 'Stockpot' sign at hotels and restaurants. This indicates that the establishment offers traditional Scottish recipes using the best of Scottish produce: Scottish soups with intriguing names like Powsowdie or Cullen Skink; Aberdeen Angus steaks or venison or game in season; salmon or trout from Scottish rivers, or herring or haddock cured in a variety of ways; and a choice of some 30 varieties of Scottish cheese—these are some of the 'Tastes of

Scotland' which add to the enjoyment of a holiday. For your free copy of the 1987 booklet, write to: Taste of Scotland Ltd, 23 Ravelston Terrace, Edinburgh EH4 3EU.

LICENSING LAWS

Currently in Scotland, the hours that public houses and hotel bars are open to serve drinks are the same all over the country. 'Pubs' are open from 1100 to 1430 and from 1700 to about 2300 hours, Monday to Saturday inclusive and most are now licensed to open on Sundays. In addition, some establishments may have obtained extended licences for afternoon or late night opening.

Hotel bars have the same hours as 'pubs', and are open on Sundays from 1230 to 1430 and 1830 to 2300. Residents in licensed hotels may have drinks served at any time. Some restaurants and hotels have extended licences allowing them to serve drinks with meals until 0100 in the morning. Persons under the age of 18 are not allowed to drink in licensed premises.

CHURCHES

The established Church of Scotland is Presbyterian, but the Roman Catholic and other denominations have very considerable numbers of adherents. The Episcopal Church of Scotland is in full communion with the Church of England, and uses a similar form of worship. In the far north and west of Scotland, particularly in the islands, many people belong to the Free Church of Scotland, and appreciate it when their views on the Sabbath as a day when there should be no recreational or other unnecessary activity, are respected by visitors. Times of services of the various denominations are usually intimated on hotel notice boards, as well as outside the churches and, of course, visitors are always welcome.

USEFUL INFORMATION ABOUT SCOTLAND

COMING FROM OVERSEAS?

Visitors to Scotland from overseas require to observe the same regulations as for other parts of the U.K. As a general rule they must have a valid passport and, in certain cases, visas issued by British Consular authorities overseas: check with a local Travel Agent, or where appropriate, the overseas offices of the British Tourist Authority.

Currency: Overseas visitors who require information about the import and export of currency, cars, or other goods, on personal purchases and belongings, shopping concessions, etc., should consult a Travel Agent or Bank or the overseas offices of the B.T.A.

Driving: Motorists coming from overseas who are members of a motoring organisation in their own country may obtain from them full details of the regulations for importing cars, motor cycles, etc., for holiday and touring purposes into the U.K. They can drive in Britain on a current Driving Licence from their own country, or with an international Driving Permit, for a maximum period of 12 months. Otherwise, a British Driving Licence must be obtained: until the Driving Test is passed it is essential to be accompanied by a driver with a British licence.

Seat belts: Drivers and front seat passengers **must** wear safety belts while driving in Britain, by law.

VAT: Value Added Tax, currently charged at 15% on many goods, can sometimes be reclaimed by overseas visitors who buy items for export. Visitors should ask the shopkeeper about the retail export schemes before making a purchase, and will be required to fill in special forms.

SCOTTISH YOUTH HOSTELS

There are 80 youth hostels in Scotland offering simple, low-cost self catering accommodation to all people, but especially the young. Youth Hostels may be in a castle or in a mansion, or a timber building way out in the wild. All have dormitories, washrooms, common room and kitchen. Some hostels also offer accommodation for families with children under five.

Further details can be obtained from the Scottish Youth Hostels Association, 7 Glebe Crescent, Stirling, FK8 2JA. Tel: Stirling (0786) 72821.

DOGS

Where dogs are permitted, owners are asked to take responsibility for pets' behaviour. In particular, please keep dogs under control in the presence of farm animals. Look for the 🐕 symbol in the entries to identify those establishments which accept dogs.

RABIES

Britain is *very* concerned to prevent the spread of rabies. Strict quarantine regulations apply to animals brought into Britain from abroad and severe penalties are enforced if they are broken or ignored. Dogs and cats are subject to 6 months quarantine in an approved quarantine centre. Full details from the Department of Agriculture and Fisheries for Scotland, Chesser House, 500 Gorgie Road, Edinburgh EH11 3AW. The restrictions do not apply to animals from Eire, Northern Ireland, the Isle of Man or the Channel Islands.

SCOTLAND'S TOURIST AREAS

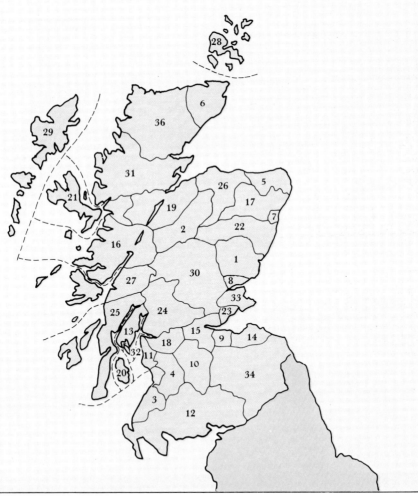

DETAILS OF SOME OF THE ATTRACTIONS OF THESE AREAS ARE TO BE FOUND ON THE FOLLOWING PAGES.

SCOTLAND'S TOURIST AREAS

1
Angus

Angus is situated on the east coast of Scotland between two rivers, the Tay and the North Esk. From the North Sea edge, with cliffs and harbours set to north and south by miles of golden sands, it stretches inland through picturesque villages and scenic glens to the foothills of the eastern Grampians. The six towns — Arbroath, Brechin, Carnoustie, Forfar, Kirriemuir and Montrose — have many interesting individual attractions and the entire district is rich in historical, literary and architectural features. A warm welcome awaits visitors to the area which offers a wide variety of recreations and pursuits together with the opportunity to relax in bracing sea breezes or balmy country air, and all compactly contained within an approximate 100-mile boundary.

2
Aviemore and Spey Valley

Dominated by tree-clad, craggy mountains, river, loch and stream, the Spey Valley offers a unique welcome. Come climbing and ski-ing in the mighty Cairngorms, sailing and canoeing on rivers and lochs and angling in the famous River Spey. History abounds with ruined castles and a relic of the Jacobite rebellion, the formidable Ruthven Barracks. Folk and clan museums, wildlife and nature parks, osprey, reindeer and breathtaking scenery provide a land of contrast. Accommodation in hotels, guest and farmhouses, caravan and campsites and the attractions of modern holiday complexes such as the Aviemore Centre offer all the year round Highland hospitality.

3
Ayrshire and Burns Country

Ayrshire and Burns Country, situated on the south-west coast of Scotland, offers something for everyone. The area's rich and colourful heritage is depicted by the many castles, both ruined and otherwise, scattered throughout the district. Robert Burns, Scotland's National Poet, was born at Alloway, the starting point for the Burns Heritage Trail. With fifteen golf courses, including three championship ones, Turnberry, Troon and Prestwick, the area is aptly described as a paradise for any golfer. With no shortage of good accommodation and entertainment facilities, why not visit ABC Land and see for yourself that it's just too good to miss!

4
Ayrshire Valleys

The Ayrshire Valleys Tourist Board Area— Kilmarnock and Loudoun and Cumnock and Doon Valley is the very heart of Scotland. Every year more and more tourists discover the special appeal of the Ayrshire Valleys. Much of the history of Scotland is here in stone and in reputation. From this area came individuals who contributed massively to the progress of mankind, inventions bringing benefits world wide, industrial innovation and literature. This heritage together with the gentle scenic beauty and the warm hospitality of Ayrshire make the Ayrshire Valleys increasingly popular for the tourist who seeks the real Scotland.

5
Banff and Buchan

Banff and Buchan is the unspoiled shoulder of Scotland which divides the North Sea from the Moray Firth. Magnificent cliffs, nesting places of the puffin, tower over picturesque fishing villages and sandy inlets. Inland, uncrowded roads lead you through the fertile, rolling countryside to the beauty of Aden Country Park, the baroque splendour of Duff House and to Fyvie Castle, the pride of the Castles of the north east. Eight good golf courses, the finest bowling greens, riding, fishing and windsurfing add to the range of activities available. The friendly local folk will welcome you with a cheery smile to a wide range of comfortable and good value accommodation, ranging from snug hotels to beach-side caravans.

Tourist Information Centres in these areas and addresses to write for further information are on pages xx to xxvi.

SCOTLAND'S TOURIST AREAS

6
Caithness

The John O'Groats Peninsula is an area of captivating contrasts. Here, craggy cliffs, spectacular rock stacks, historic harbours and beautiful beaches all contribute to some of the most magnificent coastal scenery in Europe. Many sea birds nest at Duncansby Head, and elsewhere you can see otters, seals and foxes. Caithness is a treasure house for historians, with mediaeval churches, mysterious stone circles, cairns, brochs and castles towering on cliff tops. In Thurso and Wick—the main towns in northern Scotland—you'll find a good selection of shops, and craftsmen producing woollens, pottery and the famous Caithness Glass.

7
City of Aberdeen

Aberdeen, 'Britain in Bloom' winner, Chelsea gold medal winner. All year round amazing floral displays delight the visitor — in the breathtaking Winter Gardens, or by roads, rivers, offices and houses, in parks and gardens, where crocuses, daffodils or roses carpet the ground. But there is much more to Aberdeen than flowers. A historic city with royal charters from the 12th century, Aberdeen has fascinating areas and buildings to explore; interesting museums and art galleries to browse in; sports a-plenty to try; shops and restaurants to visit; events and festivals to experience; entertainment — and Britain's most beautiful theatre — to enjoy. Aberdeen — The Flower of Scotland.

8
City of Dundee

An idyllic setting along the north bank of the River Tay Estuary, with the backcloth of the Grampian Mountains, gives Dundee one of the healthiest locations in the world. Apart from the benefits of the river — sea angling, salmon and trout fishing and sailing — it is also one of the best golf centres in the world.

Within an hour's drive there are over 40 golf courses including St Andrews, Carnoustie and Gleneagles. Three under-cover shopping malls, ample central parking. Steeped in history, Dundonians are also very friendly and proud of their parks and gardens.

9
City of Edinburgh

Edinburgh, Scotland's beautiful capital and international Festival City, is full of historic and romantic interest. It is surrounded by hills, woodlands and rivers and also features an extensive coastline. The City is dominated by its ancient fortress towering above gardens which during the summer feature a full programme of musical entertainment including Highland and Scottish country dancing. Explore the treasures of the Royal Mile or enjoy quality shopping on Princes Street. For the young, and not so young, there is always something interesting to see or do. A warm welcome awaits you.

10
Clyde Valley

The Clyde Valley — Scotland's Garden Centre linking the districts of Hamilton, Motherwell and Clydesdale stretches south east from the outskirts of Glasgow to the Lowther Hills, following the River Clyde and the A74 almost to the Border. Traditionally an area renowned for its healthy air, today the Clyde Valley is able to boast some of Scotland's best known history and scenery. Like New Lanark, Europe's most important industrial archaeological site; the famous Clydeside Orchard Country — blossom, pick-your-own fruit and garden centres. Elsewhere — castles, nature reserves, visitor centres, museums, shopping centres and acres of beautiful countryside to explore. Planning to tour Scotland? Base yourself here — Edinburgh, Glasgow, The Trossachs, Borders, Burns Country and Ayrshire are all within easy driving distance. With good road and rail connections, discovering the Clyde Valley couldn't be easier.

Tourist Information Centres in these areas and addresses to write for further information are on pages xx to xxvi.

SCOTLAND'S TOURIST AREAS

11
Cunninghame

On Scotland's west coast — encompassing north Ayrshire and the islands of Arran and Cumbrae, this area is rich in natural beauty. The mainland coastline has many fine beaches, with superb golf courses backing them. The islands have a magic of their own: peace, tranquility, yet plenty to do from cycling to mountain climbing. The Magnum Leisure Centre, with twin flumes, in Irvine's beachpark, ranks as one of the largest in Europe, and the coastal resorts of Saltcoats, Ardrossan and Largs have much to offer including Largs' world famous Viking Festival.

12
Dumfries and Galloway

This is a relatively undiscovered corner of Scotland, but for the discerning tourist looking for beaches and hills; castles and abbeys, museums and gardens; sea angling and salmon fishing; or a winter holiday away from the rigours of ski-ing: it is an area you are unlikely to forget. One of Scotland's principal highways, the A74, cuts through the area from south to north. So why don't you leave the headlong flight to others and take yourself off the dual carriageway into the quiet and meandering byways of Dumfries and Galloway. You will not regret it!

13
Dunoon and The Cowal Peninsula

Holidaying on an island stirs the romantic blood. Cowal is an island — well almost! The majority of visitors travel on one of the two short ferry crossings from Gourock to Dunoon, but you can 'Take the High Road' and be in Dunoon in under two hours from Glasgow. Being slightly off-the-beaten-track of the 'doing Scotland' tourist brigade, the Cowal Peninsula is a peaceful corner of Argyll where you can travel on quiet, uncluttered roads, where you can relax and enjoy our magnificent scenery,

our mountains, our seascapes, our lochs and glens, and the steeply wooded hillsides of the Argyll Forest Park.

14
East Lothian

East Lothian is an area rich in contrasts which provides just about everything for the family. You can be assured of a genuine welcome, good food, unspoilt scenery, historic sites, perfect stretches of golden sand, the opportunity for recreation or the relief of doing simply nothing. Hotels and guest houses, with 14 golf courses on their doorstep, specialise in catering for the golfer and his family. East Lothian — an experience you will treasure for a lifetime.

15
Forth Valley

Crowned by the magnificent Forth Bridges, Forth Valley has a wealth of history: neolithic Cairnpapple; the Antonine Wall in Falkirk; Scotland's ancient capital, Dunfermline; quaint 17th century burgh, Culross; picturesque Linlithgow Palace, birthplace of Mary Queen of Scots; elegant stately homes, The Binns, Dalmeny and Hopetoun Houses; and relics of the industrial age, the canals and Bo'ness Steam Railway. Enjoy the countryside in the beautiful parks at Muiravonside, Lochore Meadows and Beecraigs. And remember, Forth Valley is just half an hour away from Edinburgh or Glasgow and makes an ideal centre for visiting Edinburgh Castle or Glasgow's Burrell Collection.

16
Fort William and Lochaber

All the delights of Scotland and the Highlands come together in Lochaber, an area of 1,755 square miles with Fort William at the centre. From Glencoe in the south to the Small Isles of Muck, Rhum, Eigg and Canna in the west, Lochaber encompasses many of Scotland's

Tourist Information Centres in these areas and addresses to write for further information are on pages xx to xxvi.

SCOTLAND'S TOURIST AREAS

superlatives including Ben Nevis, Britain's highest mountain, and Loch Morar, the deepest loch. The land of 'bens, glens and heroes', Lochaber is resonant with Scottish history. And there's always something to do in Fort William, with its many shops, hotels, restaurants and leisure facilities.

17
Gordon

You have to be prepared for enchantment if you choose to come to Gordon District. Gordon's countryside varies from the sandy beaches of Balmedie on the east coast to the upland terrain of the western part of Strathdon. Follow the Castle Trail and visit restored castles and romantic ruins. Age-old crafts are being revived and visitors are welcome. But Gordon is not just for the spectator — it is a paradise for anglers, golfers, skiers, hillwalkers, railway enthusiasts and malt whisky drinkers. Your holiday in Gordon District can be as quiet and relaxing or as energetic and lively as you care to make it.

18
Greater Glasgow

Glasgow, Scotland's largest city, is the cultural capital of Scotland. It is home to Scottish Opera, Scottish National Orchestra, Scottish Ballet and the Scottish Theatre Company and a priceless collection of art treasures in a number of museums. Of the top twenty tourist attractions in the country, Glasgow has six including the magnificent Burrell Collection, Scotland's No. 1 attraction. The area is also ideal for shopping and entertainment. With its many first-class hotels and excellent communications by road, rail and air, Greater Glasgow is an ideal touring base from which to explore the rest of Scotland.

19
Inverness, Loch Ness and Nairn

In Inverness, the Capital of the Highlands, the shopping and accommodation are excellent, while entertainment sparkles more brightly each year. Nearby the famous monster haunts Loch Ness and the Caledonian Canal offers passage to all types of craft. Nairn, a long time favourite for family holidays, with its glorious beaches and long hours of sunshine, is also a mecca for golfers. At Culloden Moor and Cawdor Castle the history of the area comes alive. Visit this hub of the Highlands for a combination of the best of the past and of today.

20
Isle of Arran

A Hebridean refugee sheltering in the Firth of Clyde, the Isle of Arran is only an hour's sail from the mainland port of Ardrossan, which connects with rail and road traffic. Towering mountains in the north, soft rolling lands in the south, sixty miles of glorious coastline with sub-tropical palms, glens, inland lochs and waterfalls — a veritable photographer's paradise. Past and present merge when you gaze across the Firth once scoured by the Vikings and crossed by Bruce and his 300. The energetic will appreciate the Island's hillwalking and climbing — the only problem is where to start.

21
The Isle of Skye and South West Ross

A short ferry trip from South West Ross, Skye has over 900 miles of coastline rich in bays and towering cliffs, dominated by the great ridge of the Cuillin Mountains. Rich in Bonnie Prince Charlie's history it has a romantic but awe-inspiring atmosphere which can only be felt by visiting this remarkable island. The old way of life is reflected in the Black House Museums, contemporary crafts are plentiful and unusual, from candle-making to hand-weaving. With South West Ross so close on the main land, rich too in its own history — the whole area 'comes well recommended'.

Tourist Information Centres in these areas and addresses to write for further information are on pages xx to xxvi.

SCOTLAND'S TOURIST AREAS

22
Kincardine and Deeside

Kincardine and Deeside extends a heartfelt welcome and invites you to a feast of ever changing spectacle and colour — from the regal splendour of Balmoral Castle, the Scottish summer residence of the Royal Family to the thrilling sights and sounds of the world famous Braemar Gathering, to the homeland of the sparkling Dee famous for its salmon fishing. Lush pine-clad hillsides rise from its banks, while along its length a wonderland of romantic castles speak of the sometimes turbulent past. Our coastline is as varied as it is beautiful. Kincardine and Deeside is an experience you will never forget.

23
Kirkcaldy

Kirkcaldy and District is an area rich in heritage which has been preserved to ensure you will remember your stay. In Kirkcaldy, with its fine views across the Firth of Forth, you can trace the lives of Adam Smith, the philosopher, or Robert Adam, the architect; or admire the skill of the local Wemyss Ware pottery. There are many picturesque seaside villages in the area including the holiday towns of Burntisland, Kinghorn and Leven, while inland there is plenty of scope for walks and golf. If you want to travel further afield, the attractions of the East Neuk of Fife, Perth, Falkland Palace and Loch Leven are just a short drive away.

24
Loch Lomond, Stirling and the Trossachs

Bridging the gap between highlands and lowlands lies the scenic splendour of Loch Lomond and the Trossachs combining with the excitement of historic Stirling. Underlying the visual impact, feel the brooding atmosphere of the area's heritage; the land of folk hero Rob Roy McGregor, the stirring site of

Bannockburn, and the castle homes of Scotland's royalty and aristocracy. Couple this with some of today's fascinating visitor attractions; lose yourself in the tranquility of a boat trip on one of the lochs; or walk the unspoilt country paths, all before coming home to Scottish hospitality within a superb choice of accommodation.

25
Mid Argyll, Kintyre and Islay

Situated in the South West Highlands, this holiday area has over 1,000 miles of coastline, heavily indented with attractive sea lochs and natural harbours — a yachtsman's paradise. Hillwalking and loch fishing, golf and archaeology, sub-tropical gardens and bird watching — a gentle countryside to enjoy these varied pursuits. Blessed with a temperate climate the Atlantic seaboard on Kintyre and Islay provides a habitat for many species of wintering birds, especially geese. Enjoy the colourful sub-tropical gardens which flourish on Gigha and at Crarae, all year round golf, the ultimate seclusion of exploration on Jura — holidays to suit everyone.

26
Moray

Moray District lies on the sunny southern shores of the Moray Firth, midway between Aberdeen and Inverness, embracing the ancient bishopric whose symbol is the magnificent ruined Cathedral of Elgin. Along the coast sandy beaches alternate with villages whose traditional architecture is a link with the prosperous times of the fishing industry. Inland the fertile farmlands of Moray rise gently through extensive forest and beyond the River Spey — famed among salmon fishermen — to the high Cairngorm Mountains. Moray is the heart of the whisky industry, with almost half of Scotland's distilleries within its borders, many of them open to visitors.

Tourist Information Centres in these areas and addresses to write for further information are on pages xx to xxvi.

SCOTLAND'S TOURIST AREAS

27
Oban, Mull and District

Oban is the gateway to a world of tranquillity — to the enchantment of the highlands and the Hebrides. Sail away to the dreaming isles of Mull, Coll, Tiree, Staffa and the Holy Isle of Iona — or escape to the naturalists' paradise of Colonsay. Explore the land of Lorne — the grandeur of its mountains, winding lochs, whispering forests — villages, castles, gardens — and, of course, the town of Oban itself. Wherever you go you will find traditional hospitality in the friendly shops, the Highland Games and Ceilidhs — and, from country house to country cottage, holiday accommodation to suit all tastes.

28
Orkney

Separated by a mere six miles from mainland Scotland, the low lying fertile islands that comprise Orkney have an abundance of treasures. Here is the richest historic area in Scotland, some sites being of European importance. Orkney is home to over one million seabirds and has nine RSPB reserves. The lochs of Orkney provide wild brown trout and no permits are required. The surrounding waters provide good sea angling with record-breaking Skate and Halibut. Scapa Flow and its sunken German warships is Europe's best dive site. Add to this the genuine friendliness and hospitality of the people and you can be assured of an island adventure in Britain's Treasure Islands.

29
Outer Hebrides

Due to their separation from the mainland of Scotland the Outer Hebrides have a unique character all of their own. This splintered sweep of islands, stretching 130 miles from the Butt of Lewis to Barra Head incorporates six immensely beautiful holiday islands. On the west coasts there are long stretches of pasture land with wild flowers and miles of clean sandy beaches. The eastern coasts are rugged with cliffs and small bays which have an atmosphere all their own. The islands are ideal for ornithology and archaeology, for fishing and sea angling, for the photographer, or the holidaymaker seeking peace and tranquillity.

30
Perthshire

Break away to Perthshire, the heartland of Scotland, and explore one of Europe's most beautiful holiday regions. Over 2,000 square miles of Highland lochs, hidden glens and historic lowlands are yours to discover. Whether you come by rail, air or road, we know you'll come back again to enjoy our unrivalled hospitality, superb sporting facilities, and relaxing way of life. Sir Walter Scott once wrote, "If an intelligent stranger were asked to describe the most varied and most beautiful province in Scotland, it is probable that he would name the country of Perthshire". Our visitors all agree.

31
Ross and Cromarty

Explore the coast of Wester Ross and you'll discover breathtaking mountains and great cliffs. Wander through East Ross and the Black Isle, and you'll be amid gentle hills, woods and charming Highland villages. Coast to coast — there's plenty to surprise and interest you. The incredible sub-tropical Inverewe Gardens, Torridon's mighty peaks and Hugh Miller's Cottage in Cromarty. Visit Strathpeffer, the Victorian spa village or Ullapool and enjoy a pleasure cruise to the Summer Isles. Golfers, walkers and fishers can always find new experiences or alternately just laze on sandy beaches such as the Golden Sands at Gairloch.

Tourist Information Centres in these areas and addresses to write for further information are on pages xx to xxvi.

SCOTLAND'S TOURIST AREAS

32
Rothesay and Isle of Bute

The Isle of Bute has long been one of Scotland's favourite holiday retreats, set in the heart of the glorious Firth of Clyde. Safe, sandy beaches adorn the coastline. There are enough entertainments and facilities in Rothesay alone to amuse the whole family. There's golf on three courses, each enjoying spectacular views; sailing and cruising; walking, cycling and bowling. Delve into Bute's rich history at the ancient Castle and the Bute Museum. All this just 30 minutes by ferry from Wemyss Bay (serving Central Scotland and the motorways) or only 5 minutes across the Kyles of Bute from Colintraive (Argyll).

33
St Andrews and North East Fife

North East Fife, approximately one hour from Edinburgh by road or rail, lies between the Firth of Forth and the River Tay. The coastline from Lundin Links to Crail — 'The East Neuk' — is a chain of delightful fishing villages and forms part of Scotland's Fishing Heritage Trail. Inland, the many places of interest to visitors are linked by a network of quiet country roads centred on the market town of Cupar. The university town and holiday resort of St Andrews is famous too as the 'Home of Golf' and the Old Course is the venue for many international tournaments.

34
Scottish Borders

In Scotland's south-eastern corner, the Scottish Borders is a land of rolling hills, wooded river valleys, prosperous farmland and rugged castles. A link with the region's turbulent past is evidenced by the hilltop ruins of castles and keeps, while the ruined abbeys remind the visitor of a more peaceful era, and there are houses from various times. The thriving woollen textile industry produces quality knitwear and tweeds. The River Tweed, famous for its salmon fishing, threads its way through the region, and provides a superb setting for many of the towns and villages of the region.

35
Shetland

The enchanting Shetland islands lie almost as close to Norway as to Scotland and the Viking heritage lives on in culture, dialect and place names. A scattered mosaic of 100 islands or skerries, there is so much to see and explore. Nature abounds — the cliffs are teeming with birds, the lochs are filled with trout, ponies roam the hills, and seals and otters frequent the bays. Transport to Shetland is easy with frequent daily flights and drive-on drive-off ferries. For a holiday abroad in Britain, visit Shetland — the natural holiday choice.

36
Sutherland

Sutherland is a scenic area of great beauty, with mystical sea-lochs, magnificent mountains, crystal-clear streams, rugged coastline, picturesque villages and vibrant moorlands laced with quiet meandering roads. Visit Dunrobin Castle with its fairytale turrets, marvel at our range of peaks and discover the huge sea cliffs near Cape Wrath and awesome Smoo Cave. You won't believe how clean and extensive our beaches are: fishing, golf, climbing and walking are well provided for — Royal Dornoch golf course is ranked in the top 10 in the world! So come north and visit us soon. Getting to Sutherland couldn't be easier on the new A9.

Tourist Information Centres in these areas and addresses to write for further information are on pages xx to xxvi.

TOURIST INFORMATION CENTRES

i Scotland has about 160 local Tourist Information Centres dispersed throughout many towns and villages. These Centres offer you a friendly welcome, information and help with:
* places to stay
* places to see
* things to do
* routes to take
* local events
* detailed literature

PLACES TO STAY

Almost all Centres have accommodation booking services offering both LOCAL BED-BOOKING and the BOOK-A-BED-AHEAD scheme for hotels, guest houses, and bed and breakfast.

Even at short notice, many Centres can also help you book a self catering holiday in their areas, using up-to-date lists of available accommodation. Centres marked with an asterisk * in the next few pages offer this service.

PLACES TO SEE

All Centres have friendly and well-informed staff ready to tell you about castles and abbeys, museums, walks and trails and all the special delights in the area. Many Centres have displays of local attractions and posters giving details of opening times and charges.

THINGS TO DO

Local bus, rail, ferry and air time-tables are usually available for consultation and staff will be delighted to offer their suggestions on the best way to get you to your destination. They may, too, offer you suggestions of ways you'd never thought of, like the Postbus service.

ROUTES TO TAKE

There are always maps and advice available to ensure that you discover all the delights of the local countryside for yourself. Staff will help you plan your day trips to see the sights and to take the most attractive routes in the area.

LOCAL EVENTS

Tourist Information Centres are always the best place to find out what's on in the area, particularly special events, festivals and important happenings. They get detailed day-to-day information to make sure you don't miss something which would make your stay in the area an even more memorable one.

DETAILED LITERATURE

All the information services of these Centres are backed up by a wide range of publications, some free, some saleable, which are available to you. Many Centres produce their own publications and all can offer you the local area booklets and those published by the Scottish Tourist Board.

SCOTTISH TOURIST INFORMATION CENTRES

Call in for more information on Scotland.
London: 19 Cockspur Street, tel: 01-930 8661/2/3
Southwaite: M6 Service Area, Cumbria (south of Carlisle)
Edinburgh: 14 South St Andrew Street

TOURIST INFORMATION CENTRES

1

Angus

ARBROATH ✉ ⊨
Angus Tourist Board
Information Centre
Market Place
Tel: Arbroath (0241) 72609/76680
Jan-Dec

BRECHIN
Angus Tourist Board
Information Centre
St. Ninian's Place
Tel: Brechin (03562) 3050
June-Sept
✉ Arbroath

CARNOUSTIE ⊨
Angus Tourist Board
Information Centre
24 High Street
Tel: Carnoustie (0241) 52258
Jan-Dec
✉ Arbroath

FORFAR
Angus Tourist Board
Information Centre
The Myre
Tel: Forfar (0307) 67876
June-Sept
✉ Arbroath

KIRRIEMUIR
Angus Tourist Board
Information Centre
Bank Street
Tel: Kirriemuir (0575) 74097
June-Sept
✉ Arbroath

MONTROSE ⊨
Angus Tourist Board
Information Centre
212 High Street
Tel: Montrose (0674) 72000
Jan-Dec
✉ Arbroath

2

Aviemore and Spey Valley

AVIEMORE * ✉ ⊨
Aviemore and Spey Valley
Tourist Board
Main Road
Tel: Aviemore (0479) 810363
Jan-Dec

BOAT OF GARTEN * ⊨
Boat Hotel Car Park
Tel: Boat of Garten (047983) 307
May-Sept
✉ Aviemore

CARRBRIDGE * ⊨
Information Centre
Village Car Park
Tel: Carrbridge (047 984) 630
May-Sept
✉ Aviemore

GRANTOWN-ON-SPEY * ⊨
Information Centre
54 High Street
Tel: Grantown-on-Spey (0479) 2773
Jan-Dec
✉ Aviemore

KINGUSSIE * ⊨
Information Centre
King Street
Tel: Kingussie (054 02) 297
May-Sept
✉ Aviemore

NEWTONMORE * ⊨
Information Centre
Main Street
Tel: Newtonmore (054 03) 274
May-Sept
✉ Aviemore

RALIA PICNIC SITE * ⊨
Nr. Newtonmore
Tel: Newtonmore (054 03) 253
April-Oct
✉ Aviemore

3

Ayrshire and Burns Country

AYR ✉ ⊨
Information Centre
39 Sandgate
Tel: Ayr (0292) 284196 (24-hr
answering service)
Jan-Dec

CULZEAN CASTLE ⊨
Tel: Kirkoswald (065 56) 293
Apr-Oct
✉ Ayr

GIRVAN ⊨
Information Centre
Bridge Street
Tel: Girvan (0465) 4950
Apr-Oct
✉ Ayr

PRESTWICK ⊨
Information Centre
Boydfield Gardens
Tel: Prestwick (0292) 79946
June-Sept
✉ Ayr

PRESTWICK AIRPORT ⊨
British Airports Authority
Information Desk
Tel: Prestwick (0292) 79822
Jan-Dec
✉ Ayr

TROON ⊨
Information Centre
Municipal Buildings
South Beach
Tel: Troon (0292) 317696
Apr-Oct
✉ Ayr

4

Ayrshire Valleys

CUMNOCK ⊨
Tourist Information Centre
Glaisnock Street
Tel: Cumnock (0290) 23058
Jan-Dec
✉ Kilmarnock

NEW CUMNOCK ⊨
Tourist Information Centre
Town Hall
Tel: New Cumnock (0290) 38581
April-Sept
✉ Kilmarnock

DALMELLINGTON ⊨
Tourist Information Centre
Tel: Dalmellington (0292) 550145
April-Sept
✉ Kilmarnock

DARVEL ⊨
Tourist Information Centre
April-Sept
Tel: Darvel (0560) 22780
✉ Kilmarnock

KILMARNOCK ✉ ⊨
Ayrshire Valley Tourist Board
Tourist Information Centre
62 Bank Street
Tel: Kilmarnock (0563) 39090
Jan-Dec

5

Banff and Buchan

BANFF * ✉ ⊨
Information Centre
Collie Lodge
Tel: Banff (026 12) 2419
Mid Apr-Mid Oct

FRASERBURGH ✉ ⊨
Information Centre
Saltoun Square
Tel: Fraserburgh (0346) 28315
Mid May-Sept
✉ Banff

✉ Shows that you can write to the Centre for information during its normal months of opening. In some cases an alternative Centre is shown for written enquiries. Information correct at August 1986.

TOURIST INFORMATION CENTRES

FYVIE 🛏️
Information Centre
Fordoun
Tel: Fyvie (06516) 597
End Apr-Sept
✉️ Banff

PETERHEAD 🛏️
Information Centre
Arbuthnot Museum
St Peter Street
Tel: Peterhead (0779) 71904
July-Aug incl.
✉️ Banff

6
Caithness

JOHN O' GROATS 🛏️
Information Centre
Tel: John o' Groats (095 581) 373
May-Sept

THURSO 🛏️
Information Centre
Car Park
Riverside
Tel: Thurso (0847) 62371
May-Sept

WICK ✉️ 🛏️
Caithness Tourist Board
Whitechapel Road
off High Street
Tel: Wick (0955) 2596
Jan-Dec

7
City of Aberdeen

ABERDEEN ✉️ 🛏️
City of Aberdeen
Tourist Board
St Nicholas House
Broad Street
Tel: Aberdeen (0224) 632727/637353
Telex: 73366
Jan-Dec

Tourist Information Kiosk 🛏️
(local bed-booking only)
Concourse
Railway Station
Guild Street
Jan-Dec

8
City of Dundee

DUNDEE ✉️ 🛏️
Information Centre
Nethergate Centre
Tel: Dundee (0382) 27723
Jan-Dec

9
City of Edinburgh

EDINBURGH ✉️ 🛏️
City of Edinburgh Tourist
Information and Accommodation
Service
Waverley Market
Princes Street
Tel: 031-557 2727
Telex: 727143 (Mon-Fri only)
Jan-Dec

EDINBURGH AIRPORT ✉️
City of Edinburgh
Tourist Information and
Accommodation Service
Tel: 031-333 2167
Jan-Dec

10
Clyde Valley

ABINGTON 🛏️
'Little Chef'
A74 Northbound
Tel: Crawford (086 42) 436
May-Sept

BIGGAR 🛏️
Information Centre
High Street
Tel: Biggar (0899) 21066
May-Sept

Nr HAMILTON 🛏️
(M74 Northbound)
Roadchef Service Area
Tel: Hamilton (0698) 285590
May-Sept

LANARK ✉️ 🛏️
Clyde Valley Tourist Board
Horsemarket
Tel: Lanark (0555) 61661
Jan-Dec

LESMAHAGOW 🛏️
The Resource Centre
New Trows Road
Tel: Lesmahagow (0555) 894449
May-Sept

MOTHERWELL 🛏️
The Library
Hamilton Road
Tel: Motherwell (0698) 51311
May-Sept

11
Cunninghame

LARGS ✉️ 🛏️
Information Centre
Promenade KA30 8BE
Tel: Largs (0475) 673765
Jan-Dec

MILLPORT 🛏️
Information Centre
Guildford Street
Tel: Millport (0475) 530753
April-Oct
✉️ Largs

12
Dumfries and Galloway

CASTLE DOUGLAS * ✉️ 🛏️
Information Centre
Markethill
Tel: Castle Douglas (0556) 2611
Easter-Oct

DALBEATTIE * ✉️ 🛏️
Information Centre
Car Park
Tel: Dalbeattie (0556) 610117
Easter-Oct

DUMFRIES * ✉️ 🛏️
Information Centre
Whitesands
Tel: Dumfries (0387) 53862
Easter-Oct

GATEHOUSE OF FLEET * ✉️ 🛏️
Information Centre
Car Park
Tel: Gatehouse of Fleet
(05574) 212
Easter-Oct

GRETNA * ✉️ 🛏️
Information Centre
Annan Road
Tel: Gretna (0461) 37834
Easter-Oct

KIRKCUDBRIGHT * ✉️ 🛏️
Information Centre
Harbour Square
Tel: Kirkcudbright (0557) 30494
May-Sept

LANGHOLM * ✉️ 🛏️
Town Hall
Tel: Langholm (0541) 80976
Easter-Oct

---

* **Self Catering Late Booking Service operated.**   🛏️ **Local Bed-booking and Book-a-bed Ahead.**

xxi

TOURIST INFORMATION CENTRES

MOFFAT * ✉ 🏨
Information Centre
Church Gate
Tel: Moffat (0683) 20620
Easter-Oct

NEWTON STEWART * ✉ 🏨
Information Centre
Dashwood Square
Tel: Newton Stewart (0671) 2431
Easter-Oct

STRANRAER * ✉ 🏨
Information Bureau
Port Rodie
Tel: Stranraer (0776) 2595

13

Dunoon and The Cowal Peninsula

DUNOON ✉ 🏨
Dunoon & Cowal
Tourist Board
7 Alexandra Parade
Tel: Dunoon (0369) 3785
Jan-Dec

14

East Lothian

DUNBAR ✉ 🏨
Information Centre
Town House
High Street
Tel: Dunbar (0368) 63353
Jan-Dec

MUSSELBURGH ✉ 🏨
Brunton Hall
East Lothian
Tel: 031-665 6597
June-mid Sept

NORTH BERWICK * ✉ 🏨
Information Centre
Quality Street
Tel: North Berwick (0620) 2197
Jan-Dec

PENCRAIG 🏨
A1
East Linton
Tel: Pencraig (0620) 860063
Mid May-mid Sept
✉ Dunbar

15

Forth Valley

DUNFERMLINE 🏨
Information Centre
Glen Bridge Car Park
Tel: Dunfermline (0383) 720999
May-Sept
✉ Linlithgow

FORTH ROAD BRIDGE 🏨
Information Centre
Tel: Inverkeithing (0383) 417759
Easter-Sept
✉ Linlithgow

KINCARDINE BRIDGE 🏨
Tourist Information Centre
Pine 'n' Oak
Kincardine Bridge Road
Airth, Falkirk
Tel: Airth (032 483) 422
May-Sept
✉ Linlithgow

LINLITHGOW ✉ 🏨
Burgh Halls
The Cross
Tel: Linlithgow (0506) 844600
Jan-Dec

16

Fort William and Lochaber

BALLACHULISH 🏨
Tourist Office
Tel: Ballachulish (08552) 296
April-Sept
✉ Fort William

FORT WILLIAM * ✉ 🏨
Fort William and Lochaber
Tourist Board
Tel: Fort William (0397) 3781
Jan-Dec

MALLAIG 🏨
Information Centre
Tel: Mallaig (0687) 2170
April-Sept
✉ Fort William

SALEN
Tourist Office
Tel: Salen (096785) 622
Mid June-mid Sept
✉ Fort William

17

Gordon

ALFORD 🏨
Information Centre
Railway Museum
Station Yard
Tel: Alford (0336) 2052
Apr-Sept
✉ Aberdeen

ELLON 🏨
Information Caravan
Market Street Car Park
Tel: Ellon (0358) 20730
Mid May-Sept
✉ Aberdeen

HUNTLY 🏨
Information Centre
The Square
Tel: Huntly (0466) 2255
Mid May-Sept
✉ Aberdeen

INVERURIE 🏨
Information Centre
Town Hall, Market Place
Tel: Inverurie (0467) 20600
Mid May-Sept
✉ Aberdeen

18

Greater Glasgow

GLASGOW ✉ 🏨
Tourist Information Centre
35-39 St. Vincent Place
Tel: 041-227 4880
Telex: 779504
Jan-Dec

PAISLEY 🏨
Town Hall
Abbey Close
Tel: 041-889 0711
Jan-Dec
✉ Glasgow

GOUROCK 🏨
Information Centre
Municipal Buildings
Shore Street
Tel: Gourock (0475) 31126
Jan-Dec

GREENOCK ✉ 🏨
Information Centre
Municipal Buildings
23 Clyde Street
Tel: Greenock (0475) 24400

✉ Shows that you can write to the Centre for information during its normal months of opening. In some cases an alternative Centre is shown for written enquiries. Information correct at August 1986.

19

Inverness, Loch Ness and Nairn

DAVIOT ✉
by Inverness
Daviot Wood Information Centre
Tel: Daviot (046385) 203
April-Sept
✉ Inverness

FORT AUGUSTUS ✉
Information Centre
Car Park
Tel: Fort Augustus (0320) 6367
May-Sept
✉ Inverness

INVERNESS * ✉ ✉
Inverness, Loch Ness and
Nairn Tourist Board
23 Church Street
Tel: Inverness (0463) 234353
Telex: 75114
Jan-Dec

NAIRN ✉
Information Centre
62 King Street
Tel: Nairn (0667) 52753
May-Sept
✉ Inverness

20

Isle of Arran

BRODICK, Isle of Arran * ✉ ✉
Tourist Information Centre
The Pier
Tel: Brodick (0770) 2140/2401
Jan-Dec

21

The Isle of Skye and South West Ross

BROADFORD, Isle of Skye * ✉
The Isle of Skye and
South West Ross
Tourist Board
Tel: (047 12) 361/463
Easter-Sept
✉ Portree

KYLE OF LOCHALSH * ✉
The Isle of Skye and
South West Ross Tourist Board
Tel: Kyle (0599) 4276
Easter-Sept
✉ Portree

PORTREE, Isle of Skye * ✉ ✉
The Isle of Skye and
South West Ross Tourist Board
Tourist Information Centre
Tel: Portree (0478) 2137
Jan-Dec

SHIEL BRIDGE ✉
Information Caravan
Tel: Glenshiel (0599) 81264
Easter-Sept
✉ Portree

22

Kincardine and Deeside

ABOYNE * ✉ ✉
Information Caravan
Ballater Road Car Park
Tel: Aboyne (0339) 2060
Easter-Sept

BALLATER * ✉ ✉
Information Centre
Station Square
Tel: Ballater (0338) 55306
Easter-mid Oct

BANCHORY * ✉ ✉
Information Centre
Dee Street Car Park
Tel: Banchory (033 02) 2000
Easter-Sept

BRAEMAR * ✉ ✉
Information Centre
Balnellan Road
Tel: Braemar (033 83) 600
Easter-Oct

STONEHAVEN * ✉ ✉
Information Centre
The Square
Tel: Stonehaven (0569) 62806
Easter-Sept

23

Kirkcaldy

BURNTISLAND ✉
4 Kirkgate
Tel: Burntisland (0592) 872667
Jan-Dec

KIRKCALDY
Information Centre
Esplanade
Tel: Kirkcaldy (0592) 267775
Jan-Dec

LEVEN ✉
Information Centre
South Street
Tel: Leven (0333) 29464
Jan-Dec

24

Loch Lomond, Stirling and The Trossachs

ABERFOYLE ✉ ✉
Information Centre
Main Street
Tel: Aberfoyle (087 72) 352
Apr-Sept

BALLOCH ✉ ✉
Information Centre
Balloch Road
Tel: Alexandra (0389) 53533
Apr-Sept

BANNOCKBURN ✉
Motorway Services Area
by Stirling
Tel: (0786) 814111
Mar-Oct

CALLANDER ✉ ✉
Tourist Information Centre
Leny Road
Tel: Callander (0877) 30342
Apr-Sept

DUNBLANE ✉ ✉
Tourist Information Centre
Stirling Road
Tel: Dunblane (0786) 824428
Apr-Sept

HELENSBURGH ✉ ✉
Tourist Information Centre
The Clock Tower
Tel: Helensburgh (0436) 2642
Apr-Sept

KILLIN ✉ ✉
Tourist Information Centre
Main Street
Tel: Killin (056 72) 254
Apr-Sept

STIRLING ✉ ✉
Tourist Information Centre
Dumbarton Road
Tel: Stirling (0786) 75019
Jan-Dec

TARBET, Loch Lomond ✉ ✉
Information Caravan
Pier Road
Tarbet
Loch Lomond
Tel: Arrochar (03012) 260
Apr-Sept
✉ Stirling

---

* **Self Catering Late Booking Service operated.**   ✉ **Local Bed-booking and Book-a-bed Ahead.**

TOURIST INFORMATION CENTRES

TILLICOULTRY ✉ 🛏
Information Centre
Clock Mill
Upper Mill Street
Tel: Tillicoultry (0259) 52176
Apr-Sept

TYNDRUM ✉ 🛏
Information Centre Car Park
Tel: Tyndrum (083 84) 246
Apr-Sept

25

Mid Argyll, Kintyre and Islay

BOWMORE, Isle of Islay 🛏
Information Centre
Tel: (049 681) 254
Apr-mid Oct
✉ Campbeltown

CAMPBELTOWN * ✉ 🛏
Mid Argyll, Kintyre & Islay
Tourist Board
Tel: Campbeltown (0586) 52056
Jan-Dec

INVERARAY 🛏
Information Centre
Tel: Inveraray (0499) 2063
Apr-mid Oct
✉ Campbeltown

LOCHGILPHEAD 🛏
Information Centre
Tel: Lochgilphead (0546) 2344
Apr-mid Oct
✉ Campbeltown

TARBERT, Loch Fyne 🛏
Information Centre
Tel: Tarbert (088 02) 429
Apr-mid Oct
✉ Campbeltown

26

Moray

CULLEN 🛏
20 Seafield Street
Information Centre
Tel: Cullen (0542) 40757
June-Sept
✉ Elgin

DUFFTOWN 🛏
Information Centre
The Clock Tower
The Square
Tel: Dufftown (0340) 20501
May-Sept
✉ Elgin

ELGIN * ✉ 🛏
Information Centre
17 High Street, IV30 1EG
Tel: Elgin (0343) 3388/2666
Jan-Dec

FORRES 🛏
Information Centre
Falconer Museum
Tolbooth Street
Tel: Forres (0309) 72938
May-Sept
✉ Elgin

KEITH 🛏
Information Centre
Church Road
Tel: (054 22) 2634
June-Sept
✉ Elgin

TOMINTOUL 🛏
Information Centre
The Square
Tel: Tomintoul (080 74) 285
Apr-Oct
✉ Elgin

27

Oban, Mull and District

OBAN * ✉ 🛏
Oban, Mull and District
Tourist Board
Argyll Square
Tel: Oban (0631) 63122
Jan-Dec

TOBERMORY ✉ 🛏
Isle of Mull
Information Centre
48 Main Street
Tel: Tobermory (0688) 2182
Jan-Dec (9-11 in winter months)

28

Orkney

KIRKWALL ✉ 🛏
Orkney Tourist Board
Information Centre
Broad Street KW15 1NX
Tel: Kirkwall (0856) 2856
Jan-Dec

STROMNESS 🛏
Information Centre
Ferry Terminal Building
Pierhead
Tel: Stromness (0856) 850716
May-Sept
(also 2 hours per day, Oct-Apr)
✉ Kirkwall

29

Outer Hebrides

CASTLEBAY, Isle of Barra 🛏
Information Centre
Tel: Castlebay (087 14) 336
May-Sept
✉ Stornoway

LOCHBOISDALE 🛏
Isle of South Uist
Information Centre
Tel: Lochboisdale (087 84) 286
May-Sept
✉ Stornoway

LOCHMADDY 🛏
Isle of North Uist
Information Centre
Tel: Lochmaddy (08763) 321
May-Sept
✉ Stornoway

STORNOWAY, Isle of Lewis ✉ 🛏
Outer Hebrides Tourist Board
Administration and Information
Centre
4 South Beach Street
Tel: Stornoway (0851) 3088
Jan-Dec

TARBERT, Isle of Harris 🛏
Information Centre
Tel: Harris (0859) 2011
May-Sept
✉ Stornoway

30

Perthshire

ABERFELDY ✉ all year 🛏
Aberfeldy and District Tourist
Association
8 Dunkeld Street
Tel: Aberfeldy (0887) 20276
Easter-mid Sept

AUCHTERARDER * ✉ all
year 🛏
Auchterarder and District
Tourist Association
High Street
Tel: Auchterarder (076 46) 3450
Apr-Oct (Oct-Apr open 1000-1400
daily)

BLAIRGOWRIE * ✉ all year 🛏
Blairgowrie and District Tourist
Association
Wellmeadow
Tel: Blairgowrie (0250) 2960
Jan-Dec

✉ **Shows that you can write to the Centre for information during its normal months of opening. In some cases an alternative Centre is shown for written enquiries.** Information correct at August 1986.

TOURIST INFORMATION CENTRES

CRIEFF * ✉ 🛏 all year
Crieff and District Tourist Association
James Square
Tel: Crieff (0764) 2578
Apr-Oct
(Nov-Mar, open 4 hrs per day)

DUNKELD ✉ all year 🛏
Dunkeld and Birnam Tourist
Association
The Cross
Tel: Dunkeld (035 02) 688
Easter-Oct

GLENSHEE ✉ all year
Information Officer
Glenshee Tourist Association
Corsehill
Upper Allan Street
Blairgowrie
Tel: BLairgowrie (0250) 5509

KINROSS ✉ all year 🛏
Kinross-shire Tourist Association
Information Centre
Kinross Service Area,
off Junction 6, M90
Tel: Kinross (0577) 63680
(62585 when closed)
Apr-Oct

PERTH * ✉ all year 🛏
Perth Tourist Association
The Round House
Marshall Place
Tel: Perth (0738) 22900/27108
Jan-Dec

PITLOCHRY * ✉ all year 🛏
Pitlochry and District
Tourist Association
22 Atholl Road
Tel: Pitlochry (0796) 2215/2751
Jan-Dec

31

Ross and Cromarty
GAIRLOCH ✉ 🛏
Ross & Cromarty Tourist Board
Information Office
Achtercairn
Gairloch IV21 2DN
Tel: Gairloch (0445) 2130
Jan-Dec

NORTH KESSOCK ✉ 🛏
Ross & Cromarty Tourist Board
Tourist Office
North Kessock IV1 1XB
Tel: Kessock (046 373) 505
Jan-Dec

STRATHPEFFER 🛏
Ross & Cromarty Tourist Board
Information Centre
The Square
Tel: Strathpeffer (0997) 21415
Easter, May-Sept
✉ North Kessock

ULLAPOOL 🛏
Ross & Cromarty Tourist Board
Information Centre
Tel: Ullapool (0854) 2135
Easter-Sept
✉ Gairloch

32

Rothesay and Isle of Bute
ROTHESAY, Isle of Bute ✉ 🛏
Rothesay & Isle of Bute Tourist
Board
The Pier
Tel: Rothesay (0700) 2151
Jan-Dec

33

St. Andrews and North East Fife
ANSTRUTHER 🛏
East Neuk Information Centre
Scottish Fisheries Museum
Tel: (0333) 310628
May-Sept
✉ St Andrews

CUPAR 🛏
Information Centre
Fluthers Car Park
Tel: Cupar (0334) 55555
Mid June-Sept
✉ St Andrews

ST ANDREWS ✉ 🛏
Information Centre
South Street
Tel: St Andrews (0334) 72021
Jan-Dec

34

Scottish Borders
COLDSTREAM * ✉ 🛏
Henderson Park
Tel: Coldstream (0890) 2607
Apr-Oct

EYEMOUTH * ✉ 🛏
Auld Kirk
Tel: Eyemouth (0390) 50678
Apr-Oct

GALASHIELS * ✉ 🛏
Bank Street
Tel: Galashiels (0896) 55551
Apr-Oct

HAWICK * ✉ 🛏
Common Haugh
Tel: Hawick (0450) 72547
Apr-Oct

JEDBURGH * ✉ 🛏
Information Centre
Murray's Green
Tel: Jedburgh (0835)
63435/63688
Feb-Nov

KELSO * ✉ 🛏
Turret House
Tel: Kelso (0573) 23464
Apr-Oct

MELROSE * ✉ 🛏
Priorwood Gardens, nr. Abbey
Tel: Melrose (089 682) 2555
Apr-Oct

PEEBLES * ✉ 🛏
Chambers Institute
High Street
Tel: Peebles (0721) 20138
Apr-Oct

SELKIRK * ✉ 🛏
Halliwell's House
Tel: Selkirk (0750) 20054
Apr-Oct

35

Shetland
LERWICK, Shetland ✉ 🛏
Shetland Tourist Organisation
Information Centre
Tel: Lerwick (0595) 3434
Telex: 75119
Jan-Dec

36

Sutherland
BETTYHILL 🛏
Information Centre
Tel: Bettyhill (064 12) 342
May-Sept
✉ Dornoch

---

* **Self Catering Late Booking Service operated.**   🛏 **Local Bed-booking and Book-a-bed Ahead.**

TOURIST INFORMATION CENTRES

BONAR BRIDGE 🛏
Information Centre
Tel: Ardgay (08632) 333
May-Sept
✉ Dornoch

DORNOCH ✉ 🛏
Sutherland Tourist Board
The Square
Tel: Dornoch (0862) 810400
Jan-Dec

DURNESS 🛏
Information Centre
Tel: Durness (097 181) 259
April-Oct
✉ Dornoch

HELMSDALE 🛏
Information Centre
Tel: Helmsdale (043 12) 640
May-Sept
✉ Dornoch

LAIRG 🛏
Information Centre
Tel: Lairg (0549) 2160
May-Sept
✉ Dornoch

LOCHINVER 🛏
Information Centre
Tel: Lochinver (057 14) 330
April-Oct
✉ Dornoch

✉ Shows that you can write to the Centre for information during its normal months of opening. In some cases an alternative Centre is shown for written enquiries. Information correct at August 1986.

MAPS

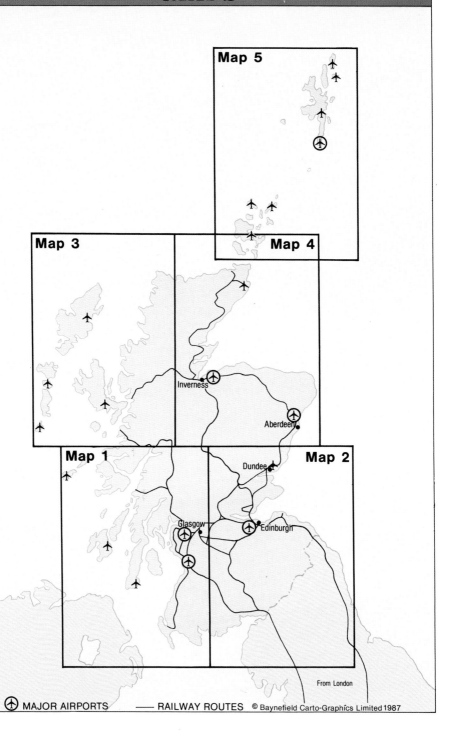

Map 5

Map 3

Map 4

Map 1

Inverness

Aberdeen

Dundee

Glasgow

Edinburgh

Map 2

From London

⊕ MAJOR AIRPORTS ── RAILWAY ROUTES © Baynefield Carto-Graphics Limited 1987

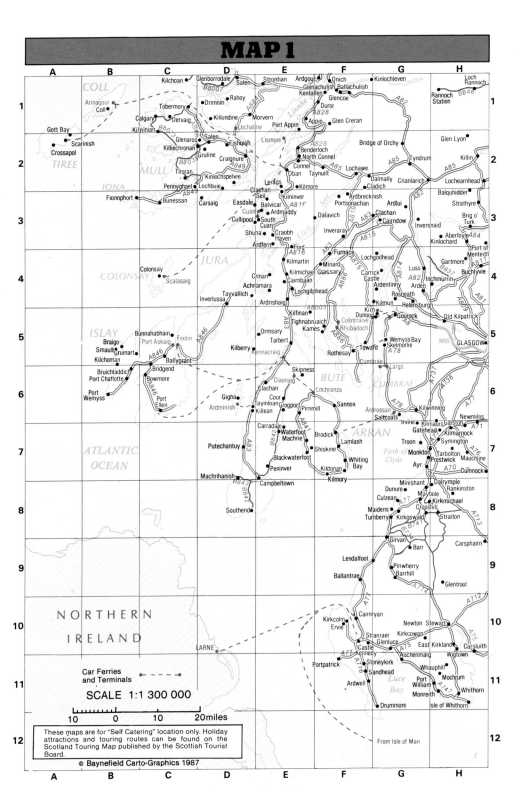

MAP 2

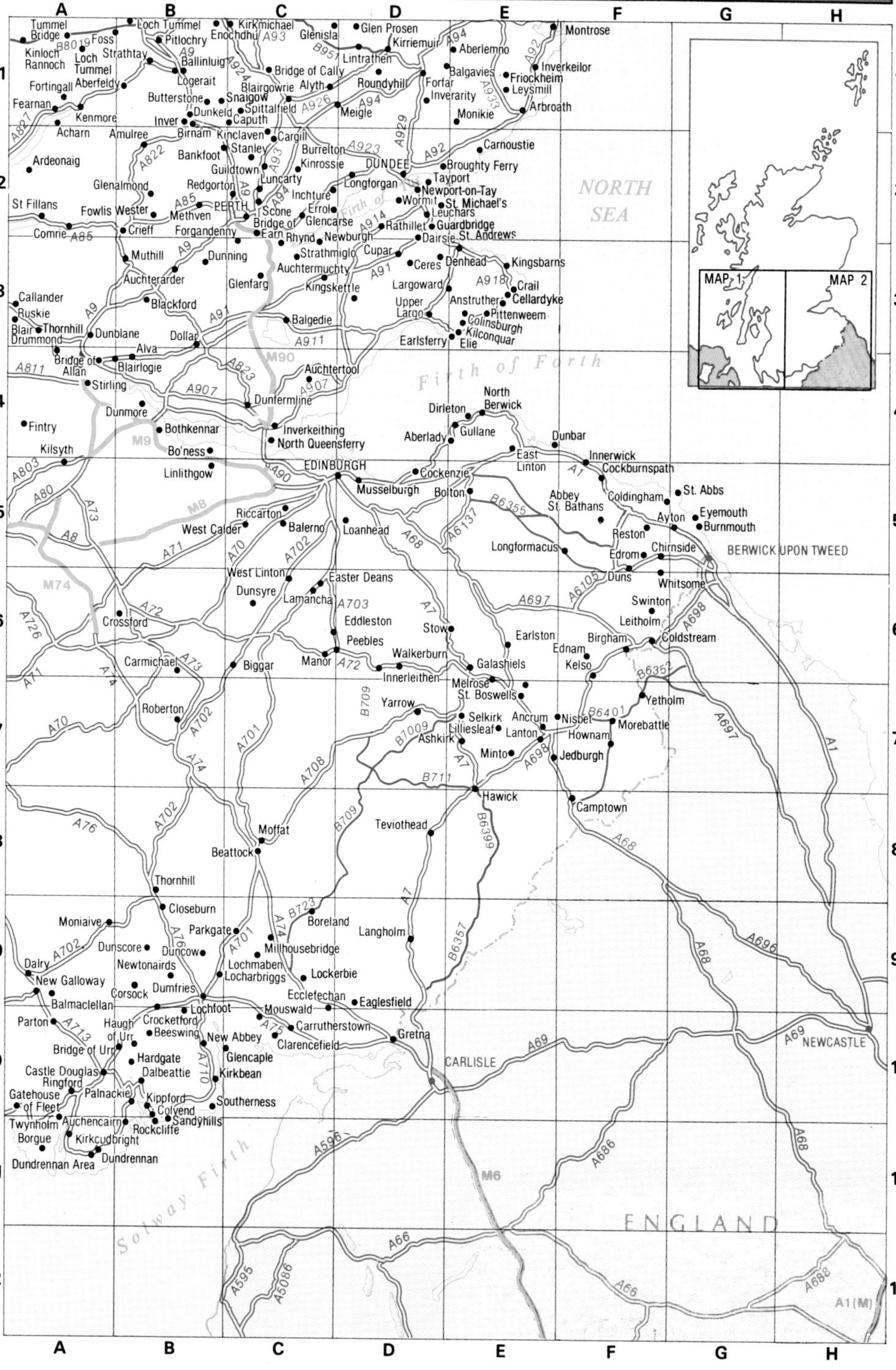

NORTH SEA

ENGLAND

MAP 1   MAP 2

BERWICK UPON TWEED

NEWCASTLE

CARLISLE

Firth of Forth

Solway Firth

EDINBURGH

PERTH

DUNDEE

Tummel Bridge, Loch Tummel, Kirkmichael, Enochdhu, Glenisla, Glen Prosen, Montrose
Kinloch Rannoch, Foss, Pitlochry, Kirriemuir, Aberlemno, Inverkeilor, Friockheim
Fortingall, Loch Tummel, Ballinluig, Strathtay, Bridge of Cally, Lintrathen, Forfar, Leysmill
Fearnan, Aberfeldy, Logierait, Blairgowrie, Alyth, Roundyhill, Inverarity, Arbroath
Kenmore, Inver, Butterstone, Snaigow, Spittalfield, Meigle, Monikie
Acharn, Amulree, Birnam, Dunkeld, Caputh, Carnoustie
Ardeonaig, Kinclaven, Cargill, Burrelton, Broughty Ferry
St Fillans, Glenalmond, Bankfoot, Stanley, Luncarty, Inchture, Longforgan, Tayport, Newport-on-Tay
Fowlis Wester, Guildtown, Redgorton, Scone, Glencarse, Wormit, St Michael's, Leuchars
Comrie, Crieff, Methven, Forgandenny, Bridge of Earn, Errol, Rhynd, Rathillet, Guardbridge
Muthill, Dunning, Newburgh, Dairsie, St Andrews
Auchterarder, Glenfarg, Strathmiglo, Cupar, Denhead, Kingsbarns
Blackford, Auchtermuchty, Kingskettle, Ceres, Largoward, Crail
Callander, Dollar, Balgedie, Upper Largo, Anstruther, Cellardyke
Ruskie, Thornhill, Colinsburgh, Pittenweem
Blair Drummond, Dunblane, Alva, Kilconquhar
Bridge of Allan, Blairlogie, Auchtertool, Earlsferry, Elie
Stirling, Dunfermline
Dunmore, Dirleton, North Berwick
Fintry, Bothkennar, Inverkeithing, Aberlady, Gullane, Dunbar
Kilsyth, Bo'ness, North Queensferry, East Linton, Innerwick, Cockburnspath
Linlithgow, Cockenzie, Coldingham, St Abbs
Riccarton, Musselburgh, Bolton, Abbey St Bathans, Ayton, Eyemouth, Burnmouth
West Calder, Balerno, Loanhead, Reston, Chirnside
Longformacus, Edrom, Duns, Whitsome
West Linton, Easter Deans, Longyester, Swinton
Dunsyre, Lamancha, Eddleston, Stow, Earlston, Birgham, Leitholm, Coldstream
Crossford, Carmichael, Biggar, Manor, Peebles, Walkerburn, Galashiels, Ednam, Kelso
Roberton, Innerleithen, Melrose, St Boswells, Yetholm
Yarrow, Selkirk, Ancrum, Nisbet, Morebattle
Ashkirk, Lilliesleaf, Lanton, Hownam
Minto, Jedburgh
Hawick, Camptown
Teviothead
Moffat
Beattock
Thornhill
Closeburn
Moniaive, Parkgate, Boreland, Langholm
Dalry, Duncow, Millhousebridge, Lockerbie
New Galloway, Newtonairds, Lochmaben, Locharbriggs, Ecclefechan, Eaglesfield
Balmaclellan, Corsock, Dumfries, Lochfoot, Mouswald, Gretna
Parton, Crocketford, Carrutherstown
Castle Douglas, Beeswing, New Abbey, Clarencefield
Ringford, Haugh of Urr, Glencaple
Gatehouse of Fleet, Bridge of Urr, Hardgate, Dalbeattie, Kirkbean
Twynholm, Palnackie, Kippford, Colvend, Southerness
Borgue, Auchencairn, Rockcliffe, Sandyhills
Dundrennan Area, Kirkcudbright, Dundrennan

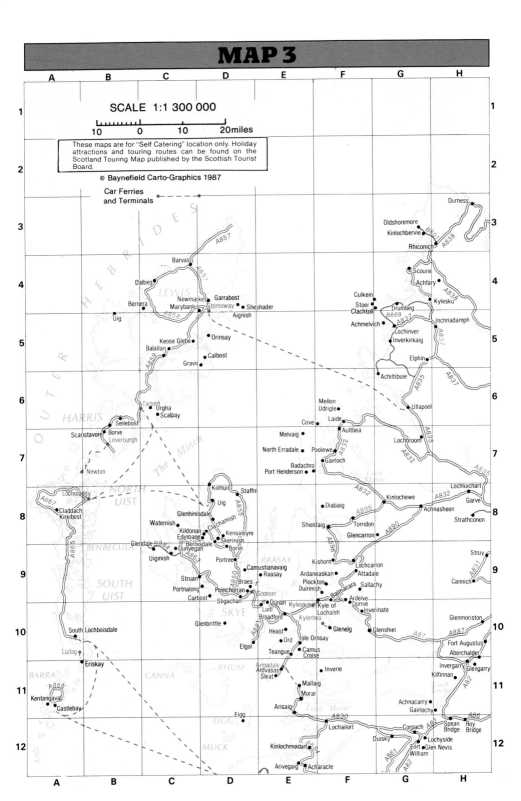

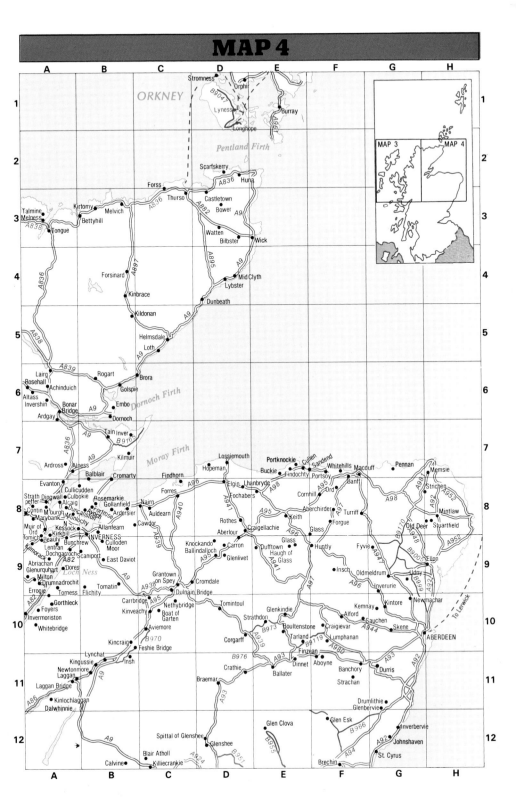

MAP 4

ORKNEY

Stromness
Orphir
B9047
Lyness
Burray
Longhope
A961

Pentland Firth

MAP 3   MAP 4

Scarfskerry
A836   Huna
Forss
Castletown
Thurso   Bower   A9
A836   A882
Kirtomy
Talmine   Melvich
Melness   Bettyhill
A838   Tongue
Watten
Bilbster   Wick
A895
Forsinard
A897   Mid Clyth
Lybster
Kinbrace
A9   Dunbeath
Kildonan

Helmsdale
Loth
A9
A839
Lairg   Rogart   Brora
Rosehall
Achinduich   Golspie
Altass   Dornoch Firth
Invershin   Bonar   Embo
Ardgay   Bridge   A9   Dornoch
Tain Inver
A836   B9165   Kilmuir
Ardross   Alness   Moray Firth
Balblair   Cromarty
Evanton   Findhorn   Lossiemouth   Portknockie   Cullen   Sandend
Strath Dingwall   Culbokie   Hopeman   Buckie   Whitehills   Macduff   Pennan
peffer   Alcaig   Rosemarkie   Forres   Elgin   Lhanbryde   Findochty   Portsoy   Banff   Memsie
Contin   M'burgh   Gollanfield   Nairn   A96   Fochabers   A98   Strichen
Marybank   Duncanston   Fortrose   A940   Cornhill   Ord   A952
Muir of   Kirkhill   Ardersier   Auldearn   A95   Keith   Aberchirder   Turriff   Mintlaw
Ord   Kessock   Allanfearn   Cawdor   Rothes   Forgue   Old Deer   Stuartfield
Tomich   Beauly   INVERNESS   Aberlour   Craigellachie   Glass   A948   A952
Kiltarlity   Bunchrew   Culloden   A939   Knockando   Carron   Glass   Huntly   Fyvie   Ellon
Abriachan   Dochgarroch   Moor   Ballindalloch   Dufftown   Haugh of   Insch   Oldmeldrum   Udny
Glenurquhart   Scaniport   East Daviot   Glenlivet   Glass   A941   B9000
Milton   Dores   Grantown   Cromdale   Inverurie   Newmachar
Drumnadrochit   Tomatin   on Spey   Insch   A96   Kintore   To Lerwick
Errogie   Flichity   A938   Dulnain Bridge   Tomintoul   Kemnay   Kintore   Newmachar
Gorthleck   Carrbridge   A95   Glenkindie   Alford   Sauchen   ABERDEEN
Foyers   Kinveachy   Nethybridge   Strathdon   B973   Boultenstone   Craigievar   Skene
Invermoriston   Boat of   Garten   Tarland   Lumphanan   A944
Whitebridge   Aviemore   Corgarff   A939   B9119   Finzean   A980   Durris
Kincraig   B970   Crathie   A93   Dinnet   Aboyne   Banchory
Lynchat   Feshie Bridge   B976   Ballater   Strachan
Kingussie   Insh   Crathie   Braemar   Drumlithie
Newtonmore   A9   Glenbervie
Laggan   Inverbervie
Laggan Bridge   A86   Glen Clova   Glen Esk   B966   Inverbervie
Kinlochlaggan   Johnshaven
Dalwhinnie   Spittal of Glenshee   Glenshee   A92   St. Cyrus
A9   Blair Atholl   Brechin   A94
Calvine   Killiecrankie   A924   B951   B955

MAP 5

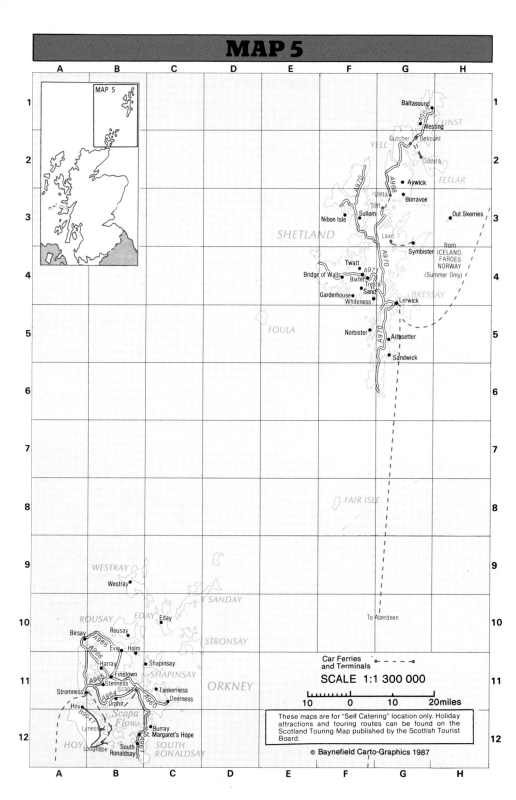

MAP 5

A B C D E F G H

1 — Baltasound, Westing, UNST

Gutcher · Belmont
YELL
Oddsta
2 — FETLAR

Aywick
Uista
Burravoe
Tort
Sullom
Out Skerries 3
Nibon Isle

SHETLAND

Laxo

Symbister
from ICELAND,
FAROES
NORWAY
(Summer Only)

Twatt
A970
Bridge of Walls
Bixter Tresta
Gardenhouse· Sand
Whiteness
BRESSAY
Lerwick

4

FOULA

Norbister
Aithsetter 5
A970
Sandwick

6

7

FAIR ISLE 8

WESTRAY 9
Westray·

SANDAY

ROUSAY EDAY· Eday
Rousay
Birsay Evie STRONSAY To Aberdeen 10
Holm

Harray
A966 Shapinsay
Finstown SHAPINSAY
Stromness· Stenness Tankerness ORKNEY
A964 Scapa Deerness
Orphir A960
Hoy
Scapa
Flow
Lyness Burray
St. Margaret's Hope
HOY Longhope South SOUTH
Ronaldsay RONALDSAY

Car Ferries and Terminals ·- - - - -

SCALE 1:1 300 000

10   0   10   20miles

These maps are for "Self Catering" location only. Holiday
attractions and touring routes can be found on the
Scotland Touring Map published by the Scottish Tourist
Board.

© Baynefield Carto-Graphics 1987

See line entry, page 188

River View Park, Kippford 11

Six Norwegian-style timber lodges in secluded garden setting with beautiful views over Urr Estuary. Equipped to a high standard for 2-6 persons. Colour TV, fridge, cots available, bed linen can be hired. Suitable semi-disabled. Off-season short stays welcome.
AA recommended. Member of Association of Scotland's Self-Caterers.
Details from Mrs G. McLellan, River View Park, Kippford, nr. Dalbeattie DG5 4LG. Tel: 055-662 204.

Luxury Log Cabins 12

BALNAKILLY · KIRKMICHAEL · PERTHSHIRE · 025 081 281

Balnakilly offers an excellent family holiday and the very best in self-catering on its private 1500-acre estate which has its own Swimming Pool, Tennis Court, Fishing, Shooting and **B.H.S. Approved Riding Centre.** Accommodation to suit all tastes and budgets, which are all individually sited amidst the most beautiful scenery and wildlife.
From a Commended 5 Crown new Norwegian House and four 4 Crown Log Cabins to traditional 3 Crown Highland Cottages.

 See line entry, page 205

Lochinver Holiday Lodges 13
Lochinver, Sutherland IV27.   Tel. 05714 282

An experience to savour, seven luxury lodges nestle against the trees in lovely Strathan bay, provide all the comforts of home. Your near neighbours could very well be seal, otter, deer and seabirds. The Scenery is matchless—majestic mountains, tranquil lochs and white sandy beaches.
Truly an idyllic setting for an unforgettable holiday. Village shops, hotel, restaurants nearby.
(£192-£478). No pets allowed.
ASSC, AA Listed   STB 🏵🏵🏵🏵 Highly Commended

 See line entry, page 234

Esplanade Court, OBAN 14

Purpose-built holiday apartments beautifully situated overlooking the sea and surrounding islands. Each apartment completely self-contained with central heating throughout. Bed linen and all equipment provided. Colour TV in each lounge. Elevator to all floors. Laundry room with automatic equipment. Private parking free. Special off-season terms.
🏵🏵🏵🏵 Highly Commended.
For colour brochure and tariff write, with S.A.E. to:
Mr NICOLSON, Esplanade Court, The Esplanade, Oban, Argyll.

 See line entry, page 254

Beechwood Holiday Homes 15
PORTREE, ISLE OF SKYE

Five modern bungalows. Well equipped with dish-washers, fridges, colour TVs etc. Bed linen supplied. Each sleeps five plus convertible couch. Five larger units opening Spring of 1987. Shops, swimming pool, tennis, squash, boat trips and hill-walking nearby. Rock climbing, sea angling and pony trekking on Island. Also museums, craft shops etc. Day trips to Outer Isles in season.
Telephone: (0478) 2634   🏵🏵🏵🏵 Commended

Glasgow Garden Festival '88

The Glasgow Garden Festival in 1988 guarantees to provide something for everyone. In addition to six themed parks, a varied and colourful programme of open air concerts, live displays and conferences will be staged from April-September.

Look for the sign that sets the standard in Scotland

The Thistle Commendation is awarded to holiday caravan parks in Scotland by the Scottish Tourist Board after rigorous inspection by the National Caravan Council and the National Federation of Site Operators – very impressive but what does it mean to you?

Booking your holiday at a Thistle Park ensures that all facilities are of the highest standard. That the caravans are modern, with all the comforts of home, and the park has a comprehensive range of facilities, for example laundry, shop, and information service. Many Parks have swimming pools and entertainment too.

So look for the sign that sets the standard for a carefree caravan holiday in Scotland.

COMMENDATION SCHEME

For further information contact
The Scottish Tourist Board, PO Box 15
Edinburgh EH1 1UY   Telephone 031-332 2433

SCOTLAND
SELF CATERING
ACCOMMODATION 1987

ABBEY ST BATHANS, by Duns Berwickshire Map Ref. 2F5

Abbey St Bathans
situated in the Scottish Borders

A secluded valley in a beautiful setting between the Lammermuir Hills and the coast, 6 miles from Duns. Ideal for walking, riding and fishing.
Bankend House, sleeps 8;
Retreat Cottage, sleeps 5;
Priory and Whiteadder Cottages, sleeps 4.
Full particuars from: **Mrs J. J. Dobie, Abbey St Bathans, Duns, Berwickshire. Tel. (036 14) 242; or Scottish Country Cottages, Suite 2d Churchill Way, Bishopbriggs, Glasgow. Tel. (041-772) 5920.**

1 house, 3 cottages, 1-2 pub rms, 2-5 bedrms, sleeps 4-8, min let weekend, £100-£220, Jan-Dec, bus 7 mls, rail 20 mls, airport 55 mls

🛌 ⓦ E ↵ 🖂 🗏 ▢ ◎ ⊡ ℃ 🗗 ⬛ ☺ ❄ �dog 🅿 🐕 🏛 † ⌂   ♪ ∪ ⟷ ⊱ ↗ ⁄ ® 🐾 🔥

Mrs J J Dobie, Abbey St Bathan's House, Duns, Berwickshire
☎ *Abbey St Bathans (03614) 242*
Built of local stone, on private estate in secluded Lammermuir Valley. Many outdoor activities.

ABERCHALDER, by Invergarry Inverness-shire Map Ref. 3H10

1 bedsit, sleeps 2-3, £56-£62, Jan-Dec, bus nearby, rail 28 mls, airport 50 mls

🛌 ⓦ E ↵ 🖂 🗏 ◎ ⊡ 🗗 ⬛ ☺ ❄ 🐕 🅿 †   ♪ ∪ ⁄ ✕ 🐾 🔥

Miss Ellice, Taigh-an-Lianach, Aberchalder Farm, Invergarry, Inverness-shire
☎ *Invergarry (08093) 287*

ABERCHIRDER Banffshire Map Ref. 4F8

1 house, 2 pub rms, 3 bedrms, sleeps 6, £130-£160, Apr-Oct, bus 2 mls, rail 10 mls, airport 45 mls

🛌 ⓦ E ↵ 🖂 🗏 ◎ ⊡ ℃ 🗗 ▢ ⬛ ☺ ❄ 🐕 🅿 🐕 🏛 †   ♪ ∪ ↗

T Burnett-Stuart, The Marble Workshop, Portsoy, Banffshire
☎ *Portsoy (0261) 42404/(04665) 801 (eve)*

1 cottage, 1 pub rm, 3 bedrms, sleeps 9, £40-£50, Apr-Oct, bus 1 ml, rail 10 mls, airport 40 mls

🛌 ⓦ E ↵ 🖂 🗏 ◎ ⊡ 🗗 ▢ ⬛ ❄ 🐕 🅿 🐕 🏛 † ⌂   ♪ ∪ ✕ 🐾 🔥

Mrs S Bowie, Monedie, Aberchirder, Banffshire
☎ *Aberchirder (04665) 287*

1 house, 1 cottage, 1 pub rm, 2 bedrms, sleeps 6, min let weekend, £65-£75, Jan-Dec, bus nearby, rail 8 mls

🛌 ⓦ E ↵ 🖂 ◎ ⊡ 🗗 ▢ ⬛ ☺ ❄ 🐕 🅿 🐕 🏛   ♪ ∪ ⚓ ⊱ ↗ ⁄ ⛷ 🎿 🛷 ✕ 🐾 Ⓣ

4 caravans, sleeps 6, min let weekend, £50-£80, May-Sep, bus nearby, rail 8 mls

🖂 ▢ ⬛ ☺ 🐕 🅿 🐕 🏛 † ⌂ ⊛   ♪ ∪ ⚓ ⊱ ↗ ⁄ ⛷ 🎿 🛷 ✕ 🐾 Ⓣ

Limehillock Development Ltd, Willsholm, 1 South Street, Aberchirder, Huntly, Aberdeenshire, AB5 5TR
☎ *Grange (05425) 291/2*

Prices shown are for guidance only. Please send SAE with each enquiry.

ABERDEEN Map Ref. 4G10

up to
COMMENDED
♛ ♛

King Street/Kepplestone/Viewfield Road 50 flats, 1 pub rm, 6 bedrms, sleeps 6, £120-£150, Jul-Sep, bus nearby, rail 2 mls, airport 5 mls

  ♿ WC E ⇥ 📻 🅰 🖳 🗄 🌀 🖲 📞 🗄 ✏ 🔌 ⊙ 🅿 ◆ 🧭   🔍 ✕ 💼 🆃

Robert Gordon's Institute of Technology, Schoolhill, Aberdeen, AB9 1FR
☎ *Aberdeen (0224) 633611 ext 381*
Student flats in residential area in west end of city. On bus route for city centre.

(See colour ad. 1 p. xxxiii)

Hillhead Halls 100 flats, 1 pub rm, 5-6 bedrms, sleeps 5-6, £161-£173, mid Mar-mid Apr, Jul-Sep, bus nearby, rail 2 mls, airport 6 mls

  ♿ WC E 📻 🅰 🖳 🗄 🌀 🗄 📦 ✏ 🔌 🅿 ∥ 🐎 🎞 ◆ 🧭   🎣 🔍 ⚓ 🎿 ∪ ⚲ ▸ 🆁 ✕
💼 🍴 🆃

University of Aberdeen, Conference Office, Kings College, Regent Walk, Aberdeen, AB9 1FX
☎ *Aberdeen (0224) 480241 Ext 5171 Telex 73458*

1 flat, 1 pub rm, 2 bedrms, sleeps 3, min let 2 weeks, £70-£95, Jul-Sep, bus nearby, rail 1 ml, airport 7 mls

  ♿ WC E ⇥ 📻 🅰 🖳 🗄 🌀 🗄 📞 📦 🧺 ✳ 🅿 🐎 †   🎿 ∪ ⚓ ⚲ ▸ ✕ 💼

Mrs M Black, 9 Devanha Gardens South, Aberdeen, AB1 2UG
☎ *Aberdeen (0224) 595872*

2 cottages, 1 pub rm, 2 bedrms, sleeps 5, £81-£130, Jan-Dec, bus 2 mls, rail 5 mls, airport 7 mls

  ♿ WC E ⇥ 🅰 🖳 🗄 🌀 🗄 📦 🗄 🧺 ⊙ ✳ 🐾 🅿 🐎 🎞   🎣 🔍 ▸ 💼 🔭

Mrs Haggart, Bodachra, Dyce, Aberdeen, AB2 0AR
☎ *Aberdeen (0224) 704210*

2 flats, 1 pub rm, 1-2 bedrms, sleeps 4-5, £95-£120, Jan-Dec, bus nearby, airport 5 mls

  ♿ WC E ⇥ 🅰 🗄 🌀 🗄 📦 🗄 🧺 ⊙ 🅿 †   ✕ 💼

Mrs R Buchanan, 6 Endrick Place, Summerhill, Aberdeen, AB2 6EF
☎ *Aberdeen (0224) 637449/319991*

20 flats, 1 pub rm, 6 bedrms, sleeps 6, £145, Jul-Sep, bus 400 yds, rail 3 mls, airport 4 mls

  ♿ WC E ⇥ 📻 🅰 🖳 🗄 🌀 🗄 🗄 🧺 ⊙ 🐾 🅿 🐎 † 🧭   🎣 🔍 ✕ 💼

Aberdeen College of Education, Hilton Place, Aberdeen, AB9 1FA
☎ *Aberdeen (0224) 483386*

VAT is shown at 15%: changes in this rate may affect prices.

ABERFELDY Perthshire Map Ref. 2B1

1 house, 2 pub rms, 4 bedrms, sleeps 8, min let weekend, from £65, Jan-Dec

Mrs D D McDiarmid, Castle Menzies Home Farm, Aberfeldy, Perthshire, PH15 2LY
☎ Aberfeldy (0887) 20260

---

3 caravans, sleeps 6-8, min let 1 night (low season), £60-£90, Apr-Sep, bus 5 mls, rail 14 mls

Mrs May Scott, Donafuil Farm, Keltneyburn, Aberfeldy, Perthshire, PH15 2LE
☎ Kenmore (08873) 371

---

6 houses, 1 flat, 1 gothic tower, 1-2 pub rms, 3 bedrms, sleeps 4-8, £100-£300, Apr-Oct

Finlayson Hughes, Bank House, 82 Atholl Road, Pitlochry, Perthshire, PH16 5BL
☎ Pitlochry (0796) 2512

---

2 cottages, 1 pub rm, 2 bedrms, sleeps 3-6, min let weekend (low season), from £65, Jan-Dec, bus 1 ml, rail 14 mls

Mrs J MacDiarmid, Mains of Murthly, Aberfeldy, Perthshire, PH15 2EA
☎ Aberfeldy (0887) 20427

---

1 flat, 2 pub rms, 3 bedrms, sleeps 7, £95, May-Oct, bus nearby, rail 16 mls
(recreation centre)

D M MacLeod, Beechfield, Old Crieff Road, Aberfeldy, Perthshire
☎ Aberfeldy (0887) 20520/20905

---

1 house, 1 pub rm, 3 bedrms, sleeps 7, min let 1 night, £150-£200, Jan-Dec, bus ½ ml, rail 14 mls, airport 80 mls

Mrs I Ferguson, Maskeliya, Crieff Road, Aberfeldy, Perthshire
☎ Aberfeldy (0887) 20431

by ABERFELDY Perthshire Map Ref. 2B1

2 houses, 2 pub rms, 3-4 bedrms, sleeps 5-8, from £75, Mar-Oct, bus ½ ml, rail 10 mls

Mrs C Thomson, West Park Farm, Aberfeldy, Perthshire, PH15 2EQ
☎ Strathtay (08874) 224

ABERFOYLE Perthshire Map Ref. 1H3

1 cottage, 2 pub rms, 3 bedrms, sleeps 5, £95-£175, Apr-Oct, bus 400 yds, rail 17 mls, airport 34 mls
(cycling)

Mrs A E R Martin, 30 Broadstone Park, Inverness
☎ Inverness (0463) 237949

　　　　Prices shown are for guidance only. Please send SAE with each enquiry.

by ABERFOYLE Perthshire Map Ref. 1H3

1 cottage, 2 pub rms, 3 bedrms, sleeps 5, min let weekend (low season), £80-£200, Jan-Dec, bus nearby(postbus), rail 20 mls, airport 35 mls

Mrs L Stott, Creag Darach, Milton of Aberfoyle, Perthshire
☎ *Aberfoyle (08772) 476*

ABERLADY East Lothian Map Ref. 2E4

COMMENDED

1 cottage, 1 pub rm, 3 bedrms, sleeps 7, £120-£185, Jan-Dec, bus nearby, rail 3 mls, airport 23 mls

Mr Binnie, Kilspindie House Hotel, Aberlady, East Lothian
☎ *Aberlady (08757) 319*
Detached with it's own small garden. Run as part of the Kilspindie House Hotel.

ABERLEMNO, by Forfar Angus Map Ref. 2E1

1 cottage, 1 pub rm, 2 bedrms, sleeps 4-6, £65-£100, Jul-Oct, bus 1 ml, rail 10 mls, airport 22 mls

(beautiful walks)

The Hon Mrs R Leslie Melville, Balgarrock, Aberlemno, Forfar, Angus
☎ *Aberlemno (030783) 219*

ABOYNE Aberdeenshire Map Ref. 4F11

Aboyne Loch Caravan Park 8 chalet/log cabins, 1 pub rm, 2 bedrms, sleeps 4, min let 3 nights, £80-£180, Apr-Oct, bus nearby

(gliding)

8 caravans, sleeps 6, min let 3 nights, £70-£165, Apr-Oct, bus nearby, rail 29 mls, ferry 29 mls, airport 29 mls

(gliding)

Aboyne Loch Caravan Park, Aboyne, Aberdeenshire, AB3 5BR
☎ *Aboyne (0339) 2244*

COMMENDED

1 cottage, 2 pub rms, 2 bedrms, sleeps 4-5, £130-£140, Jan-Dec, bus nearby

(gliding)

Mrs D Tanner, St Katherine's, Aboyne, Aberdeenshire
☎ *Aboyne (0339) 2551*
Modern two storied house with small garden in quiet location. Well placed for touring Royal Deeside.

---

1 bungalow, 1 pub rm, 2-3 bedrms, sleeps 4-6, min let 1 night, £110-£150, Jan-Dec, bus 300 yds, rail 30 mls, airport 30 mls

(gliding)

Mrs D J Barber, St Lesmo Tower, Aboyne, Aberdeenshire, AB3 5HH
☎ *Aboyne (0339) 2197/(033981) 249 (day)*

---

5 houses, 3 cottages, 1 pub rm, 2-4 bedrms, sleeps 4-8, £95-£155, Mar-Oct, rail 30 mls

Mrs Ross, Estate Office(STB), Dinnet, Aboyne, Aberdeenshire, AB3 5LL
☎ *Dinnet (033985) 341/342*

by ABOYNE Aberdeenshire Map Ref. 4F11

1 cottage, 2 pub rms, 3 bedrms, sleeps 6, £92-£127, Mar-Oct, bus 1 ml, rail 25 mls, airport 25 mls

Mr & Mrs A D M Farquharson, Finzean House, Finzean, Banchory, Kincardineshire, AB3 5ED
☎ *Feughside (033045) 229*

COMMENDED
♛ ♛ ♛

1 cottage, 1 pub rm, 1 bedrm, sleeps 2, £55-£84, Jan-Dec, bus nearby, rail 30 mls, airport 30 mls

Mrs I Strachan, Oldyleiper, Birse, Aboyne, Aberdeenshire, AB3 5BY
☎ *Aboyne (0339) 2232*
Converted farm cottage in quiet country setting. Convenient for touring Royal Deeside.

ABRIACHAN Inverness-shire Map Ref. 4A9

COMMENDED
♛ ♛ ♛

1 house, 1-2 pub rms, 2-3 bedrms, sleeps 6, min let weekend, £68-£138, Apr-Oct, bus 2 mls, rail 12 mls, airport 16 mls

Achabuie Holidays, Achbuie, Abriachan, Inverness-shire, IV3 6LE
☎ *Dochgarroch (046386) 285*
Close to working croft. Peaceful position high above Loch Ness. Superb views.

ACHARACLE Argyll Map Ref. 3E12

3 caravans, sleeps 6, min let weekend, from £65, Apr-Oct, bus 1½ mls, rail 15 mls
(windsurfing)
Mrs M Macaulay, Dalilea Farm House, Acharacle, Argyll, PH36 4JX
☎ *Salen (096785) 253*

3 caravans, sleeps 6, min let weekend, £55-£60, Apr-Oct, bus nearby, rail 21 mls

Mrs M Cameron, Ardshealach, Acharacle, Argyll, PH36 4JL
☎ *Salen (096785) 209*

1 house, 2 pub rms, 3 bedrms, sleeps 5, from £95, Apr-Oct

Bell-Ingram, Durn, Isla Road, Perth, PH2 7HF
☎ *Perth (0738) 21121*

Glencripesdale House 1 cottage, 1 pub rm, 1 bedrm, sleeps 4, £70-£120, Jan-Dec

Glencripesdale House, Loch Sunart, Acharacle, Argyll, PH36 4JH
☎ *Salen (096785) 263*

Prices shown are for guidance only. Please send SAE with each enquiry.

1 flat, 4 cottages, 1 pub rm, 1-2 bedrms, sleeps 2-5, min let weekend (low season), from £80, Jan-Dec, bus 3 mls, rail 15 mls

♿ ⓦⓒ E ↩ ⌐ ⌀ ▯ ⌀▢ ≠ ⊢ P ⌂ ⊞ † ◉   ◔ ♩ △ ⌣ ∕ T (table tennis)

Mr R Stead, Eilean Shona, Acharacle, Argyll, PA36 4LR
☎ *Salen (096785) 249*
Units situated on Island of Eilean Shona . Access by private ferry. Sea views.

ACHARN, by Aberfeldy Perthshire Map Ref. 2A1

6 houses, 1 pub rm, 2-3 bedrms, sleeps 4-8, min let weekend, £95-£285, Jan-Dec, bus 7 ½ mls, rail 21 mls, airport 80 mls

♿ ⓦⓒ E ↩ ⌀ ▦ ▯ ▢ ◎ ▯▢ ≠ ⌐ ⊙ ✳ ⊢ P ⌂ ⊞ ⋀   ♩ ∪ △ ⊢ ∕ ⪼ ⪚ ✗ ▤ ▥ T

A & J Duncan Millar, Loch Tay Lodges, Remony, Aberfeldy, Perthshire, PH15 2HR
☎ *Kenmore (08873) 465*
Converted listed building in picturesque highland village. Sailing, fishing and many lovely walks.

ACHFARY Sutherland Map Ref. 3H4

1 house, 4 cottages, 2-3 pub rms, 2-4 bedrms, sleeps 3-7, £73-£145, Apr-Oct, bus 1 ml, rail 30 mls

♿ ⓦⓒ E ↩ ⌀ ◎ ▯ ⌐ ▢ ◪ ⊙ ✳ ⊢ P ⌂ ⊞ †   ♩ ▥

The Factor, Estate Office, Achfary, by Lairg, Sutherland, IV27 4PQ
☎ *Lochmore (097184) 221*
Units of individual character, on large shooting estate amidst rugged scenery of N.W. Sutherland.

ACHILTIBUIE Ross-shire Map Ref. 3G6

1 cottage, 2 pub rms, 4 bedrms, sleeps 8, £80-£150, Apr-Oct, rail 80 mls

♿ ⓦⓒ E ↩ ⌐ ⌀ ◎ ▯▢ ▢ ◪ ⊙ ✳ ⊢ P ⌂ ⊞ †   ♩ ⪚ ✗ ▥

Mrs Macgillivray, Cluny Mains, Laggan, by Newtonmore, Inverness-shire, PH20 1BS
☎ *Laggan (05284) 228*

---

1 house, 2 pub rms, 3 bedrms, sleeps 6, £87-£168, Apr-Oct, bus 22 mls

♿ ⓦⓒ E ↩ ⌐ ⌀ ▦ ▯ ▯ ◎ ▢ ▯▢ ≠ ◪ ⊙ ✳ P †   ♩ △ ⪚ ✗ ▥

Mrs Strachan, Oldyleiper, Birse, Aboyne, Aberdeenshire
☎ *Aboyne (0339) 2232*
Recently modernised house in elevated, peaceful site. Fine views to Summer Isles and Dundonnel Hills.

---

1 cottage, 2 pub rms, 3 bedrms, sleeps 5-6, £85-£130, Mar-Nov, bus ½ ml, rail 60 mls, airport 90 mls

♿ ⓦⓒ E ↩ ⌀ ▯ ⌀ ▯ ▢ ≠ ◪ ⊙ ✳ ⊢ P ⌂ ⊞ †   ♩ △ ⪚ ✗ ▥

Mrs H Mackenzie, Achnahaird, Achiltibuie, Ross-shire
☎ *Achiltibuie (085482) 348*

---

1 chalet/log cabin, 1 pub rm, 2 bedrms, sleeps 4-6, min let 1 night, £85-£160, Jan-Dec, bus 2 ½ mls, rail 55 mls

♿ ⓦⓒ E ↩ ⌐ ⌀ ▦ ◎ ▯▢ ◪ ⊙ ⊢ P ⌂ ⊞ ⋀   ♩ △ ⌣ ⪼ ✗ ▥ ▤ (sea cruises)

Mr M W Macleod, Dornie House, Achiltibuie, by Ullapool, Ross-shire
☎ *Achiltibuie (085482) 271*

VAT is shown at 15%: changes in this rate may affect prices.

by ACHILTIBUIE Ross-shire Map Ref. 3G6

COMMENDED
♛♛♛

1 chalet/log cabin, 1 pub rm, 2 bedrms, sleeps 4, £80-£150, Feb-Nov, bus 1 ½ mls, rail 50 mls

♿ 🚾 E 📷 🏠 🎹 🗄 ◎ 🗄 🗄 🛒 ⊙ ❋ 🐎 P 🐕 ▥ 🛒 † 🏔   🎵 ⚡ ✕ 🧺 🔭 T

Mrs W MacLeod, Tigh Uisdean, Polglass, Achiltibuie, Ross-shire
☎ *Achiltibuie (085482) 266*
Modern; high isolated site with superb views over sea to Summer Isles. Village 1 mile (2km).

---

up to
COMMENDED
♛♛♛

Port Beag Chalets 8 chalet/log cabins, 1 pub rm, 2-3 bedrms, sleeps 6, min let 1 night, £84-£195, Mar-Nov, bus 4 mls, rail 35 mls, airport 95 mls

♿ 🚾 E 🛒 📷 🏠 🎹 🗄 ◎ 🗄 📞 🗄 📷 🚿 🛒 ⊙ ❋ 🐎 P 🐕 ▥ 🛒 † 🏔   🎵 ⚠ ⚡ ✕ 🧺

Mr & Mrs D A MacLeod, Port Beag Chalets, Altandhu, Achiltibuie, Ullapool, Ross-shire, IV26 2YG
☎ *Achiltibuie (085482) 279*
Units of varying design and style, on private site near shore. Fine views of Summer Isles.

ACHINDUICH, by Lairg Sutherland Map Ref. 4A6

1 cottage, 1 pub rm, 2 bedrms, sleeps 4, £47-£68, Apr-Oct, bus 7 mls, rail 2 ½ mls, airport 51 mls

♿ 🚾 E 🛒 🏠 🎹 ◎ 🗄 🚿 🛒 ⊙ ❋ P 🐕 † 🎵 ∪ ▸ ✕ 🔭

Mrs M A Macleod, Achinduich, Lairg, Sutherland, IV27 4EX
☎ *Invershin (054982) 250*

ACHMELVICH, by Lochinver Sutherland Map Ref. 3G5

Hillhead Caravan Site 6 caravans, sleeps 6, min let 3 nights, from £60, Apr-Sep, bus 1 ½ mls, rail 48 mls, airport 110 mls

🚿 📞 P 🏔   🎵 ∪ ⚠ ⚡ ∕ ⌕ ✕ 🧺 (hill walking, mountaineering)

D H Macleod, Hillhead, Lochinver, Sutherland, IV27 4JA
☎ *Lochinver (05714) 206*

ACHNACARRY AREA Inverness-shire Map Ref. 3G11

3 cottages, 1 lodge, 1-3 pub rms, 2-7 bedrms, sleeps 4-11, from £105, Apr-Oct, rail 15 mls

♿ 🚾 E 🛒 🏠 ◎ 🚿 🗄 🗄 📷 ❋ 🐎 P 🐕 ▥ †   🎵 ⚠

West Highland Estates Office, 33 High Street, Fort William, Inverness-shire, PH33 6DJ
☎ *Fort William (0397) 2433/2434*

ACHNAMARA Argyll Map Ref. 1E4

APPROVED
♛

1 house, 1 pub rm, 3 bedrms, sleeps 5, from £60, Jan-Dec, bus 9 mls

♿ 🚾 E 🏠 ◎ 🗄 ❋ 🐎 P 🐕 ▥ †   🎵 ⚠ ⚡ ▸ ∕ 🧺

Forestry Commission, Forest Holidays, Dept SC1, 231 Corstorphine Road, Edinburgh, EH12 7AT
☎ *031 334 0303*
Semi detached, on small forestry estate. Quiet location with good views over Loch Sween.

ACHNASHEEN Ross-shire Map Ref. 3G8

1 bungalow, 1 pub rm, 3 bedrms, sleeps 5, £80-£150, Apr-Oct, rail 330 yds

♿ 🚾 E 🛒 📷 🏠 🎹 🗄 ◎ 🗄 🗄 📷 🛒 ⊙ ❋ 🐎 P 🐕 ▥ †   🎵 ∕ R ✕ 🧺 🍴 T

Achnasheen Hotel, Achnasheen, Ross-shire
☎ *Achnasheen (044588) 243*

AIGNISH Isle of Lewis, Western Isles Map Ref. 3D4

1 flat, 1 pub rm, 2 bedrms, sleeps 4-5, £60-£80, Jan-Dec, bus nearby, ferry 4 ½ mls, airport 2 mls

A MacSween, 21 Aignish, Point, Isle of Lewis, Western Isles
☎ *Garrabost (0851) 870258*

AIRIDHBHRUAICH Isle of Lewis, Western Isles Map Ref. 3C5

1 cottage, 2 pub rms, 2 bedrms, sleeps 4, max £55, Jan-Dec, bus nearby, ferry 17-18 mls, airport 20 mls

Mrs C Macdonald, 66 Balallan, Lochs, Isle of Lewis, Western Isles

AITHSETTER, Cunningsburgh Shetland Map Ref. 5G5

1 cottage, 1 pub rm, 2 bedrms, sleeps 4, £45-£65, Jan-Dec, bus ½ ml, ferry 10 mls, airport 15 mls

Mrs I J Rendall, 7 Helendale Drive, Lerwick, Shetland
☎ *Lerwick (0595) 3485*

ALCAIG, by Conon Bridge Ross-shire Map Ref. 4A8

2 cottages, 1 pub rm, 3 bedrms, sleeps 6-7, £50-£100, May-Sep, bus 1 ml, rail 3 mls, airport 17 mls

Mrs M MacDuff-Duncan, Alcaig, Conon Bridge, Ross-shire, IV7 8HS
☎ *Dingwall (0349) 61220*
On private driveway with fine views over open farmland. Good touring base.

ALFORD Aberdeenshire Map Ref. 4F10

1 castle, 3 pub rms, 5 bedrms, sleeps 9, £360, Jan-Dec, bus 1 ml, rail 12 mls, airport 27 mls

Mr Mark Tennant, 8 New Square, Lincoln's Inn, London, WC2A 3QP
☎ *01 242 4986*

Haughton House 5 flats, 1 bungalow, 1 pub rm, 1-2 bedrms, sleeps 2-8, min let 2 nights, £85-£115, Apr-Oct, bus 1 ml, rail 7 mls, airport 25 mls

2 caravans, sleeps 6, min let 2 nights, £75-£80, Apr-Oct, bus 1 ml, rail 7 mls, airport 25 mls

(putting green, narrow gauge railway)
The Warden, Haughton Caravan Park, Montgarrie Road, Alford, Aberdeenshire, AB3 8NA
☎ *Alford (0336) 2107*

by ALFORD Aberdeenshire Map Ref. 4F10

1 cottage, 1 pub rm, 2 bedrms, sleeps 6, £55-£95, Jan-Dec, bus 5 mls, rail 32 mls, airport 35 mls

Mrs M Alexander, Croft of Elphillock, Glenkindie, Alford, Aberdeenshire, AB3 8SE
☎ *Kildrummy (03365) 266*

VAT is shown at 15%: changes in this rate may affect prices.

1 cottage, 1 pub rm, 2 bedrms, sleeps 6, min let weekend, £50-£95, Jan-Dec, bus 3 mls, rail 19 mls, airport 35 mls

Mrs E Hendry, Knowehead, Glenkindie, Aberdeenshire, AB3 8SH
☎ *Kildrummy (03365) 334*

---

1 cottage, 2 pub rms, 4 bedrms, sleeps 8, £75-£125, Apr-Oct, bus ½ ml, rail 30 mls, airport 30 mls

Lt Col C D Craigie Halkett, Cushnie House, Cushnie, by Alford, Aberdeenshire, AB3 8LB
☎ *Muir of Fowlis (03364) 321*

---

1 cottage, 2 pub rms, 2 bedrms, sleeps 6, £60-£90, Apr-Dec, bus 7 mls, rail 28 mls, airport 26 mls

Mr Colin Wallace, Brideswell, Cushnie, by Alford, Aberdeenshire, AB3 8LD
☎ *Muir of Fowlis (03364) 266*

ALLANFEARN, by Inverness Inverness-shire Map Ref. 4B8

1 cottage, 1 pub rm, 3 bedrms, sleeps 4, £90-£150, Apr-Oct, bus 1 ml, rail 5 mls, airport 4 mls

Mrs I MacGillivray, Bothy Hill, Allanfearn, by Inverness, Inverness-shire
☎ *Inverness (0463) 236260*

ALNESS Ross-shire Map Ref. 4B7

1 house, 2 cottages, 1-2 pub rms, 4 bedrms, sleeps 8, £92-£345, May-Oct

Mrs F Agnew, Drumarbin, Swordale Road, Evanton, Ross-shire
☎ *Evanton (0349) 830179*

---

1 house, 1 pub rm, 2 bedrms, sleeps 4, £55-£75, Apr-Oct, bus 500 yds, rail 300 yds

Mrs Dzialdowski, 12 Market Street, Alness, Ross-shire
☎ *Alness (0349) 883047*

ALTASS Sutherland Map Ref. 4A6

1 house, 3 pub rms, 5 bedrms, sleeps 9, £80-£110, Apr-Nov, bus 2 mls, rail 8 mls, airport 60 mls

Mrs Colin Gilmour, Shenaval, Altass, by Lairg, Sutherland, IV27 4EU
☎ *Rosehall (084984) 204*

ALVA Clackmannanshire Map Ref. 2B4

1 cottage, 1 pub rm, 2-3 bedrms, sleeps 4-6, £85, Jun-Sep, bus nearby, rail 7 mls

Mrs L Muir, Burnside Farm, Alva, Clackmannanshire, FK12 5HT
☎ *Alva (0259) 60229*

ALVES Moray Map Ref. 4D8

8 caravans, sleeps 6-8, min let 1 night, £60-£105, Apr-Oct, bus 1 ml, rail 6 mls

North Alves Caravan Park, Alves, Elgin, Moray, IV30 3XD
☎ *Alves (034385) 223*

ALYTH Perthshire Map Ref. 2C1

1 bungalow, 2 pub rms, 2 bedrms, sleeps 4-6, min let weekend, £80-£120, Jan-Dec, bus 6 mls, rail 22 mls, airport 60 mls

Mrs Langlands, Dalbhraddan Farm, Kilry, by Alyth, Perthshire, PH11 8HN
☎ *Lintrathen (05756) 246*

---

1 cottage, 1 pub rm, 2 bedrms, sleeps 4-6, min let weekend, from £115, Apr-Oct, bus 1 ½ mls, rail 20 mls

Mr & Mrs Brian Groom, East Tullyfergus Farm, Alyth, Perthshire
☎ *Alyth (08283) 3251*

---

by ALYTH Perthshire Map Ref. 2C1

1 cottage, 1 pub rm, 2 bedrms, sleeps 5, min let weekend, £50-£80, Mar-Dec, bus 5 mls, rail 24 mls

Mrs Nicoll, Easter Craig, Alyth, Blairgowrie, Perthshire, PH11 8HN
☎ *Lintrathen (05756) 280*

---

1 house, 2 cottages, 1-2 pub rms, 2-3 bedrms, sleeps 4-6, £80-£150, Jan-Dec, bus 2 mls

Maxwell H Wilson, Conifers, Blairmore Drive, Rosemount, Blairgowrie, Perthshire
☎ *Blairgowrie (0250) 2961*

---

1 cottage, 1 bungalow, 1 pub rm, 2 bedrms, sleeps 6, min let weekend, £60-£80, Apr-Oct, bus 2 mls

Mrs Ferguson, Fyal Farm, Bamff Road, Alyth, Perthshire
☎ *Alyth (08283) 2997*

AMULREE Perthshire Map Ref. 2B2

2 houses, 1 bungalow, 1-2 pub rms, 3-4 bedrms, sleeps 5-9, min let weekend, £65-£140, Apr-Oct, bus 15 mls, rail 25 mls, airport 50 mls

The Caretaker, Auchnafree, Amulree, Dunkeld, Perthshire, PH8 0EH
☎ *Amulree (03505) 233*

ANSTRUTHER Fife Map Ref. 2E3

1 flat, 1 cottage, 1 bunkhouse, 1 pub rm, 2 bedrms, sleeps 4-12, min let weekend, £95-£140, Jan-Dec, bus nearby, rail 14 mls, airport 50 mls

(diving facilities)

L G Pennington, West Pitkierie Farm, Anstruther, Fife
☎ *Anstruther (0333) 310768*

VAT is shown at 15%: changes in this rate may affect prices.

COMMENDED
♛♛♛

5 flats, 2 pub rms, 2-3 bedrms, sleeps 4-8, min let weekend (low season), £101-£224, Jan-Dec, bus nearby, rail 12 mls, airport 50 mls

🕭♿ E ⬅ ☏ ⌂ ▦ 🛏 ◎ ⬜ ☎ ⬛ ◻ 🗑 ⚡ ⬛ ☉ ❄ ♜ P ∥ ☞ 🛋 ➡ † 🏠 🔍 ⬥ ↖
🦆 ✿ ♩ ∪ △ ⚓ ↗ ✎ ✕ 🎒 ♫ Ⓣ (abseiling, cycles, windsurfing, canoeing)

Crispin Heath, East Neuk Outdoors, 25 High Street East, Anstruther, Fife, KY10 3DQ
☎ *Anstruther (0333) 311929*

Family holidays in listed victorian house overlooking sands and old harbour. Extensive leisure.

---

1 caravan, sleeps 7-8, £55-£139, Apr-Oct, bus nearby, rail 9 mls

🕭♿ E ☏ ⌂ ⌀ ⬜ ☎ ◻ 🗑 ⚡ P † 🏠 🔍 ✦ ⬥ 🦆 ♩ ∪ △ ⚓ ↗ ✕ 🎒 Ⓣ

Mrs Helen Milne, 103 Balunie Drive, Dundee, Angus
☎ *Dundee (0382) 43954/454363*

---

1 flat, 1 pub rm, 1 bedrm, sleeps 5, £80-£100, Mar-Oct, bus nearby, rail 14 mls

🕭♿ E ☏ ⌀ ▦ 🛏 ◎ ⬜ 🗑 ⚡ ⬛ ☉ P ☞ † ⬥ ✦ 🦆 ♩ △ ⚓ ↗ ✕ 🎒

Mrs C Anderson, The Old Schoolhouse, School Road, Anstruther, Fife
☎ *Anstruther (0333) 310472*

APPIN Argyll Map Ref. 1E1

Overlooking Sea Loch...
APPIN HOLIDAY HOMES
APPIN · ARGYLL
Resident proprietors:
Mr & Mrs I. Weir (063173) 287

Ten new timber bungalows, three traditional cottages (fully furnished and equipped, bed linen, and colour TV included), and eight fully serviced residential caravans set apart right on lochside. Superb homes in a superb setting midway **OBAN-FORT WILLIAM.** Magnificent views. **FREE FISHING** (salt and freshwater). Boats available. Sailing, hill-walking, bird watching. Truly a nature lover's paradise. Recreation room, telephone. Good parking. Baby-sitting service. Ideal for families, also honeymoons! Pony-trekking and licensed Inn nearby. Good touring centre. Open all year round. Special Spring, Autumn and Winter terms. Highly recommended. Please send SAE for free colour brochure giving number in party and dates required. Immediate reply assured.
APPIN HOLIDAY HOMES (DEPT. S.), APPIN, ARGYLL PA38 4BQ. Tel: (063173) 287.

up to
COMMENDED
♛♛♛

Appin Holiday Homes 10 chalet/log cabins, 1 cottage, 1 bungalow, 1-2 pub rms, 2 bedrms, sleeps 2-6, min let weekend (low season), £85-£230, Jan-Dec, bus nearby, rail 16 mls

🕭♿ E ⬅ ☏ ⌀ ▦ 🛏 ◎ ⬜ ☎ ⬛ ☉ ❄ P ∥ ☞ 🛋 ➡ † 🏠 🔍 ♩ ∪ △ ⚓ ✕
🎒 Ⓣ (rowing)

8 caravans, sleeps 2-6, min let weekend (low season), £75-£175, Apr-Oct, bus nearby, rail 16 mls

🕭♿ E ☏ ⌀ ⌀ ⬜ ☎ ◻ ☉ P ☞ 🛋 ➡ 🏠 🔍 ✦ ♩ ∪ △ ⚓ ↗ ⚱ ✕ 🎒 (rowing boats for hire)

Mr & Mrs I Weir, Appin Holiday Homes, Dungrianach, Appin, Argyll
☎ *Appin (063173) 287*

Timber bungalows and traditional cottages with excellent views over Loch Creran to hills beyond.

Prices shown are for guidance only. Please send SAE with each enquiry.

Kinlochlaich House & Gardens
APPIN · ARGYLL   Tel: 063 173 342

Overlooking Loch Linnhe, midway between Oban and Fort William, five properties sleeping 2 up to 6, furnished to a high standard. Open Christmas to October. Special attractions include West Highlands largest Garden Centre, ski-ing (Glencoe), climbing, sailing, water ski-ing, surfboarding, fishing, pony-trekking and touring. Activities can be organised for children.

SAE or telephone for brochure:
D. E. HUTCHISON, KINLOCHLAICH HOUSE, APPIN, ARGYLL.
PA38 4BD

AWAITING INSPECTION

4 flats, 1 cottage, 1 pub rm, 1-2 bedrms, sleeps 2-6, min let 2 nights (low season), from £52, Dec-Oct, bus nearby, rail 18 mls

Mr D E Hutchison, Kinlochlaich House, Appin, Argyll, PA38 4BD
☎ *Appin (063173) 342*

---

2 cottages, 1-2 pub rms, 3-4 bedrms, sleeps 6-9, £60-£140, Jan-Dec, bus nearby, rail 20 mls, airport 80 mls

M L Fletcher, Park Farm, Charsfield, Woodbridge, Suffolk, IP12 4LY
☎ *Charsfield (047337) 207*

---

up to COMMENDED

1 flat, 2 apartments, 1 pub rm, 1-3 bedrms, sleeps 4-8, min let 1 night (ex Easter, Jul/Aug), £55-£190, Jan-Dec, bus nearby, rail 20 mls, airport 100 mls

Mrs Mathieson, Appin House, Appin, Argyll
☎ *Appin (063173) 207*
Units of individual character and design adjoining historic country house. Large garden. Superb view.

APPLECROSS Ross-shire Map Ref. 3E9

Applecross Campsite 7 caravans, sleeps 4-8, min let 1 night, £47-£170, Apr-Oct, rail 20 mls

Mr Goldthorpe, Applecross Campsite, Applecross, Ross-shire
☎ *Applecross (05204) 284(reception)*

ARBROATH Angus Map Ref. 2E1

Red Lion Caravan Site 44 caravans, sleeps 6, min let 3 nights, from £70, Apr-Oct

Red Lion Caravan Site, Dundee Road, Arbroath, Angus
☎ *Arbroath (0241) 72038*

---

1 flat, 1 pub rm, 2-3 bedrms, sleeps 4-6, £108-£246, Jan-Dec, bus 1 ml, rail 4 mls, airport 20 mls

Mr G H Coulson, Kelly Castle, Arbirlot, Arbroath, Angus
☎ *Arbroath (0241) 72383*

ARDANEASKAN Ross-shire Map Ref. 3F9

1 cottage, 1 pub rm, 2 bedrms, sleeps 6, from £40, Mar-Nov, bus 5 mls, rail 10 mls, airport 70 mls

2 caravans, sleeps 6, min let 1 night, from £30, Mar-Nov, bus 5 mls, rail 10 mls, airport 70 mls

Mrs MacKay, Oak Dale, Ardaneaskan, Lochcarron, Ross-shire, IV54 8YL
☎ *Lochcarron (05202) 281*

ARDBRECKNISH Argyll Map Ref. 1F3

Ardbrecknish Loch Awe

DELIGHTFUL self catering COTTAGES AND APARTMENTS for 2 to 12 in ENCHANTING 17th-century country house with superb situation in peaceful lochside garden and woodland grounds in an area of outstanding natural beauty. OWNER/ARCHITECT DESIGNED conversion, COMORTABLE and WELL-EQUIPPED with TVs, bed linen and cots. INDOOR and OUTDOOR FACILITIES include games rooms, badminton and putting lawns, trim trail, adventure and toddlers' play areas, barbecues, laundry and visitors' library. SECLUDED BEACHES. EXCELLENT OPPORTUNITIES for FISHING, MOTOR and SAIL BOATING and WILDLIFE STUDY. IDEAL walking, climbing, trekking and touring centre in the heart of Argyll. OPEN ALL YEAR ROUND.

Enquiries and bookings to: **Donald & Beth Wilson, Ardbrecknish House, Loch Aweside, by Dalmally, Argyll PA33 1BH. Tel. (08663) 223.**

COMMENDED

9 flats, 1-2 pub rms, 1-5 bedrms, sleeps 2-12, min let weekend (low season), £40-£330, Jan-Dec, bus 8 mls, rail 8 mls

D J & B D Wilson, Ardbrecknish House, Lochaweside, by Dalmally, Argyll
☎ *Kilchrenan (08663) 223*
Historic country house converted into architect designed units of individual character by lochside.

ARDELVE Ross-shire Map Ref. 3F9

4 cottages, 1 pub rm, 2 bedrms, sleeps 4-6, £75-£135, Jan-Dec, bus ¼-½ ml, rail 8 mls

Mrs Helen V Allan, Arras, Drumossie, Inverness, IV1 2BB
☎ *Inverness (0463) 230403*

1 bungalow, 1 pub rm, 3 bedrms, sleeps 6, £80-£95, Apr-Oct, bus ¼ ml, rail 7 mls, airport 70 mls

1 caravan, sleeps 6, £55-£60, Apr-Oct, bus ¼ ml, rail 7 mls, airport 70 mls

Mrs Catherine A MacDonald, Tigh-na-Bruaich, Leachkin Road, Inverness, IV3 6NW
☎ *Inverness (0463) 221467*

Prices shown are for guidance only. Please send SAE with each enquiry.

ARDEN Dunbartonshire Map Ref. 1G4

Lomond Castle Hotel & Leisure Centre 55 chalet/log cabins, 1 cottage, 1 pub rm, 2-3 bedrms, sleeps 2-6, min let 2 nights, £85-£295, Jan-Dec, bus nearby, rail 1 ½ mls, airport 15 mls

Hoseasons Holidays, Sunway House, Lowestoft, Suffolk, NR32 3LT
☎ *Lowestoft (0502) 62292*

ARDENTINNY, by Dunoon Argyll Map Ref. 1G4

Glenfinart Park 4 caravans, sleeps 4-6, min let 1 night, £70-£110, Apr-Oct, bus nearby, rail 14 mls, ferry 12 mls, airport 30 mls

June & Robin Worters, Glenfinart Park, Ardentinny, by Dunoon, Argyll, PA23 8TS
☎ *Ardentinny (036981) 256*

The Anchorage Holiday Complex 1 chalet/log cabin, 1 pub rm, 3 bedrms, sleeps 6, £150-£220, Apr-Oct, bus nearby, rail 14 mls, ferry 12 mls, airport 20 mls

Mrs I G Morrison, Anchorage, Ardentinny, by Dunoon, Argyll, PA23 8TR
☎ *Ardentinny (036981) 288*

STRONCHULLIN HOLIDAY COTTAGES

Four exceptional cottages beautifully situated with magnificent views of Loch Long and the Firth of Clyde. Built to a very high standard, these cottages sleep six people and stand in their own ground adjacent to the working farm of Stronchullin. Ideal for hill-walking, pony-trekking, sea angling or salmon fishing. Booking a holiday will automatically qualify for free entry to Benmore Botanical Gardens or to Blairmore Golf Club. **Three bedrooms to sleep six people with linen provided, large lounge, shower, fully equipped kitchen, electric heating, colour TV, Low season £110, High season £220. T. B. Marshall, Stronchullin Farm, Ardentinny, by Dunoon, Argyll PA23 8TD. Telephone: (036981) 246.**

4 cottages, 1 pub rm, 3 bedrms, sleeps 6, min let 3 nights, £102-£207, Mar-Dec, bus ¼ ml, rail 12 mls, ferry 9 mls, airport 29 mls

Mr T B Marshall, Stronchullin Farm, Ardentinny, by Dunoon, Argyll, PA23 8TP
☎ *Ardentinny (036981) 246*

ARDEONAIG, by Killin Perthshire Map Ref. 2A2

1 chalet/log cabin, 1 pub rm, 2 bedrms, sleeps 6, from £148, Apr-Oct

Bell-Ingram, Durn, Isla Road, Perth, PH2 7HF
☎ *Perth (0738) 21121*

ARDERSIER Inverness-shire Map Ref. 4B8

2 caravans, sleeps 6-8, £30-£70, Jan-Dec, bus ½ ml, rail 4 mls, airport 4 mls

Mrs M Miller, Bemuchlye, Ardersier, Inverness-shire, IV1 2QR
☎ *Ardersier (0667) 62354*

VAT is shown at 15%: changes in this rate may affect prices.

1 cottage, 2 pub rms, 3 bedrms, sleeps 6, £115-£125, May-Sep, bus nearby

Miss E Third, Long Forgon, Wood Dalling, Norwich, Norfolk
☎ *01 578 2298/Saxthorpe (026387) 316*

ARDFERN Argyll Map Ref. 1E3

4 cottages, 1 pub rm, 2 bedrms, sleeps 4-6, from £80, Jan-Dec, bus 2 mls, rail 25 mls

Mrs Littler, Loch Craignish Holiday Cottages, Ardfern, by Lochgilphead, Argyll, PA31 8QN
☎ *Barbreck (08525) 671*

---

3 cottages, 1 pub rm, 2-4 bedrms, sleeps 2-7, £60-£170, Apr-Oct, bus nearby, rail 25 mls, airport 100 mls

N L Boase, Ardlarach, Ardfern, by Lochgilphead, Argyll, PA31 8QR
☎ *Barbreck (08525) 284/270*

---

1 cottage, 2 pub rms, 4 bedrms, sleeps 8, min let weekend, £95-£235, Jan-Dec, bus 1 ½ mls, rail 25 mls, airport 100 mls

Mrs Wilson, High Auchensail, Cardross, Dumbartonshire, G82 5HN
☎ *Cardross (0389) 841297*

ARDGAY Sutherland Map Ref. 4A6

2 cottages, 1 pub rm, 2 bedrms, sleeps 4-5, from £120, Apr-Oct

Finlayson Hughes, Bank House, 82 Atholl Road, Pitlochry, Perthshire, PH16 5BL
☎ *Pitlochry (0796) 2512*

---

1 cottage, 1 pub rm, 3 bedrms, sleeps 6, from £45, Apr-Oct, bus ¼ ml, rail ¼ ml, airport 40 mls

Mrs M C Maclaren, The Poplars, Ardgay, Sutherland, IV24 3BG
☎ *Ardgay (08632) 302*

---

1 cottage, 1 wing of house, 1-2 pub rms, 2-4 bedrms, sleeps 2-8, min let 2 nights, £100-£125, Jan-Dec, bus 10 mls, rail 4 mls

Mr & Mrs P Jones, Strathkyle House, Culrain, by Ardgay, Sutherland, IV24 3DP
☎ *Invershin (054982) 203/238*

ARDGOUR Argyll Map Ref. 1F1

1 cottage, 1 pub rm, 3 bedrms, sleeps 5, from £150, Apr-Nov, bus 13 mls, rail 13 mls

West Highland Estates Office, 33 High Street, Fort William, Inverness-shire
☎ *Fort William (0397) 2433/2434*

Prices shown are for guidance only. Please send SAE with each enquiry.

ARDLUI Dunbartonshire Map Ref. 1 G3

Ardlui Hotel and Caravan Park
ARDLUI · LOCH LOMOND
DUNBARTONSHIRE
Telephone: 030 14 243

Nestling in the midst of magnificent scenery at the head of Loch Lomond, the Ardlui Caravan Park stands on the shore commanding a superb panoramic view of this most famous of Scottish Lochs.

Our fleet of luxury holiday caravans are 6 or 8 berth, well equipped and connected to mains services with W.C., Shower, Fridge, and Colour TV.

Hotel on site is fully licensed with two lounge bars serving meals, and restaurant open to non-residents.

Laundry, children's play area, boat hire, slipway, moorings, shop, and petrol station.

Ardlui is an ideal centre for touring, boating, water ski-ing, fishing, hill-walking and mountaineering.

Brochure on request to: Ardlui Hotel and Caravan Park, Loch Lomond, Dunbartonshire. Tel: (030 14) 243.

Ardlui Caravan Park 5 caravans, sleeps 6-8, min let 2 nights, £120-£180, mid Mar-Oct, bus nearby, rail nearby, airport 36 mls

Ardlui Caravan Park, Ardlui, Loch Lomond, Dunbartonshire, G83 7EB
☎ *Inveruglas (03014) 243*

ARDMADDY Argyll Map Ref. 1 E3

1 house, 1 flat, 3 cottages, 1-3 pub rms, 1-4 bedrms, sleeps 2-10, min let weekend (low season), £50-£300, Jan-Dec, bus 1 ½ mls, rail 12 mls, airport 15 mls

Mrs C H Struthers, Ardmaddy Castle, by Oban, Argyll, PA34 4QY
☎ *Balvicar (08523) 353*

ARDMAIR, by Ullapool Ross-shire Map Ref. 3G6

1 caravan, sleeps 5-6, £40-£45, Apr-Sep

Mrs I Mitchell, Ardmair Bay, by Ullapool, Ross-shire
☎ *Ullapool (0854) 2060*

ARDRISHAIG Argyll Map Ref. 1 E4

1 caravan, sleeps 6, min let weekend, from £60, Apr-Oct, bus nearby, rail nearby

Mrs M Graham, Maryville, Brackley Park, Ardrishaig, Argyll, PA38 8EU
☎ *Lochgilphead (0546) 2236*

---

1 cottage, 1-2 pub rms, 2 bedrms, sleeps 4, £90-£120, Easter-Nov, bus ½ ml, rail 50 mls

Mr M Murray, Kilmahumaig, Crinan, Lochgilphead, Argyll
☎ *Crinan (054683) 238*

ARDROSS Ross-shire Map Ref. 4A7

1 cottage, 1 pub rm, 2 bedrms, sleeps 3, min let 3 nights, £30-£70, Jan-Dec, bus 5 mls, rail 5 mls, airport 35 mls

Miss J Robertson, The Old House of Ardross, Ardross, by Alness, Ross-shire
☎ *Alness (0349) 882906*

ARDVASAR Isle of Skye, Inverness-shire Map Ref. 3E11

COMMENDED

1 cottage, 1 pub rm, 2 bedrms, sleeps 4-5, £70-£150, Jan-Dec, bus nearby, rail 5 mls, ferry ¾ ml, airport 16 mls

(countryside ranger service)

Mrs R C Bidwell, Point of Sleat, Ardvasar, Isle of Skye, Inverness-shire
☎ *Ardvasar (04714) 242/217*
Modern chalet bungalow, with granite chip garden. Double glazed throughout.

COMMENDED

1 chalet/log cabin, 1 pub rm, 2 bedrms, sleeps 4, £160-£200, Jan-Dec, bus ¼ mls, rail 26 mls

(guided nature trails)

Dr A J & Mrs R L Wright, Manninagh, Mold Road, Bodfari, Denbigh, Clwyd, LL16 4DS
☎ *Bodfari (074575) 363*
Modern A-frame unit in high position above village. Spectacular views across sound to Mallaig.

ARDWELL Wigtownshire Map Ref. 1F11

APPROVED

Ardwell Chalets 6 chalet/log cabins, 1 pub rm, 2 bedrms, sleeps 4-6, min let weekend (low season), £40-£120, Jan-Dec, bus nearby, rail 10 mls, airport 100 mls

Mrs M McFadzean, Killaser, Ardwell, by Stranraer, Wigtownshire
☎ *Ardwell (077686) 294*
Finnish designed wooden units. Direct access to beach. Near small village.

ARISAIG Inverness-shire Map Ref. 3E11

Gorten Sands Caravan Site 6 caravans, sleeps 6, min let weekend, £75-£180, Apr-Sep, bus ¾ ml, rail 2 mls, ferry 8 mls, airport 100 mls

Mr A Macdonald, Gorten Sands Caravan Site, Gorten Farm, Arisaig, Inverness-shire
☎ *Arisaig (06875) 283*

2 chalet/log cabins, 1 house, 1 cottage, 1-2 pub rms, 2-4 bedrms, sleeps 6-8, from £85, Apr-Oct, bus 3 mls

Mr Henderson, Traigh Farm, Arisaig, Inverness-shire, PH39 4NT
☎ *Arisaig (06875) 645*

2 cottages, 1 pub rm, 2 bedrms, sleeps 6, £110-£210, Apr-Oct, bus ½ ml, rail 1 ml, ferry 4 mls

6 caravans, sleeps 6, £70-£130, Apr-Oct, bus ½ ml, rail 1 ml, ferry 4 mls

Mr A Gillies, Kinloid Farm, Kilmartin, Arisaig, Inverness-shire
☎ *Arisaig (06875) 666*

1 chalet/log cabin, 1 cottage, 1-3 pub rms, 2-3 bedrms, sleeps 4-6, min let 3 nights, £45-£180, Jan-Dec, rail 1 ml, ferry 7 mls

  [symbols]

2 caravans, sleeps 4-6, min let weekend, £35-£65, Apr-Oct, rail 1 ml, ferry 7 mls

  [symbols]

L & S E Kent, Achnaskia, Arisaig, Inverness-shire, PH39 4NS
☎ *Arisaig (06875) 606*

ARIVEGAIG, by Acharacle Argyll Map Ref. 3E12

1 cottage, 2 pub rms, 2 bedrms, sleeps 4, from £75, May-Oct, rail 20 mls

  [symbols]

Mrs Borthwick, 10 Ash Road, Parkhall, Dalmuir, Dunbartonshire
☎ *Duntocher (0389) 72596*

ASHKIRK Selkirkshire Map Ref. 2E7

2 apartments, 1 pub rm, 2 bedrms, sleeps 2-5, min let weekend, £144-£180, Mar-Dec, bus ¼ ml, rail 45 mls, airport 45 mls

  [symbols]

Miss Amos, The Woll, Ashkirk, Selkirkshire
☎ *Ashkirk (0750) 32222/32269*

---

2 cottages, 1 pub rm, 3 bedrms, sleeps 6, £80-£100, May-Oct, bus ¾ ml, rail 44 mls, airport 45 mls

  [symbols]

Mrs Hogg, Headshaw Farm, Ashkirk, by Selkirk, Selkirkshire
☎ *Ashkirk (0750) 32233*
Terraced sandstone cottages on a working farm in rural setting halfway between Hawick and Selkirk.

ATTADALE, by Strathcarron Ross-shire Map Ref. 3F9

1 house, 4 cottages, 1-3 pub rms, 2-6 bedrms, sleeps 4-10, min let 2 weeks (high season), £90-£180, Mar-Nov, rail 1 ml

  [symbols]

Mrs Ewen Macpherson, Attadale, by Strathcarron, Ross-shire, IV54 8YX
☎ *Lochcarron (05202) 217/01 603 0895*

AUCHENBOWIE, by Stirling Stirlingshire Map Ref. 2A4

Auchenbowie Caravan Site 8 caravans, sleeps 4-6, min let 1 night, £60-£100, Apr-Oct, bus ½ ml, rail 3 ½ mls, airport 35 mls

  [symbols]

R Forsyth Esq, Easterton Service Station, Stirling Road, Denny, Stirlingshire
☎ *Denny (0324) 822142*

AUCHENCAIRN Kirkcudbrightshire Map Ref. 2B11

2 houses, 1 flat, 2 cottages, 1-2 pub rms, 1-3 bedrms, sleeps 2-7, min let weekend, £60-£170, Jan-Dec, bus 2 mls, rail 23 mls, airport 80 mls

  [symbols]

Mrs Rollinson, The Mews, Balcary, by Auchencairn, Kirkcudbrightshire, DG7 1QZ
☎ *Auchencairn (055664) 263*

VAT is shown at 15%: changes in this rate may affect prices.

1 cottage, 1 pub rm, 2 bedrms, sleeps 6, £60-£100, Apr-Oct, bus 2 mls, rail 23 mls

♿ wc E 🚗 🖊 🕐 ◉ 📺 🛏 🔌 ✳ 🐎 P 🐴 🛋 † ⚓ ✕ 🧺 🎣

Mrs E Hendry, Rascarrel Farm, Auchencairn, Castle Douglas, Kirkcudbrightshire, DG7 1RJ
☎ *Auchencairn (055664) 214*

AUCHENCAIRN AREA Kirkcudbrightshire Map Ref. 2B11

APPROVED
♛ ♛ ♛

2 houses, 2 cottages, 1 pub rm, 2-3 bedrms, sleeps 3-6, from £60, Apr-Oct

♿ wc E 🚗 🖊 🕐 ◉ 📺 🛏 🔌 ✳ 🐎 P 🐴 🛋 † 🎣 ⛵ ⛰ ⚓ ⚡

G M Thomson & Company, 27 King Street, Castle Douglas, Kirkcudbrightshire, DG7 1AB
☎ *Castle Douglas (0556) 2701*

AUCHENMALG Wigtownshire Map Ref. 1G11

1 bungalow, 3 pub rms, 3 bedrms, sleeps 6, £80-£170, Mar-Oct, bus 5 mls, rail 15 mls, airport 60 mls

♿ wc E 🚗 🖊 🕐 ◉ 🖊 📺 🛏 🔌 ☉ ✳ 🐎 P 🐴 🛋 † 🏠 🔔 🎣 ⛵ ⛰ ⚓ ⚡ ✕ 🧺 🍷 T

9 caravans, sleeps 4-6, £65-£132, Mar-Oct, bus 5 mls, rail 15 mls, airport 60 mls

♿ wc E 🖊 🕐 🖊 🔌 📞 📺 📷 🔌 ☉ 🐎 P † 🏠 🔔 🎣 ⛵ ⛰ ⚓ ⚡ ✕ 🧺 T

Cock Inn Caravan Park, Auchenmalg, Newton Stewart, Wigtownshire
☎ *Auchenmalg (05815) 227*

Craig Lodge
AUCHENMALG, GLENLUCE, WIGTOWNSHIRE. 058 15 236

This 19th-century Shooting Lodge has been converted into modern, comfortable, self-contained flats. Spacious grounds provide play area for children and private foreshore ensures safe bathing. Nearby are good golf courses, sea/river/loch fishing and pony trekking. Flats all-electric and fully equipped to high standard. Sleeping 4/8. Resident caretaker.
Prices £50-£160. Brochure from Hon. Mrs Agnew , Sweethaws Farm, Crowborough, Sussex TN6 3SS. Tel. (08926) 5045.

6 flats, 2 bungalows, 1-2 pub rms, 2-3 bedrms, sleeps 4-8, min let weekend (low season), £50-£160, Jan-Dec, bus nearby, rail 17 mls

♿ wc E 🚗 🖊 🛏 🔌 🕐 ◉ 📺 📞 🔌 📷 🔌 ☉ ✳ 🐎 P 🐴 🛋 🚗 † 🏠 🎣 ⛵ ⛰ ⚓ ✕ 🧺

Hon Mrs Andrew Agnew, Sweethaws Farm, Crowborough, Sussex, TN6 3SS
☎ *Crowborough (08926) 5045*

AUCHINLECK Ayrshire Map Ref. 1H7

Laurienne Caravan Site 2 caravans, sleeps 4, min let weekend, £50-£55, Apr-Oct, bus 1 ml, rail 1 ml, airport 15 mls

♿ wc E 🖊 🖊 🔌 🐎 P 🏠 🎣 ⚓ 🎣 ⛵ ⛰ ⚓ ⚡ ✕ 🧺 (birdwatching)

Mr D MacDonald, Laurienne, Birnieknowe, Auchinleck, Ayrshire
☎ *Cumnock (0290) 20272*

1 caravan, sleeps 6, from £65, Mar-Oct, bus ¼ ml, rail 1 ml

♿ wc E 🕐 🔌 🖊 🔌 ✳ 🐎 P 🖊 🐴 🛋 🚗 † 🏠 ✕ 🧺 🎣

Mrs R McKinley, Hillend of Heateth, Catrine Road, Auchinleck, Ayrshire
☎ *Cumnock (0290) 22086*

Prices shown are for guidance only. Please send SAE with each enquiry.

AUCHTERARDER Perthshire Map Ref. 2B3

1 house, 1 cottage, 1 pub rm, 2 bedrms, sleeps 4-6, min let weekend (low season), £70-£150, Jan-Dec, bus ½ ml, rail 1 ½ mls, airport 35 mls

Mrs Bayne, Castlemains, Auchterarder, Perthshire, PH3 1DX
☎ *Auchterarder (07646) 2475*

---

1 house, 1 pub rm, 3 bedrms, sleeps 6, £90-£140, Jan-Dec, bus 4 mls, rail 8 mls, airport 40 mls

Mrs Hamish Macrae, Trinity Gask House, Auchterarder, Perthshire, PH3 1LJ
☎ *Madderty (076483) 369*

---

1 flat, 1 pub rm, 3 bedrms, sleeps 5, £200-£450, Jan-Dec, bus 1 ml, rail 1 ml, airport 40 mls

Mrs P M Taylor, 4 Rosefield, Kippington Road, Sevenoaks, Kent, TN13 2LP
☎ *Sevenoaks (0732) 455725*

---

1 cottage, 1 pub rm, 2 bedrms, sleeps 2-4, min let weekend, £70-£90, Jan-Dec, bus nearby, rail 1 ml

Mrs Strang, Oakbank, Montrose Road, Auchterarder, Perthshire
☎ *Auchterarder (07646) 2082*

---

1 flat, 1 pub rm, 3 bedrms, sleeps 6, min let 2 nights, £160-£240, Jan-Dec, rail ½ ml, airport 30 mls

Mrs E Jardine, R L Burges Ltd, Burnfield Avenue, Glasgow, G46 7TL
☎ *041 637 2301*

AWAITING INSPECTION

1 flat, 1 pub rm, 4 bedrms, sleeps 8-10, min let 3 nights, £150-£220, Jan-Dec, bus 300 yds, rail 2 mls, airport 40 mls

(bowling green, clay pigeon shooting)

1 caravan, sleeps 4/5, min let 2 nights/weekend, £60-£80, Apr-Oct, bus 300 yds, rail 2 mls, airport 40 mls

(bowling green, clay pigeon shooting)

Mrs J L White, Drumcharry, 1 Montrose Road, Auchterarder, Perthshire, PH3 1BZ
☎ *Auchterarder (07646) 2608*

Nether Coul Caravans 1 caravan, sleeps 6, min let 1 night, £45-£55, Jan-Dec, bus nearby, rail 3 mls, airport 45 mls

Mrs S Robertson, Nether Coul, Auchterarder, Perthshire, PH3 1NT
☎ *Auchterarder (07646) 3119*

VAT is shown at 15%: changes in this rate may affect prices.

1 caravan, sleeps 8, min let 3 nights, £90-£110, Apr-Nov, bus 500 yds, rail 1 ½ mls, airport 30 mls

  ♿ WC E 🏠 📷 🧺 🍳 ⬜ ❄ P † ⚊   🚲 🔍 🎿 🎣 ⛵ ⚓ ⛷ ✗ ➰ T

Mrs Nicholls, Castlebrae Nursery, Auchterarder, Perthshire
☎ *Auchterarder (07646) 3865*

---

2 cottages, 1-2 pub rms, 1 bedrm, sleeps 2, min let 3 nights, £50-£70, Apr-Oct, bus 1 ml, rail 3 mls, airport 35 mls

  ♿ WC E ⟲ 🏠 📷 📀 ⊚ ⬜ ⚊ ❄ 🐴 P   🔍 🎿 🎣 ⛵ ⛷ ✗ ➰

Mrs P S Stewart, Nurses' Lane, Comrie, Perthshire
☎ *Comrie (0764) 70341*

---

1 cottage, 1 pub rm, 2 bedrms, sleeps 5, min let weekend, £80-£110, Apr-Oct, bus nearby, rail 2 mls, airport 38 mls

  ♿ WC E ⟲ 📷 ⬛ 📀 ⊚ ⬜ ⬜ ⬛ ☀ ❄ P 🐴 ▦ † ⚊   🔍 🎣 ⛵ ⛷ 🏹 ✗ ➰ 🎿

(parachuting, hillwalking)

Mrs R W Dalglish, East Third, Auchterarder, Perthshire, PH3 1NJ
☎ *Auchterarder (07646) 2357*

---

1 flat, 1-2 pub rms, 3-4 bedrms, sleeps 6-7, min let 3 nights, £450-£650, Jan-Dec, bus 1 ml, rail 2 mls, airport 40 mls

  ♿ WC E ⟲ 🏠 📷 ⬛ 🗄 📀 ⊚ 🗄 📞 ⬜ 📺 ✂ ⬛ ☀ ❄ P ∥ 🐴 ▦ ⟲ †   🔍 🎣 ⛵ ⛷
🏹 🎿 R ✗ ➰ ❗ T

Mrs Fotheringham, The Spinney, Auchterarder, Perthshire
☎ *Auchterarder (07646) 2542*

---

2 houses, 1 pub rm, 6 bedrms, sleeps 4-8, £85-£165, Apr-Oct

  ♿ WC E ⟲ 📷 ⊚ 📞 ⬜ 📺 ⚊ ☀ 🐴 P 🐴 †

Finlayson Hughes, Bank House, 82 Atholl Road, Pitlochry, Perthshire, PH16 5BL
☎ *Pitlochry (0796) 2512*

AUCHTERMUCHTY Fife Map Ref. 2C3

Weaver's House AUCHTERMUCHTY
NORTH FIFE

This is one of our two warm and comfortable houses in Auchtermuchty. Both houses are to STB 4 Crowns standard and are Commended and have colour TV, dishwasher, washing machine and tumble dryer. Auchtermuchty is a good centre for golf or for exploring a surprising amount of Scotland. Prices include linen, towels, gas and electricity and are £225-£285 per week for up to 6 people.
Brochure from Mrs S C Dunlop, 6 Gladgate, Auchtermuchty, Fife KY14 7AY Scotland. Tel. 0337 28496.

1 house, 1 cottage, 1-2 pub rms, 3 bedrms, sleeps 5-6, min let 1 night, £145-£285, Jan-Dec, bus nearby, rail 5 mls, airport 40 mls

  ♿ WC E ⟲ 🏠 📷 ⬛ 🗄 🧺 📞 ⬜ 📺 ✂ ⚊ ⊚ ☀ 🏹 🐴 ▦   🔍 🎿 ⛵ ⛷ ✗ ➰ T

Elizabeth J Dunlop, 6 Gladgate, Auchtermuchty, Fife, KY14 7AY
☎ *Auchtermuchty (0337) 28496*
Warm, comfortable, traditional style houses with private gardens, in friendly, rural town.

1 cottage, 2 pub rms, 2 bedrms, sleeps 4, £120-£180, Jan-Dec, bus nearby, rail 5 mls, airport 35 mls

[symbols]

Mrs M Galloway, Cherry Trees, Kemp Road, Swanland, East Yorkshire, HU14 3LZ
☎ *Hull (0482) 631526*

AUCHTERTOOL Fife Map Ref. 2C4

Clentrie Farm 1 cottage, 1 pub rm, 3 bedrms, sleeps 6, £95-£115, Jan-Dec, bus 1 ml, rail 4 mls, airport 15 mls

[symbols] (windsurfing)

Mrs Mitchell, Clentrie Farm, Auchtertool, by Kirkcaldy, Fife, KY2 5XG
☎ *Lochgelly (0592) 782155*

AULDEARN, by Nairn Map Ref. 4C8

COMMENDED

1 cottage, 1 pub rm, 2 bedrms, sleeps 4-5, min let weekend, £63-£150, Apr-Nov, rail 6 mls, airport 10 mls

[symbols]

Mrs J Ker, Broomton, Auldearn, Nairn, IV12 5LB
☎ *Brodie (03094) 223*
On working farm. Excellent views to Moray Firth.

AULTBEA, by Achnasheen Ross-shire Map Ref. 3F7

1 caravan, sleeps 5, min let weekend, £30-£60, Apr-Oct, bus nearby, rail 40 mls, airport 85 mls

[symbols]

Mrs MacAskill, Drumchork, Aultbea, by Achnasheen, Ross-shire
☎ *Aultbea (044582) 373(exc Sun)*

COMMENDED

1 cottage, 1 pub rm, 4 bedrms, sleeps 8, £75-£130, Jan-Dec, bus nearby, rail 45 mls, airport 90 mls

[symbols]

Mrs I Donald, Kerrisdale, 4 Muirfield Rd, Inverness, IV2 4AY
☎ *Inverness (0463) 235489*
Stone built, modernised, with beamed lounge. Situated in village with excellent views over Loch Ewe.

SCOTTISH TRAVEL CENTRE
14 South St. Andrew Street
Opening early 1987.
Plan your trip round Scotland! Maps, guides, books, accommodation, car hire, travel tickets, bureau de change and a friendly welcome.
Right in the heart of Edinburgh

Aultbea
Highland Lodges
Drumchork, Aultbea, Ross-shire IV22 2HU
Telephone: (044-582) 233

Unashamed luxury, all home comforts, beautifully fitted out with carpeting, heating, colour TV. Large bedrooms (all beds have duvets). Spacious lounge with balcony; separate fully fitted kitchen; bathroom with coloured suite. Each lodge has its own road access and parking area. All this in a superb setting with stunning views over loch Ewe and beyond to the Hebrides. A scenic spectacular of seascape, mountain and forest from Torridon Hills to Sutherland Hills. The nearby hamlet of Aultbea offers everyday requirements, boating/fishing trips and beautiful beaches nearby. Wonderful walking country, a paradise for ornithologists and photographers; golf nearby, river, loch and sea fishing; the ideal touring base.

Contact Bob and Margaret Chapman for colour brochure. Early booking discount plus package/bargain offers.

COMMENDED
❀ ❀ ❀

Aultbea Lodges 10 chalet/log cabins, 1 pub rm, 2 bedrms, sleeps 6, min let 3 nights (low season), £88-£273, Jan-Dec, bus 400 yds, rail 37 mls, airport 85 mls

♿ ⌨ E �foot 🍳 📺 🛏 ◉ 🗄 🗄 📠 ⚡ 🛋 ☺ 🐴 🅿 🐕 🛏 🚗   ✂ ⚓ ▲ ↙ ✦ ✗ 🔌 T

Mr & Mrs R D Chapman, Torliath House, Drumchork, Aultbea, Achnasheen, Ross-shire, IV22 2HU
☎ *Aultbea (044582) 233*
Peacefully situated complex with spectacular views over Loch Ewe.

AVIEMORE Inverness-shire Map Ref. 4C10

1 caravan, sleeps 6, min let 2 nights, from £40, Jan-Dec, bus 3 mls, rail nearby

🏠 E 🚿 🐴 🅿   🍷 ✂ ♾ 🎿 ⛵ ⛵ ▲ ↗ 🎣 🔌

Mrs E M Grant, Avielochan, Aviemore, Inverness-shire, PH22 1QD
☎ *Aviemore (0479) 810884/810282*

---

1 cottage, 1 pub rm, 3 bedrms, sleeps 6-9, £120-£250, Jan-Dec, bus ½ ml, rail 500 yds

♿ ⌨ E 🚶 🍳 ◉ 📺 📞 ⚡ 🛋 ☺ ❄ 🐴 🅿 🐕 🛏 †   ⛵ ▲ ↗ ✦ 🎣 ✗ 🔌

Mr Gavin Alston, Balvaird, Gateside, Fife, KY14 7SR
☎ *Glenfarg (05773) 249*

---

1 bungalow, 1 pub rm, 3 bedrms, sleeps 6, £100-£180, Jan-Dec, bus nearby, rail ¾ ml

♿ ⌨ E 🚶 🍳 📺 ◉ 🗄 🗄 📠 ⚡ 🛋 ☺ ❄ 🅿 † 🍷 ✂ ♾ 🎿 ⛵ ▲ ↗ ✦ 🎣 ✗ 🔌
T

Thomas Murray, 4 Kenmure Road, Whitecraigs, Giffnock, Glasgow, G46 6TU
☎ *041 639 1443*

---

4 chalet/log cabins, 1 house, 3 flats, 2 pub rms, 1-3 bedrms, sleeps 4-10, min let 2 nights, £150-£300, Jan-Dec, bus nearby, rail 300 yds, airport 38 mls

♿ ⌨ E 🚶 ⌂ 🍳 📺 🛏 ◉ 🗄 🗄 📠 ⚡ 🛋 ☺ ❄ 🐴 🅿 ⚡ 🐕 🛏 † ⏚ ● 🎯   🍷 ✂ ♾
🎿 ⛵ ▲ ↗ 🎣 ® ✗ 🔌 🎣 🎵 T

Stakis Aviemore Chalets, Aviemore Centre, Aviemore, Inverness-shire, PH22 1PF
☎ *Aviemore (0479) 810624*

Prices shown are for guidance only. Please send SAE with each enquiry.

Ladbroke Freedom Inn 93 flats, 3 pub rms, 93 bedrms, sleeps 4, min let 1 night, £100-£200, Jan-Dec, bus 400 yds, rail 400 yds, airport 35 mls

Ladbroke Freedom Inn, Aviemore Centre, Aviemore, Inverness-shire, PH22 1PF
☎ *Aviemore (0479) 810781*

COMMENDED
♛♛♛♛

2 flats, 1 cottage, 1 bungalow, 1 pub rm, 2 bedrms, sleeps 4-5, min let 2 nights, £80-£220, Jan-Dec, bus 1 ml, rail 1 ml, airport 35 mls

Inverdruie & Glasnacardoch Properties, Aviemore, Inverness-shire, PH22 1QR
☎ *Aviemore (0479) 810357*
Warm and comfortable accommodation of individual character , 1 mile (2km) from village.

APPROVED
♛♛

1 cottage, 1 pub rm, 3 bedrms, sleeps 6, from £80, May-Nov, bus ¼ ml, rail ½ ml

Mrs G Clark, 2 Barncroft Way, St Albans, Herts, AL1 5QZ
☎ *St Albans (0727) 67029*
End terrace railway cottage in village overlooking main and steam lines to birch woods beyond.

Craigellachie House Flats & Chalets 7 chalet/log cabins, 2 flats, 1 cottage, 1 pub rm, 1-3 bedrms, sleeps 4-7, min let 2 nights, £110-£400, Jan-Dec, bus 800 yds, rail 800 yds, airport 45 mls

(mountain biking, ice rink, cinema)

8 caravans, sleeps 4-6, min let 2 nights, £100-£200, Dec-Oct, bus ¾ ml, rail ¾ ml

Mr & Mrs H M D Mcwilliam, Craigellachie House, Aviemore, Inverness-shire, PH22 1PX
☎ *Aviemore (0479) 810236*

---

2 houses, 3 pub rms, 4-5 bedrms, sleeps 10, £180-£400, Jan-Dec, bus ¾ ml, rail ¾ ml, airport 35 mls

Cairngorm Holiday Homes, Parklands, Queens Drive, Oxshott, Leatherhead, Surrey, KT22 0PF
☎ *Oxshott (037284) 3333*

---

1 bungalow, 1 pub rm, 3 bedrms, sleeps 7, min let weekend, £130-£180, Jan-Dec, bus ½ ml, rail ½ ml, airport 30 mls

Mrs Grant, 19 Craig Na Gower Avenue, Aviemore, Inverness-shire, PH22 1RW
☎ *Aviemore (0479) 810318*

HIGHLY COMMENDED
♛ ♛ ♛ ♛

8 chalet/log cabins, 1 pub rm, 2-3 bedrms, sleeps 4-8, min let 5 nights, £185-£620, Jan-Dec, bus nearby, rail 1 ml, airport 35 mls

[symbols]

Barratt Multi-Ownership & Hotels Ltd, Dalfaber Estate, Aviemore, Inverness-shire, PH22 1ST
☎ *Aviemore (0479) 811244*

Units of individual design, character and appeal. Wide range of recreational facilities.

---

1 house, 3 flats, 3 cottages, 1-3 pub rms, 1-5 bedrms, sleeps 2-10, min let weekend, from £100, Jan-Dec, bus nearby, rail nearby, airport 30 mls

[symbols]

Maureen Hendry, Aviemore Holiday Houses, P.O. Box 2, Aviemore, Inverness-shire
☎ *Aviemore (0479) 811177*

---

1 bungalow, 1 pub rm, 2 bedrms, sleeps 4-5, £105-£160, Jan-Dec, bus nearby, rail 1 ml, airport 25 mls

[symbols]

Mrs D J McAdam, Ard Choille, Mugdock, Glasgow, G62 8LQ
☎ *041 956 4824*

---

1 bungalow, 2 pub rms, 3 bedrms, sleeps 8, from £140, Jan-Dec, bus 400 yds, rail 1 ml, airport 40 mls

[symbols]

Mr Morris, 63 West Coates Road, Cambuslang, Glasgow, G72 8AE
☎ *041 641 3474*

---

2 cottages, 2 pub rms, 2-3 bedrms, sleeps 6, min let 2-3 nights (low season), £105-£295, Jan-Dec, bus 1 ½ mls, rail 2 ½ mls, airport 40 mls

[symbols]

Mrs J P Grant, Rothiemurchus Estate Office, Dell of Rothiemurchus, by Aviemore, Inverness-shire, PH22 1QH
☎ *Aviemore (0479) 810647(day)/810428(eve)*

---

1 bungalow, 1 pub rm, 2 bedrms, sleeps 2-6, min let 3 nights, £95-£200, Jan-Dec, bus 1 ml, rail 1 ml, airport 34 mls

[symbols] (birdwatching)

Miss Hedley, Coylum House, Aviemore, Inverness-shire, PH22 1RD
☎ *Aviemore (0479) 810213*

High Range Self Catering Chalets 5 chalet/log cabins, 1 pub rm, 1-2 bedrms, sleeps 2-6, min let 2 nights, from £120, Jan-Dec, bus 500 yds, rail 500 yds, airport 40 mls

[symbols]

High Range Self Catering Chalets, Aviemore, Inverness-shire, PH22 1PT
☎ *Aviemore (0479) 810636*

1 caravan, sleeps 4, min let 2 nights, £50-£70, Jan-Dec, bus nearby, rail 1 ml, airport 32 mls

Mrs D McCormick, Junipers, 5 Dell Mhor, Aviemore, Inverness-shire
☎ *Aviemore (0479) 810405*

---

1 cottage, 1 pub rm, 2 bedrms, sleeps 3, £120-£170, Dec-Oct, bus nearby, rail nearby

Mr & Mrs J H Baxter, Loramore, Grampian Road, Aviemore, Inverness-shire
☎ *Aviemore (0479) 810304*

---

1 house, 1 pub rm, 2 bedrms, sleeps 7, min let 2 nights, £80-£150, Jan-Dec, bus nearby, rail 1 ½ mls, airport 25 mls

Mrs Lambert, Balmellie Cottage, Balmellie Rd, Turriff, Aberdeenshire
☎ *Turriff (0888) 63270*

---

1 house, 1 pub rm, 1 bedrm, sleeps 2-4, min let 2 nights, from £130, Jan-Dec, bus ½ ml, rail 2 mls

5 caravans, sleeps 4-8, min let 2 nights, £60-£95, Dec-Oct, bus ½ ml, rail ½ ml

Mrs J C Andrews, 1 Willow Vale, Archiestown, Moray
☎ *Carron (03406) 468*

---

28 houses, 37 flats, 1 pub rm, 1-2 bedrms, sleeps 4-6, min let 2 nights, £220-£650, Jan-Nov, bus 500 yds, rail 500 yds, airport 30 mls

Interlude Houses Ltd, Scandanavian Village, Aviemore Centre, Aviemore, Inverness-shire, PH22 1PF
☎ *Aviemore (0479) 810852*

---

1 cottage, 1 pub rm, 4 bedrms, sleeps 6, min let weekend, £90-£120, Jan-Dec, bus nearby, rail 1 ½ mls, airport 35 mls

Mr W G Mackintosh, Grainish Farm, Aviemore, Inverness-shire, PH22 1QD
☎ *Aviemore (0479) 810225*

---

1 flat, 1 bungalow, 2 pub rms, 1-2 bedrms, sleeps 4-8, min let weekend, £85-£150, Jan-Dec, bus nearby, rail 1 ml, airport 30 mls

Mrs I B Porter, 18 Lochart Place, Aviemore, Inverness-shire, PH22 1SW
☎ *Aviemore (0479) 811152*

---

1 cottage, 1 pub rm, 3 bedrms, sleeps 6-8, £140-£230, Jan-Dec, bus 500 yds, rail 1 ml, airport 30 mls

(ice, roller skating)

Mr M Rawlings, Dell Farm Flat, Rothiemurchus, Aviemore, Inverness-shire
☎ *Aviemore (0479) 811008*

VAT is shown at 15%: changes in this rate may affect prices.

1 flat, 1 pub rm, 3 bedrms, sleeps 5-6, min let 2 nights, £120-£150, Jan-Dec, airport 30 mls

Mrs F Finlayson, Dunromin, Craig na Gower Avenue, Aviemore, Inverness-shire
☎ *Aviemore (0479) 810698*

COMMENDED

4 bungalows, 1 pub rm, 2 bedrms, sleeps 4-6, min let 2 nights, £250-£360, Dec-Oct

Balavoulin Guest House, Grampian Road, Aviemore, Inverness-shire, PH22 1RL
☎ *Aviemore (0479) 810672*
Well equipped including own patio area in secluded setting near centre of village.

---

1 house, 1 pub rm, 1 bedrm, sleeps 3-4, £110-£120, Jul-Sep, bus nearby, rail 1 ml, airport 34 mls

Miss Moira Tonkin, 1 Spey Avenue, Dalfaber, Aviemore, Inverness-shire
☎ *Aviemore (0479) 810013/810365*

Campgrounds of Scotland 15 caravans, sleeps 6, min let 1 night, £115-£240, Dec-Oct, bus nearby, rail 1 ½ mls, airport 30 mls

Campgrounds of Scotland, Coylumbridge, Aviemore, Inverness-shire
☎ *Aviemore (0479) 810120*

---

20 caravans, sleeps 6-8, min let 2 nights, £80-£138, Dec-Oct, bus 3.5 mls, rail 3.5 mls

Dalraddy Caravan Park, Aviemore, Inverness-shire
☎ *Aviemore (0479) 810330*

---

1 bungalow, 1 pub rm, 2 bedrms, sleeps 6-7, min let 2 nights, £90-£170, Jan-Dec, bus 1 ml, rail 1 ml

Mrs H MacKinnon, Home Farm, Craigend, Houston, Bridge of Weir, Renfrewshire
☎ *Bridge of Weir (0505) 613665*

---

1 bungalow, 1 pub rm, 1 bedrm, sleeps 4, min let 4 nights, £90-£150, Jan-Dec, bus nearby, rail 1 ml, airport 30 mls

Mr G Robson, 5 Killernmont Road, Bearsden, Glasgow, G61 2JB
☎ *041 942 2712*

---

1 bungalow, 2 pub rms, 3 bedrms, sleeps 6, £125-£245, Jan-Dec, bus nearby, rail 1 ml, airport 25 mls

Mrs D J McAdam, Ard Choille, Mugdock, Glasgow, G62 8LQ
☎ *041 956 4824*

Prices shown are for guidance only. Please send SAE with each enquiry.

Speyside Caravan Park 1 caravan, sleeps 6-7, min let weekend, £85-£175, Dec-Oct, bus 500 yds, rail 500 yds, airport 36 mls

Mrs A Armitt, 21 Myrtlefield, Aviemore, Inverness-shire
☎ *Aviemore (0479) 810480*

---

1 house, 1 pub rm, 1 bedrm, sleeps 4, min let weekend, £100-£175, Jan-Dec, bus nearby, rail 1 ml, airport 36 mls

Mr W Rodman, c/o Sue Smith, Tigh-na-shee, Dalfaber Road, Aviemore, Inverness-shire, PH22 1PH

Speyside Caravan Park 2 caravans, sleeps 4-6, min let 1 night, £70-£120, Dec-Oct, bus ½ ml, rail ½ ml

Miss Fiona Wilson, 27 Corrour Road, Dalfaber, Inverness-shire
☎ *Aviemore (0479) 811417/811137*

by AVIEMORE Inverness-shire Map Ref. 4C10

1 cottage, 1 pub rm, 4 bedrms, sleeps 8, £160-£260, Jan-Dec, bus nearby, rail 2 ½ mls, airport 40 mls

Mrs C Gordon, Kintail, Coylumbridge, by Aviemore, Inverness-shire
☎ *Aviemore (0479) 810475*

---

1 house, 1 cottage, 1-2 pub rms, 2-3 bedrms, sleeps 4-6, min let weekend, £85-£150, Jan-Dec, bus nearby, rail 3 mls, airport 30 mls

Mrs C Baxter, Thrums, Nethybridge, Inverness-shire
☎ *Nethybridge (047982) 634*

COMMENDED

1 cottage, 2 pub rms, 2 bedrms, sleeps 6, min let weekend, £150-£185, Jan-Dec, bus 1 ml, rail 1 ml

Mr R M Clyde, Luineag, Coylumbridge, by Aviemore, Inverness-shire, PH22 1QU
☎ *Aviemore (0479) 810642(eve)/(047986) 261*
Traditional stone building converted to holiday home, in mature pine tree setting on edge of town.

AVOCH Ross-shire Map Ref. 4B8

1 cottage, 2 pub rms, 2 bedrms, sleeps 3-4, £60-£80, Jan-Dec, bus nearby, rail 10 mls, airport 15 mls

Mr J MacDonald, Springfield, Culbokie, Ross-shire
☎ *Culbokie (034987) 603*

VAT is shown at 15%: changes in this rate may affect prices.

AYR Map Ref. 1G7

Heads of Ayr Caravan Park 10 caravans, sleeps 6-8, min let 2 nights, £60-£170, Mar-Oct, bus nearby, rail 5 mls, airport 6 mls

♿ 🚾 ⛺ E 📻 🖊 🖉 🗂 🛏 📞 🖵 📷 🚿 ▪ ☉ 🐴 P 🐕 🏠 🎣 ⚓ ✕ 🧺

J S & A Semple, Heads of Ayr Caravan Park, Dunure Road, Ayr, KA7 4HX
☎ *Alloway (0292) 42269*

---

1 house, 2 pub rms, 4 bedrms, sleeps 8, £100-£185, Jan-Dec, bus 300 yds, rail nearby, airport 4 mls

♿ 🚾 E 🛒 🖊 🖉 📞 🖵 📷 ▪ ❄ 🐴 P 🐕 🏠 † 🎣   ♪ U △ ⚓ ⛵ 🚲 ✕ 🧺

Mrs B Mccartney, 7 St Andrews Street, Ayr, KA7 3AH
☎ *Ayr (0292) 265655*

Sundrum Castle Holiday Park 103 caravans, sleeps 4-7, min let 2 nights, £69-£195, Apr-Sep, bus ½ ml, rail 4 mls

♿ 🚾 E 🖊 🖉 🗂 🖉 🖵 📞 🖵 📷 🎣 ▪ ☉ 🐴 P 🐕 🏠 🛒 🎣 ⚓ 🎡   🎣 ♪ U △
⚓ ✕ 🧺

Hoseasons Holiday Ltd, Sunway House, Lowestoft, Suffolk, NR32 3LT
☎ *Lowestoft (0502) 62292/(0292) 261464*

---

9 flats, 1 pub rm, 1-3 bedrms, sleeps 4-6, min let 3 nights, from £80, Jan-Dec, bus nearby, rail 600 yds

♿ 🚾 E 🛒 🖊 🖉 🗂 ◎ 📞 🖵 📷 ▪ ☉ ❄ 🐕 🏠 †   ✕ 🧺

J & A Moran, Belmar Holiday Flats, 17 Charlotte Street, Ayr, KA7 1DZ
☎ *Ayr (0292) 282663*

---

1 flat, 1 pub rm, 1 bedrm, sleeps 5, £70, Jan-Dec, bus ¼ ml, rail ½ ml, airport 3 mls

♿ 🚾 E 🛒 🖊 🖉 ▦ 🗂 ◎ 📞 🖵 🎣 ▪ ❄ 🐴 P 🎣 🐕 🏠 🛒 †   🎣 🎣 ⚓ 🎿 ♪ U
△ ⚓ ⛵ ✕ 🧺

Mrs Sheila Tracey, Ardgowan Guest House, 7 Eglinton Terrace, Ayr, KA7 1JJ
☎ *Ayr (0292) 269287*

---

by AYR Map Ref. 1G7

Crofthead Caravan Park 4 caravans, sleeps 4-6, min let weekend, £80-£140, Apr-Oct, bus ½ ml, rail 2 mls

♿ 🚾 E 🖊 🖉 🗂 🖉 📞 🖵 📷 🎣 ▪ ☉ ❄ P 🏠 ⚓   🎣 🎣 ♪ ⚓ ⛵ ✕ 🧺

Mr & Mrs Scott, Croft Head Caravan Park, Ayr, KA6 6EN
☎ *Ayr (0292) 263516*

<table><tr><td>AWAITING INSPECTION</td><td>Skeldon Caravan Park 2 houses, 1 pub rm, 2 bedrms, sleeps 6, min let 2 nights, £50-£140, Apr-Sep, bus ½ ml, rail 6 mls, airport 10 mls</td></tr></table>

♿ 🚾 E 🖊 🖉 ◎ 📞 🗂 🎣 ▪ ☉ 🐴 P 🐕 🏠 🛒 🎣 🏠 🎡   🎣 🎣 ♪ U △ ⚓ ✕ 🧺

1 caravan, sleeps 6, min let 2 nights, £70-£150, Apr-Sep, bus ½ ml, rail 6 mls, airport 10 mls

♿ 🚾 E 🖊 🖉 🖉 🗂 📞 🖵 📷 🎣 ☉ 🐴 P 🐕 🏠 🛒 † 🏠 🎡   🎣 🎣 ♪ U △ ⚓ ✕
🧺

Skeldon Caravan Park, c/o Mrs C Henderson, Treeview, Hollybush, by Ayr, Ayrshire, KA6 7EB
☎ *Dalrymple (029256) 202*

AYTON Berwickshire Map Ref. 2G5

1 cottage, 2 pub rms, 2 bedrms, sleeps 4, £81-£104, Apr-Oct, bus 2 mls, rail 7 mls

♿ 🚾 E 🛒 🖉 ▦ ◎ 📞 🖵 🎣 ▪ ❄ 🐴 P 🐕 🏠 🛒 † 🏠   🎣 🎣 ⚓ 🎿 ♪ U △ ⚓
✕ 🧺 🍴

Mrs J Y Cowan, Bastleridge, Ayton, Eyemouth, Berwickshire, TD14 5RN
☎ *Ayton (08907) 81318*

Prices shown are for guidance only. Please send SAE with each enquiry.

BADACHRO Ross-shire Map Ref. 3E7

up to
APPROVED

3 houses, 1 pub rm, 2 bedrms, sleeps 5, from £47, Jan-Dec, bus 3 mls, rail 30 mls

Mrs E Grigor, Dry Island, Badachro, Gairloch, Ross-shire, IV21 2AB
☎ *Badachro (044583) 317*
2 modern bungalows near Badachro, fine views; 1 isolated crofter's cottage, access by footpath only.

---

4 flats, 2 pub rms, 2-3 bedrms, sleeps 6-8, £67-£270, Mar-Oct, bus 3 mls, rail 35 mls, airport 90 mls

Glencairn Holidays Ltd, Brae House, 6 Canonbury Terrace, Fortrose, Ross-shire, 1V10 8TT
☎ *Fortrose (0381) 20127*

---

1 flat, 1 pub rm, 2 bedrms, sleeps 4-6, £70-£110, Apr-Oct, bus 3 mls, rail 30 mls

A H Irving, 84 Beechwood Avenue, Clarkston, Glasgow, G76 7XG
☎ *041 639 7074*

COMMENDED

1 house, 2 pub rms, 2 bedrms, sleeps 4, £70-£140, Jan-Dec, rail 30 mls, airport 74 mls

Mrs J P Percy, 16 Elgood Avenue, Northwood, Middlesex
☎ *Northwood (09274) 21293*
Modern, in centre of village. Elevated position allows excellent views across the bay.

---

2 chalet/log cabins, 1 house, 1 cottage, 1-2 pub rms, 2-5 bedrms, sleeps 4-10, min let nights (low season), £60-£230, Jan-Dec, bus 3 mls, rail 28 mls, airport 75 mls
(skippered sailing trips)

Mr Iain Thomson, Badachro Self-Catering, Hillcrest, Badachro, Gairloch, Ross-shire, IV21 2AA
☎ *Badachro (044583) 291*

---

1 bungalow, 1 pub rm, 2 bedrms, sleeps 5, from £100, Jan-Dec

Mrs Tallach, 17 Port Henderson, Badachro, Gairloch, Ross-shire
☎ *Badachro (044583) 278*

---

1 house, 2 pub rms, 4 bedrms, sleeps 7, from £140, Apr-Oct, bus 1 ml, rail 30 mls, airport 75 mls

Mrs M C McKenzie, 141 Rivermead Court, Ranelagh Gardens, London, SW6 3SE
☎ *01 736 1493*

---

1 chalet/log cabin, 0 , 1 pub rm, 2 bedrms, sleeps 4, £60-£120, Jan-Dec, bus 3 mls, rail 30 mls, airport 75 mls

Mrs A H Moore, Tigh an Uillt, Badachro, Gairloch, Ross-shire, IV21 2AA
☎ *Badachro (044583) 212*

VAT is shown at 15%: changes in this rate may affect prices.

BALALLAN Isle of Lewis, Western Isles Map Ref. 3C5

1 flat, 1 pub rm, 1 bedrm, sleeps 1-5, £35-£50, May-Sep, bus nearby, ferry 15 mls, airport 17 mls

Mrs M A Macdonald, 27 Balallan, Balallan, Isle of Lewis, Western Isles
☎ *Balallan (085183) 328*

BALBLAIR Ross-shire Map Ref. 4B7

Ferry Inn Caravan Site 1 chalet/log cabin, 2 pub rms, 3 bedrms, sleeps 6, from £100, Mar-Dec, bus nearby

6 caravans, sleeps 6-8, min let nightly, £50-£55, Apr-Oct, bus nearby

Mr John H Hercher, Ferry Inn, Balblair, Ross-shire
☎ *Poyntzfield (03818) 250*

BALERNO Midlothian Map Ref. 2C5

2 flats, 1 pub rm, 2 bedrms, sleeps 4-5, min let 3 nights, from £100, Jan-Dec, bus ¼ ml, rail 4 mls, airport 6 mls

Mrs Irvine, Larchgrove, Balerno, Midlothian, EH14 7BD
☎ *031 449 7103*

BALGAVIES, by Forfar Angus Map Ref. 2D1

1 cottage, 1 pub rm, 3 bedrms, sleeps 7, £80-£120, Jan-Dec, bus ½ ml, rail 10 mls, airport 20 mls

Mrs P Gandy, Castle Cottage, Balgavies, Forfar, Angus, DD8 2TH
☎ *Letham (030781) 535*

BALGEDIE Kinross-shire Map Ref. 2C3

Eagle Chalets Ltd.
STAN-MA-LANE, BALGEDIE, NEAR PERTH,
Telephone: Scotlandwell (059-284) 257
Located in an area of great landscape value with many facilities nearby.

Full details and colour brochure from:
Andrew Sneddon, Eagle Chalets Ltd., Balgedie,
Kinross KY13 7HE. Tel: (059-284) 257.

18 chalet/log cabins, 1 cottage, 1 pub rm, 2-3 bedrms, sleeps 4-8, min let 3 nights (low season), £70-£200, Jan-Dec, bus nearby, rail 12 mls, airport 28 mls
(gliding, curling (Winter))

Eagle Chalets Ltd, Stan-ma-Lane, Balgedie, Kinross, KY13 7HE
☎ *Scotlandwell (059284) 257*

BALLACHULISH Argyll Map Ref. 1F1

1 bungalow, 1 pub rm, 3 bedrms, sleeps 2-6, from £110, Apr-Oct, bus nearby, rail 12 mls, airport 80 mls

👦 📺 E ⇥ ⌨ ◐ ▦ ⊡ ◉ ☐ ▭ ◙ ◪ ☉ ✳ ✝ **P** ⛄ ▥ † ♪ ∪ △ ⤦ ⇵ ⤢ ⤣ ✗
📘 ⅀ (climbing)

Mrs J McLauchlan, Gorteneorn, Ballachulish, Argyll, PA39 4JQ
☎ *Ballachulish (08552) 263*

BALLANTRAE Ayrshire Map Ref. 1F9

Laggan House Leisure Park 4 chalet/log cabins, 1 flat, 1 bungalow, 1 pub rm, 2 bedrms, sleeps 4-6, min let weekend (low season), £60-£160, Mar-Oct, bus 3 mls, rail 13 mls

👦 📺 E ⇥ ◐ ⊡ ⌀ ◻ ☎ ▭ ◙ ∕ ◪ ☉ ✝ **P** ⛄ ▥ ◭ ♦ ❂ ♪ ∪ △ ▣ ✗ ⅀ ❢
T

Mr & Mrs Finch, Laggan House Leisure Park, Ballantrae, Ayrshire, KA26 0LL
☎ *Ballantrae (046583) 229*

1 cottage, 1 bungalow, 1 pub rm, 3 bedrms, sleeps 4-6, min let weekend (low season), £50-£120, Jan-Dec, bus 2 mls, rail 15 mls, airport 35 mls

👦 📺 E ⇥ ⌨ ◐ ▦ ◉ ☐ ▭ ◙ ◪ ☉ ✳ ✝ **P** ⛄ ▥ † ✎ ♪ △ ⤦ ⇥ ✗ ⅀ ❢

Mrs Audrey Young, Balnowlart Farm, Ballantrae, Ayrshire
☎ *Ballantrae (046583) 227*

BALIG FARM HOLIDAY COTTAGES
J. & R STEVENSON LTD.
BALIG, BALLANTRAE, AYRSHIRE
Telephone. 046583 214
Up to 🏆 🏆 🏆 Commended

4 Luxury Farm Cottages: Ranging from 2-bedroom cottages which can sleep up to 6 (2 can be linked to sleep up to 12), to our super-luxury "Whim Cottage" with 3 bedrooms, sun lounge and central heating, which can sleep up to 8.
Also: 2 Superb Lodges: In a traditional 17th century Scottish Farmhouse (sleeps up to 10 each), with period furnishings and huge, open fireplaces.
All furnished and equipped to a very high standard and within 300m of our private, sandy beach, set in breathtaking countryside and a short distance to Championship Golf Courses, Fishing, Shooting, Sailing, Swimming and Pony Trekking etc. The perfect location for a peaceful, relaxing holiday in the beautiful Burns' Country.

up to
COMMENDED
🏆 🏆 🏆 🏆

2 houses, 3 cottages, 1 bungalow, 1-2 pub rms, 2-4 bedrms, sleeps 6-12, min let weekend (low season), £60-£200, Jan-Dec, bus 300 yds, rail 11 mls, airport 35 mls

👦 📺 E ⇥ ⌨ ◐ ▦ ⊡ ◉ ◻ ☎ ▭ ◙ ∕ ☉ ✳ ✝ **P** ∕ ⛄ ▥ ➜ † ◭ ✎ ♪ ∪
⤦ ⤢ ✗ ⅀ ❢

J & R Stevenson Ltd, Balig, Ballantrae, Ayrshire
☎ *Ballantrae (046583) 214*

In beautiful countryside on 600 acre farm next to a fishing port. Private beach, safe swimming.

1 cottage, 1 pub rm, 2 bedrms, sleeps 5, min let 1 night, £45-£150, Jan-Dec, bus 2½ mls, rail 15 mls, airport 45 mls

👦 📺 E ⇥ ◐ ▦ ⊡ ◉ ☐ ▭ ◙ ◪ ✳ ✝ **P** ⛄ ▥ † ❢

Mrs Rosemary Stevenson, Meadowpark Farm, Ballantrae, by Girvan, Ayrshire, KA26 0PD
☎ *Ballantrae (046583) 263*

1 cottage, 2 pub rms, 3 bedrms, sleeps 5-6, £50-£140, Jan-Dec, bus 2 mls, rail 14 mls, airport 40 mls

Mrs Scott, Sunnyside, Colmonell, by Girvan, Ayrshire, KA26 0JU
☎ *Colmonell (046588) 207*
Attractive cottage on hill farm with rural views. 2 miles to beach, good walking, salmon fishing.

1 cottage, 2 pub rms, 3 bedrms, sleeps 6, min let weekend, £55-£150, Jan-Dec, bus 4 mls, rail 16 mls, airport 40 mls

Mrs Scott, Balkissock, Ballantrae, Girvan, Ayrshire, KA26 0LP
☎ *Ballantrae (046583) 296*

BALLATER Aberdeenshire Map Ref. 4E11

1 house, 2 cottages, 1-2 pub rms, 2-4 bedrms, sleeps 4-7, £100-£155, Mar-Oct, rail 30 mls

Mrs Ross, Estate Office(STB), Dinnet, Aboyne, Aberdeenshire, AB3 5LL
☎ *Dinnet (033985) 341/342*

1 cottage, 1 pub rm, 2 bedrms, sleeps 3-4, £45-£70, mid Apr-Oct, bus nearby, rail 42 mls, airport 44 mls

Mrs M Lindsay, Gordon Cottage, Church Square, Ballater, Aberdeenshire, AB3 5QH
☎ *Ballater (0338) 55205/(0337) 40210*

2 flats, 1 pub rm, 2 bedrms, sleeps 2-4, £125-£135, Apr-Oct, bus nearby, rail 42 mls, airport 42 mls

C D Franks, Darroch Learg Hotel, Braemar Road, Ballater, Aberdeenshire, AB3 5UX
☎ *Ballater (0338) 55443*

1 cottage, 1 bungalow, 1-2 pub rms, 2-4 bedrms, sleeps 4-6, min let long weekend, £70-£140, Jan-Dec, bus nearby, rail 42 mls, airport 45 mls

Mr & Mrs Nimmo, Morvada Guest House, Ballater, Aberdeenshire
☎ *Ballater (0338) 55501*
Modern bungalow and traditional cottage in grounds of guest house. Near village centre.

2 cottages, 2 pub rms, 4 bedrms, sleeps 6, £110-£120, Apr-Oct, bus 1 ½ mls, rail 40 mls, airport 40 mls

Glenmuick Estate Office, Messrs Savills, 12 Clerk Street, Brechin, Angus, DD9 6AE
☎ *Brechin (03562) 2187*

1 flat, 1 cottage, 1-2 pub rms, 3 bedrms, sleeps 2-8, £70-£150, Apr-Oct

Mrs R McIlwain, Tangley House, Braemar Road, Ballater, Aberdeenshire, AB3 5RQ
☎ *Ballater (0338) 55624*

Prices shown are for guidance only. Please send SAE with each enquiry.

1 cottage, 1 pub rm, 3 bedrms, sleeps 7, £120-£150, Apr-Oct, bus nearby, rail 44 mls, airport 44 mls

Mr J Murray, 10 Bridge Street, Ballater, Aberdeenshire, AB3 5QP
☎ *Ballater (0338) 55409 (day)/55459 (eve)*

---

1 wing of house, 1 pub rm, 3 bedrms, sleeps 6, min let weekend, £150-£400, Jan-Dec, bus 1 ml, rail 42 mls, airport 42 mls

Mr D J Thompson, Monaltrie House, Ballater, Aberdeenshire, AB3 5RX
☎ *Ballater (0338) 55869(eve)*

BALLINDALLOCH Banffshire Map Ref. 4D9

1 hostel, 2 pub rms, 3 bedrms, sleeps 14, £5 (per person/night), Dec-Oct, bus 1 ml, rail 35 mls

Loch Insh Watersports, Insh Hall, Kincraig, Kingussie, Inverness-shire, PH21 1NU
☎ *Kincraig (05404) 272*

---

1 cottage, 1 pub rm, 4 bedrms, sleeps 6-7, £70-£80, Apr-Oct, bus ¼ ml, rail 20 mls

Mrs R McOnie, Auldich, Ballindalloch, Banffshire, AB3 9AB
☎ *Ballindalloch (08072) 220*

BALLINLUIG Perthshire Map Ref. 2B1

1 caravan, sleeps 6, min let 1 night, £55-£60, Easter-Oct, bus ½ ml, rail 5 mls

Mrs Carol Hutchison, Ballintuim Farm, Tulliemet, Pitlochry, Perthshire, PH9 0NY

---

1 cottage, 2 pub rms, 3 bedrms, sleeps 6-7, £80-£150, Apr-Nov, bus 1 ml, rail 5 mls

Mrs A Bell, Cuil-an-Duin, Ballinluig, Perthshire, PH9 0NN
☎ *Ballinluig (079682) 287*

BALLINTUIM Perthshire Map Ref. 2C1

Ballintuim Hotel & Caravan Park 8 caravans, sleeps 6, min let 2 nights (low season), £60-£150, Jan-Dec, bus nearby, rail 15 mls

Mr P Chisholm, Ballintuim Hotel & Caravan Park, Ballintuim, Bridge of Cally, Perthshire, PH10 7NH
☎ *Bridge of Cally (025086) 276*

BALLOCH Dunbartonshire Map Ref. 1H4

Tullichewan Caravan Park 6 caravans, sleeps 6-8, min let 2 nights, £90-£220, Jan-Dec, bus 500 yds, rail ¼ ml, airport 15 mls

(boardsailing, hillwalking)

Tullichewan Caravan Park, Old Luss Road, Balloch, Dunbartonshire, G83 8QP
☎ *Alexandria (0389) 59475*

VAT is shown at 15%: changes in this rate may affect prices.

35

BALLYGRANT Isle of Islay, Argyll Map Ref. 1C5

3 flats, 1 pub rm, 1-3 bedrms, sleeps 4-7, min let 3 nights (low season), £75-£140, Jan-Dec, bus nearby, ferry 3 mls, airport 11 mls

 ⚹ ♿ WC E ⛽ ♦ 📺 ⚙ 🖥 🎛 ◎ 🖵 🗗 🔌 ☉ 🐴 🅿 ∥ 🛏 ⛺ †   🎣 ➤ ✕ 🧺 T

Mrs C Bell, Knocklearach, Ballygrant, Isle of Islay, Argyll
☎ *Port Askaig (049684) 209/656*

BALMACARA Ross-shire Map Ref. 3F10

Balmacara Holiday Homes

Balmacara Holiday Homes are on the shores of Lochalsh at Balmacara, just 3 miles from Kyle of Lochalsh and the ferry to Skye. Eilean Donan Castle is only 6 miles away, as is Loch Carron. Inverness is 80 miles. Fort William and Ben Nevis 77 miles. Homes have 2 bedrooms, lounge-and-dining-room, kitchen, bathroom. Sleep 6. Double glazing, central heating, TV. Fully equipped, including linen. Free entrance to Eilean Donan Castle for two people.
Package includes: 7 or 14 nights self-catering accommodation. March-Nov. £95-£235 per week. Minimum let 1 week.
RONALD MACPHEE, 8 Heriot Road, Lenzie G66 5AY
Telephone: 041-776 3802

6 cottages, 2 pub rms, 2 bedrms, sleeps 6, £75-£235, Apr-Nov, bus nearby, rail 3 mls, ferry 3 mls, airport 10 mls

 ♿ WC E ⛽ ♦ 📺 ⚙ 🖥 🎛 ◎ 🖵 📞 🗗 🔌 ☉ ❄ 🐴 🅿 🛏 ⛺ ⚖   🎣 🌙 ➤ ✕ 🧺 T

Mr MacPhee, 8 Heriot Road, Lenzie, Glasgow
☎ *041 776 3802*

BALMACLELLAN Kirkcudbrightshire Map Ref. 2A9

1 house, 2 cottages, 1 pub rm, 3-6 bedrms, sleeps 6-10, min let long weekend, £100-£200, Jan-Dec, bus 2 mls, rail 25 mls, airport 50 mls

 ♿ WC E ⛽ ♦ 📺 ⚙ 🖥 🎛 ◎ 🖵 🗗 🔌 ☉ ❄ 🐴 🅿 🛏 ⚖ † ⚖   ☍ 🎣 🌙 ⚓ ➤ 🪜 ✕ 🧺 ⚘

Mr P J Douglas, Balmaclellan House, by Castle Douglas, Kirkcudbrightshire, DG7 3PW
☎ *New Galloway (06442) 230*

---

1 house, 2 pub rms, 3 bedrms, sleeps 6, min let weekend, £100-£120, Jan-Dec, bus 1½ mls

 ♿ WC E ⛽ ⚙ 🖥 ◎ 🖵 🗗 🔌 ☉ ❄ 🐴 🅿 🛏 ⚖ †   🎣 🌙 ⚓ ➤ 🪜 ✕ 🧺 ⚘

Mr T T McCrow, Troquhain, Balmaclellan, Castle Douglas, Kirkcudbrightshire, DG7 3QH
☎ *New Galloway (06442) 212*

BALQUHIDDER Perthshire Map Ref. 1H3

1 cottage, 1 bungalow, 1 pub rm, 2 bedrms, sleeps 5-6, £100-£200, Jan-Dec, rail 30 mls, airport 60 mls

 ♿ WC E ⛽ ⚙ 🖥 🎛 ◎ 🖵 🗗 🔌 ☉ ❄ 🅿 🛏 ⚖ ⚖   🎣 ⚓ 🪜 ✕ 🧺 T

Miss Jill Bristow, Holiday Cottages (Scotland) Ltd, Lilliesleaf, Melrose, Roxburghshire, TD6 9JD
☎ *Lilliesleaf (08357) 424/425/320*

---

1 cottage, 1 pub rm, 2 bedrms, sleeps 7, min let weekend, £60-£170, Jan-Dec, bus ¼ ml, rail 27 mls, airport 60 mls

 ♿ WC E ⛽ ⚙ 🖥 ◎ 🖵 🗗 🔌 ☉ ❄ 🅿 🛏 ⚖ †   🎣 🌙 ⚓ ➤ 🪜 ✕ 🧺

Mrs Cato, Coshnachie, Balquhidder, Lochearnhead, Perthshire, FK19 8NZ
☎ *Strathyre (08774) 258*

AWAITING INSPECTION

2 cottages, 1 pub rm, 2 bedrms, sleeps 6, £70-£190, Jan-Dec, bus 1 ml, rail 28 mls

Hilary Prendergast, The Sawmill, Balquhidder, by Lochearnhead, Perthshire, FK19 8NY
☎ *Strathyre (08774) 218/645*

---

2 cottages, 2 pub rms, 3 bedrms, sleeps 6, min let weekend, £60-£140, Jan-Dec, bus 5 mls, rail 23 mls, airport 53 mls

Mrs Hendry, Immeroin, Balquhidder, Lochearnhead, Perthshire, FK19 8PF
☎ *Strathyre (08774) 254*

COMMENDED
👑 👑 👑

1 house, 1 bungalow, 2 pub rms, 3-4 bedrms, sleeps 6-7, £116-£220, Mar-Nov, bus 2 mls, rail 30 mls, airport 70 mls

(windsurfing, canoeing)

Mrs P L M Barber, 7A Matham Road, East Molesey, Surrey, KT8 0SX
☎ *01 941 3904*
Modern bungalow, traditional house, each with attractive garden. Small parish, lovely scenery.

by BALQUHIDDER Perthshire Map Ref. 1H3

1 flat, 1 pub rm, 2 bedrms, sleeps 4, £85-£100, Jan-Dec

Mrs V Pickering, Auchtubhmor House, Balquhidder, Perthshire, FK19 8NZ
☎ *Strathyre (08774) 632*

BALTASOUND Unst, Shetland Map Ref. 5G1

5 chalet/log cabins, 1 pub rm, 2-4 bedrms, sleeps 3-7, £50-£100, Jan-Dec, bus nearby, airport 1 ml

T J Ellis, Hagdale Lodge, Baltasound, Unst, Shetland
☎ *Baltasound (095781) 584*

BALVICAR Argyll Map Ref. 1E3

Balvicar Chalets 08523 221
BALVICAR FARM, by OBAN, ARGYLL
Seven modern and comfortable chalets delightfully situated beside the sea on a small stock-rearing farm 15 miles from Oban. All-electric, 2 bedrooms, bathroom, kitchen/lounge. Colour TV. Boat available. Shop 1 mile, eating-out facilities 3 miles.
The area is ideal for walking, bird-watching and sailing.
From £65-£170 accommodating up to five persons, discounts for two persons.

COMMENDED
👑 👑 👑

Balvicar Chalets 7 chalet/log cabins, 1 pub rm, 2 bedrms, sleeps 1-6, min let weekend, £65-£170, Mar-Nov, bus 1 ml, rail 15 mls

Mr & Mrs A MacAskill, Balvicar Chalets, Balvicar Farm, Balvicar, by Oban, Argyll, PA34 4TE
☎ *Balvicar (08523) 221*
Individual units on private site with spectacular views over sea loch to hills beyond.

BANCHORY Kincardineshire Map Ref. 4F11

Banchory Lodge Caravan Site 4 caravans, sleeps 4-6, min let 2 nights, £112-£137, Apr-Oct, bus nearby, rail 19 mls, airport 19 mls

Banchory Lodge Caravan Site, Dee Street, Banchory, Kincardineshire, AB3 3HT
☎ *Banchory (03302) 2246*

Silver Ladies Caravan Park 7 caravans, sleeps 4-6, min let 3 nights, £70-£160, Apr-Oct, bus 2 mls, rail 15 mls, airport 15 mls

J G & I Anderson, Silver Ladies Caravan Park, Strachan, Banchory, Kincardineshire, AB3 3NL
☎ *Banchory (03302) 2800*

Feughside Caravan Park 2 caravans, sleeps 6, min let weekend, £80-£130, Apr-Oct, bus nearby, rail 18 mls, airport 25 mls

Mrs S Hay, Feughside Caravan Site, Strachan, Banchory, Kincardineshire, AB3 3NT
☎ *Feughside (033045) 669*

APPROVED

1 cottage, 1 pub rm, 1 bedrm, sleeps 2, £85-£115, Jan-Dec, bus nearby, rail 16 mls, airport 16 mls

J M & M Carnie, Pitmachie, Watson Street, Banchory, Kincardineshire
☎ *Banchory (03302) 4424*
Suitably furnished with small garden and superb views of Kerloch Hills.

by BANCHORY Kincardineshire Map Ref. 4F11

COMMENDED

Woodend of Glassel 7 chalet/log cabins, 1 pub rm, 1-2 bedrms, sleeps 3-5, min let weekend (low season), £80-£120, Apr-end Oct, bus 3 mls, rail 20 mls, airport 20 mls

Enquiries to: Woodend of Glassel, A J Kostulin, Rose Cottage, Glassel, AB3 4DB
☎ *Torphin (033982) 562*
In woodland setting with views to hills and Royal Deeside valley. Hill and forest walks. Cycle hire.

1 caravan, sleeps 8, £60-£70, Apr-Oct, bus 1 ml, rail 9 mls, airport 20 mls

Mrs J G Adron, Maryfield Farm, Tilquhillie, Banchory, Kincardineshire
☎ *Banchory (03302) 2037*

BANFF Map Ref. 4F7

Banff Links Caravan Site 4 caravans, sleeps 4-9, min let 1 night, £40-£120, May-Sep, bus nearby, rail 35 mls, airport 38 mls

Mrs E Christie, Asleid Cottages, New Deer, Turriff, Aberdeenshire, AB4 8XR
☎ *New Deer (07713) 321*

Banff Links Caravan Site 4 caravans, sleeps 6, min let weekend (low season), £55-£130, May-Sep, bus nearby, rail 17 mls, airport 42 mls

Mr Alistair Scott, Farldon, Market Hill Road, Turriff, Aberdeenshire, AB5 7AZ
☎ *Turriff (0888) 63524*

1 cottage, 1 pub rm, 3 bedrms, sleeps 6-8, £58-£104, Apr-Oct, bus 1 ml, rail 20 mls, airport 40 mls

L J Mackay & Co, Linganbo Farm, King Edward, Banff, AB4 3NS
☎ *Eden (02616) 219*

Banff Links Caravan Site 3 caravans, sleeps 6-10, min let weekend (low season), £60-£135, May-Oct, bus nearby, rail 20 mls, airport 45 mls

Heather Ewen, 4 Laburnum Lane, Longside, Peterhead, Aberdeenshire
☎ *Longside (077982) 428*

---

1 cottage, 2 pub rms, 2 bedrms, sleeps 4-5, £45-£115, Mar-Nov, bus nearby, rail 47 mls, airport 41 mls

Ian Bird, c/o Carmelite House, Low Street, Banff, AB4 1AY
☎ *Banff (02612) 2152*

Banff Links 1 caravan, sleeps 6, min let weekend, £45-£75, May-Sep, bus ¼ ml

Mrs G Robb, 61 Aulton Court, Seaton Crescent, Aberdeen, AB2 1WF
☎ *Aberdeen (0224) 493751*

Banff Links 1 caravan, sleeps 4, min let weekend, £65-£85, May-Sep, bus nearby

Mr G MacKay, 3 Culbeuchly Cottages, Banff, AB4 3JR
☎ *Whitehills (02617) 631*

by BANFF Map Ref. 4F7

1 cottage, 1 pub rm, 2 bedrms, sleeps 6, £50-£80, Apr-Oct, bus 1 ml, rail 42 mls, airport 40 mls

Mrs Margaret Gill, Burnside Farm, Longmanhill, by Banff, Banffshire, AB4 3RL
☎ *Macduff (0261) 32755*

---

1 bungalow, 1 pub rm, 3 bedrms, sleeps 6, £50-£90, Apr-Oct, bus 3 mls, rail 20 mls, airport 40 mls

Mr C Dawson, Lochagan, Banff
☎ *Boyndie (02618) 213*

VAT is shown at 15%: changes in this rate may affect prices.

BANKFOOT Perthshire Map Ref. 2B2

Ⓗunters Ⓛodge

Family Cabin Holidays
Hunters Lodge, Bankfoot, Perthshire.   Tel. 0738 87 325
AA Listed   ♛♛ **Commended**

These privately owned Log Cabins are situated in the grounds of
Hunters Lodge Hotel in the heart of Scotland. An ideal centre for
Touring. Excellent sporting facilities and golfing. Enjoy good Scottish
fayre and hospitality in the hotel. Children's games room. Bar snacks a
speciality. Winner BBC's Best Pub Grub Award. Children most
welcome. "Toytown Special" menu.

COMMENDED
♛♛

6 chalet/log cabins, 1 pub rm, 2 bedrms, sleeps 1-6, min let 1 night, £175-£215, Jan-Dec,
bus nearby, rail 8 mls

👥 Ⓦ E ⊠ ⌂ ▦ ▯ ⌀ ◻ ☏ ▱ ◻ ⟋ ◻ ☺ ✳ ♞ Ⓟ ⫽ ⟲ ▥ ↴ ⟑ ◖ ❀   ◐ ✦
∪ ⚠ ❭ ⟋ Ⓡ ✖ ⬛ ❣ Ⓣ (2 lane skittle alley)

Mr Bruce Hunter, Hunters Lodge, Bankfoot, Perthshire, PH1 4DX
☎ *Bankfoot (073887) 325*

Pine units on village edge. Bar, restaurant, games room, barbeques at adjoining hotel.
Touring base.

---

1 flat, 1 pub rm, 2 bedrms, sleeps 4, £70, Apr-Oct, rail 7 mls

👥 Ⓦ E ⊠ ⌂ ▯ ⌀ ◻ ◎ ◻ ▱ ▰ ☺ ✳ Ⓟ   ✦ ❭ ⟰

Mrs M Paton, Drummond House, Main Street, Bankfoot, Perth, Perthshire, PH1 4AB
☎ *Bankfoot (073887) 407/220*

---

1 cottage, 1 pub rm, 2 bedrms, sleeps 6, from £75, Apr-Oct, bus 500 yds, rail 8 mls

👥 Ⓦ E ⊠ ⌂ ▦ ▯ ◎ ◻ ▱ ◻ ▰ ☺ ✳ ♞ Ⓟ ⟲ ▥ † ⟑   ◐ ✦ ∪ ❭ ✖ ⬛
(bowling green)

Mrs C Mackay, Blair Cottage, Main Street, Bankfoot, Perth, Perthshire, PH1 4AB
☎ *Bankfoot (073887) 338*

---

2 cottages, 1 pub rm, 2-4 bedrms, sleeps 4-8, min let weekend, £60-£90, Jan-Dec, bus 1
¼ mls, rail 10 mls

👥 Ⓦ E ⊠ ⌂ ◎ ◻ ▱ ▰ ☺ ♞ Ⓟ ⟲ ▥   ✦ ❭ ✖ ⬛ ⚘

Mrs J Paton, Meikle Obney, Bankfoot, Perthshire, PH1 4AS
☎ *Bankfoot (073887) 232*

BARR, by Girvan Ayrshire Map Ref. 1G9

♛♛

1 part house, 1 pub rm, 3 bedrms, sleeps 6, £65-£130, May-Oct, bus 2 mls, rail 9 mls

👥 Ⓦ E ⊠ ⌂ ▦ ▯ ◎ ◻ ▱ ⟋ ▰ ☺ ✳ ♞ Ⓟ ⟲ ▥ †   ⟁ ⟲ ◐ ✦ ⚠ ⚲ ❭ ✖ ⬛
⚘

Mrs V Dunlop, Glengennet Farm, Barr, by Girvan, Ayrshire, KA26 9TY
☎ *Barr (046586) 220*

BARRHILL Ayrshire Map Ref. 1G9

1 cottage, 2 pub rms, 2 bedrms, sleeps 4, £40-£65, Jan-Dec, bus nearby, rail 1 ml

👥 Ⓦ E ⊠ ⌂ ▦ ◎ ◻ ▱ ◻ ▰ ☺ ✳ ♞ Ⓟ ⟲ † ⟑   ✦ ✖ ⬛

Mrs Agnew, Ward Farm, Barrhill, Girvan, Ayrshire
☎ *Barrhill (046582) 289*

Prices shown are for guidance only. Please send SAE with each enquiry.

by **BARRHILL** Ayrshire Map Ref. 1G9

4 cottages, 1-2 pub rms, 2-3 bedrms, sleeps 4-7, min let weekend (low season), £70-£180, Jan-Dec, bus 6 mls, rail 6 mls, airport 70 mls

2 caravans, sleeps 3-5, min let weekend (low season), £60-£115, Jan-Dec, bus 6 mls, rail 6 mls, airport 70 mls

Drumlanford Est, per Michael Barne & Ptnrs, 14 Alloway Place, Ayr, KA7 2AA
☎ *Ayr (0292) 268181*

BARVAS Isle of Lewis, Western Isles Map Ref. 3C4

1 chalet/log cabin, 1 pub rm, 3 bedrms, sleeps 6, min let weekend, £45-£85, Jan-Dec, bus nearby, ferry 11 mls, airport 13 mls

Mrs C A Smith, 8 Lower Barvas, Lower Barvas, Isle of Lewis, Western Isles
☎ *Barvas (085184) 334*

BEAULY Inverness-shire Map Ref. 4A8

1 cottage, 1 pub rm, 2 bedrms, sleeps 4, £50-£100, Apr-Oct, bus 4 mls, rail 16 mls

Mrs C M Guthrie, 41 Barrow Point Avenue, Pinner, Middlesex, HA5 3HD
☎ *01 866 5026*

Cruivend Caravan Park 2 caravans, sleeps 6, min let 1 night, £60-£120, Mar-Oct, bus nearby, rail 10 mls

Mr & Mrs Dilks, Cruivend Caravan Park, Beauly, Inverness-shire, IV4 7BE
☎ *Beauly (0463) 782367*

---

2 chalet/log cabins, 1 cottage, 1 pub rm, 2-3 bedrms, sleeps 4-7, min let weekend, £60-£160, Jan-Dec, bus 1 ½ mls, rail 3 mls, airport 21 mls

Mr J M MacLennan, Inchrory, Beauly, Inverness-shire, IV4 7EY
☎ *Beauly (0463) 782352/870474*

AWAITING INSPECTION

3 bungalows, 1 pub rm, 3 bedrms, sleeps 7, min let weekend, £35-£130, Jan-Dec, rail 5 mls, airport 16 mls

Mr I MacKay, 12 Torgormack, by Beauly, Inverness-shire, IV4 7AQ
☎ *Beauly (0463) 782296*

VAT is shown at 15%: changes in this rate may affect prices.

DUNSMORE LODGES
By Beauly, Inverness-shire IV4 7EY   0463 782424

Four miles west of Beauly, nine attractive lodges set well apart in wooded hillside locations, each enjoying a high degree of privacy and view to the South. Warm, well insulated and furnished and equipped to a high standard. Dogs welcome. This beautiful part of the Highlands abounds with facilities for recreation and makes an ideal touring centre with Inverness only 15 miles away. Free colour brochure. ♛ ♛ ♛ ♛ **Highly Commended**

HIGHLY COMMENDED ♛ ♛ ♛ ♛

Dunsmore Lodges 9 chalet/log cabins, 1 pub rm, 2-3 bedrms, sleeps 4-7, £80-£215, Jan-Dec, bus 3 mls, rail 7 mls, airport 23 mls

D J Turner, Dunsmore Lodges, by Beauly, Inverness-shire, IV4 7EY
☎ Beauly (0463) 782424
Built and equipped to high standards. Privacy and comfort in well spaced wooded setting on hillside.

♛ ♛

2 chalet/log cabins, 1 pub rm, 2 bedrms, sleeps 4-6, £70-£115, Mar-Nov, bus 1 ml, rail 1 ½ mls, airport 16 mls

1 caravan, sleeps 6, min let weekend (low season), from £60, Apr-Oct, bus 1 ml, rail 1 ½ mls, airport 16 mls

Mrs M M Ritchie, Rheindown Farm, by Beauly, Inverness-shire, IV4 7AB
☎ Beauly (0463) 782461

---

2 caravans, sleeps 6, min let 1 night, £48-£114, Apr-Oct, bus 1 ½ mls, rail 2 mls, airport 20 mls

Mrs J Aiton, Dunmore House, Beauly, Inverness-shire, IV4 7AB
☎ Beauly (0463) 782660

Lovat Bridge Caravan Site 6 caravans, sleeps 4-8, min let weekend, £80-£160, Mar-Oct, bus nearby, rail 3 mls, airport 14 mls

Lovat Bridge Caravan Site, Beauly, Inverness-shire, IV4 7AY
☎ Beauly (0463) 782374

---

by BEAULY Inverness-shire Map Ref. 4A8

1 house, 1 pub rm, 3 bedrms, sleeps 6, £70-£125, Mar-Nov, bus ½ ml, rail 1 ml

Miss C M Henderson, Teandalloch Farm, by Beauly, Inverness-shire, IV4 7AA
☎ Muir-of-Ord (0463) 870291

---

1 cottage, 2 pub rms, 3 bedrms, sleeps 6, £50-£110, Mar-Oct, bus 2 mls, rail 6 mls, airport 20 mls

Mrs I MacDonald, Lower Aultvaich, by Beauly, Inverness-shire, IV4 7AN
☎ Muir-of-Ord (0463) 870560

Prices shown are for guidance only. Please send SAE with each enquiry.

BEESWING Kirkcudbrightshire Map Ref. 2B10

3 caravans, sleeps 5-8, min let 1 night, from £45, Mar-Oct, bus nearby, rail 8 mls

A Eckstein, Beeswing Caravan Park, Drumjohn Moor, Kirkgunzeon, Kirkcudbrightshire, DG2 8JL
☎ *Kirkgunzeon (038776) 242*

COMMENDED
♛ ♛ ♛

1 cottage, 1 pub rm, 1 bedrm, sleeps 2, min let 1 night, £50-£100, Jan-Dec, bus 400 yds, rail 6 mls, airport 75 mls

Mrs C M Schooling, Locharthur House, Beeswing, Dumfries, Kirkcudbrightshire
☎ *Dumfries (0387) 76235*
Of individual character, attached to georgian house. Large garden, excellent views of countryside.

BENDERLOCH Argyll Map Ref. 1E2

1 cottage, 1 pub rm, 2 bedrms, sleeps 4, £75-£100, Apr-Oct, bus 300 yds, rail 2 mls, airport 1 ml

E T F Spence, Dun-na-Mara, Ledaig, Oban, Argyll, PA37 1RT
☎ *Ledaig (063172) 233*

Tralee Bay Holidays 32 caravans, sleeps 4-7, min let 1 night, £50-£240, Apr-Oct, bus 1 ml, rail 3 mls, airport 2 mls

(Gliding)
Tralee Bay Holidays, Benderloch, by Oban, Argyll, PA37 1QR
☎ *Ledaig (063172) 255*

3 caravans, sleeps 4-6, min let 1 night, £40-£110, Apr-Oct

Margaret MacColl, 2 Keil Crofts, Benderloch, by Oban, Argyll, PA37 1QS
☎ *Ledaig (063172) 388*

3 caravans, sleeps 6, £80-£120, Apr-Oct, bus 1 ml, rail 9 mls

Mrs M MacPherson, Planetree, 4 Keil Croft, Benderloch, by Oban, Argyll
☎ *Ledaig (063172) 451*

BERNERA Isle of Lewis, Western Isles Map Ref. 3C4

1 cottage, 1 pub rm, 3 bedrms, sleeps 6, £35-£80, Jan-Dec, bus 2 mls, ferry 28 mls, airport 32 mls

Mrs Elsa Hutchison, 5 Hacklete, Great Bernera, Isle of Lewis, Western Isles
☎ *Great Bernera (085174) 269*

BERNISDALE, by Portree Isle of Skye, Inverness-shire Map Ref. 3D8

1 house, 4 bedrms, sleeps 8, £98-£130, Mar-Oct, bus nearby, rail 45 mls, ferry 45 mls, airport 40 mls

Mrs M Grant, Post Office House, Bernisdale, Portree, Isle of Skye, Inverness-shire, IV51 9NS
☎ *Skeabost Bridge (047032) 204*

VAT is shown at 15%: changes in this rate may affect prices.

1 cottage, 1 pub rm, 2 bedrms, sleeps 5, £100-£145, Mar-Nov, bus nearby, rail 40 mls, ferry 40 mls, airport 30 mls

Mr C Beaton, Totardor, Struan, Isle of Skye, Inverness-shire, IV5 9QX
☎ *Struan (047072) 229*

---

1 bungalow, 1 pub rm, 3 bedrms, sleeps 5-6, £80-£95, Apr-Oct, bus 1 ml, rail 30 mls, ferry 30 mls, airport 25 mls

Mrs Anne Montgomery, 36-37 Mains, Bernisdale, by Portree, Isle of Skye, Inverness-shire, IV51 9NS
☎ *Skeabost Bridge (047032) 280*

COMMENDED

2 cottages, 1 pub rm, 2 bedrms, sleeps 5, £70-£125, Jan-Dec, bus 800 yds, rail 40 mls, ferry 40 mls, airport 35 mls

Mr K C Mackinnon, Daldon, Bernisdale, Isle of Skye, Inverness-shire
☎ *Skeabost Bridge (047032) 331*
Modern bungalows in small crofting village. Private access to secluded site on shore of Loch Snizort.

---

1 cottage, 2 pub rms, 2 bedrms, sleeps 6, £50-£120, Mar-Dec, bus nearby

Mrs E M MacDonald, Rubislaw, 34 Bernisdale, Portree, Isle of Skye, Inverness-shire
☎ *Skeabost Bridge (047032) 212*

---

1 cottage, 1 pub rm, 2 bedrms, sleeps 5-6, £100-£130, Jan-Dec, bus 400 yds, ferry 9 mls

Mrs Macleod, Roselea, 1 Glen Bernisdale, by Portree, Isle of Skye, Inverness-shire
☎ *Skeabost Bridge (047032) 349*

BETTYHILL Sutherland Map Ref. 4B3

COMMENDED

1 house, 2 pub rms, 3 bedrms, sleeps 6, £55-£100, Jan-Dec, bus ¾ ml, rail 32 mls, airport 55 mls

Mrs A Todd, Hoy Farm, Halkirk, Caithness, KW12 6UU
☎ *Halkirk (084783) 544*
Modernised, crofting house, in remote elevated position. Overlooks Torisdale Sands and River Naver.

---

by BIGGAR Lanarkshire Map Ref. 2C6

1 cottage, 1-2 pub rms, 2 bedrms, sleeps 5-6, £65-£90, mid May-Oct, bus ½ ml, rail 18 mls, airport 24 mls

Mrs M Wannop, Muirburn, Skirling, by Biggar, Lanarkshire, ML12 6HL
☎ *Skirling (08996) 224*

BILBSTER Caithness Map Ref. 4D3

1 cottage, 2 pub rms, 2 bedrms, sleeps 6, from £40, Jan-Dec, bus 5 mls, rail 5 mls, airport 5 mls

Mrs M Adamson, Lealands Farm, Bilbster, Wick, Caithness
☎ *Watten (095582) 237*

BIRGHAM, by Coldstream Berwickshire Map Ref. 2F6

1 cottage, 2 pub rms, 2 bedrms, sleeps 4, £60-£70, Apr-Oct, bus nearby, rail 18 mls, airport 50 mls

Mrs Mitchell, Birgham Haugh, Coldstream, Berwickshire
☎ *Birgham (089083) 223*

BIRNAM, by Dunkeld Perthshire Map Ref. 2B1

COMMENDED

1 cottage, 1 pub rm, 2 bedrms, sleeps 4, min let weekend, £80-£175, Jan-Dec, bus $\frac{1}{4}$ ml, rail $\frac{1}{2}$ ml

Mrs Court, 51 Bennochy Road, Kirkcaldy, Fife, KY2 5QZ
☎ *Kirkcaldy (0592) 264369*
Former coach house, now listed building. Sheltered patio and south facing garden. Near Birnam Woods.

Erigmore House Caravan Park 4 flats, 2 cottages, 1-2 pub rms, 1-3 bedrms, sleeps 2-7, min let weekend, £65-£210, Mar-Nov, bus nearby, rail 400 yds, airport 40 mls

30 caravans, sleeps 6-8, min let weekend, £65-£220, Mar-Nov, bus nearby, rail 400 yds, airport 40 mls

Erigmore House Caravan Park, Birnam,Dunkeld, Perthshire, PH8 9XX
☎ *Dunkeld (03502) 236*

BIRSAY Orkney Map Ref. 5A10

1 cottage, 1 pub rm, 3 bedrms, sleeps 6, min let weekend, £80-£182, Jan-Dec, ferry 17 mls, airport 22 mls

Mrs K Reid, Orkney Self Catering, Finstown, Orkney, KW17 2EQ
☎ *Finstown (085676) 397*

by BIXTER West Mainland, Shetland Map Ref. 5F4

1 cottage, 2 pub rms, 2 bedrms, sleeps 4, £50-£75, Jan-Dec, bus 3 mls, ferry 20 mls, airport 35 mls

Mrs A E Ferrie, Kvernbakki, Aith, by Bixter, West Mainland, Shetland, ZE2 9NB
☎ *Bixter (059581) 265*

BLACKFORD Perthshire Map Ref. 2B3

1 house, 2 pub rms, 3 bedrms, sleeps 6-8, min let 2 nights, £60-£90, Apr-Oct, bus 1 ml, rail 2 mls

Mrs Lennox, East Kirkton Farm, Auchterarder, Perthshire, PH3 1DY
☎ *Auchterarder (07646) 2549*

AWAITING
INSPECTION

1 cottage, 3 pub rms, 1 bedrm, sleeps 5, £75-£105, Jun-Oct, bus nearby, rail 2 mls, airport 30 mls

Mr Ellis, 15 Riccarton Crescent, Currie, Edinburgh, EH14 5PB
☎ *031 449 2953*

VAT is shown at 15%: changes in this rate may affect prices.

BLACKWATERFOOT Isle of Arran Map Ref. 1E7

Seafield Holiday Flats 3 flats, 1 cottage, 1 pub rm, 1-2 bedrms, sleeps 2-6, min let weekend, £50-£115, Jan-Dec, bus nearby, ferry 12 mls

Mr & Mrs R B Walker, Seafield, Blackwaterfoot, Isle of Arran
☎ *Shiskine (077086) 209*

1 caravan, sleeps 6, min let 1 night, £50-£110, Jan-Dec, bus nearby, ferry 10 mls

---

1 caravan, sleeps 4-6, min let weekend, £60-£120, Jan-Dec, bus nearby, ferry 11 mls

Mr & Mrs W McConnell, Rock Hotel, Blackwaterfoot, Isle of Arran
☎ *Shiskine (077086) 225*

---

1 caravan, sleeps 6, £85-£135, Apr-Oct, ferry 10 mls

Mr Lochrie, The Greannan Hotel, Blackwaterfoot, Isle of Arran
☎ *Shiskine (077086) 200*

---

1 cottage, 1 pub rm, 2 bedrms, sleeps 6, min let weekend, from £60, Jan-Dec, bus nearby

(bowling green)

Mrs S M Bannatyne, 7 Torr-Righe, Shiskine, Isle of Arran
☎ *Shiskine (077086) 377*

BLAIR ATHOLL Perthshire Map Ref. 4C12

River Tilt Caravan Park 10 caravans, sleeps 2-8, min let 2 nights, £100-£200, Jan-Dec, bus nearby, rail 1 ml

(barbecue, bowling)
River Tilt Caravan Park, Bridge of Tilt, Blair Atholl, Perthshire, PH18 5TE
☎ *Blair Atholl (079681) 467*

Blair Castle Caravan Park 25 caravans, sleeps 6-8, min let 3 nights, £85-£160, Apr-Oct, bus 500 yds, rail 500 yds

Blair Castle Caravan Park, Blair Atholl, Perthshire
☎ *Blair Atholl (079681) 263*

HIGHLY COMMENDED

5 cottages, 1 pub rm, 1-3 bedrms, sleeps 2-8, min let 3 nights, £125-£315, Jan-Dec, bus nearby, rail 1 ml

(bowls)

Vale of Atholl Country Cottages, Bridge of Tilt, Blair Atholl, Perthshire, PH18 5TE
☎ *Blair Atholl (079681) 467*
Converted farm units set around south facing landscaped garden; each with patio furniture.

BLAIR DRUMMOND Perthshire Map Ref. 2A4

1 cottage, 1 pub rm, 2 bedrms, sleeps 4-5, £70-£100, Jun-Sep, bus ¼ ml

Mrs J Inglis, Briarlands Farm, Blair Drummomd, Perthshire, FK9 4UP
☎ *Doune (0786) 841309*

BLAIRGOWRIE Perthshire Map Ref. 2C1

1 bungalow, 1 pub rm, 3 bedrms, sleeps 6, £80-£100, Mar-Nov, bus nearby, rail 15 mls, airport 50 mls

Mrs S D Bell, Ardmuir, Coupar Angus Road, Rosemount, Blairgowrie, Perthshire, PH10 6LU
☎ *Blairgowrie (0250) 3238*

WWW

1 cottage, 1 pub rm, 1 bedrm, sleeps 4, min let weekend, £55-£60, Apr-Oct, bus 3 mls, rail 7 mls, airport 45 mls

1 caravan, sleeps 6-8, min let weekend, £50-£55, Apr-Oct, bus 3 mls, rail 7 mls, airport 45 mls

Mrs H Wightman, Bankhead Cottage, Clunie, Blairgowrie, Perthshire, PH10 6SG
☎ *Essendy (025084) 281*

Altamount Chalets 18 chalet/log cabins, 1 pub rm, 1-3 bedrms, sleeps 2-8, min let 2 nights/weekend, £80-£225, Jan-Dec, bus nearby, rail 15 mls

Altamount Chalets, Coupar Angus Road, Blairgowrie, Perthshire, PH10 6JN
☎ *Blairgowrie (0250) 3324*

6 cottages, 1 pub rm, 2-3 bedrms, sleeps 4-8, £65-£140, Apr-Oct, bus 2 mls, rail 18 mls

Mrs Courts, Rosemount Farm, Parkhead Rd., Blairgowrie, Perthshire, PH10 6LP
☎ *Blairgowrie (0250) 2339*

2 caravans, sleeps 2, min let weekend, £32-£35, Apr-Sep, bus nearby, rail 20 mls

Mrs J Smith, Cleveland, Rattray, by Blairgowrie, Perthshire, PH10 7HF
☎ *Blairgowrie (0250) 3692*

COMMENDED WW

1 bungalow, 2 pub rms, 3 bedrms, sleeps 6, £95-£125, May-Oct, bus nearby, rail 14 mls, airport 22 mls

Mr L I R Abbott, Birchbank, Montgomerie Terrace, Skelmorlie, Ayrshire, PA17 5DT
☎ *Wemyss Bay (0475) 521057*
Detached timber clad bungalow with large garden in quiet area. Approx 2 miles/3km from Blairgowrie.

Blairgowrie Caravan Park 6 caravans, sleeps 6, min let 1 night, £75-£150, Jan-Dec, bus 300 yds, rail 14 mls, airport 55 mls

Mr C Wood, Blairgowrie Caravan Park, Hatton Rd, Rattray, Blairgowrie, Perthshire
☎ *Blairgowrie (0250) 2941*

VAT is shown at 15%: changes in this rate may affect prices.

4 bedsits, 3 pub rms, 6 bedrms, sleeps 2-6, min let weekend, £45-£65, Jan-Dec, bus nearby, rail 14 mls

Mr & Mrs Hayes, Cruachan, Victoria Street, Rattray, Blairgowrie, Perthshire, PH10 7AG
☎ Blairgowrie (0250) 4133

COMMENDED
♛ ♛ ♛

2 flats, 1 pub rm, 1 bedrm, sleeps 2-4, min let weekend, £80-£100, Jan-Dec, bus nearby, rail 16 mls, airport 20 mls

Mrs J Roper, Glenshieling Guest House, Hatton Road, Rattray, Blairgowrie, Perthshire, PH10 7HZ
☎ Blairgowrie (0250) 4605
Conversion of former lodge in grounds of guest house. Town centre within easy reach.

---

6 flats, 1-2 bedrms, sleeps 2-4, min let weekend, £80-£160, Jan-Dec, bus nearby

Mr B G Cale, Queen's Hotel, 21 High Street, Blairgowrie, Perthshire, PH10 6ET
☎ Blairgowrie (0250) 2217

Eastfield House 1 house, 4 flats, 1 pub rm, 2-3 bedrms, sleeps 4-9, min let weekend, £55-£195, Jan-Dec, bus nearby, rail 18 mls, airport 20 mls

Mr Peter Russell, Eastfield, New Road, Rattray, Blairgowrie, Perthshire, PH10 7DJ
☎ Blairgowrie (0250) 2105

---

by BLAIRGOWRIE Perthshire Map Ref. 2C1

2 cottages, 1 pub rm, 3 bedrms, sleeps 8, £82-£155, Mar-Nov, bus 4 mls, rail 16 mls

Mrs Bruce, Riverside Holiday Homes, Drumkilbo Mains, Meigle, Perthshire, PH12 8QS
☎ Meigle (08284) 213

---

1 cottage, 2 pub rms, 2 bedrms, sleeps 6, min let weekend, £75-£250, Jan-Dec, bus 3 mls

(hang gliding, canoeing)

Mrs A Renfrew, Kynballoch, Blairgowrie, Perthshire, PH10 7PE
☎ Blairgowrie (0250) 2329

---

1 house, 4 flats, 1-2 pub rms, 2-3 bedrms, sleeps 4-8, min let weekend (low season), from £135, Jan-Dec, bus 2 mls, rail 16 mls, airport 18 mls

(putting green, barbeque)

Mrs M Nicholson, Craighall Sawmill House, Rattray, Blairgowrie, Perthshire, PH10 7JB
☎ Blairgowrie (0250) 3956   (See colour ad. 2 p. xxxiii)

1 cottage, 1 pub rm, 2 bedrms, sleeps 7, min let weekend (low season), £60-£85, Apr-Jan, bus 4 mls, rail 20 mls, airport 20 mls

Mrs Church, Easter Drimmie, Blairgowrie, Perthshire, PH10 7JD
☎ *Bridge of Cally (025086) 359*

AWAITING INSPECTION

2 houses, 1 pub rm, 2-3 bedrms, sleeps 5-10, min let 4 nights, £150-£230, Jan-Dec, bus 1 ml, rail 15 mls, airport 20 mls

Mr & Mrs L Blair-Oliphant, Ardblair Castle, Blairgowrie, Perthshire
☎ *Blairgowrie (0250) 3155*

---

1 flat, 4 pub rms, 2 bedrms, sleeps 4-5, min let weekend, £80-£130, Jan-Dec, bus 400 yds, rail 10 mls

Mr Rix, Cargil House, Cargill, Blairgowrie, Perthshire, PH2 6DT
☎ *Meikleour (025083) 334*

---

1 bungalow, 1 pub rm, 3 bedrms, sleeps 5-6, £80-£145, Jan-Dec

Finlayson Hughes, Bank House, 82 Atholl Road, Pitlochry, Perthshire, PH16 5BL
☎ *Pitlochry (0796) 2512*

BLAIRLOGIE Stirlingshire Map Ref. 2A4

1 bungalow, 1 pub rm, 3 bedrms, sleeps 5, min let weekend, £90-£110, Jan-Dec, bus nearby, rail 3 mls, airport 30 mls

Mrs S F Snowie, East Gogar, Blairlogie, Stirlingshire, FL9 5QB
☎ *Alloa (0259) 723240/215028*

BLAIRMORE Argyll Map Ref. 1G4

Gairletter Caravan Park 4 caravans, sleeps 6, min let 2 nights, £65-£85, Apr-Oct, bus nearby, rail 10 mls, ferry 10 mls, airport 40 mls

Gairletter Caravan Park, Blairmore, by Dunoon, Argyll
☎ *Ardentinny (036981) 208*

BO'NESS West Lothian Map Ref. 2B4

1 caravan, sleeps 10, min let weekend, £120-£150, Jan-Dec, rail 3 mls, airport 15 mls

Mrs B Kirk, Kinglass Farm, Bo'ness, West Lothian
☎ *Bo'ness (0506) 822861*

BOAT OF GARTEN Inverness-shire Map Ref. 4C10

1 cottage, 1 pub rm, 2 bedrms, sleeps 5, from £70, Mar-Oct, bus nearby, rail 6 mls

Mrs I Anderson, Spey Vale, Drumullie Road, Boat of Garten, Inverness-shire, PH24 3BD
☎ *Boat of Garten (047983) 248*

VAT is shown at 15%: changes in this rate may affect prices.

20 caravans, sleeps 6, min let 1 night, £115-£240, Dec-Oct, bus nearby, rail 5 mls, airport 30 mls

♿ 🚻 E 🏠 ⓐ 🎏 ⊘ 🗑 ⚲ 🛏 🗄 🔲 ☎ ⊙ ❄ 🐴 P ∥ 🛷 ▥ ⛺ † ⛰ 🔍 🌐   🎣 🚲 🐟
🏹 🎣 ∪ △ ↾ ∕ ⚞ ✕ 🏋 T D

Campgrounds of Scotland, Boat of Garten, Inverness-shire
☎ *Boat of Garten (047983) 652*

👑 👑 👑 👑

1 flat, 1 pub rm, 2 bedrms, sleeps 4, £70-£80, Mar-Oct, bus nearby, rail 6 ½ mls

♿ 🚻 E 🛏 ⓐ ⊘ 🔲 🗄 🔲 ⚲ ☎ ⊙ ❄ P 🛷 ▥ †   🔍 🎣 ∪ △ ↾ ⚞ ✕ 🏋

Mr G Keir, 4 High Terrace, Boat of Garten, Inverness-shire
☎ *Boat of Garten (047983) 262*

---

1 flat, 2 pub rms, 3 bedrms, sleeps 6-8, £100-£150, Apr-Oct, bus nearby, rail 6 mls

♿ 🚻 E 🛏 🏠 ⓐ ▥ ⊘ 🔲 🗄 ⚡ ⚲ ☎ ⊙ ❄ 🐴 P 🛷 ▥ †   🔍 🎣 ∪ △ ↾ ∕ ✕ 🏋

Mrs J Crawford, 2 Belle Isle Avenue, Uddingston, Glasgow
☎ *Uddingston (0698) 813141*

---

4 chalet/log cabins, 1 pub rm, 2 bedrms, sleeps 6, min let 2 nights, £95-£200, bus nearby, rail 8 mls, airport 30 mls

♿ 🚻 E 🛏 ⓐ ▥ 🗄 ⊘ 🔲 🗄 ⊙ P   🎣 ∪ △ ↾ ⚞ ✕ 🏋 🏇 T

Mr W B & Mrs Grant, Mains of Garten Farm, Boat of Garten, Inverness-shire, PH24 3BY
☎ *Boat of Garten (047983) 228*

---

1 cottage, 1 pub rm, 2 bedrms, sleeps 4-6, min let weekend (low season), £85-£140, Jan-Dec, bus ½ ml, rail 7 mls, airport 30 mls

♿ 🚻 E 🛏 🏠 ⓐ 🔲 🗄 🔲 ⚲ ☎ ⊙ ❄ P †   🔍 🎣 ∪ △ ↾ ⚞ ✕ 🏋 🏇

5 caravans, sleeps 6, min let weekend (low season), £65-£95, Dec-Oct, bus ½ ml, rail 7 mls, airport 30 mls

E ⊘ 🔲 ⊙ P   🎣 ∪ △ ↾ ⚞ ✕ 🏋 🏇

Mrs Margaret M Grant, Mullingarroch Croft, Boat of Garten, Inverness-shire, PH24 3BY
☎ *Boat of Garten (047983) 645*

---

1 chalet/log cabin, 1 cottage, 1 pub rm, 1-2 bedrms, sleeps 2-6, min let 2 nights, £70-£126, Jan-Dec, bus 1 ml, rail 7 mls, airport 32 mls

♿ 🚻 E 🛏 ⓐ ▥ 🗄 🔲 🗄 ⚲ ☎ ⊙ ❄ P 🛷 ▥   🔍 🎣 ∪ △ ↾ ⚞ ✕ 🏋 (canoe hire & instruction)

Mrs B A Davison, Locheil, Drumullie, by Boat of Garten, Inverness-shire, PH24 3BX
☎ *Boat of Garten (047983) 603*

Boat of Garten Site 1 caravan, sleeps 6, min let 1 night (low season), £58-£75, Dec-Oct, bus nearby, rail 4 mls, airport 25 mls

🏠 E ⊘ 🔲 🗑 🗄 ⚲ ☎ ⊙ 🐴 P † ⛰ 🔍 🌐   🎣 🚲 🐟 🔍 🎣 ∪ △ ↾ ∕ ⚞ ⚟ ✕ 🏋 T

Mr H M McKerrow, 5d Spylaw Park, Edinburgh, EH13 0LS
☎ *031 441 7903/445 4488*

---

1 cottage, 1 pub rm, 1 bedrm, sleeps 2, £65-£75, Apr-Oct, bus nearby, rail 5 mls, airport 24 mls

♿ 🚻 E 🏠 ⓐ ▥ 🗄 🔲 🗄 ⚲ ☎ ⊙ ❄ 🐴 P 🛷 † ⛰   🎣 ∪ △ ↾ ⚞ ✕ 🏋

Miss S R Wilson, Fasdail, Boat of Garten, Inverness-shire, PH24 3BW
☎ *Boat of Garten (047983) 221*

Prices shown are for guidance only. Please send SAE with each enquiry.

1 cottage, 1 pub rm, 3 bedrms, sleeps 5, min let weekend, £85-£130, Feb-Nov, bus 400 yds, rail 7 mls, airport 37 mls

Miss K M Grant, West Cullachie, Boat of Garten, Inverness-shire, PH24 3BY
☎ *Nethybridge (047982) 226*

---

1 house, 2 pub rms, 3 bedrms, sleeps 8, £160-£300, Jan-Dec, bus ½ ml, rail 5 mls

Charles Herd, Craigour, Gullane, East Lothian, EH31 2DH
☎ *Gullane (0620) 843240*

COMMENDED
👑👑👑

1 cottage, 2 pub rms, 2 bedrms, sleeps 6, min let weekend, £100-£180, Jun-Sep, bus ½ ml, rail 5 mls

Mrs L Nicholl, The Carrbridge Gift Shop, Carrbridge, by Aviemore, G61 2SE
☎ *Carrbridge (047984) 320*
Semi detached, of highland character, close to main A95. Enclosed garden & garage. Views to mountains.

---

1 bungalow, 2 pub rms, 2 bedrms, sleeps 6, £80-£160, Jan-Dec, bus nearby, rail 5 mls, airport 27 mls

Mr & Mrs Gregson, Heatherlea Guest House, Boat of Garten, Inverness-shire
☎ *Boat of Garten (047983) 674*

---

1 cottage, 1 pub rm, 3 bedrms, sleeps 6, min let weekend, £50-£130, Jan-Dec, bus 500 yds, rail 5 mls, airport 34 mls

Mrs Maureen H Smyth, Conifer Cottages, Chapelton, Boat of Garten, Inverness-shire, PH24 3BU
☎ *Boat of Garten (047983) 327*

---

up to APPROVED
👑👑

2 chalet/log cabins, 1 pub rm, 3 bedrms, sleeps 5, min let weekend, £70-£140, Jan-Dec, bus nearby, rail 5 mls, airport 30 mls

Mr R M Sim, Moorfield House Hotel, Deshar Road, Boat of Garten, Inverness-shire
☎ *Boat of Garten (047983) 646*
Two chalets to rear of small hotel in centre of highland village.

👑👑👑

1 bungalow, 1 pub rm, 3 bedrms, sleeps 6, £150-£200, May-Nov, bus 400 yds, rail 6 mls

Mrs I Souter, 10 Cliff Park, Cults, Aberdeen, Aberdeenshire, AB1 9JT
☎ *Aberdeen (0224) 867000*

---

1 house, 2 pub rms, 5 bedrms, sleeps 9, min let weekend, from £140, Jan-Dec, bus nearby, rail nearby, airport 30 mls

Maureen Hendry, Aviemore Holiday Houses, P.O.Box 2, Aviemore, Inverness-shire
☎ *Aviemore (0479) 811177*

VAT is shown at 15%: changes in this rate may affect prices.

1 cottage, 2 pub rms, 3 bedrms, sleeps 6, min let weekend, £100-£180, Jan-Dec, bus nearby, rail 5 mls, airport 36 mls

⬛⬛⬛⬛⬛⬛⬛⬛⬛⬛⬛⬛⬛⬛⬛⬛⬛⬛⬛⬛⬛⬛⬛⬛⬛⬛⬛⬛⬛⬛⬛⬛

Mrs L Kay, 6 Brewster Drive, Forres, Moray
☎ *Forres (0309) 73816*

---

1 flat, 1 pub rm, 2 bedrms, sleeps 4-6, min let weekend, £100-£150, Apr-Oct, bus nearby, rail 10 mls, airport 30 mls

⬛⬛⬛⬛⬛⬛⬛⬛⬛⬛⬛⬛⬛⬛⬛⬛⬛⬛⬛⬛⬛⬛⬛⬛⬛
(birdwatching, steam railway)

Mr Brian Taylor, Easter Cullachie, Boat of Garten, Inverness-shire
☎ *Boat of Garten (047982) 298 (after 6pm)*

---

1 house, 2 pub rms, 3 bedrms, sleeps 8, £100-£150, Apr-Oct

⬛⬛⬛⬛⬛⬛⬛⬛⬛⬛⬛⬛⬛⬛⬛⬛⬛⬛⬛⬛⬛⬛⬛⬛⬛⬛

Mr & Mrs A Connelly, 37 Duncan Avenue, Arbroath, Angus, DD11 2DA
☎ *Arbroath (0241) 74189*

BOLTON East Lothian Map Ref. 2E5

1 cottage, 2 pub rms, 3 bedrms, sleeps 6, min let 1 night, £120-£160, Apr-Oct, bus nearby, rail 6 mls, airport 26 mls

⬛⬛⬛⬛⬛⬛⬛⬛⬛⬛⬛⬛⬛⬛⬛⬛⬛⬛⬛⬛⬛⬛⬛⬛⬛⬛⬛⬛⬛⬛⬛⬛

Mrs N D Steven, Under Bolton, Haddington, East Lothian, EH41 4HL
☎ *Gifford (062081) 318*
Traditional stone cottage in rural hamlet, convenient for coast and local golf courses.

BONAR BRIDGE Sutherland Map Ref. 4A6

1 cottage, 1 pub rm, 2 bedrms, sleeps 4, £70-£110, Mar-Oct

⬛⬛⬛⬛⬛⬛⬛⬛⬛⬛⬛⬛⬛⬛⬛⬛⬛⬛⬛

Finlayson Hughes, Bank House, 82 Atholl Road, Pitlochry, Perthshire, PH16 5BL
☎ *Pitlochry (0796) 2512*

BORELAND, by Lockerbie Dumfriesshire Map Ref. 2C9

1 house, 1 pub rm, 3 bedrms, sleeps 6, min let weekend, £70-£85, Apr-Oct, bus 9 mls, rail 9 mls

⬛⬛⬛⬛⬛⬛⬛⬛⬛⬛⬛⬛⬛⬛⬛⬛⬛⬛⬛⬛⬛⬛⬛⬛

Mrs Elliot, Barton Lodge, Steeple Aston, Oxfordshire, OX5 3QH
☎ *Steeple Aston (0869) 47219*

BORGUE Kirkcudbrightshire Map Ref. 2A11

1 cottage, 1 pub rm, 2 bedrms, sleeps 5, £60-£100, Apr-Oct

⬛⬛⬛⬛⬛⬛⬛⬛⬛⬛⬛⬛⬛⬛⬛⬛⬛⬛⬛⬛⬛⬛⬛

Mrs Gray, Ingleston Farm, Borgue, Kirkcudbrightshire
☎ *Borgue (05577) 208*
Semi detached traditional stone unit on working farm in rural setting.

1 cottage, 2 pub rms, 2 bedrms, sleeps 5, min let weekend, £55-£85, Jan-Dec, bus nearby, rail 30 mls, airport 100 mls

   ⛐ ⓦⓒ E ... [icons]

Mrs S Jennings, Minto, Twynholm, Kirkcudbright, DG6 4SZ
☎ *Borgue (05577) 331*

BORGUE AREA Kirkcudbrightshire Map Ref. 2A11

2 houses, 5 cottages, 1 pub rm, 2-3 bedrms, sleeps 4-6, from £60, Apr-Oct

   ⛐ ⓦⓒ E ... [icons]

G M Thomson & Company, 27 King Street, Castle Douglas, Kirkcudbrightshire, DG7 1AB
☎ *Castle Douglas (0556) 2701*

BORVE, by Portree Isle of Skye, Inverness-shire Map Ref. 3D9

1 caravan, sleeps 4-6, min let 1 night, £45-£55, Jan-Dec, bus 400 yds, rail 38 mls, ferry 38 mls, airport 30 mls

   ⛐ ⓦⓒ E ... [icons]

Mrs Morrison, Dunalan, 28 Borve, Skeabost Bridge, by Portree, Isle of Skye, Inverness-shire
☎ *Skeabost Bridge (047032) 366*

---

1 flat, 2 pub rms, 4 bedrms, sleeps 2-9, min let weekend, £100-£150, Jan-Dec, bus nearby, rail 45 mls, ferry 40 mls, airport 32 mls

   ⛐ ⓦⓒ E ... [icons]

Mrs M Macdonald, Moorside, Borve, by Portree, Isle of Skye, Inverness-shire
☎ *Skeabost Bridge (047032) 301*

BOTHKENNAR, by Airth Stirlingshire Map Ref. 2B4

1 cottage, 2 pub rms, 3 bedrms, sleeps 6, min let weekend, from £80, Jan-Dec, bus 1 ml, rail 2 mls, airport 25 mls

   ⛐ ⓦⓒ E ... [icons]

Mrs A Paterson, The Mains of Powfoulis, Bothkennar, Falkirk, Stirlingshire, FK2 8PP
☎ *Airth (032483) 410*

BOULTENSTONE, by Strathdon Aberdeenshire Map Ref. 4E10

1 caravan, sleeps 6, min let weekend, £60-£100, Apr-Oct, bus 3 mls, rail 40 mls, airport 40 mls

   ⛐ ⓦⓒ E ... [icons]

Boultenstone Hotel, Boultenstone, by Strathdon, Aberdeenshire, AB3 8XQ
☎ *Strathdon (09752) 254*

BOWER, by Wick Caithness Map Ref. 4D3

1 house, 1 pub rm, 2 bedrms, sleeps 4-6, £40-£60, Apr-Oct, bus 1 ml, rail 10 mls

   ⛐ ⓦⓒ E ... [icons]

Mrs M Macadie, Bower Tower, Bower, Wick, Caithness
☎ *Gillock (095586) 252*

BOWMORE Isle of Islay, Argyll Map Ref. 1C6

4 flats, 1 pub rm, 1-2 bedrms, sleeps 4-6, min let weekend, £70-£175, Jan-Dec, bus nearby, ferry 10 mls, airport 6 mls

   ⛐ ⓦⓒ E ... [icons]

Islay Rhind, c/o Mrs F McNeill, 19 Elder Crescent, Bowmore, Isle of Islay, Argyll
☎ *Bowmore (049681) 532*

VAT is shown at 15%: changes in this rate may affect prices.

1 bungalow, 1 pub rm, 3 bedrms, sleeps 5-6, £69-£138, Jan-Dec, bus 2 mls, ferry 10 mls, airport 6 mls

  ♿ 🚻 E 🚗 🏠 ◎ 📺 📻 🛏 ❄ 🐎 🅿 🐕 🏚 † 🐄

Mrs J V Abbott, Duich Farm, Bowmore, Isle of Islay, Argyll
☎ *Bowmore (049681) 497*

---

1 cottage, 1 pub rm, 3 bedrms, sleeps 7, £60-£140, Jan-Dec, bus nearby, ferry 10 mls, airport 5 mls

  ♿ 🚻 E 🚗 📱 🏠 🍴 📞 ◎ 📺 📻 📻 🚿 🛏 ❄ 🐎 🅿 🐕 † 🏚   🎵 ⛵ 🏹 ⚓ 🎿 🚴 🎣 ✕ 🐟

Mrs E G Lindsay, 51A Jamieson Street, Bowmore, Isle of Islay, Argyll
☎ *Bowmore (049681) 478*

BRAEMAR Aberdeenshire Map Ref. 4D11

1 cottage, 1 pub rm, 2 bedrms, sleeps 5-6, min let 5 nights (low season), £130, mid Dec-mid Oct, bus ½ ml, rail 49 mls, airport 58 mls

  ♿ 🚻 E 🚗 🏠 🍴 📞 ◎ 📺 📻 📻 🛏 ☺ ❄ 🐎 🅿 🐕 🏚 † 🏚   🎵 ⛵ 🏹 🎣 🎿 ✕ 🐟

Mr & Mrs W J O Rose, 9 Glenshee Road, Braemar, Aberdeenshire, AB3 5YQ
☎ *Braemar (03383) 275*

---

1 bungalow, 1 pub rm, 3 bedrms, sleeps 6, from £145, Jan-Dec, bus nearby

  ♿ 🚻 E 🏠 🍴 📞 ◎ 📺 📻 📻 🛏 ☺ ❄ 🅿 🐕 †   🎵 ⛵ 🏹 🎣 🎿 ✕ 🐟

Mrs Ramsay, 410 Great Western Road, Aberdeen
☎ *Aberdeen (0224) 316115*

---

1 cottage, 2 pub rms, 2 bedrms, sleeps 4, £115-£138, Apr-Oct

  ♿ 🚻 E 🚗 🏠 ◎ 📺 🚿 🅿 🐕 †   ✕

Savills, 12 Clerk Street, Brechin, Angus
☎ *Brechin (03562) 2187*

---

1 cottage, 1 pub rm, 2 bedrms, sleeps 2-4, £85-£110, Jan-Dec, bus ¼ ml, rail 60 mls, airport 60 mls

  ♿ 🚻 E 📱 🏠 🍴 📞 ◎ 📺 📞 📻 🚿 🛏 ☺ ❄ 🅿 †   🏄 🎵 ⛵ 🏹 🎣 🎿 ✕ 🐟

Mrs Sutherland, Birchwood, Chapel Brae, Braemar, Aberdeenshire
☎ *Braemar (03383) 681*

BRAES Isle of Skye, Inverness-shire Map Ref. 3D9

1 caravan, sleeps 6, min let 1 night, £55-£60, Apr-Oct, bus 5 mls, rail 36 mls, ferry 35 mls, airport 30 mls

  ♿ 🚻 E 📱 🏠 🍳 ❄ 🐎 🅿 † 🐄

Mrs M Bruce, Cruachanlea, 3 Lower Ollach, Braes, by Portree, Isle of Skye, Inverness-shire
☎ *Sligachan (047852) 233*

BRAES, by Portree Isle of Skye, Inverness-shire Map Ref. 3D9

1 house, 1 pub rm, 4 bedrms, sleeps 6-7, £60-£140, Apr-Nov, bus 5 mls, rail 34 mls, ferry 34 mls

  ♿ 🚻 E 🏠 ◎ 📺 🚿 🛏 ❄ 🅿 🐕 †   🦅 🦆 🔍 🌳 🎵 ⛵ ⚓ 🎿 🚴 🎣 🐟 🐄

Mrs J D Bengough, White Lodge, Church Street, Sidbury, Devon, EX10 0SB
☎ *Sidbury (03957) 214*

     Prices shown are for guidance only. Please send SAE with each enquiry.

BRAIGO AREA Isle of Islay, Argyll Map Ref. 1B5

16 cottages, 3 bedsits, 1 pub rm, 1-3 bedrms, sleeps 2-8, min let long weekend, £66-£264, Jan-Dec, bus 6 mls, ferry 15 mls, airport 15 mls

⅃ ⌇ E ↩ ⌨ ◎ ⌂ ... □ ⌗ ☀ ⋆ ⊙ ... ♘ ⛺ ⊞ ↩ ⌂ ✆ ... (windsurfing, sub-aqua, birdwatching)

Iolair Estate Company, 31 Bellairs, Sutton, by Ely, Cambridgeshire, CB6 2RW
☎ *Ely (0353) 777349*

---

by BRECHIN Angus Map Ref. 4F12

2 cottages, 1 pub rm, 2-3 bedrms, sleeps 4-6, £80-£160, Jan-Dec, bus ½ ml, rail 15 mls, airport 50 mls

⅃ ⌇ E ↩ ⌨ ◎ ⌂ □ ◎ □ ⌂ ◎ ☀ ⋆ ♘ P ⛺ ⊞ † ⌂ ...

Blakes Holidays, Wroxham, Norwich, NR12 8DH
☎ *Wroxham (06053) 2917*
Traditional stone built units in grounds of victorian lodge. High position overlooks Carse of Gowrie.

BRIDGE OF ALLAN Stirlingshire Map Ref. 2A4

1 flat, 1 pub rm, 2 bedrms, sleeps 4, min let weekend, £60-£110, Jan-Dec, bus nearby, rail 1 ml

⅃ ⌇ E ↩ ⌂ ⊞ □ ⌂ □ ⌗ ⌂ ♘ ⛺ † ... ∪ ⌂ ✗ ...

Mrs Murdoch, Ardshiel, Stirling Road, Dunblane, Perthshire, FK15 9EZ
☎ *Dunblane (0786) 822150*

BRIDGE OF CALLY Perthshire Map Ref. 2C1

Stroneaird 1 bungalow, 2 pub rms, 3 bedrms, sleeps 5, £85-£90, Apr-Oct, bus 400 yds, rail 21 mls

⅃ ⌇ E ↩ ⌂ ◎ □ ⌂ ⌂ ☀ ♘ P ⛺ ⊞ † ... ⌂ ∪ ✗ ...

Mrs A Powrie, Airlie Cottage, Middle Road, Rattray, Blairgowrie, Perthshire, PH10 7EL
☎ *Blairgowrie (0250) 3671*

---

1 house, 3 pub rms, 3 bedrms, sleeps 5, from £100, Apr-Sep, bus 6 mls, rail 21 mls

⅃ ⌇ E ↩ ⌂ ⌂ ◎ □ □ ⌂ ⌗ ⌂ ☀ ♘ P ⛺ † ... ∪ ✗ ...

Bell-Ingram, Durn, Isla Road, Perth, PH2 7HF
☎ *Perth (0738) 21121*

COMMENDED
👑 👑 👑

2 houses, 1-2 pub rms, 2-3 bedrms, sleeps 6-8, min let weekend, £86-£235, Jan-Dec, bus 8 mls, rail 26 mls, airport 65 mls

⅃ ⌇ E ↩ ⌂ ⊞ □ ◎ □ ⌂ ⌂ ◎ ☀ ⋆ ♘ P ⛺ ⊞ ⌂ ... ⌂ ∪ ⌂ ...

Mr B F L Vivian, Glenshee Highland Lodges, Auchenflower, Bridge of Cally, Blairgowrie, Perthshire, PH10 7LQ
☎ *Bridge of Cally (025086) 240*
Self contained units converted from old coaching inn. 11 mls(18 km) from Glenshee ski slopes.

---

1 flat, 1 cottage, 1-2 pub rms, 2-3 bedrms, sleeps 2-6, min let weekend, £70-£130, Jan-Oct, bus ½ ml, rail 14 mls

⅃ ⌇ E ↩ ⌂ ⊞ □ ◎ □ □ ⌂ ⌗ ⌂ ◎ ☀ P ⛺ ⊞ ↩ ⌂ ... ∪ ✗ ...

Mrs E C Mear, Merklands, Ballintuim, Bridge of Cally, Perthshire, PH10 7NN
☎ *Strathardle (025081) 218*

VAT is shown at 15%: changes in this rate may affect prices.

BRIDGE OF EARN Perthshire Map Ref. 2C2

8 chalet/log cabins, 1-2 pub rms, 2-3 bedrms, sleeps 4-8, min let 2-3 nights, £85-£250, Jan-Dec, bus nearby, rail 4 mls, airport 40 mls

&♿E→⌀▦🏠◎🖥📞🗄◪↯📦☺❄🐎🅿//🛏🏛⌂ 📶↝🛋⚲🎿
🎣∪◭🏹⁄🧰✗🧺Ⓣ

Mr Somers, River Edge Chalets, Bridge of Earn, Perth, Perthshire, PH2 9AB
☎ *Bridge of Earn (0738) 812370*
Canadian red cedar bungalows in secluded position by the River Earn.

BRIDGE OF ORCHY Argyll Map Ref. 1G2

1 cottage, 1 pub rm, 3 bedrms, sleeps 6, from £70, Apr-Oct, bus 300 yds, rail 3 ½ mls

&♿E→⌀◎🖥☺🐎🅿🛏🏛† 🛴

D M Mackinnon & Co, Bank of Scotland Buildings, Oban, Argyll, PA34 4LN
☎ *Oban (0631) 63014*

BRIDGE OF WALLS West Mainland, Shetland Map Ref. 5F4

2 flats, 1 pub rm, 1-2 bedrms, sleeps 4-6, min let 5 nights, £30-£60, Jan-Dec, bus nearby, ferry 25 mls, airport 14 mls

&♿E→⌀🖥◎🖥📦❄🐎🅿🛏🏛 📶🎣∪⚓✗🧺🛴

Mrs L Hobbin, 14 Gardentown, Symbister, Whalsay, Shetland
☎ *Symbister (08066) 432*

BRIDGEND Isle of Islay, Argyll Map Ref. 1C6

1 house, 1 cottage, 1 pub rm, 2-4 bedrms, sleeps 6-10, min let weekend, £50-£200, Jan-Dec, ferry 10 mls, airport 10 mls

&♿E→🗄⌀◎↯🖥📦🖥📦☺❄🐎🅿🛏🏛† 🛴

Mrs Porter, West Carrabus Farm, Bridgend, Isle of Islay, Argyll
☎ *Bowmore (049681) 261*

BRIG O'TURK Perthshire Map Ref. 1H3

1 caravan, sleeps 5, min let 3 nights, £60-£70, Apr-Oct, bus 6 mls, airport 48 mls

&♿E🗄⌀↯🖥☺🐎🅿† ✗🧺

Mrs J Glen, The Colloch, Brig O'Turk, by Callander, Perthshire
☎ *Callander (0877) 30277*

BROADFORD Isle of Skye, Inverness-shire Map Ref. 3E10

2 caravans, sleeps 4-6, £50-£60, Apr-Oct, bus 500 yds, rail 8 mls, ferry 8 mls, airport 4 mls

&♿E🗄⌀↯🖥📦🐎🅿†⌂ ∪✗🧺🛴

Mr D J Fletcher, Ashgrove, Blackpark, Broadford, Isle of Skye, Inverness-shire, IV49 9AE
☎ *Broadford (04712) 327*

---

1 caravan, sleeps 6, min let 3 nights, £70-£80, Jan-Dec, bus 400 yds, rail 8 mls, ferry 8 mls

&♿E🗄↯🖥📦🐎🅿† ✗🧺

Mrs C Macrae, Hillcrest, Blackpark, Broadford, Isle of Skye, Inverness-shire
☎ *Broadford (04712) 375*

---

2 flats, 1-2 pub rms, 2-5 bedrms, sleeps 4-9, £113-£210, Mar-Oct, rail 8 mls, ferry 8 mls, airport 5 mls

&♿E→🗄⌀🖥◎🖥📦🖥📦☺❄🐎🅿🛏🏛 ∪◭↝✗🧺

Mr G A Campbell, Rhvellen, Broadford, Isle of Skye, Inverness-shire
☎ *Broadford (04712) 415*

Prices shown are for guidance only. Please send SAE with each enquiry.

BRODICK Isle of Arran Map Ref. 1F7

27 chalet/log cabins, 1 pub rm, 2 bedrms, sleeps 2-6, £45-£130, Apr-Sep, bus 300 yds, ferry 1 ml

Arran Ranchettes, Auchrannie, Brodick, Isle of Arran
☎ *Brodick (0770) 2235*

---

1 chalet/log cabin, 1 cottage, 1-2 pub rms, 1-2 bedrms, sleeps 4-6, £65-£110, Apr-Oct, bus nearby, ferry ½ ml

Mrs I MacMillan, Glenard, Brodick, Isle of Arran
☎ *Brodick (0770) 2318*

COMMENDED

Brodick Castle 2 flats, 1 pub rm, 2-3 bedrms, sleeps 4-6, £95-£250, Mar-Oct, ferry 2 mls

National Trust For Scotland, 5 Charlotte Square, Edinburgh, EH2 4DU
☎ *031 226 5922*
Apartments in castle with fine views over bay. Walking, golf, tennis, sea angling, trekking locally.

---

1 cottage, 1 pub rm, 2 bedrms, sleeps 4, min let weekend (low season), from £40, Jan-Dec, bus ½ ml, ferry 1 ml

Mrs McNicol, Rannoch, Brodick, Isle of Arran, KA27 8BY
☎ *Brodick (0770) 2335*

---

1 house, 1 cottage, 1-3 pub rms, 2-5 bedrms, sleeps 2-8, £80-£160, Apr-Oct, bus nearby, ferry ¼ ml

Miss A Smith, Tighnamara Cottage, Brodick, Isle of Arran, KA27 8AN
☎ *Brodick (0770) 2340/2538*

---

1 flat, 1 bungalow, 1-2 pub rms, 3-4 bedrms, sleeps 4-8, £50-£265, Jan-Dec, rail nearby, ferry ¼ ml

Mrs S Currie, The Homestead, West Mayish, Brodick, Isle of Arran
☎ *Brodick (0770) 2268/2315*

---

1 cottage, 1 pub rm, 2 bedrms, sleeps 5, £80-£135, Apr-Oct, bus nearby, ferry nearby

Peatland Properties, High Greenas, Hurst, Richmond, North Yorkshire
☎ *Richmond (0748) 84592*

---

1 cottage, 2 pub rms, 4 bedrms, sleeps 6, £75-£150, Apr-Sep, bus nearby, ferry 1 ml

Mrs D Wilkie, Cala Sona, 25 Alma Park, Brodick, Isle of Arran
☎ *Brodick (0770) 2353*

1 flat, 1 cottage, 1 pub rm, 1-2 bedrms, sleeps 4, min let weekend, from £60, Jan-Dec, bus 1 ml, ferry 1 ml

⟨symbols⟩

1 caravan, sleeps 4, min let weekend, from £60, Apr-Oct, bus 1 ml, ferry 1 ml

⟨symbols⟩

Mrs J MacLure, The Sheilin, Corriegills, Brodick, Isle of Arran
☎ *Brodick (0770) 2456*

---

4 flats, 1 pub rm, 1-3 bedrms, sleeps 2-7, min let 1 night, £80-£150, Jan-Dec, bus nearby, ferry nearby

⟨symbols⟩

Mr Walker, The Island Hotel, Brodick, Isle of Arran
☎ *Brodick (0770) 2585*

---

1 flat, 2 pub rms, 3 bedrms, sleeps 6, min let weekend, £60-£150, Jan-Dec, bus ¼ ml, ferry ¼ ml

⟨symbols⟩

E F & I Johnston, The Book & Card Centre, Shore Road, Brodick, Isle of Arran
☎ *Brodick (0770) 2288/(077086) 254*
In village overlooking Brodick Bay. Direct access to beach. Tastefully furnished.

---

1 bungalow, 2 pub rms, 3 bedrms, sleeps 6-10, £200-£260, Mar-Oct, bus nearby, ferry ¼ ml

⟨symbols⟩

Mr I Waller, Altanna Hotel, Brodick, Isle of Arran
☎ *Brodick (0770) 2232*

by BRODICK Isle of Arran Map Ref. 1F7

Altbeg Cottages 3 cottages, 2 pub rms, 2-3 bedrms, sleeps 6, £80-£100, Apr-Nov, ferry 1 ml

⟨symbols⟩

Altbeg Cottages, Room 355, 93 Hope Street, Glasgow
☎ *041 884 2706/Brodick (0770) 2386*
Attractive semi detached units of character. 1 mile/2km from Brodick Pier. Quiet rural area.

BRORA Sutherland Map Ref. 4C6

COMMENDED

2 chalet/log cabins, 1 pub rm, 2 bedrms, sleeps 4-6, £90-£150, Jan-Dec, bus ½ ml, rail 1½ mls

⟨symbols⟩

Mr & Mrs I M Sutherland, 5 Crown Square, Murkle, Thurso, Caithness, KW14 8ST
☎ *Castletown (084782) 287*
Traditional wooden units in high position with uninterrupted views of Moray Firth.

---

1 cottage, 2 pub rms, 3 bedrms, sleeps 5, £64-£119, Mar-Oct, rail 2 mls

⟨symbols⟩

Sutherland Estates Office, Duke Street, Golspie, Sutherland, KW10 6RR
☎ *Golspie (04083) 3268*

1 cottage, 1 pub rm, 3 bedrms, sleeps 6, min let weekend, £60-£85, Jan-Dec, bus 400 yds, rail 2 mls, airport 75 mls

 ♿ 🚾 E ⬅ ⌀ ▥ ▯ ◎ ▯ ⬛ 🄿 ⌛ 🏛 †   📡 ⚲ 🎣 ∪ ⧊ ⚓ ► ✗ 🗝 🔭

Mrs R M McCall, Inverbrora, Brora, Sutherland, KW9 6NJ
☎ *Brora (0408) 21208*

---

1 cottage, 2 pub rms, 2 bedrms, sleeps 5, £75-£100, Jan-Dec, bus 1 ml, rail 1 ml, airport 70 mls

 ♿ 🚾 E ⬅ ⌀ ▥ ▯ ◎ ▯ ▢ / ⬛ ☉ ❋ 🐎 🄿 ⌛ †   🎣 ∪ ⧊ ⚓ ► ⁄ ✗ 🗝 🔭

Mrs Barbara Macleod, Ashburn, Strathsteven, Brora, Sutherland, KW9 6ML
☎ *Brora (0408) 21334*

---

by BROUGHTY FERRY Angus Map Ref. 2D2

GAGIE HOUSE

By Dundee, Angus, DD4 0PR. TEL: 082 621 207

GAGIE HOUSE is the centre of a working fruit and sheep farm, 5 miles from Dundee, in a delightful wooded setting. There is an interesting and unusual flat in the historic mansion house (sleeps 5) and a charming cottage in its own garden in the grounds (sleeps 10), both well equipped and with colour television. Many varieties of soft fruit for you to pick. Excellent base for touring hills, golfing or beach.

1 flat, 1 cottage, 1-2 pub rms, 3-5 bedrms, sleeps 5-10, £90-£140, Jun-Sep, bus ¼ ml, rail 4 mls, airport 6 mls

 ♿ 🚾 E ⬅ 🕯 ⌀ ▥ ◎ ▯ 🗆 ▢ ⬛ ☉ ❋ 🐎 🄿 ⌛ 🏛 †   ⚲ 🏹 🎣 ∪ ⧊ ⚓ ► 🗝 🔭
(pick your own soft fruit)

Mr & Mrs F Smoor, Gagie House, by Dundee, Angus, DD4 0PR
☎ *Tealing (082621) 207*

BRUICHLADDICH Isle of Islay, Argyll Map Ref. 1B6

1 cottage, 1 pub rm, 3 bedrms, sleeps 6-8, min let weekend, £50-£160, Jan-Dec, bus nearby, ferry 20 mls, airport 15 mls

 ♿ 🚾 E 🕯 ⌀ ▥ ▯ ◎ ▯ 🗆 ▢ / ⬛ ☉ ❋ 🐎 🄿 ∥ ⌛ 🏛 ⬅ ⛰   🎣 ∪ ⧊ ► ✗ 🗝

Mrs Epps, Caberfeidh, Bruichladdich, Isle of Islay, Argyll
☎ *Port Charlotte (049685) 343*

---

by BRUICHLADDICH Isle of Islay, Argyll Map Ref. 1B6

2 cottages, 1 pub rm, 1-3 bedrms, sleeps 2-6, min let 2 nights, £50-£165, Jan-Dec, bus nearby, ferry 15 mls, airport 15 mls

 ♿ 🚾 E ⬅ ⌀ ▥ ▯ ◎ ▯ 🗆 ⬛ ☉ 🐎 🄿 ⌛ 🏛   🎣 ⚓ ✗ 🗝 🔭 (birdwatching)

G & M Jackson, Coultorsay Farm, Bruichladdich, Isle of Islay, Argyll, PA49 7UN
☎ *Port Charlotte (049685) 444*

BUCHLYVIE Stirlingshire Map Ref. 1H4

1 cottage, 1 pub rm, 1 bedrm, sleeps 2-4, £60-£130, Apr-Oct, bus ¼ ml, rail 14 mls

 ♿ 🚾 E 🕯 ⌀ ▥ ◎ ▯ 🗆 ⬛ ❋ 🄿 †   ∪ ⧊ ► ✗ 🗝

Mrs Rosemary Rollinson, Ballamenoch, Buchlyvie, Stirlingshire
☎ *Buchlyvie (036085) 225*

VAT is shown at 15%: changes in this rate may affect prices.

BUCKIE Banffshire Map Ref. 4E7

1 flat, 1 pub rm, 1 bedrm, sleeps 2-4, from £40, Jan-Dec, bus nearby, rail 12 mls, airport 55 mls

Mrs E Scott, 2 Ianstown Terrace, Buckie, Banffshire, AB5 1SJ
☎ Buckie (0542) 33511

---

2 cottages, 1 pub rm, 2 bedrms, sleeps 4-6, min let weekend (low season), £64-£145, Apr-Oct, bus 1 ½ mls, rail 13 mls, airport 60 mls

W McD Simpson (Dept STB), Blantyre Holiday Homes Ltd, West Bauds, Findochty, Buckie, Banffshire, AB5 2EB
☎ Buckie (0542) 31773

COMMENDED
👑 👑 👑

3 houses, 2 pub rms, 3 bedrms, sleeps 8-9, £80-£150, Apr-Oct, bus nearby, rail 13 mls, airport 60 mls

Mrs Scott, Buckpool Harbour Holiday Homes, Captains House, Land Street, Buckie, Banffshire, AB5 1QS
☎ Buckie (0542) 33292
Recently restored 'fisher type' units. Large garden to Harbour Park; play area. Views of Moray Firth.

by BUCKIE Banffshire Map Ref. 4E7

2 chalet/log cabins, 1-2 pub rms, 2 bedrms, sleeps 2-8, min let 3 nights (low season), £80-£200, Jan-Dec, rail 22 mls, airport 55 mls

Mrs Anthea M Craig, Maryhill Log Cabins, The Old Monastery, Drybridge, Buckie, Banffshire, AB5 2JB
☎ Buckie (0542) 32660

---

1 house, 1 cottage, 1-2 pub rms, 1-3 bedrms, sleeps 6, £100-£170, Apr-Oct, bus 1 ½ mls, rail 6 mls, airport 45 mls

(gliding)

MacKay's Agency, 30 Frederick Street, Edinburgh, EH2 2JR
☎ 031 225 3539

BUNCHREW, by Inverness Inverness-shire Map Ref. 4A8

3 flats, 1 pub rm, 2-3 bedrms, sleeps 5-7, £105-£195, Jan-Dec, bus ½ ml, rail 4 mls, airport 9 mls

Bunchrew House Hotel, Bunchrew, Inverness, Inverness-shire, IV3 6TA
☎ Inverness (0463) 234917

BUNNAHABHAIN Isle of Islay, Argyll Map Ref. 1C5

2 cottages, 1 pub rm, 1 bedrm, sleeps 1-4, min let 4 nights, £65-£100, Jan-Dec, bus nearby, ferry 5 mls, airport 19 mls

Mr A B Lawtie, Bunnahabhain Distillery, Bunnahabhain, Port Askaig, Isle of Islay, Argyll, PA46 7RP
☎ Port Askaig (049684) 646/277   (See colour ad. 3 p. xxxiii)

AWAITING INSPECTION	4 cottages, 2 pub rms, 2-3 bedrms, sleeps 4-6, min let 3 nights, £100-£300, Jan-Dec, bus 4 mls, ferry 4 ¾ mls, airport 20 mls

Mr Lawtie, Bunnahabhain Distillery, Bunnahabhain, Isle of Islay, Argyll
☎ *Port Askaig (049684) 646/277*

BURGHEAD Moray Map Ref. 4D7

Burghead Caravan Site 2 caravans, sleeps 6, min let 2 nights, £50-£90, Apr-Sep, bus nearby, rail 8 mls, airport 30 mls

Mr Donald R Grant, Old Post Office, Relugas, Dunphail, Forres, Moray, IV36 0QL
☎ *Dunphail (03096) 233*

BURNMOUTH Berwickshire Map Ref. 2G5

1 house, 1 pub rm, 3 bedrms, sleeps 8, min let weekend (low season), £50-£75, Jan-Dec, bus ¼ ml, rail 6 mls

Mrs Foster, Harbour View, Burnmouth, Berwickshire, TD14 5ST
☎ *Ayton (08907) 81213*

---

2 houses, 1-2 pub rms, 2 bedrms, sleeps 4-6, £65-£115, Jan-Dec, bus nearby, rail 6 mls, airport 60 mls

Mrs C J Miller, Station House, Burnmouth, Eyemouth, Berwickshire
☎ *Ayton (08907) 81500*

BURRAVOE Yell, Shetland Map Ref. 5G3

1 house, 1 pub rm, 3 bedrms, sleeps 6, £55-£65, Jan-Dec, bus nearby

Mr & Mrs E Oddie, 29 Norstane, Lerwick, Shetland
☎ *Lerwick (0595) 5604*

BURRAY Orkney Map Ref. 5C12

4 flats, 1 pub rm, 3 bedrms, sleeps 6, £60-£150, Jan-Dec, bus nearby, ferry 7 mls, airport 10 mls

Sands Motel, Burray, Orkney
☎ *Burray (085673) 298*

---

4 houses, 2 flats, 1 pub rm, 1-4 bedrms, sleeps 2-8, min let weekend, £45-£120, Jan-Dec, ferry 7-27 mls, airport 15 mls

(sub-aqua diving)

Mrs Duncan, Briarlea, Burray, Orkney, KW17 2SS
☎ *Burray (085673) 225/253*

BURRELTON Perthshire Map Ref. 2C2

1 cottage, 1 pub rm, 3 bedrms, sleeps 6, £75-£130, Apr-Oct

Finlayson Hughes, Bank House, 82 Atholl Rd, Pitlochry, Perthshire, PH16 5BL
☎ *Pitlochry (0796) 2512*

VAT is shown at 15%: changes in this rate may affect prices.

1 bungalow, 1 pub rm, 3 bedrms, sleeps 6, £100-£150, Jan-Dec, bus 300 yds, rail 12 mls, airport 14 mls

Mrs G M Duthie, Langlands Lodge, Woodside, by Coupar Angus, Blairgowrie, Perthshire, PH13 9NP
☎ *Burrelton (08287) 330*

BUTTERSTONE, by Dunkeld Perthshire Map Ref. 2B1

2 flats, 2 cottages, 1-2 pub rms, 2-3 bedrms, sleeps 3-5, £50-£95, Apr-Oct, bus 4 mls, rail 5 mls

Mrs M H Bruges, Laighwood, Dunkeld, Perthshire, PH8 0HB
☎ *Butterstone (03504) 241*

---

1 house, 1-2 pub rms, 2-3 bedrms, sleeps 6, min let weekend, £145-£190, Jan-Dec, bus 7 mls, rail 7 mls, airport 65 mls

Lt Col A M Lyle, Riemore Lodge,Butterstone, Dunkeld, Perthshire, PH8 0HP
☎ *Butterstone (03504) 205*

CAIRNBAAN Argyll Map Ref. 1E4

1 caravan, sleeps 4-6, £45-£75, Apr-Oct, bus 2 mls

Mrs Anderson, Barnekill Farm, Cairnbaan, by Lochgilphead, Argyll
☎ *Lochgilphead (0546) 2262*

---

1 cottage, 1 pub rm, 2 bedrms, sleeps 4, £60-£80, May-Oct, bus nearby

Mrs Turner, Peinmore, Skeabost Bridge, Isle of Skye, Inverness-shire
☎ *Skeabost Bridge (047032) 263*

---

1 house, 2 pub rms, 3 bedrms, sleeps 6, min let weekend, £100-£180, Apr-Oct, bus 1 ml

Mrs Campbell, 17a The Butts, Brentford, Middlesex, TW8 8BJ

CAIRNDOW Argyll Map Ref. 1G3

1 house, 3 cottages, 1 bungalow, 1-3 pub rms, 1-5 bedrms, sleeps 2-12, £50-£250, Apr-Oct, rail 11 mls, airport 50 mls

The Factor, Cairndow Estate, Strone, Cairndow, Argyll, PA26 8BQ
☎ *Cairndow (04996) 284*

CAIRNRYAN Wigtownshire Map Ref. 1F10

10 chalet/log cabins, 1 pub rm, 2 bedrms, sleeps 6, min let 2 nights, £50-£110, Apr-Oct, bus nearby, rail 7 mls

10 caravans, sleeps 4-6, min let 2 nights, £25-£30, Apr-Oct, bus nearby, rail 7 mls

Cairnryan Caravan & Chalet Park, Cairnryan, Wigtownshire
☎ *Cairnryan (05812) 231*

CALBOST, Lochs Isle of Lewis, Western Isles Map Ref. 3D5

1 house, 2 pub rms, 5 bedrms, sleeps 10, £90-£120, Jan-Dec, bus $\frac{1}{4}$ ml, ferry 30 mls, airport 30 mls

🚗♿ 🚾 E ⬛ ⬛ ⬛ ⬛ ⬛ ⬛ ⬛ ⬛ ⬛ ⬛ ⬛ ⬛ ⬛ ⬛ ⬛ ⬛

A MacLeod, Park House, Marybank, Stornoway, Isle of Lewis, Western Isles
☎ *Stornoway (0851) 2308*

CALGARY Isle of Mull, Argyll Map Ref. 1C1

2 cottages, 1 pub rm, 3 bedrms, sleeps 6, £85-£145, Apr-Oct, bus nearby, ferry 27 mls

R S Robertson, 210 Wilton Street, Glasgow, G20 6BL
☎ *041 946 2565*

---

1 cottage, 2 pub rms, 2-3 bedrms, sleeps 6, £100-£125, Jan-Dec, bus $\frac{1}{2}$ ml, airport 21 mls

Mr Bartholomew, Beathaich, Calgary, Isle of Mull, Argyll, PA75 6QT
☎ *Dervaig (06884) 240*

---

1 cottage, 2 pub rms, 2 bedrms, sleeps 5, £90-£135, Jan-Dec, bus nearby, ferry 23 mls

R Stevenson-Jones, Beul-an-Ath, Dervaig, Isle of Mull, Argyll, PA75 6QS
☎ *Dervaig (06884) 337/(09277) 63924*

---

2 stable flats, 1 pub rm, 2 bedrms, sleeps 4-6, min let weekend (low season), £30-£140, Mar-Oct, bus nearby, ferry 27 mls

Mrs Harvey, Frachadil Farm, Calgary, Isle of Mull, Argyll, PA75 6QQ
☎ *Dervaig (06884) 265/Kelso (0573) 24852*

CALLANDER Perthshire Map Ref. 2A3

Tannochbrae Chalet Park 22 chalet/log cabins, 2 pub rms, 2 bedrms, sleeps 4-6, min let 3 nights, £60-£225, Jan-Dec, bus nearby, rail 12 mls

Hoseasons Holidays, Sunway House, Lowestoft, Suffolk, NR32 3LT
☎ *Lowestoft (0502) 62292*

---

2 cottages, 1-2 pub rms, 3 bedrms, sleeps 6, min let weekend, £70-£120, Jan-Dec, bus 400 yds, rail 16 mls

Callandrade Estate, 80 Main Street, Callander, Perthshire, FK17 8BD
☎ *Callander (0877) 30059*

AWAITING
INSPECTION

Invertrossachs Hideaway 1 chalet/log cabin, 2 cottages, 2 pub rms, 2 bedrms, sleeps 4-5, min let weekend (low season), £60-£225, Jan-Dec, bus 6 mls, rail 22 mls, airport 50 mls

Fiona Snow, Invertrossachs Hideaway, Invertrossachs, by Callander, Perthshire
☎ *Callander (0877) 30010*

---

1 house, 1 pub rm, 3 bedrms, sleeps 6, £100-£160, Apr-Oct, bus 250 yds, rail 16 mls

Mrs M Malone, Aveland Lodge, Callander, Perthshire, FK17 8EN
☎ *Callander (0877) 30039*

---

1 flat, 1 pub rm, 2 bedrms, sleeps 4, min let weekend (low season), £50-£95, Apr-Oct, bus 300 yds, rail 16 mls, airport 45 mls

Mrs Gray, The Rectory, 10 Rosemount Park, Blairgowrie, Perthshire, PH10 6TZ
☎ *Blairgowrie (0250) 4583*

---

1 bungalow, 2 pub rms, 3 bedrms, sleeps 6, £110-£150, Jan-Dec, bus 300 yds, rail 16 mls

Mrs Cameron, Tulipan Lodge, Tulipan Crescent, Callander, Perthshire, FK17 8AR
☎ *Callander (0877) 30572*

---

2 cottages, 3 pub rms, 2 bedrms, sleeps 4-6, £90-£165, Apr-Oct, bus 1 ml, rail 17 mls, airport 45 mls

Mrs L Edmunds, Pogles Wood, Leny, Callander, Perthshire, FK17 8HA
☎ *Callander (0877) 30024*

AWAITING INSPECTION

Leny Estate 6 chalet/log cabins, 4 pub rms, 2 bedrms, sleeps 6, min let weekend (low season), £160-£260, Jan-Dec, bus 1 ml, rail 15 mls, airport 36 mls

Mr Roebuck, Leny House, Callander, Perthshire
☎ *Callander (0877) 31078*

👑👑👑

1 bungalow, 2 pub rms, 4 bedrms, sleeps 7, £130-£220, Jan-Dec, bus ¼ ml, rail 16 mls, airport 22 mls

Mrs J Donald, Trean Farm, Callander, Perthshire, FK17 8AS
☎ *Callander (0877) 31160*

---

1 flat, 1 pub rm, 2 bedrms, sleeps 4, £100-£140, Jan-Dec, bus nearby, airport 45 mls

Mrs Smillie, Auchyle, Stirling Road, Callander, Perthshire
☎ *Callander (0877) 31062*

---

by CALLANDER Perthshire Map Ref. 2A3

1 cottage, 2 pub rms, 3 bedrms, sleeps 5, £100-£150, Jan-Dec, bus nearby, rail 20 mls, airport 52 mls

(bird watching, hillclimbing)

Mrs M L Duff, Ardchullarie Lodge, Callander, Perthshire
☎ *Strathyre (08774) 233*

CALVINE Perthshire Map Ref. 4B12

2 cottages, 1 pub rm, 3 bedrms, sleeps 5-6, min let weekend (low season), from £60, Mar-Oct, bus 9 mls, rail 9 mls

Mrs E Martin, Blairfettie, Calvine, Pitlochry, Perthshire, PH18 5UF
☎ *Calvine (079683) 210*

1 cottage, 2 pub rms, 2 bedrms, sleeps 5, min let weekend, from £95, Mar-Oct, rail 7 mls

Wendy Stewart, Clachan of Struan, Calvine, Perthshire, PH18 5UB
☎ *Calvine (079683) 207*

1 cottage, 1 pub rm, 3 bedrms, sleeps 6, £85-£105, May-Oct, bus 4 mls, rail 4 mls

Mrs Macdonald, Invervack Farm, Calvine, Pitlochry, Perthshire, PH18 5UD
☎ *Calvine (079683) 217*

1 cottage, 2 pub rms, 2 bedrms, sleeps 4, £90-£175, Apr-Oct

Finlayson Hughes, Bank House, 82 Atholl Road, Pitlochry, Perthshire, PH16 5BL
☎ *Pitlochry (0796) 2512*

CAMPBELTOWN Argyll Map Ref. 1E7

Kilchrist Castle Cottages 6 cottages, 1 pub rm, 1-3 bedrms, sleeps 2-6, £96-£173, Apr-Oct, bus 600 yds, airport 3 mls

Col & Mrs W T C Angus, Kilchrist Castle, Campbeltown, Argyll, PA28 6PH
☎ *Campbeltown (0586) 53210*

1 cottage, 2 bedrms, sleeps 4, £90-£145, Jan-Dec, bus ¼ ml, airport 3 mls

G E Staples, Oatfield House, Campbeltown, Argyll, PA28 6PH
☎ *Campbeltown (0586) 52601*
Self contained unit attached to Oatfield House and grounds. Overlooks rich farmlands and distant sea.

by CAMPBELTOWN Argyll Map Ref. 1E7

1 house, 2 pub rms, 3 bedrms, sleeps 6, £100-£200, Apr-Oct, bus nearby, airport 4 mls

Blakes Holidays, Wroxham, Norwich, NR12 8DH
☎ *Wroxham (06053) 2917*

CAMPTOWN Roxburghshire Map Ref. 2F8

APPROVED

1 cottage, 1 pub rm, 4 bedrms, sleeps 8, min let 3 nights, £58-£161, Apr-Oct, bus 2 mls, rail 50 mls, airport 50 mls

Mrs M M Anderson, Edgerston Tofts, Camptown, Jedburgh, Roxburghshire, TD8 6NF
☎ *Camptown (08354) 276*
Secluded setting with lovely Cheviot views and walks. Good touring base, plenty scope for children.

CAMUS CROISE, Isle Ornsay Isle of Skye, Inverness-shire Map Ref. 3E10

APPROVED
♕ ♕

1 house, 2 pub rms, 2 bedrms, sleeps 5, £60-£100, Jan-Dec, bus 400 yds, rail 14 mls, ferry 14 mls, airport 11 mls

Miss M M Fraser, Old Post Office House, Isle Ornsay, Isle of Skye, Inverness-shire
☎ *Isle Ornsay (04713) 201*
Modernised croft house in its own grounds overlooking Sound of Sleat.

---

1 cottage, 1 pub rm, 2 bedrms, sleeps 4-5, min let weekend, £70-£90, Jan-Dec, bus 1 ml, rail 15 mls, ferry 15 mls, airport 10 mls

Mr Patrick Walsh, 31 Camus Cross, Isle Ornsay, Isle of Skye, Inverness-shire
☎ *Isle Ornsay (04713) 265*

CAMUSTIANAVAIG, by Portree Isle of Skye, Inverness-shire Map Ref. 3D9

1 caravan, sleeps 4-6, min let 2 nights, £45-£50, Apr-Oct, bus 2 mls, rail 30 mls, ferry 30 mls, airport 20 mls

Mrs Hutcheson, Braes Salmon Station, Camustianavaig, Braes, Isle of Skye, Inverness-shire, IV51 9LQ
☎ *Sligachan (047852) 318*

CANNICH, by Beauly Inverness-shire Map Ref. 3H9

Kerrow Cottages 1 house, 1 cottage, 1-3 pub rms, 2-4 bedrms, sleeps 4-8, £100-£190, Apr-Oct, bus 2 mls, rail 27 mls, airport 34 mls

Mrs S McRae, Kerrow House, Cannich, Strathglass, Inverness-shire, IV4 7NA
☎ *Cannich (04565) 243*

---

6 chalet/log cabins, 1 pub rm, 3 bedrms, sleeps 6-8, £87-£220, Apr-Oct, rail 30 mls, airport 40 mls

Amaro Cottage Holidays, 22 High Street, Alton, Hants
☎ *Alton (0420) 88892 Telex 858963*

Glen Affric Chalet Park 12 chalet/log cabins, 1 pub rm, 3 bedrms, sleeps 6, min let weekend, £80-£230, Apr-Oct, bus 250 yds, rail 27 mls, airport 27 mls

A & M Farquhar, Glen Affric Chalet Park, Drumnadrochit, Inverness-shire, IV3 6TJ
☎ *Drumnadrochit (04562) 224*

CARBOST Isle of Skye, Inverness-shire Map Ref. 3D9

2 cottages, 2 pub rms, 3 bedrms, sleeps 5-8, min let 2 weeks, £75-£130, Jan-Dec, bus ¼ ml, rail 35 ml, ferry 34 mls, airport 28 ml

Mrs E R Wakefield, Glendrynoch Lodge, Carbost, Isle of Skye, Inverness-shire, IV47 8SX
☎ *Carbost (047842) 209*

---

1 bungalow, 2 pub rms, 4 bedrms, sleeps 6, £100-£120, Apr-Dec, bus nearby, rail 25 mls, ferry 25 mls, airport 20 mls

(hillwalking, climbing)

Miss M Steele, 75 Fife Street, Keith, Banffshire, AB5 3EG
☎ *Keith (05422) 2072*

CARGILL Perthshire Map Ref. 2C2

Beech Hedge Restaurant and Caravan Park 1 chalet/log cabin, 1 pub rm, 2 bedrms, sleeps 6, min let 1 night, £81-£115, Apr-Oct, bus nearby, rail 10 mls

8 caravans, sleeps 6, min let 1 night, £46-£98, Apr-Oct, bus nearby, rail 10 mls

Mr M Rowan, Beech Hedge Restaurant & Caravan Park, Perth, PH2 6DU
☎ *Meikleour (025083) 249*

---

1 cottage, 1 pub rm, 2 bedrms, sleeps 7, £65-£85, Apr-Oct, bus nearby, rail 10 mls

Mrs M Livingston, Mains of Cargill, Cargill, Perth, Perthshire, PH2 6DU
☎ *Meikleour (025083) 235*

CARMICHAEL Lanarkshire Map Ref. 2B6

COMMENDED

Carmichael Estate 1 cottage, 1 pub rm, 2 bedrms, sleeps 4, £80-£150, Jan-Dec, bus ½ ml, rail 5 mls, airport 30 mls

Mr Richard Carmichael of Carmichael, Carmichael Estate Office, West Mains, Carmichael, by Biggar, Lanarkshire, ML12 6PG
☎ *Tinto (08993) 336*
Attractive stone cottage in country estate. Good touring base and excellent walking.

CARNOUSTIE Angus Map Ref. 2E2

1 bedsit, 1 bedrm, sleeps 2, from £35, May-Sep, bus nearby, rail nearby, airport 14 mls

Mrs J Samson, 37 Kinloch Street, Carnoustie, Angus, DD7 7EL
☎ *Carnoustie (0241) 53526*

---

1 cottage, 2 pub rms, 2 bedrms, sleeps 4-6, £70-£150, Jan-Dec, bus nearby, rail 300 yds, airport 14 mls

Mrs L J Wolfe, 39 Carlogie Road, Carnoustie, Angus, DD7 6ER
☎ *Carnoustie (0241) 53150*

CARRADALE Argyll Map Ref. 1E7

Shore Holiday Homes 1 cottage, 1 bungalow, 1-2 pub rms, 3-4 bedrms, sleeps 8-10, min let weekend, from £60, Jan-Dec, bus nearby, airport 20 mls

4 caravans, sleeps 6, min let weekend, from £60, Apr-Sep, bus nearby, airport 20 mls

Mr R Galbraith & Mrs M Galbraith, The Barnes, Carradale, Argyll
☎ *Carradale (05833) 274*

up to HIGHLY COMMENDED ✿✿✿✿

1 house, 3 flats, 3 cottages, 1-2 pub rms, 1-4 bedrms, sleeps 2-10, £55-£210, Jan-Dec (flat), Apr-Oct (cottages), bus 800 yds, airport 13 mls

Mrs M MacAlister Hall, Torrisdale Castle, Carradale, by Campbeltown, Argyll, PA28 6QT
☎ *Carradale (05833) 233*
Properties of individual character on privately owned wooded estate within easy reach of the beach.

---

1 house, 2 pub rms, 5 bedrms, sleeps 6-10, min let weekend, £80-£180, Apr-Oct, bus nearby, rail 90 mls, airport 20 mls

Miss J Paterson, Lochpark House, Carradale, Argyll
☎ *Carradale (05833) 225*

---

1 house, 1 pub rm, 4 bedrms, sleeps 4-8, £80-£150, Jan-Dec, bus nearby, airport 14 mls

Mrs Campbell, Whitegables, Carradale, Argyll
☎ *Carradale (05833) 641*

---

1 house, 2 pub rms, 4 bedrms, sleeps 6-8, from £80, Apr-Oct

Mrs Galbraith, Ardcraig, Carradale, by Campbeltown, Argyll
☎ *Carradale (05833) 227*

Carradale Bay Caravan Site 3 caravans, sleeps 4-5, min let 2 nights, £65-£99, Apr-Sep, bus ¼ ml

Mrs Hurst, Wallis Hunter Extras, The Steading, Carradale, Argyll
☎ *Carradale (05833) 683*

---

1 cottage, 1 bungalow, 1 pub rm, 2-3 bedrms, sleeps 6, £60-£150, Jan-Dec, bus 300 yds, ferry 18 mls, airport 20 mls

Mrs Oman, Bayview, Carradale, Argyll
☎ *Carradale (05833) 361*

---

1 cottage, 1 pub rm, 2 bedrms, sleeps 4, min let weekend, £100-£120, Apr-Oct

Mr T K Paterson, Carloonan, Mawcarse, Milnathort, Kinross-shire
☎ *Kinross (0577) 62816*

CARRBRIDGE Inverness-shire Map Ref. 4C10

COMMENDED ✿✿✿

Fairwinds Hotel & Chalets 6 chalet/log cabins, 13 hotel rooms, 1-2 pub rms, 2-3 bedrms, sleeps 4-6, min let 2 nights, £130-£285, Xmas-Oct, bus nearby, rail ½ ml, airport 20 mls

Fairwinds Hotel & Chalets, Carrbridge, Inverness-shire, PH23 3AA
☎ *Carrbridge (047984) 240*
Wooden units surrounded by mature pinewoods in 6 acres of parkland near village. Ski slopes 13 mls.

1 bungalow, 1 pub rm, 3 bedrms, sleeps 6, from £100, Jan-Dec, bus 2 mls, rail 2 mls, airport 27 mls

Mrs A J Macdonald, Keppoch, Roy Bridge, Inverness-shire
☎ Spean Bridge (039781) 240

Lochanhully Lodges 50 chalet/log cabins, 1 pub rm, 3 bedrms, sleeps 6, min let 1 night, £140-£290, Dec-Oct, rail 1 ml, airport 24 mls

(dry-slope skiing)

Lochanhully Lodges, Carrbridge, Inverness-shire
☎ Carrbridge (047984) 234

2 chalet/log cabins, 1-3 pub rms, 3 bedrms, sleeps 6, from £100, May-Nov

Mrs E Mitchell, Ellanard, Station Road, Carrbridge, Inverness-shire
☎ Carrbridge (047984) 224

1 bungalow, 1 pub rm, 2 bedrms, sleeps 2-6, £90-£160, Jan-Dec, bus nearby, rail 500 yds

Ard Na Coille Guest House, Station Road, Carrbridge, Inverness-shire
☎ Carrbridge (047984) 239

1 bungalow, 1 pub rm, 3 bedrms, sleeps 6, £100, Jan-Dec, bus $\frac{1}{4}$ ml, rail $\frac{1}{4}$ ml

Mr Pain, 1 Birch Road, Killearn, by Glasgow
☎ Killearn (0360) 50752

1 house, 2 pub rms, 5 bedrms, sleeps 1-9, min let weekend, £95-£195, Jan-Dec, bus $\frac{1}{2}$ ml, rail 1 ml

Mr & Mrs F G Allan, Longwall, Auchterhouse, by Dundee, Angus
☎ Auchterhouse (082626) 282

1 bungalow, 1 pub rm, 3 bedrms, sleeps 6, £110-£190, Jan-Dec, bus $\frac{1}{2}$ ml, rail $\frac{1}{4}$ ml, airport 25 mls

Mrs Helen L Key, Kirkside, Kirkton of Tealing, by Dundee, Angus, DD4 0RD
☎ Tealing (082621) 342

1 chalet/log cabin, 1 pub rm, 2 bedrms, sleeps 1-6, min let 1 night, £95-£250, Jan-Dec, bus $\frac{1}{2}$ ml, rail 1 ml, airport 25 mls

Flightmaster International Travel Ltd, 32A Castle Street, Edinburgh, EH2 3HT
☎ 031 225 9933

VAT is shown at 15%: changes in this rate may affect prices.

1 bungalow, 2 pub rms, 1 bedrm, sleeps 5, min let 1 night (Winter), £80-£140, Jan-Dec, bus nearby, rail ¾ ml

Mr & Mrs D Menzies, 62 Culcabock Avenue, Inverness
☎ *Inverness (0463) 222119*

---

1 cottage, 2 pub rms, 2 bedrms, sleeps 4-6, £100-£140, May-Oct

Mountain Thyme Guest House, Station Road, Carrbridge, Inverness-shire
☎ *Carrbridge (047984) 696*

---

1 house, 1 pub rm, 5 bedrms, sleeps 8, min let 3 nights, £120-£220, Jan-Dec, bus 1 ml, rail 1 ml, airport 27 mls

Mrs L McKimmie, Hair at Unit 10, Shopping Centre, Main Road, Aviemore, Inverness-shire
☎ *Aviemore (0479) 810711*

CARRICK CASTLE Argyll Map Ref. 1G4

14 motel units, 1 bedrm, sleeps 2-4, £60-£135, Jan-Dec, bus nearby, rail 20 mls, airport 60 mls

Carrick Castle Hotel, Lochgoilhead, Argyll
☎ *Lochgoilhead (03013) 251*

---

5 chalet/log cabins, 1 pub rm, 2 bedrms, sleeps 6, min let 2 nights, £70-£140, Jan-Dec, bus nearby, rail nearby

Mr Murray, Darroch Mhor Chalet & Watersport Centre, Carrick Castle, Lochgoil, Argyll
☎ *Lochgoilhead (03013) 249*

CARRON, by Aberlour Moray Map Ref. 4D9

Carron Estate 2 houses, 1 pub rm, 3 bedrms, sleeps 5-6, min let weekend, £65-£105, Mar-Oct, bus 1 ml, rail 17 mls

Alban Timber Ltd,, Rothes Estate Office, Station St, Rothes, Aberlour, Moray, IV33 7AZ
☎ *Rothes (03403) 267/(03406) 250 (eve)*

---

1 cottage, 1 pub rm, 3 bedrms, sleeps 4-5, £40-£90, Apr-Oct, bus 300 yds, rail 15 mls, airport 60 mls

Mrs E Kelly, 4 Beech Walk, Elgin, Moray, IV30 2BA
☎ *Elgin (0343) 45706*

CARSAIG Isle of Mull, Argyll Map Ref. 1D4

COMMENDED
♛ ♛ ♛

1 cottage, 2 pub rms, 3 bedrms, sleeps 8, £120-£200, Apr-Nov, bus 4 mls, rail 30 mls, ferry 20 mls

Mrs A McLean, Pier Cottage, Pennyghael, Carsaig, Isle of Mull, Argyll
☎ *Pennyghael (06814) 216*
Set in quiet location on seashore overlooking Jura. Good base for fishing, walking, touring island.

CARSLUITH Kirkcudbrightshire Map Ref. 1H10

1 chalet/log cabin, 1 pub rm, 2 bedrms, sleeps 7, min let 3 nights, £80-£150, Jan-Dec, bus nearby, rail 35 mls, ferry 35 mls, airport 70 mls

Mr & Mrs J Henry, Rambank, Carsluith, Newton Stewart, Kirkcudbrightshire
☎ *Creetown (067182) 216*

CARSPHAIRN Kirkcudbrightshire Map Ref. 1H9

1 cottage, 2 pub rms, 3 bedrms, sleeps 6, min let weekend, from £86, Mar-Dec, bus 1 ml, rail 25 mls, airport 70 mls

Miss Jill Bristow, Holiday Cottages (Scotland) Ltd, Lilliesleaf, Melrose, Roxburghshire, TD6 9JD
☎ *Lilliesleaf (08357) 424/425/320*

CASTLE DOUGLAS Kirkcudbrightshire Map Ref. 2A10

up to COMMENDED

1 house, 4 flats, 1 cottage, 1 pub rm, 1-3 bedrms, sleeps 2-6, min let 1 night, £45-£210, Jan-Dec, bus ½ ml

R H Ball, Barncrosh Farm, Castle Douglas, Kirkcudbrightshire, DG7 1TX
☎ *Bridge of Dee (055668) 216*
Selection of units on working farm. Peaceful country setting just off A75. Castle Douglas 6mls(10km)

1 house, 1 pub rm, 3 bedrms, sleeps 7-8, £60-£110, Apr-Oct

Mrs Borland, Castle Hill Farm, Gelston, Castle Douglas, Kirkcudbrightshire
☎ *Bridge of Dee (055668) 223*

AWAITING INSPECTION

2 apartments, 1-2 bedrms, sleeps 4-6, £60-£160, Mar-Nov, bus 1 ½ mls

Mr & Mrs Hunter, Dunjop House, Bridge of Dee, Kirkcudbrightshire
☎ *Bridge of Dee (055668) 271*

7 houses, 1 flat, 1-3 pub rms, 2-4 bedrms, sleeps 4-8, £80-£335, Apr-Oct

Gelston Castle Estate, Douganhill, Palnackie, Castle Douglas, Kirkcudbrightshire
☎ *Palnackie (055660) 268*

Crumquhill Farm 1 chalet/log cabin, 1 pub rm, 1 bedrm, sleeps 2-7, min let weekend, £35-£50, Jan-Dec, bus 1 ml, rail 23 mls, airport 30 mls

Y G Hutton, Crumquhill Farm, Ringford, Castle Douglas, Kirkcudbrightshire, DG7 2AL
☎ *Ringford (055722) 231*

2 cottages, 2 pub rms, 3 bedrms, sleeps 6, £85-£135, Apr-Nov, bus 1 ml, rail 23 mls, airport 48 mls

Mrs Wright, Risk farm, Bridge of Dee, Castle Douglas, Kirkcudbrightshire
☎ Bridge of Dee (055668) 218

---

1 cottage, 1 pub rm, 3 bedrms, sleeps 8, £80-£130, Jan-Dec, bus ½ ml

Mrs Edgar, Kelton Mains Farm, Castle Douglas, Kirkcudbrightshire
☎ Castle Douglas (0556) 2120

---

1 cottage, 1 pub rm, 1 bedrm, sleeps 4, min let weekend, £45-£95, Jan-Dec, bus nearby, rail 24 mls, airport 48 mls

Mr J E Yates, Dolmynach, Parton, Castle Douglas, Kirkcudbrightshire, DG7 3NE
☎ Parton (06447) 246

---

1 cottage, 1 pub rm, 2 bedrms, sleeps 5, £70-£120, Jan-Dec, bus 3 mls, rail 20 mls, airport 90 mls

Mrs E Biggar, Grange, Castle Douglas, Kirkcudbrightshire
☎ Haugh of Urr (055666) 205

CASTLE DOUGLAS AREA Kirkcudbrightshire Map Ref. 2A10

up to
COMMENDED
👑 👑 👑

20 houses, 2 cottages, 2 bungalows, 1-2 pub rms, 2-5 bedrms, sleeps 4-8, from £70, Apr-Oct

G M Thomson & Company, 27 King Street, Castle Douglas, Kirkcudbrightshire, DG7 1AB
☎ Castle Douglas (0556) 2701

CASTLEBAY Isle of Barra, Western Isles Map Ref. 3A11

2 cottages, 1-3 pub rms, 1-3 bedrms, sleeps 5-10, £45-£130, Jan-Dec, bus nearby, ferry 4 mls, airport 4 mls

Dr C Bartlett, 1 The Green, Frimley Green, Camberley, Surrey
☎ Deepcut (0252) 835123

CASTLETOWN Caithness Map Ref. 4D3

1 cottage, 1 pub rm, 2 bedrms, sleeps 4, £60-£100, May-Oct, bus nearby, rail 5 mls, airport 15 mls

Mrs D Swanson, Marldon, Murray Square, Castletown, Caithness
☎ Castletown (084782) 322

CAWDOR Nairn Map Ref. 4B8

1 house, 2 cottages, 1 pub rm, 3-4 bedrms, sleeps 6-9, £60-£180, Apr-Nov, bus 4 mls, rail 9 mls, airport 8 mls

Mr & Mrs C R Thompson, Outfield, Abernyte, Inchture, Perthshire, PH14 9RA
☎ Inchture (0828) 86444

Prices shown are for guidance only. Please send SAE with each enquiry.

CELLARDYKE, by Anstruther Fife Map Ref. 2E3

1 house, 1 pub rm, 4 bedrms, sleeps 8-9, £75-£150, Jun-Oct, rail nearby

Mr G McKenzie, 18 Dove Street, Cellardyke, Fife
☎ Anstruther (0333) 310225

CERES Fife Map Ref. 2D3

1 cottage, 1 pub rm, 2 bedrms, sleeps 4, from £70, Apr-Oct, bus ¾ ml, rail 3 mls, airport 40 mls

Mrs Ronaldson, Denhead Farm, Ceres, Fife
☎ Ceres (033482) 298

CLACHAMISH, by Portree Isle of Skye, Inverness-shire Map Ref. 3D8

1 cottage, 2 pub rms, 3 bedrms, sleeps 6, £60-£100, Apr-Oct, bus nearby, ferry 40 mls, airport 35 mls

Mrs Nicolson, Drumorel, Tayinloan, Clachamish, by Portree, Isle of Skye, Inverness-shire
☎ Edinbane (047082) 215

1 flat, 2 pub rms, 3 bedrms, sleeps 6, min let 3 nights, £70-£150, Jan-Dec, bus 500 yds, ferry 35 mls, airport 30 mls

Mrs N McKillop, 5 Knott, Clachamish, Isle of Skye, Inverness-shire
☎ Edinbane (047082) 213

CLACHAN SEIL Argyll Map Ref. 1E3

AWAITING INSPECTION

2 bungalows, 3 pub rms, 2-3 bedrms, sleeps 6, min let weekend, £81-£180, Jan-Dec, bus nearby, rail 14 mls

N & E Kenyon, Seil Island Cottages, Clachan Seil, by Oban, Argyll
☎ Balvicar (08523) 440

1 chalet/log cabin, 2 pub rms, 2 bedrms, sleeps 4, min let weekend, £65-£125, Jan-Dec, bus nearby, rail 14 mls

Mary Norris, Creag-an-Roin, Clachan Seil, Argyll
☎ Balvicar (08523) 339

(canoe)

CLACHAN, by Tarbert Argyll Map Ref. 1E6

Kirkland Caravan Site 9 caravans, sleeps 6-8, min let 1 night, £60-£70, Apr-Oct

Mr McCheyne, Kirkland Caravan Site, Clachan, Argyll
☎ Clachan (08804) 200

CLACHTOLL Sutherland Map Ref. 3G4

1 house, 1 pub rm, 3 bedrms, sleeps 6, min let 2 weeks, max £150, Apr-Aug, bus 5 mls, rail 45 mls, airport 105 mls

(ornithology)

Mr & Mrs R Boothman, Ellergill, Low Bentham, by Lancaster, North Yorkshire, LA2 7DZ
☎ Bentham (0468) 61377

CLADICH, by Dalmally Argyll Map Ref. 1F2

1 house, 1 pub rm, 3 bedrms, sleeps 6-7, £50-£125, Jan-Dec, rail 5 mls, airport 70 mls

Mr McArthur, Fernpoint Hotel, Inveraray, Argyll
☎ *Inveraray (0499) 2170*

by COCKBURNSPATH Berwickshire Map Ref. 2F5

1 caravan, sleeps 6, min let weekend, £30-£45, Apr-Oct, bus 6 mls, rail 14 mls

Mrs C Morrison, Middle Monynut Farm, Cockburnspath, Berwickshire, TD13 5YL
☎ *Abbey St Bathans (03614) 234*

COLDINGHAM Berwickshire Map Ref. 2F5

6 chalet/log cabins, 3 cottages, 1-2 pub rms, 2-3 bedrms, sleeps 4-6, min let weekend, £85-£175, Mar-Nov, bus 2 mls, rail 14 mls, airport 50 mls

Dr Edward J Wise, West Loch House, Coldingham, Berwickshire, TD14 5QE
☎ *Coldingham (08907) 71270*
Small country estate set around Coldingham Loch. Fishing available to guests.

1 house, 1 pub rm, 1 bedrm, sleeps 4, £50-£90, Jan-Dec, bus nearby, rail 11 mls, airport 50 mls

Mrs M V Laidlaw, Courtburn House, Coldingham, Berwickshire
☎ *Coldingham (08907) 71266*

COLDSTREAM Berwickshire Map Ref. 2F6

1 cottage, 1 pub rm, 3 bedrms, sleeps 6, £65-£80, Jun-Sep, bus 2 $\frac{1}{2}$ mls, rail 15 mls, airport 50 mls

Mrs Mather, Printonan, Duns, Berwickshire, TD11 3HX
☎ *Leitholm (089084) 378*

1 cottage, 1 pub rm, 2 bedrms, sleeps 4-5, min let weekend, £50-£85, Jan-Dec, bus 8 mls, rail 20 mls

Mrs S Walker, Springwells, Greenlaw, Duns, Berwickshire
☎ *Leitholm (089084) 216*

1 cottage, 1 pub rm, 3 bedrms, sleeps 6, min let weekend, £55-£90, Jan-Dec, bus nearby, rail 15 mls, airport 50 mls

Mrs S Letham, Fireburn Mill, Coldstream, Berwickshire
☎ *Coldstream (0890) 2722/2124*

by COLDSTREAM Berwickshire Map Ref. 2F6

1 house, 2 cottages, 1-2 pub rms, 2-3 bedrms, sleeps 4-7, £30-£150, Jan-Dec, bus 1 ml, rail 11 mls, airport 56 mls

Capt J D Hotham, Milne Graden Cottages, Milne Graden, Coldstream, Berwickshire
☎ *Berwick-upon-Tweed (0289) 82245*

Prices shown are for guidance only. Please send SAE with each enquiry.

COLINSBURGH Fife Map Ref. 2E3

2 cottages, 1 pub rm, 2 bedrms, sleeps 4, min let 2 weeks, £99-£116, mid Jun-end Sep, bus nearby, rail 10 mls, airport 40 mls

Lady Crawford, Balcarres, Colinsburgh, Fife
☎ *Colinsburgh (033334) 206*

---

1 cottage, 1 pub rm, 2 bedrms, sleeps 5, £40-£80, Jan-Dec, bus nearby, rail 20 mls, airport 45 mls

Mrs Dingwall, 3 Glebe Road, Newton Mearns, Glasgow, G77 6DU
☎ *041 639 3458*

COLL SANDS Isle of Lewis, Western Isles Map Ref. 3D4

Broadbay Caravan Site 10 caravans, sleeps 4-8, £40-£60, Apr-Oct, bus nearby, ferry 5 mls, airport 6 mls

Broadbay Caravan Site, Coll Sands, Stornoway, Isle of Lewis, Western Isles
☎ *Stornoway (0851) 2053*

COLL, Isle of Argyll Map Ref. 1B1

1 chalet/log cabin, 1 house, 2 flats, 1 bungalow, 1 pub rm, 2-4 bedrms, sleeps 4-8, £50-£150, Jan-Dec, ferry 5 mls

Mrs Stewart, Estate Office, Isle of Coll, Argyll, PA78 6TB
☎ *Coll (08793) 339*

COLONSAY, Isle of Argyll Map Ref. 1C4

4 houses, 9 flats, 11 cottages, 2 bungalows, 1-2 pub rms, 1-5 bedrms, sleeps 2-20, £70-£275, Jan-Dec, ferry $3\frac{1}{2}$ mls

Mrs E McNeill, Machrins Farm, Isle of Colonsay, Argyll
☎ *Colonsay (09512) 312*

COMMENDED
♔♔

3 chalet/log cabins, 1 pub rm, 2 bedrms, sleeps 5-6, min let 2 nights, £55-£285, Jan-Dec, ferry $\frac{1}{4}$ ml

Mr K Byrne, Isle of Colonsay Hotel, Isle of Colonsay, Argyll, PA61 7YP
☎ *Colonsay (09512) 316*
Modern; serviced chalets on Hebridean Island , within grounds of hotel. Near church, shop and beach.

COLVEND Kirkcudbrightshire Map Ref. 2B10

1 chalet/log cabin, 1 pub rm, 1 bedrm, sleeps 6, £50-£75, Apr-Oct, bus $\frac{3}{4}$ ml, rail 18 mls

Mrs Hamilton, Stranmillis, Port O'Warren, Colvend, Kirkcudbrightshire
☎ *Rockcliffe (055663) 274*

VAT is shown at 15%: changes in this rate may affect prices.

1 cottage, 2 pub rms, 2 bedrms, sleeps 4, min let weekend (low season), £70-£100, Apr-Oct, bus 4 mls, rail 18 mls, airport 80 mls

♿ E ◎ ♪ ⚹ 🐎 P ♫ † ⚱   ⚲ ♪ U ⛵ ⚓ ↟ ⚡ ✗ 🧺 ⛳
(windsurfing)

Mrs Coon, Ballencrieff Cottage, Ballencrieff Toll, Bathgate, West Lothian
☎ *Bathgate (0506) 632728*

COLVEND AREA Kirkcudbrightshire Map Ref. 2B10

3 houses, 1 flat, 3 cottages, 2 bungalows, 1-2 pub rms, 2-4 bedrms, sleeps 4-8, from £60, Apr-Oct

♿ E ◎ ♪ ⚹ P ♫ †   ♪ ⛵ ⚓ ↟ ✗ 🧺

G M Thomson & Company, 27 King Street, Castle Douglas, Kirkcudbrightshire, DG7 1AB
☎ *Castle Douglas (0556) 2701*

COMRIE Perthshire Map Ref. 2A2

1 cottage, 2 pub rms, 2 bedrms, sleeps 4, from £85, Jan-Dec, bus ½ ml, rail 20 mls, airport 50 mls

♿ E ◎ ♪ ▣ ◎ ⚹ 🐎 P ♫   ⚲ ♪ U ⛵ ↟ ⚡ ✗ 🧺

Mr P J Bickmore, Comrie House, Comrie, Perthshire, PH6 2LR
☎ *Comrie (0764) 70640*

---

1 cottage, 1 pub rm, 3 bedrms, sleeps 6, £70-£115, Apr-Oct

♿ E ◎ ♪ ⊙ ⚹ P ♫ †   ♪ U ⛵ ↟ ∕ ⚡ ⚡

Finlayson Hughes, Bank House, 82 Atholl Road, Pitlochry, Perthshire, PH16 5BL
☎ *Pitlochry (0796) 2512*

---

1 chalet/log cabin, 1 pub rm, 2 bedrms, sleeps 4, £25-£100, Jan-Dec, bus ¼ ml, rail 17 mls

♿ E ♪ ▣ ◎ ⊙ ⚹ 🐎 P †   ♪ U ⛵ ↟ ∕ ⚡ ⚡ ✗ 🧺

Mrs J R Mitchell, Coneyhill, Comrie, Perthshire, PH6 2LR
☎ *Comrie (0764) 70248*

---

1 cottage, 3 bedrms, sleeps 5, £100-£125, Apr-Oct, bus nearby, rail 12 mls, airport 50 mls

♿ E ♪ ▣ ⚹ 🐎 P †   ♪ ⛵ ↟ ∕ ✗ 🧺

Mrs S D MacDonald, c/o McLarty, Kilmore, Comrie, Perthshire
☎ *Comrie (0764) 70669*

---

1 cottage, 1 pub rm, 3 bedrms, sleeps 6-8, £125-£175, Apr-Oct, bus nearby, rail 25 mls

♿ E ♪ ▣ ▣ ◎ ⊙ ⚹ 🐎 P ♫ † ⚱   ♪ ⛵ ↟ ∕ ⚡ ✗ 🧺
T

Mrs Denson, 1 Cameron Road, North Camp, Aldershot, Hants
☎ *Aldershot (0252) 333707*

---

1 house, 2 pub rms, 2 bedrms, sleeps 4, from £100, Apr-Oct

♿ E ♪ ◎ ⚹ P †   ♪ ⛵ ⚡ ✗ 🧺 ⛳

Bell-Ingram, Durn, Isla Road, Perth, PH2 7HF
☎ *Perth (0738) 21121*

Prices shown are for guidance only. Please send SAE with each enquiry.

1 cottage, 2 pub rms, 2 bedrms, sleeps 3-4, £100-£125, Jan-Dec, bus 500 yds, rail 24 mls, airport 55 mls

 ♿ ᴡᴄ E 🚲 🚗 ◎ 🗐 🗖 🗐 🚿 🛋 ☉ ❄ Ⓟ ♨ 🏛 †   🦢 ᴥ 🎣 🎿 ⛰ ▸ 🏌 ⛷ ✕ 🐄 🐴 Ⓣ

Mrs J E Robb, Carroglen Farm, Comrie, Perthshire, PH6 2LY
☎ *Comrie (0764) 70377*

---

by COMRIE Perthshire Map Ref. 2A2

1 cottage, 4 pub rms, 2 bedrms, sleeps 4, £65-£85, Apr-Oct, bus ½ ml, rail 20 mls

 ♿ ᴡᴄ E 🚲 🚗 🗄 ◎ 🗐 🗖 ☉ ❄ Ⓟ ♨ 🏛 🚲 † 🏔 ᴥ   🦢 🦆 ᴥ 🎣 🎿 ⛵ ⛰ ▸ 🏌 ⛷ ✕ 🐄 🐴 Ⓣ

Mrs S M O'Grady, Carse of Lennoch, by Comrie, Perthshire
☎ *Comrie (0764) 70383*

CONNEL Argyll Map Ref. 1E2

1 house, 2 cottages, 2-3 pub rms, 3 bedrms, sleeps 6-7, £65-£300, Jan-Dec, bus ¼ ml, rail 2 mls, ferry 2 mls, airport 85 mls

 ♿ ᴡᴄ E 🚲 🗄 ▦ ◎ 🗐 📞 🗖 🛋 ☉ ❄ Ⓟ ♨ † 🏔   🦢 🦆 ᴥ 🎣 🎿 ⛵ ⛰ ⚓ ▸ 🏌 ⛷ ✕ 🐄

Highland Hideaways (Alexander Dawson), 5/7 Stafford Street, Oban, Argyll, PA34 5NJ
☎ *Oban (0631) 62056/63901*

---

1 bungalow, 2 pub rms, 3 bedrms, sleeps 6, £110-£180, Apr-Oct, bus ¼ ml, rail ½ ml, ferry 5 mls

 ♿ ᴡᴄ E 🚲 🐾 🗄 ▦ ◎ 🗐 🗖 🗐 🚿 🛋 ☉ ❄ Ⓟ ♨ †   🎣 🎿 ⛵ ⛰ ▸ ✕ 🐄

Robert Ritchie, Red Lodge, Barcaldine, by Oban, Argyll
☎ *Oban (0631) 72246*

CONTIN Ross-shire Map Ref. 4A8

1 bungalow, 1 pub rm, 3 bedrms, sleeps 5, £52-£93, Apr-Oct, bus 400 yds, rail 7½ mls, airport 30 mls

 ♿ ᴡᴄ E 🚲 🗄 ◎ 🗐 🛋 ❄ 🐾 Ⓟ ♨ 🏛 †   🎣 ⛵ ⛰ ▸ ✕ 🐄

J R Mayne, Nessdale, 32 Island Bank Road, Inverness, IV2 4QS
☎ *Inverness (0463) 230959*
Detached bungalow/cabin in birch wood on quiet road. Enclosed garden area.

VAT is shown at 15%: changes in this rate may affect prices.

CRAIGDARROCH CHALETS
Contin, by Strathpeffer

Situated on a wooded slope, facing south from Strathconon, offering, in the adjacent countryside, trout and salmon fishing, golf, pony trekking and hill climbing.

An excellent centre to see the west and north by easy day trips.

Accommodating 4/6 persons in fully furnished rooms with easily worked, very well equipped kitchen, full electric cooker, refrigerator etc. Colour TV in lounge. All linen and towels supplied. Cot available when ordered.

Pets welcome. 2 ★★ hotel adjacent offering full service of bar and meals.

Bookings weekly from Saturday, April to October.

Member of the Association of Scotland's Self Caterers.

Tel: (0997) 21584 or write for brochure.

4 chalet/log cabins, 1 pub rm, 2 bedrms, sleeps 6, £120-£165, Apr-Oct, bus 1 ml, rail 8 mls, airport 25 mls

R E Hendry, 12 Craigdarroch Drive, Contin, by Strathpeffer, Ross-shire, IV14 9EL
☎ *Strathpeffer (0997) 21584*
'A' frame units in birch woodland, all with picture windows and balconies.

---

2 cottages, 1-2 pub rms, 3 bedrms, sleeps 6, £70-£160, Mar-Dec, bus ½ ml, rail 8 mls, airport 30 mls

Mrs E A Fraser, Torachilty Farm, Contin, Ross-shire, IV14 9EG
☎ *Strathpeffer (0997) 21440*
Recently modernised units on working farm. Quiet, good walking area and touring base

---

4 chalet/log cabins, 1-3 pub rms, 2-3 bedrms, sleeps 4-6, min let 3 nights, £60-£120, Jan-Dec, bus nearby, rail 7 mls

Mr A S Finnie, Riverside Chalets Caravan Site, Contin, Strathpeffer, Ross-shire, IV14 9ES
☎ *Strathpeffer (0997) 21351*

---

1 house, 2 pub rms, 3 bedrms, sleeps 9, min let weekend, £92-£138, Apr-Oct, bus 3 mls, rail 25 mls, airport 35 mls

Mrs Cuthbert, Scatwell Farm, Comrie, Contin, by Strathpeffer, Ross-shire, IV14 9EN
☎ *Scatwell (09976) 234*

CORGARFF Aberdeenshire Map Ref. 4D10

1 bungalow, 1 pub rm, 2 bedrms, sleeps 4-5, min let weekend, £60-£90, Jan-Dec, bus 6 mls, rail 35 mls, airport 50 mls

(hillwalking)

Mr N Anderson, 201 Hardgate, Aberdeen
☎ *Aberdeen (0224) 573952/(03306) 348*

by CORNHILL Banffshire Map Ref. 4F8

1 cottage, 1 pub rm, 2 bedrms, sleeps 4-5, from £85, Apr-Oct, bus 2 ½ mls

Mrs B N Murray, Still Cottage, Glenbarry, by Cornhill, Banffshire, AB4 2HJ
☎ Knock (046686) 279

CORPACH, by Fort William Inverness-shire Map Ref. 3G12

The Bunkhouse 1 flat, 1 bunk house, 1 pub rm, 2 bedrms, sleeps 5-6, min let 4 nights, £80-£180, Jan-Dec, bus nearby, rail nearby

(canoeing, windsurfing)

Corpach Chandlers & Sailing School, Corpach, by Fort William, Inverness-shire
☎ Corpach (03977) 245/467

CORSOCK Kirkcudbrightshire Map Ref. 2A9

6 chalet/log cabins, 2 pub rms, 1-2 bedrms, sleeps 2-6, min let weekend (low season), £46-£115, Jan-Dec, bus 14 mls, rail 20 mls, airport 80 mls

Mr & Mrs N Gray, Caldow Lodge, Corsock, Kirkcudbrightshire, DG7 3EB
☎ Corsock (06444) 286

1 cottage, 2 wings of house, 1-3 pub rms, 1-3 bedrms, sleeps 2-8, min let weekend, £70-£150, Apr-Oct, bus 10 mls, rail 20 mls, airport 80 mls

Glaisters Lodge, Corsock, Kirkcudbrightshire, DG7 3DU
☎ Corsock (06444) 245

COUR, by Campbeltown Argyll Map Ref. 1E6

2 houses, 4 cottages, 1 bothy, 1-2 pub rms, 1-4 bedrms, sleeps 2-12, min let 2 weeks (high season), £58-£253, Jan-Dec, bus 17 mls, rail 80 mls, airport 25 mls

Maj G S Nickerson, Cour, by Campbeltown, Argyll, PA28 6QL
☎ Skipness (08806) 236/233

COVE Ross-shire Map Ref. 3F6

1 chalet/log cabin, 3 pub rms, 3 bedrms, sleeps 6, £160-£280, Jan-Dec, bus 8 mls, rail 40 mls, airport 90 mls

H F Armstrong, Coney Berry, Elvendon Road, Goring On Thames, Oxon
☎ Goring-on-Thames (0491) 872800

Sonas 1 house, 2 pub rms, 3 bedrms, sleeps 9-11, min let 4 nights, from £66, Jan-Nov, bus 8 mls, rail 43 mls, airport 100 mls

3 caravans, sleeps 6, min let 4 nights, from £60, Apr-Oct, bus 8 mls, rail 43 mls, ferry 63 mls, airport 100 mls

Mrs A E Ella, Sonas, Cove, by Achnasheen, Ross-shire, IV22 2LT
☎ Poolewe (044586) 203

VAT is shown at 15%: changes in this rate may affect prices.

79

CRAIGELLACHIE Banffshire Map Ref. 4D8

Elchies Caravan & Camping Park 1 caravan, sleeps 6, £65-£75, Apr-Oct, bus 2 ½ mls, rail 15 mls

  ♿ E ⊘ ⬜ 🖵 🛒 ⊙ 🐾 🅿 †   🎣 ⚲ ∪ ▸ ✗ 🧺

Mr D Hughes, The Firs, Elchies, Craigellachie, Banffshire, AB3 9SL
☎ Carron (03406) 414

CRAIGNURE Isle of Mull, Argyll Map Ref. 1D2

Shieling Holiday Centre 12 cottage tents, 1 pub rm, 2 bedrms, sleeps 4-6, min let weekend, from £80, May-Sep, bus 800 yds, ferry 800 yds

  ⊘ 🐾 🏇 🖿 🛒 † 🏔 🔍 ⊛   🥄 ∪ △ ⚓ ▸ ✗ 🧺 T (landscape painting, adventure playground)

David Gracie, Shieling Holidays (2A), 25 Regent Terrace, Edinburgh, EH7 5BS
☎ Craignure (06802) 496/031 556 0068 (low season)

---

1 house, 2 pub rms, 3 bedrms, sleeps 6, £135-£160, Apr-Oct, bus 300 yds, ferry 1 ½ mls

  ♿ 🚾 E ⬢ ⊘ ▦ ◎ ⬜ 🖵 ✂ 🛒 ❋ 🐾 🅿 🏇 †   🥄 ∪ ▸ ✗ 🧺

West Highland Estates Office, 7 Argyll Street, Oban, Argyll
☎ Oban (0631) 63617

CRAIL Fife Map Ref. 2E3

1 flat, 1 pub rm, 2 bedrms, sleeps 5, min let weekend, £70-£120, Apr-Oct, bus nearby, rail 20 mls

  ♿ 🚾 E ⬢ ⊘ ▦ ⊘ ⬜ 🖵 ◎ ✂ 🛒 ⊙ ❋ 🐾 🅿 🏇 🖿 †   🎣 ⚲ 🥄 △ ⚓ ▸ 🛶 ✗ 🧺

Marak Partnership, 2 Carmelaws, Linlithgow, West Lothian, EH49 6BU
☎ Linlithgow (0506) 842579

COMMENDED
♛ ♛ ♛ ♛

1 bungalow, 1 pub rm, 2 bedrms, sleeps 4, min let weekend, £70-£135, Jan-Dec, bus nearby, rail 15 mls

  ♿ 🚾 E ⬢ ⊘ ▦ 🖳 ◎ ⬜ 🖵 ◎ ✂ 🛒 ⊙ ❋ 🐾 🅿 🏇 🖿 † 🏔   🥄 ∪ △ ⚓ ▸ ✗ 🧺

Mrs P L Taylor, 3 The Glebe, Crail, Fife, KY10 3UJ
☎ Crail (0333) 50845
Modern, centrally heated with private gardens. Quiet position in picturesque fishing village.

Sauchope Links Caravan Park 5 caravans, sleeps 6-8, min let 3 nights, £80-£196, Apr-Oct, bus 1 ml

  ♿ 🚾 E 🖤 ⊘ ⊘ ⬜ 📞 ⬜ 🖵 ✂ 🛒 ⊙ 🐾 🅿 🏇 🖿 🏔 🔍   🥄 ∪ △ ⚓ ▸ ✗ 🧺 T

Largo Leisure Parks Ltd, Rankeilour House, Cupar, Fife, KY15 5RG
☎ Letham (033781) 233

---

1 flat, 1 pub rm, 1 bedrm, sleeps 4, £100-£120, Jun-Oct, bus nearby, rail 16 mls, airport 50 mls

  ♿ 🚾 E 🖤 🖤 ⊘ ▦ 🖳 ◎ ⬜ 🖵 ✂ 🛒 ⊙ ❋ 🅿 🏇 🖿 †   ⚲ 🥄 △ ⚓ ▸ ✗ 🧺

Mrs J Auchinlech, 2 Castle Street, Crail, Fife, KY10 3SQ
☎ Crail (0333) 50538

CRAOBH HAVEN Argyll Map Ref. 1E3

1 flat, 8 cottages, 1 pub rm, 1-3 bedrms, sleeps 2-6, min let 1 night, from £143, Jan-Dec, bus nearby, rail 25 mls, ferry 25 mls, airport 100 mls

  ♿ 🚾 E 🖤 ⊘ ▦ 🖳 ◎ ⬜ 🖵 ◎ ✂ 🛒 ⊙ ❋ 🐾 🅿 ∥ 🏇 🖿 🛒 🏔 ⊛   🥄 ∪ △ ⚓
▸ ✂ 🛶 R ✗ 🧺 ▾ T

Craobh Haven Cottages, Craobh Haven, by Lochgilphead, Argyll, PA31 8QR
☎ Barbreck (08525) 266/222

CRATHIE Aberdeenshire Map Ref. 4D11

1 cottage, 2 pub rms, 2 bedrms, sleeps 4, £90-£110, Apr-Oct, bus nearby, rail 51 mls, airport 51 mls

🕭 ⌨ E ⛵ ▨ ▦ ◎ ◎ 🗄 ⌸ ▣ ✂ ▱ ☉ ✳ 🐾 🅿 ☡ ▦ † ⌂ ✕ 🐄

Mrs M Mathers, Cairnaquheen, Crathie, Ballater, Aberdeenshire
☎ *Crathie (03384) 229*

CREETOWN Wigtownshire Map Ref. 1H10

Creetown Caravan Park 15 caravans, sleeps 6, min let 1 night, £70-£140, Mar-Oct, bus nearby, rail 30 mls, airport 70 mls

🕭 ⌨ E ▨ ▨ ✂ 🗄 ⌸ ▣ ▱ ☉ 🐾 🅿 ☡ ▦ ⛵ ⌂ ✿ 🎣 ✕ 🐄 🆃

Mrs B McMillan, Creetown Caravan Park, Creetown, Wigtownshire
☎ *Creetown (067182) 377*

---

by CREETOWN Wigtownshire Map Ref. 1H10

Cassencarie Holiday Park 8 caravans, sleeps 6-8, min let 2 nights, £60-£180, Easter-Sep, bus 800 yds, rail 32 mls, ferry 32 mls

🕭 ⌨ ⛵ E ▨ ▨ ✂ 🗄 ☎ ⌸ ▣ ✂ ▱ ☉ ✳ 🐾 🅿 ☡ ▦ † ⌂ ✿ 🌐 🎣 ⚓ 🏊 ⛵ ⛴ △ ▸ ✕ 🐄

Cassencarie Holiday Park (TBG), Creetown, Wigtownshire
☎ *Creetown (067182) 264*

CRIANLARICH Perthshire Map Ref. 1G2

2 chalet/log cabins, 1 wing of house, 1 pub rm, 2-3 bedrms, sleeps 6-9, min let weekend (low season), £60-£200, Mar-Nov, bus ½ ml, rail 1 ½ mls, airport 55 mls

🕭 ⌨ E ⛵ ▨ ▨ 🗄 ◎ 🗄 ⌸ ▣ ▱ 🐾 🅿 ☡ ▦ † ⛵ ✕ 🐄 🔔

Mrs C S R Christie, Lochdochart, Crianlarich, Perthshire, FK20 8QS
☎ *Crianlarich (08383) 274*

COMMENDED
👑 👑 👑 👑

Portnellan Highland Lodges 8 chalet/log cabins, 1 pub rm, 2-3 bedrms, sleeps 4-8, min let 3 nights, £99-£195, Mar-Dec, bus nearby, rail 1 ½ mls, airport 45 mls

🕭 ⌨ E ⛵ ▨ ▦ 🗄 ◎ 🗄 ☎ ▣ ✂ ▱ ☉ ✳ 🐾 🅿 ✂ ▱ ▦ ⌂ ⚓ ⛵ 🏊 △ ▸ ✓ 🏂 🛷 🆁 ✕ 🐄 🍴 🆃 (bicycle hire)

Trevor & Elaine Taylor, Portnellan House, Crianlarich, Perthshire, FK20 8QS
☎ *Crianlarich (08383) 284*

Modern pine units on private estate. Superb views. 12 Munros within 10 miles (16km). Game sports.

VAT is shown at 15%: changes in this rate may affect prices.

1 house, 2 pub rms, 3-4 bedrms, sleeps 8, from £100, Apr-Oct, bus 4 ½ mls, rail ½ ml

(table tennis)

Mrs Cannon, Auchessan Estate, Crianlarich, Perthshire, FK20 8QS
☎ *Killin (05672) 518*

CRIEFF Perthshire Map Ref. 2B2

up to
HIGHLY COMMENDED

Loch Monzievaird Chalets 13 chalet/log cabins, 1 pub rm, 2-3 bedrms, sleeps 2-8, min let 1 night, from £80, Jan-Dec, bus 500 yds, rail 10 mls, airport 30 mls

Alan Colquhoun, Loch Monzievaird Chalets, Ochtertyre, Crieff, Perthshire, PH7 4JR
☎ *Crieff (0764) 2586*
On wooded hill overlooking secluded loch. Fishing, Shetland ponies, play area and nature trail.

---

2 cottages, 1 pub rm, 2 bedrms, sleeps 6, min let weekend, £40-£80, Apr-Nov, bus 2 mls, rail 17 mls

Mrs Dron, Mid Crieffvechter, Crieff, Perthshire, PH7 2QJ
☎ *Crieff (0764) 2381*

COMMENDED

Crieff Hydro Chalets 15 chalet/log cabins, 1 cottage, 1 pub rm, 2 bedrms, sleeps 6, min let 2 nights, £190-£340, Jan-Dec, bus 1 ml, rail 12 mls, airport 50 mls

Crieff Hydro Limited, Crieff, Perthshire, PH7 3LQ
☎ *Crieff (0764) 2401*
Wooden units on sunny wooded hillside in grounds of hotel. Free use of hotel leisure facilities.

---

1 cottage, 1 pub rm, 2 bedrms, sleeps 4, £40-£60, Apr-Oct, bus ¼ ml, rail 10 mls, airport 50 mls

Mrs G Wilkie, Stronachlachar, Milnab Terrace, Crieff, Perthshire, PH7 4ED
☎ *Crieff (0764) 2531*

Crieff Holiday Village 3 chalet/log cabins, 1 pub rm, 2 bedrms, sleeps 6, min let 1 night, from £80, Jan-Dec, bus 300 yds, rail 9 mls, airport 18 mls

30 caravans, sleeps 4-8, min let 1 night, from £60, Jan-Dec, bus 300 yds, rail 9 mls, airport 18 mls

Crieff Holiday Village, Turret Bank, Crieff, Perthshire, PH7 4JN
☎ *Crieff (0764) 3513*

---

1 flat, 1 pub rm, 2 bedrms, sleeps 6, £100-£110, Jan-Dec, bus nearby, rail 10 mls, airport 50 mls

Mr Hoskins, Leven House Hotel, Comrie Road, Crieff, Perthshire, PH7 4BA
☎ *Crieff (0764) 2529*

Prices shown are for guidance only. Please send SAE with each enquiry.

1 bungalow, 1 pub rm, 3 bedrms, sleeps 6, £90-£120, Jan-Dec, bus ¼ ml, rail 9 mls, airport 50 mls

Mr G Graham, 16 Dollerie Crescent, Crieff, Perthshire, PH7 3EF
☎ *Crieff (0764) 2020/3104*

---

1 flat, 1 pub rm, 4 bedrms, sleeps 6, min let weekend, £40-£100, Jan-Dec, bus nearby

Mrs N A Ricketts, The Bungalow, Ardvreck, Crieff, Perthshire, PH7 4EU
☎ *Crieff (0764) 3367*

COMMENDED
♔ ♔

Mill House Caravan Site 1 flat, 1 pub rm, 1 bedrm, sleeps 4, £85-£100, Jan-Nov, bus nearby, rail 6 mls, airport 40-50 mls

1 caravan, sleeps 4, £60-£75, Jan-Nov, bus nearby, rail 6 mls, airport 40-50 mls

Mr Kelly, Mill House Caravan Site, South Bridgend, Crieff, Perthshire, PH7 4DH
☎ *Crieff (0764) 4700*
Recently modernised on ground floor of 18C house. Access through caravan park to banks of River Earn.

---

3 houses, 3 pub rms, 1-6 bedrms, sleeps 4-10, £100-£175, Apr-Oct

Finlayson Hughes, Bank House, 82 Atholl Road, Pitlochry, Perthshire, PH16 5BL
☎ *Pitlochry (0796) 2512*

---

by CRIEFF Perthshire Map Ref. 2B2

Dollerie Estate 1 chalet/log cabin, 1 house, 4 cottages, 1 annexe to mansion-house, 1-3 pub rms, 2-5 bedrms, sleeps 4-10, £70-£275, Mar-Dec, bus 1 ml, rail 14 mls, airport 35 mls

Mr A G Murray, Dollerie House, Crieff, Perthshire, PH7 3NX
☎ *Crieff (0764) 3234*

---

1 house, 2 pub rms, 3 bedrms, sleeps 6, £60-£110, Apr-Oct, bus 4 mls, rail 11 mls, airport 40 mls

Mrs J Drysdale, Brill House, 23 The Green, Brill, by Aylesbury, Buckinghamshire, HP18 9RU
☎ *Brill (0844) 238206*

---

1 house, 2 pub rms, 5 bedrms, sleeps 12, min let weekend, £100-£190, Mar-Oct, bus nearby, rail 15 mls, airport 56 mls

J Scott, Easter Dowald, Crieff, Perthshire, PH7 3QX
☎ *Crieff (0764) 3285*

---

1 house, 2 pub rms, 3 bedrms, sleeps 5, min let weekend, £45-£75, Apr-Oct, bus 2 mls, rail 6 mls

G B Thom, Ferneyfold Cottage, Madderty, Crieff, Perthshire, PH7 3PE
☎ *Madderty (076483) 351*

VAT is shown at 15%: changes in this rate may affect prices.

1 house, 1 cottage, 1-2 pub rms, 1-3 bedrms, sleeps 4, from £50, Apr-Oct, bus 2 ½ mls, rail 11 mls

&♿ 🚾 E ⏬ 🗑 ◎ ▯ ☎ 🖥 🗄 🛄 ✳ 🅿 ▮ 🌳 🏢   🧦 ∪

Bell-Ingram, Durn, Isla Road, Perth, PH2 7HF
☎ *Perth (0738) 21121*

COMMENDED
👑👑👑

1 cottage, 1 pub rm, 2 bedrms, sleeps 4, min let weekend (April), £55-£95, Apr-Oct, bus 1 ml, rail 7 mls, airport 40 mls

&♿ 🚾 E ⏬ 🗑 🖥 ◎ ▯ 🗄 🛄 ☉ ✳ 🅿 🌳 🏢 †   🧦 ∪ ⊢ 🛒

Mrs C Strang, Kintocher, by Crieff, Perthshire
☎ *Madderty (076483) 258*
Semi detached units with enclosed garden on working farm. Excellent views over surrounding farmland.

CRINAN Argyll Map Ref. 1E4

COMMENDED
👑👑👑

3 flats, 1-2 pub rms, 1-2 bedrms, sleeps 2-6, min let weekend, £55-£180, Jan-Dec, bus 8 mls, rail 35 mls, airport 80 mls

&♿ 🚾 E ⏬ 🖻 🗑 🖥 ◎ ▯ 🛄 ☉ ✳ 🅿 🌳 🏢   🧦 ∪ ⛰ ⚓ ⊢ 🎣 🏹 ✕ 🎿

Mike Murray, Kilmahumaig, Crinan, by Lochgilphead, Argyll, PA31 8SW
☎ *Crinan (054683) 238*
Apartments of individual character and style, converted from farm steading. Peaceful location.

---

1 cottage, 2 pub rms, 3 bedrms, sleeps 6, £100-£195, Jan-Dec, bus 8 mls, rail 30 mls

&♿ 🚾 E ⏬ 🗑 ◎ ▯ 🗄 🛄 ☉ ✳ 🐴 🅿 🌳 🏢 †   🧦 ∪ ⛰ ⚓ ⊢ 🎣 🏹 ✕ 🎿

Mrs Walker, The Change House, Crinan Ferry, by Lochgilphead, Argyll, PA31 8QH
☎ *Kilmarton (05465) 232*

CROCKETFORD Kirkcudbrightshire Map Ref. 2B10

Brandedleys

CROCKETFORD, BY DUMFRIES.   TEL. 055 669 250

Quiet exclusive self-catering units set in parkland with magnificent views over Galloway Hills and Loch. The two cottages, chalets and 12 Luxury Thistle Award caravans form part of a small Caravan Park with very complete facilities, including Swimming Pool (heated in season), Tennis Court, Minigolf, Games Room, TV Lounge, Children's Play Area, Bar and Restaurant for all meals. All the units have first-class views, all are fully serviced including colour TV. Bedrooms in the farmhouse are also available for letting and touring units are welcome.

2 chalet/log cabins, 2 cottages, 1-2 pub rms, 1-2 bedrms, sleeps 2-7, min let weekend, £75-£240, Mar-Jan, bus 250 yds, rail 9 mls

&♿ 🚾 E 🖻 🗑 🖥 🖥 ◎ ▯ ☎ 🗄 🛄 ☉ ✳ 🐴 🅿 🌳 🏢 ⛰ 🔍 🌐   ⚲ 🔍 🧦 ∪ ⛰ ⊢ Ⓡ ✕ 🛒 🍷 Ⓣ

12 caravans, sleeps 6-8, min let 2 nights, £68-£195, Mar-Oct, bus nearby, rail 9 mls

&♿ 🚾 🛏 E 🖻 🗑 🖥 🗄 🖻 ▯ ☎ 🗄 🛄 ✂ 🛄 ☉ ✳ 🐴 🅿 🌳 🏢 ⛰ 🔍 🌐   ⚲ 🔍 🧦 ∪ ⛰ ⚓ ⊢ ✕ 🛒 Ⓣ Ⓓ

Mr & Mrs McDonald, Brandedleys, Crocketford, by Dumfries, Kirkcudbrightshire, DG2 8RG
☎ *Crocketford (055669) 250*

---

1 house, 2 pub rms, 3 bedrms, sleeps 5-9, min let weekend, £90-£140, Jan-Dec, bus nearby, rail 10 mls, airport 90 mls

♿ 🚾 E ⛽ 📻 📱 📺 🖥 ◎ ⬚ ⬜ 💿 ✂ ⚓ ❄ 🐴 P ⌚ 🏠 🚲 † ⬛ 🐟 ✎ 🎿 ↗ Ü ⚠ ⚓ ▸ ✗ 🎒 T

G I Davidson, The Anvil, Crocketford, Dumfries, Kirkcudbrightshire
☎ Crocketford (055669) 651

CROMARTY Ross-shire Map Ref. 4B7

APPROVED ♛♛

4 cottages, 1 pub rm, 3 bedrms, sleeps 6, min let weekend (low season), from £55, May-Oct, bus ¾ ml, rail 22 mls, airport 26 mls

♿ 🚾 E ⛽ 📱 📺 ◎ ⬜ ⚓ ❄ 🐴 P ⌚ 🏠 🅰 🌐   ✎ ⚓ ✗ 🎒 🏌 (bowls)

Mrs V Macpherson, Cromarty Mains, Cromarty, Ross-shire
☎ Cromarty (03817) 232
Terraced units on working farm. Short walk to village shops and picturesque harbour. Views over Firth.

CROMDALE, by Grantown-on-Spey Moray Map Ref. 4C9

1 house, 2 pub rms, 4 bedrms, sleeps 7, from £130, Apr-Sep, bus 1 ½ mls, rail 17 mls, airport 45 mls

♿ 🚾 E ⛽ 📻 📱 📺 ◎ ⬜ 📞 💿 ✂ ⚓ ☺ ❄ 🐴 P ⌚ †   ✎ Ü ▸ ⁄ 🏋 🎒 🏌

Mrs Rutter, Latyers, Westmead, Roehampton, London, SW15 5BH
☎ 01 788 2180

CROSSAPOL Isle of Tiree, Argyll Map Ref. 1A2

1 house, 1 pub rm, 2 bedrms, sleeps 5, min let weekend, £75-£110, Apr-Oct, ferry 3 ½ mls, airport ½ ml

♿ 🚾 E ⛽ 📻 📱 📺 🖥 ◎ ⬜ 💿 ✂ ⚓ 🐴 P ⌚ 🏠 †   ✎ ⚠ ▸ 🎒 🏌 T

1 caravan, sleeps 8, min let weekend, £35-£55, Jan-Dec, ferry 3 ½ mls, airport ½ ml

♿ 🚾 E ⛽ ⚓ 🐴 P ⌚ 🏠 †   ✎ ⚠ ▸ 🎒 🏌 T

Mrs M Davies, Viewfield, Crossapol, Isle of Tiree, Argyll
☎ Scarinish (08792) 458

CROSSHILL Ayrshire Map Ref. 1G8

2 cottages, 2 pub rms, 2 bedrms, sleeps 4-6, min let weekend, £45-£100, Apr-Oct, bus 1 ml, rail 2 mls

♿ 🚾 E ⛽ 📱 📺 ◎ ⬜ ✂ ☺ ❄ 🐴 P ⌚ 🏠 ⛏   ✎ Ü ⚠ ⚓ ▸ ⁄ ✗ 🎒 🏌

D McFadzean, Dalduff Farm, Crosshill, Maybole, Ayrshire
☎ Crosshill (06554) 271

CULBOKIE Ross-shire Map Ref. 4A8

1 cottage, 1 pub rm, 2 bedrms, sleeps 4, £75-£95, Jan-Dec, bus nearby, rail 6 mls, airport 16 mls

♿ 🚾 E ⛽ 📻 📱 📺 ◎ ⬜ ⚓ ☺ ❄ 🐴 P ⌚ 🏠 ⛏ † 🅰   ✎ 🎒 🏌

Mrs M Rhind, Woodholme, Culbokie, Ross-shire, IV7 8JH
☎ Culbokie (034987) 218

CULKEIN Sutherland Map Ref. 3F4

COMMENDED ♛♛

1 house, 1 pub rm, 3 bedrms, sleeps 6, from £80, May-Oct, bus 10 mls, rail 55 mls, airport 100 mls

♿ 🚾 E ⛽ 📱 📺 ◎ ⬜ ⚓ ☺ ❄ P ⌚ † 🅰   ✎ ⚓ 🏌

Mr D MacKenzie, Dhunan, Culkein, Sutherland, IV27 4JG
☎ Stoer (05715) 268
Modernised, remotely situated in crofting area. Excellent views over Eddrachillis bay and mountains.

VAT is shown at 15%: changes in this rate may affect prices.

3 chalet/log cabins, 1 pub rm, 2 bedrms, sleeps 6, from £70, Apr-Oct

♿ 🚾 E 👁 🖊 ◎ 🗄 ▭ ☕ P 🛏 ▦   ✎ ⚓ 🔔 ♨

Mrs F T Mirtle, Old School House, Culkein, Lochinver, Sutherland, IV27 4JG
☎ *Stoer (05715) 232*

---

3 chalet/log cabins, 3 pub rms, 2-3 bedrms, sleeps 4-8, £100-£195, Apr-Oct, bus 10 mls, rail 50 mls

♿ 🚾 E ➡ 👁 🖊 ▦ ◎ 🗄 ▭ ☕ ❋ 🐕 P 🛏 ▦ † ✎ △ ⚓ 🔳

Mrs V Macleod, 7 Mount Stuart Road, Largs, Ayrshire, KA30 9ES
☎ *Largs (0475) 672931*

CULLEN Banffshire Map Ref. 4E7

1 cottage, 2 pub rms, 2 bedrms, sleeps 6, min let weekend, £60-£160, Jan-Dec, bus ½ ml, rail 15 mls

♿ 🚾 E ➡ 🖊 ▦ 🗄 🖊 🗄 ▭ ◎ ❋ 🐕 P 🛏 ▦ † ✎ △ ⚓ ▶ ✗ 🔔 (bowling)

Mrs Sarah J Grant, Earlsfield, Kennethmont, Insch, Aberdeenshire, AB5 6YQ
☎ *Kennethmont (04643) 207*

CULLEN BAY   Telephone: 0542 40777
Seafield Estate Office Cullen, Banffshire AB5 2UW
44 six-berth residential caravans for hire.
Sheltered rural site adjoining beach and
picturesque Seatown of Cullen.
Open APRIL to OCTOBER.

Seafield Estate Caravan Site 44 caravans, sleeps 6, min let 3 nights, £64-£155, Apr-Oct, bus nearby, rail 13 mls, airport 60 mls

♿ 🚾 E 👁 🖊 ▭ 🖊 📞 🗄 ▭ ◎ 🐕 P 🛏 ▦ † ⛰ ✎ ⚓ ▶ ⁄ ✗ 🔔

The Factor, The Earl of Seafield's Estate Office, Cathay Terrace, Cullen, Buckie, Banffshire, AB5 2UW
☎ *Cullen (0542) 40777*

---

1 cottage, 1 pub rm, 3 bedrms, sleeps 6, £75-£150, Apr-Oct, bus 300 yds, rail 15 mls, airport 55 mls

♿ 🚾 E ➡ 🖊 ▦ 🖊 🗄 📞 ▭ 🗄 ▭ 🐕 🛏 ▦ † ⌇ ✎ ⚓ ▶ ✗ 🔔 (bowling green)

Mr D Blair, 2 Westburn Court, Buckie, Banffshire, AB5 1EF
☎ *Buckie (0542) 33904*

---

1 house, 1 pub rm, 4 bedrms, sleeps 6-8, £55-£150, Jan-Dec, bus nearby, rail 12 mls, airport 58 mls

♿ 🚾 E ➡ 🖊 🗄 🖊 🗄 ▭ ▭ ◎ ❋ P ∥ 🛏 ▦ † ⌇ ✎ △ ⚓ ▶ ✗ 🔔

Mr & Mrs John Ross, 12 South Castle Street, Cullen, Buckie, Banffshire, AB5 2RT
☎ *Cullen (0542) 41133*

---

1 house, 2 pub rms, 3 bedrms, sleeps 7, £50-£150, Jan-Dec, bus 500 yds, rail 13 mls, airport 48 mls

♿ 🚾 E ➡ 👁 🖊 🖊 🗄 ▭ 🗄 ∥ ◎ ❋ 🐕 P 🛏 ▦ † ☎ ⌇ ⌇ ✎ U △ ⚓ ▶ ⁄ ✗ 🔔 🔳

Mrs Slater, 122 Seatown, Cullen, Buckie, Banffshire, AB5 2SN
☎ *Cullen (0542) 40783*

Prices shown are for guidance only. Please send SAE with each enquiry.

CULLICUDDEN Ross-shire Map Ref. 4B8

Wester Brae Chalets 2 chalet/log cabins, 2 lodges, 1 pub rm, 2-3 bedrms, sleeps 4-7, min let weekend, £60-£180, Apr-Dec, bus 2 mls, rail 9 mls, airport 20 mls

Mrs Phillips, Wester Brae, Culbokie, by Dingwall, Ross-shire, IV7 8JU
☎ *Culbokie (034987) 609*

CULLIPOOL Isle of Luing, Argyll Map Ref. 1D3

1 cottage, 2 pub rms, 3 bedrms, sleeps 6, £85-£110, Jan-Dec, bus nearby, rail 18 mls, ferry 2 mls

Mrs B Wilson, 5 Woburn Rise, Woodthorpe, Nottingham, NG5 4PS
☎ *Nottingham (0602) 264209*

1 cottage, 1 pub rm, 2 bedrms, sleeps 4, £70-£80, Mar-Oct, bus nearby

Willison MacQueen, Greenhill Cottage, Cullipool, Isle of Luing, Argyll
☎ *Luing (08524) 255*

CULLODEN MOOR Inverness-shire Map Ref. 4B9

1 cottage, 1 pub rm, 2 bedrms, sleeps 5, £75-£80, Apr-Oct, bus 2 ½ mls, rail 7 mls, airport 6 mls

Mrs E M C Alexander, Culdoich Farm, Culloden Moor, Inverness-shire, IV1 2EP
☎ *Inverness (0463) 790268*
Traditional stone unit on arable and livestock farm. Near Culloden Battlefield, close to Inverness.

2 chalet/log cabins, 2 cottages, 1-3 pub rms, 2-4 bedrms, sleeps 4-6, min let weekend, £100-£150, Jan-Dec, bus 1 ml, rail 7 mls, airport 10 mls

Clava Lodge Holiday Homes, Culloden Moor, Inverness-shire, IV1 2EJ
☎ *Inverness (0463) 790405/790228*

by CULZEAN Ayrshire Map Ref. 1G8

1 flat, 2 pub rms, 1 bedrm, sleeps 2-4, min let weekend (low season), £60-£110, Jan-Dec, bus 2 mls, rail 8 mls

Messrs Michael Barnes & Partners, 14 Alloway Place, Ayr, KA7 2AA
☎ *Ayr (0292) 268181*

by CUMNOCK Ayrshire Map Ref. 1H7

1 bungalow, 1 pub rm, 3 bedrms, sleeps 6, £120-£140, Jan-Dec, bus nearby, rail 5 mls, airport 15 mls

Mrs MacNab, Garlaff Farm, Skares, by Cumnock, Ayrshire
☎ *Cumnock (0290) 20349*

CUPAR Fife Map Ref. 2D3

2 cottages, 1 pub rm, 2-3 bedrms, sleeps 3-6, from £70, May-Sep, bus ¾ ml, rail 1 ml, airport 11 mls

Mrs M Addison-Scott, Kinloss House, Cupar, Fife, KY15 4ND
☎ *Cupar (0334) 52218*

VAT is shown at 15%: changes in this rate may affect prices.

2 cottages, 1 pub rm, 2 bedrms, sleeps 4, min let weekend, £50-£85, Jan-Dec, bus 1 ml, rail 4 mls

Mrs G W Lambie, Craigsanquhar Farm, Cupar, Fife, KY15 4PZ
☎ *Cupar (0334) 52391*

1 cottage, 1 pub rm, 2 bedrms, sleeps 3-8, min let weekend, £30-£90, Apr-Oct, bus 2 mls, rail 5 mls, airport 40 mls

Mrs W Roxburgh, Cantyhall Farm, Letham, Cupar, Fife
☎ *Letham (033781) 212*

by CUPAR Fife Map Ref. 2D3

1 bungalow, 2 pub rms, 3 bedrms, sleeps 6, £100-£120, Jun-Sep, bus ½ ml, rail 5 mls, airport 17 mls

Mr J Milne, Muirhead Farm, by Cupar, Fife
☎ *Ceres (033482) 234*

DALAVICH, by Oban Argyll Map Ref. 1F3

APPROVED Listed

Lochaweside Forest Cabins 44 chalet/log cabins, 12 houses, 1-2 pub rms, 2-3 bedrms, sleeps 5-6, min let 3 nights, from £60, Mar-Jan, bus 16 mls, rail 15 mls

Forestry Commission, Forest Holidays, Dept SC1, 231 Corstorphine Road, Edinburgh, EH12 7AT
☎ *031 334 0303*
Units of different style and character, seperately sited on wooded estate overlooking Loch Awe.

DALBEATTIE Kirkcudbrightshire Map Ref. 2B10

Galla Caravan Park 7 caravans, sleeps 4-6, min let 2 nights, £35-£105, Apr-Oct, bus ¼ ml, rail 15 mls, airport 58 mls

Galla Caravan Park, Haugh of Urr Road, Dalbeattie, Kirkcudbrightshire, DG5 4LD
☎ *Dalbeattie (0556) 610425*

2 bungalows, 1 pub rm, 2 bedrms, sleeps 4-6, £80-£100, Apr-Oct, bus nearby, rail 11 mls, airport 60 mls

J Johnston, Lower Porterbelly, Dalbeattie, Kirkcudbrightshire, DG5 4NJ
☎ *Kirkgunzeon (038776) 245*

3 cottages, 1-2 pub rms, 2-3 bedrms, sleeps 4-5, min let long weekend (low season), £70-£160, Jan-Dec, bus ¼ ml, rail 14 mls, airport 60 mls

Mr Gavin Bain, Munches Estate, Castle Douglas, Kirkcudbrightshire, DG7 1PD

Prices shown are for guidance only. Please send SAE with each enquiry.

by DALBEATTIE Kirkcudbrightshire Map Ref. 2B10

1 chalet/log cabin, 1 pub rm, 3-4 bedrms, sleeps 4-6, min let weekend, £50-£80, Mar-Oct, bus 3 mls, rail 15 mls

🏠📶E♿📁◎🗄️🔌☺🔥🅿️🌀🍳† 🔍🎣⛵♨️⚓🎿/✕🖼️🔥 (gliding)

Mrs Richardson, Meikle Cloak Farm, Dalbeattie, Kirkcudbrightshire, DG5 4NP
☎ *Dalbeattie (0556) 610368*

DALBEG Isle of Lewis, Western Isles Map Ref. 3C4

1 chalet/log cabin, 1 pub rm, 2 bedrms, sleeps 5, £35-£40, Jan-Dec, bus 400 yds, ferry 24 mls, airport 28 mls

🏠📶E♿📁🗄️🔌📁⚓🔥🅿️† 🎣⚓✕🖼️🔥

Mrs MacKay, 1 Dalbeg, Dalbeg, Isle of Lewis, Western Isles
☎ *Shawbost (085171) 265*

DALCROSS, by Inverness Inverness-shire Map Ref. 4B8

COMMENDED

2 cottages, 1 pub rm, 3 bedrms, sleeps 4-6, £86-£138, May-Oct, bus 1 ml, rail 8 mls, airport 3 mls

🏠📶E♿📁🗄️🔌◎🗄️📞🔌☺❄️🔥🅿️🌀🍳 🔥

Robert M Pottie, Easter Dalziel Farm, Dalcross, by Inverness, IV1 2JL
☎ *Ardersier (0667) 62213*
Tastefully decorated, in peaceful setting on working farm near Inverness. Central for touring.

DALMALLY Argyll Map Ref. 1F2

Craig Lodge · DALMALLY · ARGYLL
Telephone: 083 82 216
One wing of the Lodge has been divided into 3 large self-catering houses each sleeping 8-10 persons. There is also a bungalow nearby sleeping 6.
Facilities include:
Salmon and Trout Fishing ● Lovely Garden for Children
Sandy Bathing Pool in River ● Pool Table and Table Tennis
Colour brochure, etc. from:
Mr and Mrs C. S. Macfarlane-Barrow (ref. STB).

2 houses, 1 bungalow, 2 pub rms, 3-4 bedrms, sleeps 6-10, min let weekend, £80-£280, Jan-Dec, bus 1 ml, rail 2 mls, airport 70 mls

🏠📶E♿📁◎🗄️🔌📁⚓☺❄️🔥🅿️🌀🍳🔥🔍 ⛵♨️⚓🎿/✕🖼️🔥
Ⓣ

C S McFarlane Barrow, Craig Lodge, Dalmally, Argyll, PA33 1AR
☎ *Dalmally (08382) 216*

1 cottage, 1 cottage annex, 1 pub rm, 2-3 bedrms, sleeps 4-6, £35-£140, Jan-Dec, bus 2 mls, rail 4 mls, airport 70 mls

🏠📶E♿📁◎🗄️🔥🅿️🌀🍳† 🎣♨️🔥Ⓣ (climbing, rambling)

Mr & Mrs Keay, Succoth, Dalmally, Argyll
☎ *Dalmally (08382) 250*

by DALMALLY Argyll Map Ref. 1F2

AWAITING INSPECTION

4 cottages, 1-2 pub rms, 1-4 bedrms, sleeps 2-8, £50-£200, Apr-Oct, bus 4 mls, rail 5 mls, airport 70 mls

🏠📶E♿📁🗄️◎🗄️🔌❄️🔥🅿️🌀🍳 🎣♨️/🔥

Mrs D Fellowes, Inistrynich, Lochaweside, by Dalmally, Argyll, PA33 1BQ
☎ *Dalmally (08382) 256*

VAT is shown at 15%: changes in this rate may affect prices.

DALRY, by Castle Douglas Kirkcudbrightshire Map Ref. 2A9

3 flats, 1 cottage, 1-2 pub rms, 3-4 bedrms, sleeps 5-7, £50-£115, Mar-Oct, bus 2 mls, rail 36 mls

Mrs Forbes, Dinning House, Gargunnock, Stirlingshire, FK8 3BQ
☎ *Gargunnock (078686) 289*

---

2 cottages, 1 pub rm, 3 bedrms, sleeps 6, £45-£80, May-Sep, bus 5 mls, rail 30 mls, airport 30 mls

Mrs M Fergusson, Barlaes Farm, St John's Town of Dalry, Castle Douglas, Kirkcudbrightshire, DG7 3TZ
☎ *Dalry (06443) 251*

COMMENDED
👑👑

1 cottage, 1 pub rm, 2 bedrms, sleeps 5, min let weekend, £65-£135, Apr-Nov, bus 14 mls, rail 23 mls, airport 40 mls

Miss S Harrison, Grennan Mill, St John's Town of Dalry, Kirkcudbrightshire, DG7 3XQ
☎ *Dalry (06443) 297*
Post war stone building in grounds and to rear of Grenan house. Overlooks restored watermill.

---

4 cottages, 1-2 pub rms, 1-3 bedrms, sleeps 2-6, £60-£140, Mar-Oct, bus 2 mls, rail 28 mls, airport 70 mls

Mrs R Gordon, Glenlee Holiday Houses, New Galloway, Castle Douglas, Kirkcudbrightshire, DG7 3SF
☎ *Dalry (06443) 445*

---

1 chalet/log cabin, sleeps 4, £60-£80, Jan-Dec, bus nearby, rail 28 m:s, airport 30 mls

Mrs M B Bone, Moat Park, St John's Town of Dalry, Kirkcudbrightshire
☎ *Dalry (06443) 208*

DALRYMPLE Ayrshire Map Ref. 1H8

Doon Valley Caravan Site 25 caravans, sleeps 6-8, min let 1 night, £100-£150, Jan-Dec, bus nearby

Doon Valley Caravan Site, Dalrymple, by Ayr, Ayrshire, KA6 6EF
☎ *Dalrymple (029256) 242*

DALWHINNIE Inverness-shire Map Ref. 4B11

1 house, 1 pub rm, 3 bedrms, sleeps 6-8, £90-£150, Jan-Dec, rail nearby, airport 60 mls

Mrs Cameron, 19 Riverford Crescent, Conon Bridge, Dingwall, Ross-shire
☎ *Dingwall (0349) 63500*

DAVIOT (EAST) Inverness-shire Map Ref. 4B9

Auchnahillin Caravan Park

DAVIOT (EAST) · INVERNESS-SHIRE. Tel: (046-385) 223
Superb range of 2-8 berth luxury caravans available on our park which has attained the Thistle Award for four consecutive years. Enjoy the peaceful location surrounded by magnificent scenery yet only 10 minutes drive from Inverness and 20 minutes from Aviemore.
Excellent site amenities. Live entertainment most Friday nights. Ideal for families with young children. **From £45 to £170 per week.**

10 caravans, sleeps 2-8, min let weekend/3 nights, £40-£160, Dec-Oct, bus nearby, rail 7 mls, airport 12 mls

🏃♿ ⅏ E 📠 ⬚ ⌀ 🛢️ 📺 🖫 ✂ ⬛ ⊙ 🐓 🅿 ⛳ 🏢 ⚙ ❦   T

Mr & Mrs C Ponty, Auchnahillin Caravan Park, Daviot (East), Inverness-shire, IV1 2XQ
☎ *Daviot (046385) 223*

Auchnahillin 1 caravan, sleeps 8, £70-£135, Apr-Sep, bus nearby, rail 7 mls, airport 9 mls

♿ ⅏ E 📠 ⬚ ⌀ 🛢️ 📺 🖫 ✂ ⬛ ⊙ 🐓 🅿 ⛳ 🏢 † 🏢 ❦ ❀   ♪ ∪ ⚓ ⬦ ⌁ ∤ ⚐ ⚐
✕ T

Mr D Green, 58 Drummond Road, Inverness
☎ *Inverness (0463) 232468*

DEERNESS Orkney Map Ref. 5C11

1 cottage, 1 pub rm, 4 bedrms, sleeps 8, from £60, Jan-Dec

♿ ⅏ E ⬧ ⌀ 🍴 ◎ 🛢️ 📺 🖫 ⬛ 🐓 🅿 ⛳ 🏢 †   ⚏ 🎣

Mrs M Foubister, Esnaphy, Deerness, Orkney, KW17 2QH
☎ *Deerness (085674) 322*

DENHEAD, by St Andrews Fife Map Ref. 2D3

1 cottage, 1 pub rm, 2 bedrms, sleeps 3, £65-£100, Jun-Oct, bus 5 mls, rail 2 mls

♿ ⅏ E ⬧ ⌀ 🍴 ◎ 🛢️ 📺 🖫 ✂ ⬛ ❄ 🐓 🅿 ⫽ ⛳ 🏢   ⚲ ♪ ∪ ⚓ ⬦ ✕ 🎣

Mrs S L Underwood, Inchdairnie Holiday Properties Ltd, Denhead, by St Andrews, Fife
☎ *Strathkinness (033485) 342*

DERVAIG Isle of Mull, Argyll Map Ref. 1C1

Glen Houses 10 houses, 1 pub rm, 2 bedrms, sleeps 4-5, min let 3 nights, £70-£180, Mar-Oct, bus ¼ ml, rail 30 mls, ferry 23 mls, airport 12 mls

♿ ⅏ E ⬧ ⌀ 🍴 ◎ 🛢️ 📺 🖫 ⬛ ⊙ 🐓 🅿 ⛳ 🏢 ⬧ 🏢   ♪ ∪ ⚓ ⬦ ⌁ ∤ ✕ 🎣 T

Mr J G King, Glen Houses, Hawthorn Cottage, Dervaig, Tobermory, Isle of Mull, Argyll, PA75 6QJ
☎ *Dervaig (06884) 270/(0688) 2422/2435*

---

1 cottage, 1 pub rm, 2 bedrms, sleeps 4, from £50, Jan-Dec, bus nearby, ferry 25 mls, airport 14 mls

♿ ⅏ E ⬧ ⌀ 🍴 ◎ 🛢️ 📺 🖫 ⬛ 🐓 🅿 ⛳ 🏢 † 🏢   ♪ ∪ ⚓ ⬦ ⌁ ✕ 🎣

Col and Mrs C K Finlay, West Ardhu, Dervaig, Isle of Mull, Argyll, PA75 6QR
☎ *Dervaig (06884) 236*

AWAITING INSPECTION

1 house, 2 pub rms, 3 bedrms, sleeps 6, £60-£180, Mar-Nov, bus 1 ml, ferry 26 mls

Mrs Galbraith, Croig, Dervaig, Isle of Mull, Argyll, PA75 6QS
☎ *Dervaig (06884) 219*

---

1 chalet/log cabin, 1 pub rm, 1 bedrm, sleeps 2, £39-£86, Jan-Dec, bus nearby, ferry 20 mls, airport 13 mls

Mr D Stewart, Achnadrish Lodge, Dervaig, by Tobermory, Isle of Mull, Argyll, PA75 6QF
☎ *Dervaig (06884) 287*

---

3 houses, 1 flat, 4 cottages, 1-5 pub rms, 1-6 bedrms, sleeps 2-10, min let weekend, £95-£290, Jan-Dec, bus 2 mls, ferry 8 mls, airport 10 mls

Quinish Estate, Dervaig, Isle of Mull, Argyll
☎ *Dervaig (06884) 223*

Torr a Mhanaich Vocational Holidays 2 houses, 1-2 pub rms, 2-3 bedrms, sleeps 5-6, £98-£160, Apr-Oct, bus 500 yds, rail 23 mls, ferry 23 mls

Mrs R Whitehouse, Glebe House, Dervaig, Isle of Mull, Argyll
☎ *Dervaig (06884) 315*

👑👑👑👑👑

1 bungalow, 2 pub rms, 3 bedrms, sleeps 6-8, £100-£170, Jan-Dec, bus ¼ ml, ferry 24 mls

P J C Sumner, Buttercliff, Winscombe Hill, Winscombe, Avon
☎ *Winscombe (093484) 2219*

---

1 caravan, sleeps 6, min let 1 night, £50-£90, Apr-Oct, bus 300 yds, rail 37 mls, ferry 26 mls

Mrs Morrison, Penmore Mill, Dervaig, Isle of Mull, Argyll
☎ *Dervaig (06884) 242*

DIABAIG Ross-shire Map Ref. 3F8

1 cottage, 1 bungalow, 1 pub rm, 2 bedrms, sleeps 4, £65-£95, Mar-Oct, bus nearby, rail 30 mls, airport 90 mls

(hillwalking)

Mrs R M MacKay, Hebron House, Seabank Road, Nairn, IV12 4EU
☎ *Nairn (0667) 53888/52459*

---

1 caravan, sleeps 4, min let 3 nights, £15-£25, Mar-Nov, bus 500 yds, rail 31 mls

Mrs Isabella Ross, Ben Bhraggie, Diabaig, Torridon, Ross-shire, IV22 2HE
☎ *Diabaig (044581) 268*

Prices shown are for guidance only. Please send SAE with each enquiry.

DINGWALL Ross-shire Map Ref. 4A8

1 cottage, 1 pub rm, 2 bedrms, sleeps 4, min let weekend, £80-£90, Apr-Oct, bus 1 ½ mls, rail 1 ½ mls, airport 15 mls

♿ 🚾 E 📠 ⌀ 🖥 ◉ ▯ ♨ ❄ 🄿 🔥 † ⚱   🍴 🔍 🎣 🏌 ⛵ ⛴ ⚓ ► ✗ 🐾 🎿

Mrs Yvonne Mayer, 10 Cloudesley Place, London, N1 0JA
☎ *01 278 5086*

---

by DINGWALL Ross-shire Map Ref. 4A8

2 flats, 2 cottages, 1 pub rm, 2-3 bedrms, sleeps 4-7, £60-£204, Easter-Oct, bus nearby, rail 2 ½ mls, airport 24 mls

♿ 🚾 E ➹ 📠 ⌀ ◉ ▯ ♨ ▮ ◉ ❄ 🐾 🄿   🍴 🔍 🎣 🏌 ⛵ ⛴ ⚓ ► ✎ ⚖ ✗ 🐾 🅃

I R McCrae, Fodderty Lodge, by Dingwall, Ross-shire, IV15 9UE
☎ *Strathpeffer (0997) 21207*
Part of Fodderty Lodge, a former 1730 country manse, now 'B' listed. Large tree-lined garden.

DINNET, by Aboyne Aberdeenshire Map Ref. 4E11

1 cottage, 2 pub rms, 2 bedrms, sleeps 4, £80-£120, Jan-Dec, bus nearby, rail 35 mls, airport 35 mls

♿ 🚾 E ➹ 📠 ⌀ 🖥 ▯ ◉ ▯ ☏ ▯ ▯ 🔥 ♨ ▮ ◉ ❄ 🐾 🄿 ✎ 🔥 🏛 †   🍴 🍸 🔍 🎣
🏌 ⛴ ► ✎ ⚖ ✗ 🐾 🅃 (gliding, nature reserve)

Mrs H M Donald, Crannach, Dinnet, by Aboyne, Aberdeenshire, AB3 5JY
☎ *Dinnet (033985) 249*
Comfortable, well equipped. Varied leisure and sightseeing facilities in the area.

---

1 chalet/log cabin, 3 cottages, 1-2 pub rms, 2-6 bedrms, sleeps 4-12, £90-£390, Apr-Oct, rail 4 mls

♿ 🚾 E ➹ 📠 ⌀ 🖥 ▯ 🔥 ☏ ♨ ❄ 🐾 🄿 🔥 🏛 †   ⛴ ⚓ ✗ 🐾

Glen Tanar Sportings Company, Glen Tanar, Aboyne, Aberdeenshire, AB3 5EU
☎ *Aboyne (0339) 2451*

DIRLETON East Lothian Map Ref. 2E4

2 cottages, 1 pub rm, 1-2 bedrms, sleeps 2-4, £90-£170, Jan-Dec, bus nearby, rail 2 mls

♿ 🚾 E ➹ ⌀ 🖥 ▯ ✎ ▯ ✎ ♨ ◉ ❄ 🐾 🄿 🔥 🏛   🍴 🍸 🍸 🔍 🎣 🏌 ⛵ ⛴ ⚓ ► ✗
🐾 🅃 (bowls)

Mrs Morrison, 78 Inverleith Place, Edinburgh, EH3 5PA
☎ *031 552 6308*
Modernised, stone built on village green facing castle. Large garden. Near golf, beach, nature park.

DOCHGARROCH Inverness-shire Map Ref. 4A9

5 cottages, 2 pub rms, 2-3 bedrms, sleeps 3-5, £50-£90, Apr-Oct, bus ½ ml, rail 5 mls, airport 15 mls

♿ 🚾 E ➹ ⌀ ◉ ✎ ▯ 🔥 🄿 🔥 🏛 †   ⛴ ► 🐾

Miss J Taylor, Dochfour Estate Office, Dochgarroch, Inverness, IV3 6JP
☎ *Dochgarroch (046386) 218*

DORES Inverness-shire Map Ref. 4A9

Loch Ness Log Cabins 3 chalet/log cabins, 2 pub rms, 2 bedrms, sleeps 6, min let weekend (low season), £85-£200, Jan-Dec

♿ 🚾 E ➹ ⌀ 🖥 ▯ ◉ ▯ ▯ ✎ ◉ 🔥 🄿 🔥 🏛   ⛴ ⚓ ⚖ ✗ 🎿

Mr & Mrs A I Cameron, Drummond Farm, Dores, Inverness-shire, IV1 2TX
☎ *Dores (046375) 251*

VAT is shown at 15%: changes in this rate may affect prices.

DORNIE Ross-shire Map Ref. 3F10

2 chalet/log cabins, 1 pub rm, 2 bedrms, sleeps 4, £86, Apr-Oct, bus ½ ml, rail 8 mls

D F MacRae, Rock House, Dornie, Ross-shire, IV40 8DX
☎ Dornie (059985) 268

---

1 cottage, 1 pub rm, 3 bedrms, sleeps 5, £95-£125, Apr-Oct, bus 1 ml, rail 7 mls, airport 74 mls

Mrs C Sim, 17 Kyle Drive, Giffnock, Glasgow, Renfrewshire, G46 6ES
☎ 041 637 9972(tel enq only)

DORNOCH Sutherland Map Ref. 4B6

1 cottage, 2 pub rms, 3 bedrms, sleeps 6-7, from £50, Apr-Oct, bus nearby, rail 13 mls

Mrs E A Ross-Harper, 172 Rolleston Road, Burton on Trent, Staffs, DE13 OLE
☎ Burton on Trent (0283) 61168
Terraced house on quiet street, 250 yards from town square. Near beach.

---

1 cottage, 1 pub rm, 3 bedrms, sleeps 6, from £58, Apr-Oct, bus 1 ml, rail 14 mls, airport 50 mls

Mrs J C McHardy, Achley Farm, Dornoch, Sutherland, IV25 3HS
☎ Dornoch (0862) 810303

---

3 cottages, 1-2 pub rms, 2-3 bedrms, sleeps 6, min let weekend, £75-£185, Jan-Dec, bus nearby, rail 10 mls, airport 50 mls

Mr D Holt, Skibo Castle Estate, Clashmore, by Dornoch, Sutherland
☎ Whiteface (086288) 236

---

1 house, 3 pub rms, 4 bedrms, sleeps 8, £120-£150, Jan-Dec, bus 500 yds, rail 14 mls, airport 60 mls

Mrs M Alford, Tigh Ruaraidh, Well Street, Dornoch, Sutherland
☎ Dornoch (0862) 810415

---

1 house, 1 pub rm, 4 bedrms, sleeps 6-7, from £140, Apr-Oct, bus nearby, rail 15 mls, airport 50 mls

Mr A Ross, Ardshave, Dornoch, Sutherland
☎ Golspie (04083) 3732

---

3 chalet/log cabins, 4 cottages, 1 pub rm, 2 bedrms, sleeps 4-6, min let weekend, from £70, Mar-Oct, bus 1 ml, rail 14 mls, airport 65 mls

Mrs E M Grant, Pitgrudy, Dornoch, Sutherland, IV25 3HY
☎ Dornoch (0862) 810291

2 cottages, 1 pub rm, 2 bedrms, sleeps 4, min let weekend (low season), £65-£95, Apr-Oct, bus 1 ½ mls, rail 8 mls, airport 50 mls

♿ 📶 E 🧺 🗄 📺 ◉ 🍳 🗄 🛏 ☺ ❋ 🐕 🅿 � 🛏 ♨ ⚠ ♪ ∪ ▸ ✗ 🛒 ⛽

Mrs A Burnett, Pulrossie Farm, Dornoch, Sutherland, IV25 3RL
☎ *Whiteface (086288) 206*

Seaview Farm Caravan Park 2 caravans, sleeps 4, £42-£48, May-Sep, bus nearby, rail 14 mls

⊘ ◖ ◉ 🐕 🅿   ♪ △ ⚡ ✗ 🛒 ⛽

Mr T R Preston, Seaview Farm Caravan Park, Hilton, Dornoch, Sutherland, IV25 3PW
☎ *Dornoch (0862) 810294/(0349) 852749*

Heatherwood Park 13 bungalows, 1 pub rm, 2-3 bedrms, sleeps 5-7, min let 3 nights, £92-£253, Jan-Dec, bus nearby, rail 12 mls, airport 65 mls

♿ 📶 E 🧺 🗄 🖥 📺 ◉ 🗄 ◖ 🗄 ☺ ❋ 🐕 🅿 🗐 ♨ ⚠ ⌇ ✎ 🎣 ♪ ∪ ⚡ ▸ ✗ 🛒
🅣

Heatherwood Park, Dornoch, Sutherland, IV25 3QJ
☎ *Dornoch (0862) 810596*

---

1 house, 3 pub rms, 3 bedrms, sleeps 6, £150-£200, Apr-Oct

♿ 📶 E 🧺 🏠 🗄 🖥 ◉ 🗄 🗐 🖨 ☺ ❋ 🅿 ♨ †   ✗ 🛒

Mrs S Michie, 35 Dunmuir Road, Castle Douglas, Kirkcudbrightshire
☎ *Castle Douglas (0556) 2132*

---

by DORNOCH Sutherland Map Ref. 4B6

3 houses, 2 cottages, 1 pub rm, 2-3 bedrms, sleeps 4-6, min let weekend, £80-£220, Apr-Oct, Jan-Dec (2 houses); bus ½ ml, rail 15 mls, airport 55 mls

♿ 📶 E 🧺 🏠 🗄 🖥 🗄 📺 ◉ 🗄 ◖ 🗐 🖨 ☺ ❋ 🐕 🅿 🗐 ♨ † ⚠ ⌇ 🎣 ♪ ∪ △
⚡ ▸ ✎ ✗ 🛒 ⛽ 🅣

Mrs Noel Mackintosh, Embo House, Dornoch, Sutherland, IV25 3PP
☎ *Dornoch (0862) 810260*
Estate cottages and apartments of individual character in wings of 'A' category historic house.

DOUNE Perthshire Map Ref. 2A3

1 cottage, 1 pub rm, 2 bedrms, sleeps 5, £85-£95, Jun-Sep, bus 8 mls, rail 6 mls, airport 35 mls

♿ 📶 E 🧺 🗄 ◉ 🗄 ◖ 🖨 ❋ 🅿 ♨ ⚠ † ⚠   ♪ ∪ △ ✗ 🛒

Mrs Wordie, The Row, Dunblane, Perthshire
☎ *Doune (0786) 841200*

DRIMNIN, Morvern Argyll Map Ref. 1D1

1 cottage, 1 pub rm, 3 bedrms, sleeps 6, min let weekend, £80-£200, Jan-Dec

♿ 📶 E 🧺 🏠 🗄 🖥 🗄 ◖ ⁄ 🖨 ☺ ❋ 🐕 🅿 🗐 ⚠   ♪ ∪ △ ⚡ ⁄ 🅣

Mrs B Garvey, 17 Southfield Avenue, Bury, Lancashire
☎ *061 764 9866*

APPROVED
♕

1 house, 1 pub rm, 3 bedrms, sleeps 6, min let weekend, £75-£180, Jan-Dec, rail 25 mls, ferry 12 mls

♿ 📶 E 🧺 🗄 📺 ◉ 🗄 🗄 🖨 ☺ ❋ 🐕 🅿 🗐 ♨   ♪ △ ⚡ ⁄ ⛽

Mrs E MacDonald, Fasgadh, Drimnin, by Oban, Argyll
☎ *Drimnin (096782) 247*
Traditional farmhouse on working sheep farm; access by farm track. Coastal and forest walks.

VAT is shown at 15%: changes in this rate may affect prices.

DRINNISHADER Isle of Harris, Western Isles Map Ref. 3C6

Laig House Caravan Site 1 caravan, sleeps 4, min let 3 nights, £28-£30, Apr-Oct, bus nearby, ferry 4 ½ mls, airport 42 mls

Angus MacDonald, 10 Drinnishader, Drinnishader, Isle of Harris, Western Isles
☎ *Drinnishader (085981) 207*

DRUMBEG Sutherland Map Ref. 3G4

APPROVED

1 cottage, 1 pub rm, 3 bedrms, sleeps 8, min let 3 nights (low season), £80-£195, Jan-Dec, bus nearby, rail 60 mls, airport 100 mls

Elizabeth Johnson, Low Alwinton, Harbottle, Morpeth, Northumberland, NE65 7BE
☎ *Rothbury (0669) 50224*
Stone built, modernised, highland croft house. On picturesque coastal route, near village.

1 cottage, 1 pub rm, 3 bedrms, sleeps 6, from £110, Jan-Dec, bus nearby

Mrs M MacRae, Springfield, Culkein, Drumbeg, Sutherland, IV27 4NL
☎ *Drumbeg (05713) 243*

1 chalet/log cabin, 1 pub rm, 2 bedrms, sleeps 6, £80-£100, Jan-Dec, bus nearby

Mr & Mrs Smales, Brae Cottage, Drumbeg, Sutherland, IV27 4NW
☎ *Drumbeg (05713) 219*

1 chalet/log cabin, 1 pub rm, 2 bedrms, sleeps 4, £70-£140, Jan-Dec, bus 1 ml, rail 52 mls

Mrs C Mackenzie, 307 Culkein, Drumbeg, Sutherland, IV27 4NL
☎ *Drumbeg (05713) 258*

DRUMLITHIE Kincardineshire Map Ref. 4G11

1 cottage, 2 pub rms, 2 bedrms, sleeps 5, min let weekend, £100, Apr-Oct, bus nearby, rail 7 mls

Mr A R Mowat, Mackenzie & Dunn SSC, 6 Clifton Terr, Edinburgh, EH12 5ET
☎ *031 337 4242*

DRUMMORE Wigtownshire Map Ref. 1G11

1 cottage, 1 pub rm, 2 bedrms, sleeps 6, min let weekend (low season), £45-£100, Jan-Dec, bus 3 mls, rail 20 mls, airport 80 mls

(bowling, tennis)

Mrs J R Ramsay, Mid Muntloch Farm, Drummore, Wigtownshire, DG9 9HL
☎ *Drummore (077684) 225*

Kilstay Caravan Site 2 caravans, sleeps 6, min let weekend, £45-£55, Apr-Oct, bus nearby, rail 17 mls, airport 70 mls

Peter M Irving, Cruachan, Kilstay, Drummore, Stranraer, Wigtownshire, DG9 9QT
☎ *Drummore (077684) 397/249*

Clashwhannon Caravan Site 6 caravans, sleeps 6, min let weekend, £65, Apr-Oct, bus nearby, rail 20 mls, ferry 20 mls, airport 70 mls

Clashwhannon Caravan Site, Drummore, by Stranraer, Wigtownshire
☎ *Drummore (077684) 374*

---

1 cottage, 1 pub rm, 3 bedrms, sleeps 6, £60-£90, Apr-Oct, bus 3 mls, rail 20 mls

Mrs McGarvie, Auchneight Farm, Drummore, Wigtownshire
☎ *Drummore (077684) 222*

DRUMNADROCHIT Inverness-shire Map Ref. 4A9

up to
COMMENDED
🌸🌸🌸🌸

Achmony Holiday Chalets 9 chalet/log cabins, 1 pub rm, 2 bedrms, sleeps 4, min let weekend, £70-£180, Apr-Oct, bus ½ ml, rail 15 mls, airport 24 mls

Mrs E MacKintosh, Achmony Holiday Chalets, Drumnadrochit, Inverness-shire, IV3 6UX
☎ *Drumnadrochit (04562) 357*
Woodland setting high above village. Magnificent views of surrounding area towards Loch Ness. **(See colour ad. 4 p. xxxiii)**

Ancarraig Chalets 12 chalet/log cabins, 2 bedrms, sleeps 4-6, min let weekend, £65-£208, Mar-Oct, bus 4 mls, rail 14 mls

Hoseasons Holidays, Sunway House, Lowestoft, Suffolk, NR32 3LT
☎ *Lowestoft (0502) 62292*

COMMENDED
🌸🌸🌸

1 chalet/log cabin, 2 bungalows, 1 pub rm, 3 bedrms, sleeps 6, min let weekend, £80-£180, Mar-Oct, bus nearby, rail 15 mls, airport 20 mls

Mrs W D Ross, Strone, Drumnadrochit, Inverness-shire, IV3 6XL
☎ *Drumnadrochit (04562) 351*
Modern units, individually sited overlooking Loch Ness. Near Castle Urquhart; 1 ml (2km) to village.

VAT is shown at 15%: changes in this rate may affect prices.

1 house, 1 pub rm, 3 bedrms, sleeps 8, £100-£150, Apr-Oct, bus 1 ml, rail 16 mls, airport 25 mls

Miss C Dixon-Carter, Easter Balnabaan, Drumnadrochit, Inverness-shire, 1V3 6UX
☎ Drumnadrochit (04562) 310

---

1 cottage, 2 pub rms, 2 bedrms, sleeps 6, min let weekend, £75-£150, Jan-Dec, bus nearby, rail 15 mls, airport 20 mls

Mrs C Campbell, Cruachan, Milton, Drumnadrochit, Inverness-shire, IV3 6UA
☎ Drumnadrochit (04562) 628

---

1 bungalow, 1 pub rm, 2 bedrms, sleeps 4, £100-£155, Jan-Dec, bus nearby

Mrs Jean MacKenzie, Schoolhouse, Drumnadrochit, Inverness-shire
☎ Drumnadrochit (04562) 300

---

1 house, 2 pub rms, 4 bedrms, sleeps 6, min let weekend, from £100, Apr-Oct, bus ½ ml, rail 15 mls

Duncan Fraser, Pitkerrald, Drumnadrochit, Inverness-shire
☎ Drumnadrochit (04562) 240

---

by DRUMNADROCHIT Inverness-shire Map Ref. 4A9

COMMENDED

Borlum Farm Cottages 2 cottages, 1 pub rm, 3 bedrms, sleeps 6, £95-£200, mid Mar-Oct, bus nearby, rail 15 mls, airport 25 mls

Capt & Mrs A D MacDonald-Haig, Borlum Farm, Drumnadrochit, Inverness-shire, IV3 6XN
☎ Drumnadrochit (04562) 220
In quiet surroundings on working farm. Near Urquhart Castle and Loch Ness. Good base for West Coast.

DUFFTOWN Banffshire Map Ref. 4E9

1 cottage, 1 pub rm, 2 bedrms, sleeps 4, min let weekend, £65-£90, Jan-Dec, bus 1 ml, rail 10 mls, airport 50 mls

Mrs J Smart, Errolbank, 134 Fife Street, Dufftown, Keith, Banffshire, AB5 4DP
☎ Dufftown (0340) 20229

---

1 house, 1 pub rm, 5 bedrms, sleeps 8, £80-£95, Apr-Oct, bus nearby, rail 10 mls, airport 54 mls

Mrs Violet Thomson, 14 Fife Street, Dufftown, Banffshire, AB5 4AL
☎ Dufftown (0340) 20266

---

1 cottage, 1 pub rm, 3 bedrms, sleeps 7, min let weekend (low season), £50-£105, May-Oct, bus nearby, rail 20 mls, airport 40 mls

Mrs Kathleen Martin, Gamekeeper's Cottage, Shougle, Birnie, Elgin, Moray, IV30 3RP
☎ Longmorn (034386) 285

Prices shown are for guidance only. Please send SAE with each enquiry.

1 flat, 1 pub rm, 2 bedrms, sleeps 4-5, min let weekend, £40-£75, Jan-Dec, rail 9 mls, airport 54 mls

🦽 ⑭ E 🍴 🛏 ⑦ 🎞 🖵 ◎ 🖵 🖵 ▰ ☺ ❊ 🐕 🅿 🐃 🎞 ✝ ⚙   📻 🔍 ♪ 🤸 ▸ ✕ 🧺
(bowling)

Mrs A M Brown, Ashville, Church Street, Dufftown, Keith, Banffshire, AB5 4AR
☎ *Dufftown (0340) 20265/20342*

---

1 bungalow, 2 pub rms, 3 bedrms, sleeps 6, min let weekend, £80-£150, Jan-Dec, bus nearby, rail 10 mls

🦽 ⑭ E 🍴 🛏 ⑦ 🎞 🖵 ◎ 🖵 🖵 🖸 💈 ▰ ☺ ❊ 🅿 🦮 ✝   🔍 ♪ ▸ ✕ 🧺

Mrs Mary M Robertson, Bregach, Glenrinnes, Dufftown, Keith, Banffshire
☎ *Dufftown (0340) 20818*

by DUFFTOWN Banffshire Map Ref. 4E9

1 house, 2 pub rms, 3 bedrms, sleeps 5-8, £80-£125, Jun-Oct, rail 40 mls, airport 60 mls

⑭ E 🍴 ⑦ 🎞 🖵 ◎ 🖵 🖸 💈 ▰ ☺ ❊ 🐕 🅿 🐃 🎞 ✝ ⚙   ♪ 🤸 🏄 ▸ 🎿 🐂 🧺

Mrs E Strathdee, Wester Auchmore, Glenrinnes, Dufftown, Keith, Banffshire, AB5 4DD
☎ *Dufftown (0340) 20854*

DUIRINISH Ross-shire Map Ref. 3F9

Duirinish Lodge Holidays
By KYLE, ROSS-SHIRE IV40 8BE   Tel. 059 984 268

Enjoy a peaceful, relaxed holiday in one of our very well equipped Scandinavian Log Chalets situated on the Lochalsh Peninsula, 4 miles from the ferry to Skye. Castles and gardens to visit, hills to climb, pony-trekking, small boat sailing, wild flowers in abundance, birdlife, etc. Try visiting us April/May for the beauty of spring, quiet roads and long days.
AA 👑 👑 👑 **Commended.**

COMMENDED
👑 👑 👑

Duirinish Lodge Holidays 7 chalet/log cabins, 1 pub rm, 2-3 bedrms, sleeps 4-6, min let 2 nights, £60-£215, Mar-Nov, bus 4 mls, rail 2 mls

🦽 ⑭ E 🍴 ⑦ 🎞 🖵 ◎ 🖵 🖵 ▰ ☺ 🐕 🅿 🐃 🎞 ⚙   ♪ 🤸 🏄 🎿 ✕ 🧺 Ⓣ

Duirinish Lodge Holidays, Dept STB, Duirinish, by Kyle, Ross-shire, IV40 8BE
☎ *Plockton (059984) 268*
Scandinavian log units in peaceful, wooded setting surrounded by burn and hill. Skye Ferry 4mls/6kms.

DUISKY, by Fort William Inverness-shire Map Ref. 3G12

COMMENDED
👑 👑

1 chalet/log cabin, 1 pub rm, 2-3 bedrms, sleeps 4-7, £65-£135, Jan-Dec, bus 6 mls, rail 9 mls, airport 100 mls

🦽 ⑭ E 🍴 ⑦ 🎞 🖵 ◎ 🖵 🔔 💈 ▰ ☺ ❊ 🐕 🅿 🐃 🎞 ⚙   ♪ 🤸 🏄 🎿 ▸ 🎿 🐂

Mrs J Cox, The Old School, Duisky, by Fort William, Inverness-shire, PH33 7AW
☎ *Kinlocheil (039783) 227*
Wooden lodge in own grounds overlooking Loch Eil. Boating and fishing available.

DULNAIN BRIDGE Moray Map Ref. 4C9

1 cottage, 2 pub rms, 3 bedrms, sleeps 6, min let weekend, £120-£145, Mar-Oct, bus 10 mls, rail 10 mls, airport 20 mls

🦽 ⑭ E 🍴 ⑦ 🎞 ◎ 🖵 🔔 🖵 🖸 💈 ▰ ☺ ❊ 🅿 🐃 🎞 ✝ ⚙   📻 🦌 🚣 🔍 🏹 ♪ 🤸 🏄
▸ 🎿 🐂 🎿 ✕ 🧺 🐄

Mrs C J R Whittle, Easter Laggan, Dulnain Bridge, by Grantown-on-Spey, Moray, PH26 3NT
☎ *Dulnain Bridge (047985) 283*

VAT is shown at 15%: changes in this rate may affect prices.

1 cottage, 1 pub rm, 3 bedrms, sleeps 6, from £105, Jan-Dec, bus 2 mls, rail 14 mls, airport 35 mls

Mrs J Ross, Ballintomb Farm, Dulnain Bridge, by Grantown-on-Spey, Moray, PH26 3LS
☎ *Dulnain Bridge (047985) 334*

---

1 house, 1 pub rm, 2 bedrms, sleeps 6, min let weekend, from £70, Jan-Dec, bus ½ ml, rail 12 mls, airport 30 mls

Mrs R Allan, Easter Curr, Dulnain Bridge, Moray
☎ *Dulnain Bridge (047985) 282*

---

2 cottages, 1 pub rm, 1-2 bedrms, sleeps 3-5, min let weekend, £60-£90, Jan-Dec, bus nearby, rail 7 mls, airport 30 mls

Mr & Mrs J C Allan, Post Office, Dulnain Bridge, Grantown-on-Spey, Moray
☎ *Dulnain Bridge (047985) 331*

---

1 cottage, 1 pub rm, 4 bedrms, sleeps 15, min let weekend, £200-£250, Jan-Dec, bus ½ ml, rail 5 mls

Skye of Curr Hotel, Dulnain Bridge, Grantown-on-Spey, Moray
☎ *Dulnain Bridge (047985) 345*

---

1 house, 1 cottage, 1-2 pub rms, 3-4 bedrms, sleeps 6-8, min let 3 nights, from £100, Jan-Dec, bus 1 ml, rail 8 mls

Mrs Hamilton, Tullochgribban Mains, Dulnain Bridge, by Grantown-on-Spey, Moray
☎ *Dulnain Bridge (047985) 333*

---

1 cottage, 1 pub rm, 1 bedrm, sleeps 4, £50-£60, Mar-Nov, bus nearby, rail 6 mls, airport 36 mls

Mrs Henderson, Broomlands, Dulnain Bridge, Inverness-shire
☎ *Dulnain Bridge (047985) 255*

---

1 house, 1 pub rm, 2 bedrms, sleeps 4, £70-£80, Jan-Dec, bus 500 yds, rail 12 mls, airport 35 mls

Mrs M Mackenzie, Tigh-Na-Hath, Dulnain Bridge, by Grantown-on-Spey, Moray, PH26 3NU
☎ *Dulnain Bridge (047985) 266*

---

1 bungalow, 2 pub rms, 2 bedrms, sleeps 7, £80-£100, May-Sep, bus 1 ml, rail 10 mls

Mrs E McCafferty, Parkhead Cottage, Dulnain Bridge, Moray
☎ *Dulnain Bridge (047985) 219*

DUMFRIES Map Ref. 2B9

1 cottage, 1 pub rm, 2 bedrms, sleeps 6-8, max £100, Apr-Oct, bus 1 ml, rail 4 mls

Mrs J Butlin, Guillyhill, Holywood, Dumfries, DG2 0RJ
☎ *Newbridge (0387) 720353*

Prices shown are for guidance only. Please send SAE with each enquiry.

2 cottages, 1 pub rm, 5-6 bedrms, sleeps 4-6, min let 3 nights, £120-£160, Apr-Oct, bus nearby, rail ¾ ml, airport 32 mls

🔥♿ E ⚡ ◉ ⊙ ▢ ▢ ▣ ▦ ☺ ❋ 🐕 P ⟳ ▦ 🏔   ♩ ∪ △ ⚃ ↟ ✗ 🖹 ⅚ T

Mr & Mrs Hunter, Fountainbleau Farm, Lockerbie Road, Dumfries
☎ *Dumfries (0387) 53760*

Nunland Park 5 chalet/log cabins, 1 pub rm, 2 bedrms, sleeps 6, min let weekend, £120-£200, Feb-Oct, bus 300 yds, rail 3 ½ mls

🔥♿ E 🔥 ▦ ▢ ◉ ⊙ ▢ ▢ ⁄ ▦ ☺ 🐕 P ⟳ 🔥 🏔 ● ⊕   ⤳ ⟿ ◵ 🌲 ♩ ∪ △ ↟
✗ 🖹 ⅚ T (horse riding & stabling (for own horse))

Mr & Mrs Reid, Nunland, Crocketford Road, Dumfries
☎ *Dumfries (0387) 73214*

DUMFRIES AREA Map Ref. 2B9

6 houses, 2 cottages, 1 bungalow, 1-2 pub rms, 2-4 bedrms, sleeps 5-8, from £70, Apr-Oct

🔥♿ E ⚡ ◉ ⊙ ▢ ▢ ▦ ❋ 🐕 P ⟳ ▦   ♩ ✗ 🖹

G M Thomson & Company, 27 King Street, Castle Douglas, Kirkcudbrightshire, DG7 1AB
☎ *Castle Douglas (0556) 2701*

by DUNBAR East Lothian Map Ref. 2E4

1 cottage, 1 pub rm, 2 bedrms, sleeps 4-5, £75-£92, Jan-Dec, bus 2 mls, rail 3 mls, airport 30 mls

🔥♿ E ⚡ ◉ ⊙ ▢ ▢ ▣ ▦ ❋ P ⟳ ▦ † 🏔   ♩ ∪ ↟ 🖹 ⅚

W H Henderson, Pleasants, Dunbar, East Lothian, EH42 1RE
☎ *Dunbar (0368) 63737*

---

1 house, 2 cottages, 1-2 pub rms, 2-3 bedrms, sleeps 4-8, £70-£185, Jan-Dec, bus 1 ½ mls, rail 2 ½ mls, airport 40 mls

🔥♿ E ⚡ ◉ ▦ ▣ ▦ ◉ ⊙ ▢ ▢ ▣ ▦ ☺ ❋ 🐕 P ⟳ ▦ 🔥 † 🏔 ⊕   ⤳ ⟿ ◵ ♩ ∪
△ ↟ ⁄ ✗ 🖹

Mrs Moira Marrian, Bowerhouse, Dunbar, East Lothian, EH42 1RE
☎ *Dunbar (0368) 62293*

DUNBEATH Caithness Map Ref. 4D4

1 cottage, 2 pub rms, 2 bedrms, sleeps 4, £67-£107, Apr-Oct, bus nearby, rail 16 mls, airport 21 mls

🔥♿ E ⚡ 🔥 ▦ ▦ ▣ ◉ ⊙ ▢ ▢ ▣ ⁄ ▦ ☺ ❋ 🐕 P ⟳ ▦ † 🏔   ⤳ ⟿ ◵ ♩ ∪ ⚃
↟ ✗ 🖹

Mrs Hazel Lindsay, Tigh A Mhuilinn, Dunbeath, Caithness, KW6 6EG
☎ *Dunbeath (05933) 259*

---

1 caravan, sleeps 6-8, min let 1 night, £40-£45, Apr-Oct, bus nearby, rail 20 mls, airport 20 mls

🔥♿ E ▣ ⁄ 🐕 P † 🏔   ♩ ∪ △ ⚃ ↟ ✗ 🖹 ⅚ T

Mrs J Polanska, Knockinnon, Dunbeath, Caithness
☎ *Dunbeath (05933) 347*

DUNBLANE Perthshire Map Ref. 2A3

2 flats, 3 cottages, 3 pub rms, 2-3 bedrms, sleeps 4-6, £95-£130, Jun-Sep, bus 1 ml, rail 1 ml, airport 40 mls

Kippendavie Estate Office, 5 High Street, Dunblane, Perthshire, FK15 0EE
☎ *Dunblane (0786) 822233/823413*
Converted farmworkers house on private estate in quiet countryside. Good touring base.

---

1 flat, 1 pub rm, 2 bedrms, sleeps 4, £100-£140, Jan-Dec, bus nearby, rail 400 yds, airport 40 mls

Mr K Hay, 16 Clarendon Place, Stirling
☎ *Stirling (0786) 74323*

DUNCANSTON Ross-shire Map Ref. 4A8

1 cottage, 1 pub rm, 3 bedrms, sleeps 6, £50-£70, Apr-Oct, bus nearby, rail 6 mls, airport 16 mls

Mrs A Hannan, Shalom, Dunvournie, Culbokie, by Dingwall, Ross-shire, IV7 8JB
☎ *Culbokie (034987) 246*
On working farm with delightful views over Cromarty Firth and surrounding hills. Central for touring.

DUNCOW, by Dumfries Dumfriesshire Map Ref. 2B9

1 bungalow, 1 pub rm, 3 bedrms, sleeps 6, £70-£80, May-Sep, bus nearby, rail 5 mls

Mrs M Cairnie, Gateside, Duncow, Dumfries, Dumfriesshire
☎ *Amisfield (0387) 710285*

DUNDEE Angus Map Ref. 2D2

Hillside Student Flats 8 flats, 1 pub rm, 6-8 bedrms, sleeps 6-8, from £50, Jul-Aug, bus 300 yds, rail 2 ½ mls, airport 1 ½ mls

Irene Donaldson, Student Services, Duncan of Jordanstone College of Art, Dundee, Angus
☎ *Dundee (0382) 23261*

Peterson & Wimberley Houses 60 houses, 1 pub rm, 4-7 bedrms, sleeps 4-7, £29 (per person), Jul-Sep, bus nearby, rail nearby

(windsurfing)

Residences Office, University of Dundee, Perth Road, Dundee, Angus, DD1 4HN
☎ *Dundee (0382) 23181 ext 4040*

DUNDONNELL Ross-shire Map Ref. 3G7

1 caravan, sleeps 6, min let 1 night, max £50, Mar-Oct, rail 34 mls

Mrs A Ross, 4 Camusnagaul, Dundonnell, by Garve, Ross-shire
☎ *Dundonnell (085483) 237*

DUNDRENNAN AREA Kirkcudbrightshire Map Ref. 2A11

2 houses, 2 cottages, 1 bungalow, 1 pub rm, 3 bedrms, sleeps 6-7, from £80, Apr-Oct

♿ ᵂᶜ E 🖐 🗠 ◎ 🗐 🗖 🧺 ☼ 🐴 🅿 🖋 🎞 †　🎣 ∪ ⚓ ⚲ ►

G M Thomson & Company, 27 King Street, Castle Douglas, Kirkcudbrightshire, DG7 1AB
☎ *Castle Douglas (0556) 2701*

DUNFERMLINE Fife Map Ref. 2C4

1 house, 2 pub rms, 6 bedrms, sleeps 10, £100-£180, Jan-Dec

♿ ᵂᶜ E 🖐 ⌜ 🗠 🎞 ◎ 🗐 ✆ 🗖 🗐 ✏ 🧺 ☉ ☼ 🐴 🅿 🖋 🎞 †

Finlayson Hughes, Bank House, 82 Atholl Road, Pitlochry, Perthshire, PH16 5BL
☎ *Pitlochry (0796) 2512*

DUNKELD Perthshire Map Ref. 2B1

1 house, 1 pub rm, 4 bedrms, sleeps 6, min let weekend, £95-£140, Apr-Oct, rail 7 mls

♿ ᵂᶜ E 🖐 🗠 ◎ 🗐 🗖 🧺 ☉ ☼ 🐴 🅿 🖋 🎞 † ⩜　🎣 ⚓ ► ⚲ ✗ 🎿

Mr Boyne, Balmacneil Farm, Dunkeld, Perthshire, PH8 0LB
☎ *Ballinluig (079682) 213*

---

2 caravans, sleeps 4-6, min let weekend, £50-£70, Apr-Oct, bus 1 ml, rail 3 mls

♿ ᵂᶜ E ⌜ 🗠 ✏ ✆ ☉ 🐴 🅿 † ⩜　🎣 ► 🎿

Mrs J Mathieson, Inchmagrannachan Farm, Dunkeld, Perthshire, PH8 0JS
☎ *Dunkeld (03502) 372*

---

4 cottages, 1 pub rm, 2 bedrms, sleeps 4, £50-£95, Mar-Nov, bus 1 ml, rail 12 mls, airport 65 mls

♿ ᵂᶜ E 🖐 🗠 🗓 ◎ 🗐 🗖 🗐 🧺 ☼ 🐴 🅿 　 ☍ 🎣 ∪ ►

Mrs R Steuart Fothringham, Fothringham House, by Forfar, Angus, DD8 2JP
☎ *Inverarity (030782) 231*

---

4 houses, 1 cottage, 1 bungalow, 1-2 pub rms, 2-5 bedrms, sleeps 6-10, £100-£205, Mar-Oct

♿ ᵂᶜ E 🖐 ⌜ 🗠 🎞 ◎ 🗐 ✆ 🗖 🗐 🧺 ☉ ☼ 🐴 🅿 🖋 🎞 † ⩜　🎣 ∪ ⚓ ► 🎿 🎿

Finlayson Hughes, Bank House, 82 Atholl Road, Pitlochry, Perthshire, PH16 5BL
☎ *Pitlochry (0796) 2512*

---

1 house, 1 bungalow, 2 pub rms, 3-4 bedrms, sleeps 5-8, £75-£130, Apr-Oct, bus 4 mls, rail 4 mls

♿ ᵂᶜ E 🖐 🗠 🗓 ◎ 🗐 🗖 🗐 🧺 ☼ 🅿 🖋 🎞 　 ☍ 🎣 ► 🎿

Mrs Fotheringham, Ballinloan, Trochry, Dunkeld, Perthshire, PH8 0BS
☎ *Trochry (03503) 246*

TRY A "TASTE OF SCOTLAND"
Look for the stockpot—
sign of good food,
a warm welcome
and value for money!

VAT is shown at 15%: changes in this rate may affect prices.

DUNAIRD CABINS
Birnam

"Far from the madding crowd" — yet so convenient. Escape from today's frenetic lifestyle to the peace and tranquillity of our clean, comfortable, octagonal cabins in a woodland setting near "The Mouth of the Highlands". We are only a few minutes' walk from historic Birnam and Dunkeld whose facilities ensure an enjoyable holiday whilst the nearby A9 and rail link make this an ideal centre for touring.

**Apply to Mrs M. DONALD,
Dunaird Cabins, St Mary's Road, Birnam,
Dunkeld. Tel: Dunkeld (03502) 262**

AWAITING INSPECTION

Dunaird House Cabins 10 chalet/log cabins, 1 pub rm, 2 bedrms, sleeps 6, min let 2 nights, £70-£235, Jan-Dec, bus nearby, rail 400 yds, airport 50 mls

Mrs M Donald, Dunaird Cabins, St Mary's Road, Birnam, Dunkeld, Perthshire, PH8 0BJ
☎ *Dunkeld (03502) 262*

---

by DUNKELD Perthshire Map Ref. 2B1

10 chalet/log cabins, 1 pub rm, 3 bedrms, sleeps 8, min let weekend, £150-£270, Jan-Dec, bus 4 mls, rail 4 mls, airport 27 mls

Butterstone Log Cabins Ltd, Butterstone, Dunkeld, Perthshire, PH8 0HA
☎ *Butterstone (03504) 234/205*

2 houses, 1 annexe, 1-2 pub rms, 2-3 bedrms, sleeps 4-6, from £110, Jan-Dec, rail 5 mls

Bell-Ingram, Durn, Isla Road, Perth, PH2 7HF
☎ *Perth (0738) 21121*

DUNNING Perthshire Map Ref. 2B3

2 cottages, 1-2 pub rms, 1-4 bedrms, sleeps 4-8, £95-£295, Jan-Dec, bus ½ ml, rail 10 mls, airport 40 mls

Mrs W Marshall, Dalreoch, Dunning, Perth, Perthshire, PH2 0QJ
☎ *Dunning (076484) 368*

DUNOON Argyll Map Ref. 1G5

3 chalet/log cabins, 3 flats, 1 cottage, 1 pub rm, 1-2 bedrms, sleeps 2-4, min let 3 nights, £65-£160, Jan-Dec, bus nearby, rail 3 mls, ferry ½ ml, airport 23 mls

Mrs J Allan, Claymore, Wellington Street, West Bay, Dunoon, Argyll
☎ *Dunoon (0369) 2658*

Stratheck International Caravan Park 6 caravans, sleeps 6, min let weekend, £69-£140, Apr-Oct, bus ½ ml, rail 8 mls, ferry 6 mls, airport 30 mls

Stratheck International Caravan Park, Loch Eck, Dunoon, Argyll, PA23 8SG
☎ *Kilmun (036984) 472*

Prices shown are for guidance only. Please send SAE with each enquiry.

1 flat, 1 pub rm, 3 bedrms, sleeps 5, £85-£100, Feb-Nov, bus nearby, ferry 1 ml

♿ ⌨ E 🛏 🖉 ⊚ ▣ 🖵 ⎘ ✦ ⧉ ❋ ⛱ 🏢 † ⛷ ⚲ ♪ △ ⚓ ↱ ✕ 🦞

Mrs G Ewart, Cherrytree House, Hornby, Gt Smeaton, Northallerton, N Yorks
☎ *Gt Smeaton (060981) 603*

---

2 chalet/log cabins, 1-2 pub rms, 2-3 bedrms, sleeps 2-6, min let weekend (by arrangement), £75-£275, Apr-Oct, bus nearby, rail 3 mls, ferry ¾ ml, airport 26 mls

♿ ⌨ E 🛏 🖉 ▤ 🖳 ⊙ 🖵 ▢ 🖵 ⎘ ✦ ◉ ❋ 🐕 🅿 ⧉ ⛱ 🏢 ⤵ ⛰ ◍ 🍃 ⛷ ⛷ 🐎 ⚲ 🐟 ♪ ∪ △ ⚓ ↱ ✓ 🍴 Ⓡ ✕ 🦞 🍽 ♫ Ⓣ (hillclimbing trails)

Janet & Keith Lamanque, c/o Singing Pines, A4 Hafton Estate, Hunters Quay, by Dunoon, Argyll, PA23 8HP
☎ *Dunoon (0369) 6876*

---

by DUNOON Argyll Map Ref. 1G5

Cowal Caravan Park 14 caravans, sleeps 6, min let 2 nights, £48-£108, Jan-Dec, bus nearby, rail 2 mls, ferry nearby, airport 20 mls

♿ ⌨ E 🖳 🖉 🖳 🖉 🖵 ▢ 🖵 ▢ ⧉ ◉ ❋ 🅿 † ⛷ 🐎 ⚲ 🐎 ♪ ∪ △ ⚓ ↱ ✓ ⇶ ⇶ ✕ 🦞 Ⓣ

Mr & Mrs A B Garner, Cowal Caravan Park, Hunters Quay, Dunoon, Argyll, PA23 8JY
☎ *Dunoon (0369) 4259*

Freedom is Yours . . .

LAMONT LODGES, RASHFIELD, DUNOON, ARGYLL PA23 8QY
Telephone: Kilmun (0369 84) 205
4 and 5 Crown Self-Catering. Beautiful, relaxing and comfortable base for your holiday explorations, with freedom of access to hill, shore and lochside. Spacious log cabins, 2/3 bedroomed, sleeping 2-8. Colour TV, washer/drier, dishwasher. Fully carpeted.
FREE: Welcome tray, children's swimming, garden entry, maps, guides, club memberships. FREE UNLIMITED GOLF. Open all year.
From £96 to £295 per week.

---

up to
COMMENDED
👑👑👑👑👑

18 chalet/log cabins, 1 pub rm, 2-3 bedrms, sleeps 4-8, min let weekend, £96-£295, Jan-Dec, bus nearby, rail 6 mls, ferry 3 mls, airport 35 mls

♿ ⌨ E 🛏 🖉 ▤ 🖳 ⊙ 🖵 ▢ 🖵 ▢ ✦ ▢ ◉ ❋ 🐕 🅿 ⛱ 🏢 ⤵ ⛰ ◍ ⛷ ⛷ 🐎 ⚲ 🐟 ♪ ∪ △ ⚓ ↱ ✓ ⇶ ✕ 🦞 Ⓣ

Lamont Country Lodges, Rashfield, Dunoon, Argyll, PA23 8QT
☎ *Kilmun (036984) 205/641*
Magnificently set in Benmore National Forest Park. Woodland garden, forest walks, fishing, free golf.

Loch Eck Caravan Park 4 caravans, sleeps 4-6, min let weekend, £60-£120, Apr-Oct, bus nearby, rail 10 mls, ferry 9 mls, airport 30 mls

♿ ⌨ 📠 E 🖉 🖉 🖵 📞 🖵 ▢ 🖵 ◉ ❋ 🐕 🅿 ◍ ⚲ 🐎 ⛷ 🐎 ⚲ 🐎 ♪ ∪ △ ⚓ ↱ ✓ ⇶ ⇶ ✕ (boat launching)

Mr & Mrs T J Forster, Loch Eck Caravan Park, Loch Eck, by Dunoon, Argyll
☎ *Kilmun (036984) 447*

Invereck Caravan Park 2 caravans, sleeps 4-6, min let 3 nights, £55-£90, Apr-Oct, bus nearby, rail 5 mls, ferry 4 mls, airport 25 mls

♿ E 🖉 🖵 ▢ ◉ 🐕 🅿 ⚲ ♪ ∪ △ ⚓ ↱ ✓ ✕ 🦞 Ⓣ

Invereck Caravan Park, by Dunoon, Argyll
☎ *Dunoon (0369) 6395/Kilmun (036984) 208*

COMMENDED
👑👑👑👑

Hafton Country Club 58 chalet/log cabins, 1-2 pub rms, 2-3 bedrms, sleeps 4-7, min let weekend (low season), £95-£325, Jan-Dec, bus nearby, rail 3 mls, ferry 1 ml, airport 26 mls

[symbols] (putting)

Hafton Country Club, Hafton House, Hunter's Quay, by Dunoon, Argyll, PA23 8HP
☎ *Dunoon (0369) 6205*

Woodland or loch view site. Lots to do if you wish, use of superb country house facilities.

(See ad. on p. 106)

DUNS Berwickshire Map Ref. 2F5

1 cottage, 1 pub rm, 3 bedrms, sleeps 6, £50-£90, Jun-Oct, bus 2 mls, rail 15 mls

[symbols]

Mrs A Thomson, Mungoswalls, Duns, Berwickshire, TD11 3LT
☎ *Duns (0361) 83278*

1 cottage, 1 pub rm, 3 bedrms, sleeps 7, min let weekend, £40-£100, Jan-Dec, bus 4 mls, rail 12 mls

[symbols]

Mrs J Biggar, The Heugh, Kimmerghame, Duns, Berwickshire
☎ *Duns (0361) 83781*

1 cottage, 1 pub rm, 4 bedrms, sleeps 9, min let weekend, £20-£90, Jan-Dec, bus 1 ½ mls, rail 17 mls, airport 50 mls

[symbols]

Mrs Staniforth, 18 North Park Terrace, Edinburgh, EH4 1DP
☎ *031 332 6371*

DUNSCORE Dumfriesshire Map Ref. 2B9

1 bungalow, 1 pub rm, 3 bedrms, sleeps 7, min let weekend, £70-£80, Apr-Oct, bus ½ ml, rail 13 mls, airport 50 mls

[symbols]

Mrs Wharton, Snade, Dunscore, Dumfriesshire
☎ *Dunscore (038782) 296*

1 cottage, 1 pub rm, 1 bedrm, sleeps 2-4, £60-£90, Jan-Dec, bus 1 ml

[symbols]

Mr Zan Kirk, Low Kirkbride, Auldgirth, Dumfriesshire, DG2 0SP
☎ *Dunscore (038782) 252*

DUNSYRE Lanarkshire Map Ref. 2C6

COMMENDED
👑👑👑

2 cottages, 1 pub rm, 2-3 bedrms, sleeps 4-6, £105-£210, Jan-Dec, rail 10 mls, airport 25 mls

[symbols]

Lee & Carnwath Estates, Estate Office, Carnwath, Lanarkshire, ML11 8JY
☎ *Carnwath (0555) 840273*

Under personal supervision of the owners. In small village on private estate.

DUNURE Ayrshire Map Ref. 1G8

AWAITING INSPECTION

1 cottage, 1 pub rm, 2 bedrms, sleeps 6-8, from £90, Jun-Sep, bus nearby, rail 5 mls, airport 10 mls

Mrs Reid, Lagg Farm, Dunure, Ayrshire, KA7 4LE
☎ *Dunure (029250) 647*

VAT is shown at 15%: changes in this rate may affect prices.

DUNVEGAN Isle of Skye, Inverness-shire Map Ref. 3C9

3 houses, 1-2 pub rms, 3-4 bedrms, sleeps 6-8, £75-£140, Mar-Oct, bus 1 ml, rail 50 mls, ferry 50 mls, airport 40 mls

♿ 🚾 E 🔌 📀 ◎ 📺 ⬚ 🔳 ❄ ♉ P 🐴 🏛 †   ♪ ∪ △ ∡ ✕ 🐕 🎣

K F S Mackenzie, F.R.I.C.S, 9 Millbank Street, Nairn
☎ *Nairn (0667) 53493*

MILLBURN HOUSE

Very comfortable flat consisting of 1 public room and 4 bedrooms. Central heating, kitchen (electric cooker), TV.

Situated on the lovely Isle of Skye at the head of Loch Dunvegan, there is plenty to see and do with fishing, pony-trekking, sailing and golf nearby.

For further information contact Mrs E. Campbell, Millburn House, Dunvegan, Isle of Skye, Inverness-shire. Tel: Dunvegan (047022) 210.

1 flat, 1 pub rm, 4 bedrms, sleeps 5-7, £120-£150, Jan-Dec, bus nearby, rail 45 mls, ferry 42 mls, airport 40 mls

♿ 🚾 E 🔌 ♉ 📀 🖥 ⬚ ◎ 📺 📞 ⬚ 🔳 📀 ✦ ♉ ❄ P 🐴 🏛 🔌 † 🏛 ✪ ♞ ⚓ ♪ ∪ △ ▸ ✕ 🐕 🎣

Mrs E Campbell, Millburn House, Dunvegan, Isle of Skye, Inverness-shire
☎ *Dunvegan (047022) 210*

2 flats, 1-2 pub rms, 2-3 bedrms, sleeps 4-7, £125-£140, Jan-Dec, bus 2 mls, rail 48 mls, ferry 48 mls

♿ 🚾 E 🔌 ♉ 🏛 ◎ 📺 📞 📀 ✦ ♉ P 🐴 🏛   ♪ ∪ ∡

Mrs M Roberts, Orbost House, Dunvegan, Isle of Skye, Inverness-shire, IV51 9RS
☎ *Dunvegan (047022) 207*

1 house, 1 pub rm, 3 bedrms, sleeps 6, £75-£110, Jan-Dec, bus 2 mls, rail 52 mls, ferry 52 mls, airport 48 mls

♿ 🚾 E 🔌 ♉ 🏛 ◎ 📺 🔳 📀 ◉ ♉ P 🐴 🏛 †   ♪ ∪ ✕

Mrs S Macleod, Howlands Farm, South Road, Durham City, County Durham, DH1 3TQ
☎ *Durham (0385) 63143*

1 flat, 2 pub rms, 2 bedrms, sleeps 4-5, £115-£130, Apr-Oct, bus ½ ml, rail 50 mls, ferry 48 mls

♿ 🚾 E 🔌 ♉ 🏛 🔳 📺 ⬚ 📀 ❄ ♉ P 🐴 🏛 †   ♪ ∪ ∡ ✕ 🐕

Mrs P Morrison, Ardnorn, Roskhill, Dunvegan, Isle of Skye, Inverness-shire
☎ *Dunvegan (047022) 354*

Prices shown are for guidance only. Please send SAE with each enquiry.

1 bungalow, 2 pub rms, 3 bedrms, sleeps 6, £100-£170, Jan-Dec, bus nearby, rail 50 mls, ferry 50 mls, airport 40 mls

Mr D MacGregor, Broughfold, Natland, by Kendal, Cumbria
☎ *Kendal (0539) 21055*

1 bungalow, 1 pub rm, 4 bedrms, sleeps 8, £85-£130, Jan-Dec, bus nearby, rail 44 mls, ferry 44 mls, airport 38 mls

Mrs Dorothy Henderson, The Manse, Kirk Street, Campbeltown, Argyll
☎ *Campbeltown (0586) 52759*

by DUNVEGAN Isle of Skye, Inverness-shire Map Ref. 3C9

2 flats, 1 pub rm, 1-2 bedrms, sleeps 2-6, £80-£165, Mar-Oct, ferry 46 mls

Mrs I E Beevers, Roskhill Guest House, Roskhill, Dunvegan, Isle of Skye, Inverness-shire
☎ *Dunvegan (047022) 317*

DURNAMUCK, by Dundonnell Ross-shire Map Ref. 3F6

1 caravan, sleeps 7, £85-£95, Feb-Nov, bus 1 ml, rail 30 mls, airport 75 mls

(sea cruises arranged)
Mrs S G Reeves, Seaview, Durnamuck, Dundonnell, Ross-shire, IV23 2QZ
☎ *Dundonnell (085483) 221*

DURNESS Sutherland Map Ref. 3H3

1 flat, 1 pub rm, 1 bedrm, sleeps 2-3, £70-£80, May-Oct

Mrs W Stewart, Ceol-na-Mara, Lerin, Durness, Sutherland
☎ *Durness (097181) 240*

2 chalet/log cabins, 1 pub rm, 2 bedrms, sleeps 4, from £70, Mar-Oct, bus nearby

Mrs M Hames, Old Manse, Sangamore, Durness, Sutherland
☎ *Durness (097181) 223*

DUROR, by Appin Argyll Map Ref. 1F1

1 cottage, 2 pub rms, 3 bedrms, sleeps 6, from £130, Easter-Oct, bus nearby, rail 15 mls, ferry 30 mls, airport 80 mls

Mrs F C Worthington, Lag-na-Ha Cottage, Duror, Argyll
☎ *Duror (063174) 207*

DURRIS, by Banchory Kincardineshire Map Ref. 4G11

1 cottage, 1 pub rm, 1 bedrm, sleeps 2-4, £80, May-Oct, bus 2 mls

Mrs P Gould, Woodlands Cottage, Woodlands of Durris, Banchory, Kincardineshire, AB3 3BG
☎ *Drumoak (03308) 625*

EARLSFERRY, by Elie Fife Map Ref. 2E3

1 flat, 1 pub rm, 4 bedrms, sleeps 8-10, from £200, Jan-Dec, bus 2 mls, rail 20 mls, airport 50 mls

J A L James, The Lodge, Steyning Road, Rottingdean, Brighton, Sussex
☎ *Brighton (0273) 32170*

EARLSTON Berwickshire Map Ref. 2E6

1 cottage, 1 pub rm, 2 bedrms, sleeps 4, £70-£175, Mar-Nov, bus 1 ½ mls, rail 36 mls, airport 40 mls

Mrs Barlow, The Park, Earlston, Berwickshire, TD4 6AB
☎ *Earlston (089684) 267*

EASDALE, by Oban Argyll Map Ref. 1D3

1 chalet/log cabin, 1 cottage, 1 pub rm, 2 bedrms, sleeps 4-6, £60-£120, Apr-Oct, bus nearby, rail 16 mls

Mrs Barbara Nathan, The Old Inn, Easdale, by Oban, Argyll
☎ *Balvicar (08523) 209*

1 cottage, 1 pub rm, 2 bedrms, sleeps 5, £85-£130, Apr-Oct, bus 500 yds, rail 16 mls

Mrs J Forster, Corriegorm, Killin, Perthshire
☎ *Killin (05672) 201*

1 cottage, 1 pub rm, 2 bedrms, sleeps 4, min let weekend, £60-£120, Apr-Oct, bus nearby

Mrs Chadwick, Kinvara, Ganavan, by Oban, Argyll
☎ *Oban (0631) 62786*

EAST LINTON East Lothian Map Ref. 2E4

1 cottage, 1 pub rm, 2 bedrms, sleeps 5, from £60, Apr-Oct, bus 5 mls, rail 5 mls, airport 30 mls

Mrs D Gardner, Stonelaws Farm, East Linton, East Lothian, EH40 3DX
☎ *Whitekirk (062087) 207*

EASTER DEANS, by Peebles Peeblesshire Map Ref. 2C6

1 house, 2 pub rms, 3 bedrms, sleeps 8, £80-£210, Apr-Oct, bus 1 ml, rail 12 mls, airport 15 mls

Mrs J P Campbell, Glenrath Farm, Kirkton Manor, Peeblesshire
☎ *Kirkton Manor (07214) 221*

ECCLEFECHAN Dumfriesshire Map Ref. 2C9

1 cottage, 1 pub rm, 2 bedrms, sleeps 4-6, £50-£70, May-Oct, bus ½ ml, rail 4 mls, airport 80 mls

♿ 🚾 E + ⊘ ◎ □ ☐ ▨ ☉ ✼ P ➬ 📺 † ♪ ▸ 🚲 🐃

Mrs J D Clark, Whins Farm, Ecclefechan, Lockerbie, Dumfriesshire, DG11 3LW
☎ *Ecclefechan (05763) 257*

EDAY Orkney Map Ref. 5C10

3 cottages, 1 pub rm, 1-2 bedrms, sleeps 4-5, £35-£100, Jan-Dec, ferry 5 mls, airport 1 ½ mls

♿ 🚾 E + 🎣 ⊘ 🛏 📦 ◎ □ ☎ ☐ ▨ ☉ ✼ 🐎 P ⁄ ➬ 📺 🛒 † ∪ ⛵ ⚓ ✗ 🐃

Mrs D W G Cockram, Fersness Farm, Isle of Eday, Orkney
☎ *Eday (08572) 262*

EDDLESTON Peeblesshire Map Ref. 2C6

1 cottage, 1 pub rm, 2 bedrms, sleeps 4, £60-£95, May-Oct, bus 300 yds, rail 14 mls, airport 15 mls

♿ 🚾 E + ⊘ 📦 ◎ □ ☐ ▨ ☉ ✼ 🐎 P † ↯ ⚲ ∪ ▸ ✗

Mrs D Jeffrey, Linnfall, Eddleston, Peeblesshire, EH45 8QX
☎ *Eddleston (07213) 228*

APPROVED ♛♛

1 cottage, 4 pub rms, 3 bedrms, sleeps 8, min let weekend, £60-£80, Jan-Dec, bus 4 mls, rail 27 mls, airport 27 mls

♿ 🚾 E + ⊘ 📦 ◎ □ ☐ ▨ 🐎 P ➬ 📺 † ⌂ ↯ ⚲ ⚲ ✡ ∪ ⛵ ⚓ ▸ ╱ 🐃

Mrs J A Gascoigne, Harehope Farm, Eddleston, Peeblesshire
☎ *Eddleston (07213) 243*
Original farmhouse adjoining owners home. Peaceful location, about 1 ml(2 km) from road.

---

1 cottage, 1 pub rm, 2 bedrms, sleeps 4, £58-£69, Apr-Oct, bus 1 ml, rail 19 mls, airport 19 mls

♿ 🚾 E + ⊘ ◎ □ ☐ ▨ ☉ ✼ 🐎 P ➬ 📺 † ⌂ ↯ ✡ ∪ ⛵ ⚓ ╱ ✗ 🚲 🐃

Mrs Brockie, Wormiston Farm, Eddleston, Peeblesshire
☎ *Eddleston (07213) 272*

COMMENDED ♛♛♛

1 bungalow, 1 pub rm, 3 bedrms, sleeps 8, £70-£90, Jan-Dec, bus ½ ml, rail 19 mls, airport 20 mls

♿ 🚾 E + 🎣 ⊘ 📦 🛏 ◎ □ ☐ ▨ ☎ ✼ 🐎 P ➬ 📺 † ⌂ ↯ ⚲ ✡ ∪ ⛵ ⚓ ▸ ✗ 🚲 🐃

Mrs A Smellie, Hattonknowe Farm, Eddleston, Peeblesshire
☎ *Eddleston (07213) 282*
Modern, on 700 acre farm (arable, sheep, cattle). Own garden. Fine views towards Peebles.

EDINBANE Isle of Skye, Inverness-shire Map Ref. 3D8

1 bungalow, 2 pub rms, 3 bedrms, sleeps 6, £70-£110, May-Oct

♿ 🚾 E + ⊘ ◎ □ ▨ P ➬ 📺 † ⌂ ∪ ⛵ ⚓ ✗ 🚲 🐃

Miss N Mackinnon, 2 Birkhall Drive, Bearsden, Glasgow, G61 1DB
☎ *041 942 4195*

---

by EDINBANE Isle of Skye, Inverness-shire Map Ref. 3D8

1 flat, 1 pub rm, 1 bedrm, sleeps 4, min let 3-4 nights, £110, Apr-Oct, bus 1 ½ mls, rail 38 mls, ferry 38 mls, airport 35 mls

Mrs B Creed, Three Rowans, Kildonan, Arnisort, Edinbane, Isle of Skye, Inverness-shire
☎ *Edinbane (047082) 286*

EDINBURGH Map Ref. 2D5

2 houses, 6 flats, 1-2 pub rms, 1-4 bedrms, sleeps 1-6, min let 2 weeks, £120-£400, Jun-Sep

Dundas Property Agency, 61/63 Broughton Street, Edinburgh, EH1 3RJ
☎ *031 556 8363*

---

1 flat, 1 pub rm, 3 bedrms, sleeps 6, £150-£200, Apr-Oct, bus nearby, rail 2 mls, airport 10 mls

Miss Karen Campbell, Glenrath Farm, Kirkton Manor, Peebles
☎ *Kirkton Manor (07214) 221*

---

5 flats, 1 pub rm, 1 bedrm, sleeps 2-6, min let 2 nights, £35-£50, Jan-Dec, bus nearby, rail 3 mls, airport 6 mls

Mr & Mrs Hepburn, No 5, 5/7 Abercorn Terr, Portobello, Edinburgh, EH15 2DD
☎ *031 669 1044*

COMMENDED
👑 👑 👑 👑

42 flats, 1 cottage, 1 pub rm, 1-3 bedrms, sleeps 2-6, min let 1 night, £98-£297, Jan-Dec, bus nearby, rail 1 ml, airport 5 mls

Keyplan Apartments, Linton Court, Murieston Road, Edinburgh, EH11 2JJ
☎ *031 337 4040*
Serviced units, 1 mile (2km) S.W. of city centre. Convenient bus route to city. Resident caretaker.

---

1 flat, 1 pub rm, 2 bedrms, sleeps 4, £90-£100, Jul-Sep, bus 300 yds, rail 2 mls, airport 6 mls

Mr & Mrs F Westbury, 116 Braid Road, Edinburgh, EH10 6AS
☎ *031 447 3695*

---

1 flat, 1 pub rm, 1 bedrm, sleeps 4, £60-£120, Jan-Dec, bus nearby, rail 3 ½ mls, airport 10 mls

Mrs M Abbey, Baronscourt, 7 Milton Road East, Edinburgh, EH15 2ND
☎ *031 669 6900*

1 flat, 1 pub rm, 2 bedrms, sleeps 6, min let 3 nights, £120-£145, Jul-Sep, bus nearby, rail ½ ml, airport 10 mls

 ♿ ♿ E ⌀ □ ◎ □ ☎ ⌶ ◙ ✂ ▬ ☺ 🍴 ⌸ † ✗ ▣

Mrs C J Raven, 30 Great King Street, Edinburgh, EH3 6QH
☎ 031 556 2912

COMMENDED
♛ ♛ ♛

1 cottage, 2 pub rms, 2 bedrms, sleeps 4-5, min let 3 nights, £100-£160, Jan-Dec, bus nearby, rail ¼ ml

 ♿ ♿ E ⌀ □ ▦ ⌸ ⌀ □ ☎ ⌸ ✂ ▬ ☺ ✳ 🐾 🅿 †

Mrs Chalmer, Estate Office, Kinlochlaggan, by Newtonmore, Inverness-shire
☎ *Laggan (05284) 300*
Terraced cottage in residential area close to Haymarket station. Convenient for city centre. Garden.

---

2 flatlets, 1 pub rm, 1 bedrm, sleeps 2, min let 1 night, £120-£150, Jan-Dec, bus nearby, rail 1 ml, airport 6 mls

 ♿ ♿ E ⌀ □ ◎ □ ☎ ⌸ ▬ ☺ ✳ ⟁ ⌘ ⚲ ✗ ⋃ ⟁ ▸ ✗ ▣ Ⓣ

Mrs Forbes, 27 West Relugas Road, Edinburgh, EH9 2PW
☎ 031 667 7670

EDINBURGH
West End Apartments

★ Ideally situated in Edinburgh's West End a few minutes walk from Princes Street.

★ The property forms part of a fine Victorian terrace within the Edinburgh New Town Conservation Area and comprises studio, 1 and 2 bedroom apartments providing superbly appointed accommodation for 2-6 persons.

★ All apartments have private bathroom and are fully equipped with modern kitchen facilities, refrigerator, washing machine, colour TV, duvets and bed linen.

★ Unrestricted parking and frequent bus services.

For further information and brochure telephone
031-332 0717 *or write to:*

Mr & Mrs B. Mathieson, 2 Learmonth Terrace, EDINBURGH EH4 1PQ.

COMMENDED
♛ ♛ ♛ ♛

5 flats, 1 pub rm, 1-2 bedrms, sleeps 2-6, min let 2 nights, £90-£300, Jan-Dec, bus nearby, rail 1 ml, airport 7 mls

 ♿ ♿ E ⌀ □ ▦ ⌸ ◎ □ ☎ ⌶ ◙ ✂ ▬ ☺ ☮ 🍴 ⌸ † ⟁ ⌘ ⚲ ✗ ⌶ ⋃ ⟁ ⌁ ▸
⌁ ✗ ▣ Ⓣ

Mr & Mrs B Mathieson, 2 Learmonth Terrace, Edinburgh, EH4 1PQ
☎ 031 332 0717
Victorian terraced house close to West End within easy reach of city centre. Unrestricted parking.

NORTHESK
Self Catering Apartments
23 PILRIG STREET, EDINBURGH EH6 5AL
City Centre · Fully Equipped
Maid Service · Parking
Personally supervised · Open all year
Telephone: 031-554 4205

4 flats, 6 apartments, 1 pub rm, 1-3 bedrms, sleeps 2-6, min let 2 nights, from £80, Jan-Dec, bus nearby, rail 1 ml, airport 5 mls

♿ ⓦ E ➡ 📞 📁 🖥 📺 🎚 🌀 🛁 🍽 📞 🗄 ⚡ 🧳 ☺ ❄ ∥ 🦮 🏕 † ▶ 🏋 ✕ 🐾 ⊤

Mrs Robertson, North Esk Apartments, 23/48 Pilrig Street, Edinburgh, EH6 5AL
☎ *031 554 4205*

HIGHLY RECOMMENDED FLATS IN THREE CLASSICALLY ELEGANT GEORGIAN HOUSES IN CENTRAL EDINBURGH.

The houses at Inverleith Row enjoy a unique position overlooking the famous Royal Botanic Gardens. The house at 21 Northumberland Street is only three blocks from Edinburgh's main thoroughfare, Princes Street. See our highly competitive rates in the line entries.

Tel: 050 683 4999.
Mrs J S Armstrong, Hope Park, Blackness EH49 7NE.

9 flats, 1 pub rm, 2-4 bedrms, sleeps 4-6, £80-£150, Jun-Sep, bus nearby, rail 1-2 mls, airport 8 mls

♿ ⓦ E ➡ 📞 📁 🖥 📺 🎚 🌀 🛁 🍽 📞 🧳 ☺ ❄ 🐴 🅿 🗄 🏕 † ⚰ 🦌 🐿 🐕 🎣 ⛵ ∪ ⚠ ▶ 🏋 ✕ 🐾

Mrs J S Armstrong, Hope Park, Blackness, West Lothian, EH49 7NE
☎ *Philipstoun (050683) 4999*

---

1 flat, 1 pub rm, 3 bedrms, sleeps 4, £100-£130, Jul-Sep, bus nearby, rail 1 ml, airport 5 mls

♿ ⓦ E ➡ 📁 📺 🛁 📞 🗄 🌅 🧳 ❄ 🅿 🗄 🏕 † 🦌 🐿 ⛵ ∪ ⚠ ≠ ▶ ✕ 🐾

Mr Patrizio, 37 Gowanbrae Drive, Dunfermline, Fife, KY12 7RL
☎ *Dunfermline (0383) 723302*

---

1 flat, 1 pub rm, 3 bedrms, sleeps 5, £100-£150, Jul-Sep, bus nearby, rail 2 mls, airport 6 mls

♿ ⓦ E ➡ 📁 📺 🎚 🛁 📞 🗄 🌅 🧳 🗄 † 🦌 🐿 🐿 🔫 ⛵ ∪ ⚠ ≠ ▶ ✕ 🐾

Mr Cantlay, 21 Morningside Grove, Edinburgh, EH10 5QB
☎ *031 447 5566*

---

1 flat, 1 pub rm, 1 bedrm, sleeps 2-4, £90-£125, Jul-Sep, bus nearby, rail 1 ml, airport 4 mls

♿ ⓦ E ➡ 📁 🖥 📺 🌀 📞 🗄 🌅 ⚡ 🧳 ☺ † 🦌 🐿 🐿 🔫 ∪ ▶ ✕ 🐾 ⊤

Mrs E Conway, 11 Clarendon Place, Stirling, FK8 2QW
☎ *Stirling (0786) 75951*

Prices shown are for guidance only. Please send SAE with each enquiry.

1 flat, 1 pub rm, 3 bedrms, sleeps 4, from £90, Jul-Oct, bus nearby, rail 1 ml

🔥🚾E⛏🏠🖥🗄🛏🍴🖻📞🗄🛒🔔🐎🅿🛢🏛† 🎣🛥⛵🏇🗡×🎿♟

Mrs Wright, 45 Salisbury Road, Edinburgh, EH16 5AA
☎ *031 667 1264*

Glen House Apartments
22-26 GLEN STREET · EDINBURGH · EH3 9JE
Booking Address: Whitmuir, Selkirk TD7 4PZ. Tel. 0750-21728
Near the centre of this exciting and beautiful Capital City located in a quiet street, we have 13 fully modernised apartments (studio, 1, 2, or 3 bedrooms) in a building listed for architectural interest. All-electric fitted kitchens; bathrooms with showers. Close to Castle, Theatres, Museums and Restaurants. Colour TV, linen, laundry, telephone, etc. Open all year.
From £80.50 per week. Mini-breaks from £46. Brochure Ref. 708.

Glen House Apartments 13 flats, 1 pub rm, 1-3 bedrms, sleeps 2-6, min let 2 nights, £104-£345, Jan-Dec, bus nearby, rail 1 ml, airport 8 mls

🔥🚾E⛏🏠🖥🗄🛏🍴🗄📞🗄🛢⚡🛒🔆🐎🐎🗄🛒🏛† 🎣🎣🛥🔍🏇🗡
🛥⛵⚓🗡🎣×🎿♟🇹

Mrs Hilary Dunlop, Whitmuir, Selkirk, TD7 4PZ
☎ *Selkirk (0750) 21728*

---

1 flat, 3 pub rms, 3 bedrms, sleeps 6, min let weekend, £200-£250, Jul-Sep, bus nearby, rail nearby

🔥🚾E⛏🏠🖥🗄🛏🍴🗄📞🗄🛢⚡🛒🔆🗄🛒🏛† 🔍🏇🗡🛥⛵⚓🗡×🎿♟🇹

Mr B C Goss, Bruce House, Gordonstoun School, Gordonstoun, Morayshire
☎ *Hopeman (0343) 830453*

---

6 flats, 1 pub rm, 1-4 bedrms, sleeps 16, £90-£150, Jan-Dec, bus 400 yds, rail 1 ½ mls, airport 7 mls

🔥🚾E⛏🏠🖥🗄🛏🍴🗄📞🗄🛢⚡🛒🔆🐎🛒🏛† 🎣🛥🔍🗡🛥⛵⚓🗡🅁
×🎿♟🇹

Mr Forbes, 9 Lauriston Park, Edinburgh, EH3 9JA
☎ *031 229 9530*

---

1 flat, 2 pub rms, 3 bedrms, sleeps 5, min let 2 weeks, £185-£205, Jul-Sep, bus nearby, rail 1 ml, airport 10 mls

🔥🚾E⛏🏠🗄🛏🍴🗄📞🗄🛒🔆🛒† 🎣🛥🔍🏇🗡×🎿♟

Mrs Cameron, 12 Crawford Road, Edinburgh, EH16 5PQ
☎ *031 667 0606*

---

1 flat, 1 pub rm, 2 bedrms, sleeps 2-4, £140-£190, Jan-Dec, bus nearby, rail 1 ml, airport 8 mls

🔥🚾E⛏🏠🖥⚓🗄🛒🗄🛒🔆🐎🅿🛒🏛†🏛 🗡🛥⚓🗡×🎿♟🇹

Mrs Adamson, 11 Lynedoch Place, Edinburgh, EH3 7PX
☎ *031 225 1647*

HIGHLY COMMENDED
👑👑👑

1 flat, 1 pub rm, 2 bedrms, sleeps 4, £120-£220, Jan-Dec, bus nearby, rail 2 mls, airport 6 mls

🔥🚾E⛏🏠🖥🗄🛏🍴🗄📞🗄🛒🔆❄🅿† 🗡🛥⚓🗡×🎿♟🇹

Dr K T Gruer, 13 Winton Loan, Edinburgh, EH10 7AN
☎ *031 445 2841(eve)*
Modern, in residential area of Murryfield. Near rugby stadium, ice/curling rink, and Edinburgh Zoo.

AWAITING INSPECTION

1 flat, 1 pub rm, 2 bedrms, sleeps 5, £105-£180, Jan-Dec, bus ¼ ml, rail 1 ml

Mrs S Ryan, 1 Woodgate, Cringleford, Norwich, Norfolk, NR4 6XT
☎ Norwich (0603) 54279

---

1 flat, 1 pub rm, 2 bedrms, sleeps 4, £130-£145, Jun-Oct, bus 300 yds, rail 2 mls, airport 4 mls

(artificial ski slope)

Mrs D Brown, 1 Easter Belmont Road, Edinburgh, EH12 6EX
☎ 031 337 3888

---

1 flat, 1 pub rm, 3 bedrms, sleeps 5-7, from £120, Jun-Sep, bus nearby, rail 1 ml, airport 7 mls

Mrs Forsyth, 5 Ravelston Place, Edinburgh
☎ 031 332 6625

COMMENDED

4 flats, 1 pub rm, 2 bedrms, sleeps 4-5, min let 1 night, £160-£275, Jan-Dec, bus nearby, rail 1 ¼ mls, airport 7 mls

Mrs Sayles, 37/7 Lochrin Place, Tollcross, Edinburgh, EH3 9RB
☎ 031 228 2819

Modern block in city centre. 100 yards from King's Theatre, 10 minutes walk from city's West End.

---

2 houses, 1-2 pub rms, 4-7 bedrms, sleeps 4-10, min let weekend, £35-£50, Jan-Dec, bus 400 yds, rail 1 ml, airport 6 mls

Miss E McLean, 67 Hailes Gardens, Edinburgh, EH13 0JN
☎ 031 441 2638

AWAITING INSPECTION

1 cottage, 1 pub rm, 2 bedrms, sleeps 5, £95-£150, Jan-Dec, bus nearby, rail 5 mls, airport 5 mls

Mrs Donachie, P & S Donachie, 64 St John's Road, Edinburgh
☎ 031 334 2860

---

1 flat, 1 pub rm, 2 bedrms, sleeps 4, £125-£150, Jul-Sep, bus nearby, rail 1 ml, airport 10 mls

Miss Hardie, Top Flat(right), 4 Marchmont Crescent, Edinburgh, EH9 1HN
☎ 031 229 2181

---

1 flat, 1 pub rm, 3 bedrms, sleeps 5, £180-£237, Jul-Sep, bus nearby, rail 250 yds, airport 8 mls

Mrs Helen Allan, SBN Doormanlaan 5, 2243AH Wassenaar, The Netherlands
☎ 010 31 1751 10269

32 flats, 1 pub rm, 3-4 bedrms, sleeps 3-4, £90-£115, mid Jul-mid Sep, bus 250 yds, rail 3 mls, airport 3 mls

♿ ⓦ E 🚶 �TV ◎ 🍽 🛋 🅿 ⛳   🎣 🏊 ⛰ 🚣 ⛵ ⛷ ✗ 🧺

The Secretary, Queen Margaret College, Clerwood Terrace, Edinburgh, EH12 8TS
☎ *031 339 8111*

---

1 flat, 1 pub rm, 1 bedrm, sleeps 2-4, £135-£175, Jan-Dec, bus nearby, rail 2 mls, airport 8 mls

♿ ⓦ E 📻 🖥 🚶 📺 🍴 🔟 🔲 🍽 ✂ 🛋 ☺ ❄ 🎵 🐕 🍽 🚶 ✝ 🏔   🎣 🏊 ⛳ 🏊 ⛰ 🚣 ⛵ ⛷
▸ 🏊 🇹

Mrs M Hayward, 16 Woodburn Terrace, Edinburgh, EH10 4SJ
☎ *031 447 4802*

EDNAM, by Kelso Roxburghshire Map Ref. 2F6

1 cottage, 1 pub rm, 2 bedrms, sleeps 4-6, min let weekend, from £85, Apr-Sep, bus nearby, rail 18 mls, airport 40 mls

♿ ⓦ E 🚶 🍴 🖥 ◎ 🔲 🛋 ❄ 🐴 🅿 🍽 🚶 ✝ 🏔   🎣 🏊 ⛳ ⛰ 🚣 ⛵ ▸ ✗ 🧺 🌸

Mrs A Stewart, Cliftonhill, Ednam, by Kelso, Roxburghshire
☎ *Kelso (0573) 25028*

EDROM, by Duns Berwickshire Map Ref. 2F5

1 part house, 1 pub rm, 3 bedrms, sleeps 5, min let weekend, £60-£80, Jan-Dec, bus ¼ ml, rail 12 mls

♿ ⓦ E 🚶 🍴 🔟 ◎ 🔲 ☎ 🔲 🖥 🛋 ❄ 🐴 🅿 🎵 ✝   🎣 🚣 ▸ 🧺

Miss D B C Macpherson, 2 Manse Cottages (North), Edrom, by Duns, Berwickshire, TD11 3PX
☎ *Chirnside (089081) 704*

EIGG, Isle of Inverness-shire Map Ref. 3D12

4 chalet/log cabins, 2 houses, 8 cottages, 1-2 pub rms, 1-3 bedrms, sleeps 2-10, £58-£320, Jan-Dec, ferry ½ ml passengers only

♿ ⓦ 🚶 📻 🍴 🔟 ❄ 🐴 🐕 🍽 🚶 🏔 🔍 🌀   🚣 🚣 ⛵ ⛷ ✗ 🧺 🇹

Eigg Holiday Bookings, Maybank, Udny, Ellon, Aberdeenshire, AB4 0PQ
☎ *Udny (06513) 2367*

---

1 cottage, 1 pub rm, 3 bedrms, sleeps 7, £60-£95, Jan-Dec, ferry 4 mls

♿ ⓦ 🚶 🍴 ◎ ❄ 🎵 ✝   🚣 🚣 ⛵ ⛷ 🧺 🌸

Mr A J MacKinnon, Cleadale, Isle of Eigg, Inverness-shire, PH42 4RL
☎ *Mallaig (0687) 82433*

ELGIN Moray Map Ref. 4D8

Palmers Cross 11 chalet/log cabins, 4 cottages, 1 pub rm, 1-4 bedrms, sleeps 2-8, £71-£213, Apr-Oct, bus ½ ml, rail 1 ml, airport 27 mls

♿ ⓦ E 🚶 📻 🍴 🖥 ◎ 🔟 🔲 🖥 ✂ 🛋 ☺ ❄ 🐴 🅿 🍽 🚶 🏔 🌀   🚣 🚣 ⛵ ⛷ ▸ ✗
🧺 🇹

Lossie Holiday Homes, c/o Miss J Bristow, Thorncroft, Lilliesleaf, Melrose, Roxburghshire, TD6 9JD
☎ *Lilliesleaf (08357) 424/425/320*

Riverside Caravan Park 4 caravans, sleeps 4-6, min let 1 night, £75-£140, Apr-Oct, bus nearby, rail 1 ml

♿ ⓦ 🛖 E 📻 🍴 🔟 ☎ 🔲 🖥 ✂ 🛋 ☺ 🅿 ✝ 🏔 🔍   🚣 🚣 ⛵ ▸ ✗ 🧺

Riverside Caravan Park, West Road, Elgin, Moray, 1V30 3UN
☎ *Elgin (0343) 2813*

---

by ELGIN Moray Map Ref. 4D8

1 cottage, 2 pub rms, 4 bedrms, sleeps 8, min let weekend, £45-£145, Jan-Dec, bus nearby, rail 3 mls, airport 30 mls

♿ ♿ E 🛏 🚗 🖥 🔘 🗄 🖵 📷 🔥 ⊙ ❄ 🐴 P 🐎 🏠 † ⚲ ✕ 🧺 T

Mrs Harper, Ardgilzean, Elgin, Moray, IV30 3XT
☎ *Elgin (0343) 3075/7141*

---

2 cottages, 1 pub rm, 3 bedrms, sleeps 6-8, £80-£165, Jan-Dec, bus ½ ml, rail 4 mls, airport 30 mls

♿ ♿ E 🛏 🚗 🖥 🗄 🔘 🗄 🖵 📷 ⊙ ❄ 🐴 P 🐎 🏠 ⚲ 🌐 🎣 🐟 🔍 🌲 🎣 🗑 ⛵ ♂
🚣 🧺 🚲 T

Mrs Roy Petrie, Rosehaugh Farm, Elgin, Moray, IV30 3XW
☎ *Elgin (0343) 7355*

North East Farm Chalets
(JOINT MARKETING)
SHERIFFSTON, ELGIN, MORAY
Telephone: (0343 84) 2695 (Lhanbryde)

Five A-frame chalets, identical in design, furnished by Habitat; sited in beautiful, rural locations, on four working farms near Elgin and Keith. Enjoy all the comforts of modern purpose-built accommodation and the traditional, warm, old-fashioned welcome of your farmer hosts. Ideal for children. Personal attention. Accessible by public transport. Excellent local facilities both indoor and outdoor, and within easy reach of lovely uncrowded beaches. Try our special Moray golf holidays, or just relax in peace and quiet!

For full particulars, brochure, tariff and availability contact: Mrs J. M. Shaw, Sheriffston, Elgin, Moray IV30 3LA. Tel. 0343 84 2695.

3 chalet/log cabins, 1 pub rm, 2 bedrms, sleeps 6, min let weekend, from £65, Mar-Jan, bus 300 yds, rail 3 ½ mls, airport 40 mls

♿ ♿ E 🛏 🚗 🖥 🗄 🔘 🗄 🖵 ⚲ ⊙ ❄ 🐴 P 🐎 🏠 🛏 † ⚲ 🎣 🐟 🔍 🌲 🎣 ⛵ ♂
🚣 ♂ 🚲 ✕ 🧺 🚲 T

North East Farm Chalets, Mrs J M Shaw, Sheriffston, Elgin, Moray, IV30 3LA
☎ *Lhanbryde (034384) 2695*

---

1 flat, 1 pub rm, 3 bedrms, sleeps 9, £100-£160, Jun-Sep, bus 1 ½ mls, rail 3 mls, airport 35 mls

♿ ♿ E 🛏 🚗 🔘 🗄 📞 🖵 📷 ⚲ ⊙ ❄ P 🐎 🏠 † 🎣 🐟 🔍 🌲 🎣 ⛵ ♂ 🚣 ✕ 🧺
(bowling, gymnasium)

Mrs M McConnachie, Easter Calcots, Elgin, Moray, IV30 2NZ
☎ *Lhanbryde (034384) 2254*

---

1 bungalow, 1 pub rm, 3 bedrms, sleeps 4-6, min let weekend, £50-£120, Jan-Dec, bus ½ ml, rail 3 mls, airport 34 mls

♿ ♿ E 🛏 🚗 🖥 🔘 🗄 📞 🖵 📷 ⚲ ❄ 🐴 P 🐎 🏠 🛏 † ⚲ 🎣 🌲 🎣 ⛵ ♂ 🚣 ✕ 🧺

Mrs I Miller, Findrassie House, Elgin, Moray, IV30 2PS
☎ *Elgin (0343) 7292*

Prices shown are for guidance only. Please send SAE with each enquiry.

1 cottage, 1 pub rm, 2 bedrms, sleeps 6-8, min let 1 night, £45-£65, Jan-Dec, bus ¼ ml, rail 5 mls, airport 40 mls

Mrs W Cruickshank, Coleburn Farm, Longmorn, Elgin, Moray, IV30 3SN
☎ *Longmorn (034386) 248*

---

1 house, 2 pub rms, 2 bedrms, sleeps 6, £85-£100, Apr-Oct, bus nearby, rail 4 mls, airport 30 mls

Mrs F G Archer, Ardgye Lodge, Elgin, Moray, IV30 3UP
☎ *Alves (034385) 356*

ELGOL Isle of Skye, Inverness-shire Map Ref. 3D10

COMMENDED

1 bungalow, 2 pub rms, 3 bedrms, sleeps 6, £75-£125, Apr-Oct, bus nearby, rail 24 mls, ferry 23 mls, airport 20 mls

Mrs Pickering, 3 Monkend Terrace, Croft-on-Tees, Darlington, Co Durham, DL2 2SQ
☎ *Darlington (0325) 721042*

Modern unit in hamlet. Own garden. High position, superb views to the Small Isles and Ardnamurchan.

---

1 cottage, 2 pub rms, 3 bedrms, sleeps 6, £25-£100, Jan-Dec, bus nearby, rail 23 mls, ferry 22 mls, airport 20 mls

Mrs J Stewart, Grafton, Pell Green, Wadhurst, Sussex
☎ *Wadhurst (089288) 2180*

ELIE Fife Map Ref. 2E3

1 studio, sleeps 4-5, min let weekend, £60-£95, Jan-Dec, bus ¼ ml

Mrs J Stirrat, Higham Farm, Newburgh, Fife
☎ *Newburgh (0337) 40356*

---

1 house, 1 flat, 1-2 pub rms, 2-3 bedrms, sleeps 4-6, £50-£200, Jan-Dec, bus nearby, rail 15 mls, airport 40 mls

(bike hire)

Mrs Boak, Elms Guest House, Park Place, Elie, Fife, KY19 1DH
☎ *Elie (0333) 330404*

---

by ELIE Fife Map Ref. 2E3

2 houses, 6 flats, 6 cottages, 1-3 pub rms, 1-4 bedrms, sleeps 2-10, £50-£300, Jan-Dec, bus nearby, rail 15 mls, airport 45 mls

(windsurfing)

Mrs S Pattullo, The Park, Bank Street, Elie, Fife
☎ *Elie (0333) 330219*

ELLON Aberdeenshire Map Ref. 4H9

1 cottage, 1 pub rm, 2 bedrms, sleeps 4-5, min let weekend, £35-£90, Jan-Dec, bus 1 ml, rail 20 mls, airport 20 mls

Mrs J M Shivas, Hayhillock, Ellon, Aberdeenshire, AB4 9DH
☎ *Ellon (0358) 20318*

VAT is shown at 15%: changes in this rate may affect prices.

1 flat, 1 pub rm, 1 bedrm, sleeps 4, min let weekend, £60-£120, Jan-Dec, bus nearby, rail 15 mls, airport 16 mls

(bowling)

Mrs Watt, L'Entente Cordiale Bureau, Dunstown, Mintlaw, Aberdeenshire, AB4 7UJ
☎ *Longside (077982) 249*

ELPHIN Sutherland Map Ref. 3G5

1 cottage, 1-2 pub rms, 2 bedrms, sleeps 4, min let weekend, £40-£80, Jan-Dec, bus ½ ml, rail 30 mls

Mrs M Strang, Birchbank, Knockan, Elphin, by Lairg, Sutherland
☎ *Elphin (085484) 215*

ELVANFOOT Lanarkshire Map Ref. 2B7

1 cottage, 1 pub rm, 2 bedrms, sleeps 6, min let weekend, £40-£120, Jan-Dec, bus 1 ml

Mrs MacArthur, Nunnerie, Elvanfoot, by Biggar, Lanarkshire
☎ *Elvanfoot (08645) 224*

EMBO Sutherland Map Ref. 4B6

1 house, 1 pub rm, 3 bedrms, sleeps 6, min let weekend (low season), £60-£120, Jan-Dec, bus nearby

Mr J Cumming, Balnafettack Farmhouse, Leachkin Road, Inverness
☎ *Inverness (0463) 237837*

Grannie's Heilan' Hame 62 caravans, sleeps 6-8, min let weekend, £60-£200, Apr-Oct, bus nearby, rail 15 mls, airport 55 mls

Grannies Heilan Hame & Co, Embo, Dornoch, Sutherland, IV25 3QD
☎ *Dornoch (0862) 810260*

ENOCHDHU, by Blairgowrie Perthshire Map Ref. 2B1

2 houses, 1 cottage, 1-3 pub rms, 2-8 bedrms, sleeps 6-15, from £92, Apr-Oct, rail 10 mls

(hillwalking, birdwatching)

Bell-Ingram, Durn, Isla Road, Perth, PH2 7HF
☎ *Perth (0738) 21121*

ERISKAY, Isle of South Uist, Western Isles Map Ref. 3A11

1 cottage, 1 pub rm, 3 bedrms, sleeps 6-8, £100, Jan-Dec, ferry ½ ml, airport 30 mls

Mrs C Rusk, 10 Port Patrick, Isle of Eriskay, South Uist, Western Isles
☎ *Eriskay (08786) 233*

Prices shown are for guidance only. Please send SAE with each enquiry.

1 house, 1 pub rm, 4 bedrms, sleeps 6, min let weekend, £100-£150, Jan-Dec, ferry ½ ml, airport 30 mls

Mrs C Rusk, 10 Port Patrick, Isle of Eriskay, South Uist, Western Isles
☎ Eriskay (08786) 233

ERROGIE Inverness-shire Map Ref. 4A10

AWAITING
INSPECTION

1 chalet/log cabin, 1 pub rm, 2 bedrms, sleeps 5, min let weekend, £85-£190, Jan-Dec, bus 1 ml, rail 19 mls, airport 26 mls

1 caravan, sleeps 6, min let weekend, £45-£85, Apr-Oct, bus 1 ml, rail 19 mls, airport 26 mls

Mrs Janet Sutherland, 1 Aultnagoire, Errogie, Inverness-shire, IV1 2UH
☎ Gorthleck (04563) 641

ERROL Perthshire Map Ref. 2C2

2 cottages, 1 pub rm, 3 bedrms, sleeps 6, £75-£100, Jan-Dec, bus nearby, rail 11 mls, airport 10 mls

Mr George Aimer, The Horn, Errol, Perth, Perthshire, PH2 7SR
☎ Rait (08217) 237(day)/(0250) 3196(eve)

---

1 bungalow, 1 pub rm, 3 bedrms, sleeps 5, £150-£200, Jul-Sep, bus nearby, rail 3 mls

Mrs J P Angus, Flatfield, Errol, Perth, Perthshire, PH2 7RW
☎ Errol (08212) 334

ERVIE, by Stranraer Wigtownshire Map Ref. 1F10

2 cottages, 1-2 pub rms, 2-4 bedrms, sleeps 6-12, min let weekend, £60-£100, Apr-Oct, bus 8 mls, rail 8 mls, ferry 8 mls, airport 70 mls

Mrs J Douglas, Mains of Airies, Ervie, by Stranraer, Wigtownshire
☎ Kirkcolm (077685) 4226

ETTRICK VALLEY Selkirkshire Map Ref. 2D7

2 caravans, sleeps 4-6, £50, Apr-Oct, bus 12 mls, rail 50 mls

Mrs Dodds, West Deloraine, Ettrick Valley, Selkirkshire, TD7 5HR
☎ Ettrick Valley (0750) 62263

EVANTON Ross-shire Map Ref. 4A7

1 bungalow, 1 pub rm, 3 bedrms, sleeps 6, min let weekend, £55-£85, Apr-Oct, bus 1 ml, rail 4 mls

Miss Isobel Robertson, Struan, Swordale Road, Evanton, Ross-shire, IV16 9XA
☎ Evanton (0349) 830655

VAT is shown at 15%: changes in this rate may affect prices.

1 cottage, 1 pub rm, 3 bedrms, sleeps 6, £60-£100, Mar-Oct, bus ¾ ml, rail 7 mls

Mr J Fraser, Lower Park, Evanton, Ross-shire
☎ *Evanton (0349) 830269*

Black Rock Caravan Site 2 caravans, sleeps 6-8, from £100, Apr-Oct, bus nearby, rail 2 mls, airport 20 mls

Mr Donald, Black Rock Caravan Site, c/o Spar Shop, Evanton, Ross-shire
☎ *Evanton (0349) 830213*

EVIE Orkney Map Ref. 5B10

1 house, 1 cottage, 1-3 pub rms, 1-3 bedrms, sleeps 4-6, £40-£150, Jan-Dec, bus nearby, ferry 15 mls, airport 18 mls

Mr Kidd, Lower Quoys, Evie, Orkney
☎ *Evie (085675) 325*

---

1 flat, 1 pub rm, 1 bedrm, sleeps 2-5, from £50, Jan-Dec, bus ¼ ml, ferry 1 ml, airport 21 mls

(birdwatching)

Mr & Mrs J Goddin, Woodwick House, Evie, Orkney, KW17 2PQ
☎ *Evie (085675) 330*

EYEMOUTH Berwickshire Map Ref. 2G5

Northburn Caravan Park 200 caravans, sleeps 4-8, min let 2 nights, from £65, mid Mar-Oct, bus nearby, rail 8 mls, airport 50 mls

(air compressor/scuba diving)

James Wood & Son, Northburn Caravan Park, Eyemouth, Berwickshire
☎ *Eyemouth (08907) 50808/51050/50426*

AWAITING INSPECTION

3 flats, 1 pub rm, 1-2 bedrms, sleeps 3-7, min let weekend, £70-£125, Apr-Oct, bus nearby, rail 9 mls, airport 50 mls

Mrs Dougal, 60 High Street, Eyemouth, Berwickshire
☎ *Eyemouth (08907) 50536*

FEARNAN Perthshire Map Ref. 2A1

1 house, 2 bungalows, 1-2 pub rms, 2-3 bedrms, sleeps 4-6, £95-£180, Jan-Dec, Apr-Oct

Finlayson Hughes, Bank House, 82 Atholl Road, Pitlochry, Perthshire, PH16 5BL
☎ *Pitlochry (0796) 2512*

---

2 houses, 5 cottages, 1-2 pub rms, 2-3 bedrms, sleeps 6-10, min let weekend, £75-£220, Jan-Dec, bus 9 mls, rail 25 mls, airport 70 mls

Mr I Menzies, Boreland Farm, Fearnan, Aberfeldy, Perthshire, PH15 2PG
☎ *Kenmore (08873) 212*

Prices shown are for guidance only. Please send SAE with each enquiry.

1 house, 2 pub rms, 6 bedrms, sleeps 9, from £270, Apr-Oct, bus 4 mls, rail 21 mls

♿ 🚾 E 🛴 ⓜ ◎ ▯ ☐ ✳ 🅿 🐎 † ♪ ∪ ⛟ ▸ 🛍

Bell-Ingram, Durn, Isla Road, Perth, PH2 7HF
☎ *Perth (0738) 21121*

---

1 house, 1 pub rm, 2 bedrms, sleeps 5, £90-£140, Mar-Nov, rail 15 mls, airport 60 mls

♿ 🚾 E 🛴 ⓜ ▦ ☐ ☎ ☐ ☐ ✳ 🐕 🅿 🐎 ▥ † ♪ ∪ ⛟ ⟋ ⤢ ✕ 🛍

Mrs F Fraser, Slade House, Carmyllie, by Arbroath, Angus
☎ *Carmyllie (02416) 215*

FESHIE BRIDGE Inverness-shire Map Ref. 4B10

1 bungalow, 2 pub rms, 3 bedrms, sleeps 5, £100-£150, Apr-Oct, bus 2 mls, rail 7 mls, airport 40 mls

♿ 🚾 E 🛴 🏠 ⓜ ▯ ◎ ☐ ☐ ✄ ☎ ☉ ✳ 🐕 🅿 🐎 ▥ † ⛰ ♪ ∪ ⛟ ⟋ ⤢ ✕ 🛍

T (gliding)

Mr D Adam, 80 Culduthel Road, Inverness
☎ *Inverness (0463) 224200*
Modern, in quiet setting by River Feshie. Within 8 mls(13 km) of Aviemore and Cairngorms.

FINDHORN Moray Map Ref. 4C7

Findhorn Bay Caravan Park 40 caravans, sleeps 2-8, min let 2 nights, £69-£144, Apr-Oct, rail 4 mls

♿ 🚾 E ⓜ ▯ ✄ ☐ ☎ ☐ ✄ ☎ ☉ 🐕 🅿 🐎 ▥ 🛴 † ⛰ ♪ ∪ ⛟ ⤢ ✕ 🛍

Findhorn Bay Caravan Park, Findhorn, Forres, Moray, IV36 0TY
☎ *Findhorn (0309) 30203*

Findhorn Sands Caravan Park 9 caravans, sleeps 6-8, min let long weekend, £63-£117, Apr-Oct, bus 5 mls, rail ¼ ml

E ✄ ☐ ☉ 🐕 🅿 ⛰ 🔍 🎣 ⛟ ⤢ ✕ 🛍

Findhorn Sands Caravan Park, Findhorn, Forres, Moray, IV36 0YZ
☎ *Findhorn (0309) 30324*

---

1 chalet/log cabin, 1 pub rm, 2 bedrms, sleeps 8, £40-£180, Jan-Dec, bus ¼ ml, rail 5 mls, airport 25 mls

♿ 🚾 E 🏠 ⓜ ▦ ◎ ☐ ✄ ☎ ☉ ✳ 🅿 🐎 ▥ † ✄ 🔍 ♪ ∪ ⛟ ⤢ ✕ 🛍 T

Mrs Susan Gibb, St Boniface, Fortrose, Ross-shire, IV10 8SX
☎ *Fortrose (0381) 20750*

---

1 flat, 1 pub rm, 2 bedrms, sleeps 6, £80-£150, May-Oct, bus nearby, rail 5 mls, airport 25 mls

♿ 🚾 E 🛴 🏠 ⓜ ▦ ▯ ◎ ☐ ☐ ✄ ☎ ☉ ✳ 🐕 🅿 🐎 ▥ † ✄ 🔍 🎣 ♪ ∪ ⛟
⤢ ▸ ⤢ ✕ 🛍

Mrs A Philp, The Old Smiddy, Findhorn, Forres, Moray, IV36 0YE
☎ *Findhorn (0309) 30275*

FINDOCHTY Banffshire Map Ref. 4E7

1 cottage, 1 pub rm, 3 bedrms, sleeps 6, min let weekend (low season), £75-£155, Jan-Dec, bus nearby, rail 15 mls, airport 55 mls

♿ 🚾 E 🛴 ⓜ ◎ ☐ ☎ ☐ ☐ ☉ ✳ 🐕 🅿 🐎 ▥ ✄ ♪ ⛟ ⤢ ✕ 🛍

Mr A Scott, Faraldon, 8 Markethill Rd, Turriff, Aberdeenshire, AB5 7AZ
☎ *Turriff (0888) 63524*

VAT is shown at 15%: changes in this rate may affect prices.

FINSTOWN Orkney Map Ref. 5B11

1 house, 5 bungalows, 1-2 pub rms, 2-3 bedrms, sleeps 4-8, £80-£160, Jan-Dec, bus nearby, ferry 7 mls, airport 10 mls

Mrs K Reid, Orkney Self Catering, Finstown, Orkney, KW17 2EQ
☎ *Finstown (085676) 397*

---

2 flats, 1 pub rm, 2 bedrms, sleeps 4-6, £60-£110, Apr-Oct, bus nearby, rail 6 mls, airport 10 mls

Mrs Kirkness, Calvyden, Finstown, Orkney
☎ *Finstown (0856) 76303*

FINTRY Stirlingshire Map Ref. 2A4

Culcreuch Castle Lodges 8 lodges, 1 pub rm, 3 bedrms, sleeps 6, min let 3 nights, £55-£240, Jan-Dec, bus 6 mls, rail 17 mls, airport 29 mls

Culcreuch Castle Country Park, Fintry, Stirlingshire, G63 0LW
☎ *Fintry (036086) 228*

FINZEAN Kincardineshire Map Ref. 4F11

1 flat, 2 pub rms, 2 bedrms, sleeps 4, £70-£100, Jan-Dec, bus nearby, rail 25 mls, airport 23 mls

Mrs T M Proudfoot, East Lodge, Finzean, by Banchory, Kincardineshire
☎ *Feughside (033045) 333*

FIONNPHORT Isle of Mull, Argyll Map Ref. 1B3

1 cottage, 2 pub rms, 2 bedrms, sleeps 2-5, £100-£180, Apr-Oct, bus 1 ¼ mls, ferry 37 mls

Mrs Campbell, Fidden Cottage, Fionnphort, Isle of Mull, Argyll
☎ *Fionnphort (06817) 427*

FLICHITY Inverness-shire Map Ref. 4B9

4 chalet/log cabins, 4 cottages, 1-2 pub rms, 1-3 bedrms, sleeps 2-8, min let 3 nights, £85-£225, Mar-Oct, bus 1 ml, rail 12 mls, airport 16 mls

Maj A C Humfrey, Brin Holiday Homes, Balvoulin, Abererder, Inverness, Inverness-shire
☎ *Farr (08083) 283*   **(See colour ad. 5 p. xxxiii)**

FOCHABERS Moray Map Ref. 4E8

Burnside Caravan Site 1 cottage, 1 pub rm, 3 bedrms, sleeps 6, min let 3 nights, £80-£95, Apr-Oct, bus nearby

Christies (Fochabers) Ltd, The Nurseries, Fochabers, Moray, IV32 7PF
☎ *Fochabers (0343) 820362*

by FOCHABERS Moray Map Ref. 4E8

Orton Estate 16 cottages, 1-2 pub rms, 1-4 bedrms, sleeps 2-7, £42-£121, Apr-Oct, bus ½ ml-2 mls, rail 7 mls, airport 40 mls

Orton Management Co Ltd, Estate Office, Orton, Fochabers, Moray, 1V32 7QE
☎ Orton (034388) 240

Spey Bay Caravan Site 1 flat, 3 apartments, 1 pub rm, 1-2 bedrms, sleeps 3-4, min let 3 nights, £95-£110, Jan-Dec, bus 3 mls

Spey Bay Hotel, Spey Bay, Fochabers, Moray, IV32 7PY
☎ Fochabers (0343) 820424

FORD, by Lochgilphead Argyll Map Ref. 1E3

3 cottages, 1 pub rm, 1-4 bedrms, sleeps 2-7, £30-£130, Jan-Dec

Mrs W Cairns, Finchairn, Ford, by Lochgilphead, Argyll, PA31 8RJ
☎ Ford (054681) 223

FORFAR Angus Map Ref. 2D1

2 cottages, 2 pub rms, 2-3 bedrms, sleeps 5-7, min let weekend, £50-£125, Jan-Dec, bus 1 ml, rail 10 mls, airport 20 mls

Lady Maitland, Mid Dod, Burnside, Forfar, Angus
☎ Forfar (0307) 62766
Traditional stone units on working farm. Lovely woodland walks. Market town 3 mls. Good touring base.

by FORFAR Angus Map Ref. 2D1

Memus Caravan Park 2 caravans, sleeps 4-6, min let weekend, £40-£50, Apr-Oct, bus 5 mls, rail 20 mls, airport 20 mls

Memus Caravan Park, Memus, Memus, by Forfar, Angus
☎ Foreside (030786) 258

FORGANDENNY Perthshire Map Ref. 2C3

3 cottages, 1-2 pub rms, 1-3 bedrms, sleeps 3-6, £74-£145, Jun-Oct, bus 1 ml, rail 6 mls, airport 38 mls

Mr D Pentland, Rossie Farmhouse, Forgandenny, Perth, Perthshire, PH2 9EH
☎ Bridge of Earn (0738) 812081

FORGUE, by Huntly Aberdeenshire Map Ref. 4F8

1 cottage, 1 pub rm, 2 bedrms, sleeps 5, min let weekend (low season), £45-£65, Apr-Oct, bus 8 mls, rail 8 mls, airport 40 mls

Mrs Ingram, Bogton, Forgue, by Huntly, Aberdeenshire, AB5 6HN
☎ Ythanwells (04647) 237

VAT is shown at 15%: changes in this rate may affect prices.

by FORRES Moray Map Ref. 4C8

1 chalet/log cabin, 1 pub rm, 3 bedrms, sleeps 6, min let weekend, £65-£195, Apr-Oct, bus ½ ml, rail 4 mls, airport 15 mls

Mrs E Fraser, Thornhall, Dyke, Forres, Moray, IV36 0TL
☎ *Brodie (03094) 283/Forres (0309) 73320*

COMMENDED

4 chalet/log cabins, 1 pub rm, 2 bedrms, sleeps 2-5, min let 3 nights, £65-£210, Apr-Dec, bus 4 ½ mls, rail 4 ½ mls, airport 23 mls

Mrs D Du Boulay, Tulloch Holiday Lodges, Rafford, Forres, Moray, IV36 0RU
☎ *Forres (0309) 73311*

Modern, cedar units in peaceful woodland. Information kiosk, childrens' play area. Near sandy beach. **(See colour ad. 6 p. xxxiv)**

---

1 cottage, 1 pub rm, 3 bedrms, sleeps 6, min let 2-3 nights, £95-£170, Mar-Nov, bus 2 mls, rail 4 ½ mls, airport 18 mls

Mrs W Falconer, Snab of Moy, Dyke, Forres, Moray, IV36 0TL
☎ *Brodie (03094) 280*

COMMENDED

1 house, 2 cottages, 1-2 pub rms, 1-4 bedrms, sleeps 2-8, min let weekend, from £60, Jan-Dec, bus 1 ml, rail 4 mls, airport 25 mls

Mrs G M Mackay, Forres Holiday Cots, Easter Lawrenceton, by Forres, Moray, IV36 0RL
☎ *Forres (0309) 73501*

Traditional country units, superb views to Moray Firth and hills. Garden and play area. Near beach.

---

1 cottage, 1 pub rm, 3 bedrms, sleeps 6, min let weekend, £60-£100, Jan-Dec, bus 3 mls, rail 3 mls, airport 20 mls

Mrs M A James, Braemar, Rafford, Forres, Moray, IV36 0RT
☎ *Forres (0309) 73676*

---

1 cottage, 1 pub rm, 3 bedrms, sleeps 6, £85-£140, Mar-Oct, bus 1 ml, rail 5 mls, airport 15 mls

Mrs Jean M Taylor, Wellhill Farm, Dyke, Forres, Moray, IV36 0TL
☎ *Brodie (03094) 228*

---

1 house, 3 pub rms, 5 bedrms, sleeps 23, min let weekend, £2 per person/night, Jan-Dec, bus 2 mls, rail 4 mls, airport 25 mls

Director of Recreation, Moray District Council, 30-32 High Street, Elgin, Moray, IV30 1BX
☎ *Elgin (0343) 45121*

FORSINARD Sutherland Map Ref. 4B4

2 cottages, 1 pub rm, 3 bedrms, sleeps 5-6, from £55, Apr-Oct, bus 5 mls, rail 10 mls, ferry 20 mls, airport 40 mls

🔥 ♿ E ➰ ⓪ ▥ ▯ ◉ ▯ ▱ ☺ ⍭ 🅿 ⅗ ▥   ∪ ▸ 🐟 ⅖

Mrs A Douglas, Bighouse, Halladale, Forsinard, Sutherland, KW13 6YU
☎ *Halladale (06417) 251*

FORT WILLIAM Inverness-shire Map Ref. 3G12

1 flat, 1 pub rm, 1 bedrm, sleeps 4, £80-£100, Jan-Dec, rail 2 mls

🔥 ♿ E ⋒ ⓪ ▯ ◉ ▯ ▱ ✠ ▱ ☺ 🅿 †   ⋨ 𝈄 ⦚ ✧ ∪ ⋪ ▸ ✕ ⅖

Mrs Thompson, Smirisary, Achintore Road, Fort William, Inverness-shire
☎ *Fort William (0397) 2918*

LOCHY CARAVAN PARK
CAMAGHAEL · FORT WILLIAM
Telephone: (0397) 3446

Ultra-modern fleet of luxury "Thistle" Award caravans. All caravans have toilets, showers, fridges, colour TVs, gas, electricity plus hot and cold running water as standard. The caravans are well spaced out and the park offers one of the best views of Ben Nevis and surrounding mountains. The park is very peaceful but offers a well stocked shop, restaurant, very modern toilets and laundry.

Prices start at £100 per week but discounts apply at various times of the year. Please enquire to Mrs A. K. Brown for full colour brochure.

Lochy Caravan Park 20 caravans, sleeps 6, min let 3 nights, £115-£185, Apr-Nov, bus 600 yds, rail 2 ½ mls

🔥 ♿ E ⋒ ⓪ ▯ ⌀ ▯ ☏ ▱ ▣ ✠ ▱ ☺ ⍭ 🅿 ⅗ ▥   ⋨ 𝈄 ⦚ ✧ ∪ △ ▸ ✕ ⅖ Ⓣ

Mrs M B Brown, Lochy Caravan Park, Camaghael, Fort William, Inverness-shire, PH33 7NF
☎ *Fort William (0397) 3446/5252*

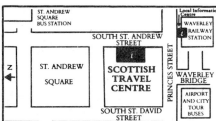

VAT is shown at 15%: changes in this rate may affect prices.

Great Glen Lodges
TORLUNDY · FORT WILLIAM PH33 6SW · 0397 3015

Superbly situated on working Highland Farm with breathtaking views of Ben Nevis. The 8 Scandinavian Chalets are pine panelled internally throughout, attractively furnished and equipped to a high standard. Launderette and pay-phone on site. Pony trekking on the estate.

Just North of Fort William. Ideal centre for a family holiday, walks.

STB ♚ ♚ ♚ Commended   Pets welcome. Tranquillity. Sleeps 4/6.

COMMENDED
♚ ♚ ♚

Great Glen Chalets 8 chalet/log cabins, 1 pub rm, 2 bedrms, sleeps 4-6, min let 3 nights, £110-£245, Apr-Oct, bus 1 ml, rail 3 mls, airport 60 mls

Great Glen Holidays, Torlundy, Fort William, Inverness-shire, PH33 6SW
☎ *Fort William (0397) 3015*
Each chalet set amidst pine and silver birch trees, with clear views of Ben Nevis.

---

1 flat, 2 pub rms, 1 bedrm, sleeps 4, min let 1 night, £70, Jan-Dec, bus nearby, rail 1 ½ mls

Mrs M Wardle, 16 Perth Place, Upper Achintore, Fort William, Inverness-shire
☎ *Fort William (0397) 4392*

---

up to APPROVED
♚ ♚

Achintee Farm 2 flats, 1 cottage, 1-2 bedrms, sleeps 4-8, min let weekend, £85-£160, Jan-Dec, bus 1 ½ mls, rail 2 mls

Mr F A Collins, Achintee Farm, Glen Nevis, Fort William, Inverness-shire
☎ *Fort William (0397) 2240*
Stone built units in shadow of Ben Nevis overlooking Glen Nevis.

COMMENDED
♚ ♚ ♚

Innseagan Apartments 6 apartments, 1 pub rm, 1 bedrm, sleeps 4, min let 3 nights, £105-£210, Jan-Dec, bus nearby, rail 1 ½ mls, airport 65 mls

Innseagan Holidays, Achintore Road, Fort William, Inverness-shire, PH33 6RW
☎ *Fort William (0397) 2452*
All units have balconies with superb views of Loch Linnhe and mountains.

(See colour ad. 7 p. xxxiv)

COMMENDED
♚ ♚ ♚

Glen Nevis Holiday Cottages 12 cottages, 1 pub rm, 2 bedrms, sleeps 5, min let 2 nights, £140-£245, Mar-Dec, bus 2 ½ mls, rail 2 ½ mls

30 caravans, sleeps 2-6, min let 2 nights, £85-£195, Apr-Sep, bus 2 mls, rail 2 ½ mls

Glen Nevis Holiday Caravans, Glen Nevis Holiday Cottages, Glen Nevis, Fort William, Inverness-shire, PH33 6SX
☎ *Fort William (0397) 2191*
Traditional units in landscaped park close to mighty Ben Nevis. Shop on site and restaurant nearby. **(See ad. on p. 129)**

---

1 flat, 1 pub rm, 2 bedrms, sleeps 6-8, £100-£200, Jan-Dec, bus nearby, rail 1 ml

Mr A R MacDonald, Garry Valtos, 4 Fife Place, Fort William, Inverness-shire
☎ *Fort William (0397) 4255*

1 house, 1 pub rm, 3 bedrms, sleeps 6, £70-£205, Jan-Dec, bus 300 yds, rail ¾ ml

Mrs R A Rumney, Glasdrum, Argyll Road, Fort William, Inverness-shire
☎ Fort William (0397) 2272

---

by FORT WILLIAM Inverness-shire Map Ref. 3G12

2 cottages, 1 pub rm, 2 bedrms, sleeps 6, £58-£155, Jan-Dec, bus 20 mls, rail 7 mls

Mr A Gray, Alana, 7 Blaich, Fort William, Inverness-shire, PH33 7AN
☎ Corpach (03977) 697

Linnhe Caravan Park
Dept STA1
CORPACH · FORT WILLIAM
Telephone: 03977-376

Luxury holiday caravans for hire on this quiet award-winning park. Set in beautiful surroundings with magnificent views over Loch Eil. All caravans have mains services, refrigerator and television. Most have showers. Free gas and electricity. Direct access to the beach. Private dinghy park and launching slip. Playground and barbecue area. Pets welcome. Ideal base for touring the Best of the Highlands.

To celebrate this, our Silver Jubilee Year, we are presenting a commemorative bottle of wine for each booking of a week or more.
Free colour brochure on request.

Linnhe Caravan Park Ltd 77 caravans, sleeps 6, min let 2 nights, £90-£200, Apr-Sep, bus 1 ml, rail 1 ½ mls

T (barbecue area, dinghy park)

Linnhe Caravan Park Ltd, Corpach, by Fort William, Inverness-shire
☎ Corpach (03977) 376

---

4 chalet/log cabins, 1 pub rm, 2 bedrms, sleeps 6, £100-£170, Apr-Oct, bus 300 yds, rail ½ ml

2 caravans, sleeps 4-6, £90-£155, Apr-Oct, bus 300 yds, rail ½ ml

Mrs C Campbell, Rowanlea, Corpach, by Fort William, Inverness-shire, PH33 7LX
☎ Corpach (03977) 586

HOLIDAY SCOTLAND 1987
The most exciting collection of easy-to-book top value holidays in Scotland!

Get a free brochure now from your travel agent.

Prices shown are for guidance only. Please send SAE with each enquiry.

Mossfield Holiday Flats
MOSSFIELD, LOCHYSIDE, FORT WILLIAM
Telephone: 0397 3087/3309

Mossfield Holiday Flats are approximately 3 miles from Fort William. A regular bus service operates to and from the town. Each flat is self-contained with its own bedroom(s), kitchen, sitting room, shower or bathroom/toilet and commands a panoramic view of Ben Nevis and the surrounding hills. Ample parking space and garden.

From £60 per week   Sleeps 2-5

COMMENDED
👑👑

Mossfield Holiday Flats 4 flats, 1 pub rm, 1-2 bedrms, sleeps 2-5, min let 1 night, from £50, Jan-Dec, bus nearby, rail 3 mls, airport 60 mls

Mrs M Cassidy, Glendoune, 1 Grange Terrace, Fort William, PH33 6JQ
☎ *Fort William (0397) 3087/3309*
Modern, purpose built, in quiet residential area. Excellent views of Ben Nevis, 3 mls from town.

FORTINGALL Perthshire Map Ref. 2A1

AWAITING INSPECTION

1 cottage, 2 pub rms, 2 bedrms, sleeps 4-5, £60, Apr-Oct

Mrs Fraser, Duneaves, Drumclog Avenue, Milngavie, Glasgow, G62 8NA
☎ *041 956 2949*

FORTROSE Ross-shire Map Ref. 4B8

AWAITING INSPECTION

1 house, 1 pub rm, 3 bedrms, sleeps 6-8, £50-£120, Apr-Oct, bus ½ ml, rail 12 mls, airport 15 mls

Mrs M Strachan, 53 Ranmoor Crescent, Sheffield, South Yorkshire, S10 3EW
☎ *Sheffield (0742) 305677*

COMMENDED
👑👑👑

1 flat, 1 pub rm, 4 bedrms, sleeps 6, min let 4 nights, £65-£140, Jan-Dec, bus nearby, rail 12 mls, airport 20 mls

Mrs A Jack, The Oaks, Canonbury Terrace, Fortrose, Ross-shire
☎ *Fortrose (0381) 20664*
Spacious, recently refurbished flat in centre of Royal Burgh. Attractive garden. Washing machine.

VAT is shown at 15%: changes in this rate may affect prices.

FOSS, by Pitlochry Perthshire Map Ref. 2A1

Glengoulandie Deer Park
GLENGOULANDIE · FOSS · by PITLOCHRY · Tel. 08873 509
Three self-catering units, sleeping 5-8, situated amidst mountains; central for tourer, adjoining a Wildlife Park and rainbow trout fishing pool.
Within 7 miles of swimming, squash, tennis, snooker, pony-trekking, golf, sailing, sailboarding and canoeing.

Glengoulandie Deer Park 1 house, 1 cottage, 1-2 pub rms, 2-4 bedrms, sleeps 5-8, £50-£120, Apr-Oct, bus 9 mls, rail 17 mls, airport 70 mls

H S & Mrs J McAdam, Glengoulandie, Foss, by Pitlochry, Perthshire, PH16 5NL
☎ Kenmore (08873) 509

FOWLIS WESTER, by Crieff Perthshire Map Ref. 2B2

1 cottage, 2 pub rms, 2 bedrms, sleeps 4-6, min let weekend, £100-£140, Apr-Oct, bus 500 yds, rail 12 mls, airport 40 mls

Mrs M Drysdale, Newmilne, Fowlis Wester, Crieff, Perthshire
☎ Madderty (076483) 362

FOYERS Inverness-shire Map Ref. 4A10

Near Loch Ness   Tel: 04563 200
G. C. Latham,
Wester Muirnich, Gorthleck, Inverness IV1 2YS
Traditional crofters' cottages in the scenic Loch Ness area. Fully equipped, sleeping 4-7, open all year. Bicycle hire, pony trekking, golf, illustrated information about walks and activities. Ideal touring centre for north. Mysterious Loch Ness 5 mins. drive, Inverness, Capital of the Highlands, 40 mins. drive.
Telephone or send stamp for colour brochure. Important: please state dates preferred and number in party.

up to
COMMENDED

1 flat, 4 cottages, 1 pub rm, 2 bedrms, sleeps 4-6, min let weekend (low season), £60-£195, Jan-Dec, bus nearby, rail 18 mls, airport 25 mls

[T] (bicycle hire)

G C Latham, Wester Muirnich, Gorthleck, Inverness-shire, IVI 2YS
☎ Gorthleck (04563) 200
Traditional stone units in rural setting above Loch Ness. Walking, fishing and cycle hire.

COMMENDED

2 flats, 1 pub rm, 2 bedrms, sleeps 4-5, min let 1 night (low season), £40-£110, Jan-Dec, bus nearby, rail 16 mls, airport 25 mls

Mrs L E Fraser, 2 Elmbank, Lower Foyers, Inverness-shire, IV1 2YF
☎ Gorthleck (04563) 610
In peaceful quiet village, upper-storey units above owner's home on ground floor. Views over Loch Ness.

4 flats, 2 cottages, 1 pub rm, 2 bedrms, sleeps 6, min let weekend, £45-£125, Jan-Dec, bus nearby, rail 19 mls, airport 23 mls

Patmac Holiday Enterprises, 103 Church Street, Inverness, IV1 2ES
☎ *Inverness (0463) 231683*

---

2 chalet/log cabins, 1 pub rm, 3 bedrms, sleeps 6-8, £60-£120, Apr-Sep, bus ¼ ml, rail 20 mls, airport 25 mls

Mr K Glass, Foyers Bay House, Foyers, Inverness-shire
☎ *Gorthleck (04563) 624*

FRASERBURGH Aberdeenshire Map Ref. 4H7

1 flat, 2 pub rms, 2 bedrms, sleeps 4-5, £35-£60, Jan-Dec, bus 400 yds, rail 800 yds

Mrs Crawford, 36 Victoria Street, Fraserburgh, Aberdeenshire
☎ *Fraserburgh (0346) 23661*

---

2 flats, 1 pub rm, 2 bedrms, sleeps 4, min let 1 night, £70-£120, Jan-Dec, bus nearby, rail 40 mls, airport 40 mls

Mrs M Greig, 131 Charlotte Street, Fraserburgh, Aberdeenshire, AB4 5LS
☎ *Fraserburgh (0346) 28365*

FRIOCKHEIM Angus Map Ref. 2E1

2 caravans, sleeps 4-6, £70-£95, Apr-Sep, bus 2 mls, rail 8 mls, airport 20 mls

Little Kinnell Country Caravan Park, Little Kinnell, Friockheim, Angus
☎ *Friockheim (02412) 388*

FURNACE Argyll Map Ref. 1F4

1 cottage, 1 pub rm, 2 bedrms, sleeps 4-6, £70-£130, Apr-Oct, bus nearby

Mrs E MacCallum, Thornwood, Furnace, Argyll, PA32 8UX
☎ *Furnace (04995) 673*

FYVIE Aberdeenshire Map Ref. 4G9

1 chalet/log cabin, 1 pub rm, 2 bedrms, sleeps 6, min let weekend, £60-£70, Apr-Oct, bus 2 mls, airport 27 mls

Mrs E Milne, Burnside, Gourdas, Fyvie, by Turriff, Aberdeenshire, AB5 8SA
☎ *Fyvie (06516) 387*

GAIRLOCH Ross-shire Map Ref. 3F7

3 chalet/log cabins, 1 pub rm, 3 bedrms, sleeps 6, £50-£195, Jan-Dec, bus nearby, rail 28 mls, airport 80 mls

(bowling green)

Mr H Davis, Creag Mor Hotel, Gairloch, Ross-shire
☎ *Gairloch (0445) 2068*

VAT is shown at 15%: changes in this rate may affect prices.

Sands Holiday Centre 4 caravans, sleeps 6, £100-£170, Apr-Oct, bus 4 mls, rail 33 mls, airport 80 mls

 ♿ ᵂᶜ E 📻 🖊 ⊘ 🔥 📞 ⊡ 🖳 🗑 ∥ ▄ ⊙ 🄿   ♪ 🔺 ⚖ ⌐ 🐾 🔔

P J & W Cameron, Gairloch Sands Holiday Centre, Gairloch, Ross-shire, IV21 2DL

☎ Gairloch (0445) 2152

COMMENDED
♛ ♛ ♛ ♛

1 house, 3 pub rms, 4 bedrms, sleeps 8-10, £168-£275, Apr-Oct, bus 400 yds, rail 29 mls, airport 77 mls

♿ ᵂᶜ E ➡ 🖊 🔥 🍳 ◎ ⊡ 🗑 ∥ ▄ ✻ 🄿 ⌛ 🖿 †   ♒ 🔍 ♪ 🔺 ⚖ ⌐ / 🏊 ✗ 🔔 🅃

Mrs I Macdonald, Tigh-an-Uillt, 48 Culduthel Road, Inverness, IV2 4HQ

☎ Inverness (0463) 232308/237313

Modern, architect designed house, delightfully situated overlooking the sea with grounds to shore.

AWAITING INSPECTION

1 cottage, 2 pub rms, 3 bedrms, sleeps 5, min let 2 weeks (high season), £45-£65, Apr-Oct, bus nearby

♿ ᵂᶜ E ➡ 🔥 🍳 ◎ ⊡ 🖳 ▄ ✻ 🐴 🄿 ⌛ 🖿 † ⌂   ♪ ∪ 🔺 ⚖ ⌐ ✗ 🔔

Mrs D D MacKenzie, Inchgowan, Gairloch, Ross-shire

☎ Gairloch (0445) 2012

---

1 chalet/log cabin, 1 pub rm, 1 bedrm, sleeps 2-3, min let weekend, £55-£75, Apr-Oct, bus ½ ml, rail 30 mls

♿ ᵂᶜ E ➡ 🖊 🔥 ⊘ ⊡ 🖳 ⊙ ✻ 🄿 †   ♪ 🔺 ⚖ ⌐ ✗ 🔔 🔔

3 caravans, sleeps 6, min let weekend, £80-£130, Apr-Oct, bus ½ ml, rail 30 mls

♿ ᵂᶜ E 📻 🔥 🖊 ⊘ ⊡ 🖳 ⊙ ✻ 🄿 †   ♪ 🔺 ⚖ ⌐ ✗ 🔔 🔔

Mrs J Fraser, Ploverdale, 14 Mihol Road, Strath, Gairloch, Ross-shire, IV21 2BX

☎ Gairloch (0445) 2484

COMMENDED
♛ ♛ ♛ ♛

1 bungalow, 2 pub rms, 6 bedrms, sleeps 11, £100-£290, Apr-Oct, bus 220 yds, rail 30 mls

♿ ᵂᶜ E ➡ 🔥 ▦ ◎ ⊡ 🖳 🗑 ▄ ⊙ ✻ 🐴 🄿 ∥ ⌛ 🖿 † ⌂   🔍 ♪ 🔺 ⚖ ⌐ ✗ 🔔

(cycle & canoe hire nearby)

Mr R Forbes, 3 Fernoch Drive, Lochgilphead, Argyll

☎ Lochgilphead (0546) 2637

Spacious modern house in popular coastal village facing the sea. Some bedrooms with washbasin.

---

1 house, 1 cottage, 1 pub rm, 3-4 bedrms, sleeps 6-8, from £50, Jan-Dec, bus nearby, rail 25 mls

♿ ᵂᶜ E ➡ 📻 🔥 ▦ ◎ ⊡ 🖳 🗑 ∥ ▄ ⊙ ✻ 🐴 🄿 ⌛ 🖿   ♪ 🔺 ⚖ ⌐ / ✗ 🔔

Mr J A MacRae, 4 Braeside, Gairloch, Ross-shire, IV21 2BG

☎ Gairloch (0445) 2300

Prices shown are for guidance only. Please send SAE with each enquiry.

Gairloch Sands
SELF-CATERING APARTMENTS

Gairloch Sands stands overlooking the sands of Gairloch Bay.

Each of the 20 comfortable self catering apartments for 2, 4 or 6 persons has a balcony or patio with the same superb view and each has a large comfortably furnished lounge/dining room, colour TV, bathroom and kitchen. Crockery, cutlery, linen, towels and continental quilts are all provided.

A children's play area and games room, superb sandy beaches, safe sea bathing, loch fishing, golf and sea angling are available. The Restaurant, Bar, Tennis, Boat Hire and Highland entertainment facilities at Gairloch Hotel are only a few minutes away.

Weekly rentals start at £70.

For further information and brochures: Gairloch Sands Self Catering Apartments, Gairloch, Ross-shire IV21 2BJ. Tel: 0445 2001

Gairloch Sands 20 flats, 1 pub rm, 1-2 bedrms, sleeps 2-6, min let 4 nights, £70-£215, Jan-Dec, bus nearby, rail 40 mls, airport 80 mls

(windsurfing)

Gairloch Sands, Gairloch, Ross-shire, IV21 2BJ
☎ *Gairloch (0445) 2001*

---

1 house, 3 cottages, 1-2 pub rms, 3-4 bedrms, sleeps 6-7, £75-£175, Jan-Dec, bus 1-7 mls, rail 26 mls

Mrs B J Reese, Gillymere, Horseshoe Lane, Ash Vale, Aldershot, Hants
☎ *Aldershot (0252) 25119*
Modernised, on traditional croft. On edge of village within easy reach of amenities.

---

1 house, 2 pub rms, 3 bedrms, sleeps 7, £75-£95, Apr-Oct

Mr R MacKenzie, 16 Strath, Gairloch, Ross-shire
☎ *Gairloch (0445) 2230*

---

5 flats, 1 pub rm, 2-3 bedrms, sleeps 4-6, min let 3 nights (low season), £100-£215, Jan-Dec, bus nearby

Millcroft Hotel, Gairloch, Ross-shire, IV21 2BT
☎ *Gairloch (0445) 2376*

---

1 house, 2 pub rms, 4 bedrms, sleeps 8, £60-£180, Jan-Dec, bus 5 mls, rail 35 mls, airport 75 mls

J MacDonald, 8 View Place, Inverness
☎ *Inverness (0463) 231975*
Secluded cottage with large attractive garden in peaceful setting. Good holiday base.

---

1 cottage, 1 pub rm, 2 bedrms, sleeps 5-6, £100-£150, Jan-Dec, bus nearby, rail 30 mls, airport 80 mls

♿ ᵂᶜ E 👜 🄰 🏢 ◉ 🔲 ▢ ⚡ 🔌 ⊙ ❉ 🅿 † ⚲ 🥄 △ ⚼ ↑ ✗ 🗻

Mrs P R Lyon, Camalaig, Dunvegan, Isle of Skye, Inverness-shire
☎ *Dunvegan (047022) 355*

---

1 bungalow, 1 pub rm, 3 bedrms, sleeps 6-7, from £130, Jan-Dec

♿ ᵂᶜ E 👜 🄰 🏢 ◉ 🔲 ▢ 🄾 🔌 ⊙ ❉ 🅿 ⛟ 🛏 † 🥄 △ ⚼ ↑ ✗ 🗻

Mrs J MacKenzie, MacKenzie & MacLennan, The Garage, Gairloch, Ross-shire
☎ *Gairloch (0445) 2255*

Glencairn Holidays
GAIRLOCH · WESTER ROSS
Telephone: 0381-20127

GLENCAIRN modern apartments and houses are magnificently situated with spectacular sea views. The accommodation is luxuriously equipped providing all the comforts of home — fully carpeted, heated and tastefully furnished. Colour TV and bed linen is provided. Kitchens have cookers, fridges, washing machines, tumble dryers and dishwashers in some properties.

The area provides superb hill-walking, safe sandy beaches, golf, fishing and Inverewe Gardens is only a few miles away.

From our Reception Centre a warm welcome awaits you; hire from our wide range of sporting equipment, sailing dinghies, fishing/pleasure boats, sailboards, canoes and bicycles, browse in our Craft Shop or enjoy a snack in the Centre's delightful Coffee Shop.

For further details and free colour brochure telephone (0381) 20127.

up to
HIGHLY COMMENDED
👑 👑 👑 👑 👑

2 houses, 2 pub rms, 3 bedrms, sleeps 6-8, £114-£314, Mar-Oct, bus 1 ml, rail 35 mls, airport 90 mls

♿ ᵂᶜ E 👜 🄰 🏢 🔲 ◉ 🔲 🕯 🔲 ▢ 🔌 ⚓ ⊙ ❉ 🐾 🅿 ⛟ 🛏 † ⚲ 🥄 △ ⚼ ↑ ✗ 🗻 🔲 ⊤

Glencairn Holidays Ltd, Brae House, 6 Canonbury Terrace, Fortrose, Ross-shire, IV10 8TT
☎ *Fortrose (0381) 20127*

Well furnished modern units. Good sea views, watersports, walking, wildlife etc.

---

1 house, 1 pub rm, 3 bedrms, sleeps 6, £100-£150, Apr-Oct, bus 400 yds, rail 30 mls, airport 75 mls

♿ ᵂᶜ E 👜 🄰 🏢 🔲 ◉ 🔲 🔲 ▢ ⚓ ⊙ ❉ 🐾 🅿 ⛟ † 🥄 △ ⚼ ↑ ✗ 🗻

Mrs A MacKenzie, Somerled, Charleston, Gairloch, Ross-shire
☎ *Gairloch (0445) 2243*

---

1 house, 2 pub rms, 3 bedrms, sleeps 6, £50-£160, Jan-Dec, bus nearby, rail 28 mls, airport 80 mls

♿ ᵂᶜ E 👜 🄰 🏢 🔲 ◉ 🔲 🔲 ▢ 🔌 ⚓ ⊙ ❉ 🐾 🅿 ⛟ 🛏 † ⚲ 🥄 △ ⚼ ↑ ✓ ✗ 🗻 🔲 ⊤

Mrs A K Mackenzie, No4 Strath, Gairloch, Ross-shire, IV21 2BX
☎ *Gairloch (0445) 2047*

GAIRLOCHY Inverness-shire Map Ref. 3H11

1 house, 2 pub rms, 4 bedrms, sleeps 8, from £80, Jan-Dec, bus 4 mls, rail 4 mls

7 caravans, sleeps 6-8, from £70, Mar-Oct, bus 4 mls, rail 4 mls

Mrs M Stevenson, Post Office House, Achnacarry, Spean Bridge, Inverness-shire
☎ *Gairlochy (039782) 218*

Gairlochy Caravan Park 4 caravans, sleeps 6, min let 1 night, £60-£110, Apr-Sep, bus 3 mls, rail 2 mls

Mr J Anderson, Gairlochy Caravan Park, Spean Bridge, Inverness-shire, PH34 4EQ
☎ *Gairlochy (039781) 711*

GALASHIELS Selkirkshire Map Ref. 2E6

COMMENDED

2 houses, 1 pub rm, 3 bedrms, sleeps 6, £105-£150, May-Sep, bus nearby, rail 35 mls, airport 35 mls

Ogilvie Dickson Holiday Homes, 23 Paton Street, Galashiels, Selkirkshire, TD1 3AT
☎ *Galashiels (0896) 3496*
Modern houses of individual character. Seperately sited in residential area of two Border towns.

GALSTON Ayrshire Map Ref. 1H7

COMMENDED

1 house, 1 pub rm, 3 bedrms, sleeps 6-7, min let weekend, £85-£140, Jan-Dec, bus 5 mls, rail 12 mls, airport 12 mls

Mrs Bone, Auchencloigh Farm, Galston, Ayrshire
☎ *Galston (0563) 820567*
Quietly situated on family run farm. Panoramic views of surrounding countryside.

by GARDENSTOWN Banffshire Map Ref. 4G7

1 caravan, sleeps 4-6, min let weekend, £30-£70, Jan-Dec, bus 1 ml, rail 30 mls, airport 35 mls

D Schofield, Bankhead Croft, Gamrie, Banff, Banffshire, AB4 3HN
☎ *Gardenstown (02615) 584*

by GARELOCHHEAD Dunbartonshire Map Ref. 1G4

1 cottage, 1 pub rm, 2 bedrms, sleeps 4-6, £80-£140, Apr-Oct, bus nearby, rail 2 mls, airport 25 mls

W P Swan, Mambeg House, Mambeg, Gareloch, Dunbartonshire, G84 OEN
☎ *Garelochhead (0436) 810136*

GARRABOST, by Stornoway Isle of Lewis, Western Isles Map Ref. 3D4

1 house, 2 pub rms, 3 bedrms, sleeps 4-6, £80-£100, Apr-Oct, bus nearby, ferry 5 mls, airport 2 ½ mls

Mrs K Macarthur, 3 Garrabost, Point, Isle of Lewis, Western Isles, P86 OPL
☎ *Garrabost (0851) 870236*

VAT is shown at 15%: changes in this rate may affect prices.

GARTMORE Perthshire Map Ref. 1H4

1 caravan, sleeps 6, £55-£65, Mar-Oct, bus 400 yds, rail 22 mls, airport 28 mls

& ⓦ E ⌂ ⊘ ⬚ ☼ ⁑ ℙ † ⚟ ✕ ⬛

Mrs J B Billett, Glenhead, Gartmore, Stirling, FK8 3RP
☎ *Aberfoyle (08772) 261*

COMMENDED
♛ ♛ ♛ ♛

1 bungalow, 1 pub rm, 2 bedrms, sleeps 5, £75-£160, Apr-Oct, bus ¼ ml, rail 20 mls, airport 28 mls

& ⓦ E ⌀ ⌂ ▦ ⬚ ◎ ⬚⬚ ⬚ ▱ ☉ ☼ ⁑ ℙ ⌛ ▦ † ⚟ ♪ ∪ △ ⊳ ⚓ ✕ ⬛

Mrs Prescott, Dalnacreoch, Gartmore, Aberfoyle, Stirling, FK8 3RP
☎ *Aberfoyle (08772) 285*
Modernised, on edge of peaceful village. Large garden. Central heating. Well behaved pets welcome.

---

by **GARVE** Ross-shire Map Ref. 3H8

2 chalet/log cabins, 1 pub rm, 1-2 bedrms, sleeps 4, £60-£120, Jan-Dec, bus nearby, rail 1 ml

& ⓦ E ⬚ ⌀ ▦ ⌂ ⊘ ⬚⬚ ◿ ▱ ☼ ⁑ ℙ ⌛ † ♪ ∪ ⊳ ✕ ⬛

Mr & Mrs R A Miller, Tigh-na-Drochit, Garve, Ross-shire, IV23 2PU
☎ *Garve (09974) 256*

INCHBAE LODGE CHALET
INCHBAE, by GARVE, ROSS-SHIRE Tel: 09975 269
For those who prefer the freedom of a Self Catering Holiday there is one Chalet in the grounds of Inchbae Lodge. The Chalet has two bedrooms, spacious lounge, kitchen and bathroom. All towels and linen are provided. You may also use the facilities of the Hotel including bar, bar meals and highly rated restaurant.

1 chalet/log cabin, 1 pub rm, 2 bedrms, sleeps 4-6, £120-£160, Apr-Oct, bus nearby, rail 6 mls, airport 30 mls

& ⓦ E ⬚ ⌀ ⌂ ⊘ ⬚⬚ ☎ ▱ ☉ ☼ ⁑ ℙ ⌛ ▦ † ⚟ ⊕ ♪ ∪ △ ⚓ ⊳ ⌿ ⚓ ⒭ ✕ ♨
Ⓣ

Mr Mitchell, Inchbae Lodge, by Garve, Ross-shire
☎ *Aultguish (09975) 269*

GATEHEAD, by Kilmarnock Ayrshire Map Ref. 1H7

1 cottage, 1 pub rm, 2 bedrms, sleeps 2-4, min let weekend, £90-£130, Apr-Oct, bus 300 yds, rail 4 mls

& ⓦ E ⬚ ⌀ ▦ ⌂ ⊘ ⬚⬚ ☎ ⬚ ▱ ◿ ▱ ☉ ☼ ⁑ ℙ ⫽ ⌛ ▦ ⟿ † ⚟ ● ⚞ ⚘ ⚲
⚘ ♪ ∪ △ ⊳ ⚓ ✕ ⬛ Ⓣ

Mrs Hunt, The Courtyard, Mid Fairlie, Gatehead, Kilmarnock, Ayrshire
☎ *Drybridge (0563) 850266*

GATEHOUSE OF FLEET Kirkcudbrightshire Map Ref. 2A10

Auchenlarie Holiday Farm 50 caravans, sleeps 4-7, min let 2 nights, £70-£190, Apr-Oct, bus nearby, rail 4 mls, airport 60 mls

& ⓦ E ▨ ⊘ ⊘ ⬚ ☎ ⬚ ▱ ◿ ▱ ☉ ⁑ ℙ ⌛ ▦ † ⚟ ● ⊕ ⚞ ⚲ ♪ ∪ △ ⊳
✕ ⬛ ⬚ Ⓣ (amusement centre)
Auchenlarie Holiday Farm, Gatehouse of Fleet, Kirkcudbrightshire, DG7 2EX
☎ *Mossyard (055724) 251*

Prices shown are for guidance only. Please send SAE with each enquiry.

2 houses, 2 flats, 1 bungalow, 1-3 pub rms, 3-5 bedrms, sleeps 6-9, min let weekend (low season), £60-£160, Jan-Dec, rail 32 mls, airport 89 mls

Mrs Murray Usher, Cally Estate Office, Gatehouse of Fleet, Kirkcudbrightshire
☎ *Gatehouse (05574) 200*

---

1 cottage, 3 pub rms, 4 bedrms, sleeps 4-8, min let 2 weeks, £90-£180, Jan-Dec, car essential

Mrs Johnstone, Meikle Cullendoch, Dromore Farm, Gatehouse, Kirkcudbrightshire
☎ *Gatehouse (05574) 338*

---

1 house, 2 pub rms, 4 bedrms, sleeps 8, £30-£150, Jan-Dec, bus nearby, rail 30 mls, airport 80 mls

Mrs Case, Halls Farm, Silchester, by Reading, Berks, RG7 2NH
☎ *Basingstoke (0256) 881680*

---

1 house, 1 pub rm, 3 bedrms, sleeps 6-7, min let weekend, £30-£110, Jan-Dec, bus nearby, rail 33 mls, airport 60 mls

Mrs A M Johnstone, Dromore, Gatehouse of Fleet, Kirkcudbrightshire
☎ *Gatehouse (05574) 338*

---

2 cottages, 3 bungalows, 1-2 pub rms, 2-3 bedrms, sleeps 4-6, min let weekend (low season), £60-£125, Jan-Dec, bus 3 mls, rail 35 mls, airport 90 mls

(special interest courses, Spring/Autumn)

Mrs B Gilbey, Rusko, Gatehouse of Fleet, Castle Douglas, Kirkcudbrightshire, DG7 2BS
☎ *Gatehouse of Fleet (05574) 215*

---

1 cottage, 1 pub rm, 2 bedrms, sleeps 3-4, £55-£70, Apr-Sep, bus 500 yds

Mrs M Lee, Sarsbank, Old London Road, Chipping Norton, Oxon, OX7 5UX
☎ *Chipping Norton (0608) 2885*

GATEHOUSE OF FLEET AREA Kirkcudbrightshire Map Ref. 2A10

up to
COMMENDED

20 houses, 3 cottages, 1-2 pub rms, 2-6 bedrms, sleeps 4-16, from £70, Apr-Oct

G M Thomson & Company, 27 King Street, Castle Douglas, Kirkcudbrightshire, DG7 1AB
☎ *Castle Douglas (0556) 2701*

VAT is shown at 15%: changes in this rate may affect prices.

GIGHA, Isle of Argyll Map Ref. 1D6

GIGHA ENTERPRISES
Isle of Gigha, Argyll
Tel. 05835 254

The lovely isle of Gigha (pronounced Gee-a) is the innermost of the Hebrides, just 3 miles from mainland Argyll, only 2½ hours drive from Glasgow with a regular daily ferry service from Tayinloan.

Achamore House, set in the midst of a unique Rhododendron and Azalea garden, has been completely redecorated and furnished to the highest standards and is available for let as a whole or in 2 parts: the main house accommodates 15, the nursery wing 5.

Three modernised stone cottages with gas cooking and heating are comfortably furnished and ideal for family holidays.

The Gigha Hotel, renowned for superb home fare, offers meals to non-residents; the Boathouse serves coffee, tea and snacks.

Brochure on request.

COMMENDED

2 houses, 1 flat, 2 cottages, 1-4 pub rms, 1-8 bedrms, sleeps 4-15, £115-£800, Jan-Dec, ferry ½-1 ½ mls

Gigha Enterprises, Gigha Hotel, Isle of Gigha, Argyll
☎ Gigha (05835) 254
Seperately sited on small island, units varying in character, design and appeal.

GIRVAN Ayrshire Map Ref. 1G9

1 flat, 1 pub rm, 2 bedrms, sleeps 5, £75-£150, Jan-Dec, bus nearby, rail ½ ml

Mrs Moyra M Hay, 50 Dalrymple Street, Girvan, Ayrshire, KA26 9BT
☎ Girvan (0465) 4421/2378

---

1 flat, 1 pub rm, 1 bedrm, sleeps 4, min let weekend, from £40, Jan-Dec

D Iannarelli, 21 Louisa Drive, Girvan, Ayrshire
☎ Girvan (0465) 2277

---

by GIRVAN Ayrshire Map Ref. 1G9

Jeancroft Holiday Park 50 caravans, sleeps 4-6, min let 2 nights, £60-£110, Mar-Oct, bus 500 yds, rail 3 mls, airport 18 mls

Mr Russell, Jeancroft Caravan Park, Dipple, by Girvan, Ayrshire, KA26 9JW
☎ Turnberry (06553) 288

Prices shown are for guidance only. Please send SAE with each enquiry.

GLASGOW Map Ref. 1H5

Jordanhill College

Set in 120 acres of parkland, 10 minutes from city centre, self-catering accommodation with fully equipped kitchens, linen and including swimming, tennis, table tennis, squash, games hall and sports pitch. Resident sports coaches.

Visit the pleasures and treasures of Glasgow, tour Burns' country and West Highlands. A friendly and welcoming staff will ensure a unique holiday. Accommodation in units of 3-6 from £131, inclusive of VAT, per week.

For full details: Mr D. C. Wilkie, Jordanhill College of Education 76 Southbrae Drive, GLASGOW G13 1PP. Tel: 041-959 1232, Ext. 292.

7 flats, 3 pub rms, 29 bedrms, sleeps 3-6, min let 1 night, £150-£296, Apr, Jun-Sep, bus ¼ ml, rail ½ ml, airport 7 mls

Mr D Wilkie, Jordanhill Clge of Education, 76 South Brae Drive, Glasgow, G13 1PP
☎ *041 959 1232 ext 292*

2 flats, 1 pub rm, 1-2 bedrms, sleeps 2-3, £150-£250, Jan-Dec, bus nearby, rail ½ ml, airport 8 mls

Harvey & Donaldson, 153 Buchanan Street, Glasgow, G1 2JX
☎ *041 221 7211*

Garnett Hall 24 flats, 1 pub rm, 4-6 bedrms, sleeps 4-6, £150-£170, Jun-Sep, bus nearby, rail ½ ml, airport 8 mls

University of Strathclyde, Garnett Hall, Cathedral Street, Glasgow
☎ *041 552 4400 ext 3560*

Forbes Hall 20 flats, 1 pub rm, 4-6 bedrms, sleeps 4-6, £150-£170, Jun-Sep, bus nearby, rail ½ ml, airport 8 mls

University of Strathclyde, Forbes Hall, Rottenrow East, Glasgow
☎ *041 552 4400 ext 3560*

Maclay Hall 124 bedsits, 4 pub rms, 1 bedrm, sleeps 1-3, min let 1 night, £40, mid Mar-mid Apr, Jul-mid Sep, bus 500 yds, rail 2 mls, airport 10 mls

Conference & Vacation Office, University of Glasgow, 52 Hillhead St, Glasgow, G12 8PZ
☎ *041 330 5385*

VAT is shown at 15%: changes in this rate may affect prices.

GLASS, by Huntly Aberdeenshire Map Ref. 4E9

2 houses, 2 cottages, 2 pub rms, 2-4 bedrms, sleeps 4-8, min let weekend, £50-£150, Jan-Dec, bus nearby, rail 6 mls, airport 45 mls

Mrs T Ingleby, Aswanley, Glass, by Huntly, Aberdeenshire, AB5 4XJ
☎ *Glass (046685) 262*

GLEN CLOVA Angus Map Ref. 4E12

1 cottage, 1 pub rm, 2 bedrms, sleeps 6, min let weekend, £50-£65, Apr-Oct, bus nearby(postbus), rail 25 mls, airport 25 mls

Mrs Hood, Middlehill Farm, Glen Clova, Kirriemuir, Angus
☎ *Cortachy (05754) 262*

GLEN CRERAN Argyll Map Ref. 1F1

2 houses, 2 cottages, 2 pub rms, 2-6 bedrms, sleeps 5-13, £60-£300, Apr-Feb, bus 5 mls, rail 25 mls, airport 100 mls

Mr P D Zvegintov, Glencreran Estate, Rosebank, Appin, Argyll
☎ *Appin (063173) 401*

GLEN ESK Angus Map Ref. 4F12

1 cottage, 1 pub rm, 2 bedrms, sleeps 4, £50-£70, May-Nov, bus 12 mls, rail 18 mls, airport 40 mls

Mrs M Main, Keenie Farm, Glenesk, Brechin, Angus, DD9 7YS
☎ *Tarfside (03567) 228*

1 chalet/log cabin, 1 cottage, 1 pub rm, 2-3 bedrms, sleeps 6-7, from £50, Apr-Oct, bus 14 mls, rail 25 mls

Mrs A C McIntosh, Dalbrack, Tarfside, Glen Esk, Brechin, Angus, DD9 7YY
☎ *Tarfside (03567) 233*

3 cottages, 1 pub rm, 2-4 bedrms, sleeps 4-6, £65-£225, Apr-Oct, bus 20 mls, rail 30 mls, airport 90 mls

(hillwalking)

The Factor, Dalhousie Estates Office, Brechin, Angus
☎ *Brechin (03562) 4566*

GLEN LYON Perthshire Map Ref. 1H2

4 houses, 1 cottage, 1-2 pub rms, 2-7 bedrms, sleeps 4-10, £70-£350, Apr-Oct

Finlayson Hughes, Bank House, 82 Atholl Road, Pitlochry, Perthshire, PH16 5BL
☎ *Pitlochry (0796) 2512*

2 flats, 1 cottage, 2 pub rms, 2-4 bedrms, sleeps 4-6, min let weekend, from £65, Jan-Dec, bus 6 mls, rail 28 mls

Mrs M O Graham, Invervar Lodge, Glen Lyon, Perthshire
☎ *Glen Lyon (08877) 203*

Prices shown are for guidance only. Please send SAE with each enquiry.

GLEN PROSEN Angus Map Ref. 2D1

1 flat, 4 cottages, 1-2 pub rms, 1-3 bedrms, sleeps 2-7, min let weekend, £60-£185, Jan-Dec, bus post bus, rail 30 mls, airport 30 mls

 ♿ ᵂᶜ E ⬛ ⊚ ▦ ▢ ◉ ◱ ▢ ▣ 🔌 ☉ ✲ 🐎 🅿 🛇 ▥ †   🛇 🎣 ∪ ⌐ 🏊 🛥 (cycle hire)

Mrs P MacLean, Balnaboth, Glenprosen, Kirriemuir, Angus, DD8 4SA
☎ *Cortachy (05754) 302*

Situated on estate in secluded Angus Glen. Pony trekking, fishing, cross country skiing, cycle hire.

GLENACHULISH, Ballachulish Argyll Map Ref. 1F1

House-in-the-Wood Holidays
GLENACHULISH · BALLACHULISH · ARGYLL PA39 4JZ

A large 5-bedroomed cottage by Loch Linnhe or 6-berth chalets beautifully set in natural woodland make good bases from which to explore the Highlands and Islands. Fishing, Riding, boating and places to eat out are all available locally. It is excellent walking country—pets are welcome and we are open all year.
Write or phone for brochure.   **TEL: 08552 379**

4 chalet/log cabins, 2 houses, 1 cottage, 1 pub rm, 1-6 bedrms, sleeps 4-15, min let weekend (low season), £60-£300, Jan-Dec, bus nearby, rail 12 mls, airport 90 mls

 ♿ ᵂᶜ E ⬛ ▸ ⊚ ▦ ◉ ◱ ▢ ⌁ 🔌 ☉ ✲ 🐎 🅿 🛇 ▥ †   🎣 ∪ △ 🛥 ⌐ 🏊 ✕ 🛥 Ⓣ

The House In The Wood Holidays, Glenachulish, Ballachulish, Argyll, PA39 4JZ
☎ *Ballachulish (08552) 379*

Units of different character and design set in 5 acres of natural woodland, close to Loch Linnhe.

GLENAROS Isle of Mull, Argyll Map Ref. 1D2

AWAITING INSPECTION

2 houses, 3 cottages, 1 bungalow, 1-2 pub rms, 2-6 bedrms, sleeps 4-10, min let weekend (low season), £70-£210, Jan-Dec, bus 400 yds, ferry 7-14 mls, airport 3 mls

 ♿ ᵂᶜ E ⬛ ▸ ⊚ ▢ ⊙ 🐎 🛇 ▥ †   🎣 ∪ △ 🛥 ⌐ ✓ ✕ 🛥 🐾 Ⓣ

Mrs D Scott, Glenaros, Aros, Isle of Mull, Argyll, PA72 6JP
☎ *Aros (06803) 337/340*

GLENBERVIE Kincardineshire Map Ref. 4G11

1 bungalow, 1 pub rm, 2 bedrms, sleeps 4, £60-£95, Apr-Oct, bus 1 ml, rail 8 mls, airport 24 mls

 ♿ ᵂᶜ E ⬛ ▸ ⊚ ▢ 🔌 ☉ ✲ 🅿 †   🎣 ∪ ⌐ ✕ 🛥

Mrs J S Hodson, 17 Sandy Lane, Orpington, Kent, BR6 0DY
☎ *Orpington (0689) 32960*

GLENBORRODALE Argyll Map Ref. 1D1

1 chalet/log cabin, 1 pub rm, 2 bedrms, sleeps 5, £60-£120, Apr-Oct, bus nearby, rail 27 mls

 ♿ ᵂᶜ E ⬛ ⊚ ◉ ▢ 🔌 ☉ ✲ 🐎 🅿 🛇 ▥ †   🎣 △ 🛥 ✕

Mr G A Hunter, Hunterscolt, Glenborrodale, Acharacle, Argyll, PH36 4JP
☎ *Glenborrodale (09724) 219*

---

1 house, 1 pub rm, 3 bedrms, sleeps 7, min let weekend, £161-£218, Mar-Oct

 ♿ ᵂᶜ E ⬛ ⊚ ◱ ⌁ ◱ ▢ ▢ 🔌 ☉ ✲ 🐎 🅿 🛇 ▥ ◂ † ⛰   🎣 ∪ △ ⌐ Ⓡ ✕ 🍴 Ⓣ

The Clan Morrison Hotel, Glenborrodale, Acharacle, Argyll, PH36 4JP
☎ *Glenborrodale (09724) 232*

VAT is shown at 15%: changes in this rate may affect prices.

GLENBRITTLE Isle of Skye, Inverness-shire Map Ref. 3D10

1 cottage, 1 pub rm, 3 bedrms, sleeps 6, £98-£132, Apr-Oct, bus 9 mls, rail 45 mls, ferry 45 mls, airport 35 mls

👤♿ⓌⒸ E ⛽ 📻 Ⓜ ◎ ◻ 🄿 †   ✂ 🔌 🛒 ⛽

Mrs G Macrae, Glenbrittle, Isle of Skye, Inverness-shire, IV47 8TA
☎ *Carbost (047842) 232*

GLENCAPLE Dumfriesshire Map Ref. 2C10

1 cottage, 1 pub rm, 2 bedrms, sleeps 6, £50-£80, Apr-Oct, bus nearby, rail 4 mls, airport 80 mls

♿ⓌⒸ E 📻 Ⓜ ◎ ◻ 🍴 🄰 ⚲ ☼ ✻ ♘ 🄿 🐎 🎴 † 🏔   🎣 🦢 🔍 ✈ ✂ ∪ ➤ ✖ 🛒 ⛽

Mrs Murray, Conheath, Glencaple, Dumfriesshire, DG1 4UB
☎ *Glencaple (038777) 205*

GLENCOE Argyll Map Ref. 1F1

COMMENDED
👑 👑 👑

Torren Cottages 3 cottages, 1 pub rm, 3 bedrms, sleeps 6-8, min let 2 nights, £115-£250, Jan-Dec, bus 2 mls, rail 16 mls, airport 85 mls

♿ⓌⒸ E ⛽ 📻 Ⓜ 🏠 🍴 ◎ ◻ 🍴 🄰 🚭 🄰 ⚲ ☼ ✻ ♘ 🄿 🐎 🎴 🏔   ✂ ∪ ⚠ ⚡ ✦ 🕱 ⚡ ✖ 🛒 🅃

Mrs V A B Sutherland, The Moss, Pier Road, Rhu, Helensburgh, Dunbartonshire, G84 8LH
☎ *Rhu (0436) 820274/(08552) 207*
Modern, architect designed units in secluded woodland location on riverbank. Superb views of hills.

---

4 chalet/log cabins, 1 pub rm, 2 bedrms, sleeps 6, min let 2 nights (low season), £75-£150, Jan-Dec, bus ¼ ml, rail 18 mls

♿ⓌⒸ E 📻 Ⓜ 🏠 ◎ 🍴 🄰 🚭 ☼ ♘ 🄿 🐎 🎴   ✂ ∪ ⚠ ⚡ ✦ 🕱 🅁 ✖ 🛒 🍷 🎵
(hillwalking, climbing, canoeing)

Eileen & Peter Daynes, Clachaig Inn, Glencoe, Argyll, PA39 4HX
☎ *Ballachulish (08552) 252*

Glencoe Bunkhouses 2 bunkhouses, 1 alpine barn, sleeps 1-70, min let 1 night, £14-£18 (per person), Jan-Dec, bus 1 ½ mls, rail 15 mls

♿ⓌⒸ 📻 Ⓜ ◎ ⚲ 🄰 🚭 ✻ ♘ 🄿 🐎 🎴 † 🏔 🌐   ✂ ∪ ⚠ ⚡ ➤ ✦ 🕱 ⚡ ✖ 🛒 ⛽ 🅃
(climbing)

H MacColl, Leacantuim Farm Bunkhouses, Glencoe, Argyll
☎ *Ballachulish (08552) 256*

Invercoe Caravan Site 5 caravans, sleeps 8, £64-£126, Easter-Oct, bus nearby, rail 14 mls, airport 88 mls

♿ⓌⒸ E 📻 Ⓜ ⚲ ◎ 🍴 🄰 ◻ 🄰 ⚲ ☼ ♘ 🄿 🏔   ✂ ∪ ⚠ ⚡ ✖ 🛒 🅃 (cycles for hire)
M Brown, Invercoe Caravan Site, Glencoe, Argyll
☎ *Ballachulish (08552) 210*

Prices shown are for guidance only. Please send SAE with each enquiry.

GLENDALE Isle of Skye, Inverness-shire Map Ref. 3C9

COMMENDED
👑 👑 👑 👑

5 cottages, 2 pub rms, 3 bedrms, sleeps 5, min let 4 nights, £100-£145, Jan-Dec, bus ½ ml, rail 60 mls, ferry 60 mls, airport 55 mls

Mrs Worts & Mrs Gohin, Pliaborough Ltd, Orchard Works, Warners End Rd, Hemel Hempstead, Herts, HP1 1SN
☎ *Hemel Hempstead (0442) 55761*

Modernised croft house in 8 acres of ground to river. Double glazed picture windows; scenic views.

GLENDARUEL Argyll Map Ref. 1F4

Glendaruel Caravan Park 4 caravans, sleeps 6, min let 2 nights, £75-£150, Apr-Oct, bus ½ ml, ferry 18 mls

Mrs Q Craig, Glendaruel Caravan Park, Glendaruel, Argyll
☎ *Glendaruel (036982) 267*

GLENELG Ross-shire Map Ref. 3F10

Lamont Chalets 5 chalet/log cabins, 1 bungalow, 1 pub rm, 2-3 bedrms, sleeps 4-8, min let 1 night (low season), £45-£150, Jan-Dec, bus 8 mls, rail 25 mls, airport 25 mls

1 caravan, sleeps 6, min let 1 night (low season), £36-£50, Mar-Oct, bus 8 mls, rail 25 mls, airport 25 mls

Mr & Mrs M J Lamont, Creagmhor, Glenelg, by Kyle, Ross-shire
☎ *Glenelg (059982) 231*

1 cottage, 2 pub rms, 4 bedrms, sleeps 7, £150-£200, May-Jul, bus 2 mls, rail 30 mls, airport 75 mls

(birdwatching, sea bathing, hillwalking)

Mrs J Ellice, Scallasaig, Glenelg, Ross-shire
☎ *Glenelg (059982) 217*

GLENFARG Perthshire Map Ref. 2C3

2 cottages, 1-2 pub rms, 2 bedrms, sleeps 4-6, £75-£110, Jan-Dec, bus 3 mls, rail 9 mls

Mrs S R Christie, Rossie Ochil, Forgandenny, Perthshire, PH2 9DH
☎ *Glenfarg (05773) 307*

1 cottage, 1 pub rm, 2 bedrms, sleeps 4, £60-£140, Jan-Dec, bus ¾ ml, rail 10 mls

(gliding)

Mrs J D S Baillie, Colliston, Glenfarg, Perthshire, PH2 9PE
☎ *Glenfarg (05773) 434*

GLENFORSA Isle of Mull, Argyll Map Ref. 1D2

1 caravan, sleeps 6, min let 4 nights, £75-£95, Apr-Oct, bus nearby, rail 20 mls, ferry 10 mls, airport ½ ml

Mrs MacGillvray, Pennygowan Farm, Glenforsa, Isle of Mull, Argyll
☎ *Aros (06803) 335*

VAT is shown at 15%: changes in this rate may affect prices.

145

GLENGARRY, by Invergarry Inverness-shire Map Ref. 3H11

APPROVED

1 cottage, 1 pub rm, 3 bedrms, sleeps 6, min let weekend (low season), £85-£135, Apr-Oct, bus 9 mls, rail 30 mls, airport 55 mls

Mrs M Cameron, South Lodge, Glenfintaig, by Spean Bridge, Inverness-shire, PH34 4DX
☎ *Spean Bridge (039781) 349/243*
Wooden unit set high above and overlooking Loch Garry. Fishing permit available.

GLENHINISDALE, by Portree Isle of Skye, Inverness-shire Map Ref. 3D8

1 cottage, 1 pub rm, 2 bedrms, sleeps 5-7, £55-£65, Apr-Oct, bus 2 mls, ferry 6 mls

Mrs Isobel Nicolson, 2 Peinloch, Glenhinisdale, Snizort, by Portree, Isle of Skye, Inverness-shire
☎ *Uig (047042) 343*

GLENISLA Perthshire Map Ref. 2C1

2 cottages, 1 pub rm, 2 bedrms, sleeps 5-6, min let weekend, £50-£80, Jan-Dec, bus 7 mls, rail 23 mls, airport 23 mls

Mrs D Clark, Purgavie Farm, Glenisla, Kirriemuir, Perthshire
☎ *Lintrathen (05756) 213*

APPROVED

1 bedsit, 1 bedrm, sleeps 2-4, min let weekend, £100, Jan-Dec, bus 10 mls, rail 30 mls, airport 70 mls

[T] (hang-gliding, roller skiing)

Mr H Davidson, Kirkside House Hotel, Kirkton of Glenisla, Perthshire, PH11 8PH
☎ *Glenisla (057582) 278*
Adjacant to small, glen inn overlooking River Isla.

Glenmarkie Lodge · Glenisla
GLENMARKIE LODGE, GLENISLA, PERTHSHIRE PH11 8QB
Telephone: 057582 219
Spacious, comfortable, self-contained apartments, some sleeping up to 8 people.Situated amidst magnificent scenery in the unspoilt beauty of the Angus glens.
Central laundry, recreation room, colour TV in all apartments.
From £95 per apartment weekly according to season and apartment size.
Weekends by arrangement. Write or telephone for brochure.

COMMENDED

3 flats, 1 pub rm, 1-3 bedrms, sleeps 4-8, min let weekend, £95-£175, Jan-Dec, bus 10 mls, rail 25 mls, airport 25 mls

Glenmarkie Lodge, Glenisla, by Blairgowrie, Perthshire, PH11 8QB
☎ *Glenisla (057582) 219*
Units in magnificent victorian shooting lodge in secluded glen. Super scenery, many outdoor pursuits.

---

1 house, 1 cottage, 1 pub rm, 3 bedrms, sleeps 6-8, £68-£164, Mar-Nov

Mr I M Ogston, Post Office, Woodend, Glenisla, by Blairgowrie, Perthshire, PH11 8PQ
☎ *Glenisla (057582) 221*

GLENKINDIE Aberdeenshire Map Ref. 4E10

Glenkindie Estate 4 cottages, 1-2 pub rms, 2-3 bedrms, sleeps 4-6, from £75, Jan-Dec, bus 1 ml

Bell-Ingram, Durn, Isla Road, Perth, PH2 7HF
☎ *Perth (0738) 21121*

GLENLIVET Banffshire Map Ref. 4D9

1 cottage, 2 pub rms, 2 bedrms, sleeps 6, £70-£90, Apr-Oct, bus 1 ml, rail 35 mls

Mrs Pauline Davidson, Riverstone, Ballindalloch, Banffshire, AB3 9DA
☎ *Glenlivet (08073) 219*

Glenlivet Holiday Lodges
GLENLIVET · BALLINDALLOCH AB3 9DR · 080 73 209
Excellent Lodges, Chalets and Cottages with magnificent panoramic views in peaceful setting in the heart of Speyside. Accommodation of various sizes sleeping from 2-8, and include continental quilts, with bed linen.
Relax after a day's walking, fishing, climbing, golfing, pony-trekking, ski-ing, touring, in the comfortable lounge bar "The Poacher's Retreat".

up to
COMMENDED

Glenlivet Holiday Lodges 10 chalet/log cabins, 2 cottages, 1 pub rm, 2-3 bedrms, sleeps 2-8, min let 3 nights, £115-£320, Dec-Oct, bus 8 mls, rail 17 mls, airport 53 mls

Mrs S N T Godfrey, Glenlivet Holiday Lodges, Glenlivet, Ballindalloch, Banffshire, AB3 9DR
☎ *Glenlivet (08073) 209*
Varying styles of units amidst rolling upland scenery. Spectacular views.

1 house, 2 pub rms, 4 bedrms, sleeps 6-8, £80-£150, May-Oct, rail 27 mls, airport 70 mls

Mrs D McColville, 12 Three Rivers Walk, Newmill, Elgin, Moray, IV30 2AG
☎ *Elgin (0343) 2762*

GLENLUCE Wigtownshire Map Ref. 1G10

Glenluce Caravan Park 18 caravans, sleeps 4-6, min let 2 nights, £83-£115, Apr-Oct, bus nearby, rail 10 mls, airport 50 mls

Glenluce Caravan Park, Glenluce, Wigtownshire
☎ *Glenluce (05813) 412/437*

Whitecairn Farm Caravan Park 20 caravans, sleeps 4-8, min let 2 nights, £49-£115, Apr-Oct, bus 1 ½ mls, rail 11 mls, ferry 11 mls

Mr & Mrs Rankin, Whitecairn Farm Caravan Park, Glenluce, Newton Stewart, Wigtownshire, DG8 0NZ
☎ *Glenluce (05813) 267*

1 bungalow, 2 pub rms, 2 bedrms, sleeps 4-5, £50-£100, Apr-Oct, bus ¾-1 ml, rail 12 mls

  🚽⚿ E ⇥ ⌀ ◎ 🗍 ⬚ ⬛ ▲ ☉ ❋ 🐾 P ⌇ 🏛 †   ⏲ ∪ ⬥ ⚲ ↯ ✗ 🐎 ฿

Mrs Rankin, 45 West View Road, Sutton Coldfield, West Midlands
☎ 021 378 1844

GLENMORISTON Inverness-shire Map Ref. 3H10

2 chalet/log cabins, 1 pub rm, 2 bedrms, sleeps 4-6, £98-£163, Mar-Oct, bus nearby, rail 37 mls, airport 40 mls

  🚽⚿ E ⇥ ⌀ ▥ 🗍 ⬚ ◎ 🗍 ⬚ 🗍 ▲ ☉ ❋ 🐾 P ⌇ 🏛 †   ⏲ ↯

Mrs M C Grant, Dundreggan, Glenmoriston, Inverness-shire, IV3 6YJ
☎ *Dalreichart (0320) 40207*

1 chalet/log cabin, 1 pub rm, 3 bedrms, sleeps 6, min let weekend, £122-£185, Mar-Oct, bus 8 mls, rail 35 mls, airport 48 mls

  🚽⚿ E ⇥ ⌀ ▥ 🗍 ◎ 🗍 ⬚ 🗍 ▲ ☉ 🐾 P ⌇ 🏛 ◿   ⏲ R 🐎 T

Blakes Holidays, Wroxham, Norwich, NR12 8DH
☎ *Wroxham (06053) 2917*

GLENSHEE Perthshire Map Ref. 4D12

5 cottages, 1-3 pub rms, 2-4 bedrms, sleeps 3-8, min let weekend (low season), £46-£104, Jan-Dec, bus 15 mls, rail 30 mls, airport 70 mls

  🚽⚿ E ⇥ ⌀ ◎ 🗍 🗍 ✂ ▲ ☉ ❋ 🐾 P ⌇ 🏛 †   ⏲ ∪ ↳ ⚲ ✗ 🐎

M MacKenzie Smith, Dalreoch, Enochdhu, Blairgowrie, Perthshire, PH10 7PF
☎ *Strathardle (025081) 280*

Dalnaglar Castle
GLENSHEE · PERTHSHIRE · (025 082) 232
Dalnagar is a fairytale castle situated in the heart of Glenshee near Royal Deeside and Pitlochry. It can accommodate large parties and on the estate are 4 recently converted cottages, each with its own character.
AA RECOMMENDED
Fishing, walking, pony trekking, horse riding and golfing can be enjoyed nearby.

up to COMMENDED
👑 👑 👑 👑

4 cottages, 1 east wing of castle, 1-2 pub rms, 2-11 bedrms, sleeps 2-40, min let weekend, £100-£900, Jan-Dec, bus 14 mls, rail 30 mls, airport 70 mls

  🚽⚿ E ⇥ ⌀ ⌀ 🗍 ◎ 🗍 ↳ ⬚ ▲ ☉ ❋ 🐾 P ⌇ 🏛 †   ⏲ ∪ ↳ ⚲ ✗ T

Mrs M N Burke, Dalnaglar Castle, Glenshee, Blairgowrie, Perthshire, PH10 7LP
☎ *Blacklunans (025082) 232*
Old style units in grounds of fairy tale style castle. Also castle accommodation for winter skiers.

3 cottages, 2 pub rms, 2 bedrms, sleeps 2-7, min let 3 nights, £80-£170, Jan-Dec, bus 13 mls, rail 22 mls, airport 35 mls

  🚽⚿ E ⇥ ⌀ ⌀ 🗍 ◎ 🗍 ⬚ ▲ ☉ ❋ 🐾 P ⌇ 🏛 †   ⏲ ∪ ↳ ⚲ ✗ T

Mr & Mrs J C Harvey, Drumore Self-Catering, Blacklunans, Blairgowrie, Perthshire, PH10 7LA
☎ *Blacklunans (025082) 218*

1 cottage, 1 bungalow, 1-2 pub rms, 3-4 bedrms, sleeps 6-8, min let weekend (low season), £70-£120, Jan-Dec, bus 11 mls, rail 26 mls

Mrs K Imlay, Easter Bleaton Farm, Blacklunans, Blairgowrie, Perthshire, PH10 7LJ
☎ Blacklunans (025082) 282

1 cottage, 1 pub rm, 1 bedrm, sleeps 4, min let weekend, £65-£80, Jan-Dec, bus 12 mls, rail 30 mls, airport 70 mls

Mrs A B Houstoun, Lintrathen Lodge, Kirriemuir, Angus, DD8 5JJ
☎ Lintrathen (05756) 228

1 bungalow, 2 pub rms, 2 bedrms, sleeps 4, £100-£145, Apr-Oct, bus 20 mls

MacKay's Agency, 30 Frederick St, Edinburgh, EH2 2JR
☎ 031 225 3539

GLENSHIEL Ross-shire Map Ref. 3F10

2 houses, 1 cottage, 2-3 pub rms, 3-9 bedrms, sleeps 6-15, £65-£230, Apr-Oct, rail 15 mls

Miss J Taylor, Dochfour Estate Office, Inverness, IV3 6JP
☎ Dochgarroch (046386) 218

1 cottage, 1 pub rm, 2 bedrms, sleeps 5, £50-£80, Apr-Oct, bus 1 ml, rail 16 mls

Mrs A MacRae, Shiel Bridge, Glenshiel, Kyle, Ross-shire

GLENTROOL, by Bargrennan Wigtownshire Map Ref. 1H9

APPROVED

Galloway Forest Park 6 houses, 1 pub rm, 3 bedrms, sleeps 5, min let 3 nights, from £66, Apr-Oct, bus nearby, rail 30 mls, airport 60 mls

(hillwalking, forest trails)

Forestry Commission, Forest Holidays, Dept SC1, 231 Corstorphine Rd, Edinburgh, EH12 7AT
☎ 031 334 0303
Semi detached cottages in rural village. Former forestry worker's homes.

GLENURQUHART Inverness-shire Map Ref. 4A9

5 chalet/log cabins, 1 pub rm, 3 bedrms, sleeps 6-8, min let 3 nights, £121-£193, Apr-Nov, bus nearby, rail 20 mls, airport 26 mls

Mrs Lyon, Kilmartin Estates Ltd, Kilmartin Farm, Glenurquhart, Inverness-shire, IV3 6TN
☎ Glenurquhart (04564) 327

Tor Croft Holiday Chalets 5 chalet/log cabins, 1 pub rm, 2 bedrms, sleeps 6, min let weekend, £70-£200, Apr-Oct, bus 3 mls, rail 18 mls, airport 27 mls

Mrs E MacKintosh, Achmony, Drumnadrochit, Inverness-shire, IV3 6UX
☎ Drumnadrochit (04562) 357

VAT is shown at 15%: changes in this rate may affect prices.

149

GOLSPIE Sutherland Map Ref. 4B6

2 cottages, 1-2 pub rms, 2-3 bedrms, sleeps 4-5, £64-£119, Mar-Oct, rail 1 ½ mls

Sutherland Estates Office, Duke Street, Golspie, Sutherland, KW10 6RR
☎ *Golspie (04083) 3268*

APPROVED

1 bungalow, 1 pub rm, 3 bedrms, sleeps 5, £50-£120, Jan-Dec, bus 1 ½ mls, rail 1 ½ mls, airport 60 mls

Mr J M L Scott, Priory House, Priory Road, Stamford, Lincolnshire
☎ *Stamford(0780)63365(eve/wknd)52075(day)*
Traditional style timber bungalow in woodland setting behind village. Superb views over sea and hills.

1 house, 1 cottage, 2 pub rms, 3-4 bedrms, sleeps 7-12, from £100, Jan-Dec, bus 1 ml, rail 3 mls

Mrs N Grant, Deo Greine, Backies, Golspie, Sutherland, KW10 6SE
☎ *Golspie (04083) 3106*

COMMENDED

3 chalet/log cabins, 1 pub rm, 1-2 bedrms, sleeps 2-4, min let weekend, £100-£160, mid Apr-mid Oct, bus 400 yds, rail 500 yds, airport 70 mls

J D Norris, Golf Links Hotel, Golspie, Sutherland, KW10 6TT
☎ *Golspie (04083) 3408*
Semi detached units in grounds of small hotel. Overlooks hotel lawn. Within easy reach of golf course.

by GOLSPIE Sutherland Map Ref. 4B6

1 house, 1 cottage, 1-2 pub rms, 2-3 bedrms, sleeps 5-8, min let weekend, £60-£120, Jan-Dec, bus nearby, rail 1 ml, airport 60 mls

Mrs Mccall, Culmaily Farm, Golspie, Sutherland, KW1 6TA
☎ *Golspie (04083) 3275/3154*

GORTHLECK Inverness-shire Map Ref. 4A10

1 cottage, 1 pub rm, 3 bedrms, sleeps 6, £50-£90, Mar-Oct, bus ¼ ml

Mrs Fraser, Gorthleck Mains, Gorthleck, Inverness-shire
☎ *Gorthleck (04563) 282*

GOTT BAY Isle of Tiree, Argyll Map Ref. 1A2

Tiree Lodge Hotel 5 flats, 1 pub rm, 1 bedrm, sleeps 5, min let 1 night, £60-£120, Jan-Dec, ferry 1 ml, airport 6 mls

Tiree Lodge Hotel, Gott Bay, Isle of Tiree, Argyll
☎ *Scarinish (08792) 368*

GOURDON Kincardineshire Map Ref. 4G12

Gourdon Caravan Park 10 caravans, sleeps 4-6, min let weekend, £42-£105, Apr-Oct, bus nearby, rail 10 mls

Mrs K Greaves, Gourdon Caravan Park, Gourdon, Montrose, Kincardineshire, DD10 0LA
☎ Gourdon (0561) 61475

GOUROCK Renfrewshire Map Ref. 1G5

Cloch Caravan Park 35 caravans, sleeps 4-6, min let 2-3 nights, £61-£181, Apr-Oct, bus 300 yds, rail 2 ½ mls, airport 35 mls

Cloch Caravans, The Cloch, Gourock, Renfrewshire, PA19 IBA
☎ Gourock (0475) 32675

GRANTOWN-ON-SPEY Moray Map Ref. 4C9

COMMENDED
♔♔

1 house, 1 pub rm, 3 bedrms, sleeps 6, £60-£115, Apr-Oct, bus 250 yds, rail 11 mls, airport 35 mls

(bowling)

Mrs G G Turnbull, Reidhaven, Grantown-on-Spey, Moray
☎ Grantown-on-Spey (0479) 2061
Self contained wing of victorian house. Close to woods and River Spey. Near town centre. Own garden.

---

1 cottage, 2 pub rms, 3 bedrms, sleeps 6, min let 2 weeks, from £60, Apr-Oct, bus ¼ ml, rail 15 mls, airport 25 mls

Mrs J R Allan, 35 Heriot Row, Edinburgh, EH3 6ES
☎ 031 225 3581

---

3 caravans, sleeps 6, min let 2 nights, from £45, Apr-Oct, bus 3 mls, rail 22 mls, airport 32 mls

Mr J Miller, Rynaballoch Farm, Cromdale, Grantown-on-Spey, Moray, PH26 3LW
☎ Advie (08075) 231

---

2 caravans, sleeps 6-8, min let 1 night, from £50, Apr-Oct, bus 1 ml, rail 15 mls, airport 35 mls

Mrs M Shand, Lyne Macgregor, Grantown-on-Spey, Moray, PH26 3PR
☎ Grantown-on-Spey (0479) 2473

COMMENDED
♔♔

1 house, 1 pub rm, 3 bedrms, sleeps 6-7, £60-£150, Jan-Dec, bus nearby, rail 14 mls

Mrs E Mackay, 8 Merchiston Gardens, Edinburgh, EH10 5DD
☎ 031 337 4591

---

1 cottage, 3 pub rms, 2 bedrms, sleeps 4, £80-£105, Apr-Oct, bus 1 ml, rail 14 mls, airport 36 mls

Mrs J Bulmer, Honeywood, Westwood Road, Windlesham, Surrey
☎ Ascot (0990) 22125/(0479) 2966 (May-Sep)

VAT is shown at 15%: changes in this rate may affect prices.

COMMENDED

5 houses, 1 pub rm, 3 bedrms, sleeps 6, min let 3 nights, £90-£245, Jan-Dec, bus nearby, rail 14 mls, airport 30 mls

Mr & Mrs Lawson, Arnish, Market Road, Grantown-on-Spey, Moray, PH26 3HP
☎ *Grantown-on-Spey (0479) 2339*
Modern, purpose built lodges on private secluded site near centre of small town. Ample parking.

Grantown-on-Spey Caravan Site 1 caravan, sleeps 5, min let weekend, £60-£85, Apr-Oct, bus ¼ ml, rail 15 mls, airport 34 mls

Mrs Butcher, Mondhuie, Nethybridge, Inverness-shire, PH25 3DF
☎ *Nethybridge (047982) 331*

1 house, 2 pub rms, 3 bedrms, sleeps 6-8, min let weekend, £95-£160, Jan-Dec, bus nearby, rail 11 mls, airport 40 mls

Miss Linda MacLennan, 13 High Street, Grantown-on-Spey, Moray
☎ *Aviemore (0479) 810176(day)/3011(eve)*

1 flat, 1 pub rm, 2 bedrms, sleeps 4-5, £70-£110, Jan-Dec

Mr Nigel Boyd, 14 Ailsa Drive, Giffnock, Glasgow, G46 6RL
☎ *041 638 8745*

1 cottage, 1 pub rm, 3 bedrms, sleeps 6, £85-£130, Apr-Nov, bus 1 ml, rail 15 mls, airport 30 mls

Mrs R Donaldson, The Hawthorn, Old Spey Bridge, Grantown-on-Spey, Moray
☎ *Grantown-on-Spey (0479) 2016*

1 house, 1 pub rm, 3 bedrms, sleeps 6, £100-£150, May-Oct, bus 500 yds, rail 12 mls

Mrs M Mellor, Lilac Cottage, Roundyhill, Forfar, Angus, DD8 1QD
☎ *Kirriemuir (0575) 72478/(0307) 67422*

by GRANTOWN-ON-SPEY Moray Map Ref. 4C9

1 house, 2 pub rms, 3 bedrms, sleeps 6, min let weekend, £90-£150, Mar-early Jan, bus 1 ml, rail 12 mls, airport 30 mls

Mrs P M Laing, Craggan, Grantown-on-Spey, Moray
☎ *Grantown-on-Spey (0479) 2120*

GRAVIR Isle of Lewis, Western Isles Map Ref. 3D5

1 cottage, 1 pub rm, 2 bedrms, sleeps 8, from £59, Jan-Dec, bus 1 ml, ferry 28 mls, airport 30 mls

Mrs Nellie A Kennedy, 7 Orinsay, Lochs, Isle of Lewis, Western Isles
☎ *Gravir (085188) 394*

GRETNA Dumfriesshire Map Ref. 2D10

1 house, 1 pub rm, 3 bedrms, sleeps 6-9, min let weekend, £70-£100, Jan-Dec, bus nearby

G Rome, Nivenhill, Gretna, Dumfriesshire
☎ *Gretna (0461) 38338*

GROGPORT, by Carradale Argyll Map Ref. 1E6

1 house, 1 cottage, 2-3 pub rms, 1-5 bedrms, sleeps 2-10, £60-£250, Jan-Dec, bus 4 mls, rail 70 mls, airport 22 mls

Mr Arthur, Grogport Old Manse, Grogport, by Carradale, Argyll
☎ *Carradale (05833) 255*

GRULINE Isle of Mull, Argyll Map Ref. 1D2

1 flat, 2 cottages, 1 pub rm, 1-2 bedrms, sleeps 2-8, min let 2 nights, £91-£150, Mar-Oct, bus 3 mls, ferry 14 mls, airport 4 mls

Mr W G Thomson, Gruline Home Farm, by Salen, Aros, Isle of Mull, Argyll, PA71 6HR
☎ *Aros (06803) 437*
Variety of units in country location, 3 mls (5 km) from shops, post office, garage and eating places.

1 cottage, 1 pub rm, 3 bedrms, sleeps 6, £80-£142, May-Oct, bus 3 mls, ferry 13 mls

Mrs M J B Scott, The Vicarage, Thorp Arch, Wetherby, Yorkshire
☎ *Boston Spa (0937) 842430*

2 flats, 1 pub rm, 2 bedrms, sleeps 4-6, £25-£150, Jan-Dec, bus 2 ½ mls, ferry 6 mls, airport 3 mls

(birdwatching)
2 caravans, sleeps 6, £25-£140, Jan-Dec, bus 2 ½ mls, ferry 6 mls, airport 3 mls

Mrs Gunning, Torlochan, Gruline, Isle of Mull, Argyll
☎ *Aros (06803) 380*

GUARDBRIDGE, by St Andrews Fife Map Ref. 2D2

1 cottage, 1 pub rm, 2 bedrms, sleeps 4, £80-£100, Jun-Sep, bus nearby, rail 2 mls, airport 12 mls

Mrs H Christie-Douglas, Seggie House, Cupar Road, Guardbridge, by St Andrews, Fife, KY16 0UP
☎ *Leuchars (033483) 209*

GULLANE East Lothian Map Ref. 2E4

1 flat, 1 pub rm, 2 bedrms, sleeps 4-6, min let 2 weeks, from £115, Jan-Dec

East Lothian Co-operative Society Ltd, 1-9 Church Street, Tranent, East Lothian
☎ *Tranent (0875) 610551*

VAT is shown at 15%: changes in this rate may affect prices.

153

by HADDINGTON East Lothian Map Ref. 2E5

MONKSMUIR CARAVAN PARK

Haddington.   Tel: (0620) 860 340

Centrally situated in beautiful East Lothian, with miles of sandy beaches, trout fishing nearby. Delightful small site on A1 with easy access by car to Edinburgh. 12 golf courses within 12 miles.

Golf Package available £21 for 5 days golf on four different courses: North Berwick East: Dunbar, Winterfield; Haddington, Amisfield; Musselburgh, Monktonhall.

Accommodation is in our luxury 4/6 berth Caravans which have colour TV, fridge, showers, flush toilets, electricity, gas cookers, gas fires and are fully equipped to STB standards. There is a shop, cafe, launderette, showers, public telephone, children's play area on the site.

AA ▶ ▶ ▶   RAC Listed

Monksmuir Caravan Park 5 caravans, sleeps 4-6, min let 1 night, £50-£180, Apr-Oct, bus nearby, rail 8 mls

 ♿ ᵂᶜ E 🏠 📷 🎣 ▯ 🔌 🛏 📺 🖊 ☕ ☺ P ✂ 🎿 ⛰ ⛳   🎣 ♉ J ∪ ⚓ ▸ T

Mr & Mrs Inglis, Monksmuir Caravan Park, by Haddington, East Lothian, EH41 3SB
☎ *East Linton (0620) 860340*

HARRAY Orkney Map Ref. 5B11

1 caravan, sleeps 4, min let weekend, from £35, Apr-Oct, bus nearby, ferry 8 mls, airport 12 mls

 ♿ ᵂᶜ 📷 ▯ 🎣 P †   J ▸ ✗ ▣ 🐴

Mrs C Copland, Appiehouse, Harray, Orkney, KW17 2JR
☎ *Harray (085677) 224*

HAUGH OF GLASS, by Huntly Aberdeenshire Map Ref. 4H9

1 cottage, 1 pub rm, 2 bedrms, sleeps 4-5, £45-£65, Apr-Oct, bus nearby, rail 7 mls, airport 40 mls

 ♿ ᵂᶜ E 🛒 📷 ▯ 🎣 ◎ ▯ ▯ 🖊 ☕ ☺ ❄ 🐴 P ✂ 🎿 †   J ∪ ▸

Mrs J Hay, Edinglassie, Huntly, Aberdeenshire, AB5 4YD
☎ *Glass (046685) 274*

   Prices shown are for guidance only. Please send SAE with each enquiry.

Woodburn House Caravan Park 9 caravans, sleeps 4-6, min let weekend, £45-£150, Apr-Oct, bus nearby, rail 15 mls, airport 50 mls

     [symbols]

Mr & Mrs Alexander, Woodburn House, Haugh of Urr, Castle Douglas, Kirkcudbrightshire, DG7 3JR
☎ *Haugh of Urr (055666) 217*

HAUGH OF URR AREA Kirkcudbrightshire Map Ref. 2B10

2 cottages, 2 bungalows, 1 pub rm, 3 bedrms, sleeps 5-7, from £70, Apr-Oct

     [symbols]

G M Thomson & Company, 27 King Street, Castle Douglas, Kirkcudbrightshire, DG7 1AB
☎ *Castle Douglas (0556) 2701*

---

by HAWICK Roxburghshire Map Ref. 2E8

Hazeldean Holiday Centre 12 chalet/log cabins, 1 pub rm, 2-3 bedrms, sleeps 5-6, min let weekend, £124-£263, Jan-Dec, bus 3 mls, rail 50 mls, airport 50 mls

     [symbols]

Hazeldean Holiday Centre, Hassendeanburn, Denholm, Hawick, Roxburghshire
☎ *Denholm (045087) 373*   **(See colour ad. 8 p. xxxiv)**

HELMSDALE Sutherland Map Ref. 4C5

1 cottage, 1 pub rm, 1 bedrm, sleeps 2, £55, Jan-Dec, bus nearby, rail 400 yds

     [symbols]

Mrs E McAngus, Glebe House, Sutherland Street, Helmsdale, Sutherland, KW8 6LQ
☎ *Helmsdale (04312) 682*

---

by HELMSDALE Sutherland Map Ref. 4C5

1 cottage, 2 pub rms, 3 bedrms, sleeps 6, min let weekend (low season), £50-£100, Jan-Dec, bus nearby, rail 6 mls

     [symbols]

Mrs E A Shale, Loth School House, by Helmsdale, Sutherland, KW8 6HP
☎ *Helmsdale (04312) 285*

HOLM Orkney Map Ref. 5B11

6 chalet/log cabins, 1 pub rm, 1-3 bedrms, sleeps 2-7, min let weekend, £60-£200, Jan-Dec, bus nearby, ferry 15 mls, airport 5 mls

     [symbols]

Commodore Motel, St Mary's, Holm, Orkney, KW17 2RU
☎ *Holm (085678) 319*

HOPEMAN Moray Map Ref. 4D7

8 chalet/log cabins, 6 flats, 1 pub rm, 1-2 bedrms, sleeps 4-6, min let weekend, £50-£120, Apr-Oct, bus ½ ml, rail 6 mls, airport 40 mls

     [symbols]

Mr & Mrs K McKerron, Hopeman Lodge, Hopeman, Elgin, Moray, IV30 2YA
☎ *Hopeman (0343) 830245*

VAT is shown at 15%: changes in this rate may affect prices.

Station Caravan Park 16 caravans, sleeps 6, min let 2 nights, £49-£154, Apr-Oct, bus 400 yds, rail 6 mls

Station Caravan Park, West Beach Road, Harbour Street, Hopeman, Elgin, Moray, IV30 2RU
☎ *Hopeman (0343) 830880*

by HOPEMAN Moray Map Ref. 4D7

1 chalet/log cabin, 4 bedrms, sleeps 4, min let 2 nights, £45-£75, Apr-Oct, bus ½ ml, rail 6 mls, airport 30 mls

Mrs Elizabeth Beaton, Keam School House, Hopeman, Moray, IV30 2YB
☎ *Hopeman (0343) 830301*

HOWNAM Roxburghshire Map Ref. 2F7

1 cottage, 1 pub rm, 2 bedrms, sleeps 5, min let weekend, £65-£100, May-Oct, bus 7 mls, rail 35 mls, airport 48 mls

D Tweedie, Buchtrig, Hownam, Jedburgh, Roxburghshire, TD8 6NJ
☎ *Camptown (08354) 230*

APPROVED
♛ ♛

2 cottages, 1 pub rm, 2-3 bedrms, sleeps 4-6, min let weekend, £55-£145, Jan-Dec, bus 4 mls, rail 26 mls

Mrs J Harris, Greenhill, Hownam, by Kelso, Roxburghshire
☎ *Morebattle (05734) 505*
Stone built cottage and bothy in courtyard of former shooting lodge. Games room. Nearest village 1ml.

HOY, Isle of Orkney Map Ref. 5A11

1 chalet/log cabin, 1 pub rm, 2-3 bedrms, sleeps 5-7, min let weekend (low season), £50-£80, Apr-Oct, ferry 5 ½-13 mls, airport 24 mls

(birdwatching, hillwalking, climbing)

1 caravan, sleeps 5-7, min let weekend (low season), £40-£55, Apr-Oct, ferry 5½ mls;13 mls, airport 24 mls

(bird watching, hill walking, climbing)

Mrs D A Rendall, Glen, Rackwick, Isle of Hoy, Orkney, KW16 3NJ
☎ *Hoy (085679) 262*

1 bungalow, 1 pub rm, 3 bedrms, sleeps 10, min let 1 night, from £30, Jan-Dec, ferry 1 ml

Mrs McLaren, Northness, Lyness, Hoy, Orkney, KW16 3NY
☎ *Hoy (085679) 301*

HUNA Caithness Map Ref. 4D2

Huna Caravan Site 1 caravan, sleeps 6, min let 1 night, £50-£75, Apr-Oct, bus 17 mls, rail ¼ ml

Mr J Campbell, 15 Shore Street, Thurso, Caithness
☎ *Thurso (0847) 63524*

Prices shown are for guidance only. Please send SAE with each enquiry.

HUNTLY Aberdeenshire Map Ref. 4F9

2 bungalows, 1 pub rm, 3 bedrms, sleeps 6, min let weekend, £50-£120, Jan-Dec, bus 2 ½ mls, rail 6 mls, airport 40 mls

  🛇 ⚏ E ⇥ ⌀ ❒ ◉ ☐ ❏ ⊙ ✿ 🐾 🅿 ⛄ 🎖 † ⛰   ♪ ∪ ↾ ⁄ 🐾

Mrs Gordon, Tillyminate, Gartly, by Huntly, Aberdeenshire, AB5 4OS
☎ *Gartly (046688) 207*

---

1 chalet/log cabin, 1 pub rm, 2 bedrms, sleeps 6, £40-£120, Apr-Sep, bus 1 ml, rail 1 ml, airport 33 mls

  🛇 ⚏ E ⇥ ⌀ ▦ ❒ ◉ ☐ ❏ 🖴 ⊙ ✿ 🅿 ⛄ 🎖 † ⛰   ☂ ⚲ ♪ ∪ ↾ ✗ 🐾 🐾 T

Mrs A Stewart, Gibston House, Huntly, Aberdeenshire, AB5 4UN
☎ *Huntly (0466) 2805*

---

by HUNTLY Aberdeenshire Map Ref. 4F9

up to
COMMENDED
👑 👑 👑

Gordon Holiday Cottages 3 cottages, 1 pub rm, 1-2 bedrms, sleeps 2-6, min let weekend (low season), from £70, Jan-Dec, bus nearby, rail 5 mls, airport 35 mls

  🛇 ⚏ E 🏠 ⌀ ❒ ◉ ☐ ❏ ⁄ 🖴 ⊙ ✿ 🐾 🅿 ⛄ 🎖 ⛰ 🌐   ☂ ⚲ ♪ ∪ ↾ ⁄ ⚱
✗ 🐾 T (cycle hire)

J T Cosgrove, 118 Kidmore End Road, Emmer Green, Reading, Berks, RG4 8SL
☎ *Reading (0734) 472524/(046688) 277*
Traditional railway cottages, near level crossing. Large enclosed garden, clock golf, cycle hire.

AWAITING
INSPECTION

1 cottage, 1 pub rm, 3 bedrms, sleeps 8, min let weekend, £65-£100, Jan-Dec, bus 1 ½ mls, rail 4 mls, airport 35 mls

  🛇 ⚏ E ⇥ ⌀ ▦ ❒ ◉ ☐ ❏ ⁄ 🖴 ✿ 🐾 🅿 ⛄ 🎖 ⇥ ⛰   ☂ ⚲ ♪ ∪ ↾ ⁄ ⚱ ✗
🐾 🐾 T

Mrs Grant, Faich-Hill Farm, Gartly, by Huntly, Aberdeenshire, AB5 4RR
☎ *Gartly (046688) 240*

---

1 cottage, 1 pub rm, 3 bedrms, sleeps 2-6, min let weekend, £40-£100, Jan-Dec, bus 3 mls, rail 3 mls, airport 40 mls

  🛇 ⚏ E ⇥ ⌀ ❒ ◉ ☐ ❏ 🖴 ⁄ ⊙ ✿ 🐾 🅿 ⛄ 🎖 † ⛰   ☂ ⚲ ♪ ∪ ↾ ✗ 🐾

Mrs A J Morrison, Haddoch Farm, Huntly, Aberdeenshire, AB5 4SL
☎ *Rothiemay (046681) 217*

---

1 cottage, 1 pub rm, 3 bedrms, sleeps 6, £45-£100, Jan-Dec, bus 2 mls, rail 1 ¾ mls, airport 38 mls

  🛇 ⚏ E ⇥ ⌀ ❒ ◉ ☐ ❏ 🖴 ✿ 🅿 †   ☂ ⚲ ♪ ∪ ↾ ✗ 🐾 🐾

Mrs M Stewart, Cocklarachy, Huntly, Aberdeenshire, AB5 4RA
☎ *Huntly (0466) 2760*

---

1 caravan, sleeps 6, min let weekend, £65-£75, Apr-Oct, bus 2 ½ mls, rail 5 mls, airport 40 mls

  🛇 ⚏ E 🏠 ⌀ ❒ ◉ ☐ ❏ ⊙ ✿ 🅿 ⛄ 🎖 † ⛰   ☂ ⚲ ♪ ∪ ↾ 🐾

Mrs Wilson, Whitestones of Tillathrowie, Gartly, by Huntly, Aberdeenshire, AB5 4SB
☎ *Gartly (046688) 247*

INCHMURRIN, Island of Loch Lomond, Dunbartonshire Map Ref. 1H4

2 flats, 1 pub rm, 4-5 bedrms, sleeps 10, £200-£290, Apr-Oct, bus 3 mls, rail 3 mls, airport 15 mls

🕭 ♿ E ⛁ 🔥 🛏 🍳 ◎ 🗄 🖵 ☺ ✳ 🐕 P ⛵ 🏛 ⛰ ⚐ 🔔 ✎ ♪ ∪ ⚠ ⚓ ➤ ⚒ R ✗ ⚑
⛄ T

Mr & Mrs T F Scott, Inchmurrin Hotel, Island of Inchmurrin, Loch Lomond, Dunbartonshire, G63 0JY
☎ *Arden (038985) 245*

INCHNADAMPH Sutherland Map Ref. 3H5

AWAITING INSPECTION

1 cottage, 1 pub rm, 3 bedrms, sleeps 8, £85-£115, Apr-Oct, bus 1 ml, rail 40 mls

🕭 ♿ E ⛁ 🔥 ◎ 🗄 ✎ ⛄ ☺ ✳ 🐕 P ⛵ 🏛 † ♪ ∪ ⚠ ⚓ ✗

Mrs E A Miles, 8 Longfield Drive, West Parley, Wimborne, Dorset, BH22 8TY
☎ *Bournemouth (0202) 571739*

INCHTURE Perthshire Map Ref. 2C2

👑 👑 👑

1 cottage, 3 pub rms, 3 bedrms, sleeps 6, £45-£100, Jan-Dec, bus 1 ml, rail 11 mls

🕭 ♿ E ⛁ 🔥 🛏 ◎ 🗄 🖵 🔲 ⛄ ☺ ✳ 🐕 P ⛵ 🏛 † ♪ ∪ ⚓ ✗ ⚑ ⛄ T

C A Acheson, Easter Ballindean Farm, Inchture, Perthshire, PH14 9QS
☎ *Inchture (0828) 86256*

INNERWICK, by Dunbar East Lothian Map Ref. 2F5

👑 👑

1 cottage, 2 pub rms, 2 bedrms, sleeps 4-5, £65-£90, Mar-Oct, bus 4 mls, rail 8 mls, airport 42 mls

🕭 ♿ E ⛁ 🔥 ◎ 🗄 🖵 ✎ ⛄ ☺ ✳ 🐕 P ⛵ 🏛 † ☞ ♪ ∪ ⚓ ⛄

Mrs K Macdonald, Aikengall Farm, Innerwick, by Dunbar, East Lothian
☎ *Innerwick (03684) 249*

INSCH Aberdeenshire Map Ref. 4F9

1 house, 4 cottages, 1-2 pub rms, 2-4 bedrms, sleeps 2-9, min let 2 nights, £65-£120, Mar-Nov, Jan-Dec (2 properties), bus ¼ ml-2 mls, rail 5-6 mls, airport 25 mls

🕭 ♿ E ⛁ 📞 🔥 🛏 ◎ 🗄 🖵 🔲 ⛄ ☺ 🐕 P ⛵ 🏛 † ♪ ∪ ➤ ✗ ⚑ ⛄ T

Ardlair Holiday Properties, Ardlair, Insch, Aberdeenshire, AB5 6YR
☎ *Kennethmont (04643) 250/434 (Mrs Grant)*

---

by INSCH Aberdeenshire Map Ref. 4F9

AWAITING INSPECTION

1 house, 2 cottages, 1-2 pub rms, 2-3 bedrms, sleeps 2-8, min let weekend, £70-£160, Jan-Dec, bus 2 mls, rail 6 mls, airport 28 mls

🕭 ♿ E ⛁ 📞 🔥 🛏 🍳 ◎ 🗄 🖵 🔲 ✎ ⛄ ☺ ✳ 🐕 P ✎ ⛵ 🏛 ⛁ ⛰ ✿ ♪ ∪
☞ ⚒ ✗ ⚑ ⛄ T (cycling)

Mrs K M Yeats, Auchmar Farm, Leslie, Insch, Aberdeenshire, AB5 6PJ
☎ *Kennethmont (04643) 254*

INSH, by Kingussie Inverness-shire Map Ref. 4B11

1 chalet/log cabin, 1 pub rm, 2-3 bedrms, sleeps 4-6, min let weekend, from £75, Jan-Dec, bus 2 mls, rail 5 mls, airport 45 mls

🕭 ♿ E ⛁ 🔥 🛏 🍳 ◎ 🗄 🖵 ⛄ ☺ ✳ 🐕 P ⛵ 🏛 † ⛰ ♪ ∪ ⚠ ☞ ⚒ ✗ ⚑

Mrs A Mackintosh, Annandale, Gordon Hall, Kingussie, Inverness-shire, PH21 1NR
☎ *Kingussie (05402) 560*

Prices shown are for guidance only. Please send SAE with each enquiry.

INVER, by Dunkeld Perthshire Map Ref. 2B1

1 caravan, sleeps 2, £45-£55, Mar-Oct, bus 500 yds, rail 1 ml

Mrs Taylor, Mill Timber, Inver, by Dunkeld, Perthshire
☎ *Dunkeld (03502) 587*

INVERARAY Argyll Map Ref. 1F3

Argyll Caravan Park 11 caravans, sleeps 6-8, min let 1 night, £75-£140, Apr-Oct, bus nearby, rail 15 mls/24 mls, airport 65 mls

Argyll Caravan Park, Inveraray, Argyll, PA32 8XT
☎ *Inveraray (0499) 2285*

2 caravans, sleeps 1-8, £55-£120, Mar-Oct, bus nearby, rail 23 mls, airport 70 mls

Mrs D Crawford, Brenchoille Farm, Inveraray, Argyll
☎ *Furnace (04995) 662*

7 cottages, 1 pub rm, 1-4 bedrms, sleeps 4-10, min let weekend, £90-£270, Jan-Dec, bus 300 yds

Mrs Semple, Killean, Inveraray, Argyll
☎ *Inveraray (0499) 2474*

1 house, 2 pub rms, 4 bedrms, sleeps 8, £80-£200, Apr-Oct

Mrs MacLean, Brickmakers Cottage, Lambourn, Woodlands, Newbury, Berks
☎ *Lambourn (0488) 71474*

2 flats, 3 pub rms, 3 bedrms, sleeps 4-8, £100-£200, Jan-Dec, bus nearby, rail 15-24 mls, airport 60 mls

The Factor, Argyll Estates Office, Cherry Park, Inveraray, Argyll, PA32 8XE
☎ *Inveraray (0499) 2203*

INVERARITY, by Forfar Angus Map Ref. 2D1

AWAITING INSPECTION

2 cottages, 1 pub rm, 2-3 bedrms, sleeps 5-6, min let weekend, £75-£125, Jan-Dec, bus nearby-400 yds, rail 8-9 mls, airport 8-9 mls

Mrs E J Pate, Kincreich, Inverarity, Forfar, Angus
☎ *Inverarity (030782) 340*

1 chalet/log cabin, 1 house, 1 flat, 1 cottage, 1 bungalow, 1 pub rm, 2 bedrms, sleeps 4, min let 2 nights, £75-£85, Apr-Oct, bus ½ ml, rail 15 mls, airport 15 mls

Mrs E Marsh, Carterhaugh, Mains of Kinnettles, by Forfar, Angus
☎ *Inverarity (030782) 314*

VAT is shown at 15%: changes in this rate may affect prices.

INVERBEG, by Luss Dunbartonshire Map Ref. 1G4

Inverbeg Caravan Park 15 caravans, sleeps 6-8, min let weekend, £80-£135, Apr-Oct, bus nearby, rail 12 mls, airport 33 mls

Inverbeg Caravan Park, Inverbeg, Luss, by Alexandria, Dunbartonshire, G83 8PD
☎ *Luss (043686) 267*

INVERBERVIE Kincardineshire Map Ref. 4G12

1 cottage, 1 pub rm, 1-2 bedrms, sleeps 4-5, £55-£65, Apr-Oct, bus nearby, rail 10 mls, airport 40 mls

Mrs J P Hardiker, 14 Fishermore Road, Flixton, nr Manchester
☎ *061 747 7993*

INVERGARRY Inverness-shire Map Ref. 3H11

High Garry Lodges 4 chalet/log cabins, 1 pub rm, 3 bedrms, sleeps 6, £75-£270, Jan-Dec, bus ½ ml, rail 20 mls, airport 50 mls

Hoseasons Holidays, Sunway House, Lowestoft, Suffolk, NR32 3LT
☎ *Lowestoft (0502) 62292 (quote ref: H37)*

Great Glen Water Park 40 chalet/log cabins, 1 pub rm, 2-3 bedrms, sleeps 4-7, min let 3 nights, £69-£299, Mar-Nov, bus 400 yds, rail 12 mls, airport 47 mls

Hoseasons Holidays, Sunway House, Lowestoft, Suffolk, NR32 3LT
☎ *Lowestoft (0502) 62292/(08093) 223*

1 cottage, 3 pub rms, 2 bedrms, sleeps 6-7, £85-£110, Apr-Oct, bus nearby, rail 16 mls, airport 42 mls

Mrs C Smith, Aberchalder Farm, Invergarry, Inverness-shire
☎ *Invergarry (08093) 260*

2 cottages, 1-2 pub rms, 1-2 bedrms, sleeps 2-4, £70-£185, Apr-Oct, bus 1 ml, rail 15 mls

Reception, Glengarry Castle Hotel, Invergarry, Inverness-shire, PH35 4HW
☎ *Invergarry (08093) 254*

Faichemard Farm Chalets 4 chalet/log cabins, 2 pub rms, 3 bedrms, sleeps 6, min let weekend (low season), £60-£120, Mar-Oct, bus 2 mls, rail 16 mls

(hillwalking, birdwatching)

3 caravans, sleeps 6, min let weekend (low season), from £50, Apr-Oct, bus 2 mls, rail 16 mls

(hill walking, birdwatching)

A & D Grant, Faichemard Farm, Invergarry, Inverness-shire, PH35 4HG
☎ *Invergarry (08093) 276*

1 house, 2 pub rms, 5 bedrms, sleeps 9, £95-£250, Apr-Oct, bus 8 ½ mls, rail 24 mls, airport 55 mls

 ♿ 🚽 E 🔌 📱 ⊙ 🗆 🗔 ⚓ ✳ 🐎 🅿 🎖 ➡ † 🐾   ♐ ∪

Mr A Sturgis, 12 Onslow Road, Walton On Thames, Surrey
☎ *Walton on Thames (0932) 220379*

---

by INVERGARRY Inverness-shire Map Ref. 3H11

> **COMMENDED**
> 👑 👑

1 flat, 1 pub rm, 2 bedrms, sleeps 6, min let 3 nights, £65-£170, Jan-Dec, bus 1 ml, rail 12 mls

♿ 🚽 E 📠 📱 ⛟ 🖵 ⊙ 🗆 🗄 🗔 ⚓ ⊙ ✳ 🐎 🅿 ⅋ 🎖 ➡ † 🐾   🎣 🐟 ♐ ∪ ⚠ 🛶 ✗ 🔋

Mrs Waugh, North Laggan Farmhouse, by Spean Bridge, Inverness-shire
☎ *Invergarry (08093) 335*

Peaceful, open countryside, superb views. Warm welcome, home-made bread. Hill walking excellent.

---

1 cottage, 1 pub rm, 2 bedrms, sleeps 4, £70-£150, Apr-Nov, bus 300 yds, rail 12 mls, airport 47 mls

♿ 🚽 E 🔌 📠 📱 ⛟ ⊙ 🗆 🗔 ⁄ ⚓ ⊙ ✳ 🐎 🅿 ⅋ 🎖 †   ♐ ∪ ⚠ 🛶 ✗ 🔋

Mr M Glover, 44 Lochalsh Crescent, Milton of Campsie, Glasgow, G65 8EZ
☎ *Lennoxtown (0360) 311104/041 339 6042*

INVERGLOY, by Spean Bridge Inverness-shire Map Ref. 3H11

3 caravans, sleeps 6, min let 1 night, £95-£150, Apr-Oct, bus 400 yds, rail 5 mls

♿ 🚽 E 📠 📱 ⚓ ⁄ 🗔 ✳ 🐎 🅿   ☍ ♐ ∪ ⚠ ➤ ⚓ 🛶 ✗

Mrs M H Cairns, Invergloy House, Invergloy, by Spean Bridge, Inverness-shire, PH34 4DY
☎ *Invergloy (039784) 281*

INVERIE Inverness-shire Map Ref. 3F11

Knoydart Peninsula Estate 1 house, 2 cottages, 2-3 pub rms, 1-5 bedrms, sleeps 2-8, £85-£350, Jan-Dec

♿ 🚽 E 🔌 📠 📱 ⛟ 🖵 ⊙ ⁄ 🗆 🕿 🗆 ⁄ ⚓ ⊙ ✳ 🐎 🅿 ⅋ 🎖 †   ♐ ⚠ ⚓ ⁄ 🔋 ♥

Mrs M McKenzie, Knoydart Estate Office, Inverie, by Mallaig, Inverness-shire
☎ *Mallaig (0687) 2331*

INVERINATE Ross-shire Map Ref. 3F10

1 house, 1 pub rm, 3 bedrms, sleeps 6, £50-£100, Jan-Dec, bus nearby, rail 10 mls, airport 72 mls

♿ 🚽 E 🔌 📠 📱 ⊙ 🗆 🗔 ⚓ ⊙ ✳ 🐎 🅿 🎖 🎖 †   ♐ ⚓ ➤ ✗ 🔋

Mrs Joan Douglas, Little Dalcross, Croy, Inverness, Inverness-shire, IV1 2PS
☎ *Croy (06678) 224*

INVERKEILOR, by Arbroath Angus Map Ref. 2E1

1 cottage, 1 pub rm, 2 bedrms, sleeps 4, £70-£100, Jan-Dec, bus 3 mls, rail 5 mls

♿ 🚽 E 🔌 📱 ⊙ 🗆 🗆 ⚓ ✳ 🐎 🅿 ⅋ 🎖 🎖 ➡ †   🎣 🐟 ☍ 🎣 ♐ ∪ ⚠ ⚓ ➤ ⁄ ✗ 🔋 🎍

Mrs Middleton, Ethie Mains, Inverkeilor, Arbroath, Angus
☎ *Inverkeilor (02413) 409*

INVERKEITHING Fife Map Ref. 2C4

1 flat, 1 pub rm, 1 bedrm, sleeps 2-3, min let weekend, £80, Jan-Dec, bus nearby, rail ½ ml, airport 7 mls

 ♿ wc E ⛽ 📷 ✐ 🖥 🍴 ☎ ◎ ∅ ⛺ ▱ ⬛ ☉ ✳ 🦃 🅿 ∥ ⛵ ▥ ⚓ † ⛰   ✕ ▓ ⊤

Mrs J E Singal, Nirvaana, 54 Hope Street, Inverkeithing, Fife, KY11 1LN
☎ *Inverkeithing (0383) 413876*

INVERKIRKAIG, by Lochinver Sutherland Map Ref. 3G5

1 chalet/log cabin, 1 pub rm, 2 bedrms, sleeps 5, from £70, Mar-Nov, bus nearby, rail 50 mls, ferry 37 mls, airport 110 mls

 ♿ wc E ⛽ ✐ 🖥 🍴 ◎ ☎ ☏ 🖥 ∅ ⬛ ☉ ✳ 🦃 🅿 ⛵ ▥ † ⛰   ♪ ⚐ ⚓ ⚓

(climbing, walking, birdwatching)

Mrs Mary C Ross, Tighnuilt, Inverkirkaig, Lochinver, Sutherland, IV27 4LR
☎ *Lochinver (05714) 233*
Modern 'A' line chalet with enclosed garden. In elevated position overlooking Inverkirkaig Bay.

INVERLUSSA Isle of Jura, Argyll Map Ref. 1D4

1 house, 2 cottages, 1-2 pub rms, 2-4 bedrms, sleeps 5-8, min let weekend, £10-£300, Jan-Dec, ferry 24 mls

 ♿ wc E ⛽ ✐ 🖥 ◎ 🍴 ⬛ 🦃 🅿 ⛵ ▥ †   ♪ ∪ ✓

Mrs Nelson, Ardlussa, Isle of Jura, Argyll
☎ *Jura (049682) 224*

INVERMORISTON Inverness-shire Map Ref. 4A10

1 flat, 1 pub rm, 1 bedrm, sleeps 4, min let weekend, £60-£95, Apr-Oct, rail 30 mls, airport 50 mls

 ♿ wc E 📷 ✐ 🖥 ◎ 🍴 ▱ ⬛ ☉ ✳ 🦃 🅿 ⛵ ▥ † ⛰   ♪ ∪ ⚐ ↗ ✓ ⚓ ✕ ▓ ⊤

Mrs W Billings, Johnnie's Point, Invermoriston, Inverness-shire, IV3 6YE
☎ *Glenmoriston (0320) 51205*

<table>
<tr>
<td>

AUTUMN
WINTER
SPRING

</td>
<td>

MINI BREAKS IN A MAGIC COUNTRY
Scotland offers great value for money all the year round and particularly outwith the main holiday months.

Whether its countryside or city centre, hotel or self-catering, there are hundreds of bargains to be found.

FREE BROCHURE FROM THE SCOTTISH TOURIST BOARD

</td>
</tr>
</table>

GLENMORISTON ESTATES LTD.

Glenmoriston Nr. Inverness IV3 6YA
Telephone (0320) 51202
Telex 8954667 VBSTLX G Quote Ref. GME

Glenmoriston starts at Invermoriston Village and follows the River Moriston up through a picturesque private estate — an ideal centre for walking and touring the Highlands. There are 17 chalets and 3 cottage/bungalows within walking distance of the village, each cleverly sited to provide maximum peace and privacy, and 4 chalets and 2 cottages further up the Glen offering complete privacy. All chalets have colour TV. All are superbly equipped and furnished for a labour saving holiday, but if the cook gets fed up there is always a welcome at the Glenmoriston Arms Hotel for meals and to savour the Estate's Old Farm Whisky.

Salmon and trout fishing is available at very reasonable prices both on the river and twenty hill lochs.

Please send SAE for brochure to:
Glenmoriston Estates Ltd. (STB), Glenmoriston,
Inverness IV3 6YA. Telephone: (0320) 51202.

up to
COMMENDED
🏵 🏵 🏵

21 chalet/log cabins, 2 cottages, 3 bungalows, 1-2 pub rms, 2-3 bedrms, sleeps 4-10, min let 4 nights (low season), £75-£235, Mar-Oct, bus ½ ml, rail 27 mls, airport 32 mls

Glenmoriston Estates Limited, Glenmoriston, by Inverness, Inverness, 1V3 6YA
☎ *Glenmoriston (0320) 51202*
Selection of units on highland estate. Some close to village, others further up 'The Glen'. Fishing.

4 caravans, sleeps 6, min let 2 nights (low season), £50-£175, Mar-Oct, bus nearby, rail 28 mls, airport 38 mls

Loch Ness Caravan & Camping Park, Invermoriston, Inverness-shire, IV3 6YE
☎ *Glenmoriston (0320) 51207*

INVERNESS Map Ref. 4B8

Torvean Caravan Park 10 caravans, sleeps 6, min let long weekend, from £75, Mar-Oct, bus nearby, rail 2 mls, airport 9 mls

G N R Sutherland, Caravan Sales, Glenurquhart Road, Inverness, IV3 6JL
☎ *Inverness (0463) 220582*

Bunchrew Caravan Park 9 caravans, sleeps 6, min let 2 nights, from £60, Apr-Sep, bus nearby, rail 3 mls, airport 10 mls

Bunchrew Caravans Ltd, Bunchrew, Inverness, IV3 6TD
☎ *Inverness (0463) 237802*

1 caravan, sleeps 6, £40-£70, May-Oct, bus 1 ml, rail 3 mls

Mrs B Fraser, Rosedale, Essich Road, Inverness, IV1 2AH
☎ *Inverness (0463) 234959*

3 caravans, sleeps 6, £45-£80, Apr-Oct

Mrs H MacIntosh, 13 Inshes Holdings, Inverness, IV1 2BG
☎ *Inverness (0463) 233830*

VAT is shown at 15%: changes in this rate may affect prices.

163

COMMENDED

1 bungalow, 1 pub rm, 2 bedrms, sleeps 4, £100-£150, Jan-Dec, bus nearby, rail 2 mls, airport 10 mls

Mrs P R Lyon, Camalaig, Dunvegan, Isle of Skye, Inverness-shire, IV55 8WA
☎ *Dunvegan (047022) 355*

Modern, semi detached unit with garden. Panoramic views south eastwards over town to Beauly Firth.

---

1 flat, 1 pub rm, 2 bedrms, sleeps 3-4, £90-£115, Jan-Dec, bus nearby, rail 1 ½ mls, airport 8 mls

Mrs C M MacLeod, 42 Island Bank Road, Inverness, IV2 4QT
☎ *Inverness (0463) 224692*

---

2 flats, 1 pub rm, 1-2 bedrms, sleeps 4, £85-£110, Apr-Oct, bus nearby, rail ¾ ml, airport 8 mls

Mrs M MacKay, 24 Damfield Road, Inverness, IV2 3HU
☎ *Inverness (0463) 237984*

---

1 house, 3 pub rms, 4 bedrms, sleeps 7, from £200, Jun-Nov, bus nearby, rail 1 ½ mls

Mr & Mrs Peter W Hay, Inver Lodge, Lochinver, Lairg, Sutherland
☎ *Lochinver (05714) 318*

---

1 bungalow, 1 pub rm, 3 bedrms, sleeps 5, £70-£170, Jan-Dec, bus nearby, rail 2 mls, airport 9 mls

Mrs A Mackenzie, 6A Green Drive, Inverness
☎ *Inverness (0463) 236763*

---

1 flat, 1 pub rm, 3 bedrms, sleeps 4-6, £85-£125, Jan-Dec, bus nearby, rail ½ ml, airport 7 mls

Mrs Bonsor, Culduthel Lodge, 14 Culduthel Road, Inverness
☎ *Inverness (0463) 240089*

---

1 flat, 1 pub rm, 2 bedrms, sleeps 4, £110-£130, Apr-Sep, bus ½ ml, airport 8 mls mls

Mr I Keir, 1a Lochalsh Road, Inverness
☎ *Inverness (0463) 223521/234117*

---

by INVERNESS Map Ref. 4B8

1 house, 1 cottage, 1-3 pub rms, 2-9 bedrms, sleeps 5-15, £95-£750, Apr-Oct

Finlayson Hughes, Bank House, 82 Atholl Road, Pitlochry, Perthshire, PH16 5BL
☎ *Pitlochry (0796) 2512*

Prices shown are for guidance only. Please send SAE with each enquiry.

INVERNESS AREA Map Ref. 4B8

4 houses, 10 cottages, 2 bungalows, 1-4 pub rms, 2-6 bedrms, sleeps 4-10, £65-£450, Apr-Oct

& ⓦ E 🛏 🍴 ⊚ ⌀ ▢ 🔲 🐕 P 🛒 ▥ † 🎣 ∪ △ ↗ ⚓ 🛍

Scottish Highland Holiday Homes, Wester Altourie, Abriachan, Inverness, Inverness, IV3 6LB

☎ *Dochgarroch (046386) 247*

INVERUGLAS Dunbartonshire Map Ref. 1G3

Loch Lomond Holiday Park 6 caravans, sleeps 6, min let weekend, £90-£140, Apr-Oct, bus nearby, rail 4 mls, airport 30 mls

& ⓦ E 🔥 ⌀ ⊘ 🔲 ⊡ ⊙ 🐕 P 🛒 ▥ 🔌 ⛰ 🎣 △ T

Halley Caravans Ltd, Glasgow Road, Milngavie, Glasgow, G62 6JP

☎ *041 956 1126/Inveruglas (03014) 224* **(See colour ad. 9 p. xxxiv)**

---

by INVERURIE Aberdeenshire Map Ref. 4G9

1 cottage, 1 pub rm, 3 bedrms, sleeps 6, min let weekend, £60-£100, Jan-Dec, bus 2 mls, rail 5 mls, airport 25 mls

& ⓦ E 🛏 ⌀ ▥ 🔲 P ⊚ 🔲 ▢ ⌀ 🚿 ▢ ❋ P 🛒 ▥ † ⛰ ⚡ 🔍 🎿 🎣 ∪ ↗ ✗ 🛍 T

Mrs R Skinner, Strathorn Farm, Pitcaple, by Inverurie, Aberdeenshire, AB5 9EJ

☎ *Old Rayne (04645) 204*

---

1 caravan, sleeps 4-5, min let weekend, £55-£80, Apr-Oct, bus ½ ml, rail 5 mls, airport 15 mls

& ⓦ E 🛏 ⌀ ⊚ 🔲 ▢ ❋ P 🛒 ▥ 🔌 † ⚡ 🔍 🎿 🎣 ∪ ⚡ ✗ 🛍 T (hillwalking, bird sauctuary)

Mrs G Royle, Old Mill of Durno, Pitcaple, by Inverurie, Aberdeenshire, AB5 9ED

☎ *Pitcaple (04676) 676*

IONA, Isle of Argyll Map Ref. 1B3

1 bungalow, 1 pub rm, 3 bedrms, sleeps 6, £100-£250, Jan-Dec

& ⓦ E 🔥 ⌀ ▥ ⊚ 🔲 ▢ ▢ ⊙ ❋ 🐕 P † 🎣 ∪ △ ⚡ ✗ 🛍 T

Mr G Grant, Achavaich, Isle of Iona, Argyll

☎ *Iona (06817) 338*

IRVINE Ayrshire Map Ref. 1G7

8 caravans, sleeps 4-8, min let weekend, £58-£121, Apr-Sep, bus nearby, rail 4 mls, airport 13 mls

& ⓦ 🗓 🛏 ⌀ ⌀ ▢ 🔲 📞 🔲 ▢ ▢ ⊙ 🐕 P 🛒 ▥ † ⛰ 🔍 ⊕ 🎣 ∪ △ ⚡ ↗ 🔧 🛍 T

Mr J Sim, Cunninghamhead Estate Caravan Park, Irvine, by Kilmarnock, Ayrshire, KA3 2PE

☎ *Torranyard (029485) 238*

ISLE ORNSAY Isle of Skye, Inverness-shire Map Ref. 3E10

1 caravan, sleeps 6, £70-£100, Apr-Oct, bus nearby, rail 7-14 mls, ferry 7-14 mls, airport 10 mls

& ⓦ E 🔥 ⌀ 🔲 ⌀ 🔲 🐕 P † ⛰ 🎣 ∪ ⚡ ↗ ✗ 🛍

Mrs Prior, Duisdale, Isle Ornsay, Sleat, Isle of Skye, Inverness-shire

☎ *Isle Ornsay (04713) 212*

VAT is shown at 15%: changes in this rate may affect prices.

ISLE OF WHITHORN Wigtownshire Map Ref. 1H11

1 chalet/log cabin, 1 pub rm, 2 bedrms, sleeps 4-5, £45-£90, Apr-Oct, bus nearby

   ♿ ᴡᴄ E ⊣ ⌀ ▥ ◉ ⎕ ⊡ ◎ ▱ ✳ ⋔ **P** ♋ ▥ †   ↗ Ü △ ⚴ ⚓ ✗ 🛍

Mrs Amey, Millands Farm, Monreith, Whithorn, Wigtownshire, DG8 9LS
☎ *Port William (09887) 306*

BURROWHEAD HOLIDAY FARM

Burrowhead Holiday Farm. Spacious holiday site of over 100 acres situated on coast overlooking Luce Bay. Modern toilet blocks with showers and constant hot water. Amenities on site include launderette, shop, cocktail bar, lounge bar with entertainment. Children's supervised playroom open most evenings, amusement arcade, teenage discotheques, swimming pool and carry-out cafe, ideally situated for touring, golf, sea and fresh water fishing. Advance booking not necessary. Dogs allowed.

For details send SAE to:
Burrowhead Holiday Farm, Isle of Whithorn, Newton Stewart, Wigtownshire
or telephone Whithorn (09885) 252.

10 chalet/log cabins, 1 pub rm, 2 bedrms, sleeps 6, min let weekend, £70-£145, Apr-Oct, bus 2 mls, rail 28 mls

♿ ᴡᴄ E ⊣ ⌀ ⌀ ⎕ ⊡ ⊙ ⋔ **P** ♋ ▥ ⚖ ◕ 🟉   ↖ ᵜ Ü △ ⚴ ⚓ **R** ✗ 🛍 ♀ ♬ **T**
(sub-aqua)

Burrowhead Holiday Farm, Isle of Whithorn, Newton Stewart, Wigtownshire, DG8 8OA
☎ *Whithorn (09885) 252*

COMMENDED
♛ ♛ ♛

1 house, 2 pub rms, 3 bedrms, sleeps 8, min let weekend (low season), £50-£120, Jan-Dec, bus 300 yds, rail 30 mls, airport 70 mls

♿ ᴡᴄ E ⊣ ⌀ ▥ ⌺ ◉ ⎕ ⊡ ◎ ▱ ⊙ ✳ ⋔ **P** ♋ ▥   ᵜ ↗ Ü △ ⚴ ⚓ ✗ 🛍

1 caravan, sleeps 6, min let weekend (low season), £35-£60, Easter-Oct, bus ½ ml, rail 30 mls, airport 70 mls

♿ ᴡᴄ E ⌀ ⌺ ⌀ ⎕ ⊡ **P** ♋ ▥ †   ᵜ ↗ Ü △ ⚴ ⚓ ✗ 🛍 🛁

Mrs W Brown, Boyach Farm, Whithorn, Wigtownshire, DG8 8LA
☎ *Whithorn (09885) 324*
Terraced stone built cottage with small garden to rear overlooking harbour.

by ISLE OF WHITHORN Wigtownshire Map Ref. 1H11

COMMENDED
♛ ♛ ♛

2 cottages, 1 pub rm, 2 bedrms, sleeps 5, min let weekend (low season), £55-£75, Apr-Oct, bus 1 ml, rail 36 mls, airport 70 mls

♿ ᴡᴄ E ⊣ ⌀ ▥ ⌺ ◉ ⎕ ⊡ ▱ ⊙ ✳ ⋔ **P** ♋ ▥   ᵜ Ü △ ⚴ ⚓ ✗ 🛍 🛁

Mrs D McIlwraith, Stannock Farm, Isle of Whithorn, Wigtownshire, DG8 8JF
☎ *Whithorn (09885) 266*
Semi detached stone built units on working farm. Access via farm track, 1ml (2km) from farmhouse.

JEDBURGH Roxburghshire Map Ref. 2E7

Jedwater Caravan Park 5 caravans, sleeps 6, min let 1 night, from £50, Apr-Oct, bus nearby

♿ ᴡᴄ E ⌀ ⌀ ⌺ ⌀ ⎕ ⌾ ⎕ ⊡ ◎ ⁄ ▱ ⊙ ⋔ **P** ♋ ▥ ⟿ ⚖ ◕   ᵜ 🏳 ♀ ↗ Ü ⟼
✗

Jedwater Caravan Park, Jedburgh, Roxburghshire
☎ *Camptown (08354) 219*

Prices shown are for guidance only. Please send SAE with each enquiry.

1 cottage, 1 pub rm, 3 bedrms, sleeps 4-6, min let 3 nights, £60-£100, Apr-Oct, bus 5 mls, rail 30 mls, airport 50 mls

Mrs A A Scott, Dolphinston, Jedburgh, Roxburghshire
☎ *Camptown (08354) 225*

---

1 cottage, 1 pub rm, 3 bedrms, sleeps 6, £50-£90, Mar-Oct, bus 2 ½ mls, airport 47 mls

Mrs Betty Forster, Netherwells Farm, Jedburgh, Roxburghshire, TD8 6QZ
☎ *Jedburgh (0835) 62530*

by JEDBURGH Roxburghshire Map Ref. 2E7

up to
COMMENDED

3 houses, 2 flats, 6 cottages, 1-2 pub rms, 1-3 bedrms, sleeps 2-6, min let weekend, £95-£800, Jan-Dec, bus nearby, rail 40 mls, airport 45 mls

(free entry to woodland centre)

Lothian Estates Office, Bonjedward, Jedburgh, Roxburghshire, TD8 6UF
☎ *Jedburgh (0835) 62201*
Individual properties in rural setting all within 8 miles of Jedburgh and Queen Mary's House.

JOHNSHAVEN Kincardineshire Map Ref. 4G12

1 flat, 1 pub rm, 1 bedrm, sleeps 2-4, £55-£80, Jan-Dec, bus nearby, rail 8 mls, airport 35 mls

Mrs J P Beattie, Nirvana, South Street, Johnshaven, Montrose, Kincardineshire, DD10 0HE
☎ *Inverbervie (0561) 62533*

by KEITH Banffshire Map Ref. 4E8

2 chalet/log cabins, 1 pub rm, 2 bedrms, sleeps 6, min let weekend, from £65, Apr-Oct, bus 2 mls, rail 3 mls, airport 45 mls

North East Farm Chalets, Mrs J M Shaw, Sheriffston, Elgin, Moray, IV30 3LA
☎ *Lhanbryde (034384) 2695*

---

1 bungalow, 1 pub rm, 3 bedrms, sleeps 6, £60-£100, Jan-Dec, bus 1 ½ mls, rail 3 mls

Mrs E Morrison, Bush of Muldearie Farm, Keith, Banffshire, AB5 3YS
☎ *Keith (05422) 2669*

---

1 cottage, 2 pub rms, 4 bedrms, sleeps 6-7, £80-£150, Jan-Dec, bus 1 ml, rail 6 mls, airport 55 mls

Estate Office, Drummuir, Keith, Banffshire, AB5 3JE
☎ *Drummuir (054281) 225*

VAT is shown at 15%: changes in this rate may affect prices.

KELSO Roxburghshire Map Ref. 2F6

Maxmill Park
0573 24468
KELSO · SCOTTISH BORDERS

Luxury self-catering apartments for 2, 4 or 6/8 persons, ideal for disabled. Fully equipped to a very high standard: double glazing, central heating, linen, towels, colour TV. Telephone. Launderette on premises. Good touring centre, unspoiled walking, riding countryside. Easy access for fishing on Tweed, Teviot. Autumn to Spring Mini-Breaks. OPEN ALL YEAR.

Colour brochure: Mr and Mrs Peter Halley, Resident Proprietors.

AA Listed ♔♔ *Approved* ♔♔♔ *Commended*

up to
COMMENDED
♔♔♔

11 apartments, 1 pub rm, 1-2 bedrms, sleeps 2-8, min let weekend, £65-£220, Jan-Dec, bus nearby, rail 20 mls, airport 40 mls

Mr & Mrs Halley, Maxmill Park, Kelso, Roxburghshire
☎ *Kelso (0573) 24468*
Situated in secluded garden on town outskirts. All apartments double glazed with central heating.

♔♔♔

1 flat, 1 pub rm, 3 bedrms, sleeps 6, min let weekend, from £80, Jan-Dec, bus 300 yds, rail 20 mls, airport 45 mls

George Wright, 22 Horsemarket, Kelso, Roxburghshire
☎ *Kelso (0573) 24542*

by KELSO Roxburghshire Map Ref. 2F6

♔♔

1 cottage, 1 pub rm, 2 bedrms, sleeps 4, from £95, Apr-Oct, bus 2 mls, rail 25 mls, airport 50 mls

Mrs Somervail, Oxnam Neuk, Jedburgh, Roxburghshire
☎ *Jedburgh (0835) 63281*

KEMNAY Aberdeenshire Map Ref. 4G10

1 flat, 1 pub rm, 1-2 bedrms, sleeps 2-5, min let weekend, £70, Jan-Dec, bus 2 mls, rail 6 mls, airport 12 mls

Mrs E C Riddell, Nether Coullie, Kemnay, Aberdeenshire, AB5 9LU
☎ *Kemnay (04674) 2203*

KENMORE Perthshire Map Ref. 2A1

2 houses, 2 cottages, 1-2 pub rms, 2-3 bedrms, sleeps 4-6, £90-£180, Apr-Oct

Finlayson Hughes, Bank House, 82 Atholl Road, Pitlochry, Perthshire, PH16 5BL
☎ *Pitlochry (0796) 2512*

Prices shown are for guidance only. Please send SAE with each enquiry.

up to
COMMENDED

3 houses, 1-2 pub rms, 2-4 bedrms, sleeps 4-6, min let long weekend, £70-£180, Apr-Oct, bus ¼ ml, rail 30 mls

3 caravans, sleeps 6, min let long weekend, £60-£140, Apr-Oct, bus 20 mls, rail 6 mls
(hillwalking)

Diana & Duncan Menzies, Mains of Taymonth, Kenmore, Aberfeldy, Perthshire, PH15 2HN
☎ *Kenmore (08873) 226*

Stone units set around courtyard on home farm for Taymouth Castle. Walking, golfing, sailing locally.

Loch Tay Chalets & Watersports Centre 17 chalet/log cabins, 1 pub rm, 1-3 bedrms, sleeps 2-6, min let weekend (low season), £125-£318, Jan-Dec, bus 7 mls, rail 20 mls, airport 85 mls
(jacuzzi, solarium)

Miss P A Barratt, Croft-na-Caber, Kenmore, Perthshire, PH15 2HW
☎ *Kenmore (08873) 236*

---

2 bungalows, 2 pub rms, 3 bedrms, sleeps 6, from £88, mid Jan-Dec, bus 7 mls, rail 22 mls
(picnic site, forest walk)

Forestry Commission, Forest Holidays, Dept SC1, 231 Corstorphine Road, Edinburgh, EH12 7AT
☎ *031 334 0303*

---

by KENMORE Perthshire Map Ref. 2A1

1 cottage, 2 pub rms, 3 bedrms, sleeps 6, £70-£150, Jan-Dec, bus 4 mls, rail 27 mls, airport 80 mls
(hillwalking)

Deirdrie Knox-Browne, Ringmill House, Gannochy Farm, Perth
☎ *Perth (0738) 33773*

KENSALEYRE Isle of Skye, Inverness-shire Map Ref. 3D8

1 cottage, 1 pub rm, 2 bedrms, sleeps 4-5, £55-£75, Apr-Oct, bus nearby, ferry 7 mls

Mrs M Macinnes, Rhenetra House, Kensaleyre, by Portree, Isle of Skye, Inverness-shire, IV51 9XF
☎ *Skeabost Bridge (047032) 245*

---

1 cottage, 2 pub rms, 2 bedrms, sleeps 4, max £95, Apr-Oct, bus nearby, rail 30 mls, ferry 29 mls, airport 25 mls

1 caravan, sleeps 4-5, £50-£55, Apr-Oct, bus nearby, rail 30 mls, ferry 29 mls, airport 25 mls

Mrs M Macdonald, Macdonald Nurseries, Kensaleyre, by Portree, Isle of Skye, Inverness-shire
☎ *Skeabost Bridge (047032) 339*

KENTALLEN Argyll Map Ref. 1F1

COMMENDED

8 chalet/log cabins, 1 pub rm, 2 bedrms, sleeps 4-6, min let 3 nights, £85-£240, Jan-Dec, bus nearby, rail 15 mls

Loch Linnhe Chalets, 31 Acorn Road, Jesmond, Newcastle upon Tyne, NE2 2DJ
☎ 091 281 5744
On private site, situated at waters edge with spectacular views over Loch Linnhe to mountains beyond.

by KENTALLEN Argyll Map Ref. 1F1

1 house, 2 pub rms, 3 bedrms, sleeps 8, £100-£200, Easter-Oct, bus 15 mls, rail nearby

Mr D McArthur, Ardshiel Farm, Kentallen, Duror, by Appin, Argyll
☎ Duror (063174) 229

KENTANGAVAL Isle of Barra, Western Isles Map Ref. 3A11

1 bungalow, 2 pub rms, 3 bedrms, sleeps 10, £50-£132, Jan-Dec, ferry ½ ml, airport 10 mls

Mr Gerard A Campbell, 26 Kentangavel, Castlebay, Isle of Barra, Western Isles, PA80 5XE
☎ Castlebay (08714) 328

KEOSE GLEBE Isle of Lewis, Western Isles Map Ref. 3C5

1 house, 2 pub rms, 4 bedrms, sleeps 9, min let 2 weeks, £60-£100, Jan-Dec, bus 1 ml ferry 11 mls, airport 13 mls

M MacLeod, Keose House, Keose Glebe, Isle of Lewis, Western Isles, PA86 9JX
☎ Balallan (085183) 243

KILBERRY, by Tarbert Argyll Map Ref. 1D5

Port Ban Caravan Site 7 caravans, sleeps 6-8, min let 1 night, £47-£157, Apr-Oct, bus 15 mls, rail 56 mls

(putting)

Mr Sheldrick, Port Ban Caravan Site, Kilberry, by Tarbert, Argyll
☎ Ormsary (08803) 224

2 cottages, 1 pub rm, 2-3 bedrms, sleeps 6-8, min let weekend, £65-£130, Jan-Dec, rail 16 mls

N L Boase, Ardlarach, Ardfern, by Lochgilphead, Argyll, PA31 8QR
☎ Barbreck (08525) 270/Ormsary (08803) 237

Prices shown are for guidance only. Please send SAE with each enquiry.

KILCHOAN, by Ardnamurchan Argyll Map Ref. 1C1

Ardnamurchan Peninsula

STEADING HOLIDAYS, KILCHOAN, by ACHARACLE
ARGYLL PH36 4LH   TEL: (097 23) 262

Ardnamurchan Peninsula, between Mull and Skye, remains peaceful and unspoilt. From the heights of Ben Hiant to the wide stretch of Sanna Sands, a place for the individual and nature lover. Fishing, table tennis, summer ferry to Mull.
Quality accommodation includes croft houses, log chalets, luxury homes. All have sea views. Full details in colour brochure.

up to COMMENDED
😋 😋 😋 😋

6 chalet/log cabins, 2 houses, 1 flat, 3 cottages, 1-2 pub rms, 1-3 bedrms, sleeps 2-6, min let weekend, from £90, Jan-Dec

Mrs P Campbell, Steading Holidays, Kilchoan, Acharacle, Argyll, PH36 4LH
☎ *Kilchoan (09723) 262*

Selection of units in remote village on Ardnamurchan Peninsula. Views across sound to Isle of Mull.

---

1 cottage, 1 pub rm, 2 bedrms, sleeps 6, min let weekend, from £60, Jan-Dec, bus 5 mls, rail 30 mls, ferry 5 mls

1 caravan, sleeps 6, min let weekend, from £50, Apr-Oct, bus 5 mls, rail 30 mls, ferry 5 mls

Mrs C G Cameron, Mo Dhachaidh, Portuairk, Kilchoan, by Acharacle, Argyll, PH36 4LN
☎ *Kilchoan (09723) 285*

KILCHOMAN Isle of Islay, Argyll Map Ref. 1B6

COMMENDED
😋 😋 😋

5 cottages, 1 pub rm, 2-3 bedrms, sleeps 2-8, £80-£250, Jan-Dec, ferry 19 mls, airport 15 mls

Stuart & Lesley Taylor, Kilchoman House, Bruichladdich, Isle of Islay, Argyll, PA49 7UY
☎ *Port Charlotte (049685) 382*

Recently modernised on 40 acre private estate. Excellent views over surrounding countryside.

KILDONAN Isle of Arran Map Ref. 1F7

8 flats, 1 pub rm, 1-3 bedrms, sleeps 4-6, min let 1 night (low season), £110-£154, Apr-Oct, bus nearby, ferry 12 mls

1 caravan, sleeps 4-6, min let 1 night (low season), £110-£154, Apr-Oct, bus nearby, ferry 12 mls

Mr P Gledhill, Breadalbane Hotel, Kildonan, Isle of Arran
☎ *Kildonan (077082) 284*

---

1 cottage, 2 pub rms, 4 bedrms, sleeps 4-6, from £75, May-Oct, bus 500 yds, ferry 14 mls

Mrs Georges, 197 Okehampton Crescent, Welling, Kent
☎ *01 304 3217*

1 flat, 1 pub rm, 2 bedrms, sleeps 5, min let 5 nights, from £70, Mar-Sep, bus nearby, ferry 11 mls

1 caravan, sleeps 6, min let weekend, from £65, Mar-Oct, bus nearby, ferry 11 mls

Mrs Hoyland, Dippin House, Kildonan, Isle of Arran
☎ *Kildonan (077082) 223*

---

2 flats, 10 bungalows, 1 pub rm, 2-3 bedrms, sleeps 2-8, min let weekend, £80-£250, Jan-Dec, bus nearby, ferry 12 mls

(sub-aqua facilities)

Mr Deighton, Kildonan Hotel, Kildonan, Isle of Arran
☎ *Kildonan (077082) 207*

KILDONAN, by Edinbane Isle of Skye, Inverness-shire Map Ref. 3D8

1 flat, 2 pub rms, 2 bedrms, sleeps 4-5, £50-£110, Apr-Oct, bus nearby, rail 50 mls, ferry 50 mls, airport 45 mls

Mrs B Herbert, Kildonan, Arnisort, Edinbane, Isle of Skye, Inverness-shire, IV51 9PN
☎ *Edinbane (047082) 285*

KILFINAN, by Tighnabruaich Argyll Map Ref. 1E5

Melldalloch Lodges 20 chalet/log cabins, 1 pub rm, 2-3 bedrms, sleeps 4-6, min let weekend (low season), £82-£196, Jan-Dec, ferry 27 mls, airport 42 mls

Mr John MacColl, Melldalloch Holiday Chalets, Kilfinan, by Tighnabruaich, Argyll, PA21 2ER
☎ *Tighnabruaich (0700) 811482*

KILFINNAN, by Spean Bridge Inverness-shire Map Ref. 3H11

Kilfinnan Holiday Lodges 10 chalet/log cabins, 1 pub rm, 2-3 bedrms, sleeps 4-8, min let weekend, £130-£255, Mar-Nov, bus 3½ mls, rail 20 mls

J H P Roberts, Kilfinnan Holiday Homes, Badgers Hill, Speen, Aylesbury, Bucks
☎ *Hamden Row (024028) 289*

KILLEAN, by Tayinloan Argyll Map Ref. 1D6

Killean Estate Cottages 8 cottages, 1-2 pub rms, 2-3 bedrms, sleeps 2-6, min let 3 nights, £50-£260, Mar-Oct, bus nearby, rail 80 mls, airport 20 mls

Mr & Mrs D Attey, Newmarche House, Thorpe in Balne, Doncaster, South Yorkshire, DN6 0DY
☎ *Doncaster (0302) 883160/(05834) 238*

KILLIECHRONAN Isle of Mull, Argyll Map Ref. 1D2

1 house, 10 cottages, 1-2 pub rms, 1-3 bedrms, sleeps 2-6, min let 1 night (low season), £38-£150, Jan-Dec, ferry 12 mls, airport 5 mls

Killiechronan, 18 Maxwell Place, Stirling, FK8 1JU
☎ *Stirling (0786) 62519*
Converted farm buildings on west of island. Overlooks sea, 4 miles (6km) from village of Salen.

KILLIECRANKIE Perthshire Map Ref. 4C12

2 cottages, 1 pub rm, 1 bedrm, sleeps 3-4, min let 3 nights, £70-£120, Mar-Nov, bus nearby, rail 4 mls

(putting green)

Mrs B M S Milne, The Coach House, Druimuan, Killiecrankie, Pitlochry, Perthshire, PH16 5LG
☎ *Pitlochry (0796) 3335*

---

1 chalet/log cabin, 1 pub rm, 3 bedrms, sleeps 6, £90-£150, Apr-Oct

Finlayson Hughes, Bank House, 82 Atholl Rd, Pitlochry, Perthshire, PH16 5BL
☎ *Pitlochry (0796) 2512*

---

5 chalet/log cabins, 1 pub rm, 2 bedrms, sleeps 4-6, min let weekend (low season), £100-£220, Jan-Dec, bus 4 mls, rail 4 mls

Mr & Mrs J Stephen, The Retreat, Old Faskally, Killiecrankie, Pitlochry, Perthshire, PH16 5LR
☎ *Pitlochry (0796) 3436*

---

3 flats, 1 pub rm, 1 bedrm, sleeps 4, min let weekend/3 nights (low season), £70-£135, Jan-Dec, bus nearby, rail 3 mls

(putting green, croquet lawn)

Mrs Sanderson, Druimuan, Killiecrankie, Perthshire
☎ *Pitlochry (0796) 3214*

KILLIN Perthshire Map Ref. 1H2

Boreland Estate 1 cottage, 2 pub rms, 3 bedrms, sleeps 5, from £75, Apr-Oct, bus 1 ml, rail 14 mls

Bell-Ingram, Durn, Isla Road, Perth, PH2 7HF
☎ *Perth (0738) 21121*
Attractive cabin in quiet, private location with views to Loch Tay.

---

1 chalet/log cabin, 1 pub rm, 3 bedrms, sleeps 6, £90-£180, Jan-Dec, bus ½ ml, rail 14 mls

Mr & Mrs H Forster, Springburn, Craignavie Road, Killin, Perthshire, FK21 8SH
☎ *Killin (05672) 371*
Set in landscaped garden; picnic table. Views of river and hill. About 1 ml (2km) from village.

VAT is shown at 15%: changes in this rate may affect prices.

1 cottage, 1 pub rm, 3 bedrms, sleeps 6, min let weekend, from £85, Apr-Oct, bus 350 yds, rail 14 mls

♿ 🚾 E 🏠 🖊 ◎ ▢ 🗄 🔌 ❄ 🐎 🅿 🐕 🍳 💧 † 🏔   🔍 🎣 🛶 △ 🚴 ✗ 🎿

Mrs Twigg, No 2 Craigdarroch, Main Street, Killin, Perthshire
☎ *Killin (05672) 484*

---

1 bungalow, 2 pub rms, 2 bedrms, sleeps 5, min let weekend, £75-£180, Jan-Dec, bus nearby, rail 14 mls, airport 75 mls

♿ 🚾 E 🛒 🖊 📟 🗄 ◎ ▢ ▢ 🔌 ☺ ❄ 🐎 🅿 🐕 🍳 †   🔍 🎣 ∪ △ 🚴 ✗ 🎿
(trout fishing included)

Mrs C A Campbell, Ledcharrie Farm, Luib, by Crianlarich, Perthshire, FK20 8QT
☎ *Killin (05672) 532*

---

2 caravans, sleeps 4, £80, Apr-Oct, bus 2 mls, rail 14 mls

♿ 🚾 E 🏠 🖊 📟 ◎ ◑ ▢ ❄ 🐎 🅿 🐕 🍳   🔍 🎣 🚴 ✗ 🎿 🐾 T

Ms Lois Dommersnes, Shieling Restaurant, Killin, Perthshire, FK21 8TX
☎ *Killin (05672) 334*

---

1 bungalow, 1 pub rm, 3 bedrms, sleeps 6, min let weekend (low season), £60-£160, Jan-Dec, bus ½ ml

♿ 🚾 E 🛒 🖊 📟 🗄 ◑ ▢ ▢ ◎ 🔌 ☺ ❄ 🐎 🅿 ∥ 🐕 🍳 †   🎣 △ 🚴 ✗ 🎿 🐾 T

Peter George, 3 Pier Road, Killin, Perthshire
☎ *Killin (05672) 578*

---

by KILLIN Perthshire Map Ref. 1H2

1 bungalow, 1 pub rm, 2 bedrms, sleeps 4, min let weekend, £79-£163, Jan-Dec, bus 16 mls, rail 4 mls

♿ 🚾 E 🛒 🖊 🗄 ◑ ▢ ▢ ◎ 🔌 ❄ 🐎 🅿 🍳 †   🎣 ∪ △ 🚴 ✗ ⚓ ⚒ ✗ 🎿 🍴

Mrs P Gibson, Tomochrocher, Killin, Perthshire
☎ *Killin (05672) 527*

---

2 flats, 1 pub rm, 2 bedrms, sleeps 3-5, £98-£170, Apr-Oct, bus 2 mls, rail 12 mls, airport 70 mls

♿ 🚾 E 🛒 🖊 📟 ◎ 🗄 ▢ ∦ 🔌 ❄ 🅿 †   🔍 🎣 ∪ △ 🚴 ✗ 🎿

Miss H I Mustard, 4 Blackford Hill Grove, Edinburgh
☎ *031 667 3344/Killin (05672) 300*

Loch Tay Highland Lodges 6 chalet/log cabins, 1 pub rm, 2-3 bedrms, sleeps 4-8, min let 2 nights, from £95, Jan-Dec, bus 3 mls, rail 8 mls, airport 80 mls

♿ 🚾 E 🛒 🖊 📟 🗄 ◎ ▢ 📞 ▢ 🔌 ☺ 🐎 🅿 🐕 🍳 🏔   🎣 △ 🚴 ✗ ⚓ ✗ 🎿 🍴 T

Mr J C Booth, Loch Tay Highland Lodges, Milton Morenish, by Killin, Perthshire
☎ *Killin (05672) 323*   **(See ad. on p. 175)**

---

1 cottage, 1 pub rm, 2 bedrms, sleeps 4-5, £65-£85, Apr-Oct, bus nearby(postbus), rail 22 mls, airport 70 mls

♿ 🚾 E 🛒 🖊 📟 🗄 ◎ ▢ ▢ 🔌 ☺ ❄ 🐎 🅿 🍳 †   🎣 ∪ △ 🚴 ✗ ⚓ ⚒ ✗ 🍴

Mrs M Taylor, Dall Farm, by Killin, Perthshire, FK21 8SX
☎ *Killin (05672) 432*

LOCH TAY
HIGHLAND LODGES

Milton Morenish, by Killin,
Perthshire FK21 8TY   Tel: 05672 323.

Loch Tay Highland Lodges offer luxury self-catering accommodation in six individual lodges situated on a secluded site on the north shore of Loch Tay. From each south facing terrace, our guests have spectacular views across the loch to the mountains beyond.

The lodges are fully equipped with electric cooker, refrigerator, colour television and all cooking utensils and crockery, all linen (except towels) is provided, and all electricity is included in the rent. This unique site is newly established and offers the guest an unrivalled standard of accommodation on a beautiful centrally located site, an ideal base for a touring holiday.

The nearby Killin, provides holidaymakers with shopping facilities, restaurants and golf, while many other activities, such as fishing, swimming, boating, and hill-walking can be enjoyed at Milton Morenish.

Further details and illustrated brochure are available on request.

KILLUNDINE Argyll Map Ref. 1D1

2 cottages, 1 bungalow, 1 pub rm, 2-3 bedrms, sleeps 4-6, min let 1 night, £40-£110, Jan-Dec

William Lauder, Higher Longcombe, Totnes, Devon, TQ9 6PN
☎ *Totnes (0803) 863059*

KILMARNOCK Ayrshire Map Ref. 1H7

1 bungalow, 1 pub rm, 3 bedrms, sleeps 6-7, £75-£140, Jan-Dec, bus 1 ml I

Hillhouse Farm, Grassyards Road, Kilmarnock, Ayrshire
☎ *Kilmarnock (0563) 23370*

by KILMARNOCK Ayrshire Map Ref. 1H7

1 west wing of castle, 2 pub rms, 5 bedrms, sleeps 8, £400-£600, Apr-Oct, bus 1 ½ mls, rail 4 mls, airport 10 mls

Mr H Houison-Craufurd, Craufurdland Castle, by Kilmarnock, Ayrshire
☎ *Fenwick (05606) 402*

KILMARTIN Argyll Map Ref. 1E4

1 flat, 2 pub rms, 4 bedrms, sleeps 8, £110-£130, Jun-Sep, bus ½ ml, rail 30 mls, airport 90 mls

Mrs J M Gordon, Ri-Cruin, Kilmartin, by Lochgilphead, Argyll
☎ *Kilmartin (05465) 231*

KILMAURS, by Kilmarnock Ayrshire Map Ref. 1H6

2 cottages, 1 pub rm, 3-4 bedrms, sleeps 7-12, £75-£155, Apr-Oct, bus nearby-1 ¼mls, rail 1-2 mls, ferry 11 mls, airport 16 mls

Mrs W Steel, Aulton Farm, Kilmaurs, by Kilmarnock, Ayrshire
☎ *Kilmarnock (0563) 38208*

KILMICHAEL GLASSARY Argyll Map Ref. 1E4

1 house, 3 pub rms, 5 bedrms, sleeps 10, £120-£160, May-Sep, bus ½ ml, rail 40 mls, airport 80 mls

Mrs Jane K Gibb, Dunadd Farm, Kilmichael Glassary, Lochgilphead, Argyll, PA31 8QE
☎ *Dunadd (054684) 239*

KILMORACK, by Beauly Inverness-shire Map Ref. 4A9

1 house, 1 pub rm, 3 bedrms, sleeps 6, from £80, Apr-Oct

Mrs I Buchanan, 1 Ruisaurie, Kilmorack, by Beauly, Inverness-shire
☎ *Beauly (0463) 782334*

Prices shown are for guidance only. Please send SAE with each enquiry.

KILMORE Argyll Map Ref. 1E2

1 cottage, 2 pub rms, 3 bedrms, sleeps 6, £75-£175, Jan-Dec, bus ½ ml, rail 5 mls

Mrs P L Baber, Glenfeochan House, Kilmore, Oban, Argyll, PA34 4QR
☎ *Kilmore (063177) 273*

KILMORY Isle of Arran Map Ref. 1F7

1 house, 2 pub rms, 3 bedrms, sleeps 8, £85, Apr-Sep, bus ½ ml, ferry 17 mls

Mrs P Picken, Lenamhor, Kilmory, Isle of Arran
☎ *Sliddery (077087) 263*

1 cottage, 1 pub rm, 1 bedrm, sleeps 2, min let weekend, £45-£55, Jan-Dec, bus nearby, ferry 17 mls

Mrs M Climie, Clachaig, Kilmory, Isle of Arran
☎ *Sliddery (077087) 242*

KILMUIR Isle of Skye, Inverness-shire Map Ref. 3D8

1 chalet/log cabin, 1 house, 1 pub rm, 2-4 bedrms, sleeps 3-9, min let 3 nights, £50-£125, Jan-Dec, bus 1 ml, rail 56 mls, ferry 56 mls, airport 40 mls

Mrs M A Mackenzie, Hungladder, Bornasketaig, Kilmuir, Isle of Skye, Inverness-shire
☎ *Duntulm (047052) 279*

1 cottage, 1 pub rm, 3 bedrms, sleeps 6, £60-£80, Jan-Dec, bus nearby, rail 60 mls, ferry 5 mls

Mrs Mary Cowe, Heatherlea, Hungladder, Kilmuir, Portree, Isle of Skye, Inverness-shire, IV51 9GD
☎ *Duntulm (047052) 217*

KILMUIR Ross-shire Map Ref. 4B7

1 cottage, 2 pub rms, 3 bedrms, sleeps 6, £100-£150, Apr-Oct, bus 2 mls, rail 4 mls, airport 8 mls

Mrs L A Baillie, Greenhill, Redcastle, Muir-of-Ord, Ross-shire
☎ *Muir-of-Ord (0463) 870420*

KILNINIAN Isle of Mull, Argyll Map Ref. 1C1

1 house, 1 cottage, 1 pub rm, 2-3 bedrms, sleeps 6, £100-£190, Jan-Dec, ferry 15 mls

Mr Ian Anderson, 25 Highworth Avenue, Cambridge, CB4 2BQ
☎ *Cambridge (0223) 352860*

KILNINVER, by Oban Argyll Map Ref. 1 E3

Barndromin Farm Holiday Cottages 2 chalet/log cabins, 1 flat, 1 cottage, 1 bungalow, 1 pub rm, 2-3 bedrms, sleeps 2-7, min let weekend (low season), £80-£190, Apr-Nov, bus nearby, rail 6 mls, airport 15 mls

Mrs James T P Mellor, Barndromin Farm, Knipoch, by Oban, Argyll
☎ *Kilninver (08526) 273*

---

2 flats, 1 pub rm, 3 bedrms, sleeps 5-7, £50-£140, Jan-Dec, bus 4 mls, rail 15 mls

Mr & Mrs M Handley, Bragleenbeg House, Kilninver, by Oban, Argyll, PA34 4UU
☎ *Kilninver (08526) 283*

---

2 houses, 1 flat, 2 cottages, 1 bungalow, 1-3 pub rms, 2-4 bedrms, sleeps 4-9, £100-£300, Mar-Nov, bus nearby, rail 8 mls

T (free fishing)

David R Kilpatrick, Kilninver, by Oban, Argyll, PA34 4UT
☎ *Kilninver (08526) 272*

---

2 chalet/log cabins, 1-2 pub rms, 2-3 bedrms, sleeps 4-6, £75-£120, Jan-Dec, bus 10 mls, rail 10 mls

Mrs P Cadzow, Duachy Farm, Kilninver, by Oban, Argyll
☎ *Kilninver (08526) 244*

Lagganmore Caravans 1 caravan, sleeps 6, min let 3 nights, £84-£139, Mar-Nov, bus ½ ml, rail 10 ½ mls

Mrs P S Sandilands, Lagganmore, Oban, Argyll
☎ *Kilninver (08526) 200*

---

1 chalet/log cabin, 1 house, 1 flat, 1 cottage, 1-2 pub rms, 1-3 bedrms, sleeps 2-8, min let weekend (low season), £50-£220, Jan-Dec, bus 1 ml, rail 9 mls

Mr Inglis, Raera Farm, Kilninver, Argyll
☎ *Kilninver (08526) 271*

---

7 bungalows, 1 pub rm, 2-3 bedrms, sleeps 4-6, min let weekend (low season), £145-£290, Apr-Nov, bus 1 ½ mls, rail 12 mls

J G Beilby, Eleraig Estate, Kilninver, by Oban, Oban, PA34 4UX
☎ *Kilmelford (08522) 225/031 332 1621*   **(See colour ad. 10 p. xxxiv)**

1 cottage, 2 pub rms, 3 bedrms, sleeps 6, from £125, Apr-Oct, bus nearby, rail 12 mls

🐾♿ wc E 🛏 🍴 ▦ ◉ 🗂 📞 🗄 🖥 ▱ ⊙ ♞ 🅿 ✂ ▥ † 🎵 ⋃ ⚠ ⚓ ▸

Mrs A C Macdonald, 21 Lindisfarne Road, Newcastle-upon-Tyne
☎ *Tyneside (091) 281 1695*

---

1 bungalow, 2 pub rms, 3 bedrms, sleeps 7, £130-£195, Jan-Dec, bus 15 mls, rail 15 mls

♿ wc E 🛏 🍴 ▦ ◉ 🗂 🗄 ✦ ▱ ✳ ♞ 🅿 ✂ ▥ † 🎵 ⚠ 🧺

R K & Mrs M A Mainwaring, Oteley, Ellesmere, Salop, SY12 0PB
☎ *Ellesmere (069171) 2514*

---

1 house, 2 pub rms, 3 bedrms, sleeps 6, £100-£200, Jan-Dec, bus 1 ml, rail 9 mls, airport 100 mls

♿ wc E 🛏 🍴 ◉ 🗂 📞 🗄 ✦ ▱ ✳ ♞ 🅿 ✂ ▥ †

Mrs R Wakeford, Grove Farm, Barby, Rugby, Warwickshire, CV23 8TR
☎ *Rugby (0788) 890556*

KILTARLITY Inverness-shire Map Ref. 4A9

Glaichbea Caravan Park 1 caravan, sleeps 6, £65-£100, Apr-Oct, bus ½ ml, rail 7 ½ mls, airport 17 mls

♿ wc E 🐾 🛏 🍴 ⊘ 🗂 🗄 ✦ ▱ ⊙ ✳ 🅿 † 🎵 ⋃ ⚓

P R Johnstone, The Filling Stn & Caravan Park, Glaickbea, Kiltarlity, by Beauly, Inverness-shire, IV4 7HR
☎ *Kiltarlity (046374) 496*

---

by KILWINNING Ayrshire Map Ref. 1G6

1 cottage, 1 pub rm, 2 bedrms, sleeps 4, £70-£85, Apr-Sep, bus 1 ml, rail 4 mls, airport 12 mls

♿ wc E 🛏 🍴 ◉ 🗂 🗄 ✦ ✳ 🅿 ✂ ▥ † ⛰ 🎵 ⚓ ✗

Mrs D Campbell, Bridgend, Montgreenan, Kilwinning, Ayrshire, KA13 7RL
☎ *Torranyard (029485) 288*

In open countryside on former country estate. Stream and trout fishing available.

KINBRACE Sutherland Map Ref. 4B4

1 cottage, 1 bungalow, 1 pub rm, 3 bedrms, sleeps 4-5, from £75, Apr-Sep, bus 22 mls, rail 3 mls, airport 50 mls

♿ wc E 🛏 🍴 🏠 ◉ ⊘ 🗂 ✦ ✳ ♞ 🅿 ✂ † ⛰ 🎵 ▸ ✦ 🧺

R P Howden, Achentoul Estate Company, The Estate Office, Berriedale, Caithness, KW7 6HE
☎ *Berriedale (05935) 237*

---

1 house, 1 pub rm, 3 bedrms, sleeps 6, from £75, Apr-Oct, bus ½ ml, rail 3 mls

♿ wc E 🛏 🍴 ◉ 🗂 ✦ ✳ ♞ 🅿 ✂ ▥ † 🎵 🧳 🧺 T

Mrs Sutherland, Borrobol, Kinbrace, Sutherland
☎ *Kinbrace (04313) 268*

KINCLAVEN Perthshire Map Ref. 2C1

2 cottages, 1-2 pub rms, 3-5 bedrms, sleeps 6-10, min let long weekend, £104-£196, Apr-Dec, bus 3 mls, rail 10 mls, airport 20 mls

♿ wc E 🛏 🍴 🏠 ◉ 🗂 🗄 ✦ ⊙ ✳ ♞ 🅿 ✂ ▥ 🎣 ⛵ 🎾 🏹 🎵 ⋃ ▸ ✦ ⚓ ✗ 🧺 T

Ballathie Estates Office, Stanley, Perth, Perthshire, PH1 4QN
☎ *Meikleour (025083) 250*

KINCRAIG, by Kingussie Inverness-shire Map Ref. 4B10

ALVIE ESTATE
TEL: (054 04) 255

KINCRAIG, KINGUSSIE, INVERNESS-SHIRE PH21 1NE

4 fully equipped holiday cottages sleeping 6-8 set in peaceful rural surroundings in the heart of the Spey Valley overlooking the Cairngorms, 4 miles south of Aviemore. Linen, except towels, provided. Electricity charged by 50p coin meter. Excellent local leisure activities including fishing, shooting, ski-ing, canoeing, sailing, wind-surfing, golf, horse riding and bird watching.

Write or phone for brochure.

---

2 houses, 1 cottage, 1 bungalow, 2 pub rms, 3 bedrms, sleeps 4-9, £95-£200, Jan-Dec, bus 5 mls, rail 5 mls

Alvie Estate Office, Kincraig, by Kingussie, Inverness-shire
☎ *Kincraig (05404) 255*

Insh Hall 3 flats, 3 pub rms, 4 bedrms, sleeps 12-20, min let 2 nights, £5 per person/night, Jan-Dec, bus 1 ml, rail 7 mls, airport 40 mls
(windsurfing)

Loch Insh Watersports, Insh Hall, Kincraig, by Kingussie, Inverness-shire, PH21 1NU
☎ *Kincraig (05404) 272*

---

1 hostel, 2 pub rms, 2 bedrms, sleeps 40, min let weekend, from £35, Jan-Dec, bus 6 mls, rail 3 mls, airport 45 mls

Mrs Catriona M Ross, Meadowside House, Kincraig, Kingussie, Inverness-shire, PH21 1LX
☎ *Kincraig (05404) 247*

---

1 hostel, 2 pub rms, 10 bedrms, sleeps 2-4, £28 (per person), Jan-Dec, bus 6 mls, rail 6 mls
(gliding)

The Warden, Badenoch Christian Centre, Kincraig, Inverness-shire, PH21 1NA
☎ *Kincraig (05404) 373/221*

APPROVED
♛ ♛

5 cottages, 1 pub rm, 2-3 bedrms, sleeps 4-6, £90-£150, Jan-Dec, bus 6 mls, rail 6 mls, airport 30 mls
(gliding)

Nigel Reid, Invereshie House Hotel, Kincraig, by Kingussie, Inverness-shire, PH21 1NA
☎ *Kincraig (05404) 332*
Overlooks Loch Insh near the Cairngorms. Peacefully sited within grounds of Invereshie House Hotel.

---

1 flat, 1 pub rm, 2 bedrms, sleeps 4-6, £80-£85, Apr-Oct, bus 6 mls, rail 6 mls

Mrs D M Randerson, The Old Manse, Kincraig, by Kingussie, Inverness-shire, PH21 1NA
☎ *Kincraig (05404) 386*

Prices shown are for guidance only. Please send SAE with each enquiry.

1 house, 1 flat, 2 pub rms, 5 bedrms, sleeps 8-10, min let weekend (low season), £170-£230, Jan-Dec, bus 5 mls, rail 5 mls, airport 40 mls

Mrs A F Williamson & Miss K Hine, Alvie House, Kincraig, Inverness-shire
☎ *Kincraig (05404) 335*

KINGHORN Fife Map Ref. 2D4

Pettycur Bay Caravan Park 50 caravans, sleeps 4-6, min let 2 nights, £55-£180, Mar-Oct, bus nearby, rail ½ ml airport 15 mls

Pettycur Bay Caravan Park, Kinghorn, Fife, KY3 9YE
☎ *Kinghorn (0592) 890321*

KINGSBARNS Fife Map Ref. 2E3

2 cottages, 1 pub rm, 1-2 bedrms, sleeps 2-4, £75-£80, Apr-Oct, bus nearby, rail 12 mls, airport 20 mls

Miss M M Pilkington, Kingsbarns House, 6 The Square, Kingsbarns, by St Andrews, Fife
☎ *Boarhills (033488) 245*

KINGSKETTLE Fife Map Ref. 2D3

1 cottage, 2 pub rms, 3 bedrms, sleeps 6, min let weekend, £50-£125, Apr-Oct, bus 1 ½ mls, rail 3 mls, airport 36 mls

Mrs Alison G Simpson, 6/3 Oxgangs Street, Edinburgh, EH13 9JV
☎ *031 445 4984*

KINGUSSIE Inverness-shire Map Ref. 4B11

2 houses, 2 cottages, 1 pub rm, 2-3 bedrms, sleeps 4-6, £120-£140, Apr-end Oct, Xmas/New Year, bus 2 ½ mls, rail 2 ½ mls

Mrs L H Sandison, Killie Huntly, Kingussie, Inverness-shire, PH21 1NZ
☎ *Kingussie (05402) 270*

1 bungalow, 1 pub rm, 2 bedrms, sleeps 4, £80-£120, Jan-Dec, bus 5 mls, rail 5 mls, airport 40 mls

T (bird reserve, water sports)

Pamela Moir, Hillfoot, Insh, by Kingussie, Inverness-shire, PH21 1NU
☎ *Kingussie (05402) 531*

3 flats, 1 pub rm, 2-4 bedrms, sleeps 5-8, min let weekend, £50-£200, Jan-Dec, bus 300 yds, rail 300 yds, airport 46 mls

Mrs Crooks, Rose Cottage, Insh, by Kingussie, Inverness-shire
☎ *Kingussie (05402) 318*

1 house, 1 pub rm, 2 bedrms, sleeps 4-6, £120-£200, Jan-Dec

Mrs A Williamson, Ashwood, 103 High Street, Kingussie, Inverness-shire
☎ *Kingussie (05402) 572*

VAT is shown at 15%: changes in this rate may affect prices.

181

1 flat, 3 pub rms, 2 bedrms, sleeps 6, min let weekend, £80-£140, Jan-Dec, bus 250 yds, rail 300 yds, airport 42 mls

 ♿ �📶 E 🏠 🛋 💻 🖨 🚪 ⚬🕯 🔌 🗄 🎨 ✦ ☀️ 🐴 🅿️ ✎ ❄️ 🛏 🚼 † ⚱ 　 🧦 ∪ △ ↣
✓ ⚓ ✗ 🏋 🆃 (bowls)

Mr Neil D Thackrey, Tighvonie, West Terrace, Kingussie, Inverness-shire, PH21 1HA
☎ *Kingussie (05402) 263*

KINLOCH RANNOCH Perthshire Map Ref. 2A1

5 cottages, 1-2 pub rms, 2-4 bedrms, sleeps 4-8, min let weekend (low season), £75-£167, Mar-Nov, bus 1-4 mls, rail 18 mls, airport 80 mls

 ♿ ⏀ E 🚗 🏠 🛋 💻 🖨 ⚬ 🔌 🗄 🎨 ✦ ☀️ 🐴 🅿️ ❄️ 🛏 † 　 🎣 🧦 △ ↣ ⚓ ✎ ✗
🏋 🐾

Mrs Dunlop, Ballinloan, Dunalastair, Pitlochry, Perthshire, PH16 5PE
☎ *Kinloch Rannoch (08822) 305*

up to
HIGHLY COMMENDED
👑 👑 👑 👑

Loch Rannoch Highland Lodges 85 lodges, 1 pub rm, 1-3 bedrms, sleeps 4-8, £200-£610, Jan-Dec, rail 18 mls, airport 60 mls

 ♿ ⏀ E 🚗 🏠 🛋 💻 🖨 ⚬ 🔌 🗄 🎨 ☀️ 🐴 🅿️ ✎ 🛏 ❄️ ⚱ ● 🌍 　 🍴 📷 🔍
🎣 🧦 ∪ △ ↣ ✓ ⚓ ✎ ® ✗ 🏋 🎾 ♪ 🆃

Loch Rannoch Hotel, Kinloch Rannoch, Pitlochry, Perthshire, PH16 5PS
☎ *Kinloch Rannoch (08822) 201*
Units of varying character and style set above Loch Rannoch. Britain's first timeshare development.

2 cottages, 1-2 pub rms, 4 bedrms, sleeps 6-8, from £65, Apr-Oct, rail 8 mls

 ♿ ⏀ E 🚗 🖨 ☀️ 🐴 🅿️ 🛏 🛋 　 🍴 🧦 △ ✗ 🏋

Astel Limited, c/o J Boscawen, Strathtay Estate Office, Boltachan, Aberfeldy, Perthshire, PH15 2LB
☎ *Aberfeldy (0887) 20496*

1 wing of house, 1-2 pub rms, 3 bedrms, sleeps 4-6, £95-£150, Jan-Dec

 ♿ ⏀ E 🚗 🏠 🛋 💻 🖨 🚪 ⚬🔌 🗄 🎨 ✦ ☀️ 🐴 🅿️ ✎ 🛏 † 　 🧦 ∪ △ ↣ ✓ ⚓
⚓ ✗ 🏋

Finlayson Hughes, Bank House, 82 Atholl Road, Pitlochry, Perthshire, PH16 5BL
☎ *Pitlochry (0796) 2512*

2 cottages, 2-3 pub rms, 2 bedrms, sleeps 4-6, £97-£138, Apr-Oct, bus 300 yds, rail 18 mls

 ♿ ⏀ E 🚗 🖨 🖨 ⚬ 🗄 ✦ ☀️ 🐴 🅿️ 🛏 ❄️ ⚱ 　 🔍 🎣 🧦 ∪ △ ↣ ✓ ⚓ ✗ 🏋 🐾

Mrs S H Barclay, Innerhadden, Kinloch Rannoch, Perthshire, PH16 5QD
☎ *Kinloch Rannoch (08822) 344*

2 caravans, sleeps 4-6, min let nightly, £70, Mar-Oct, bus ½ ml, rail 18 mls, airport 70 mls

 ♿ ⏀ E 🖨 🛋 🗄 ⚬🎨 ☀️ 🐴 🅿️ ✎ 🛏 🚼 　 🍴 📷 🔍 🎣 🧦 △ ✓ ✗ 🏋 🐾 🆃
(Hillwalking, curling)
Mrs A Steffen, Cuilmore Cottage, Kinloch Rannoch, Perthshire, PH16 5QB
☎ *Kinloch Rannoch (08822) 218*

KINLOCHARD, by Aberfoyle Perthshire Map Ref. 1H3

1 cottage, 1 pub rm, 1 bedrm, sleeps 6, £30-£60, Jan-Dec, bus 1 ½ mls, rail 25 mls

 ♿ ⏀ E 🚗 🖨 💻 ⚬ 🗄 ☀️ 🐴 🅿️ 🛏 † 　 🧦 ∪ ↣ ✓ ✗ 🏋

Mr Heaton-Armstrong, Armstrong of Aberfoyle, Aberfoyle, Perthshire, FK8 3UG
☎ *Aberfoyle (08772) 221*

1 cottage, 2 pub rms, 3 bedrms, sleeps 6, £100-£140, Apr-Oct

Finlayson Hughes, Bank House, 82 Atholl Road, Pitlochry, Perthshire, PH16 5BL
☎ *Pitlochry (0796) 2512*

HIGHLY COMMENDED

10 timeshare lodges, 1 pub rm, 2 bedrms, sleeps 6-8, £300-£630, Jan-Dec, rail 23 mls, airport 35 mls

Barratt Multi-Ownership & Hotels Ltd, Forest Hills Estate, Kinlochard, Aberfoyle, Stirling, FK8 3TL
☎ *Kinlochard (08777) 277*

Time-share apartments in 22 acre grounds overlooking Loch Ard. Extensive recreational facilities.

KINLOCHBERVIE Sutherland Map Ref. 3G3

1 cottage, 2 pub rms, 3 bedrms, sleeps 7-8, min let weekend, £65-£85, Apr-Oct, bus 3 mls, rail 50 mls

Mr B Cook, 5 Upper Coatbridge Terrace, Edinburgh
☎ *031 346 0360*

AWAITING INSPECTION

1 house, 1 bungalow, 1-2 pub rms, 2-3 bedrms, sleeps 5-9, min let 2 nights, £80-£150, Jan-Dec, bus nearby, rail 50 mls

(ornithology, mountaineering, geology)

Far North Hotel, Balnakeil, Durness, Sutherland
☎ *Durness (097181) 221/(097182) 372*

---

1 house, 2 pub rms, 3 bedrms, sleeps 4-6, £86-£135, Apr-Oct, bus 5 mls, rail 50 mls

The Factor, Estate Office, Achfary, by Lairg, Sutherland, IV27 4PQ
☎ *Lochmore (097184) 221*

---

1 cottage, 1 pub rm, 1 bedrm, sleeps 3, £56-£62, Jan-Dec, bus nearby, rail 50 mls, airport 100 mls

2 caravans, sleeps 6-8, min let weekend, £56-£62, Apr-Sep, bus nearby, rail 50 mls, airport 100 mls

Mr J P MacKenzie, 152 Oldshoremore, Kinlochbervie, Sutherland, IV27 4RS
☎ *Kinlochbervie (097182) 281*

KINLOCHEWE Ross-shire Map Ref. 3G8

up to APPROVED

6 chalet/log cabins, 1 pub rm, 2 bedrms, sleeps 6, from £80, Jan-Dec, bus nearby, rail 10 mls, airport 60 mls

Kinlochewe Holiday Chalets, Kinlochewe, Ross-shire, IV22 2PA
☎ *Kinlochewe (044584) 234*

Situated by Kinlochewe Hotel, just off main road. Near National Trust Nature Reserve.

COMMENDED
👑 👑 👑

1 bungalow, 1 pub rm, 3 bedrms, sleeps 7, £110-£165, Mar-Nov, bus ½ ml, rail 8 mls

♿ ᵂᶜ E 🔌 🗇 🖥 ⊚ 🗃 🗄 ⊙ ❊ 🐕 🅿 🛋 🏢 † ⌂   🎣 ⚓ ✦ ✕ 🗝

C V Dodgson, Buttercrags, Grasmere, Cumbria, LA22 9QZ
☎ *Grasmere (09665) 259*
Modern, amidst rugged Glen Torridon scenery. 1 ml(2 km) from village.

---

1 bungalow, 2 pub rms, 4 bedrms, sleeps 8, from £130, Mar-Nov, bus ¼ ml, rail 10 mls

♿ ᵂᶜ E 🔌 🗇 🖥 ⊚ 🗃 🗄 ✂ 🗄 ⊙ ❊ 🅿 🛋 †   🎣 ✕ 🗝

Mrs M A Cross, Taransay, Kinlochewe, Achnasheen, Ross-shire
☎ *Kinlochewe (044584) 254*

---

1 bunk house, 1 pub rm, 1 bedrm, sleeps 18, min let 1 night, £30 (per person), Jan-Dec, bus nearby, rail 9 mls, airport 60 mls

♿ ᵂᶜ E 🏠 🗇 🖥 ✂ 🗄 ⊙ 🐕 🅿 🛋 †   🎣 ✦ ✕ 🗝 🆃

P Jackson, Kinlochewe Hotel, Kinlochewe, Ross-shire, IV22 2PA
☎ *Kinlochewe (044584) 253*

---

2 houses, 2-5 pub rms, 4-11 bedrms, sleeps 6-16, from £70, Jan-Dec, Nov-mid Jul, bus ½ ml, rail 12 mls, airport 60 mls

♿ ᵂᶜ E 🔌 🏠 🗇 🗄 🗄 🔔 ✂ 🗄 ❊ 🅿 🛋 🖥   🎣 ✕ 🗝 🆃

Mr Whitbread, The Old Rectory, Dennington, by Woodbridge, Suffolk
☎ *Badingham (072875) 335*

KINLOCHLAGGAN, by Newtonmore Inverness-shire Map Ref. 4A11

up to
COMMENDED
👑 👑 👑 👑

Ardverikie Estate Ltd 3 houses, 2 cottages, 1-3 pub rms, 2-6 bedrms, sleeps 2-16, min let 3 nights, £60-£350, Jan-Dec, rail 15 mls

♿ ᵂᶜ E 🔌 🏠 🗇 🗄 ⊚ ✂ 🗄 🔔 🗄 🗄 ✂ 🗄 ⊙ ❊ 🐕 🅿 🛋 🖥 🔌 †   🎣 ⛵ ⚓ ✦ 🦌 🆃

Mrs G Chalmer, The Estate Office, Kinlochlaggan, by Newtonmore, Inverness-shire
☎ *Laggan (05284) 300*
Units separately sited on large highland estate. Forest walks, sheep and deer. Loch with sandy beach.

---

1 cottage, 2 pub rms, 2 bedrms, sleeps 4, £65, May-Aug

♿ ᵂᶜ E 🔌 🗇 ⊚ 🗄 🗄 ❊ 🐕 🅿 †   🎣 ⛵

Mrs D M Morgan, 603 Gilbert House, The Barbican, London, EC2Y 8BD
☎ *01 588 3343(eve Mon-Fri)*

Prices shown are for guidance only. Please send SAE with each enquiry.

KINLOCHLEVEN Argyll Map Ref. 1G1

Mamore Holiday Lodge 2 chalet/log cabins, 1 house, 5 flats, 1-4 pub rms, 2-4 bedrms, sleeps 4-8, min let weekend, £139-£299, Jan-Dec, bus 2 mls, rail 22 mls, airport 95 mls

Mr P Bush, Mamore Lodge, Kinlochleven, Argyll
☎ *Kinlochleven (08554) 213*   (See ad. on p. 185)

Caolasnacon Caravan & Camping Park 20 caravans, sleeps 4-6, min let 1 night, £85-£140, Apr-Oct, bus nearby, rail 17 mls

The Manager, Caolasnacon Caravan & Camping Site, Kinlochleven, Argyll
☎ *Kinlochleven (08554) 279*

KINLOCHMOIDART Inverness-shire Map Ref. 3E12

1 house, 1 cottage, 1-2 pub rms, 1-6 bedrms, sleeps 2-11, £80-£320, Mar-Oct, bus $\frac{1}{2}$ ml, rail 13 mls

Mrs M D Stewart, Kinlochmoidart House, Kinlochmoidart, Inverness-shire
☎ *Salen (096785) 609*

KINTORE Aberdeenshire Map Ref. 4G10

Hillhead Caravan Park 1 cottage, 1 pub rm, 1 bedrm, sleeps 4, min let 1 night, £58-£85, Easter-Oct, bus 1 ml, rail 3 mls, ferry 13 mls, airport 10 mls

(bowls)

4 caravans, sleeps 6-8, min let 1 night, £58-£95, Easter-Oct, bus 1 ml, rail 3 mls, ferry 13 mls, airport 10 mls

(bowls)

Mr L Gray, Hillhead Caravan Park, Kintore, Aberdeenshire, AB5 0YX
☎ *Kintore (0467) 32809*

KIPPFORD Kirkcudbrightshire Map Ref. 2B10

Doonpark Caravan Park 17 caravans, sleeps 6-8, min let weekend, £65-£135, Mar-Oct, bus 3 mls, rail 18 mls

J & E Thomson, Doonpark Caravan Park, Kippford, by Dalbeattie, Kirkcudbrightshire
☎ *Kippford (055662) 259*

KIPPFORD CARAVAN PARK

KIPPFORD, by DALBEATTIE, KIRKCUDBRIGHTSHIRE
Telephone: 055 662 636

SEASIDE ½ A MILE

Award-winning family holiday park, in a hilly, part-wooded and landscaped setting. New and top quality static hire caravans fully serviced and with colour TV. Situated in small groups, and all with lovely views. Shop and launderette. Touring hook-up's and excellent toilet facilities.

NEARBY ACTIVITIES ARRANGED.

Excellent play and adventure-playgrounds. Pony trekking, sea fishing trips, loch with boat, and cycle hire are all adjacent. Windsurfing and tuition, and golf nearby. Babysitting.

STB THISTLE AWARD and TOP QUALITY Park GRADING AWARDS for quality and service.

Holiday caravan sales. Chalets for hire. Brochure by return.

Indoor heated pool at Kippford planned for 1987

A SELECT THISTLE AWARD PARK ½ A MILE FROM KIPPFORD

2 COASTAL PARKS OF QUALITY . . .

A QUIET PARK, 200 YARDS FROM ROCKCLIFFE BAY AND THE SEA. SUPERB SEA VIEWS.

CASTLE POINT CARAVAN PARK

ROCKCLIFFE by DALBEATTIE, KIRKCUDBRIGHTSHIRE. Tel: (0556) 62636/63248

200 YARDS FROM THE SEA—SMALL AND QUIET

With outstanding views of Rockcliffe Bay and the sea. Part of a small farm, there is good fishing from the rocks and bathing off the small, semi-private beaches. Activities all within 3 miles: Sailing, windsurfing and tuition, trekking, loch fishing and boat; golf. Shop 600 yards.

HIRE VANS FULLY SERVICED and COLOUR TVs.

A & B Grade vans, all with colour TV, shower, fridge, WC, H&C, etc. One and two bedroom, 4 and 6 berth.

Touring hook-up's and excellent toilet block. Launderette at our larger park (Kippford Caravan Park) 3 miles away.

Children welcome, dogs on lead, babysitting.

VAT is shown at 15%: changes in this rate may affect prices.

187

6 chalet/log cabins, 1 pub rm, 3 bedrms, sleeps 4-6, min let weekend, £70-£200, Mar-Oct, bus nearby, rail 17 mls, airport 60 mls

20 caravans, sleeps 6, min let weekend, £60-£180, Mar-Oct, bus nearby, rail 17 mls, ferry 70 mls, airport 60 mls

[D] (caravans suitable for wheelchairs)

P R Aston, Kippford Caravan Park, by Dalbeattie, Kirkcudbrightshire

☎ *Kippford (055662) 636*　　　　(See ad. on p. 187)

up to
HIGHLY COMMENDED

River View Park 6 chalet/log cabins, 1 pub rm, 2-3 bedrms, sleeps 2-6, min let 2-3 nights, £100-£280, Feb-Dec, bus ½ ml, rail 17 mls, airport 50 mls

J & G McLellan Ltd, River View Park, Kippford, Kirkcudbrightshire, DG5 4LG

☎ *Kippford (055662) 204*

Norwegian timber-style units. In lovely garden setting, overlooking the Urr Estuary.

(See colour ad. 11 p. xxxv)

KIRKBEAN Kirkcudbrightshire Map Ref. 2B10

2 caravans, sleeps 6, £63-£98, Apr-Oct, bus nearby, rail 12 mls

Mr McMyn, Kirkhouse Farm, Kirkbean, Kirkcudbrightshire, DG2 8DW

☎ *Kirkbean (038788) 206*

2 cottages, 2 pub rms, 3-7 bedrms, sleeps 7-12, £100-£140, Apr-Oct, bus 2 mls, rail 15 mls, airport 90 mls

Blackett Leisure Enterprises, Arbigland, Kirkbean, Kirkcudbrightshire, DG2 8BQ

☎ *Kirkbean (038788) 213*

1 cottage, 1 pub rm, 3 bedrms, sleeps 2-6, min let weekend, £68-£115, Apr-Oct, bus nearby, rail 15 mls

(forest trails, green bowling)

Mrs Kirkland, Cowcorse Farm, Kirkbean, Kirkcudbrightshire, DG2 8AU

☎ *Southwick (038778) 258*

KIRKCOLM, by Stranraer Wigtownshire Map Ref. 1F10

1 bungalow, 2 pub rms, 2 bedrms, sleeps 4-6, min let weekend, £60-£75, Jan-Dec, bus 1 ml, rail 12 mls

Mrs Gibson, North Park, Kirkcolm, Stranraer, Wigtownshire

☎ *Kirkcolm (077685) 666*

1 cottage, 0 , 1 pub rm, 2 bedrms, sleeps 4, £90-£100, Apr-Oct

Mrs Cannon, Barneight Farm, Kirkcowan, Wigtownshire

☎ *Kirkcowan (067183) 259*

KIRKCOWAN Wigtownshire Map Ref. 1H10

COMMENDED

1 house, 0 , 1 pub rm, 3 bedrms, sleeps 6, £85-£145, Jan-Dec, bus nearby, rail 18 mls, ferry 18 mls, airport 53 mls

 ♿ ᵂᶜ E ↵ 🏠 ▦ ◎ ☐ ▢ ◙ ✦ ▱ ☉ ❋ ♘ P ∥ ㋡ ▥ ➡ †   ✔ ⚠ ✗ 🏷 T

Mr & Mrs D McKenzie, Kirkcowan Service Station, Kirkcowan, Wigtownshire, DG8 0HQ
☎ *Kirkcowan (067183) 229*

Adjacent terraced cottages, recently modernised with large garden. In main street of quiet village.

KIRKCUDBRIGHT Map Ref. 2A11

BRIGHOUSE BAY HOLIDAY PARK
Brighouse Bay, Borgue, Kirkcudbright DG6 4TS
Tel: Borgue (05577) 267

Awarded top grades for facilities and accommodation, Brighouse Bay is one of Scotland's finest family parks. Leisure facilities include heated pool, Windsurfing and Watersports School, Pony Trekking Centre, all tide slipway, canoe, boat and bicycle hire, farm tours, parascending, jet skiing and lots more. Luxury caravans. Cottages on farm. All tourists welcome.
A Thistle Commended Park.

4 cottages, 2-3 pub rms, 2-3 bedrms, sleeps 5-8, £70-£205, Apr-Oct, bus 2 mls, rail 35 mls

♿ ᵂᶜ E ↵ 🏠 ▦ ◎ ☐ ▢ ▱ ☉ ❋ ♘ P ㋡ ▥ † ⌂   ⌇ ✔ ∪ ⚠ ⚐ ⇌ ✗ 🏷 ㏑ T

25 caravans, sleeps 4-8, min let 2 nights, £60-£175, Apr-Oct, bus 2 mls, rail 35 mls

♿ ᵂᶜ E 🏠 🛢 ▱ ☐ ☎ ▢ ◙ ▱ ☉ ♘ P ㋡ ▥ ㏑ ◕ ✪   ⌇ ✔ ∪ ⚠ ⚐ ⇌ ✗ ㏑ T D (windsurfing, parascending, jet skiing)

Brighouse Bay Holiday Park, Borgue, Kirkcudbrightshire, DG6 4TS
☎ *Borgue (05577) 267*

Seaward Caravan Park
DHOON BAY · KIRKCUDBRIGHT · (05577) 267

Awarded STB's "Thistle Commendation" annually since 1981 and holder of the highest possible classification and grading awards, Seaward is quiet, exclusive and beautifully situated with exceptional panoramic views over Kirkcudbright Bay. Amenities include heated pool, games/TV room, sauna, sunbed, mini golf, launderette, shop. Sandy beach. Activity Centre at nearby Brighouse Bay. Log chalettas and luxury caravans. All tourists welcome. A "Gillespie" Leisure Park.

11 caravans, sleeps 6-8, min let 2 nights, £72-£180, Mar-Oct, bus nearby, rail 32 mls

♿ ᵂᶜ E 🏠 🛢 ▱ ☐ ☎ ▢ ◙ ✦ ▱ ☉ ♘ P ㋡ ▥ ㏑ ◕   ⌇ ⚐ ✔ ∪ ⚠ ⚐ ⇌ ✗ T (mini golf, bicycle hire, sunbed)

Seaward Caravan Park, Dhoon Bay, Kirkcudbright
☎ *Borgue (05577) 267(off)/(0557) 31079*

---

2 flats, 2-4 pub rms, 2 bedrms, sleeps 4-6, £60-£100, Jan-Dec, bus 2 ½ mls, rail 30 mls, airport 100 mls

♿ ᵂᶜ E ↵ 🏠 ▦ ◎ ☐ ☎ ▢ ◙ ✦ ▱ ☉ ❋ P ㋡ ▥ †   ⚐ ✔ ∪ ⚠ ⚐

2 caravans, sleeps 4-6, £50-£65, Apr-Oct, bus 2 ½ mls, rail 30 mls, ferry 50 mls, airport 100 mls

♿ E 🛢 ☐ ◙ ❋ ♘ P ㋡ ▥   ⚐ ✔ ∪ ⚠ ⚐

D M Henry, The Grange, Kirkcudbright, DG6 4XG
☎ *Kirkcudbright (0557) 30519*

VAT is shown at 15%: changes in this rate may affect prices.

2 flats, 1 pub rm, 2 bedrms, sleeps 4-6, £60-£120, Apr-Sep, bus nearby, rail 27 mls

H J Clayton, Lulwind, Kirkcudbright
☎ *Kirkcudbright (0557) 30603/31146(5pm)*

---

1 cottage, 1 pub rm, 2 bedrms, sleeps 5, £60-£90, Jan-Dec, bus 3 mls

Mrs J Picken, Torrs, Kirkcudbright
☎ *Townhead (055723) 256*

---

1 flat, 2 pub rms, 3 bedrms, sleeps 6, £30-£120, Jan-Dec

J Beattie, Fludha, Tongland Road, Kirkcudbright, DG6 4UU
☎ *Kirkcudbright (0557) 30208*

---

1 flat, 1 pub rm, 1 bedrm, sleeps 2-3, £55-£75, Apr-Oct, bus nearby, rail 30 mls

Mrs Lesley M Priestley, 70 High Street, Kirkcudbright, DG6 4JX
☎ *Kirkcudbright (0557) 31022*

APPROVED
👑 👑

2 bungalows, 1 pub rm, 1-3 bedrms, sleeps 2-6, £75-£125, Jan-Dec, bus 4 mls, rail 23 mls, airport 80 mls

Mrs H Caygill, Marks, Kirkcudbright
☎ *Kirkcudbright (0557) 30854*
Units of individual character pleasantly situated on working farm. 4 miles/6 km from town.

---

2 cottages, 1 pub rm, 3-4 bedrms, sleeps 6-8, £90-£155, Jan-Dec, bus 1 ml, rail 30 mls, airport 90 mls

Mrs Dunlop, Cannee, Kirkcudbright
☎ *Kirkcudbright (0557) 30684*

---

1 flat, 1 pub rm, 2 bedrms, sleeps 4-5, min let weekend, £60-£90, Apr-Oct, bus nearby, rail 28 mls

Mrs E M Chaplin, Gladstone House, 48 High Street, Kirkcudbright
☎ *Kirkcudbright (0557) 31424*

---

1 flat, 1 pub rm, 2 bedrms, sleeps 4-6, £60-£95, Jan-Dec, bus ¼ ml

Mrs S G Irwin, 6 Queens Drive, Stokesley, Middlesbrough, T59 5HA
☎ *Stokesley (0642) 710870*

COMMENDED
👑 👑 👑

3 cottages, 1 pub rm, 2-3 bedrms, sleeps 4-6, £58-£120, Apr-Oct, bus 3 ½ mls, rail 28 mls, airport 75 mls

Mrs I M Blacklock, Little Sypland, Kirkcudbright
☎ *Kirkcudbright (0557) 30592*
Stone built units each with own garden amidst rolling Galloway farmland. 4 mls (6 km) from town.

by KIRKCUDBRIGHT Map Ref. 2A11

1 bungalow, 1 pub rm, 3 bedrms, sleeps 6, £70-£110, Jan-Dec, bus 4 mls, rail 26 mls, airport 60 mls

Mrs G Macadam, Hartburn, Kirkcudbright
☎ *Kirkcudbright (0557) 31005*

KIRKCUDBRIGHT AREA Map Ref. 2A11

up to
HIGHLY COMMENDED

7 houses, 2 cottages, 1 bungalow, 1-2 pub rms, 2-4 bedrms, sleeps 4-8, from £65, Apr-Oct

G M Thomson & Company, 27 King Street, Castle Douglas, Kirkcudbrightshire, DG7 1AB
☎ *Castle Douglas (0556) 2701*

KIRKGUNZEON Kirkcudbrightshire Map Ref. 2B10

Mossband Caravan Park 3 caravans, sleeps 4-6, min let 2 nights, £52-£98, Easter-Oct, bus nearby, rail 9 mls

G & M Graham, Mossband, Kirkgunzeon, Kirkcudbrightshire
☎ *Kirkgunzeon (038776) 280*

KIRKHILL, by Inverness Inverness-shire Map Ref. 4A8

up to
COMMENDED

Reelig Glen Estate 12 chalet/log cabins, 1 flat, 1 cottage, 2 bungalows, 1-2 pub rms, 2-3 bedrms, sleeps 4-6, £80-£189, Jan-Dec, bus ½ ml, rail 8 mls, airport 15 mls

Mr M R Fraser, Reelig Estate, Reelig Glen, Kirkhill, Inverness-shire, IV5 7PR
☎ *Drumchardine (046383) 208*
Variety of units set individually in secluded woodland on highland estate. Recreation room, Putting.

up to
COMMENDED

2 cottages, 1 pub rm, 2-4 bedrms, sleeps 4-6, £90-£165, Apr-Oct, bus ¼-5 mls, rail 8-15 mls, airport 15-22 mls

Mr E A H Fraser, Kingillie House, Kirkhill, Inverness-shire, IV5 7PU
☎ *Drumchardine (046383) 275*
One unit in hamlet of Crask of Aigas; other in grounds of Kingillie House. 8 miles (13km) Inverness.

KIRKMICHAEL Perthshire Map Ref. 2C1

Borland Farm Caravan Site 3 caravans, sleeps 6, min let weekend, £42-£48, Apr-Oct, bus ¼ ml, rail 12 mls

Mrs C Sutherland, Borland Farm, Kirkmichael, Blairgowrie, Perthshire, PH10 7NR
☎ *Strathardle (025081) 250*

2 houses, 1-2 pub rms, 2-3 bedrms, sleeps 4-8, min let weekend, £50-£230, Jan-Dec, bus nearby, rail 12 mls, airport 33 mls

(hillwalking, hang-gliding)

J & I Milne, Main Street, Kirkmichael, Blairgowrie, Perthshire, PH10 7NT
☎ *Strathardle (025081) 385*

VAT is shown at 15%: changes in this rate may affect prices.

KIRKMICHAEL, by Maybole Ayrshire Map Ref. 1G8

1 cottage, 1 pub rm, 2 bedrms, sleeps 4-6, £60-£120, Jan-Dec, bus 1 ml, rail 5 mls

Michael Barne & Partners, 14 Alloway Place, Ayr, KA7 2AA
☎ *Ayr (0292) 268181*

KIRKOSWALD Ayrshire Map Ref. 1G8

1 house, 2 pub rms, 3 bedrms, sleeps 7, £80-£150, Jan-Dec, bus nearby, rail 4 mls, ferry 30 mls, airport 18 mls

Mrs M G Henry, Kirklands, Kirkoswald, Maybole, Ayrshire
☎ *Kirkoswald (06556) 635*

KIRN, Dunoon Argyll Map Ref. 1G5

7 flats, 1 pub rm, 1 bedrm, sleeps 4-5, min let weekend, £60-£120, Jan-Dec, bus nearby, ferry 1 ml, airport 12 mls

Ian R Taylor, Dunmore Holiday Flats, Alexandra Parade, Kirn, Dunoon, Argyll, PA23 8DX
☎ *Dunoon (0369) 4205*
Situated on sea front between Hunter's Quay and Dunoon pier.

KIRRIEMUIR Angus Map Ref. 2D1

1 flat, 1 pub rm, 2 bedrms, sleeps 4-6, £50-£65, Apr-Oct, bus nearby, rail 17 mls, airport 17 mls

Mrs A Fraser, 31 Brechin Road, Kirriemuir, Angus
☎ *Kirriemuir (0575) 73141*

---

1 cottage, 2 pub rms, 3 bedrms, sleeps 7, from £95, Apr-Oct, bus 5 mls, rail 22 mls

Bell-Ingram, Durn, Isla Road, Perth, PH2 7HF
☎ *Perth (0738) 21121*

---

1 cottage, 1 pub rm, 2 bedrms, sleeps 5, £60-£85, Jan-Dec, bus 350 yds, rail 17 mls

Mrs C McCombe, Pluckerston Farm, Kirriemuir, Angus
☎ *Kirriemuir (0575) 72667*

by KIRRIEMUIR Angus Map Ref. 2D1

2 cottages, 1 pub rm, 1-2 bedrms, sleeps 2-8, min let weekend, £65-£75, Jan-Dec, bus 6 mls, rail 20 mls, airport 50 mls

Mrs F M Fleming, Easter Peel, Lintrathen, by Kirriemuir, Angus, DD8 5JJ
☎ *Lintrathen (05756) 205*

---

3 cottages, 1 pub rm, 2-3 bedrms, sleeps 3-5, £110-£160, Apr-Oct, bus nearby(postbus), rail 20 mls, airport 20 mls

Scottish Country Cottages, Suite 2d, Churchill Way, Bishopbriggs, Glasgow, G64 2RH
☎ *041 772 5920*

AWAITING INSPECTION

1 colt house, 1 pub rm, 2 bedrms, sleeps 4, £65-£135, Jan-Dec, bus 6 mls, rail 22 mls, airport 25 mls

Mrs M Marchant, The Welton, Kingoldrum, Kirriemuir, Angus
☎ *Kingoldrum (057581) 243*

KIRTOMY, by Bettyhill Sutherland Map Ref. 4B3

APPROVED
👑 👑 👑

1 cottage, 2 pub rms, 2 bedrms, sleeps 4-5, £70-£120, Jan-Dec, bus 1 ml, rail 45 mls, airport 60 mls

Mr & Mrs P K Massey, Langness, Bulstrode Way, Gerrards Cross, Bucks, SL9 7QT
☎ *Gerrards Cross (0753) 884796*
Former crofter's home in small, remote settlement. Near beach with extensive views.

KISHORN Ross-shire Map Ref. 3F9

Listed

1 chalet/log cabin, 1 pub rm, 3 bedrms, sleeps 6, from £85, Jan-Dec, rail 9 mls

Mrs H Murchison, Achintraid, Kishorn, Strathcarron, Ross-shire, IV54 8XB
☎ *Kishorn (05203) 242*

KNOCKANDO Moray Map Ref. 4D9

1 house, 2 pub rms, 3 bedrms, sleeps 8, min let weekend, £60-£85, Jan-Dec, bus 2 mls, rail 20 mls, airport 40 mls

Mrs A M Dean, Kirdellbeg, Ballindalloch, Banffshire, AB3 9BS
☎ *Ballindalloch (08072) 233*

---

1 cottage, 1 pub rm, 3 bedrms, sleeps 6, £60-£125, Jan-Dec, bus 1 $\frac{1}{4}$ mls, rail 18 mls, airport 40 mls

Mr A Franklin, 373 Wimborne Road, Oakdale, Dorset, BH15 3ED
☎ *Poole (0202) 685053*

KNOCKROME Isle of Jura, Argyll Map Ref. 1D5

1 caravan, sleeps 6, min let weekend, £40-£75, Jan-Dec

Mr C Rozga, Knockrome, Isle of Jura, Argyll, PA60 7XZ
☎ *Jura (049682) 277*

KYLE OF LOCHALSH Ross-shire Map Ref. 3F10

1 bungalow, 1 pub rm, 3 bedrms, sleeps 6, £75-£115, Jan-Dec, bus 500 yds, rail 500 yds, ferry 500 yds

P G Wright, 16 Duntrune Terrace, West Ferry, Dundee, Angus, DD5 ILF
☎ *Dundee (0382) 77462*

---

1 house, 2 pub rms, 3 bedrms, sleeps 1-7, £60-£110, Jan-Dec, bus nearby, rail nearby, ferry nearby, airport 4 mls

Mrs C M Macrae, Lovedale, Kyle of Lochalsh, Ross-shire
☎ *Kyle (0599) 4235*

VAT is shown at 15%: changes in this rate may affect prices.

KYLESKU Sutherland Map Ref. 3G4

1 cottage, 2 pub rms, 2 bedrms, sleeps 5, £65-£105, Jan-Dec, bus ¾ ml, rail 40 mls, ferry 32 mls

 ♿ 🚾 E 🚗 🏠 🖥 🖨 🧺 🍳 ✿ 🐴 P 🏇 🏭 †   🎣 ⛵ ⛱ 🏊 ✕ 🏪 🚲 (guided hillwalking)

Mrs F J Macaulay, Linne Mhuirich, Unapool, Kylesku, by Lairg, Sutherland, IV27 4HW
☎ *Kylestrome (097183) 227*

LAGGAN BRIDGE, by Newtonmore Inverness-shire Map Ref. 4A11

1 cottage, 2 pub rms, 4 bedrms, sleeps 6, from £75, Mar-Nov, bus nearby, rail 7 mls

 ♿ 🚾 E 🚗 🏠 🏭 ◎ ☉ 🖥 🖨 🔌 ☉ ✿ P 🏇 † 🚠   🎣 ⛵ ➤ 🏊 ✕ 🏪 Ⓣ

S M B Fleming, Saxon House, Molly Hurst Lane, Woolley, by Wakefield, West Yorks
☎ *Barnsley (0226) 383258*

LAGGAN, by Newtonmore Inverness-shire Map Ref. 4A11

2 cottages, 1 pub rm, 2-3 bedrms, sleeps 5-6, min let 3 days (low season), £50-£110, Mar-Nov, bus nearby, rail 7 mls, airport 55 mls

 ♿ 🚾 E 🚗 🏠 🏭 ◎ 🖥 🖨 🔌 🧺 🔌 ☉ ✿ 🐴 P 🏇 🏭 †   🎣 ⛵ ✕ 🏪 🚲

Mrs Shirley A Grant, Gaskbeg, Laggan, Newtonmore, Inverness-shire, PH20 1BS
☎ *Laggan (05284) 255*

1 cottage, 2 pub rms, 3 bedrms, sleeps 6, £80-£100, Apr-Oct, bus 6 mls, rail 6 mls, airport 45 mls

 ♿ 🚾 E 🚗 🏠 🧺 🖨 🔌 ✿ 🐴 P †   🎣 ⛵ ⛱ ➤ ✎ 🏊 ✕ 🏪 🚲

Mrs Macgillivray, Cluny Mains, Laggan, by Newtonmore, Inverness-shire, PH20 1BS
☎ *Laggan (05284) 228*

LAIDE Ross-shire Map Ref. 3F6

COMMENDED
♛ ♛

2 bungalows, 2 pub rms, 3 bedrms, sleeps 6-7, min let weekend, £110-£150, Mar-Oct, bus nearby, rail 46 mls

 ♿ 🚾 E 🚗 🏠 ◎ 🖥 🖨 🔌 ☉ ✿ 🐴 P 🏇 🏭   🎣 ⛵ ⛱ ➤ ✎ ✕ 🏪

1 caravan, sleeps 6, min let weekend, £50, Apr-Oct, bus nearby, rail 46 mls

 ♿ 🚾 E 🏠 🧺 🔌 🖨 🐴 P 🏇 🏭 †   🎣 ⛵ ⛱ ➤ ✎ ✕ 🏪

Mrs Isabel Stewart, The Sithean, Lonmore, Gairloch, Ross-shire, IV21 2DB
☎ *Gairloch (0445) 2035*
Modern units, seperately sited above village. Panoramic views over Gruinard Bay and beyond.

1 cottage, 2 pub rms, 3 bedrms, sleeps 8, £60-£150, Jan-Dec, bus 4 mls, rail 40 mls

 ♿ 🚾 E 🚗 🏠 🧺 🖨 🔌 ✿ 🐴 P 🏇 🏭 †   🎣 ⛵ ⛱ 🏪

N G A Gardner, 62 Dean Lane, Hazel Grove, Stockport, Cheshire, SK7 6DJ
☎ *Poynton (0625) 873075*

1 cottage, 1 pub rm, 3 bedrms, sleeps 6, £70-£90, Apr-Oct

 ♿ 🚾 E 🚗 🏠 ◎ 🖥 🖨 🔌 ☉ ✿ 🐴 P 🏇 🏭 🚗 †   🎣 ⛵ ⛱ ✕ 🏪

Mrs D MacLennan, Cherrytree, Laide, Achnasheen, Ross-shire, IV22 2NP
☎ *Aultbea (044582) 252*

---

1 house, 1 pub rm, 3 bedrms, sleeps 6, £80-£150, Jan-Dec, bus nearby, rail 50 mls, airport 85 mls

♿ ᵂᶜ E 🔥 ⌨ 🖥 🍽 ⌀ ⬜ ▭ ◙ ✂ ⚓ ☉ ❄ 🐎 🅿 🐟 🛏 🚽 † ⛰ 🌀   🐟 ⚲ Ⓡ ✗ 🧰
🔔 🎵 Ⓣ

Ocean View Hotel, Laide, by Aultbea, Ross-shire, IV22 2ND
☎ *Aultbea (044582) 385*

AWAITING INSPECTION	1 cottage, 2 pub rms, 3 bedrms, sleeps 6, £70-£120, May-Sep, bus 3 mls ♿ ᵂᶜ E 🔥 ⌀ ◎ ⬜ ⚓ ☉ ❄ 🅿 🐟 🍽 † 🐟 △ ▸ 🧰

Mrs M C Maxwell, Greenacres, Westhill, Inverness
☎ *Inverness (0463) 791604*

---

1 bungalow, 1 pub rm, 2 bedrms, sleeps 4, from £70, May-Sep, bus 1 ½ mls, rail 40 mls

♿ ᵂᶜ E 🚽 ⌀ 🎹 ◎ ⬜ ▭ ✂ ⚓ ☉ ❄ 🅿 🐟 † ⛰   🐟 △ ⚲ ✗ 🧰 🔭

Mrs A MacIver, Meadowbank, Achgarve, Laide, Ross-shire
☎ *Aultbea (044582) 251*

LAIRG Sutherland Map Ref. 4A6

Builnatobrach Farm Cottages
Up to 👑 👑 👑
Commended

BUILNATOBRACH · LAIRG · SUTHERLAND
Telephone: (0549) 2018

Set amidst forest, these cottages offer a peaceful retreat, yet only 5 minutes' walk from village centre. Panoramic views over Loch Shin with mountains of Sutherland in the background. An ideal base for the fisherman, birdwatcher or nature-lover. Each cottage has lounge/kitchen, 2 bedrooms, 1 double, 1 twin (extra beds on request), bathroom, fully equipped with colour TV, automatic washing machine and all bed linen.

Newly converted farm cottage with 3 bedrooms now available.

For bookings please write or ring:
Sue and David Hayhurst, Builnatobrach Farm, Lairg, Sutherland. SAE will be appreciated.

---

up to **COMMENDED** 👑 👑 👑	2 flats, 2 cottages, 1 pub rm, 2 bedrms, sleeps 2-4, £55-£190, Jan-Dec, bus 500 yds, rail 3 mls ♿ ᵂᶜ E 🚽 ⌀ 🖥 ◎ ⌀ ⬜ ▭ ◙ ⚓ ❄ 🐎 🅿 🐟 ⛰ 🐟 ∪ △ ⚲ ▸ ✗ 🧰 🔭 Ⓣ

Mr D P Hayhurst, Builnatobrach Farm, Lairg, Sutherland, IV27 4DB
☎ *Lairg (0549) 2018*
In rural setting overlooking Loch Shin, 300 yards from village.

---

3 caravans, sleeps 6-8, min let 1 night, £20-£60, Jan-Dec, bus nearby, rail ¼ ml, airport 55 mls

♿ ᵂᶜ E ⌀ 🖥 ⌀ ⬜ ▭ ◙ ⚓ ☉ ❄ 🐎 🅿 †   🐟 ∪ ✗ 🧰 Ⓣ

Mrs E K Dunbar, Cairnmuir, Riverside, Lairg, Sutherland
☎ *Lairg (0549) 2136*

👑 👑 👑	2 cottages, 1 pub rm, 3 bedrms, sleeps 5, £70-£100, Apr-Nov, bus nearby, rail 6 mls ♿ ᵂᶜ E 🚽 ⌀ 🖥 ◎ ⬜ ▭ ◙ ⚓ ☉ ❄ 🐎 🅿 ⁄ 🐟 🍽 🚽 ✎ 🐟 △ ⁄ 🧰 🔭

Mrs Magee, Colaboll Farm, Shinness, Lairg, Sutherland, IV27 4DN
☎ *Lairg (0549) 2316*

Sutherland Arms
SELF CATERING
GARDEN APARTMENTS & COTTAGE

Sutherland Arms Hotel stands overlooking Loch Shin in the peace and tranquillity of Sutherland. In the hotel grounds, our Garden Apartments and Cottage offer superb accommodation for 2, 4 or 6 persons with comfortably furnished lounge/dining room, colour TV, bathroom and kitchen. Crockery, cutlery, linen, towels and continental quilts all provided.

The Hotel's Restaurant and Bar facilities are all available and the well-stocked Scottish Craft Shop is well worth a visit. The hotel has excellent loch and river fishing and championship golf and magnificent beaches are available at Dornoch and other areas nearby.

Weekly rentals start at £70.

Write or telephone for further information and brochures to: Sutherland Arms Hotel, Lairg, Sutherland IV27 4AT. Tel: 0549-2291.

1 flat, 5 cottages, 1 pub rm, 1-2 bedrms, sleeps 2-6, £70-£205, Jan-Dec, rail 1 ½ mls, airport 60 mls

Mr D Walker, Manager, Sutherland Arms Hotel, Lairg, Sutherland, IV27 4AT
☎ *Lairg (0549) 2291*

Woodend Caravan Site 8 caravans, sleeps 6, min let 1 night, £70-£80, Apr-Sep, bus 7 mls, rail nearby

Mr & Mrs C M Ross, Woodend Caravan and Camping Site, Achnairn, Lairg, Sutherland, IV27 4DN
☎ *Lairg (0549) 2248*

---

1 cottage, 1 pub rm, 2 bedrms, sleeps 7, £80-£115, Apr-Oct

Finlayson Hughes, Bank House, 82 Atholl Rd, Pitlochry, Perthshire, PH16 5BL
☎ *Pitlochry (0796) 2512*

LAMLASH Isle of Arran Map Ref. 1F7

1 flat, 7 maisonettes, 1 pub rm, 2 bedrms, sleeps 4, £90-£160, Jan-Dec, ferry 3 ½ mls

Mr J Gordon, Ship House Maisonettes, Lamlash, Isle of Arran
☎ *Lamlash (07706) 231*

Prices shown are for guidance only. Please send SAE with each enquiry.

ISLE OF ARRAN
Dyemill Chalets · Monamhor Glen
Telephone: (07706) 419

Six superior Scandinavian chalets set in secluded site bordering on Forestry Commission woodland with delightful views of hill and glen. Double glazed and insulated. Warm and clean. Equipped to a high standard. Continental quilts and all bed linen supplied.

Chalet operation under the attentive personal supervision of the proprietors. Stamp only for brochure.

**Enquiries to: Mrs and Mrs J. T. Cowie,
The Dyemill, Monamhor Glen,
by Brodick, Isle of Arran KA27 8NU.
AA LISTED**

up to COMMENDED
♕♕♕♕

6 chalet/log cabins, 1 pub rm, 2 bedrms, sleeps 4, £75-£160, mid Apr-Sep, bus ¼ ml, ferry 4 mls

🚫 wc E 🛏 ⌀ 🖥 🗄 ◉ 🗍 📞 🔌 ⊙ ❄ P 🐎 🏛   ✎ 🎣 ∪ ⚠ ⚓ ↑ 🖊 ✗ 🧺

Mr & Mrs Cowie, The Dyemill, Mona Mhor Glen, Via Brodick, Isle of Arran, KA27 8NU
☎ Lamlash (07706) 419

Units well spaced in secluded wood setting. Millhouse seperately sited. Hill views, forest walks.

---

1 flat, 1 pub rm, 3 bedrms, sleeps 6, min let weekend, £70-£160, Feb-Oct, bus nearby, ferry 3 mls

🚫 wc E 🛏 🗟 ⌀ 🗄 ◉ 🗍 🗗 🗖 ∥ 🔌 ⊙ ❄ 🐾 🏠 P 🐎 🐕 †   🍴 🎿 ✎ 🎣 🎣 ∪ ⚠ ⚓ ↦ ✗ 🧺

1 caravan, sleeps 4, min let weekend, £30-£100, Feb-Oct, bus nearby, ferry 3 mls

🚫 wc E 🗟 ⌀ 🗄 ⊘ 🗍 🗗 🗖 ∥ 🔌 ⊙ ❄ 🐾 P † 🍴 🎿 ✎ 🎣 🎣 ∪ ⚠ ⚓ ↦ ✗ 🧺

Mrs McArthur, Blairbeg House, Lamlash, Isle of Arran
☎ Lamlash (07706) 383

COMMENDED
♕♕♕♕

4 houses, 1 pub rm, 2-3 bedrms, sleeps 4-7, min let weekend (low season), £50-£135, Jan-Dec, bus ¾ ml, ferry 4 mls

🚫 wc E 🛏 ⌀ 🖥 🗄 ◉ 🗍 🗗 🗖 ∥ 🔌 ⊙ ❄ 🐾 🏠 P 🐎 🏛 🛏 ⚙ ☺   🍴 ✎ 🎣 🎣 ∪ ⚠ ⚓ ↦ R ✗ 🧺 🔥

Mr & Mrs Muirhead, Oakbank Farm, Lamlash, Isle of Arran
☎ Lamlash (07706) 404

Newly converted farm steading on high site with easy access to shops. Owner on site. Evening Meals.

---

1 house, 2 pub rms, 3 bedrms, sleeps 5, £80-£170, Jan-Dec, bus ¼ ml, ferry 4 mls

🚫 wc E 🛏 ⌀ 🖥 🗄 ◉ 🗍 📞 🗗 🔌 ⊙ ❄ P 🐎 🏛 †   ✎ 🎣 ∪ ⚠ ⚓ ↦ 🖊 ✗ 🧺

Mr & Mrs J T Cowie, The Dyemill, Mona Mhor Glen, Via Brodick, Isle of Arran, KA27 8NU
☎ Lamlash (07706) 419

LANGHOLM Dumfriesshire Map Ref. 2D9

1 cottage, 1 pub rm, 3 bedrms, sleeps 6, £76-£160, Apr-Oct, rail 12 mls, airport 30 mls

🚫 wc E 🛏 ⌀ ◉ 🗍 ⊙ ❄ 🐾 P †   🎣 ✗

Amaro Cottage Holidays, 22 High Street, Alton, Hants
☎ Alton (0420) 88892 Telex 858963

VAT is shown at 15%: changes in this rate may affect prices.

LANTON, by Jedburgh Roxburghshire Map Ref. 2E7

COMMENDED

2 cottages, 1 pub rm, 2-4 bedrms, sleeps 5-8, min let weekend (low season), £50-£140, Mar-Oct, bus nearby

Mrs C Bruce, Bemersyde Farm, Melrose, Roxburghshire
☎ *St Boswells (0835) 23721*
Converted stone units surrounded by farm land. Each with large garden, sharing common courtyard area.

LARGOWARD Fife Map Ref. 2D3

1 cottage, 1 pub rm, 4 bedrms, sleeps 5, £80-£130, Jun-Sep, bus nearby, rail 7 mls, airport 17 mls

Mrs J Sharpus-Jones, Old Largoward Cottages, Largoward, Fife, KY9 1JA
☎ *Peat Inn (033484) 376*

LAUDER Berwickshire Map Ref. 2E6

APPROVED

1 house, 2 pub rms, 4 bedrms, sleeps 7, min let weekend, £45-£145, Jan-Dec, bus nearby, rail 26 mls, airport 35 mls

Mrs J D Durran, 11 Eskside West, Musselburgh, Midlothian, EH21 6PL
☎ *031 665 2682*
An early victorian stone built house standing at one end of small green in centre of village.

LEITHOLM Berwickshire Map Ref. 2F6

1 cottage, 1 pub rm, 3 bedrms, sleeps 6, £60-£85, Apr-Oct, bus ½ ml, rail 15 mls, airport 50 mls

Mrs M Calder, Langrig, Leitholm, Coldstream, Berwickshire
☎ *Leitholm (089084) 256*

LENDALFOOT, by Girvan Ayrshire Map Ref. 1F9

Carleton Caravan Park 5 caravans, sleeps 6, min let 1 night, £60-£90, Mar-Oct, bus ½ ml, rail 7 mls, airport 35 mls

Mr & Mrs W Hyslop, Carelton Lodge, Lendalfoot, by Girvan, Ayrshire, KA26 0JF
☎ *Lendalfoot (046589) 215*

The Meidlum 4 chalet/log cabins, 1 pub rm, 2 bedrms, sleeps 6-8, min let weekend, £50-£180, Mar-Oct, Xmas-New Year, bus nearby, rail 6 mls, airport 30 mls

Meidlum Holidays, 40 Manor Close, Sherston, by Malmesbury, Wilts, SN16 0NS
☎ *Sherston (0666) 840694*

1 cottage, 1 pub rm, 2 bedrms, sleeps 5, £75-£160, Jan-Dec, bus ½ ml, rail 9 mls

Mrs Moyra M Hay, 50 Dalrymple Street, Girvan, Ayrshire, KA26 9BT
☎ *Girvan (0465) 4421/2378*

LENTRAN Inverness-shire Map Ref. 4A9

3 cottages, 1 pub rm, 2-3 bedrms, sleeps 4-6, min let weekend (low season), £60-£120, May-Sep, bus ¼ ml, rail 6 mls, airport 12 mls

🐾♿ E 🛏 🗑 ◎ 🗂 ✂ ▱ ⊙ 🐕 🅿 🛁 🏥   ✒ ∪ ⚐ ↾ ✗ 🔋 🎠

Mrs S Lawson, The Stackyard, Pitglassie Farm, Dingwall, Ross-shire, IV15 9TR
☎ *Dingwall (0349) 62249*
Chalet-style accommodation on working farm. 1/2 mile (1km) from main A832, 6 miles (9km) Inverness.

LERAGS, by Oban Argyll Map Ref. 1E2

1 house, 1 pub rm, 2 bedrms, sleeps 8, £65-£170, Jan-Dec, bus 3 mls, rail 3 mls

🐾♿ E 🛏 🗑 ▦ ◎ 🗂 📞 ▱ ◣ 🐕 🅿 🛁 🏥 † ⚲   ⬱ 🐟 ✒ ∪ ⚐ ⚡ ✗ 🔋

Mrs M R Whitton, Kilbride Farm, Lerags, by Oban, Argyll
☎ *Oban (0631) 62878*

---

1 cottage, 2 pub rms, 4 bedrms, sleeps 2-7, min let weekend, from £50, Jan-Dec, bus 5 mls, rail 5 mls

🐾♿ E 🛏 🗑 ▦ ▱ ◎ 🗂 ▱ 🗑 ◣ ⊙ ✳ 🅿 🛁 🏥 🛏 †   ✒ ∪ ⚐ ↾ ⚡ ✗

Miss E Lees Whittick, Lerags Beg, by Oban, Argyll, PA34 4SE
☎ *Oban (0631) 62450*

LERWICK Shetland Map Ref. 5G4

1 hostel, 2 pub rms, 6 bedrms, sleeps 8, min let 1 night, £3-£4 (per person/night), mid Apr-Sep, ferry ½ ml, airport 25 mls

🐾♿ E 🗂 🖋 🗑 ▦ ▱ ◎ 🗂 📞 ▱ 🗑 ✂ ◣ ⊙ ✳ 🅿 🛁 † ● 🌐   ⬱ ⬲ 🐟 ⚲ 🎋 ✒ ∪
⚐ ⚡ ↾ ® ✗ 🔋 🆃

Lerwick Youth Hostel, Islesburgh House, King Harald St, Lerwick, Shetland, ZE1 0EQ
☎ *Lerwick (0595) 2114*

---

6 flats, 1 pub rm, 1-3 bedrms, sleeps 2-6, £120-£260, Jan-Dec, bus nearby, ferry 1 ml, airport 24 mls

🐾♿ E 🛏 🗂 🖋 🗑 ▦ ▱ ◎ 🗂 📞 ▱ 🗑 ◣ ⊙ ✳ 🐕 🅿 ∥ 🛁 🏥 ⚲   ⬱ 🐟 ⚲ 🎋 ✒
⚐ ⚡ ↾ ⚑ ⚡ ✗ 🔋 🆃 (sub-aqua)

Queens Hotel, Lerwick, Shetland
☎ *Lerwick (0595) 2826*

---

1 cottage, 1 pub rm, 2 bedrms, sleeps 6, £60-£80, Jan-Dec, bus nearby, rail 180 mls, ferry ½ ml, airport 5 mls

🐾♿ E 🗂 🗑 🗂 ◎ 🗂 ▱ ◣ ⊙ 🅿 🛁 🏥 †   ⬱ 🐟 ⚲ 🎋 ✒ ∪ ⚐ ⚡ ↾ ⚑ ⚡ ✗ 🔋
🆃 (skin diving)

Mrs S Manson, Bersa, 49 King Harald Street, Lerwick, Shetland, ZE1 0EQ
☎ *Lerwick (0595) 3782*

LEUCHARS Fife Map Ref. 2D2

Almar Bank Caravan Park 8 caravans, sleeps 5-8, min let 2 nights, £35-£90, Mar-Oct, bus nearby, rail 1 ml, airport 8 mls

🐾♿ E 🗂 🗑 🗑 🗂 🗑 ✂ ◣ ⊙ 🅿 🛁 🏥 † ⚲ 🌐   ⚲ ✒ ∪ ⚐ ⚡ ↾ ✗ 🔋

G & D Adam, Almar Villa, 6 Meadow Road, Leuchars, Fife, KY16 0EX
☎ *Leuchars (033483) 303*

VAT is shown at 15%: changes in this rate may affect prices.

1 cottage, 1 pub rm, 2 bedrms, sleeps 6, from £75, Jan-Dec, bus 3 mls, rail 3 mls, airport 12 mls

♿ ᵂᶜ E 🛏 🔌 🖥 ◎ 🗂 ⚡ 🛁 ❄ 🐕 🅿 ▸

Forestry Commission, Forest Holidays, Dept SC1, 231 Corstorphine Rd, Edinburgh, EH12 7AT
☎ *031 334 0303*

---

1 cottage, 1 pub rm, 2 bedrms, sleeps 4, £80-£110, Jun-Sep, bus 1 ½ mls, rail 2 mls, airport 12 mls

♿ ᵂᶜ E 🛏 🔌 🗄 ◎ 🗂 🗂 🗂 🛁 ❄ 🐓 🅿 🛋 🖥 † ⚰ ∪ ▸ ✕ 🦺 🐾

Mrs E Clark, Cast Farm, Leuchars, Fife, KY16 0DP
☎ *Leuchars (033483) 524*

LEYSMILL, by Arbroath Angus Map Ref. 2E1

1 house, 2 pub rms, 2 bedrms, sleeps 5, £30-£85, Jan-Dec, bus 1 ml, rail 5 mls, airport 75 mls

♿ ᵂᶜ E 🛏 🔌 🖥 🗂 🗂 🗂 🛁 ☺ ❄ 🅿 🛋 🖥 † 🎵 ⚓ ✕ 🦺

Mrs A M Ephraums, Damside, Leysmill, by Arbroath, Angus, DD11 4RS
☎ *Friockheim (02412) 226*

LILLIESLEAF, by Melrose Roxburghshire Map Ref. 2E7

1 cottage, 1 pub rm, 3 bedrms, sleeps 5, £70-£120, Apr-Oct, bus 2 mls, rail 50 mls, airport 58 mls

♿ ᵂᶜ E 🛏 🔌 🖥 🗄 ◎ 🗂 🗂 🗂 ⚡ 🛁 ☺ ❄ 🐕 🅿 🛋 🖥 † 🎵 ✕ 🦺 🐾 Ⓣ (riding centre, hillwalking)

Mrs Jane Cameron, Dimpleknone, Lilliesleaf, Melrose, Roxburghshire, TD6 9JU
☎ *Lilliesleaf (08357) 333*

LINLITHGOW West Lothian Map Ref. 2B5

CRAIGS HOLIDAY LODGES
Williamcraigs, Linlithgow, West Lothian EH49 6QF
Near Edinburgh, Craigs Holiday Lodges stand on a wooded hillside with panoramic views over the Forth Valley. Ideal for trips to Scottish Borders, Trossachs, Edinburgh. Country parks, castles, stately homes, fishing, golf, all within a few miles. Barbecue and children's play area. Chalets are fully equipped including colour TV. Bed linen supplied. A quiet rural site, ideal for children.
Telephone: Linlithgow (0506 84) 5025

Craigs Chalet Park 10 chalet/log cabins, 1 pub rm, 2 bedrms, sleeps 4-6, £75-£195, Jan-Dec, bus 1 ml, rail 1 ml, airport 14 mls

♿ ᵂᶜ E 🛏 🔌 🗄 🔄 ◎ 🗂 📞 🗂 ☺ ❄ 🐓 🅿 🛋 🖥 ⚲ 🎣 🎵 ⚓ ▸ ✕ 🦺 Ⓣ

J & G Howie, Craigs Chalet Park, Williamcraigs, Linlithgow, West Lothian, EH49 6QF
☎ *Linlithgow (0506) 845025*

Loch House Farm Site 1 caravan, sleeps 4-6, min let 1 night, £50-£70, Jan-Dec, bus nearby, rail 1 ml, airport 10 mls

E 🗄 🔌 🗂 🛁 ☺ 🐓 🅿 † 🎣 🐾 ⚲ 🎣 🎵 ∪ ⚓ ▸ ✕ 🦺 🐾

Mr A G Smart, Loch House Farm, Linlithgow, West Lothian
☎ *Linlithgow (0506) 842144*

LINTRATHEN, by Kirriemuir Angus Map Ref. 2D1

1 chalet/log cabin, 1 pub rm, 2 bedrms, sleeps 6, min let 2 nights (low season), £100-£160, Jan-Dec, bus 6 mls, rail 22 mls, airport 70 mls

♿ 🆆 E ⏬ ⌂ ■ □ ◉ □ □ ▫ ◼ ☉ ✧ ✔ ♻ † ♩ ◡ ▸ ∕ ▣ ⅞

Mrs M E Houstoun, Lintrathen Lodge, Kirriemuir, Angus
☎ *Lintrathen (05756) 228*

LITTLE DALCROSS, by Croy Inverness-shire Map Ref. 4B8

1 caravan, sleeps 4-6, £50-£80, Mar-Oct, bus 1 ml, rail 8 mls, airport 2 mls

♿ 🆆 E ⎪ ⌂ ◉ □ □ ✧ ✔ ♻ † ⅞

Mrs J Douglas, Little Dalcross, Croy, Inverness, Inverness-shire, IV1 2PS
☎ *Croy (06678) 224*

LOCH RANNOCH Perthshire Map Ref. 1H1

COMMENDED

1 cottage, 2 pub rms, 2 bedrms, sleeps 6, from £78, Jan-Dec, rail 9 mls

♿ 🆆 E ⏬ ⌂ ◼ ◉ □ ▫ ☉ ✧ ✔ ♻ ▣ ◼ † ♩ △

Forestry Commission, Forest Holidays, Dept SC1, 231 Corstorphine Rd, Edinburgh, EH12 7AT
☎ *031 334 0303*
Stone built, former keeper's cottage. Quiet location beside loch, on edge of Black Wood of Rannoch.

Loch Rannoch

Comfortable holiday cottages by the lochside. The ideal place for a peaceful holiday amidst magnificent scenery, with many interesting places to visit.
Trout fishing, birdwatching, hill and forest walks.
For brochure, write or telephone: **Mr and Mrs V. C. REDDISH, Croiscrag, Rannoch, Perthshire PH17 2QG.
Telephone: 088-23 255.**

2 flats, 5 cottages, 1-2 pub rms, 2 bedrms, sleeps 6, from £72, Mar-Oct, rail 9 mls

♿ 🆆 E ⏬ ⌂ ◼ ◉ □ ▫ ✧ ✔ ♻ ▣ ◼ ♩ △ ∕ (birdwatching)

Mr & Mrs V C Reddish, Croiscrag, Rannoch, Perthshire, PH17 2QG
☎ *Bridge of Gaur (08823) 255*

LOCH TUMMEL Perthshire Map Ref. 2A1

1 cottage, 1 pub rm, 2 bedrms, sleeps 4-6, min let 3 nights, £40-£120, Jan-Dec, bus 300 yds, rail 8 mls, airport 40 mls

♿ 🆆 E ⏬ ⌂ ◼ ◉ □ ● □ / ▫ ✧ ✔ ♻ ▣ † ⃠ ♩ ◡ △ ▸ ✕

Miss Grace Stirling, 4 Nelson Street, Dundee, Angus, DD3 8JN
☎ *Dundee (0382) 26057*

by LOCHAILORT Inverness-shire Map Ref. 3F12

1 cottage, 1 pub rm, 1 bedrm, sleeps 4-5, £65-£90, May-Oct, bus nearby, rail 8 mls

♿ 🆆 E ⌂ ◼ / □ ✔ ♻ ▣ ◼ † ♩ ◡ △ ≼ ✕ ▣ ⅞
2 caravans, sleeps 4-6, min let weekend, £60-£75, May-Oct, bus nearby, rail 8 mls

♿ 🆆 E ⌂ ◉ / □ ✧ ✔ ♻ ▣ ◼ ⃠ ◡ ✕ ▣ ⅞

Mrs M MacDonald, Seannlag, Glenuig, Lochailort, Inverness-shire
☎ *Lochailort (06877) 226*

LOCHARBRIGGS, by Dumfries Dumfriesshire Map Ref. 2B9

AWAITING INSPECTION

1 bungalow, 1 pub rm, 3 bedrms, sleeps 6, £70-£90, Jan-Dec, bus ½ ml, rail 3 mls

Mr & Mrs J H Henderson, Catherinefield Farm, Locharbriggs, Dumfries, Dumfriesshire, DG1 3PJ
☎ *Dumfries (0387) 54972*

LOCHAWE Argyll Map Ref. 1F2

3 flats, 1 pub rm, 1-2 bedrms, sleeps 2-5, £111-£265, Jan-Dec, bus ½ ml, rail ½ ml, airport 65 mls

Mr & Mrs H Douglas-Reid, St Conan's Tower, Lochawe, Argyll, PA33 1AH
☎ *Dalmally (08382) 342*

LOCHBROOM Ross-shire Map Ref. 3G7

2 caravans, sleeps 5-6, £55-£70, May-Sep, bus 4 mls, rail 25 mls, ferry 10 mls, airport 60 mls

Mrs C Cameron, Hillview, Ardindrean, Lochbroom, Ross-shire, IV23 2SE
☎ *Lochbroom (085485) 244*

---

1 cottage, 1 pub rm, 3 bedrms, sleeps 6, from £100, Apr-Oct, bus 8 mls, rail 24 mls, airport 52 mls

Mr & Mrs J E Hurst, Morton Old Rectory, Morton-on-the-Hill, Norwich, Norfolk
☎ *Norwich (0603) 860225/611212*

---

3 cottages, 1-2 pub rms, 2-3 bedrms, sleeps 6-7, £60-£140, Feb-Sep, bus 7 mls, rail 70 mls, ferry 7 mls, airport 70 mls

Inverlael Cottages, Lochbroom, by Ullapool, Ross-shire
☎ *Lochbroom (085485) 262*

---

3 caravans, sleeps 6, £65-£80, Apr-Oct, bus 5 mls, rail 30 mls, airport 65 mls

Mr Urquhart, Park View, Ardcharnich, Lochbroom, by Garve, Ross-shire
☎ *Lochbroom (085485) 270/(0854) 2677*

LOCHBUIE Isle of Mull, Argyll Map Ref. 1D2

1 house, 2 pub rms, 4 bedrms, sleeps 8, £115-£170, Jan-Dec, ferry 14 mls

Mrs A Reid, Post Office, Lochbuie, Isle of Mull, Argyll
☎ *Kinlochspelve (06804) 260*

LOCHCARRON Ross-shire Map Ref. 3F9

1 cottage, 2 pub rms, 2 bedrms, sleeps 6, min let weekend (low season), £75-£175, Jan-Dec, rail 2 mls, airport 65 mls

Mrs Inglis, The White Cottage, Lochcarron, Ross-shire, IV54 8YB
☎ *Lochcarron (05202) 311 (eve)*

Prices shown are for guidance only. Please send SAE with each enquiry.

1 house, 2 pub rms, 4 bedrms, sleeps 8, min let weekend, £184-£230, Oct-Jun, rail ½ ml, airport 60 mls

க் ᴡᴄ E ⬅ 🗑 ◎ 📺 🥃 ⚡ ⭐ ⊙ ❋ 🐎 P ⫽ ✂ ⊞ † 🔧 U ⚓ ⚓ ▸ ⟋ ✕ 🛍 🔥 T

Mr M J Knatchbull, 41 Montpelier Walk, London, SW7 1JH
☎ *01 589 8829*

LOCHEARNHEAD Perthshire Map Ref. 1H2

Loch Earn Lodges TEL: (05673) 211
LOCHEARNHEAD · PERTHSHIRE · FK19 8PT
Six comfortable Scots Log Chalets, well spaced with beautiful views of Loch Earn and the Perthshire hills. Fully equipped for 4/6 people, including colour TV, linen. Personally supervised by resident owners. Excellent touring, fishing, hill walking, water sports. Free launchings, jetty, moorings. Water ski-ing tuition. Motor boats, sailboards, canoes for hire. Loch cruises. From £80-£230 per week.
Colour brochure from Mrs C. Borland, Loch Earn Lodges, Lochearnhead, Perthshire (05673) 211.

APPROVED
👑 👑 👑

Lochearn Lodges 6 chalet/log cabins, 1 pub rm, 2-3 bedrms, sleeps 6, min let 2 nights (low season), £70-£230, Jan-Dec, bus 600 yds, rail 20 mls, airport 50 mls

க் ᴡᴄ E ⬅ 🗑 🛏 ◎ 📺 🍳 ⚡ ⬛ ⊙ ❋ 🐎 P ⫽ ✂ ⊞ ⬅ 🔧 U ⚓ ▸ ⊿ ✕ 🛍 T

Mrs Catherine Borland, Loch Earn Lodges, Lochearnhead, Perthshire, FK19 8PT
☎ *Lochearnhead (05673) 211*

In attractive high setting above Loch Earn. Close to local amenities and recreational facilities.

APPROVED
👑 👑 👑

1 cottage, 1 pub rm, 1 bedrm, sleeps 2-4, min let 2 nights, £60-£85, Apr-Oct, bus 1 ml, rail 30 mls, airport 60 mls

க் ᴡᴄ E 📻 🗑 🍳 🛏 ◎ 📺 🍳 ⬛ ⊙ ❋ 🐎 P ✂ ⊞ † 🔧 ⚓ ▸ ⟋ ⊿ ✕ 🛍 🔥 T

1 caravan, sleeps 2, min let 2 nights, £50-£75, Apr-Oct, bus 1 ml, rail 30 mls, airport 60 mls

க் ᴡᴄ E 📻 ◎ 📺 🍳 ⬛ ❋ 🐎 P ✂ ⊞ † 🔧 ⚓ ▸ ⟋ ⊿ ✕ 🛍 🔥 T

Aubrey Knowles, Earnknowe, Lochearnhead, Perthshire, FK19 8PY
☎ *Lochearnhead (05673) 238*

Timber clad in elevated position giving excellent views over Loch Earn.

HIGHLY COMMENDED
👑 👑 👑 👑

8 chalet/log cabins, 3 studios, 1 pub rm, 2-3 bedrms, sleeps 4-6, min let 2 nights, £95-£265, Apr-Oct, bus nearby (postbus), rail 16 mls, airport 60 mls

க் ᴡᴄ E ⬅ 📻 🖥 🛏 ◎ 📺 🍳 ⬛ ⊙ ❋ 🐎 P ✂ ⊞ /\ 🔍 🎣 🔧 ⚓ ▸ ⊿ ✕ 🛍 🍷 T

Lochearnhead Hotel & Lochside Cottages, Lochearnhead, Perthshire
☎ *Lochearnhead (05673) 229*

Modern, Danish pine units on lochside by hotel. Watersports centre; launching, mooring and jetty.

---

1 cottage, 2 pub rms, 2 bedrms, sleeps 6, £65-£110, Apr-Oct, bus ½ ml, rail 16 mls, airport 50 mls

க் ᴡᴄ E ⬅ 🗑 🛏 ◎ 📺 🥃 🗄 ◎ ⬛ P ✂ ⊞ † 🔧 ⚓ ▸ ✕ 🛍

Mrs MacLachlan, Castleview West, Lochearnhead, Perthshire, FK19 8PU
☎ *Lochearnhead (05673) 201*

VAT is shown at 15%: changes in this rate may affect prices.

203

1 bungalow, 3 bedrms, sleeps 4-5, min let weekend, £100-£150, Mar-Nov, bus 500 yds, rail 30 mls, airport 60 mls

Mrs Jean Parry, Pensans, 9 The Drive, Retford, Notts, DN22 6SD
☎ *Retford (07707) 700799*

LOCHFOOT Dumfriesshire Map Ref. 2B10

1 house, 1 pub rm, 1 bedrm, sleeps 5, min let weekend, from £60, Apr-Oct, bus nearby, rail 5 mls

Mrs J McCubbing, Red House, Lochfoot, Dumfriesshire
☎ *Lochfoot (038773) 253*

LOCHGILPHEAD Argyll Map Ref. 1E4

Lochgilphead Caravan Park 10 caravans, sleeps 6, min let 2 nights, from £60, Apr-Oct, bus nearby, rail 37 mls

(sports centre)

Mr MacDonald, Lochgilphead Caravan Park, Lochgilphead, Argyll
☎ *Lochgilphead (0546) 2003*

LOCHGILPHEAD AREA Argyll Map Ref. 1E4

Ellary Estate Cottages

The *Gardens Cottage*, one of the several available on Ellary Estate.

●

Send for brochure to the booking office:
Ellary, Lochgilphead, Argyll PA31 8PA or Telephone 088 03 232 or 054 685 223

AWAITING INSPECTION

5 chalet/log cabins, 9 houses, 2 flats, 4 cottages, 1-3 pub rms, 2-4 bedrms, sleeps 6-8, min let 2 nights, £90-£240, Jan-Dec

20 caravans, sleeps 6, min let 2 nights, £82-£170, Mar-Oct

Castle Sween (Holidays) Ltd, Ellary, Lochgilphead, Argyll, PA31 8PA
☎ *Ormsary (08803) 232*

Prices shown are for guidance only. Please send SAE with each enquiry.

LOCHGOILHEAD Argyll Map Ref. 1G4

6 flats, 1 pub rm, 1 bedrm, sleeps 2-4, min let 2 nights, £69-£135, Jan-Dec, bus nearby, rail 16 mls, airport 55 mls

Douglas Campbell, Failte, Lochgoilhead, Argyll, PA24 8AD
☎ *Lochgoilhead (03013) 320/444*

Corrow Cabins 12 flats, 1 pub rm, 2 bedrms, sleeps 6, min let 2 nights, £69-£135, Jan-Dec, bus nearby, rail 18 mls, airport 55 mls

Mr Douglas Campbell, Failte, Lochgoilhead, Argyll, PA24 8AD
☎ *Lochgoilhead (03013) 320/444*

---

1 cottage, 1 pub rm, 5 bedrms, sleeps 9, min let weekend, £75-£115, Apr-Oct, bus nearby, rail 11 mls, airport 50 mls

Mrs A Lee, 51 School Lane, Solihull, West Midlands
☎ *021 705 0201*

---

1 house, 4 pub rms, 4 bedrms, sleeps 8-10, £175-£230, Mar-Oct, bus 800 yds, rail 10-12 mls, airport 48 mls

Mrs P G Evans, Nuthill, Lochgoilhead, Argyll
☎ *Lochgoilhead (03013) 271*

LOCHINVER Sutherland Map Ref. 3G5

HIGHLY COMMENDED

7 lodges, 1 pub rm, 2 bedrms, sleeps 2-6, £221-£450, Jan-Dec, bus nearby, rail 45 mls, airport 100 mls

Mrs Stewart, Lochinver Holiday Lodges, Strathan, by Lochinver, Sutherland, IV27 4LR
☎ *Lochinver (05714) 282*
Uniquely situated in secluded bay with excellent sea views. Personally run site.

(See colour ad. 13 p. xxxv)

Baddidarrach Chalets 3 chalet/log cabins, 1 pub rm, 2 bedrms, sleeps 4-6, min let 3 nights, £90-£185, Jan-Dec, bus ½ ml, rail 50 mls, airport 100 mls

Mrs J C MacLeod, 74 Baddidarrach, Lochinver, by Lairg, Sutherland, IV27 4LP
☎ *Lochinver (05714) 457/274*

---

1 cottage, 1 pub rm, 2 bedrms, sleeps 2-4, from £60, Apr-Oct, bus nearby

Mrs M McCall, Bayview House, Lochinver, by Lairg, Sutherland
☎ *Lochinver (05714) 231*

HIGHLY COMMENDED

1 cottage, 2 pub rms, 1 bedrm, sleeps 2, from £75, Mar-Nov, bus ¼ ml, rail 45 mls, airport 100 mls

Mrs Joan McClelland, Baddidarroch, Lochinver, Sutherland, IV27 4LR
☎ *Lochinver (05714) 377*
Extensively modernised and refurbished, former crofter's home. On private hillside overlooking loch.

VAT is shown at 15%: changes in this rate may affect prices.

1 cottage, 1 pub rm, 2 bedrms, sleeps 4, from £120, Apr-Oct, bus 1 ml, rail 46 mls, airport 100 mls

Mrs N W MacLeod, Inverness Cottage, Lochinver, Sutherland, IV27 4LP
☎ *Lochinver (05714) 284/417*

---

1 house, 2 pub rms, 4 bedrms, sleeps 8, £100-£200, Jan-Dec, bus 3 mls, rail 40 mls

Mr I Yates, 84 Torbreck, Lochinver, Sutherland
☎ *Lochinver (05714) 312*

---

3 caravans, sleeps 6, from £50, May-Oct, bus 3 mls, rail 45 mls, airport 100 mls

Mrs M Macaskill, Hamnavoe, 2 Inverkirkaig, Lochinver, Sutherland, IV27 4LR
☎ *Lochinver (05714) 239/267*

---

1 cottage, 1 pub rm, 3 bedrms, sleeps 6, from £115, May-Oct, bus 1 $\frac{1}{2}$ mls, rail 80 mls, airport 100 mls

T A S Forster, Tradewinds, Colley Way, Reigate, Surrey, RH2 9JH
☎ *Reigate (07372) 41092*

---

1 cottage, 2 pub rms, 3 bedrms, sleeps 6, from £50, Mar-Nov, bus nearby, rail 45 mls, airport 100 mls

Dr P Mcmichael, 90 Inverleith Place, Edinburgh, EH3 5PA
☎ *031 552 4143*

by LOCHINVER Sutherland Map Ref. 3G5

up to COMMENDED

Valhalla Lodges 6 lodges, 1 pub rm, 2 bedrms, sleeps 4-6, min let weekend, from £60, Mar-Nov, bus nearby, rail 45 mls, airport 100 mls

William Hutchison, Valhalla, Inverkirkaig, Lochinver, Sutherland, IV27 4LF
☎ *Lochinver (05714) 382*
Individually sited, overlooking secluded bay and facing Inverpolly Nature Reserve. Fishing and walks.

LOCHLUICHART, by Garve Ross-shire Map Ref. 3H8

1 bungalow, 1 pub rm, 3 bedrms, sleeps 6, £100-£140, Apr-Oct, rail 1 $\frac{1}{2}$ mls

Mr & Mrs R A Bedwell, Achnaclerach, Garve, Ross-shire, IV23 2PG
☎ *Garve (09974) 207*

---

2 cottages, 1-2 pub rms, 3-4 bedrms, sleeps 5-7, £63-£109, Jan-Dec, rail 1 ml, airport 35 mls

Lady E L Melville, Lochluichart Lodge, by Garve, Ross-shire
☎ *Garve (09974) 242*

LOCHMABEN, by Lockerbie Dumfriesshire Map Ref. 2C9

Mill Loch Caravan Site 15 caravans, sleeps 4-8, £47-£101, Jan-Dec, bus 500 yds, rail 2 mls, airport 30 mls

A & E Rollinson, Primrose Cottage, Greenhill, Hightae, Lockerbie, Dumfriesshire, DG11 1JB
☎ *Lochmaben (038781) 874*

1 cottage, 1 pub rm, 3 bedrms, sleeps 6, £80-£110, Apr-Oct, bus 1 ½ mls, rail 4 mls

Mr J A Forsyth, 60 Nunholm Road, Dumfries
☎ *Dumfries (0387) 69167/54212*

1 bungalow, 1 pub rm, 3 bedrms, sleeps 6, min let weekend, from £120, Jan-Dec, bus ½ ml, rail 5 mls

Mr W Blacklock, Maxwell Bank, Lochmaben, Lockerbie, Dumfriesshire, DG11 1RJ
☎ *Lochmaben (038781) 284*

LOCHRANZA Isle of Arran Map Ref. 1E6

1 house, 2 pub rms, 3 bedrms, sleeps 6, £100-£120, Jan-Dec, bus nearby, ferry 16 mls

Mrs McAllister, Millhill, Lochranza, Isle of Arran
☎ *Lochranza (077083) 273*

1 cottage, 1 pub rm, 1 bedrm, sleeps 2-4, min let weekend, £50-£70, Apr-Oct, bus nearby, ferry 15 mls

Mrs Brown, Kincardine Lodge, Lochranza, Isle of Arran
☎ *Lochranza (077083) 267*

1 cottage, 1 pub rm, 3 bedrms, sleeps 6, min let weekend, £50-£120, Jan-Dec

Mr Stewart, Lochranza Hotel, Lochranza, Isle of Arran
☎ *Lochranza (077083) 223*

VAT is shown at 15%: changes in this rate may affect prices.

LOGIERAIT, by Pitlochry Perthshire Map Ref. 2B1

Logierait Pine Lodges
by PITLOCHRY PH9 0LH
Telephone: (0796) 82 253

Luxurious Scandinavian chalets superbly fitted out. Extremely warm and comfortable. Beautifully situated by quiet riverside with free fishing. Adjoining hotel restaurant and bar. Ideal for touring, golf, bird watching, rambling. Low season charges from **£77 per week for 2/4 berth chalet fully inclusive.** Also 4/6 berth and 6/8 berth sized chalets.

Up to ♚ ♚ ♚ Commended

up to
COMMENDED
♚ ♚ ♚

Logierait Pine Lodges 15 chalet/log cabins, 1 pub rm, 1-3 bedrms, sleeps 2-8, min let 2 nights, £77-£285, Jan-Dec, bus nearby, rail 5 mls, airport 60 mls

 🔧 ⬛ E 🔌 📻 ⌂ 💻 🛏 💿 ⌂ 🖵 ▫ ☉ ♨ 🅿 ✎ 🔥 ♨ 📺 🎿 ⛰ ⟳ ⌬ ◔ 🎋 🎣 🏊 ⚓ ►
/ Ⓡ ✕ ⚓ ♈ 🎵 Ⓣ

Mr J MacFarlane, Logierait Pine Lodges, Logierait, by Pitlochry, Perthshire, PH9 0LJ
☎ *Ballinluig (079682) 253*
Beautiful riverside setting only minutes from town centre. Ideal touring area.

LONGFORGAN, by Dundee Perthshire Map Ref. 2D2

1 caravan, sleeps 4-6, min let 3 nights, £45-£55, Apr-Oct, bus nearby, rail 7 mls, airport 7 mls

 🔧 🎛 E ⌂ 🛏 ⌂ 🖵 ☀ ♨ 🅿 † ⛰ ⟳ 🎣 ⚓ ► 🎋 🏊

Mrs M B Kettles, Wellwood, Longforgan, by Dundee, Perthshire
☎ *Longforgan (082622) 259*

---

1 cottage, 1 bedrm, sleeps 2, £55-£80, Apr-Oct, bus nearby, rail 6 mls, airport 5 mls

 🔧 ⬛ E 🔌 📻 ⌂ 💻 ◉ ⌂ 🖵 ✎ ⚓ ☉ ☀ ♨ 🅿 † ⟳ ⌬ ◔ 🎋 ► ✕ 🏊

Mrs B G Kennedy, Elevation Bungalow, Gowanbank, by Arbroath, Angus
☎ *Gowanbank (024189) 215*

LONGFORMACUS Berwickshire Map Ref. 2F5

COMMENDED
♚ ♚

1 cottage, 1 pub rm, 3 bedrms, sleeps 5, £75-£100, May-Oct, bus 10 mls, rail 25 mls, airport 35 mls

 🔧 ⬛ E 🔌 ⌂ 💻 🛏 ◉ ⌂ 🖵 ✎ ⚓ ☉ ☀ ♨ 🅿 🎿 📺 † ⛰ 🎣 ✕ 🏊

Mrs A W Pate, Horseupcleugh, Duns, Berwickshire
☎ *Longformacus (03617) 225*
Former shepherd's home situated on its own on working farm amidst rolling Lammermuir Hills.

---

1 bungalow, 1 pub rm, 3 bedrms, sleeps 6, min let weekend, from £105, Jan-Dec, bus 5 mls, rail 20 mls

 🔧 ⬛ E 🔌 ⌂ 💻 ◉ ⌂ 🖵 ⚓ 🛏 ♨ 🎿 📺 † ⟳ ◔ 🎣 ∪ ► ✕ 🏊 🍴

Mrs A Rodger, Stobswood, Duns, Berwickshire, TD11 3NT
☎ *Longformacus (03617) 226*

LOSSIEMOUTH Moray Map Ref. 4D7

Silver Sands & East Beach Caravan Sites 14 caravans, sleeps 6, min let 2 nights, £60-£120, Apr-Oct, bus nearby, rail 6 mls, airport 35 mls

 🕭 📶 E ⌂ 🗲 ∅ ∅ 🗂 📞 🗓 ✂ ☉ ⅍ 🅿 † 🏔 🔍 ❀ ⛰ ⚓ ↯ ⟟ ✗ 🐾

Mr Donald R Grant, Old Post Office, Relugas, Dunphail, Forres, Moray, IV36 0QL
☎ *Dunphail (03096) 233*

---

1 cottage, 1 pub rm, 1 bedrm, sleeps 2-4, £35-£60, Jan-Dec, bus nearby, rail 6 mls, airport 40 mls

 🕭 📶 E ➹ ∅ ▥ 🗄 ☺ ◎ 🗂 🗖 ✂ ⌂ ※ ⅍ 🅿 🛋 🍴 ➹ † 🏔 🥢 ✎ ♪ ∪ ⛰ ↯ ⟟ ⟟
 ✗ 🐾

Mrs Lesley Leiper, Rowan Brae, Stotfield, Lossiemouth, Moray, IV31 6QF
☎ *Lossiemouth (034381) 3000*

Silver Sands Leisure Park 55 caravans, sleeps 4-8, min let 2 nights, from £50, Mar-Oct, bus 1 ½ mls, rail 6 mls, airport 40 mls

 🕭 📶 E ⌂ 🗲 ∅ ∅ 🗂 📞 🗖 🗓 ⌂ ☉ ⅍ 🅿 🛋 🍴 🏔 🔍 ❀ 🥢 ✎ ♪ ∪ ⛰ ↯ ⟟ ✗ 🐾

Silver Sands Leisure Park, Covesea, West Beach, Lossiemouth, Moray, IV31 6SP
☎ *Lossiemouth (034381) 3262/3099*

3 flats, 1 annexe, 1 pub rm, 2-4 bedrms, sleeps 4-12, min let weekend, £85-£195, Jan-Dec, bus nearby, rail 6 mls, airport 35 mls

 🕭 📶 E ➹ 🗲 ∅ ▥ 🗄 ☺ ◎ 🗂 📞 🗖 🗓 ⌂ ⌂ ☉ ※ ⅍ 🅿 🛋 🍴 🏔 ♪ ∪ ⛰ ↯ ⟟ ✗
 🐾

Mr & Mrs Ian Smith, Beachview Luxury Flats, Stotfield Road, Lossiemouth, Moray, IV31 6QS
☎ *Lossiemouth (034381) 3053*

---

1 house, 2 pub rms, 3 bedrms, sleeps 6-8, £68-£100, May-Oct, bus 300 yds, rail 6 mls

 🕭 📶 E ➹ ∅ ◎ 🗂 📞 🗖 ⌂ ⌂ ☉ ※ 🅿 🛋 🍴 † ♪ ∪ ↯ ⟟ ⟟ ✗ 🐾

Mrs F C Foubister, Willowbank, Stotfield, Lossiemouth, Moray
☎ *Lossiemouth (034381) 3245*

LUIB Isle of Skye, Inverness-shire Map Ref. 3E10

1 cottage, 3 bedrms, sleeps 6, min let weekend, £100-£180, Mar-Nov, bus nearby

 🕭 📶 E ➹ 🗲 ∅ ▥ 🗄 ◎ 🗂 🗖 🗓 ⌂ ⌂ ☉ ※ ⅍ 🅿 🛋 🍴 † ♪ ⛰ ↯ ⟟ ✗ 🐾

Mrs M MacLeod, Chalma, Daviot, Inverness-shire
☎ *Deviot (046385) 239/(047032) 274*

VAT is shown at 15%: changes in this rate may affect prices.

209

LUMPHANAN Aberdeenshire Map Ref. 4F10

1 cottage, 1 pub rm, 3 bedrms, sleeps 6, min let weekend, £70-£145, Jan-Dec, bus ½ ml, rail 25 mls, airport 25 mls

Mr J S Collier, 32 Graham Park Road, Gosforth, Newcastle-upon-Tyne, NE3 4BH
☎ *091 285 3651*

---

1 caravan, sleeps 6, min let weekend, £45-£50, Jan-Dec, bus nearby, rail 27 mls, airport 27 mls

Mrs Jean Riddell, Tillylodge, Lumphanan, Aberdeenshire
☎ *Lumphanan (033983) 274*

LUNCARTY Perthshire Map Ref. 2C2

1 cottage, 1 pub rm, 2 bedrms, sleeps 6, min let nights, £70-£110, Jan-Dec, bus nearby, rail 5 mls

Mrs A Grant, Pebble Mill, Luncarty, Perth, Perthshire, PH1 3ES
☎ *Stanley (0738828) 268*

LUNDIN LINKS Fife Map Ref. 2D3

Woodland Gardens Caravan & Camping Site 4 caravans, sleeps 6, min let 1 night, £85-£110, Mar-Oct, bus ½ ml, rail 13 mls, airport 35 mls

Woodland Gardens Caravan & Camping Site, Blindwell Road, Lundin Links, Fife, KY8 5QG
☎ *Upper Largo (03336) 319*

Largo House Caravan Park 2 caravans, sleeps 6-8, min let 3 nights, £75-£155, Mar-Oct, bus ½ ml

Largo Leisure Parks Ltd, Rankeilour House, Cupar, Fife, KY15 5RG
☎ *Letham (033781) 233*

LUSS, by Alexandria Dunbartonshire Map Ref. 1G4

2 cottages, 2 pub rms, 2-3 bedrms, sleeps 4-6, £80-£150, Jan-Dec, bus nearby, rail 8 mls, airport 25 mls

Luss Estate Co, Ross Dhu, Luss, by Alexandria, Dunbartonshire, G83 8NT
☎ *Luss (043686) 650/619*

COMMENDED
👑 👑 👑

1 bungalow, 1 pub rm, 2 bedrms, sleeps 5-6, £85-£125, Easter-Oct, bus 2 mls, rail 10 mls, airport 25 mls

Mrs K R Wragg, Glenmollochan Farm, Luss, by Alexandria, Dunbartonshire, G83 8PB
☎ *Luss (043686) 246*
On hill sheep farm above village. Superb views of hills and Loch Lomond. Enclosed garden.

COMMENDED

1 cottage, 1 pub rm, 2 bedrms, sleeps 6, £90-£135, May-Oct, bus ½ ml, rail 6 mls, airport 20 mls

♿ 🚾 E ⬅ 🍴 ▢ 🖥 ◎ ▢ ▯ ⚡ ⬛ ☺ Ⓟ 🎠 🏛 † ⛰ ♪ ⛵ ⚓ ⛹ ✕ 🎿

Mrs A Lennox, Shemore Farm, Luss, Alexandria, Dunbartonshire, G83 8RH
☎ *Arden (038985) 239*

Former shepherd's home on hill sheep farm Superb views over Loch Lomond. 3 mls (5 km) village.

LYBSTER Caithness Map Ref. 4D4

1 house, 1 cottage, 2 pub rms, 3-4 bedrms, sleeps 6-8, £30-£115, Jan-Dec, bus 6 mls, rail 13 mls, airport 13 mls

♿ 🚾 E ⬅ 🍴 ▢ ▦ ▯ ◎ ⬤ ▢ ▯ ⚡ ⬛ ☺ ✳ 🐎 Ⓟ ∥ 🎠 🏛 🍼 † ♪ ∪ ⚓ ∕ 🎿 🏕

Mr E J Darmady, Camster Lodge, Lybster, Caithness, KW3 6BD
☎ *Lybster (05932) 251*

LYNCHAT, by Kingussie Inverness-shire Map Ref. 4B11

AWAITING INSPECTION

1 house, 3 pub rms, 3 bedrms, sleeps 9, min let weekend, £150-£180, Jan-Dec, rail 2 mls

♿ 🚾 E ⬅ 🎨 🍴 ▦ ▯ ◎ ▢ ▯ ⚡ ⬛ ☺ ✳ 🐎 Ⓟ 🎠 🏛 † ⛰ ♪ ∪ ⚓ ⛹ 🎿 🎿 ✕ 🏕

Mrs E Scott, Whitecroft, East Calder, Livingston, West Lothian, EH53 0ET
☎ *Mid Calder (0506) 881810*

---

by MACDUFF Banffshire Map Ref. 4F7

Wester Bonnyton Farm Site 1 chalet/log cabin, 1 pub rm, 3 bedrms, sleeps 9, min let 1 night, £70-£130, Easter-Oct, bus nearby, rail 17 mls, airport 40 mls

♿ 🚾 E ⬅ 🍴 ▯ ⌀ ▢ ▯ ▢ ⬛ ☺ Ⓟ 🎠 🏛 † ⛰ 🔍 ◉ 🎣 🚣 ⚓ 🎿 ♪ ∪ ⚓ ⚓ ⛹ ✕ 🏕 Ⓣ

15 caravans, sleeps 4-8, min let 1 night, £40-£130, Apr-Oct, bus nearby, rail 17 mls, airport 40 mls

♿ 🚾 E 🍴 ▯ ⌀ ▢ ▯ ▢ ⬛ ☺ Ⓟ 🎠 🏛 † ⛰ 🔍 ◉ 🎣 🚣 ⚓ 🎿 ♪ ∪ ⚓ ⚓ ⛹ ✕ 🏕 Ⓣ

Mrs M Rothnie, Wester Bonnyton, Gamrie, Banff, Banffshire, AB4 3EP
☎ *Macduff (0261) 32470*

MACHRIE Isle of Arran Map Ref. 1E7

5 cottages, 1-2 pub rms, 3-4 bedrms, sleeps 6, min let weekend, £95-£190, Easter-Oct, bus ½ ml, ferry 12 mls

♿ 🚾 E ⬅ 🍴 ◎ ▢ ▯ ⚡ ⬛ ☺ ✳ 🐎 Ⓟ 🎠 🏛 † 🎣 ⚓ 🚣 ♪ ∪ ⚓ ⛹ ⛹ ∕ 🎿 🏕 Ⓣ (cycling, windsurfing)

Mrs S C Gibbs, Estate Office, Dougarie, Machrie, Isle of Arran
☎ *Machrie (077084) 229/259*

---

1 house, 1 pub rm, 3 bedrms, sleeps 7, from £75, May-Oct, bus 800 yds, ferry 10 mls

♿ 🚾 E ⬅ 🍴 ◎ ▢ 📞 ▢ ⬛ ✳ Ⓟ 🎠 🏛 🍼 † ⛰ 🎣 ♪ ⚓ ⛹ 🏕

Mr & Mrs J Anderson, Hillcrest Farm, Machrie, Brodick, Isle of Arran, KA27 8DZ
☎ *Machrie (077084) 240*

---

2 caravans, sleeps 4-6, min let weekend, £35-£80, Jan-Dec, bus ½ ml, ferry 5 mls

♿ 🚾 E ⌀ ▢ ▯ ✳ 🐎 Ⓟ ⛰ 🎣 🚣 ⚓ ♪ ∪ ⚓ ⛹ 🏕

Mrs Lammie, Monyquil, String Road, by Brodick, Isle of Arran
☎ *Machrie (077084) 237*

VAT is shown at 15%: changes in this rate may affect prices.

3 flats, 1 pub rm, 2 bedrms, sleeps 4, min let weekend, from £45, Jan-Dec, bus nearby, ferry 9 mls

Mr K Hunter, Machrie House, Machrie, Isle of Arran
☎ *Machrie (077084) 223*

---

1 cottage, 2 pub rms, 3 bedrms, sleeps 7, £100-£170, Apr-Oct, bus ½ ml, ferry 8 mls

Mrs Catherine Eason, 39 Alexandra Street, Kirkintilloch, Glasgow, G66 1HE
☎ *041 776 3838*

---

1 house, 1-2 pub rms, 3 bedrms, sleeps 8, £70-£210, Jan-Dec, bus nearby, ferry 5 mls, airport 40 mls

Mr D Buchan, Pollock & Buchan, Jaegar House, 62 Buchanan Street, Glasgow, G1 3JE
☎ *041 226 3422*

MACHRIHANISH Argyll Map Ref. 1D7

1 bungalow, 1 pub rm, 3 bedrms, sleeps 6, £40-£130, Mar-Oct, bus 1 ml, rail 80 mls, airport 3 mls

Mrs MacNeal, Lossit House, Machrihanish, by Campbeltown, Argyll
☎ *Machrihanish (058681) 204*

---

1 caravan, sleeps 6, min let weekend, from £40, Apr-Oct, bus nearby, airport 3 mls

Mrs Stewart, Kingston, Machrihanish, by Campbeltown, Argyll
☎ *Machrihanish (058681) 343*

---

1 house, 2 pub rms, 6 bedrms, sleeps 12, min let long weekend, £68-£145, Mar-Oct, bus 2 mls, airport 6 mls

Mrs Marsden, Westfield, 109 Ralston Avenue, Crookston, Glasgow, G52 3NB
☎ *041 882 6088*

MAIDENS Ayrshire Map Ref. 1G8

1 cottage, 1 pub rm, 3 bedrms, sleeps 7, min let weekend, £80-£160, Apr-Oct, bus ½ ml

Mrs J McFadzean, Thomaston Farm, by Maybole, Ayrshire
☎ *Kirkoswald (06556) 217*

MALLAIG Inverness-shire Map Ref. 3E11

1 house, 2 pub rms, 3 bedrms, sleeps 6, from £60, Apr-Oct

Mrs C MacPherson, The Bungalow, Mallaig Vaig, Inverness-shire
☎ *Mallaig (0687) 2253*

MANOR Peeblesshire Map Ref. 2C6

> 2 cottages, 1 pub rm, 2 bedrms, sleeps 6, min let 3 nights, £52-£63, Easter-Oct, bus 2 mls, rail 27 mls, airport 30 mls
>
> ♿ ᵂᶜ E 🔌 📻 📶 ◉ 📺 🖥 🔥 ☀ 🐕 🅿 ⛱ 🛏 † ⛰ 🎣 🔍 ⚓ ∪ ⊢ ⛸
>
> *Mrs M Barr, Woodhouse Farm, Manor, Peeblesshire, EH45 9JN*
> ☎ *Kirkton Manor (07214) 217*

MARYBANK Ross-shire Map Ref. 4A8

> 1 cottage, 1 pub rm, 3 bedrms, sleeps 6, £70-£90, Apr-Sep
>
> ♿ ᵂᶜ E 🔌 📶 🖥 ◉ 📺 ✂ ☀ 🐕 🅿 ⛱ † ⛰ ⚓ ∪ ⊿ 🚜 ⛸
>
> *Mrs R MacLeod, Easter Balloon Farm, Marybank, Muir-of-Ord,, Ross-shire, IV6 7UW*
> ☎ *Urray (09973) 211*

MARYBANK Isle of Lewis, Western Isles Map Ref. 4A8

> 1 caravan, sleeps 6, £40-£65, Jan-Dec, bus nearby, ferry 1 ml, airport 2 mls
>
> ♿ ᵂᶜ E 📶 ⊘ 🐕 🅿 ⛱ 🛏 † ⛰ ⚓ ∪ ⊿ ✗ 🗡 ⛸
>
> *A MacLeod, Park House, Marybank, Stornoway, Isle of Lewis, Western Isles, PA86 0DD*
> ☎ *Stornoway (0851) 2308*

MARYBURGH Ross-shire Map Ref. 4A8

up to
COMMENDED
♛ ♛

> 16 cottages, 1-2 pub rms, 2-4 bedrms, sleeps 4-8, min let weekend, £50-£200, Apr-Oct, bus ½-2 mls, rail 1-4 mls, airport 20 mls
>
> ♿ ᵂᶜ E 🔌 📶 🖥 ◉ 📺 🙂 ☀ 🐕 🅿 ⛱ 🛏 † 🎣 🔍 🏹 ⚓ ∪ ⛵ ↗ ✏ 🏋 ✗ 🗡 ⛸ T
>
> *J A Gilzean, Brahan, Dingwall, Ross-shire*
> ☎ *Dingwall (0349) 61150*
> Restored units on 5000 acre estate. Trout and pike fishing, garden and forest walks, birdwatching.

MARYCULTER Kincardineshire Map Ref. 4G10

> Lower Deeside Caravan Park 4 caravans, sleeps 4-8, min let 1 night, £35-£75, Apr-Oct, bus nearby, rail 6 mls, airport 9 mls
>
> ♿ ᵂᶜ 🔲 E 📻 📶 🖥 ⊘ 🖥 📺 📞 📺 📸 ✂ 🔌 ☉ 🐕 🅿 † ⛰ 🔔 ⚓ ∪ ✗ 🗡 (childrens ATC track with bike hire)
>
> *Lower Deeside Caravan Park, Maryculter, Kincardineshire, AB1 0AX*
> ☎ *Aberdeen (0224) 733860*

MAUCHLINE Ayrshire Map Ref. 1H7

> 2 cottages, 1 pub rm, 2 bedrms, sleeps 4-6, from £45, Apr-Oct, airport N
>
> ♿ ᵂᶜ E 🔌 📶 ◉ 📺 🖥 🔌 ☉ ☀ 🅿 🛏 † ⚓
>
> *Mr H Templeton, Syke Farm, Mauchline, Ayrshire*
> ☎ *Mauchline (0290) 51252*

VAT is shown at 15%: changes in this rate may affect prices.

1 cottage, 2 pub rms, 3 bedrms, sleeps 6, £65-£85, Apr-Sep, bus 1 ½ mls, rail 2 mls, airport 15 mls

Mrs J P Templeton, Willoxton Farm, Mauchline, Ayrshire
☎ *Mauchline (0290) 51249*

MAYBOLE Ayrshire Map Ref. 1G8

1 house, 1 cottage, 1-3 pub rms, 2-4 bedrms, sleeps 2-8, min let long weekend, £54-£130, Jan-Dec, bus ½ ml, rail 4 mls, airport 16 mls

Miss S M Andrew, Bungalow, Rowanstone, Maybole, Ayrshire
☎ *Crosshill (06554) 205*

---

1 caravan, sleeps 6, from £90, Apr-Oct, bus ½ ml, rail ¾ ml, airport 10 mls

Mr & Mrs R Dalgleish, Fordhouse Farm, Maybole, Ayrshire, KA19 7SA
☎ *Maybole (0655) 83202/82264*

---

1 cottage, 1 pub rm, 2 bedrms, sleeps 2-6, min let weekend/3 nights, £60-£130, Jan-Dec, bus nearby, rail ¼ ml, airport 12 mls

Mrs L Wallace, Lyonston, Maybole, Ayrshire, KA19 7HS
☎ *Maybole (0655) 83176*
In own sheltered garden on working farm (dairy cattle, sheep, arable). 8 miles (13km) from Ayr.

MEIGLE Perthshire Map Ref. 2D1

Kings of Kinloch Holiday Lodges 5 chalet/log cabins, 1 pub rm, 2 bedrms, sleeps 6, min let 3 nights, £110-£200, Jan-Dec, bus 1 ml, rail 14 mls, airport 14 mls

Mr J G M Brown, Manager, Kings of Kinloch Hotel, Meigle, Perthshire, PH12 8QX
☎ *Meigle (08284) 273*

MELLON UDRIGLE, by Laide Ross-shire Map Ref. 3F6

Ceol na Mara 5 chalet/log cabins, 1 house, 1-3 pub rms, 3-4 bedrms, sleeps 6-8, £65-£225, Mar-Oct, bus 3 mls, rail 40 mls, airport 75 mls

Mr Tew, Ceol na Mara Ltd, South Kenwood, by Kenton, Exeter
☎ *Starcross (0626) 891672*

MELVAIG Ross-shire Map Ref. 3E7

1 house, 1 pub rm, 2 bedrms, sleeps 6, £100-£150, Jan-Dec, bus nearby, rail 39 mls, airport 93 mls

M A Alburger, 28 Melvaig, by Gairloch, Ross-shire, IV21 2EA
☎ *North Erradale (044585) 234*
Recently built house adjoining croft and set in rugged scenery.

1 bungalow, 2 pub rms, 3 bedrms, sleeps 6, min let weekend, £110-£150, Mar-Oct, bus nearby, rail 46 mls

♿ 🚾 E ⌂ ⓘ ⊚ ▤ 🗒 🗍 ▣ 🔌 ☉ ✳ 🐎 P 🍔 ☷ †   ♪ △ ⚲ ‣ ƒ

Mrs Isabel Stewart, The Sithean, Lonmore, Gairloch, Ross-shire, IV21 2DB
☎ *Gairloch (0445) 2035*
Modern, with own garden. Overlooks 'The Minch' with spectacular views across Atlantic to Hebrides.

MELVICH, by Thurso Sutherland Map Ref. 4B3

4 chalet/log cabins, 1 pub rm, 2 bedrms, sleeps 4-6, min let weekend (low season), £60-£95, Apr-Oct, bus nearby, rail 13 mls, airport 40 mls

♿ 🚾 E 📜 ⓘ ⊚ ▤ 🗒 ▣ ☉ ✳ 🐎 P 🍔 ☷   ♪ ⚲ ‣ ƒ Ⓡ ✖ ♟ ♪ ♫

Mrs Joan Ritchie, Tigh na Clash, Melvich, by Thurso, Sutherland, KW14 7YJ
☎ *Melvich (06413) 262*
Semi detached units in own ground overlooking the sea. Restaurant nearby.

MEMSIE, by Fraserburgh Aberdeenshire Map Ref. 4H7

1 bungalow, 1 pub rm, 2 bedrms, sleeps 4, £70, Jan-Dec, bus 5 mls, rail 40 mls, airport 40 mls

♿ 🚾 E ⌂ ⓘ ▤ ⊚ 🗒 ▣ ✳ 🐎 P 🍔 ☷ † ⌂   ‣ ♟ Ⓣ

Mrs Pittendrigh, Kirktown, Tyrie, Fraserburgh, Aberdeenshire
☎ *Memsie (03464) 231*

METHVEN Perthshire Map Ref. 2B2

2 houses, 2 pub rms, 2 bedrms, sleeps 4-6, £70-£90, Apr-Oct, bus nearby, rail 6 mls, airport 38 mls

♿ 🚾 E ⌂ ⓘ ▤ ⊚ ⊚ 🗒 ▣ ☉ ✳ 🐎 P 🍔 ☷   ♪ ∪ ‣ ✖ ♟

Mrs S Grant, 3 James Street, Methven, Perth, Perthshire, PH1 3QH
☎ *Methven (073884) 480*

---

1 cottage, 1 pub rm, 2 bedrms, sleeps 4, £45-£85, Jan-Dec, bus 1 ml, rail 6 mls

♿ 🚾 E ⌂ ⓘ ⊚ ⊚ 🗒 ▣ ☉ ✳ P 🍔 †   ⚲ ✖ ♟

Mrs Doig, Lawmuir Farm, Methven, Perthshire
☎ *Methven (073884) 261*

---

by METHVEN Perthshire Map Ref. 2B2

2 flats, 2 cottages, 1 pub rm, 2 bedrms, sleeps 4-5, £69-£98, Apr-Oct, bus ½ ml, rail 10 mls, airport 50 mls

♿ 🚾 E ⌂ ⓘ ⊚ ▤ 🗒 ▣ ☉ ✳ 🐎 P 🍔 ☷   ♪ ♟

Mr & Mrs MacKenzie-Smith, Newrow, Methven, Perth, Perthshire, PH1 3RE
☎ *Madderty (076483) 222*

MID CLYTH Caithness Map Ref. 4D4

1 cottage, 1 pub rm, 2 bedrms, sleeps 8, from £70, Jan-Dec, bus nearby, rail 10 mls, airport 10 mls

♿ 🚾 E ⌂ 📜 ⓘ ⊚ ▤ 🗒 ☎ ▤ 🗍 ▣ ☉ ✳ 🐎 P 🍔 ☷ † ⌂   ♪ ∪ △ ⚲ ‣ ƒ ✖
♟ Ⓣ

Mr David B Calder, 13 George Street, Thurso, Caithness
☎ *Thurso (0847) 62813*

MILLHOUSEBRIDGE, by Lochmaben Dumfriesshire Map Ref. 2C9

1 cottage, 1 pub rm, 2 bedrms, sleeps 4, £95-£175, Jan-Dec, bus nearby, rail 4 mls

♿ 🚾 E ⌂ ⌀ ▦ ▯ ◉ ☐▭ ⌁ ◗ ▦ ⊙ ❄ ♘ P ❧ ▥ ☞ ⚂ ♩ ∪ △ ↙ ⚓ ⅁ ✕ ▦ T

Scottish Country Cottages, Suite 2d, Churchill Way, Bishopbriggs, Glasgow, G64 2RH
☎ *041 772 5920*

MILLPORT Isle of Cumbrae, Bute Map Ref. 1G6

1 flat, 1 pub rm, 1 bedrm, sleeps 4, min let weekend, £40-£85, Apr-Jan, ferry 4 mls

♿ 🚾 E ⌂ ⌀ ▦ ◉ ☐▭ ▪ ❄ ♘ P ❧ ▥ † ⚲ ♩ ∪ △ ⅁ ↙ ⚓ ✕ ▦

Mrs Clark, Crossburn, Bute Terrace, Millport, Isle of Cumbrae, Bute, KA28 0BA
☎ *Millport (0475) 5303454*

MILTON, by Drumnadrochit Inverness-shire Map Ref. 4A9

1 chalet/log cabin, 1 pub rm, 2 bedrms, sleeps 5, min let weekend, £95-£195, Jan-Dec, bus 500 yds, rail 16 mls, airport 25 mls

♿ 🚾 E ⌂ ⌀ ▦ ▯ ◉ ☐▭ ▪ ⊙ P ❧ ▥ ☞ † ⚲ ♩ ∪ ⌁ ✕ ▦ T (bicycle hire)

Mrs Ellistone, Glaichmor, Milton, Drumnadrochit, Inverness-shire, IV3 6TZ
☎ *Drumnadrochit (04562) 257*
Timber chalet set on its own on south facing hillside with views over Loch Ness and countryside.

MINARD Argyll Map Ref. 1F4

2 houses, 1 pub rm, 3 bedrms, sleeps 5-6, from £80, Apr-Oct, bus 1 ml

♿ 🚾 E ☞ ⌀ ◉ ☐ ⌁ ☐ ◉ ▪ ♘ P ❧ ▥ † ♩ △ ▦ (birdwatching)

Bell-Ingram, Durn, Isla Road, Perth, PH2 7HF
☎ *Perth (0738) 21121*

MINTO Roxburghshire Map Ref. 2E7

1 cottage, 1 pub rm, 3 bedrms, sleeps 6, £60-£90, Apr-Oct, bus 4 mls, rail 50 mls, airport 50 mls

♿ 🚾 E ☞ ⌀ ▯ ◉ ☐▭ ▯ ▪ ⊙ ❄ ♘ P ❧ ▥ † ♩ ∪ △ ↙ ✕ ▦ ⚞ T

Mrs Susan Manners, Deanfoot Farm, Denholm, by Hawick, Roxburghshire
☎ *Denholm (045087) 229*

MOCHRUM, by Port William Wigtownshire Map Ref. 1H11

2 houses, 1-2 pub rms, 3-4 bedrms, sleeps 2-8, from £105, Apr-Oct

♿ 🚾 E ☞ ⌀ ◉ ☐▭ ▪ ❄ P ❧ ▥ † ⚲ ♩ ∪ △ ⌁ ↙

G M Thomson & Company, 27 King Street, Castle Douglas, Kirkcudbrightshire, DG7 1AB
☎ *Castle Douglas (0556) 2701*

---

1 cottage, 2 pub rms, 3 bedrms, sleeps 8, £85-£95, Apr-Oct, bus 1 ml, rail 25 mls, airport 70 mls

♿ 🚾 E ☞ ⌀ ▯ ◉ ☐▭ ▪ ⊙ ❄ ♘ P ❧ ▥ † ⚲ ♩ △ ↙ ✕ ▦ ⚞

Mrs MacTier, Boghouse Farm, Mochrum, Whauphill, Wigtownshire, DG8 9LU
☎ *Port William (09887) 314*

MOFFAT Dumfriesshire Map Ref. 2C8

1 house, 1-2 pub rms, 6 bedrms, sleeps 12, £75-£180, Jan-Dec, bus ¼ ml, rail 15 mls, airport 50 mls

    [symbols]

Mrs Currie, The Manse, 1 Rothes Road, Dorking, Surrey, RH4 1JW
☎ *Dorking (0306) 883652*
Stone built, detached; about 140 years old. Five minutes walk to shops. Quiet situation.

---

2 bungalows, 1 pub rm, 3 bedrms, sleeps 6, from £95, Apr-Oct

    [symbols]

G M Thomson & Company, 27 King Street, Castle Douglas, Kirkcudbrightshire, DG7 1AB
☎ *Castle Douglas (0556) 2701/2973*

COMMENDED

Heatheryhaugh Lodges 4 bungalows, 2 pub rms, 3 bedrms, sleeps 6, min let weekend (low season), £105-£225, Jan-Dec, bus ¾ ml, rail 15 mls

    [symbols]

Mr B Larmour, Heatheryhaugh, Moffat, Dumfriesshire, DG10 9LD
☎ *Moffat (0683) 20107*
Self contained units in rural setting about 2 miles/ 3km from centre of small town.

---

1 caravan, sleeps 5, min let weekend, £70-£100, Jan-Dec

    [symbols]

J & L Deas & W Gray, Barnhill Springs Country Guest House, Moffat, Dumfriesshire, DG10 9QS
☎ *Moffat (0683) 20580*

---

1 cottage, 1 pub rm, 2 bedrms, sleeps 6, £60-£90, Apr-Oct

    [symbols]

Mrs Susan Taylor, The Decor Salon, 19/20 Galloway St, Dumfries, DG2 7TL
☎ *Dumfries (0387) 54641/74205*

---

1 bungalow, 1 pub rm, 3 bedrms, sleeps 6, min let weekend, £75-£90, Mar-Oct, bus 5 mls, rail 20 mls, airport 50 mls

    [symbols]

Mrs P E Williams, Corehead Farm, Annan Water, Moffat, Dumfriesshire
☎ *Moffat (0683) 20182*

---

1 caravan, sleeps 6, min let weekend (low season), £70-£130, Mar-Nov, bus nearby, rail 16 mls, airport 50 mls

    [symbols]

Mrs J G McKenzie, Hidden Corner, Beattock Road, Moffat, Dumfriesshire
☎ *Moffat (0683) 20243*

---

1 cottage, 1 pub rm, 1 bedrm, sleeps 5, £50-£100, Jan-Dec, bus 800 yds, rail 14 mls, ferry 40 mls

    [symbols]

Mr L D Bowman, 19 King Edward Road, Jordanhill, Glasgow, G13 1QW
☎ *041 954 9914*

MONIAIVE Dumfriesshire Map Ref. 2A9

3 cottages, 1 pub rm, 2-4 bedrms, sleeps 5-8, £95-£180, Easter-end Oct, bus 3 mls, rail 20 mls, airport 70 mls

J F S Gourlay, Auchencheyne, Moniaive, Dumfriesshire, DG3 4EP
☎ *Moniaive (08482) 285*

---

1 cottage, 2 pub rms, 2 bedrms, sleeps 6, min let nights (low season), £120-£180, Jan-Dec, bus ½ ml, rail 17 mls, airport 60 mls

(bikes, badminton)

Mr McIver, Woodlea Hotel, Moniaive, Dumfriesshire, DG3 4EN
☎ *Moniaive (08482) 209*

MONKTON Ayrshire Map Ref. 1G7

2 houses, 1 pub rm, 3 bedrms, sleeps 6-7, max £80, Jul-Oct, bus 1 ml, rail 3 mls, airport 2 mls

Mrs G Lawrie, Brieryside Farm, Monkton, Prestwick, Ayrshire, KA9 2SB
☎ *Prestwick (0292) 77639*

St. Andrews Caravan Park 4 caravans, sleeps 6, £65-£150, Apr-Sep, bus 500 yds, rail ½ ML

(barbecue & beer garden)

St Andrew's Caravan Park, Monkton, by Prestwick, Ayrshire, KA9 1UA
☎ *Prestwick (0292) 79261*

MONREITH Wigtownshire Map Ref. 1H11

15 caravans, sleeps 6, min let 1 night, £40-£145, Apr-Oct, bus nearby, rail 18 mls, airport 90 mls

Monreith Sands Holiday Park, Monreith, Wigtownshire, DG8 9LJ
☎ *Port William (09887) 218*

---

1 cottage, 2 pub rms, 3 bedrms, sleeps 5, £70-£100, Mar-Nov, bus nearby, rail 26 mls

(bowling green)

Mrs P Heywood, Old Knock School, Monreith, Port William, Wigtownshire
☎ *Port William (09887) 409/414*

MONTROSE Angus Map Ref. 2E1

1 house, 1 pub rm, 2 bedrms, sleeps 6, £55-£85, Jan-Dec, bus nearby, rail ½ ml

Mrs J F Craik, Fairfield, 24 The Mall, Montrose, Angus, DD10 8NW
☎ *Montrose (0674) 72259*

---

1 flat, 1 pub rm, 2 bedrms, sleeps 6, £40-£75, May-Sep, bus 300 yds, rail 350 yds

Mrs Birrell, Birmac, Isla Road, Perth
☎ *Perth (0738) 20374*

Prices shown are for guidance only. Please send SAE with each enquiry.

MORAR Inverness-shire Map Ref. 3E11

Ardintigh Adventure Centre 1 stone bothy (dormitory), 2 wooden cabins, sleeps 8-16, from £25 (per person if 24 in group), Jan-Dec

    ♿ WC E 🏠 🖊 ✎ ✂ 🐾 ⚓   ✦ ⚠ ⚓ T

Mr Tom McClean, Invermorar House, Morar, Mallaig, Inverness-shire, PH40 4PA
☎ *Mallaig (0687) 2274*

---

1 bungalow, 2 pub rms, 2 bedrms, sleeps 4-6, £88-£218, Jan-Dec, bus nearby, rail ½ ml, ferry 2 mls, airport 120 mls

    ♿ WC E ⬇ ⟐ ▦ 🖥 ◎ 🗄 ⬜ 📷 ✂ ⬛ ☉ ❄ 🐾 P 🔥 🏚 † ✦ ⚠ ⚓ ▶ ✕ 🔧 T

Mrs Stewart, Glengorm, Morar, Mallaig, Inverness-shire
☎ *Mallaig (0687) 2165*

MOREBATTLE Roxburghshire Map Ref. 2F7

1 cottage, 1 pub rm, 1 bedrm, sleeps 3, min let weekend, £50-£55, Jan-Dec, bus 300 yds, rail 30 mls

    ♿ WC E ⬇ ⟐ 🖥 ◎ 🗄 ⬜ ⬛ ☉ ❄ P † ✦ ∪ ✕ 🔧

Mrs A Paterson, The Square, Morebattle, Kelso, Roxburghshire, TD5 8QL
☎ *Morebattle (05734) 304*

---

1 cottage, 2 pub rms, 3 bedrms, sleeps 2-6, from £80, Apr-Sep, bus nearby, rail 30 mls

    ♿ WC E ⬇ 🏠 ⟐ ◎ 🗄 ⬜ 📷 ⬛ ☉ ❄ P 🔥 🏚 † ✦ ∪ ✕ 🔧

Mrs R Paterson, The Tealing, Queen Victoria School, Dunblane, Perthshire, FK15 0JE
☎ *Dunblane (0786) 823997*
Detached cottage with garden in quiet village.

---

1 cottage, 1 pub rm, 3 bedrms, sleeps 6, min let 4 nights, £70-£90, Apr-Oct, bus ¼ ml, rail 30 mls, airport 60 mls

    ♿ WC E ⬇ ⟐ ◎ 🗄 ⬜ ✂ ⬛ 🐾 P 🔥 🏚 † ✦ ∪ ✕ 🔧 ♿

Mrs G Smith, Morebattle Mains, Morebattle, by Kelso, Roxburghshire
☎ *Morebattle (05734) 200*

VAT is shown at 15%: changes in this rate may affect prices.

MORVERN Argyll Map Ref. 1D1

Ardtornish Self Catering
**ARDTORNISH ESTATE, MORVEN,
ARGYLL PA34 5XA. Tel: (096 784) 288 (24 hrs.)**
Open all year. Self catering. Choose a secluded cottage or spacious Victorian flat, sleeping up to 12.
Prices from £75 to £350 per week.
Children welcome, and dogs. Bank fishing on hill lochs free with accommodation; a variety of other fishing by arrangement.
Ardtornish Estate covers 60 square miles of hills, woodland, rivers and lochs, with a long coastline on the Sound of Mull, and Loch Linnhe. Deer, otters, wildcats, seals and 135 recorded species of birds, 28 acres of beautiful gardens. Especially recommended April to June.
Swim, walk, hire a boat or simply relax in spectacular and peaceful countryside. Post Office and Shop in Lochaline Village 4 miles away.
Please send for brochures to Mr Leask at above address.

2 houses, 5 flats, 3 cottages, 1-3 pub rms, 2-6 bedrms, sleeps 5-20, £70-£350, Jan-Dec, car essential

♿ 🚾 E ⬛ ⬛ ⬛ ▦ ◎ ⬛ ☎ ✁ ⬛ ☼ ⬛ P ⬛ ▥ † ⛰   ♪ ⛴ △ ⬛ ⬛ ✗ ⬛ ⬛
T

Mr Austin Leask, Ardtornish Estate Office, Morvern, Argyll
☎ *Morvern (096784) 288*

MUASDALE Argyll Map Ref. 1D6

1 caravan, sleeps 4, £30-£55, Apr-Sep, bus 30 mls, airport 15 mls

⬛ ☼ ⬛ ⬛ †   ✗ ⬛

Mrs G McAllister, Tigh na Creige, Muasdale, by Tarbert, Argyll
☎ *Glenbarr (05832) 270*

MUIR-OF-ORD Ross-shire Map Ref. 4A8

APPROVED
♛♛

1 cottage, 1 pub rm, 3 bedrms, sleeps 5, £50-£105, Apr-Oct, bus 1 ½ mls, rail 1 ½ mls

♿ 🚾 E ⬛ ⬛ ◎ ⬛ ☎ ⬛ ◎ ⬛ ☼ P ⬛ ▥ † ⛰   ♪ ⛴ ✗ ⬛ ⬛

Mrs A H McLean, 43 Riccarton Mains Road, Currie, Midlothian, EH14 5NF
☎ *031 449 2448*
Traditional, with secluded garden. Open fire in lounge. Attractive countryside, views over Firth.

COMMENDED
♛♛

1 house, 1 pub rm, 3 bedrms, sleeps 6, £55-£120, Apr-Oct, bus 1 ml, rail 1 ml

♿ 🚾 E ⬛ ⬛ ⬛ ⓘ ◎ ⬛ ⬛ ◎ ✁ ⬛ ☼ ⬛ P ⬛ ▥ † ⛰   ♪ ⛴ △ ⬛ ✗ ⬛ ⬛
T

Mrs A B G Fraser, Gilchrist Farm, Muir-of-Ord, Ross-shire, IV6 7RS
☎ *Muir-of-Ord (0463) 870243*
Pleasantly situated on working farm. Ideal for Highlands touring. Inverness only 14 miles (22 km).

1 house, 1 pub rm, 3 bedrms, sleeps 6, £30-£75, Apr-Oct, bus 2 mls, rail 2 mls

♿ 🚾 E ⬛ ⬛ ⬛ ◎ ⬛ ⬛ ◎ ☼ P ⬛ ▥ † ⛰   ♪ ⛴ △ ⬛ ✗ ⬛ ⬛

Mrs C MacKenzie, Dungrianach, Corry, Muir-of-Ord, Ross-shire, IV6 7TN
☎ *Muir-of-Ord (0463) 870316*

Prices shown are for guidance only. Please send SAE with each enquiry.

1 bungalow, 2 pub rms, 3 bedrms, sleeps 6, £50-£125, Jan-Dec, bus 1 ml, rail 2 mls

Mrs S B Morrison, Easter Urray, Muir-of-Ord, Ross-shire, IV6 7UL
☎ Muir-of-Ord (0463) 870270

1 cottage, 1 pub rm, 4 bedrms, sleeps 7, £45-£85, Apr-Oct, bus nearby, rail 2 ½ mls

Mrs M MacKenzie, 11 Newmore, Muir-of-Ord, Ross-shire, IV6 7RG
☎ Dingwall (0349) 61870

by MUIR-OF-ORD Ross-shire Map Ref. 4A8

Druimorrin Caravan Park 3 caravans, sleeps 4-6, £44-£85, mid May-mid Sep, bus 2 ½ mls, rail 2 ½ mls, airport 23 mls

Mrs M C Stewart, Druimorrin Caravan & Camping Park, Orrin Bridge, Urray, Muir-of-Ord, Ross-shire, IV6 1UL
☎ Urray (09973) 252

MUNLOCHY Ross-shire Map Ref. 4A8

1 bungalow, 1 pub rm, 3 bedrms, sleeps 6, min let 2 weeks, £75-£160, Jan-Dec, bus 250 yds, rail 7 mls, airport 14 mls

Mrs MacNeill, New Bungalow, The Winter Garden, Tulloch, Dingwall, Ross-shire
☎ Dingwall (0349) 64870

MUSSELBURGH East Lothian Map Ref. 2D5

1 caravan, sleeps 2-8, min let weekend, £60-£120, Jan-Dec, bus ½ ml, rail 6 mls, airport 14 mls

(Stabling for horses available on site)
Mrs Weare, Carberry Gardens, Musselburgh, East Lothian
☎ 031 665 4486

MUTHILL Perthshire Map Ref. 2B3

1 cottage, 1 pub rm, 2 bedrms, sleeps 4-5, £55-£75, Apr-Oct, bus 1 ½ mls, rail 5 mls

Mrs B McIntosh, Kirklea, 12 Station Road, Muthill, Perthshire, PH5 2AR
☎ Muthill (076481) 374

1 cottage, 1 pub rm, sleeps 2, £35-£40, May-Sep, bus 5 mls, rail 27 mls, airport 50 mls

Mrs M Paterson, Dunruchan, Muthill, Crieff, Perthshire, PH5 2DF
☎ Muthill (076481) 306

NAIRN Map Ref. 4C8

3 caravans, sleeps 8, min let 3 nights (low season), from £70, Apr-Oct, bus ¾ ml, rail 1 ml, airport 6 mls

Mrs M Forsyth, Moravia, 8 Grant Street, Nairn, IV12 4NN
☎ Nairn (0667) 52339

VAT is shown at 15%: changes in this rate may affect prices.

1 chalet/log cabin, 1 pub rm, 2 bedrms, sleeps 4, £100-£125, Jan-Dec, bus ¼ ml, rail 1 ml, airport 8 mls

♿ Ⓦ E ➡ 🗑 ◎ 🗂 📞 🖥 📠 ⌨ ☺ ✳ 🐾 🅿 🎿 🛏 † ⚏   🍃 🔍 🎋 🥌 ∪ ↑ ✗ 🧺

(bowling, beach swimming)

Mr & Mrs P B Cruickshank, Sunny Brae, Marine Road, Nairn, IV12 4EA
☎ *Nairn (0667) 52309*

Lochloy Holiday Park 15 chalet/log cabins, 1-3 pub rms, 1-3 bedrms, sleeps 4-6, min let weekend, £122-£226, Easter-Oct, bus ¾ ml, rail 1 ml, airport 10 mls

♿ Ⓦ E ➡ 🎛 🗑 🖊 🗂 📠 ▦ ✳ 🅿 ⫻ 🎿 🛏 ⚏ ● ✿   🍃 🔍 🐚 🎋 🥌 ∪ △ ↙ ↑ ✗
🧺 Ⓣ (bus tours)

50 caravans, sleeps 2-6, min let weekend, £72-£228, mid Mar-Oct, bus ¼ ml, rail 1½ mls, airport 10 mls

♿ Ⓦ E 🎛 🗑 🖊 🗂 📞 🖥 📠 🚿 ▦ ☺ 🅿 🎿 🛏 ⚏ ● ✿   🍃 ↙ 🐚 🔍 🎋 🥌 ∪ △ ↙
↑ ⫻ ✗ 🧺 Ⓣ Ⓓ

Lochloy Holiday Park, East Beach, Nairn, IV12 4PH
☎ *Nairn (0667) 53764*

---

1 house, 1 pub rm, 1 bedrm, sleeps 3-4, £85-£120, Jan-Dec, bus ¼ ml, rail ¼ ml, airport 7 mls

♿ Ⓦ E ➡ 🎛 🗑 📠 🗂 ◎ 🗂 📞 🖥 ☺ ✳ 🐾 🎿 🛏 †   🍃 🥌 ∪ ↑ ✗ 🧺

Mrs Murray, Tullibardine, Lewiston, Drumnadrochit, Inverness-shire
☎ *Drumnadrochit (04562) 459*

NETHYBRIDGE Inverness-shire Map Ref. 4C10

Dell of Abernethy
NETHYBRIGE IN SPEY VALLEY
Warm, comfortable stone-built cottages of individual character with spacious secluded grounds within sight of Cairngorm Mountains. Peaceful local walks; interesting places to visit; a good centre for touring, and a wide variety of family activities.

 Inclusive prices with off-season discounts for small numbers.
TELEPHONE: NETHYBRIDGE 643

---

1 flat, 3 cottages, 2 bungalows, 1 pub rm, 2-3 bedrms, sleeps 3-7, min let weekend (low season), £90-£235, Jan-Dec, bus 1 ml, rail 10 mls, airport 35 mls

♿ Ⓦ E ➡ 🎛 📠 🗂 ◎ 🗂 📞 🗂 🚿 🗑 ☺ ✳ 🐾 🅿 🎿 🛏 ⚏   🍃 🔍 🎋 🥌 ∪ △ ↑
⫻ ✗ 🧺

Mr & Mrs J Fleming, Dell of Abernethy, Nethybridge, Inverness-shire, PH25 3DL
☎ *Nethybridge (047982) 643*
Stonebuilt units of individual character. Set in mature, secluded grounds, 1 mile (2km) from village.

---

2 flats, 1 pub rm, 1 bedrm, sleeps 2, min let long weekend, £51, Jan-Dec, bus nearby, rail 8 mls, airport 30 mls

♿ Ⓦ E ➡ 🎛 📠 🗂 ◎ 🗂 📞 🗑 ☺ ✳ 🐾 🅿   🥌 ∪ △ ↑ ⫻ ✗ 🧺

Mr & Mrs L D Gavin, Culreach, Grantown-on-Spey, Moray, PH26 3NH
☎ *Nethybridge (047982) 269*
Pleasantly sited, differing in character and facilities. Fine views of surrounding countryside.

Prices shown are for guidance only. Please send SAE with each enquiry.

1 house, 1 pub rm, 2 bedrms, sleeps 5, £75-£130, May-Nov, bus nearby, rail 11 mls, airport 35 mls

Mr S Davies, Farthings, The Causar, Nethybridge, Inverness-shire, PH25 3DR
☎ *Nethybridge (047982) 648/313*

---

2 houses, 2-3 pub rms, 3-4 bedrms, sleeps 7-10, min let weekend, £90-£140, Jan-Dec, bus ½ ml, rail 7 mls, airport 30 mls

Mr B W Broadhurst, Cedar House, Collinwood Road, Witham, Essex, CM8 2DY
☎ *Witham (0376) 512105*

---

up to COMMENDED
🏵 🏵 🏵 🏵

2 cottages, 4 bungalows, 1 converted smithy, 1 pub rm, 1-4 bedrms, sleeps 2-10, min let 2 nights, £70-£295, Jan-Dec, bus nearby, rail 9 mls, airport 30 mls

Mr & Mrs J B Patrick, 1 Chapelton Place, Forres, Moray
☎ *Forres (0309) 72505*
Seperately sited in village, cottages and converted smithy each with own character. Enclosed garden.

COMMENDED
🏵 🏵 🏵 🏵

1 bungalow, 1 pub rm, 3 bedrms, sleeps 5, £90-£175, Mar-Oct, bus 500 yds, rail 9 mls, airport 40 mls

Miss K M Grant, West Cullachie, Boat of Garten, Inverness-shire, PH24 3BY
☎ *Nethybridge (047982) 226*
Quiet, sheltered site on banks of River Nethy. Well kept, fenced garden. Near village and golf course.

---

1 chalet/log cabin, 1 house, 1-2 pub rms, 2-3 bedrms, sleeps 4-6, min let weekend, £80-£160, Jan-Dec, bus nearby, rail 10 mls, airport 50 mls

Mr & Mrs J Hall, Mondhuie, Nethybridge, Inverness-shire, PH25 3DF
☎ *Nethybridge (047982) 331*

Kimberley Holiday Homes 3 cottages, 1-3 pub rms, 2-4 bedrms, sleeps 5-6, min let 1 night, £80-£135, Jan-Dec, bus nearby, rail 10 mls, airport 35 mls

(birdwatching, bike hire)

James & Hilda Thomson, Kimberley Holiday Homes, Nethybridge, Inverness-shire, PH25 3ED
☎ *Nethybridge (047982) 255*

VAT is shown at 15%: changes in this rate may affect prices.

1 chalet/log cabin, 1 pub rm, 3 bedrms, sleeps 8, £120-£200, Jan-Dec, bus 600 yds, rail 9 mls, airport 34 mls

Mrs A F Buckley, 3 Hoy Place, Thurso, Caithness
☎ *Thurso (0847) 63912*

AWAITING INSPECTION

1 cottage, 1 pub rm, 2 bedrms, sleeps 4, min let weekend, £70-£100, Jan-Dec, bus 500 yds, rail 11 mls, airport 36 mls

Mr Anderson, Tigh-Na-Drochit, Nethybridge, Inverness-shire
☎ *Nethybridge (047982) 666*

COMMENDED 👑 👑 👑

1 cottage, 1 pub rm, 2 bedrms, sleeps 6, £80-£115, Jan-Dec, bus nearby, rail 11 mls, airport 30 mls

  (cycle hire)

Mrs S Smith, Tigh Beag, Nethybridge, Inverness-shire, PH25 3DR
☎ *Nethybridge (047982) 293*
Highland cottage with own large garden in quiet residential area of village.

---

1 house, 1 pub rm, 3 bedrms, sleeps 6, £110-£130, Apr-Oct, bus nearby, rail 10 mls, airport 40 mls

Mrs R Moir, Brown Hills, Fintray, Dyce, Aberdeen, AB2 0YB
☎ *Fintray (022476) 296*

---

1 cottage, 1 pub rm, 4 bedrms, sleeps 6, £99-£173, Jan-Dec, bus 1 ml, rail 10 mls, airport 33 mls

Dr J M Bryden, Coulnakyle, Nethybridge, Inverness-shire
☎ *Nethybridge (047982) 688*

CROFT GARLYNE

These spacious modern bungalows are situated in a peaceful location, overlooking the picturesque Highland village of Nethybridge. They have commanding views of the Cairngorms and across Speyside. Weekend breaks available off-season. Aviemore 12 miles, Loch Garten and famous Ospreys 3 miles, Whisky Trail 8 miles.
Great walking and fishing country!

Tel: Nethybridge 312 (evenings)

2 bungalows, 1-2 pub rms, 3 bedrms, sleeps 2-8, min let weekend, £70-£200, Jan-Dec, bus ½ ml, rail 12 mls, airport 28 mls

Mrs M Fraser, 36 Lynstock Crescent, Nethybridge, Inverness-shire, PH25 3DX
☎ *Nethybridge (047982) 312/(0786) 824957*

---

224   Prices shown are for guidance only. Please send SAE with each enquiry.

AWAITING INSPECTION	1 house/flat, 2 pub rms, 1-4 bedrms, sleeps 2-6, £100-£180, Jan-Dec, bus nearby, rail 12 mls, airport 34 mls

 ⟨symbols⟩

Mrs A McLaren, Northwood, Seafield Court, Grantown-on-Spey, Moray, PH26 3LE
☎ *Grantown-on-Spey (0479) 3365*

---

1 cottage, 1 pub rm, 2 bedrms, sleeps 6-7, min let 2 nights, £100-£170, Jan-Dec, bus ½ ml, rail 11 mls

⟨symbols⟩ (sports equipment hire)

Mr & Mrs K R Bateman, Craigmore Cottage, Nethybridge, Inverness-shire
☎ *Nethybridge (047982) 333*

COMMENDED ♕♕♕♕	1 bungalow, 1 pub rm, 2 bedrms, sleeps 6, min let weekend, £85-£135, Jan-Dec, bus nearby, rail 10 mls, airport 30 mls

 ⟨symbols⟩

Mrs S Horton, 33 Lynstock Crescent, Nethybridge, Inverness-shire
☎ *Nethybridge (047982) 679*
Modern detached bungalow with own garden in centre of village. Easy access to Spey Valley amenities.

COMMENDED ♕♕♕	1 cottage, 1 pub rm, 2 bedrms, sleeps 4, min let weekend (low season), £95-£130, Jan-Dec, bus nearby, rail 10 mls

 ⟨symbols⟩

Mr D V Johnston, Tigh na Froach, Nethybridge, Inverness-shire
☎ *Nethybridge (047982) 342*
Traditional highland cottage with garden. Secluded position yet close to village.

---

1 house, 1 pub rm, 3 bedrms, sleeps 8, min let weekend, £100-£200, Jan-Dec, bus nearby, rail 11 mls, airport 42 mls

⟨symbols⟩

Mrs G Robertson, Pitgarvie Farm, Laurencekirk, Kincardineshire
☎ *Northwaterbridge (067484) 219*

VAT is shown at 15%: changes in this rate may affect prices.

Birchfield Speyside Cottages

Newly-converted all-electric cottages, peacefully situated among pines and birches, overlooking the picturesque Highland village of Nethybridge. Mountains, rivers, lochs, forests, ideal for relaxation whether you want to flop or jog. Sleep 2-6, open-plan living room in each, comfortable bedrooms, carpeted throughout. Wonderful touring countryside; naturalists paradise. Fishing, riding, ski-ing, sailing, walking, climbing, canoeing, available within easy reach.

**Birchfield, Nethybridge, Inverness-shire PH25 3DD
Telephone: 047 982 613**

COMMENDED

3 cottages, 1 pub rm, 1-2 bedrms, sleeps 2-6, £70-£225, Jan-Dec, bus ½ ml, rail 10 mls, airport 39 mls

(riding tuition & hacking)

Mr & Mrs Rankin, Birchfield, Nethybridge, Inverness-shire, PH25 3DD
☎ *Nethybridge (047982) 613*
Comfortable accommodation in attractive rural setting. convenient for all Spey Valley amenities.

---

1 flat, 1 pub rm, 2 bedrms, sleeps 4-6, min let 1 night, £70-£130, Jan-Dec, bus nearby, rail 11 mls, airport 35 mls

Mr & Mrs T R Dunn, Duacklodge, Nethybridge, Inverness-shire, PH25 3DB
☎ *Nethybridge (047982) 284*

---

1 flat, 1 pub rm, sleeps 4, min let weekend, £70-£105, Jan-Dec, bus nearby, rail 10 mls, airport 30 mls

Mrs W Shand, Sgorgaoithe, Causer, Nethybridge, Inverness-shire, PH25 3DS
☎ *Nethybridge (047982) 262*

---

1 caravan, sleeps 8, min let weekend, £80-£120, Mar-Oct (or by arrangement), bus 3.5 mls, rail 9 mls, airport 35 mls

(cross country skiing)
Mrs J Pott, Tigh Ban, Nethybridge, Inverness-shire
☎ *Boat-of-Garten (047983) 227*

NEW ABBEY Kirkcudbrightshire Map Ref. 2B10

2 cottages, 1 pub rm, 2-3 bedrms, sleeps 4-7, £60-£100, Jan-Dec, bus ½ ml, rail 8 mls

Mr J Deans, Ingleston Farm, New Abbey, Dumfries, DG2 8DG
☎ *New Abbey (038785) 204*

---

1 cottage, 1 pub rm, 2 bedrms, sleeps 4-5, £28-£60, Jan-Dec, bus nearby, rail 7 mls

Mrs Greenshields, Abbey House, New Abbey, Kirkcudbrightshire, DG2 8BU
☎ *New Abbey (038785) 210*

NEW GALLOWAY Kirkcudbrightshire Map Ref. 2A9

5 cottages, 1-2 pub rms, 1-3 bedrms, sleeps 4-7, £75-£140, Mar-Oct, bus 2 mls, rail 28 mls, airport 70 mls

Mrs R Gordon, Glenlee Holiday Houses, New Galloway, Castle Douglas, Kirkcudbrightshire, DG7 3SF
☎ *Dalry (06443) 445*

NEW GALLOWAY AREA Kirkcudbrightshire Map Ref. 2A9

up to COMMENDED

18 houses, 5 cottages, 1 pub rm, 2-5 bedrms, sleeps 4-11, from £60, Apr-Oct

G M Thomson & Company, 27 King Street, Castle Douglas, Kirkcudbrightshire, DG7 1AB
☎ *Castle Douglas (0556) 2701*

NEWBURGH Fife Map Ref. 2C3

1 cottage, 1 pub rm, 2 bedrms, sleeps 4-6, from £70, Apr-Oct, bus $\frac{1}{4}$ ml, rail 9 mls, airport 40 mls

Mrs Adams, Woodriffe Farm, Newburgh, Fife, KY14 6DW
☎ *Newburgh (0337) 40264*

NEWMACHAR Aberdeenshire Map Ref. 4G10

1 cottage, 1 pub rm, 2 bedrms, sleeps 7, £60-£95, Jan-Dec, bus 2 mls, rail 10 mls, airport 4 mls

Mrs A Burgess, Highlands, Newmachar, Aberdeenshire, AB5 0QA
☎ *Newmachar (06517) 2241*

NEWMARKET, by Stornoway Isle of Lewis, Western Isles Map Ref. 3D4

up to COMMENDED

1 cottage, 1 bungalow, 1 pub rm, 2-3 bedrms, sleeps 4, £66-£99, Apr-Oct, ferry 2 mls, airport 4 mls

Murdo MacLeod, 31 Urquhart Gardens, Stornoway, Isle of Lewis, Western Isles
☎ *Stornoway (0851) 2458*
On crofting land, 3 miles (5km) from town. On regular bus route to town centre.

NEWMILNS Ayrshire Map Ref. 1H7

1 flat, 2 bungalows, 1 pub rm, 2 bedrms, sleeps 4, £50-£170, Jan-Dec, bus 1 $\frac{1}{2}$ mls, rail 8 mls, airport 14 mls

Mrs M K Hodge, Loudoun Mains, Newmilns, Ayrshire, KA16 9LG
☎ *Darvel (0560) 21246*

NEWPORT-ON-TAY Fife Map Ref. 2D2

1 house, 2-3 pub rms, 3-4 bedrms, sleeps 5-7, min let weekend (low season), £100-£160, Jan-Dec, bus nearby, rail 1 $\frac{1}{2}$ mls, airport 2 mls

Mr & Mrs A Ramsay, Balmore, 3 West Road, Newport-on-Tay, Fife
☎ *Newport-on-Tay (0382) 542274*

VAT is shown at 15%: changes in this rate may affect prices.

by NEWPORT-ON-TAY Fife Map Ref. 2D2

1 cottage, 1 pub rm, 1 bedrm, sleeps 2, £90-£120, Apr-Oct

🦽 ♿ E ➹ ❏ 🗐 ⌾ ⊚ ⌗ ⊡ ◉ ❄ 𝗣 †

Finlayson Hughes, Bank House, 82 Atholl Road, Pitlochry, Perthshire, PH16 5BL
☎ *Pitlochry (0796) 2512*

NEWTON STEWART Wigtownshire Map Ref. 1H10

APPROVED
👑 👑 👑

1 cottage, 1 pub rm, 2 bedrms, sleeps 5, £60-£100, May-Sep, bus ¾ ml

🦽 ♿ E ➹ 🗐 ⌾ ⊡ ⊡ ⊡ ❄ ♞ 𝗣 🛶 ▥ † ⚙   ⌇ ◔ 🎣 ↯ ⚓ ✓ 🐎 (birdwatching)

Mrs M J Templeton, Carslae Farm, Newton Stewart, Wigtownshire, DG8 9TE
☎ *Wigtown (09884) 2292*
Stone built, on working livestock farm. Enclosed garden. Open views over adjacent farmland.

Conifers Leisure Park
NEWTON STEWART
DUMFRIES & GALLOWAY
Telephone: (0671) 2107

24 Scandinavian Self-Catering Luxury Cabins (all electric). Colour TV, double-glazed, fully insulated and furnished to high standards, set in 25 acres of picturesque forest setting.

For the sportsman there is river, loch and sea angling, shooting, riding, all within easy reach; golf course adjacent.

Two saunas, health spa, solarium/sun beds and video room (with instruction tapes on golf, fly fishing, shooting and sailing).

Spend an active or relaxing time at Conifers at any time of the year and you are sure to enjoy yourself. Lots of places to wine and dine within one-mile radius including the licensed Kirroughtree Hotel adjacent.

FREE: Over one mile of salmon and sea trout fishing and golf all week for the family. (Ideal for a visit to Turnberry.)

24 chalet/log cabins, 1 pub rm, 2-3 bedrms, sleeps 4-6, min let 2 nights, £87-£225, Jan-Dec, bus 1 ml, rail 16 mls, airport 52 mls

🦽 ♿ E ➹ ❏ 🗐 ▥ ⊡ ⌾ ⊡ ⌗ ⊡ ◉ ❄ ♞ 𝗣 🛶 ▥ ⚙   ⌇ ◔ 🎣 ∪ ⚓ ↯ ► ✓
ⓡ ✗ 🔧 Ⓣ (health spa, jacuzzi)

Ian S Lowth, Conifers Leisure Parks, Kirroughtree, Newton Stewart, Wigtownshire, DG8 6AN
☎ *Newton Stewart (0671) 2107*

---

1 chalet/log cabin, 1 flat, 1 cottage, 1 pub rm, 1-2 bedrms, sleeps 2-5, min let weekend, £50-£100, Jan-Dec, bus 4 ½ mls, rail 30 mls, airport 80 mls

🦽 ♿ E ➹ 🗐 ⌾ ⊡ ❄ ♞ 𝗣 🛶 ▥ †   🎣 ∪ ⚓ ↯ ► 🚲 🐎

Mrs J Landers, Craigdistant, Newton Stewart, Wigtownshire, DG8 7BN
☎ *Newton Stewart (0671) 2461*

---

1 house, 2 pub rms, 3 bedrms, sleeps 8, min let weekend, £98-£145, Apr-Oct, bus 500 yds, rail 18 mls

🦽 ♿ E ➹ 🗐 ⊡ ⌾ ⊡ ⌇ ⌗ ⊡ ❄ 𝗣 🛶 ▥ † ⚙   🎣 ∪ ⚓ ↯ ► ✓ ✗ 🔧

Mrs C Kwiatkowska, 13 Mansfield Place, Newton Stewart, Wigtownshire, DG8 6LS
☎ *Newton Stewart (0671) 2684*

    Prices shown are for guidance only. Please send SAE with each enquiry.

9 caravans, sleeps 4-6, min let 1 night, £55-£110, Mar-Oct, bus nearby, rail 9 mls

Mrs Gaunt, Merrick Caravan Park, Bargrennan, by Newton Stewart, Wigtownshire, DG8 6RN
☎ *Bargrennan (067184) 280*

APPROVED
👑 👑

1 cottage, 1 pub rm, 3 bedrms, sleeps 6, £75-£125, Apr-Oct, bus 1 ml, rail 19 mls, airport 50 mls

Mrs L M Muir, Larg, Newton Stewart, Wigtownshire
☎ *Newton Stewart (0671) 2939*
Detached building in own grounds; ample parking. Rural setting. 1 mile (2km) from Newton Stewart.

---

1 house, 2 pub rms, 3 bedrms, sleeps 7, from £70, Apr-Oct, bus $\frac{1}{4}$ ml

Mr & Mrs McGaw, Ardvale, St Couans Road, Newton Stewart, Wigtownshire, DG8 6LU
☎ *Newton Stewart (0671) 2870*

---

1 cottage, 1 pub rm, 2 bedrms, sleeps 4, £80-£90, Apr-Oct, bus 2 mls, rail 20 mls, airport 50 mls

Mrs M Oxley, Skaith Farm, Newton Stewart, Wigtownshire, DG8 6QP
☎ *Newton Stewart (0671) 2774*

---

2 cottages, 1 pub rm, 2 bedrms, sleeps 4, £150-£175, Jan-Dec, bus nearby, rail 20 mls, airport 80 mls

Scottish Country Cottages, Suite 2d, Churchill Way, Bishopbriggs, Glasgow, G64 2RH
☎ *041 772 5920*

---

by NEWTON STEWART Wigtownshire Map Ref. 1H10

Three Lochs Caravan Park 16 caravans, sleeps 6, min let weekend, £85-£115, Apr-Oct, bus 7 mls, rail 19 mls, airport 80 mls

Mr Alan Brown, Three Lochs Caravan Park, Kirkcowan, Newton Stewart, Wigtownshire
☎ *Kirkcowan (067183) 304*

---

1 house, 4 cottages, 1-2 pub rms, 2-4 bedrms, sleeps 4-8, min let weekend (low season), £80-£250, Jan-Dec, bus 6 mls, rail 6 mls, airport 70 mls

Mrs Beale, Drumlamford, Barrhill, Ayrshire
☎ *Barrhill (046582) 220*

NEWTON STEWART AREA Wigtownshire Map Ref. 1H10

6 houses, 3 flats, 7 cottages, 1 bungalow, 1 pub rm, 1-3 bedrms, sleeps 6-7, from £70, Apr-Oct

G M Thomson & Company, 27 King Street, Castle Douglas, Kirkcudbrightshire, DG7 1AB
☎ *Castle Douglas (0556) 2701*

VAT is shown at 15%: changes in this rate may affect prices.

NEWTONAIRDS Dumfriesshire Map Ref. 2B9

2 flats, 1 pub rm, 2 bedrms, sleeps 6, min let weekend, £80-£150, Jan-Dec, bus ½ ml, rail 7 mls

Mr Higgins, Newtonairds House, Newtonairds, Dumfries, Dumfriesshire
☎ *Dunscore (038782) 312*

NEWTONMORE Inverness-shire Map Ref. 4B11

AWAITING INSPECTION

3 bungalows, 1 pub rm, 2-3 bedrms, sleeps 4-6, min let weekend, £80-£160, Mar-Nov, bus 400 yds, rail 1 ml

Mr A C Gillies Jnr, Gillies Leasing, Dalwhinnie, Inverness-shire
☎ *Dalwhinnie (05282) 267*

COMMENDED

1 bungalow, 2 pub rms, 3 bedrms, sleeps 2-6, min let weekend, £80-£160, Jan-Dec, bus 800 yds, rail 300 yds, airport 45 mls

Alastair Troup, 32 Fowgay Drive, Solihull, West Midlands, B91 3PH
☎ *021 705 3950*

Modern, with own garden. In quiet part of village, within easy reach of shops and local amemities.

Glentruim Estate 4 cottages, 1-2 pub rms, 1-3 bedrms, sleeps 2-8, min let long weekend, £86-£144, Jan-Dec, bus 3 mls, rail 3 mls, airport 60 mls

Mrs Macpherson of Glentruim, Glentruim Estate, Newtonmore, Inverness-shire, PH20 1DE
☎ *Newtonmore (05403) 221/534*

1 bungalow, 1 pub rm, 2 bedrms, sleeps 6, £75-£110, Apr-Oct, bus nearby, rail 1 ½ mls

Mrs M C Woodward, 10 Clamps Wood, East Kilbride, Lanarkshire, G74 2HB
☎ *East Kilbride (03552) 25142*

1 chalet/log cabin, 1 pub rm, 2 bedrms, sleeps 5-6, £70-£115, Jan-Dec, bus ½ ml, rail ½ ml

Mr J D Macdonald, 27 Hinchley Drive, Hinchley Wood, Esher, Surrey, KT10 0BZ
☎ *01 398 1456*

1 cottage, 1 pub rm, 3 bedrms, sleeps 5, £60-£95, Feb-Nov, bus nearby, rail ½ ml, airport 45 mls

Mrs K Macrae, Loch na Leoba, Newtonmore, Inverness-shire
☎ *Newtonmore (05403) 373*

1 house, 2 flats, 1 cottage, 1 bungalow, 1-3 pub rms, 4-6 bedrms, sleeps 5-9, £109-£230, May-Oct, bus 3-15 mls, rail 2-5 mls, airport 50-65 mls

Mrs E Drysdale, Ralia Lodge, Newtonmore, Inverness-shire
☎ *Newtonmore (05403) 248/500*

1 bungalow, 1 pub rm, 2 bedrms, sleeps 4-6, from £75, Apr-Oct, bus nearby, rail 1 ml

Mrs A R Mackintosh, Ku Ring Gai, Church Terrace, Newtonmore, Inverness-shire
☎ Newtonmore (05403) 477

---

1 house, 2 pub rms, 3 bedrms, sleeps 6-8, £105-£175, Jan-Dec, bus nearby, rail ½ ml

Mrs H Cochran, Knowes, Dunbar, East Lothian
☎ East Linton (0620) 860221

NIBON, by Hillswick North Mainland, Shetland Map Ref. 5F3

1 cottage, 1 pub rm, 2 bedrms, sleeps 2-4, £55-£65, Apr-Oct, bus 2 mls

Miss R Tulloch, Inches, Bells Road, Lerwick, Shetland
☎ Lerwick (0595) 5413

NORBISTER, by Bridge End Burra Isle, Shetland Map Ref. 5F5

1 cottage, 1 pub rm, 3 bedrms, sleeps 6, £50-£60, Jan-Dec, bus 3 mls, ferry 12 mls, airport 25 mls

Mrs W Simpson, 2 Vevoe, Brough, Whalsay, Shetland
☎ Symbister (08066) 286

NORTH BERWICK East Lothian Map Ref. 2E4

1 flat, 2 pub rms, 3 bedrms, sleeps 5, from £50, Jan-Dec

Mrs Auld, First Flat, Mafeking House, 43 Westgate, North Berwick, East Lothian
☎ North Berwick (0620) 2137

---

1 house, 1 pub rm, 3 bedrms, sleeps 6, £60-£185, Jan-Dec, bus nearby, rail nearby, airport 30 mls

Mrs E M Macdonald, Blake Holt, Browsea View Avenue, Lilliput, Poole, Dorset
☎ Canford Cliffs (0202) 707894

---

1 flat, 2 pub rms, 2 bedrms, sleeps 4, £25-£120, Apr-Oct, bus ¾ ml, rail ¾ ml

Mrs M Lowis, Fauhope, Melrose, Roxburghshire
☎ Melrose (089682) 2157

---

1 house, 1 pub rm, 3 bedrms, sleeps 6, £130-£160, Jan-Dec, bus 1 ml, rail 4 mls, airport 30 mls

Mrs D C Jackson, 1 Redholm, Greenheads Road, North Berwick, East Lothian, EH39 4RA
☎ North Berwick (0620) 3420

---

1 flat, 1 pub rm, 2 bedrms, sleeps 6, min let weekend, £60-£100, Jan-Dec, bus ½ ml, rail 1 ml, airport 30 mls

Mrs I Brown, 14 Marine Parade, North Berwick, East Lothian
☎ North Berwick (0620) 2063

VAT is shown at 15%: changes in this rate may affect prices.

1 flat, 1 pub rm, 2 bedrms, sleeps 6, min let weekend, £75-£110, Apr-Oct, bus ¼ ml, rail ½ ml, airport 40 mls

♿ ᵂᶜ E ⬅ ⬛ ⬛ ⬛ ⬛ ⬛ ⬛ ⬛ ⬛ ⬛ † ⬛ ⬛ ⬛ ⬛ ⬛ ⬛ ⬛ ⬛ ⬛ ⬛ ⬛ 🅃

Mrs Braidwood, 77 Middle Street, Brockham, Surrey
☎ *Betchworth (073784) 3508*

---

1 bedsit, sleeps 2, £45-£75, Apr-Oct, bus nearby, rail nearby

♿ ᵂᶜ E ⬅ ⬛ ⬛ ⬛ ⬛ 🅿 ⬛ † ⬛ ⬛ ⬛ ⬛

Mrs Grudley, 9A Abbey Mews, North Berwick, East Lothian
☎ *North Berwick (0620) 2426*

---

1 flat, 1 bedrm, sleeps 2-4, from £50, Jan-Dec, bus nearby, rail 400 yds

♿ ᵂᶜ E ⬅ ⬛ ⬛ ⬛ ⬛ ⬛ ⬛ ⬛ ⬛ ⬛ ⬛ ⬛ ⬛ † ⬛ ⬛ ⬛ ⬛ ⬛ ⬛ ⬛
(windsurfing)

Mr Richard Smeed, Springfield Guest House, Belhaven Road, Dunbar, East Lothian
☎ *Dunbar (0368) 62502*

NORTH CONNEL Argyll Map Ref. 1E2

1 house, 2 pub rms, 3 bedrms, sleeps 6, £75-£240, Apr-Oct, bus ¼ ml, rail 2 mls, airport 2 mls

♿ ᵂᶜ E ⬅ ⬛ ⬛ ⬛ ⬛ ⬛ ⬛ ⬛ ⬛ ⬛ ⬛ 🅿 ⬛ ⬛ † ⬛ ⬛ ⬛ ⬛ ⬛ ⬛ ⬛ ⬛
(gliding)

Ms. Allison McDougall, Lochside, North Connell, Argyll
☎ *Connel (063171) 282*
Modern detached unit with large garden, situated on ridge above Loch Etive. Excellent views.

---

1 house, 2 cottages, 1-2 pub rms, 2-3 bedrms, sleeps 4-7, £80-£200, Apr-Oct, bus 1 ½ mls, rail nearby

♿ ᵂᶜ E ⬅ ⬛ ⬛ ⬛ ⬛ ⬛ ⬛ ⬛ ⬛ 🅿 ⬛ ⬛ ⬛ ⬛ ⬛ ⬛ ⬛

Mrs M McIntyre, Eilean Beag, South Ledaig, Connel, Argyll
☎ *Connel (063171) 597*

COMMENDED
🏵 🏵 🏵 🏵

2 bungalows, 1 pub rm, 3 bedrms, sleeps 6, min let weekend, £70-£175, Jan-Dec, bus 1 ml, rail 2 mls, airport 1 ml

♿ ᵂᶜ E ⬅ ⬛ ⬛ ⬛ ⬛ ⬛ ⬛ ⬛ ⬛ ⬛ 🅿 ⬛ ⬛ ⬛ ⬛ ⬛ ⬛

Mrs Isobel Campbell, Druimbhan, North Connel, Argyll, PA37 1RA
☎ *Connel (063171) 424*
Modern units, beautifully sited overlooking Loch Etive. Ideal base for touring and visiting islands.

COMMENDED
🏵 🏵 🏵 🏵

1 cottage, 1 bungalow, 1 pub rm, 3 bedrms, sleeps 6, min let 3 nights, £70-£175, Jan-Dec, bus 2 mls, rail 3 mls

♿ ᵂᶜ E ⬅ ⬛ ⬛ ⬛ ⬛ ⬛ ⬛ ⬛ ⬛ 🅿 ⬛ ⬛ ⬛ ⬛ ⬛ ⬛

Mrs D Campbell, Achnacree Bay, North Connel, Argyll
☎ *Connel (063171) 288*
Bungalow in quiet location overlooking Loch Etive. Cottage with superb view of loch and Ben Guachan.

NORTH ERRADALE, by Gairloch Ross-shire Map Ref. 3E7

COMMENDED

1 bungalow, 1 pub rm, 3 bedrms, sleeps 6, £80-£180, Jan-Dec, bus 5 mls, rail 30 mls, ferry 55 mls, airport 80 mls

Mrs MacLennan, Westbank, Kirkhill, Inverness
☎ *Inverness (0463) 83717*
Modern unit on site of original croft. Remote location, enjoying excellent sea views to Isle of Skye.

NORTH KESSOCK Ross-shire Map Ref. 4A8

1 chalet/log cabin, 1 pub rm, 3 bedrms, sleeps 6-8, min let weekend, £70-£190, Jan-Nov, bus 1 ml, rail 3 mls, airport 10 mls

Mrs Lowe, Glaick of Kessock, North Kessock, Ross-shire
☎ *Kessock (046373) 531*

---

1 cottage, 1 pub rm, 3 bedrms, sleeps 7, £80-£100, Mar-Oct, bus nearby, rail 2 mls

Miss Sheila Rattray, Brae Farm, Dingwall, Ross-shire
☎ *Dingwall (0349) 63066*

---

1 cottage, 1 pub rm, 3 bedrms, sleeps 6, £65-£135, Apr-Sep, bus $\frac{3}{4}$ ml, rail 3 mls, airport 8 mls

Mr J MacRury, 21 Allington Road, Orpington, Kent, BR6 8AY
☎ *Orpington (0689) 38075*

---

1 caravan, sleeps 8, min let weekend, £75-£110, Apr-Oct, bus 2 $\frac{1}{2}$ mls

(windsurfing, birdwatching)
Mrs Balan, 36 Lansdown Hill, Fulwood, Preston, Lancashire, PR2 3WD
☎ *Preston (0772) 863898/(046373) 373*

NORTH QUEENSFERRY Fife Map Ref. 2C4

AWAITING
INSPECTION

6 flats, 1-2 pub rms, 1-3 bedrms, sleeps 2-7, £80-£220, Jan-Dec, bus nearby, rail 300 yds, airport 9 mls

Mrs Anderson, 1 Inverkeithing Road, Crossgate, Fife
☎ *Cowdenbeath (0383) 510666*

OBAN Argyll Map Ref. 1E2

1 house, 1 pub rm, 2 bedrms, sleeps 6, from £90, Apr-Oct, bus 6 mls, rail 6 mls

Bell-Ingram, Durn, Isla Road, Perth, PH2 7HF
☎ *Perth (0738) 21121*

COMMENDED

2 flats, 1 pub rm, 2 bedrms, sleeps 2-7, £65-£190, Jan-Dec, bus $\frac{1}{2}$ ml, rail $\frac{1}{2}$ ml

Mrs MacDonald, Mingulay, Laurel Crescent, Oban, Argyll
☎ *Oban (0631) 62627*
Modern units with garden area, in quiet residential area on Oban Hill with excellent views.

VAT is shown at 15%: changes in this rate may affect prices.

COMMENDED

12 flats, 1 pub rm, 1-2 bedrms, sleeps 1-6, £90-£220, Apr-Nov, bus ¼ ml, rail ¼ ml

Mr I Nicholson, Westbay Apartments, Esplanade, Oban, Argyll, PA34 5PW
☎ Oban (0631) 62067
Central, modern purpose built block with superb views of sea and islands. Elevator to all floors. **(See colour ad. 14 p. xxxv)**

1 chalet/log cabin, 1 pub rm, 1 bedrm, sleeps 2, £50-£60, Apr-Sep, bus ¾ ml, rail ¾ ml

A Gillespie, The Cottage, Gallanach Road, Oban, Argyll
☎ Oban (0631) 64179

HIGHLY COMMENDED

14 flats, 1 pub rm, 1-3 bedrms, sleeps 1-7, £100-£240, Apr-Nov, bus ¼ ml, rail ¼ ml

Esplanade Court Apartments, The Esplanade, Oban, Argyll, PA34 5PW
☎ Oban (0631) 62067
Modern purpose built or traditional units, some with sea and island views.

5 flats, 1 pub rm, 2-3 bedrms, sleeps 4-6, £50-£140, Jan-Dec, bus nearby, rail nearby

M A & M MacDonald, Almar, McCaig Road, Soroba, Oban, Argyll
☎ Oban (0631) 62400

1 house, 2 pub rms, 3 bedrms, sleeps 7, from £110, Apr-Oct, bus nearby, rail ¼ ml, airport 6 mls

Mr Hyland, Dun-shee, Croft Road, Oban, Argyll
☎ 041 220 5346(day)/(03552) 49569(eve)

up to COMMENDED

2 flats, 1 pub rm, 2 bedrms, sleeps 4-6, min let 3 nights (low season), £80-£200, Jan-Dec, bus ¼ ml, rail ¼ ml

Mr R Connelly, Hamilton House, Dunollie Road, Oban, Argyll
☎ Oban (0631) 62384
New purpose built apartments in central, level position close to promenade, harbour and town centre.

TRY A "TASTE OF SCOTLAND"
Look for the stockpot—
sign of good food,
a warm welcome
and value for money!

Glenquaich House

ARDCONNEL TERRACE · OBAN · 0631 63814/65604

Tastefully converted into luxury flats, Glenquaich House is situated in the town centre with superb views of Oban Bay and the Sound of Kerrera. The flats have central heating, colour TV, and bed linen is supplied.

Prices from £65 per week
(Special Short Break terms available)
Contact: J. Wallace, Glenquaich House, Ardconnel Terrace, Oban. Tel. No. 0631 63814/65604

COMMENDED
♛ ♛ ♛

4 flats, 1 pub rm, 1-2 bedrms, sleeps 2-6, £70-£210, Jan-Dec, bus ½ ml, rail ½ ml, airport 6 mls

Glenquaich House (Booking Dept), 10 Argyll Square, Oban, Argyll
☎ *Oban (0631) 63814(office)/65604(eve)*

Recently modernised apartments on Ardconnel Hill. Quiet area overlooking town and harbour.

AWAITING INSPECTION

3 flats, 1-2 pub rms, 2 bedrms, sleeps 4, £65-£160, May-Oct, bus 350 yds, rail 350 yds

Mr A D E Sharp, Dreva-Mhor, Ganavan Road, Oban, Argyll
☎ *Oban (0631) 62684*

---

10 chalet/log cabins, 4 flats, 1 pub rm, 1-2 bedrms, sleeps 4-6, min let 1 night, £136-£260, Jan-Dec, bus 1 ½ mls, rail 1 ½ mls

Soroba House Hotel, Soroba Road, Oban, Argyll
☎ *Oban (0631) 62628*

---

5 flats, 1 pub rm, 2 bedrms, sleeps 4-6, £60-£220, Jan-Dec, bus nearby, rail nearby

Kings Arms Apartments, 28 George Street, Oban, Argyll
☎ *Oban (0631) 62304*

---

1 cottage, 1 pub rm, 1 bedrm, sleeps 4, from £80, May-Sep

Mrs M K Dunlop, Rockmount, Glencruitten Road, Oban, Argyll
☎ *Oban (0631) 64647*

---

2 flats, 1 pub rm, 1-2 bedrms, sleeps 2-6, £90-£130, Apr-Sep, bus ½ ml, rail ½ ml

Mrs May, Fairhaven, Glencruitten Road, Oban, Argyll
☎ *Oban (0631) 66528*

Gallanachmore Farm Caravan Site 15 caravans, sleeps 6-8, £70-£100, Apr-Oct, bus 2 mls, rail 2 mls, ferry 2 mls

Brian & Sylvia Thompson, Gallanachmore Farm, Gallanach Road, Oban, Argyll
☎ *Oban (0631) 62425/63502*

VAT is shown at 15%: changes in this rate may affect prices.

1 house, 1 pub rm, 4 bedrms, sleeps 8-9, £50-£200, Apr-Oct

Mr D J C Leckie, 15 Lanark Place, Fort William, Inverness-shire, PH33 6JR
☎ Fort William (0397) 4361

---

4 flats, 1 pub rm, 1-2 bedrms, sleeps 2-6, £50-£165, Jan-Dec, bus nearby, rail nearby

Mr & Miss J Henderson, Neidpath, Polvinister Road, Oban, Argyll
☎ Oban (0631) 64021

---

2 flats, 1 pub rm, 2 bedrms, sleeps 2-6, min let weekend, £90-£155, Apr-Oct

Mrs S Russell, 2 Glencruitten Road, Oban, Argyll
☎ Oban (0631) 64339

---

1 cottage, 1 pub rm, 1 bedrm, sleeps 2-4, £100-£150, Apr-Oct, bus 1 ml, rail 1 ml

(bowling/putting green)

Mrs Gunn, Hollymount, Breadalbane Lane, Oban, Argyll
☎ Oban (0631) 62239

---

1 flat, 2 flatlets, 1 pub rm, 1-2 bedrms, sleeps 2-6, min let weekend, £50-£180, Apr-Oct, bus ½ ml, rail ½ ml

Mrs MacGregor, Helenslee, Dalriach Road, Oban, Argyll
☎ Oban (0631) 62240

---

1 flat, 1 pub rm, 2 bedrms, sleeps 5, £95-£200, Mar-Nov, bus nearby, rail ¼ ml, airport 7 mls

Mrs Sara A Reid, Ravenscraig, Carrington Terrace, Crieff, Perthshire
☎ Crieff (0764) 2392/3160

---

by OBAN Argyll Map Ref. 1E2

up to
COMMENDED
👑 👑 👑

14 chalet/log cabins, 5 bungalows, 1 pub rm, 2-3 bedrms, sleeps 4-6, min let 3 nights (low season), £68-£195, Apr-Oct, bus 1 ½ mls, rail 3 ½ mls

D G Wren, Lag-na-Keil Chalets, (Oban) Ltd, Lerags, by Oban, Argyll
☎ Oban (0631) 62746
On spacious wooded site in peaceful location. 4 mls (6km) from Oban.

Modern Homely Timber Bungalows

FOR TWO TO SIX PEOPLE
on
COLOGIN FARM

One of our large timber bungalows

THREE MILES SOUTH OF OBAN

yet set in a peaceful private glen under the hills in wild and open countryside. Have a real country holiday away from it all in a Cologin Bungalow.

Here you will find complete freedom — you can do something different each day, or nothing, just as you fancy. Use a dinghy (and fishing rods if you want them) on our own trout loch or on the sea loch. You can ride on one of our bikes.

Join in an informal ceilidh/barbecue or ceilidh/dance with a kilted highland piper.

The old farm and surrounding countryside abound in a variety of wildlife, from herons and hares, to roe deer and foxes, and there are ducks, hens, a nanny goat, a donkey, rabbits and a market garden on the old farm itself.

In our games room or lounge bar you can play table-tennis, darts, pool, dominoes, etc. In our area within 2 or 3 miles there are excellent facilities for golf, diving, fishing, swimming, sauna, tennis, bowls, pony-trekking, squash, sailing and walking. We have a home-made cold buffet all day in our lounge bar and there are many other good hotels and restaurants at which to enjoy dining out within 2 and 3 miles away. Our site is ideal for children.

— OPEN ALL YEAR ROUND —

THE OLD BYRE ON COLOGIN FARM —
NOW A COUNTRY PUB SERVING OUR BUNGALOWS

Every bungalow is double glazed and fully insulated, electrically heated and has an electric cooker (with oven and grill) and fridge (all electricity is included in rentals). Living rooms, bathroom, double/twin bedrooms and kitchens are all fully equipped. Colour TV is available in all bungalows, shop and laundry service on site, baby sitting available, cots and high chairs available. All linen can be hired. Details (stamp please) from:

Mrs BERYL DOVE, COLOGIN HOMES LTD., COLOGIN,
LERAGS, By OBAN, ARGYLL PA34 4SE
Telephone Oban (0631) 64501 any time.   *AA LISTED*

COMMENDED
♛ ♛ ♛

Cologin Farm 18 chalet/log cabins, 1-2 pub rms, 1-3 bedrms, sleeps 2-6, min let 1 night (low season), £75-£230, Jan-Dec, bus 1 ml, rail 3 mls

Cologin Homes Ltd, Cologin, Lerags, by Oban, Argyll, PA34 4SE
☎ *Oban (0631) 64501*

On peaceful, private site 3 miles/5km from Oban. Informal atmosphere in bar; home food all day.   **(See ad. on p. 237)**

---

3 flats, 1 pub rm, 1-2 bedrms, sleeps 2-6, min let 1 night, from £90, Jan-Dec, bus nearby, rail 2 mls, airport 2 mls

(windsurfing, diving)

Dunstaffnage Yacht Haven, Dunbeg, Oban, Argyll
☎ *Oban (0631) 66555*

OBAN AREA Argyll Map Ref. 1E2

10 houses, 10 flats, 10 cottages, 10 bungalows, 1-3 pub rms, 1-6 bedrms, sleeps 2-12, min let weekend (low season), £50-£350, Apr-Oct, airport 85 mls

Highland Hideaways (Alexander Dawson), 5/7 Stafford Street, Oban, Argyll, PA34 5NJ
☎ *Oban (0631) 62056/63901*

OLD DEER Aberdeenshire Map Ref. 4H8

1 cottage, 1 pub rm, 2 bedrms, sleeps 2-3, £85-£100, Mar-Oct, bus ½ ml

Mrs E Cook, Saplinbrae House Hotel, Old Deer, Aberdeenshire, AB4 8LP
☎ *Mintlaw (07712) 2215*

OLD KILPATRICK Dunbartonshire Map Ref. 1H5

2 houses, 1 pub rm, 2-4 bedrms, sleeps 4-8, £60-£100, Apr-Oct, bus 1 ml, rail 1 ml, airport 5 mls

Mrs S Fleming, Gavinburn Farm, Old Kilpatrick, Glasgow, G60 5NH
☎ *Duntocher (0389) 73058*

OLDMELDRUM Aberdeenshire Map Ref. 4G9

1 house, 2 pub rms, 4 bedrms, sleeps 8, £100-£200, Jan-Dec, bus ½ ml, rail 5 mls, airport 10 mls

Mrs Simmers, Ardmedden, Oldmeldrum, Aberdeenshire, AB5 0AG
☎ *Oldmeldrum (06512) 2261*

---

by OLDMELDRUM Aberdeenshire Map Ref. 4G9

COMMENDED
♛ ♛ ♛

1 cottage, 1 pub rm, 3 bedrms, sleeps 6, min let weekend (low season), £70-£100, Apr-Oct, bus 2 mls, rail 9 mls, airport 18 mls

Mrs B Milne, 2 North Bethelnie Cottages, Oldmeldrum, Aberdeenshire, AB5 0AN
☎ *Oldmeldrum (06512) 2352*

Traditional cottage with south facing garden. On mixed arable farm with scenic views of Bennachie.

ONICH, by Fort William Inverness-shire Map Ref. 1F1

Ardrhu Cottages 13 cottages, 1-2 pub rms, 2-4 bedrms, sleeps 2-8, min let 2 nights, £80-£260, Jan-Dec, bus ½ ml, rail 8 mls, airport 40 mls

Ardrhu Cottages, Onich, Inverness-shire, PH33 6SD
☎ Onich (08553) 228

Corran Caravans 9 caravans, sleeps 5-6, min let 1 night, £65-£145, Mar-Oct, bus ¼ ml, rail 9 mls

Corran Caravans, Moss Cottage, Onich, by Fort William, Inverness-shire, PH33 6SE
☎ Onich (08553) 208

Cross Cottage Caravan Site 8 caravans, sleeps 6, min let 1 night (low season), £52-£155, Jan-Oct, bus nearby, rail 11 mls

Mr J Fraser, Cross Cottage Caravan Site, 19/20 North Ballachulish, Onich, by Fort William, Inverness-shire, PH33 6RZ
☎ Onich (08553) 335

---

3 cottages, 1 pub rm, 2 bedrms, sleeps 4-6, min let weekend, £110-£220, Jan-Dec, bus 400 yds, rail 10 mls, airport 75 mls

9 caravans, sleeps 6, min let 1 night (low season), £70-£155, Easter-Oct, bus 400 yds, rail 10 mls, airport 75 mls

Mr & Mrs A Dewar, Cuilcheanna House, Onich, by Fort William, Inverness-shire, PH33 6SD
☎ Onich (08553) 226

---

4 cottages, 1-2 pub rms, 2-3 bedrms, sleeps 6, min let weekend, £80-£175, Jan-Dec, bus nearby, rail 10 mls, airport 100 mls

Mrs M MacDonald, Springwell, Onich, Fort William, Inverness-shire, PH33 6RY
☎ Onich (08553) 257

---

9 chalet/log cabins, 1 bunkhouse, 1 pub rm, 2-3 bedrms, sleeps 4-6, min let weekend, £76-£220, Jan-Dec, bus nearby, rail 9 mls, airport 70 mls

(climbing wall)

Inchree Chalets, Onich, Fort William, Inverness-shire, PH33 6SD
☎ Onich (08553) 287

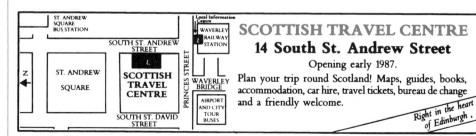
VAT is shown at 15%: changes in this rate may affect prices.

LOCH LEVEN CHALETS
ONICH, FORT WILLIAM, INVERNESS-SHIRE
Telephone: Onich (08553) 272
Resident Proprietors: David and Helen King
Seven luxury chalets on the shores of Loch Leven with magnificent views across to Glencoe. The chalets are fully equipped for 6 persons including linen, colour TV. Powerboats and sailboat available from our private pier. For the more adventurous we offer clay pigeon shooting and tuition for the beginner.
Special Low Season Offer: 3 nights for £65.

Loch Leven Chalets 7 chalet/log cabins, 1 pub rm, 2 bedrms, sleeps 6, min let 3 nights, £137-£240, Jan-Dec, bus 4 mls, rail 16 mls

David & Helen King, Loch Leven Chalets, Onich, by Fort William, Inverness-shire
☎ *Onich (08553) 272*

---

2 flats, 1 pub rm, 1 bedrm, sleeps 4-6, min let 3 nights, from £60, Jan-Dec, bus nearby, rail 10 mls, airport 90 mls

Mrs Gillian Fuller, Glenrigh House, Onich, Inverness-shire
☎ *Onich (08553) 354*

ORD Isle of Skye, Inverness-shire Map Ref. 3E10

Ord House Country Club 10 chalet/log cabins, 1 pub rm, 3 bedrms, sleeps 6, min let weekend (low season), £80-£290, Dec-Oct, bus 10 mls, rail 20 mls, ferry 20 mls, airport 20 mls

Cabin Holidays Ltd, Bull Plain, Hertford, Herts, SG14 1DY
☎ *Hertford (0992) 59933*

ORINSAY, Lochs Isle of Lewis, Western Isles Map Ref. 3D5

COMMENDED
👑 👑 👑

1 bungalow, 1 pub rm, 3 bedrms, sleeps 6, from £65, Jan-Dec, bus nearby, ferry 30 mls, airport 33 mls

1 caravan, sleeps 6, from £25, Apr-Oct, bus nearby, ferry 30 mls, airport 33 mls

Mrs A M Kennedy, 3 Orinsay, Lochs, Isle of Lewis, Western Isles
☎ *Gravir (085188) 375*
Modern, on hillside overlooking Loch Shiant and with views to Isle of Skye.

COMMENDED
👑 👑 👑

1 cottage, 2 pub rms, 3 bedrms, sleeps 6, from £55, Jan-Dec, bus nearby, ferry 30 mls, airport 30 mls

Mrs J Mont & V Brookbank, 86 High Street, Lewes, East Sussex
☎ *Lewes (0273) 472696*
Standing in own grounds overlooking Loch Shiant, in remote crofting township.

Prices shown are for guidance only. Please send SAE with each enquiry.

ORMSARY Argyll Map Ref. 1E5

Camas 13 chalet/log cabins, 1 house, 1 pub rm, 1-3 bedrms, sleeps 2-6, £70-£235, Jan-Dec

க் wc E ➡ 🏠 🖳 🛗 ⊙ 🎍 🗗 ✂ ⊙ 🐎 P 🏊 🏛 ⚒   ♪ ∪ ⚠ ⚓ ∮ ⚑ 🎣 ☎

Ormsary Estate (Holidays), Ormsary Estate Office, P.O. Box 7, Lochgilphead, Argyll, PA31 8JH
☎ *Ormsary (08803) 222*

ORPHIR Orkney Map Ref. 5B11

1 bungalow, 1 pub rm, 4 bedrms, sleeps 8, min let 2 weeks (high season), £85-£115, Mar-Jan, bus 4 mls, ferry 7 mls, airport 12 mls

க் wc E ➡ 🏠 ⊙ 🗗 🛏 ⚓ ❄ P 🏊 🏛 †   ♪ ⚓ ✗ 🎣 ☎

Mrs V Pirie, Orakirk, Orphir, Orkney, KW17 2RE
☎ *Orphir (085681) 328*

---

1 caravan, sleeps 6, min let 1 night, £20-£40, Jan-Dec, ferry 8 mls, airport 8 mls

க் wc E 🏠 🖳 ✂ 🗗 🛏 ⚓ ❄ 🐎 P ⚒ 🏊 🏛 ➡ †   ♪ ⚠ ⚓ ▸ ✗

Mrs W R Slater, Roadside Cottage, Smoogro, Orphir, Orkney, KW17 2RB
☎ *Orphir (085681) 345*

---

1 flat, 1 bedsit, sleeps 1-4, from £50, Apr-Sep, ferry 12 mls, airport 10 mls

க் wc E ➡ 🏠 🖳 ⊙ 🗗 🛏 🖻 ✂ ⚓ ⊙ 🐎 P 🏊 🏛 †   ♪ ⚠ ⚓ ✗ 🎣 ☎

Mrs S Bichan, Swanbister, Orphir, Orkney, KW15 2RB
☎ *Orphir (085681) 261*

OUT SKERRIES Shetland Map Ref. 5H3

1 chalet/log cabin, 1 pub rm, 2 bedrms, sleeps 4-5, min let 2 nights, £42, Jan-Dec, ferry ¼ ml

க் wc E ➡ 🏠 🖳 ✂ 🗗 ☎ 🗗 ⚓ ⊙ 🐎 P 🏊 🏛 † 🏛 🔍 🌐   ⚓ 🎣 ☎

Mrs K Johnson, Rocklea, East Isle, Skerries, Shetland
☎ *Out Skerries (08065) 228*

PALNACKIE, by Castle Douglas Kirkcudbrightshire Map Ref. 2B10

3 chalet/log cabins, 1-2 pub rms, 2-3 bedrms, sleeps 4-8, min let 2 nights, £70-£180, Apr-Oct, bus ¼ ml, rail 17 mls

க் wc E ➡ 🏠 ✂ 🗗 🗗 🖻 ⚓ ⊙ 🐎 P 🏊 🏛 🏛 🔍   ⚓ ♪ ∪ ⚠ ⚓ ▸ ⚓ R ✗ ♉ ♫ T

8 caravans, sleeps 4-6, min let 2 nights, £58-£160, Apr-Oct, bus ¼ ml

க் wc E 🏠 ✂ 🗗 🗗 🖻 ✂ ⚓ ⊙ 🐎 P 🏊 🏛 🏛 🔍   ⚓ ♪ ∪ ⚠ ⚓ ▸ ⚓ ✗ T

(mini golf)
Barlochan Caravan Park, c/o Booking Office, Brighouse Bay, Borgue, Kirkcudbrightshire
☎ *Borgue (05577) 267*

PARKGATE Dumfriesshire Map Ref. 2C9

2 cottages, 1 pub rm, 1-2 bedrms, sleeps 4, min let 3 nights, £65-£130, Jan-Dec, bus nearby, rail 10 mls, airport 35 mls

♿ ᴡᴄ E ⊒ ⌂ ⬛ ⌷ ◎ ▢ ☎ ▢ 🔟 ⚡ ▬ ☉ ❄ 🐴 🅿 🔄 ▦ 🚼 ⛰ ✎ ♪ ∪ ⚓ ⚓↘
✐ 🐟 🔟 T

Mr & Mrs R M Graham, Kirkland, Courance, by Lockerbie, Dumfriesshire, DG11 1TU
☎ *Parkgate (038786) 645*

PARTON Kirkcudbrightshire Map Ref. 2A10

1 cottage, 2 pub rms, 3 bedrms, sleeps 6, min let weekend, from £80, May-Oct, bus nearby, rail 20 mls, airport 60 mls

♿ ᴡᴄ E ⌂ ⬛ ▦ ⌷ ◎ ▢ ▢ ⚡ ▬ ☉ 🐴 🅿 🔄 ▦ † ♪ ∪ ⚓ ⚓↘ ⚒ ✕ 🔟 🐟

15 caravans, sleeps 6, min let weekend (low season), from £105, end Mar-early Nov, bus nearby, rail 20 mls, airport 60 mls

♿ ᴡᴄ E ⌂ ⬛ ⌷ ⊘ ▢ ☎ ▢ 🔟 ⚡ ▬ ☉ ❄ 🐴 🅿 🔄 ▦ ⛰ ✿ ♪ ⚓ ⚓↘ ⚒ ✕ 🔟
🐟 D

Mrs Penny Bryson, Boreland, Parton, Castle Douglas, Kirkcudbrightshire, DG7 3NE
☎ *Parton (06447) 282*

---

2 cottages, 1 pub rm, 2 bedrms, sleeps 5-6, min let weekend, £70-£130, Jan-Dec, bus nearby, rail 25 mls

♿ ᴡᴄ E ⌂ ⬛ ▦ ⌷ ◎ ▢ ▢ ▬ ☉ ❄ 🐴 🅿 🔄 ▦ 🚼 ⛰ ♪ ∪ ⚓ ⚒ ✕ 🔟

Mr & Mrs A K Mccrone, Carnearie, Parton, Castle Douglas, Kirkcudbrightshire, DG7 3ND
☎ *Parton (06447) 221*

PEEBLES Map Ref. 2C6

Crossburn Caravan Park 6 caravans, sleeps 6, min let 2 nights, £84-£126, Apr-Oct, bus nearby, rail 23 mls, airport 30 mls

♿ ᴡᴄ E ⌂ ⬛ ⌷ ⊘ ▢ ☎ ▢ 🔟 ⚡ ▬ ☉ 🐴 🅿 ⛰ 🔍 ✿ 🦢 🍴 ♪ ∪↘ ✕ 🔟

Earnville Caravans, Crossburn Caravan Park, Edinburgh Road, Peebles, EH45 8ED
☎ *Peebles (0721) 20501*

---

1 cottage, 1 pub rm, 2 bedrms, sleeps 5, £70-£90, Apr-Oct, bus 400 yds

♿ ᴡᴄ E ⌂ ⬛ ▦ ⌷ ◎ ▢ ▢ ▬ ☉ ❄ 🐴 🅿 🔄 ▦ † ⛰ 🦢 ✎ ♪ ∪↘ ✕ 🔟 🐟
(hillwalking, nature trails)

Mrs J W Watson, Nether Kidson Farm, Peebles, EH45 8PJ
☎ *Peebles (0721) 20269*

---

1 house, 1 pub rm, 3 bedrms, sleeps 6, from £60, Jan-Dec

♿ ᴡᴄ E ⊒ ⌂ ⬛ ⌷ ◎ ▢ ▢ ▬ ☉ 🅿 🔄 ▦ † ♪ ∪↘ 🐟

Mrs Mary Dick, Hamildean, Peebles
☎ *Drochil Castle (0721) 52247*

Prices shown are for guidance only. Please send SAE with each enquiry.

KERFIELD COACH HOUSE
KERFIELD COTTAGE, INNERLEITHEN ROAD, PEEBLES
Unique secluded 250 year old Coach House situated on the Peebles town boundary opposite Glentress Forest and a couple of hundred yards from the River Tweed. High stone-walled garden and courtyard.
Fully furnished and equipped for a relaxing holiday.
40 minutes from Edinburgh.
For full details phone: Peebles (0721) 20264.

COMMENDED

1 coach house, 1 pub rm, 2 bedrms, sleeps 4, £80-£250, Jan-Dec, bus nearby, rail 23 mls, airport 24 mls

Mrs Holmes, Kerfield Cottage, Innerleithen Road, Peebles
☎ *Peebles (0721) 20264*
Modernised, stone built unit, standing in walled courtyard. On town outskirts, near River Tweed.

Rosetta 7 caravans, sleeps 6, min let 1 night (exc Jul/Aug), £85-£110, Apr-Oct, bus ½ ml, rail 30 mls, airport 35 mls

Rosetta Caravan Park, Rosetta Road, Peebles, EH45 8PG
☎ *Peebles (0721) 20770*

APPROVED

1 flat, 1 pub rm, 2 bedrms, sleeps 5, £80-£150, Apr-Nov, bus nearby

Mr P Rogerson, Kaimend, Damside, Innerleithen, Peeblesshire
☎ *Innerleithen (0896) 830248*
Situated in town centre. Good base for touring beautiful Border countryside.

1 cottage, 1 pub rm, 3 bedrms, sleeps 8, £60-£100, Apr-Oct, bus 1 ml, rail 23 mls, airport 25 mls

Mrs Ruby Smith, Chapel Hill Farm, Peebles, EH45 8PQ
☎ *Peebles (0721) 20188*

APPROVED

1 flat, 2 pub rms, 2 bedrms, sleeps 6, £90-£120, Jan-Dec, bus nearby

Mr Norman Kerr, Kingsmuir Hotel, Springhill Road, Peebles, EH45 9EP
☎ *Peebles (0721) 20151*
Self contained unit above shop. Lounge view overlooks hills to the south.

by PEEBLES Map Ref. 2C6

up to
COMMENDED

3 cottages, 1 pub rm, 2-3 bedrms, sleeps 6-8, £55-£145, Jan-Dec, bus 6 ½ mls, rail 29 mls, airport 30 mls

Mr John P Campbell, Glenrath Farm, Kirkton Manor, Peeblesshire
☎ *Kirkton Manor (07214) 221*
Situated on busy working farm approx. 9 miles/14 km from Peebles.

1 house, 1 pub rm, 3 bedrms, sleeps 6, min let 4 nights, £75-£130, Jan-Dec, bus ¼ ml, rail 27 mls, airport 27 mls

Mrs M A Richard, Kailzie, Garden House, by Peebles
☎ *Peebles (0721) 20007*

---

1 house, 3 flats, 1 cottage, 1 pub rm, 1-2 bedrms, sleeps 2-5, min let 3 nights, £55-£200, Jan-Dec, bus nearby

Mrs C S Eaton, Sunnybrae House, Walkerburn, Peeblesshire
☎ *Walkerburn (089687) 501*

PEINCHORRAN, Braes Isle of Skye, Inverness-shire Map Ref. 3D9

1 flat, 1 pub rm, 3 bedrms, sleeps 5, min let weekend (low season), £80-£110, Jan-Dec, bus nearby, rail 40 mls, ferry 40 mls, airport 35 mls

Mrs M Macdonald, 4 Peinchorran, Braes, by Portree, Isle of Skye, Inverness-shire
☎ *Sligachan (047852) 270*

PENINVER Argyll Map Ref. 1E7

up to COMMENDED

2 houses, 1-2 pub rms, 3-4 bedrms, sleeps 8, £126-£238, Jan-Dec, bus 8 mls, airport 12 mls

Campbeltown Creamery Ltd, Witchburn Road, Campbeltown, Argyll, PA28 6JU
☎ *Campbeltown (0586) 52244*
Large farmhouse, let seperately or as a whole. Fine views over Kilbrennan Sound. Enclosed garden.

Peninver Sands Caravan Park 12 caravans, sleeps 6, min let 1 night, from £50, Apr-Oct, bus 500 yds, rail 90 mls, airport 8 mls

E & E MacCallum, Craig View, Peninver, by Campbeltown, Argyll, PA28 6QP
☎ *Campbeltown (0586) 52262*

---

1 chalet/log cabin, 1 pub rm, 3 bedrms, sleeps 7, min let weekend (low season), £95-£190, Mar-Oct, bus 300 yds, airport 8 mls

Mrs Woodier, Tom Dhu, Peninver, by Campbeltown, Argyll
☎ *Campbeltown (0586) 53281*

PENNAN Aberdeenshire Map Ref. 4G7

1 cottage, 1 pub rm, 5 bedrms, sleeps 9, £75-£140, Jan-Dec

(private walks)

Mr G Ferguson, Upper Crichie, Stuartfield, Aberdeenshire, AB4 8DX
☎ *Stuartfield (0771) 24206/24369*

PENNYGHAEL Isle of Mull, Argyll Map Ref. 1C2

1 cottage, 2 pub rms, 3 bedrms, sleeps 5, £85, Apr-Sep, bus 10-20 mls, ferry 20 mls

Mrs Fiona Love, 2 Quarry Road, Oban, Argyll
☎ *Oban (0631) 63212 (after 6pm)*

2 cottages, 2 pub rms, 3 bedrms, sleeps 6, min let 3 nights, £60-£120, Jan-Dec, bus 3 mls, rail 40 mls, ferry 26 mls, airport 44 mls

Managed Estates, 18 Maxwell Place, Stirling, FK8 1JU
☎ *Stirling (0786) 62519*

1 cottage, 1 pub rm, 2 bedrms, sleeps 6, £95-£120, Apr-Oct, bus nearby, ferry 12 mls

Mr & Mrs Cheape, Middleton, Fossoway, Kinross
☎ *Fossoway (05774) 487*

PERTH Map Ref. 2C2

1 flat, 1 pub rm, 2 bedrms, sleeps 6, £80, Jan-Dec, bus ½ ml, rail ½ ml, airport 45 mls

Mr H D McLaren, 63 Princes Street, Perth, PH2 8LH
☎ *Perth (0738) 25410/23729*

9 caravans, sleeps 4, min let 2 nights, £55-£93, Apr-Sep, bus nearby, rail ½ ml

Windsor Caravan Park, Windsor Terrace, Perth, PH2 0BA
☎ *Perth (0738) 23721*

1 cottage, 1 pub rm, 2 bedrms, sleeps 4, £60-£80, Apr-Oct, bus 1 ½ mls, rail 5 mls, airport 45 mls

Mr & Mrs Niven, Gloagburn Farm, Tibbermore, Perth, PH1 1QL
☎ *Perth (0738) 84295/84228*

by PERTH Map Ref. 2C2

APPROVED

1 cottage, 1 pub rm, 2 bedrms, sleeps 4-6, £50-£90, Jan-Dec, bus 3 mls, rail 5 mls, airport 38 mls

Mrs E Stirrat, Fingask, Rhynd, by Perth, Perthshire, PH2 8QF
☎ *Bridge of Earn (0738) 812220*
Traditional, stone built; on working farm on elevated site overlooking River Tay and Earn and hills.

PINWHERRY, by Girvan Ayrshire Map Ref. 1G9

COMMENDED

1 cottage, 2 pub rms, 3 bedrms, sleeps 6, min let weekend, from £60, Jan-Dec, bus 1 ml, rail 10 mls, airport 30 mls

Mrs A Shankland, Talberg, Burnfoot Farm, Colmonell, Girvan, Ayrshire
☎ *Colmonell (046588) 265/220*
Traditional stone semi detached cottage in rural hamlet with beautiful views of river and hills.

1 flat, 2 pub rms, 3 bedrms, sleeps 6, £50-£200, Apr-Oct, bus nearby, rail 8 mls, ferry 28 mls, airport 30 mls

Mrs Cartney, Currarie Farm, Lendalfoot, Girvan, Ayrshire, KA26 0JB
☎ *Lendalfoot (046589) 213*

PIRNMILL Isle of Arran Map Ref. 1E6

2 flats, 1 cottage, 1 pub rm, 2 bedrms, sleeps 4-6, from £75, Jan-Oct, bus nearby, ferry 18 mls

Mr & Mrs J Anderson, Hillcrest Farm, Machrie, Brodick, Isle of Arran, KA27 8DZ
☎ *Machrie (077084) 240*
Situated in small village with views to Kintyre.

PITLOCHRY Perthshire Map Ref. 2B1

2 houses, 1 flat, 1 cottage, 1 bungalow, 1-2 pub rms, 1-4 bedrms, sleeps 4-7, £90-£190, Jan-Dec, Apr-Oct

Finlayson Hughes, Bank House, 82 Atholl Road, Pitlochry, Perthshire, PH16 5BL
☎ *Pitlochry (0796) 2512*

Dalshian 3 cottages, 1 pub rm, 1-3 bedrms, sleeps 4-6, min let weekend, £70-£150, Apr-Oct, bus nearby, rail 1 ½ mls

7 caravans, sleeps 6, min let weekend, £75-£150, Apr-Oct, bus nearby, rail 1 ½ mls

Mrs H Telford, Dalshian, Perth Road, Pitlochry, Perthshire, PH16 5JS
☎ *Pitlochry (0796) 2173*

---

1 cottage, 1 pub rm, 2 bedrms, sleeps 5, £80-£100, Apr-Oct, bus nearby, rail 1 ml

Mrs G Aird, Redbank, Achterneed, Strathpeffer, Ross-shire, IV14 9EA
☎ *Strathpeffer (0997) 21312*

---

1 flat, 2 pub rms, 3 bedrms, sleeps 4, min let 3 nights, £90-£135, Jan-Dec, bus nearby, rail nearby

(curling)

Mrs E M Egglishaw, 54 West Moulin Road, Pitlochry, Perthshire, PH16 5EQ
☎ *Pitlochry (0796) 2084*

---

1 cottage, 2 pub rms, 2 bedrms, sleeps 5, £85-£180, Mar-Oct, bus ½ ml, rail 1 ml, airport 40 mls

Mrs Howman, Auchnahyle, Pitlochry, Perthshire, PH16 5JA
☎ *Pitlochry (0796) 2318*

1 cottage, 1 pub rm, 1 bedrm, sleeps 3, min let 3 nights, £75-£120, Jan-Dec, bus nearby, rail 1 ml

  (curling)

Mrs E Egglishaw, 54 West Moulin Road, Pitlochry, Perthshire, PH16 5EQ
☎ *Pitlochry (0796) 2084*

Teallach Estate 1 house, 3 pub rms, 3 bedrms, sleeps 6, £100-£325, Jan-Dec, bus ½ ml, rail ½ ml, airport 65 mls

  (curling)

Dr D G Teal, Teallach Estate, Fonab, Pitlochry, Perthshire, PH16 5ND
☎ *Pitlochry (0796) 2345*

---

1 flat, 1 pub rm, 1 bedrm, sleeps 4, £100-£210, Jan-Dec, bus 500 yds, rail 700 yds

Mrs K Dickie, The Moorings, Lower Oakfield, Pitlochry, Perthshire
☎ *Pitlochry (0796) 3014*
Open plan garden flat of individual character with own sun patio and garden. Residential area.

---

1 house, 3 pub rms, 3 bedrms, sleeps 6, min let weekend, £85-£195, Apr-Oct, bus nearby, rail nearby

Mrs R T A Ross, Firtrees, 9 Lower Oakfield, Pitlochry, Perthshire, PH16 5DS
☎ *Pitlochry (0796) 2418*

---

1 cottage, 2 pub rms, 3 bedrms, sleeps 6, from £88, Jan-Dec, rail 6 mls

Forestry Commission, Forest Holidays, Dept SC1, 231 Corstorphine Road, Edinburgh, EH12 7AT
☎ *031 334 0303*

---

by PITLOCHRY Perthshire Map Ref. 2B1

6 caravans, sleeps 4-6, £45-£125, Apr-Sep, bus 2 mls, rail 2 mls

A R Lees (Caravans), 1 Argyle Street, Dundee, Angus, DD4 7AP
☎ *Dundee (0382) 41300*

Faskally Home Farm 40 caravans, sleeps 2-6, min let weekend, £65-£180, Mar-Oct, bus nearby, rail 2 mls

E M R Hay, Faskally Caravan Park, Pitlochry, Perthshire, PH16 5LA
☎ *Pitlochry (0796) 2007/3202*

Faskally Caravan Park 1 caravan, sleeps 6, min let 1 night, £75-£120, Apr-Oct, bus 500 yds, rail 2 mls

Mrs McLaren, Limervay, East Moulin Road, Pitlochry, Perthshire, PH16 5ER
☎ *Pitlochry (0796) 2759*

VAT is shown at 15%: changes in this rate may affect prices.

2 cottages, 1 pub rm, 2-3 bedrms, sleeps 5-6, £95-£165, bus 4 mls, rail 10 mls, airport 85 mls

♿ 🚾 E ⬤ ▢ ▢ ▢ ◎ ▢ ▢ ▢ ▢ ⊙ ⌁ �P ⌬ ▦ ♪ △ T

Mrs Gifford, Foss Home Farm, by Pitlochry, Perthshire, PH16 5NQ
☎ *031 336 7789/(08824) 243(eve)*

PITTENWEEM Fife Map Ref. 2E3

AWAITING INSPECTION

Grangemuir Woodland Park Ltd 15 chalet/log cabins, 1 pub rm, 3 bedrms, sleeps 6, min let weekend, £75-£275, Mar-Nov, bus 1 ml, rail 16 mls, airport 22 mls

♿ 🚾 E ⬤ ▢ ▢ ◎ ▢ ▢ ✆ ▢ ▢ ◎ ⌁ ▢ ⊙ ✳ P ⌬ ▦ △ ● 🌐 ⬤ ♪ U △ ⋆ ▸ ✕ ☒ ♈ T

Grangemuir Woodland Park Ltd, Grangemuir, Pittenweem, Fife, KY10 2RB
☎ *Anstruther (0333) 311213*

AWAITING INSPECTION

1 house, 2 pub rms, 2 bedrms, sleeps 7-9, £80-£150, Jan-Dec, bus nearby

♿ 🚾 E ⬤ ▢ ▢ ▦ ◎ ▢ ▢ ▢ ⌁ ▢ ⊙ ✳ ⌖ P ⌬ ▦ † ⬤ ♪ U △ ⋆ ▸ ✕ ☒

Mrs J M Sneddon, Glenlusset, 21 Redwood Crescent, Bishopton, Renfrewshire
☎ *Bishopton (0505) 862398*

PLOCKTON Ross-shire Map Ref. 3F9

COMMENDED
🏆🏆🏆

1 cottage, 1 pub rm, 3 bedrms, sleeps 6, £105-£195, Jan-Dec, rail 1 ml

♿ 🚾 E ⬤ ▢ ▢ ▦ ◎ ▢ ▢ ▢ ⊙ ✳ ⌖ P ⌬ ▦ † ♪ △ ⋆ ▸ ⟋ ✕ ☒

Petmathen Projects Ltd, c/o Mrs M A White, 10 Mannerston, Blackness, by Linlithgow, West Lothian
☎ *Philpstoun (050683) 4891*
Modernised, stone built terraced unit. Near village centre, overlooking small bay and Loch Carron.

---

by PLOCKTON Ross-shire Map Ref. 3F9

1 cottage, 1 pub rm, 3 bedrms, sleeps 7, min let weekend, £100-£175, Jan-Dec, bus 6 mls, rail 2 mls

♿ 🚾 E ⬤ ▢ ▦ ◎ ▢ ✆ ▢ ⊙ ✳ P † ♪ U △ ⋆ ▸ ⟋ ✕ ☒

Mrs Hunter, 8 Buckingham Terrace, Edinburgh, EH4 3AA
☎ *031 332 9028(eve)*

POOLEWE Ross-shire Map Ref. 3F7

10 caravans, sleeps 4-8, min let 1 night, £60-£85, Apr-Oct, bus nearby, rail 36 mls

♿ 🚾 E ▢ ▢ ▢ ⌀ ▢ ▢ ⌖ P ⌬ ▦ † ✕ ☒

Mrs J Craigie, Daisybank, Poolewe, Ross-shire, IV22 2LA
☎ *Poolewe (044586) 336*

---

1 bungalow, 1 pub rm, 3 bedrms, sleeps 6, £70-£85, May-Oct, bus nearby, rail 36 mls, airport 70 mls

♿ 🚾 E ⬤ ▢ ▦ ◎ ▢ ▢ ⊙ ✳ ⌖ P ⌬ † △ ♪ △ ⋆ ▸ ✕ ☒

J C MacLennan, Whin Cottage, Kinlochewe, by Achnasheen, Ross-shire, IV22 2PA
☎ *Kinlochewe (044584) 236*

---

4 cottages, 1 pub rm, 2-3 bedrms, sleeps 4-6, £40-£115, Apr-Oct, bus $\frac{1}{4}$ ml, rail 40 mls, airport 85 mls

♿ 🚾 E ⬤ ▢ ◎ ▢ ⊙ ⌖ P ⌬ ▦ ♪ △ ⋆ ✕ ☒ 🔺

Miss V C Whitton, 5 Drummond Street, Inverness, IV1 1QF
☎ *Inverness (0463) 233001*

| APPROVED | 1 house, 2 pub rms, 5 bedrms, sleeps 10, from £55, Jan-Dec, bus nearby, rail 25 mls, airport 84 mls |

   Mr A Urquhart, Torwood, 15 Croft, Poolewe, Ross-shire, IV22 2JY
   ☎ *Poolewe (044586) 268*
   Original stone built crofter's cottage. Fine views over River Ewe and Loch Maree.

3 caravans, sleeps 4-6, min let 1 night, £60-£65, Apr-Oct

   Mrs M Newton, Andmar, 1 Londubh, Poolewe, by Achnasheen, Ross-shire
   ☎ *Poolewe (044586) 413*

| AWAITING INSPECTION | 1 bungalow, 1 pub rm, 3 bedrms, sleeps 5, £60-£180, Jan-Dec, bus 400 yds, rail 35 mls, airport 90 mls |

(cycle hire)

   J Cawthra, Gate Lodge, Inverewe, Poolewe, Ross-shire, IV22 2LG
   ☎ *Poolewe (044586) 229*

PORT APPIN Argyll Map Ref. 1E1

2 cottages, 1-2 pub rms, 3-4 bedrms, sleeps 6-8, min let weekend, £75-£160, Mar-Jan, bus 2 mls, rail 25 mls

   Mrs Pery, Ardtur Cottage, Port Appin, Argyll
   ☎ *Appin (063173) 223*

PORT CHARLOTTE Isle of Islay, Argyll Map Ref. 1B6

3 caravans, sleeps 6-7, from £50, Apr-Oct, bus nearby, ferry 18-23 mls, airport 20 mls

   Mrs D Clark, Craigfad, Port Charlotte, Isle of Islay, Argyll, PA4 7UE
   ☎ *Port Charlotte (049685) 244*

2 flats, 1 cottage, 1-2 pub rms, 1-3 bedrms, sleeps 2-8, min let 2-3 nights (low season), £55-£125, Jan-Dec, bus nearby, ferry 15-21 mls, airport 16 mls

   Lady Wilson, Cala na Ruadh, Port Charlotte, Isle of Islay, Argyll
   ☎ *Port Charlotte (049685) 289*

| up to HIGHLY COMMENDED | 5 cottages, 1 pub rm, 1-2 bedrms, sleeps 2-6, min let 2 nights, £60-£185, Jan-Dec, bus nearby, ferry 20 mls, airport 18 mls |

   Mrs S Roy, Lorgba House, Port Charlotte, Isle of Islay, Argyll, PA48 7UD
   ☎ *Port Charlotte (049685) 208*
   Individual in character, in picturesque setting. Direct access to shore. Super views across loch.

1 house, 2 pub rms, 4 bedrms, sleeps 7, £65-£120, Apr-Oct, ferry 16 mls, airport 12 mls

   Mrs S Daniel, 72 Victoria Park, Cambridge, CB4 3EL
   ☎ *Cambridge (0223) 359362*

VAT is shown at 15%: changes in this rate may affect prices.

COMMENDED
♛ ♛ ♛

1 cottage, 2 pub rms, 2 bedrms, sleeps 2-4, min let 4 nights, £65-£130, Jan-Dec, bus nearby, ferry 15 mls, airport 15 mls

🔣🔣🔣🔣🔣🔣🔣🔣🔣🔣🔣🔣🔣🔣🔣🔣🔣🔣🔣🔣🔣🔣🔣 🔣🔣🔣🔣🔣🔣 T

Mrs G Roy, Sgioba House, Port Charlotte, Isle of Islay, Argyll
☎ *Port Charlotte (049685) 334*
Purpose built, split level studio with french window to secluded garden. Easy access to sandy beach.

PORT ELLEN Isle of Islay, Argyll Map Ref. 1C6

up to
COMMENDED
♛ ♛ ♛

3 flats, 1 pub rm, 1-3 bedrms, sleeps 2-8, £40-£160, Jan-Dec, bus nearby, ferry nearby, airport 4 mls

🔣🔣🔣🔣🔣🔣🔣🔣🔣🔣🔣🔣🔣🔣🔣🔣🔣🔣🔣🔣🔣🔣🔣🔣🔣🔣🔣🔣🔣
🔣🔣 T (free cycling)

Mr McNab, Harbour Flats, Port Ellen, Isle of Islay, Argyll, PA42 7DJ
☎ *Port Ellen (0496) 2331/(055665) 435*
Situated in village by the pier with pleasant views overlooking the bay.

---

2 cottages, 1 pub rm, 1-2 bedrms, sleeps 2-6, £50-£160, Jan-Dec, bus nearby, ferry ½ ml, airport 5 mls

🔣🔣🔣🔣🔣🔣🔣🔣🔣🔣🔣🔣🔣🔣🔣🔣🔣🔣🔣🔣🔣🔣🔣🔣🔣🔣🔣🔣🔣🔣🔣

Mrs Kent, Port Ellen Pottery, Tighcargaman, Port Ellen, Isle of Islay, Argyll, PA42 7BX
☎ *Port Ellen (0496) 2345*

PORT HENDERSON Ross-shire Map Ref. 3E7

1 house, 2 pub rms, 5 bedrms, sleeps 9, from £120, Apr-Oct

🔣🔣🔣🔣🔣🔣🔣🔣🔣🔣🔣🔣🔣🔣🔣🔣🔣🔣🔣🔣🔣🔣🔣

Mrs B MacKenzie, Minchview, Port Henderson, Gairloch, Ross-shire
☎ *Badachro (044583) 278*

PORT SETON East Lothian Map Ref. 2D5

Seton Sands Caravan Park 23 caravans, sleeps 2-8, min let 2 nights, £57-£230, Apr-Oct, bus nearby, rail 2 mls, airport 15 mls

T D

Bourne Leisure Group Ltd, 51-55 Bridge Street, Hemel Hempstead, Herts, HP1 1EQ
☎ *Hemel Hempstead (0442) 48661*

Seton Sands Holiday Site 1 caravan, sleeps 6, min let long weekend, from £55, Apr-Oct, bus nearby

🔣🔣🔣🔣🔣🔣🔣🔣🔣🔣🔣🔣🔣🔣🔣🔣🔣🔣🔣🔣🔣🔣🔣🔣🔣🔣🔣🔣🔣🔣
🔣 T

Mrs N Mcleod, 27 Waverley Park, Mayfield, Dalkeith, Midlothian
☎ *031 663 1439/Port Seton (0875) 811834*

Seton Sands Caravan Park 1 caravan, sleeps 6, min let weekend, £50-£70, Apr-Oct, bus 10 mls, rail nearby

🔣🔣🔣🔣🔣🔣🔣🔣🔣🔣🔣🔣🔣🔣🔣🔣🔣🔣🔣🔣🔣

Mrs Shoniwa, 112 Pilton Avenue, Edinburgh, EH5 2HD
☎ *031 336 4446(work)/552 2155(home)*

PORT WEMYSS Isle of Islay, Argyll Map Ref. 1B6

1 house, 1 cottage, 1-2 pub rms, 2-3 bedrms, sleeps 4-6, min let weekend, £80-£150, Jan-Dec, bus nearby, ferry 25 mls, airport 25 mls

Dr A G Mackinnon, Askernish, Port Ellen, Isle of Islay, Argyll
☎ *Port Ellen (0496) 2103/(049686) 282*

PORT WILLIAM Wigtownshire Map Ref. 1H11

1 house, 1 cottage, 1-2 pub rms, 3-4 bedrms, sleeps 5-8, min let 2 weeks, £90-£175, Jan-Dec, bus 3 mls, rail 25 mls, airport 90 mls

(bowling)

J H G Korner, House of Elrig, Port William, Wigtownshire, DG8 9RF
☎ *Port William (09887) 242*

1 house, 3 pub rms, 5 bedrms, sleeps 9-10, min let weekend, £80-£140, May-Oct, bus nearby, rail 20 mls, airport 45 mls

Robinson-Wyllie Ltd, Culbae, Whauphill, Wigtownshire
☎ *Kirkinner (098884) 249*

Auchness Caravan Park 4 caravans, sleeps 8, min let weekend, £50-£90, Apr-Oct, bus 4 mls, rail 25 mls, airport 80 mls

Mrs Elsie Walker, Barwinnock Farm, Whauphill, Wigtownshire, DG8 9PX
☎ *Port William (09887) 291*

2 cottages, 2 pub rms, 3 bedrms, sleeps 6, £95-£160, Jan-Dec, bus nearby, rail 23 mls

Mrs F E Shaw, Blew House Farm, Finghall, Leyburn, North Yorkshire, DL8 5ND
☎ *Bedale (0677) 50374*

APPROVED

1 house, 3 flats, 1-2 pub rms, 1-3 bedrms, sleeps 2-6, min let weekend, £65-£150, Jan-Dec, bus 1 ml, rail 23 mls, airport 110 mls

Michael Barne & Partners, 14 Alloway Place, Ayr, KA7 2AA
☎ *Ayr (0292) 268181/2*
Fine mansion built by ancestors of present owner. Views over grounds to Galloway Hills and Irish Sea.

1 cottage, 1 pub rm, 3 bedrms, sleeps 5, £40-£90, Jan-Dec, bus 1 ml, rail 25 mls, airport 100 mls

Mr G Walker, Horsham House, Horsham Road, Cranleigh, Surrey, GU6 8DZ
☎ *Cranleigh (0483) 276149*

1 cottage, 2 pub rms, 2 bedrms, sleeps 6, £60-£130, Jan-Dec, bus nearby

Ms Carol & Kate Semple, 34A Main Road, Castlehead, Paisley, Renfrewshire
☎ *041 887 3193*

PORT OF MENTEITH Perthshire Map Ref. 2A3

up to
COMMENDED
♛♛♛♛

Lochend Chalets 14 chalet/log cabins, 1 cottage, 1 pub rm, 2-3 bedrms, sleeps 6-7, min let weekend, £80-£290, Jan-Dec, bus 2 mls, rail 16 mls

Mr & Mrs Nairn, Lochend Chalets, Lochend House, Port of Menteith, Stirling, FK8 3JZ
☎ Port-of-Menteith (08775) 268
Units set in landscaped grounds on shore of Lake of Menteith. Boating, fishing, hill walking locally.

APPROVED
♛♛

1 cottage, 1 pub rm, 2 bedrms, sleeps 6, min let weekend, £90-£135, Apr-Nov, bus nearby, rail 13 mls, airport 30 mls

Mr C W Newman, Ruskie House, Port of Menteith, Stirling, FK8 3LD
☎ Port-of-Menteith (08775) 228
Former coachhouse, convenient for Central Scotland and local recreation. Outdoor swimming pool.

Parks of Garden 2 caravans, sleeps 4-6, £65-£95, May-Sep, bus 1 ½ mls, rail 13 mls, airport 26 mls

Mrs E A Dalgleish, Parks of Garden, Port of Menteith, Stirling, FK8 3JX
☎ Kippen (078687) 315

---

1 caravan, sleeps 6, min let 1 night, £75-£90, Apr-Oct, bus nearby, rail 12 mls

Mrs Janet Moore, The Cottage, Castle Rednock, Port of Menteith, Perthsire, FK8 3LD
☎ Port of Menteith (08775) 665

PORTKNOCKIE Banffshire Map Ref. 4E7

COMMENDED
♛♛♛

5 cottages, 1 pub rm, 2-4 bedrms, sleeps 5-8, min let weekend (low season), £75-£175, Jan-Dec, bus nearby, rail 15 mls, airport 50 mls

Mr A Scott, Faraldon, 8 Markethill Road, Turriff, Aberdeenshire, AB5 7AZ
☎ Turriff (0888) 63524
Modernised cottages in Moray Coast villages, close to golf courses, fishing, beaches, Whisky Trail.

---

2 cottages, 1 pub rm, 2 bedrms, sleeps 4-6, min let weekend (low season), £64-£145, Apr-Oct, bus nearby, rail 13 mls, airport 60 mls

W McD Simpson (Dept STB), Blantyre Holiday Homes Ltd, West Bauds, Findochty, Buckie, Banffshire, AB5 2EB
☎ Buckie (0542) 31773

---

1 cottage, 2 pub rms, 4 bedrms, sleeps 7, £80-£140, Jan-Dec, bus nearby, rail 14 mls

(bowls)

Mr M McNeish, 9 Mayfield Drive, Heron Hill, Kendal, Cumbria, LA9 7NS
☎ Kendal (0539) 27362 (after 6pm)

1 cottage, 1 pub rm, 1 bedrm, sleeps 2-3, £40-£70, Jun-Sep, bus 400 yds, rail 14 mls, airport 50 mls

Mrs M Cowie, 31 Church Street, Portknockie, Buckie, Banffshire, AB5 2LN
☎ *Cullen (0542) 40356*

PORTNALONG Isle of Skye, Inverness-shire Map Ref. 3D9

1 cottage, 1 pub rm, 2 bedrms, sleeps 4-6, from £60, Mar-Oct

Mrs Mary Ann Nicolson, Donann, 7 Fernilea, Portnalong, Isle of Skye, Inverness-shire
☎ *Portnalong (047872) 275*

1 cottage, 1 pub rm, 2 bedrms, sleeps 5-6, min let weekend, from £50, Jan-Dec, bus ½ ml

Mrs C Macsween, 25 Portnalong, Carbost, Isle of Skye, Inverness-shire, IV47 8SL
☎ *Portnalong (047872) 263*

1 cottage, 1 pub rm, 2 bedrms, sleeps 5, £70-£90, Apr-Oct, bus nearby

Miss Macleod, 4 Ullinish, Struan, Isle of Skye, Inverness-shire
☎ *Struan (047072) 202*

1 bungalow, 1 pub rm, 3 bedrms, sleeps 6-8, £90-£110, Jan-Dec, bus nearby, ferry 34 mls, airport 24 mls

Mrs Robertson, 5 Distillery Cottages, Carbost, Isle of Skye, Inverness-shire
☎ *Carbost (047842) 262*

1 cottage, 1 pub rm, 2 bedrms, sleeps 5, £65-£70, Apr-Oct, bus nearby

Kenneth Macleod, 2 Fernilea, Portnalong, by Carbost, Isle of Skye, Inverness-shire

PORTPATRICK Wigtownshire Map Ref. 1F11

5 caravans, sleeps 6, min let weekend, £60-£130, Apr-Oct, bus ¼ ml, rail 8 mls

Mr C E De Looze, Sunnymeade Caravan Park, Portpatrick, by Stranraer, Wigtownshire, DG9 8LN
☎ *Portpatrick (077681) 293*

1 flat, 3 cottages, 1-2 pub rms, 1-3 bedrms, sleeps 2-6, £90-£160, Apr-Oct, bus 1 ml, rail 8 mls, airport 60 mls

E S Orr Ewing, Dunskey, Portpatrick, Stranraer, Wigtownshire, DG9 8TJ
☎ *Portpatrick (077681) 211*

3 caravans, sleeps 6-8, min let weekend, £75-£140, Apr-Sep, bus ¼ ml, rail 8 mls, airport 60 mls

(bowling)
Galloway Point Holiday Park, Portree House, Portpatrick, Wigtownshire, DG9 9AA
☎ *Portpatrick (077681) 561*

VAT is shown at 15%: changes in this rate may affect prices.

1 bungalow, 2 pub rms, 2 bedrms, sleeps 5, £50-£100, Jan-Dec, bus 4 mls, rail 6 mls, airport 55 mls

Mrs Archibald, Glaick, Leswalt, Wigtownshire
☎ *Leswalt (077687) 286*

Castle Bay Caravan Park 10 caravans, sleeps 4-6, min let weekend, £75-£130, Mar-Oct, bus ¾ ml, rail 8 mls, airport 60 mls

Castle Bay Caravan Park, Portpatrick, Wigtownshire
☎ *Portpatrick (077681) 462*

---

8 cottages, 1-3 pub rms, 2-4 bedrms, sleeps 4-8, £100-£160, Jan-Dec, bus nearby

Portpatrick Self Catering Cottage Agency, 39 Main Street, Portpatrick, Wigtownshire
☎ *Portpatrick (077681) 212*

---

1 caravan, sleeps 6, min let weekend, £65-£85, Jan-Dec

Mrs Howett, Knockinaam Wood Cottage, Portpatrick, Wigtownshire
☎ *Portpatrick (077682) 330*

PORTREE Isle of Skye, Inverness-shire Map Ref. 3D9

1 bungalow, 1 pub rm, 2 bedrms, sleeps 4, £100-£115, May-Oct, bus 1 ml, rail 36 mls, ferry 36 mls, airport 25 mls

J A Burgess, East House, 2 Fort Haven, Shoreham-by-Sea, Sussex, BN4 5HY
☎ *Shoreham (07917) 3632*

COMMENDED
👑👑👑

Beechwood Holiday Homes 5 bungalows, 1 pub rm, 2 bedrms, sleeps 7, £86-£207, Jan-Dec, bus 1 ml, rail 35 mls, ferry 35 mls, airport 30 mls

H Murray Ltd, Dunvegan Road, Portree, Isle of Skye, Inverness-shire
☎ *Portree (0478) 2634*
Modern units in 6 acre wooded site close to centre of village. Near swimming pool and amenities. **(See colour ad. 15 p. xxxv)**

---

1 chalet/log cabin, 1 pub rm, 3 bedrms, sleeps 7, £70-£140, Apr-Oct, bus 1½ mls

Mr John Mackenzie, 2 Heatherfield, Portree, Isle of Skye, Inverness-shire
☎ *Portree (0478) 2820*

---

up to
HIGHLY COMMENDED
👑👑👑👑

4 cottages, 1 pub rm, 1-2 bedrms, sleeps 2-5, £60-£190, Jan-Dec, bus ¼ ml, rail 34 mls, ferry 34 mls, airport 27 mls

Mrs Mena Wilson, Portree House, Portree, Isle of Skye, Inverness-shire
☎ *Portree (0478) 2796*
Modern units, in grounds of georgian mansion; bar/restaurant. Play area for children, swimming pool.

Prices shown are for guidance only. Please send SAE with each enquiry.

1 house, 1-2 pub rms, 4 bedrms, sleeps 8, £85-£300, Apr-Oct, rail $\frac{1}{2}$ ml, airport $\frac{1}{2}$ ml

MacKinnon Hathway, Estate and Land Agent, Main Street, Kyle of Lochalsh, Ross-shire, IV40 8AB
☎ Kyle (0599) 4567

---

1 house, 2 pub rms, 6 bedrms, sleeps 9, from £140, Jan-Dec, bus $\frac{3}{4}$ ml, rail 33 mls, ferry 33 mls, airport 25 mls

Mrs Leslie, Baile na Coille, Balmoral, Aberdeenshire, AB3 5TB
☎ Crathie (03384) 278

---

1 bungalow, 1 pub rm, 2 bedrms, sleeps 2-6, min let 3 nights, £75-£120, Jan-Dec, bus 1 ml

Mrs Thorpe, 5 Achachork, Portree, Isle of Skye, Inverness-shire
☎ Portree (0478) 2274

---

6 houses, 1 pub rm, 3 bedrms, sleeps 6, £100-£170, Jan-Dec

Rosebank Holiday Homes, Portree, Isle of Skye, Inverness-shire
☎ Portree (0478) 2788

AWAITING INSPECTION

1 cottage, 1 wing of house, 1 annexe, 1-2 pub rms, 1-2 bedrms, sleeps 4-6, £90-£170, Jan-Dec, bus nearby

Mrs Simmister, Kiltarglen, Portree, Isle of Skye, Inverness-shire
☎ Portree (0478) 2435

---

1 cottage, 1 pub rm, 2 bedrms, sleeps 4, £80-£110, Jan-Dec, bus 1 ml, rail 35 mls, ferry 34 mls, airport 30 mls

Mrs M Macdonald, 1 Woodpark, Dunvegan Road, Portree, Isle of Skye, Inverness-shire
☎ Portree (0478) 2358

---

by PORTREE Isle of Skye, Inverness-shire Map Ref. 3D9

1 house, 1 pub rm, 4 bedrms, sleeps 9, £90-£140, Jan-Dec, bus 2 $\frac{1}{2}$ mls

Mrs M MacPherson, 1 Torvaig, Portree, Isle of Skye, Inverness-shire
☎ Portree (0478) 2664

PORTSONACHAN Argyll Map Ref. 1F3

3 chalet/log cabins, 1 house, 6 flats, 3-5 pub rms, 2-4 bedrms, sleeps 4-8, £60-£225, Apr-Oct, bus 10 mls, rail 11 mls

4 caravans, sleeps 6, £45-£145, Apr-Oct, bus 10 mls, rail 10 mls

Mr & Mrs A Rose, Sonachan House, Portsonachan, by Dalmally, Argyll, PA33 1BN
☎ Kilchrenan (08663) 240(office)/243

VAT is shown at 15%: changes in this rate may affect prices.

PORTSOY Banffshire Map Ref. 4F7

1 cottage, 1 pub rm, 2 bedrms, sleeps 4, £55-£70, May-Sep, bus ½ ml, rail 17 mls

Mrs M Shearer, 27 North High Street, Portsoy, Banffshire, AB4 2PA
☎ *Portsoy (0261) 43039*

---

2 houses, 1-2 pub rms, 1-3 bedrms, sleeps 2-6, £85-£195, Apr-Oct, bus 300 yds, rail 17 mls, airport 55 mls

Mr T Burnett-Stuart, The Marble Workshop, Portsoy, Banffshire
☎ *Portsoy(0261)42404(day)/(046683)349(eve)*

---

1 cottage, 2 pub rms, 3 bedrms, sleeps 6, £115-£220, Jan-Dec, bus 250 yds

Scottish Country Cottages, Suite 2d, Churchill Way, Bishopbriggs, Glasgow, G64 2RH
☎ *041 772 5920*

---

1 chalet/log cabin, 1 pub rm, 3 bedrms, sleeps 6, £70-£150, May-Oct, bus 1 ½ mls

Mrs M Murray, Stonehousehill, Hatton, Peterhead, Aberdeenshire
☎ *Hatton (077984) 257*

---

1 house, 2 pub rms, 3 bedrms, sleeps 6, £120, Jun-Oct, bus ¼ ml, rail 15 mls, airport 50 mls

Mr Peter J Cook, 20 Caledonian Place, Aberdeen, AB1 2TT
☎ *Aberdeen (0224) 584751*

---

1 flat, 1 pub rm, 2 bedrms, sleeps 5, min let weekend (low season), £75-£155, Jan-Dec, bus 300 yds, rail 20 mls, airport 50 mls

Mr Scott, 8 Markethill Road, Turriff, Aberdeenshire
☎ *Turriff (0888) 63524*

Portsoy Links Site 1 caravan, sleeps 6-8, min let weekend, £75-£115, Apr-Sep, bus ½ ml, rail 15 mls, airport 52 mls

Mrs Geddes, Burnside, Lintmill, Cullen, Banffshire
☎ *Cullen (0542) 41141*

---

by PORTSOY Banffshire Map Ref. 4F7

1 cottage, 1 pub rm, 2 bedrms, sleeps 4, from £80, Jan-Dec, bus nearby, rail 11 mls, airport 60 mls

J Palphramand, Bogroy, Cornhill, Banff, Banffshire
☎ *Cornhill (04666) 381*

PRESTWICK Ayrshire Map Ref. 1G7

1 chalet/log cabin, 1 pub rm, 2 bedrms, sleeps 5, £40-£100, Jan-Dec, bus 300 yds, rail ¼ ml

Mrs F McClure, The Fairway, 19 Links Road, Prestwick, Ayrshire
☎ *Prestwick (0292) 70396*

PUTECHANTUY, by Campbeltown Argyll Map Ref. 1D7

6 cottages, 1-2 pub rms, 1-2 bedrms, sleeps 2-7, min let weekend, £65-£190, Mar-Jan, bus nearby, ferry 8 mls, airport 8 mls

Putechan Lodge Hotel, Putechantuy, Kintyre, Argyll, PA28 6QE
☎ *Glenbarr (05832) 266*

RAASAY, Isle of Inverness-shire Map Ref. 3E9

2 houses, 1 pub rm, 2 bedrms, sleeps 5-6, min let 3 nights, £42-£50, Jan-Dec, ferry 1 ½ mls

Mrs Jean B Bancroft, 42 Dales Lane, Whitefield, Manchester, M25 9WW
☎ *061 766 2663*

1 chalet/log cabin, 1 house, 1 pub rm, 2-3 bedrms, sleeps 5-8, £70-£180, Apr-Oct, ferry 1 ml

Mrs J R S Macrae, Suisnish House, Isle of Raasay, by Kyle, Inverness-shire
☎ *Raasay (047862) 251*

RAHOY, Morvern Argyll Map Ref. 1D2

1 house, 5 cottages, 1-4 pub rms, 2-5 bedrms, sleeps 4-10, £70-£500, Jan-Dec, bus 4 mls, rail 44 mls

(birdwatching)

Mr M Hornsby, Rahoy Cottage, Rahoy Estate, Morvern, Argyll
☎ *Morvern (096784) 287*

by RANKINSTON Ayrshire Map Ref. 1H8

1 cottage, 2 pub rms, 2 bedrms, sleeps 4-6, £80-£120, Jan-Dec, bus nearby

Mrs Alison M R Martin, Bonnyton House, by Ayr, KA6 7EW
☎ *Drongan (0292) 590209*

by RANNOCH STATION Perthshire Map Ref. 1G1

1 part house, 2 pub rms, 2 bedrms, sleeps 5, min let weekend (low season), £65-£110, Mar-Nov, bus 5 mls, rail 12 mls

5 caravans, sleeps 3-6, min let weekend (low season), £45-£90, Apr-Oct, bus 5 mls, rail 12 mls

Mr & Mrs A Barr, Learan Farm, Killiechonan, Rannoch Station, Perthshire, PH17 2QW
☎ *Bridge of Gaur (08823) 264*

VAT is shown at 15%: changes in this rate may affect prices.

RATHILLET Fife Map Ref. 2D2

1 house, 2 flats, 5 cottages, 1-2 pub rms, 2-5 bedrms, sleeps 4-10, min let weekend, £55-£250, Jan-Dec, bus 2 mls, rail 5 mls, airport 45 mls

Mrs A H B Wedderburn, Mountquhanie, Rathillet, by Cupar, Fife, KY15 4QJ
☎ *Gauldry (082624) 252*

REDGORTON Perthshire Map Ref. 2C2

1 cottage, 1 pub rm, 2 bedrms, sleeps 5, £65-£75, Apr-Oct, bus ¼ ml, rail 3 mls

Mrs Joy Niven, Innernyte Farm, Stanley, Perthshire, PH1 4QH
☎ *Stanley (073882) 8326*

RESTON, by Eyemouth Berwickshire Map Ref. 2F5

1 cottage, 1 pub rm, 3 bedrms, sleeps 6, £50-£100, Apr-Oct, bus 1 ml, rail 11 mls, airport 60 mls

Mrs M Morgan, Newlands, Sunnyside Farm, Reston, Berwickshire, TD14 5LN
☎ *Reston (08907) 61311*

---

1 house, 2 pub rms, 3 bedrms, sleeps 6, £50-£60, Apr-Oct, bus nearby, rail 8 mls

Mrs Brown, Jedlea, Preston, Duns, Berwickshire
☎ *Duns (0361) 82843*

RHICONICH Sutherland Map Ref. 3H3

1 house, 1 pub rm, 4 bedrms, sleeps 8, £100-£130, Jun-Oct, bus 1 ½ mls, rail 40 mls, airport 100 mls

Mr & Mrs D Forbes, Rhivichie, Rhiconich, by Lairg, Sutherland, IV27 4RA

RICCARTON Midlothian Map Ref. 2C5

36 flats, 1 pub rm, 3-5 bedrms, sleeps 3-6, £106-£200, Jul-Sep, bus nearby, rail 6 mls, airport 3 mls

The Controller, Heriot-Watt University, Riccarton, Midlothian, EH14 4AS
☎ *031 449 5111*

RINGFORD Kirkcudbrightshire Map Ref. 2A10

1 cottage, 1 pub rm, 2 bedrms, sleeps 6, £50-£110, Apr-Oct, bus nearby

Mrs E Smith, Culquha Farm, Ringford, Castle Douglas, Kirkcudbrightshire
☎ *Ringford (055722) 266*

Prices shown are for guidance only. Please send SAE with each enquiry.

ROCKCLIFFE Kirkcudbrightshire Map Ref. 2B11

1 house, 2 flats, 1 cottage, 1 wing of house, 1-3 pub rms, 2-5 bedrms, sleeps 2-10, min let weekend, £70-£280, Feb-Nov, bus nearby, rail 18 mls, airport 70 mls

(free fishing)

Mrs S Sinclair, Mount of Glenluffin, Rockcliffe, Dalbeattie, Kirkcudbrightshire, DG5 4QG
☎ *Rockcliffe (055663) 205*

Individual farm cottages on edge of village, about 500 yards from beach on the Colvend coast.

Castle Point Caravan Park 6 caravans, sleeps 4-6, min let weekend, £60-£150, Mar-Oct, bus 500 yds, rail 23 mls, airport 75 mls

(windsurfing & tuition)

Castle Point Caravan Park, Rockcliffe, by Dalbeattie, Kirkcudbrightshire, DG5 4QL
☎ *Rockcliffe (0556) 62636/63215*

ROCKCLIFFE AREA Kirkcudbrightshire Map Ref. 2B11

4 houses, 2 cottages, 1-2 pub rms, 1-4 bedrms, sleeps 2-9, from £60, Apr-Oct

G M Thomson & Company, 27 King Street, Castle Douglas, Kirkcudbrightshire, DG7 1AB
☎ *Castle Douglas (0556) 2701*

ROGART Sutherland Map Ref. 4B6

1 cottage, 1 pub rm, 3 bedrms, sleeps 6, £62-£105, Mar-Oct, rail 10 mls

Sutherland Estates Office, Duke Street, Golspie, Sutherland, KW10 6RR
☎ *Golspie (04083) 3268*

ROSEHALL Sutherland Map Ref. 4A6

1 cottage, 1 pub rm, 3 bedrms, sleeps 4-6, £50-£130, Apr-Oct, rail 8 mls, airport 65 mls

Mr D A Walker, Ord View Cottage, Lairg, Sutherland
☎ *Lairg (0549) 2291*

Glencassley Estate 2 cottages, 1 pub rm, 1-3 bedrms, sleeps 2-4, from £45, Apr-Oct, bus 5 mls, rail 12 mls

Bell-Ingram, Durn, Isla Road, Perth, PH2 7HF
☎ *Perth (0738) 21121*

ROSEMARKIE Ross-shire Map Ref. 4B8

3 cottages, 1 pub rm, 2 bedrms, sleeps 4-5, £50-£85, May-Oct, bus 1-2 mls, rail 15 mls, airport 20 mls

Mrs W McIver, Flowerburn Mains, Rosemarkie, Ross-shire, IV10 8SJ
☎ *Fortrose (0381) 20339*

Rosemarkie Beach 2 caravans, sleeps 4-6, £44-£49, Apr-Sep, bus 18 mls, rail 1 ml

Mrs J L Straw, Springwells Cottage, Eathie Road, Rosemarkie, Ross-shire, IV10 8UF
☎ *Fortrose (0381) 20767*

Flowerburn House Holiday Homes 4 chalet/log cabins, 1 cottage, 1 pub rm, 2 bedrms, sleeps 4-6, min let 2 nights, £80-£200, Jan-Dec, bus 2 mls, rail 15 mls, airport 20 mls

Mrs Fraser, Flowerburn House, Rosemarkie,Fortrose, Ross-shire
☎ *Fortrose (0381) 20266*

ROSNEATH, by Helensburgh Dunbartonshire Map Ref. 1G4

Rosneath Castle Caravan Park 8 caravans, sleeps 8, from £100, Apr-Oct, bus ½ ml, rail 7 ½ mls, airport 30 mls

Rosneath Castle Caravan Park, Rosneath, by Helensburgh, Dunbartonshire
☎ *Clynder (0436) 831208*

---

by ROTHES Moray Map Ref. 4D8

2 houses, 1-2 pub rms, 3-5 bedrms, sleeps 5-8, min let weekend, £70-£130, Apr-Oct, bus ¼ ml, rail 10 mls, airport 60 mls

Rothes Estate Office, Station Street, Rothes, Aberlour, Moray, IV33 7AZ
☎ *Rothes (03403) 267*

ROTHESAY Isle of Bute Map Ref. 1F5

Eskdale & Beechwood Holiday Flats 11 flats, 10 apartments, 1 pub rm, 1-3 bedrms, sleeps 2-8, min let 2 nights, £40-£180, Jan-Dec, bus 500 yds, ferry 500 yds

Mrs McIntosh, 7 & 11 Bishop Terrace, Rothesay, Isle of Bute, PA20 9HF
☎ *Rothesay (0700) 3999*

---

7 apartments, 1 pub rm, 1 bedrm, sleeps 2-8, min let weekend (low season), £45-£130, Apr-Oct, bus nearby, ferry 1 ml

Mrs K Fyfe, Innisfree, 45/46 Crichton Road, Craigmore, Rothesay, Isle of Bute
☎ *Rothesay (0700) 3762*

---

8 flats, 1 pub rm, 1-5 bedrms, sleeps 4-10, min let weekend, £90-£185, Apr-Oct, bus nearby, ferry 800 yds

Mr & Mrs R Caldwell, Ivy Court Apartments, Rothesay, Isle of Bute
☎ *Rothesay (0700) 2778*
Units on seafront overlooking bay, within 10 minutes walking distance of the pier.

---

1 cottage, 1 pub rm, 2 bedrms, sleeps 4, min let weekend, from £60, Jan-Dec, bus nearby, ferry 2 mls

Mrs J McKirdy, Wimbelton House, 26 Mountstuart Rd, Rothesay, Isle of Bute
☎ *Rothesay (0700) 4623*

Roseland Chalet Park 3 chalet/log cabins, 1 pub rm, 2 bedrms, sleeps 5, min let weekend, £50-£140, Apr-Oct, ferry 1 ml

3 caravans, sleeps 4, £40-£90, Apr-Oct, ferry 1 ml

Roseland Chalet Park, Canada Hill, Rothesay, Isle of Bute
☎ *Rothesay (0700) 4027*

Prices shown are for guidance only. Please send SAE with each enquiry.

COMMENDED
❀❀❀❀

4 flats, 1 cottage, 1 pub rm, 1-2 bedrms, sleeps 2-6, min let 2 nights, from £89, Jan-Dec, bus nearby, ferry 1 ml

(symbols) (nature trails)

Mrs G Shaw, Morningside, Mountpleasant Road, Rothesay, Isle of Bute, PA20 9HQ
☎ *Rothesay (0700) 3526*
On seafront within own garden area. Central heating, colour TV, bath and shower. Cottage with garden.

COMMENDED
❀❀❀

5 suites, sleeps 2-4, min let weekend, from £45, Jan-Dec, bus nearby, ferry 300 yds

(symbols) (scuba diving)

Guildford Court, Watergate, Rothesay, Isle of Bute
☎ *Rothesay (0700) 3770*
Compact units adjacent to harbour. Room service available.

AWAITING INSPECTION

6 flats, 1 pub rm, 2 bedrms, sleeps 3-6, min let weekend, £90-£185, Jan-Dec, bus nearby, ferry ½ ml

(symbols)

Bute Enterprises Ltd, 25 Bishop Street, Rothesay, Isle of Bute
☎ *Rothesay (0700) 4754*

---

by ROTHIEMAY Banffshire Map Ref. 4F8

1 chalet/log cabin, 1 pub rm, 2 bedrms, sleeps 4-6, min let weekend, £80-£150, Jan-Dec, bus nearby, rail 10 mls, airport 40 mls

(symbols)

Mr J C Logan, Eastertown of Mayen, Rothiemay, Huntly, Banffshire, AB5 5NL
☎ *Rothiemay (046681) 331*

ROUNDYHILL, by Glamis Angus Map Ref. 2D1

Drumshademuir Caravan Park 2 caravans, sleeps 6, £90, Apr-Oct, bus nearby

(symbols)

Drumshademuir Caravan Park, Roundyhill, by Glamis, Angus
☎ *Kirriemuir (0575) 73284*

ROUSAY Orkney Map Ref. 5B10

2 cottages, 1 pub rm, 1-2 bedrms, sleeps 2-5, min let weekend, £69-£115, Apr-Oct, ferry 6 mls

(symbols)

Alastair & Elizabeth Findlay, Fjalquoy, Rousay, Orkney
☎ *Rousay (085682) 381*

VAT is shown at 15%: changes in this rate may affect prices.

ROY BRIDGE Inverness-shire Map Ref. 3H12

Bunroy Holiday Chalets
ROY BRIDGE PH31 4AG   Tel: 039781 332

Small landscaped development overlooking River Spean. Simple, self-contained accommodation for 4. Each chalet fully equipped except linen. Toilet, W/H basin, shower, 3-plate stove with oven, fridge, 22" colour TV. River fishing, good swimming. Ideal for hillwalking, touring.
£75-£120 per week. *Will rent by night or weekend off-season. Free "Best of the Highlands" guide and map with each fortnightly booking.*
(SFM) W. McCallum, Bunroy Holiday Chalets, Roy Bridge, Inverness-shire PH31 4AG, tel 039781 332.

APPROVED
Listed

8 chalet/log cabins, 1 pub rm, 1 bedrm, sleeps 4, min let 1 night, £80-£115, Apr-Oct, bus 300 yds, rail 300 yds

1 caravan, sleeps 4, min let 1 night, £55-£75, Apr-Sep, bus 300 yds, rail 300 yds

W A McCallum, Bunroy Holiday Chalets, Roy Bridge, Inverness-shire, PH31 4AG
☎ *Spean Bridge (039781) 332*

Well maintained site near River Spean. Good views of Ben Nevis.

Kinchellie Caravan Park 6 caravans, sleeps 4-6, min let weekend, £50-£120, Apr-Oct, bus 400 yds, rail 300 yds

Kinchellie Croft Motel, Roy Bridge, Inverness-shire, PH31 4AW
☎ *Spean Bridge (039781) 265*

COMMENDED

Na Tighean Beaga 10 bungalows, 1 pub rm, 2 bedrms, sleeps 4-6, min let weekend (low season), £90-£200, Jan-Dec, bus 250 yds, rail nearby

(rod and boat hire)

C & E Matheson, East Park, Roy Bridge, Inverness-shire, PH31 4AG
☎ *Spean Bridge (039781) 370/436*

Small, family-run development spaciously set in 200 acres of silver birch and heather.

(See colour ad. 16 p. xxxvi)

---

1 bungalow, 1 pub rm, 3 bedrms, sleeps 6, min let weekend, £95-£120, Jan-Dec, bus nearby, rail ½ ml, airport 70 mls

Mrs Macdonald, Keppoch House, Roy Bridge, Inverness-shire
☎ *Spean Bridge (039781) 240*

RUSKIE, by Port of Menteith Perthshire Map Ref. 2A3

1 caravan, sleeps 2-4, min let 2 nights, £35-£40, Mar-Oct, bus nearby, rail 12 mls

Mrs J Bain, Lower Tarr Farm, Ruskie, by Port of Menteith, Stirling
☎ *Thornhill (078685) 202*

SALEN Argyll Map Ref. 1D1

2 chalet/log cabins, 1 flat, 1 pub rm, 1-2 bedrms, sleeps 2-6, £90-£170, Apr-Oct

D H & E M McEwan, Tigh Na Creagan, Salen, Argyll, PH36 4JN
☎ *Salen (096785) 270*

by SALEN Argyll Map Ref. 1D1

Resipole Caravan Park 3 caravans, sleeps 6, min let 3 nights, £100-£140, Mar-Nov, bus nearby, rail 30 mls

Mrs Sinclair, Resipole Farm, Salen, by Acharacle, Argyll, PH36 4HX
☎ Salen (096785) 235

SALEN, Aros Isle of Mull, Argyll Map Ref. 1D2

1 house, 2 pub rms, 3 bedrms, sleeps 8-9, £100-£175, Apr-Oct, bus nearby, ferry 9 mls, airport ½ ml

D J MacGillivray, Pennygown Farm, Aros, Isle of Mull, Argyll
☎ Aros (06803) 335

---

by SALEN, Aros Isle of Mull, Argyll Map Ref. 1D2

1 cottage, 2 pub rms, 3 bedrms, sleeps 9, £80-£130, Apr-Oct, bus nearby, ferry 8 mls

Mrs MacPhail, Callachally Farm, Glenforsa, Salen, Isle of Mull, Argyll
☎ Aros (06803) 424

COMMENDED 👑👑👑👑

1 cottage, 2 pub rms, 2 bedrms, sleeps 6, £70-£160, Jan-Dec, bus 1 ml, ferry 12 mls, airport 5 mls

Ms R F B Jones, Woodbourne, 76 Wokingham Road, Crowthorne, Berks
☎ Crowthorne (0344) 772174/(06803) 361
Whitewashed cottage in quiet countryside. About 1 ml (2 km) from nearest village.

SALLACHY, by Dornie Ross-shire Map Ref. 3F9

1 cottage, 1 pub rm, 3 bedrms, sleeps 6, from £70, Jan-Dec, bus 4-5 mls, rail 12 mls

Mrs J Tuach, Nonach, by Dornie, Kyle of Lochalsh, Ross-shire, IV40 8DZ
☎ Killilan (059988) 279

SALTCOATS Ayrshire Map Ref. 1G6

50 caravans, sleeps 4-6, £35-£175, Apr-Oct, bus ¼ ml, rail ¼ ml, airport 30 mls

Sandylands Leisure Estate Ltd, Auchenharvie Park, Saltcoats, Ayrshire, KA21 5JN
☎ Saltcoats (0294) 69411

SAND West Mainland, Shetland Map Ref. 5F4

2 chalet/log cabins, 1 pub rm, 2 bedrms, sleeps 4, £35-£45, Jan-Dec, bus 1 ml, ferry 25 mls, airport 50 mls

Mr Peter Hick, The Haa' Sand, Bixter, Shetland, ZE2 9NQ
☎ Reawick (059586) 284(eve)/261(day)

VAT is shown at 15%: changes in this rate may affect prices.

SANDEND, by Portsoy Banffshire Map Ref. 4F7

Sandend Caravan & Camping Park 3 caravans, sleeps 6, min let 1 night, £75-£135, Apr-Oct, bus ½ ml, rail 12 mls, airport 56 mls

    [symbols]

Sandend Caravan Park, The Old School House, Sandend, Portsoy, Banffshire
☎ *Portsoy (0261) 42660*

SANDHEAD Wigtownshire Map Ref. 1F11

2 cottages, 1 pub rm, 2 bedrms, sleeps 6, £75-£110, Jan-Dec, bus ¼ ml, rail 7 mls, airport 90 mls

    [symbols]

Mrs M Parker, Grusey House, Sandhead, Wigtownshire
☎ *Sandhead (077683) 309*

---

1 house, 2 pub rms, 4 bedrms, sleeps 11, £100-£220, Apr-Oct, bus 3 mls, rail 8 mls, airport 60 mls

    [symbols]

1 caravan, sleeps 6, £40-£45, Apr-Oct, bus 3 mls, rail 8 mls, airport 60 mls

    [symbols]

Mrs Rowan, Mid Float Farm, Sandhead, Wigtownshire
☎ *Sandhead (077683) 248*

SANDWICK Shetland Map Ref. 5A11

COMMENDED

1 cottage, 2 pub rms, 2 bedrms, sleeps 4, min let 5 nights, £45-£70, Jan-Dec, bus ½ ml, ferry 15 mls, airport 12 mls

    [symbols]

Mrs B Smith, Broonies Taing, Sandwick, Shetland
☎ *Sandwick (09505) 280*
Traditional, low bedroom ceilings and doors. Convenient for Mousa Ferry.

SANDWICK Orkney Map Ref. 5A11

1 cottage, 1 pub rm, 2 bedrms, sleeps 4-6, £80, Jan-Dec, bus 1 ml, ferry 10 mls

    [symbols] (S.S.S.I.& R.S.P.B. area)

Mrs M Johnston, Bryameadow, Twatt, Sandwick, Orkney, KW17 2JH
☎ *Sandwick (085684) 664*

SANDYHILLS, by Dalbeattie Kirkcudbrightshire Map Ref. 2B10

Your Chalet in Bonnie Galloway

Only 1 hour from the M6 at Carlisle

Luxurious self-catering log houses in outstandingly beautiful countryside. So many amenities near your holiday home. Private fishing, golf courses, a riding school and pony-trekking. Nearby (within walking distance) is Sandyhills beach. There are many places locally of historical interest to visit, too. Dogs welcome. Restaurant, two bars and laundry on site. Colour TV, centrally-heated, continental quilt and all linen provided.

For details: **BAREND PROPERTIES LTD. Barend 25, Sandyhills, Dalbeattie, Kirkcudbrightshire.**

Telephone Southwick 663/648 STD (0387 78).

up to
COMMENDED

60 chalet/log cabins, 1-2 pub rms, 2-3 bedrms, sleeps 4-10, min let weekend, from £120, Jan-Dec, bus 300 yds, rail 18 mls, airport 100 mls

Barend Properties Ltd, Sandyhills, Dalbeattie, Kirkcudbrightshire
☎ *Southwick (038778) 663*

On south facing slope overlooking man-made loch to forested area. Sandy beach only 500 yards.

---

1 cottage, 2 pub rms, 4 bedrms, sleeps 6-8, min let long weekend (low season), £56-£158, Apr-Oct, bus 5 mls, rail 18 mls

Mrs Hanbury, Drumstinchall, Dalbeattie, Kirkcudbrightshire, DG5 4PD
☎ *Southwick (038778) 279*

---

1 cottage, 1 pub rm, 3 bedrms, sleeps 7, £80-£130, Jan-Dec, bus nearby, rail 20 mls

Capt G Douglas, Anchordale, Colvend, Dalbeattie, Kirkcudbrightshire, DG5 4PU
☎ *Southwick (038778) 240*

---

3 chalet/log cabins, 2 pub rms, 3 bedrms, sleeps 2-7, min let long weekend, £130-£195, Apr-Dec, bus nearby, rail 15 mls, airport 90 mls

Mr Osborne, Barnhourie Deer Farm Chalets, Sandyhills, Kirkcudbrightshire
☎ *Southwick (038778) 650*

SANNOX Isle of Arran Map Ref. 1F6

5 flats, 1 pub rm, 1 bedrm, sleeps 2-5, min let 4 nights, £60-£150, Jan-Dec, bus nearby, ferry 7 mls

Mr & Mrs McAllister-Hall, Ingledene Hotel, Sannox, Isle of Arran
☎ *Corrie (077081) 225*

VAT is shown at 15%: changes in this rate may affect prices.

1 flat, 1 pub rm, 3 bedrms, sleeps 6, from £65, Mar-Oct, bus nearby, ferry 6 mls

Mrs J Hawkins, Ferghan Mhor, Sannox, Isle of Arran, KA27 8JD
☎ *Corrie (077081) 684*

SAUCHEN Aberdeenshire Map Ref. 4F10

1 cottage, 1 pub rm, 3 bedrms, sleeps 4, min let weekend, £50-£100, Jan-Dec, bus nearby, rail 12 mls, airport 20 mls

  (bowling green)

Mrs E Thomson, Millbank Cottage, Sauchen, by Inverurie, Aberdeenshire, AB3 7RX
☎ *Sauchen (03303) 379*

SCALPAY Isle of Harris, Western Isles Map Ref. 3C6

Eilean Glas
LIGHTHOUSE
Isle of Scalpay, Harris,
Outer Hebrides · 0859 84 345

A beautiful, remote location. Stay in former keepers' cottages, completely modernised and tastefully furnished. Enjoy peat fires, fishing trips, and a sauna. This unique place is reached by a ½-mile walk over the heather-covered moors of Scalpay. Once there, you and this tiny holiday community are assured of a rare sense of peace and timelessness.

Cottages from £115 per week.
Brochure from Eilean Glas, Scalpay, Harris, Outer Hebrides.
Please quote Ref: WTS/SC.

AWAITING INSPECTION

3 houses, 1-2 pub rms, 2-3 bedrms, sleeps 4-8, min let 1 night, £81-£207, Apr-Oct, bus 3 mls, ferry 3 mls, airport 48 mls

Mr & Mrs R J Ford-Sagers, Eilean Glas Lighthouse, Isle of Scalpay, Harris, Western Isles, PA84 3YH
☎ *Scalpay (085984) 345*

---

1 house, 2 pub rms, 3 bedrms, sleeps 5, £60-£110, Jan-Dec, ferry 2 mls, airport 42 mls

Mrs E Ross, 21 Ormidale Terrace, Edinburgh, EH12 6DY
☎ *031 337 5622*

SCANIPORT Inverness-shire Map Ref. 4B9

1 house, 3 pub rms, 4 bedrms, sleeps 8, £95-£145, Apr-Oct, bus 1 ½ mls, rail 5 mls, airport 10 mls

Miss J Taylor, Dochfour Estate Office, Dochgarroch, Inverness, IV3 6JP
☎ *Dochgarroch (046386) 218*

SCARFSKERRY Caithness Map Ref. 4D2

Pentland View Chalets 084 785 357
Pentland House, Scarfskerry, Caithness KW14 8XW
Two modern cottage-style holiday homes situated on the outskirts
of the village of Scarfskerry, a mere 25 yards from the sea and
offering spectacular panoramic views across the Pentland Firth to
the Orkney Islands. Both chalets sleep 6 and are equipped with
modern furnishings and fittings. The area generally offers all the
ingredients for a quiet and relaxing holiday.

2 chalet/log cabins, 1 pub rm, 2 bedrms, sleeps 2-6, £65-£100, Apr-Oct, bus 1 ml, rail 12 mls, airport 20 mls

Mrs T Body, Pentland View, Scarfskerry, Caithness, KW14 8XW
☎ *Barrock (084785) 357*
Modern, cottage style homes with panoramic views of sea and Orkney Isles. Quiet area by waters edge.

SCARISTAVORE Isle of Harris, Western Isles Map Ref. 3B7

1 chalet/log cabin, 1 pub rm, 3 bedrms, sleeps 6, £70-£85, Jan-Dec, ferry 15 mls

Mrs M A MacSween, Sandview, 6 Scaristavore, Scaristavore, Isle of Harris, Western Isles
☎ *Scarista (085985) 212*

SCONE Perthshire Map Ref. 2C2

Scone Palace Camping Site 20 caravans, sleeps 4-8, min let 2 nights, £70-£180, Apr-Oct, bus ½ ml, rail 3 mls, airport 20 mls

Scone Palace Holiday Caravans, Estates Office, Scone Palace, Scone, Perthshire, PH2 6BD
☎ *Scone (0738) 52308*

(See colour ad. 17 p. xxxvi)

SCOURIE Sutherland Map Ref. 3G4

1 house, 2 pub rms, 3 bedrms, sleeps 6, £80-£140, Apr-Oct, bus 400 yds, rail 43 mls, airport 100 mls

Mr J M Williams, Deers Hill, Sutton Abinger, by Dorking, Surrey, RH5 6PS
☎ *Dorking (0306) 730331*

---

1 house, 1 cottage, 2-3 pub rms, 3 bedrms, sleeps 5, £86-£135, Apr-Oct, bus ¼ ml, rail 35 mls

The Factor, Estate Office, Achfary, by Lairg, Sutherland, IV27 4PQ
☎ *Lochmore (097184) 221*

---

1 house, 2 pub rms, 4 bedrms, sleeps 7, £85-£160, Apr-Oct

Finlayson Hughes, Bank House, 82 Atholl Road, Pitlochry, Perthshire, PH16 5BL
☎ *Pitlochry (0796) 2512*

VAT is shown at 15%: changes in this rate may affect prices.

1 chalet/log cabin, 1 pub rm, 1 bedrm, sleeps 2, min let weekend, from £35, Jan-Dec, bus 300 yds, rail 45 mls, airport 100 mls

1 caravan, sleeps 4, min let weekend, £20-£35, Jan-Dec, bus 300 yds, rail 45 mls, airport 100 mls

Mr H MacLeod, Arch Cottage, Scourie, Sutherland, IV27 4TE
☎ *Scourie (0971) 2039*

SEILEBOST Isle of Harris, Western Isles Map Ref. 3B6

1 bungalow, 2 pub rms, 3 bedrms, sleeps 6, £90-£110, Apr-Oct, ferry 9 mls, airport 40 mls

Mrs M Morrison, 20 Seilebost, Seilebost, Isle of Harris, Western Isles
☎ *Scarista (085985) 250*

1 house, 2 pub rms, 4 bedrms, sleeps 7-9, from £85, Jan-Dec, ferry 10 mls, airport 47 mls

Mrs C Morrison, Post Office House, 12 Seilebost, Isle of Harris, Western Isles, PA85 3HP
☎ *Scarista (085985) 205*
Single storied house in own grounds. Overlooks village and Luskentyre Beaches.

1 bungalow, 1 pub rm, 2 bedrms, sleeps 6, £85-£95, May-Sep, ferry 9 mls, airport 50 mls

(hillwalking)

Mrs MacLennan, Sandville, Seilebost, Isle of Harris, Western Isles
☎ *Scarista (085985) 230*

SELKIRK Map Ref. 2E7

1 cottage, 1 pub rm, 2 bedrms, sleeps 6, min let weekend, max £100, Jan-Dec, bus 1 ¼ mls, rail 40 mls, airport 40 mls

Mrs J G Buglass, Middlestead, Selkirk
☎ *Selkirk (0750) 21752*

1 cottage, 1 pub rm, 2 bedrms, sleeps 2-3, min let weekend, £40-£100, Jan-Dec, bus nearby, rail 40 mls, airport 40 mls

Mrs J Millar, Nether Whitlaw, Selkirk
☎ *Selkirk (0750) 21217*
Cottage in residential area of town.

---

by SELKIRK Map Ref. 2E7

APPROVED

1 cottage, 1 pub rm, 3 bedrms, sleeps 6, min let weekend, £40-£100, Jan-Dec, bus 3 ½ mls, rail 40 mls, airport 40 mls

Mrs J Miller, Nether Whitlaw, Selkirk, TD7 4QN
☎ *Selkirk (0750) 21217*
On working farm, 4 miles from Selkirk.

WHITMUIR ESTATE
Whitmuir, Selkirk, Borders TD7 4PZ. TEL: 0750 21728

We have nine spacious fully modernised country house apartments and seven super cottages round a south-facing courtyard for 2-6 persons. Large gardens. 850 acres farmland. Private loch fishing, games rooms, sauna, laundry; linen provided. Colour TV, children and pets welcome. Shop 3 miles away.
OPEN ALL YEAR. From £80.50 p.w. Mini-Breaks from £46.
Properties throughout the Central Borders. Brochure Ref. 707.

COMMENDED

Whitmuir Estate 9 flats, 7 cottages, 1 pub rm, 1-3 bedrms, sleeps 2-6, min let 2 nights, £81-£200, Jan-Dec, bus 3 mls, rail 40 mls, airport 40 mls

Mrs Hilary Dunlop, Whitmuir, Selkirk, TD7 4PZ
☎ *Selkirk (0750) 21728*

Set around private loch, 850 acre farm estate. In and outdoor leisure pursuits. Barbecues in summer.

SHANDWICK Ross-shire Map Ref. 4B7

1 house, 1 pub rm, 3 bedrms, sleeps 6, £55-£95, Apr-Oct, bus 1 ml, rail 3 mls, airport 40 mls

Mrs J E MacKay, Station House, Muir-of-Ord, Ross-shire
☎ *Muir-of-Ord (0463) 870680*

SHAPINSAY Orkney Map Ref. 5C11

2 cottages, 1 pub rm, 2-3 bedrms, sleeps 5-6, min let weekend, £80, Jan-Dec

Mrs C Zawadzki, Balfour Castle, Shapinsay, Orkney
☎ *Balfour (085671) 282*

1 caravan, sleeps 6, min let weekend, £40-£50, Apr-Oct, ferry 2 mls

(Boat trips round islands)
Mr Groat, Houseby Cottage, Shapinsay, Orkney
☎ *Balfour (085671) 254*

SHIELDAIG Ross-shire Map Ref. 3F8

1 house, 2 pub rms, 3 bedrms, sleeps 6, from £120, Apr-Oct, bus post bus

(hillwalking, birdwatching)
Bell-Ingram, Durn, Isla Road, Perth, PH2 7HF
☎ *Perth (0738) 21121*

1 cottage, 1 bungalow, 2 pub rms, 3 bedrms, sleeps 6, min let weekend, £161-£230, May-mid Sep, bus 1 ml, rail 12 mls, airport 80 mls

Mrs M Pattinson, High Billinge House, Utkinton, Tarporley, Cheshire
☎ *Tarporley (08293) 2536*

COMMENDED
♛ ♛

1 chalet/log cabin, 2 pub rms, 3 bedrms, sleeps 5, £80-£140, May-Oct, bus 1 ½ mls, rail 18 mls

[symbols]

Mr J D Frew, 45 Pepperd Road, Caversham, Reading, Berkshire, RG4 8NR
☎ *Reading (0734) 472140*
Modern, well equipped chalet in lovely Scots pine setting. Fine views of Loch Shieldaig and beyond.

---

1 cottage, 3 pub rms, 3 bedrms, sleeps 5, £110-£190, Apr-Oct

[symbols]

Mr P Burton, 28 Three Springs Road, Pershore, Worcs, WR10 1HS
☎ *Pershore (0386) 553440*

COMMENDED
♛ ♛ ♛ ♛

1 chalet/log cabin, 2 pub rms, 3 bedrms, sleeps 5, £200-£250, Jan-Dec, rail 16 mls, airport 70 mls

[symbols] (guided nature trails)

Dr A J & Mrs R L Wright, Manninagh, Mold Road, Bodfari, Denbigh, Clwyd, LL16 4DS
☎ *Bodfari (074575) 363*
Small select development, 1 acre grounds include scots pine wood. Views over loch and mountain.

SHIELDAIG AREA Ross-shire Map Ref. 3F8

AWAITING INSPECTION

4 houses, 1 cottage, 2 bungalows, 1-2 pub rms, 1-5 bedrms, sleeps 1-13, £60-£220, Apr-Oct

[symbols]

Mackinnon Hathway, Estate and Land Agent, Main Street, Kyle of Lochalsh, Ross-shire, IV40 8AB
☎ *Kyle (0599) 4567*

SHISKINE Isle of Arran Map Ref. 1E7

1 house, 3 pub rms, 5 bedrms, sleeps 11, £60-£170, Jan-Dec, bus nearby, ferry 12 mls

[symbols]

C J E Mills, 474 Duffield Road, Allestree, Derby
☎ *Derby (0332) 558805*

SHUNA, Isle of Argyll Map Ref. 1E3

3 houses, 1 bungalow, 1-2 pub rms, 3-5 bedrms, sleeps 6-12, £73-£231, Apr-Oct, bus 1 ½ mls, rail 20 mls, ferry nearby-1 ml, airport 25 mls

[symbols]

The Hon E Gully, Island of Shuna, Arduaine, by Oban, Argyll, PA34 4SZ
☎ *Luing (08524) 244*

Prices shown are for guidance only. Please send SAE with each enquiry.

SKELMORLIE Ayrshire Map Ref. 1G5

1 flat, 1 cottage, 1 pub rm, 1-2 bedrms, sleeps 5-6, min let 2 nights, from £75, Jan-Dec, bus ½ ml, rail 2 mls, airport 30 mls

9 caravans, sleeps 6, min let 2 nights, from £75, Mar-Oct, bus ½ ml, rail 2 mls, airport 30 mls

Mrs M Stirrat, Mains Caravan Site, Skelmorlie, Ayrshire, PA17 5EW
☎ *Wemyss Bay (0475) 520794*

SKENE Aberdeenshire Map Ref. 4G10

Mains of Keir 6 caravans, sleeps 6-8, min let weekend, £40-£90, Apr-Oct, bus ½ ml, rail 7 mls, airport 7 mls

(bowling)

Mrs M Mitchell, Mains of Keir, Skene, Aberdeenshire, AB3 6VA
☎ *Aberdeen (0224) 743282*

SKIPNESS Argyll Map Ref. 1E6

2 houses, 6 cottages, 2-3 pub rms, 2-6 bedrms, sleeps 4-11, min let weekend (low season), £40-£440, Jan-Dec, bus 6 mls, rail 60 mls, airport 30 mls

Mrs M R Oakes, Skipness Castle, Tarbert, Argyll, PA29 6XU
☎ *Skipness (08806) 207/209*

3 houses, 1 flat, 1 cottage, 1-2 pub rms, 2-3 bedrms, sleeps 4-8, min let weekend, £50-£200, Jan-Dec, bus 3-6 mls, rail 60 mls, ferry 1-2 mls, airport 30 mls

Mrs S Oakes, Creggan, Skipness, by Tarbert, Argyll
☎ *Skipness (08806) 225*

SKIRINISH, by Skeabost Bridge Isle of Skye, Inverness-shire Map Ref. 3D8

1 farmhouse, 2 pub rms, 4 bedrms, sleeps 6, £110-£160, May-Dec, bus 2 mls, rail 42 mls, airport 30 mls

Mrs Charles Cameron, 3 Marine Cottages, Marine Road, Nairn
☎ *Nairn (0667) 54778/(047032) 207*

SLIGACHAN Isle of Skye, Inverness-shire Map Ref. 3D9

1 cottage, 2 pub rms, 4 bedrms, sleeps 8, min let 2 weeks, £80-£135, Jan-Dec, bus ¾ ml, rail 27 mls, ferry 26 mls, airport 20 mls

Mrs E R Wakefield, Glendrynoch Lodge, Carbost, Isle of Skye, Inverness-shire, IV47 8SX
☎ *Carbost (047842) 209*

1 house, 1-3 pub rms, 2-4 bedrms, sleeps 4-20, min let weekend, £100-£300, Jan-Dec, bus nearby, rail 24 mls, ferry 24 mls, airport 20 mls

Skye Entertainment & Leisure, Sligachan, Isle of Skye, Inverness-shire
☎ *Sligachan (047852) 303*

VAT is shown at 15%: changes in this rate may affect prices.

SMAULL AREA Isle of Islay, Argyll Map Ref. 1B5

Isle of Islay
Sliabh Mór Estate Cottages

Enjoy the beauty and tranquillity of the "Queen of the Hebrides" — the friendly isle, renowned for its healthy, relaxing holidays.

Traditional stone-built cottages, superbly equipped, on our 2,000-acre estate fringed by 8 kilometres of coast, secluded sandy bays and fine cliff views.

- Restaurant, health club (pool, saunas, solaria, polygym).
- External dancing/dining patio, shops.
- Sailboard, cycle, canoe, zodiac hire.
- Riding, sub aqua, fishing

Roam the island, discover its wealth of nature and history — or perhaps it will be bird-watching (240 species), golf or visiting whisky distilleries that makes you friends with Islay . . .

28 cottages (2-12 beds). EXCLUSIVE FLY-DRIVE COTTAGES from £120. Cottages £50-£396, all year.

Bookings, packages, brochure: Sliabh Mór Estate Co Ltd, Lower Smaull, Isle of Islay, Argyll PA44 7PT. Tel: (049 685) 555.

12 cottages, 3 bedsits, 1 pub rm, 1-3 bedrms, sleeps 2-12, min let long weekend, £66-£396, Jan-Dec, bus 6 mls, ferry 15 mls, airport 15 mls

(windsurfing, sub-aqua, birdwatching)

Iolair Estate Company, 31 Bellairs, Sutton, by Ely, Cambridgeshire, CB6 2RW
☎ *Ely (0353) 777349*

SNAIGOW, by Dunkeld Perthshire Map Ref. 2B1

1 cottage, 2 pub rms, 2 bedrms, sleeps 5-6, £95-£135, Jan-Dec, bus 4 mls, rail 5 mls, airport 25 mls

Highland Cottages, Glenshieling Guest House, Hatton Road, Blairgowrie, Perthshire, PH10 7HZ
☎ *Blairgowrie (0250) 4605*

SOUTH AYWICK East Yell, Shetland Map Ref. 5G2

2 caravans, sleeps 4-6, min let 3 nights, £20-£30, Jan-Dec, bus nearby, ferry 10 mls

Mrs E Tulloch, Pinewood Guest House, Aywick, East Yell, Shetland
☎ *Mid Yell (0957) 2077*

SOUTH CUAN Isle of Luing, Argyll Map Ref. 1E3

1 bungalow, 3 pub rms, 3 bedrms, sleeps 6, £80-£120, Apr-Oct, bus ¼ ml, rail 16 mls, ferry ¼ ml

Mrs K M Macdonald, 1 Ferry Houses, Cuan Ferry, by Oban, Argyll
☎ *Balvicar (08523) 252 (after 6pm)*

Sunnybrae Caravan Site 5 caravans, sleeps 6, min let 1 night, £50-£80, Mar-Oct, bus nearby, rail 16 mls, ferry nearby, airport 23 mls

Sunnybrae Caravan Site, South Cuan, Luing, by Oban, Argyll, PA34 4TU
☎ *Luing (08524) 274*

SOUTH LOCHBOISDALE South Uist, Western Isles Map Ref. 3A10

1 house, 3 pub rms, 6 bedrms, sleeps 12, £140-£150, Jan-Dec, ferry 6 mls, airport 28 mls

🏷🚾 E ⬛🔌🪣🔲🌙🔥🪑❄🐴🅿🏸🐎✝🏛 🎵🔵🔺🚣🎣↯🛥

Mrs Douglas Miers, c/o Boisdale House, South Lochboisdale, South Uist, Western Isles
☎ *Lochboisdale (08784) 314*

SOUTH RONALDSAY Orkney Map Ref. 5B12

1 cottage, 1 pub rm, 4 bedrms, sleeps 7, £35-£75, Jan-Dec, bus 1½ mls, ferry 7 mls, airport 10 mls

🏷🚾 E ⬛🌀◎🔲🔲🔲🛋❄🐴🔥🐎✝🏛 🔍🌲🎵🔵🔺↯🚲🚢🐴

Mrs A Cromarty, South Cara, South Ronaldsay, Orkney
☎ *St Margaret's Hope (085683) 275*

SOUTHEND Argyll Map Ref. 1D8

1 house, 2 pub rms, 4 bedrms, sleeps 8, £100-£175, Mar-Oct, bus nearby, airport 10 mls

🏷🚾 E ⬛🌿⬛🎛🔲◎🔲🌙🔥🛋☀❄🐴🅿🐎🛏✝🏛 🎵▸✖🚢▣

Blakes Holidays, Wroxham, Norwich, NR12 8DH
☎ *Wroxham (06053) 2917*

SOUTHERNESS Dumfriesshire Map Ref. 2B10

6 cottages, 1 pub rm, 1-3 bedrms, sleeps 2-6, £60-£170, Jan-Dec, bus nearby, rail 20 mls, airport 50 mls

🏷🚾 E ⬛🎛◎🔲🔲🔥🛋☀❄🐴🅿🐎🛏🏛 🎵🔵🔺↯▸🟥✖🚢❗

Michael Noble, Killylung, Holywood, Dumfries, Dumfriesshire, DG2 0RL
☎ *Newbridge (0387) 720415*
Stone built units on edge of village. Next to sandy beach and well placed for many leisure pursuits. **(See colour ad. 18 p. xxxvi)**

Southerness Holiday Village 30 caravans, sleeps 6, min let weekend, £46-£165, Mar-Oct, bus nearby, rail 17 mls

🏷🚾 E 🌿⬛◎🪣🔲🛋🔲🔥🐴🅿🐎🛏🏛🔔🌐 🦢🎵🔵🔺↯✖🚢

Southerness Holiday Village, The Estate Office, Southerness, by Dumfries, DG2 8AZ
☎ *Kirkbean (038788) 256/278/281*

---

1 cottage, 2 pub rms, 3 bedrms, sleeps 6, £60-£120, Jan-Dec, bus nearby, rail 15 mls, airport 70 mls

🏷🚾 E ⬛🌀◎🔲🔲🔥❄🐴🅿🐎✝🏛 🎵🔵🔺↯▸🟥✖🚢❗

Miss M E Brown, Colt Green, Damerham, Fordingbridge, Hants
☎ *Rockbourne (07253) 240*

SPEAN BRIDGE Inverness-shire Map Ref. 3H12

Burnbank Holiday Homes 9 chalet/log cabins, 1 pub rm, 1 bedrm, sleeps 4, £75-£115, Jan-Dec, bus ¼ ml, rail ¼ ml

🏷🚾 E 🌿⬛🎛🔲◎🔲🔲🔲🔥🛋🔥🐴🅿🐎🛏🛏 🎵🔵🔺↯▸🗡✖🚢 ▣

Mr MacLennan, Burnbank Holiday Homes, Spean Bridge, Inverness-shire, PH34 4EU
☎ *Spean Bridge (039781) 398*
Small development on the banks of the River Spean, in quiet woodland setting.

Cypress Holidays 1 chalet/log cabin, 2 cottages, 1 pub rm, 2-3 bedrms, sleeps 4-6, £90-£180, Apr-Oct, bus nearby, rail nearby

Mrs Cormack, Stroma, Drumfada Terrace, Corpach, Inverness-shire
☎ *Corpach (03977) 286*

---

2 chalet/log cabins, 1 cottage, 1 pub rm, 2 bedrms, sleeps 6, £50-£130, Mar-Oct, bus nearby, rail 300 yds

(cycle hire)

Mrs Parrish, Pine Cottage, Spean Bridge, Inverness-shire, PH34 4EP
☎ *Spean Bridge (039781) 404*

SPITTAL OF GLENSHEE Perthshire Map Ref. 4D12

8 cottages, 1-2 pub rms, 1-4 bedrms, sleeps 2-8, min let 2 nights, £63-£290, Jan-Dec, bus 22 mls, rail 36 mls, airport 80 mls

Mr S N Winton, Dalmunzie Ltd, Spittal of Glenshee, Blairgowrie, Perthshire, PH10 7QG
☎ *Glenshee (025085) 226*
Individual stone built cottages on country estate near Spittal of Glenshee.

(See colour ad. 19 p. xxxvi)

SPITTALFIELD Perthshire Map Ref. 2C1

2 cottages, 1 pub rm, 3 bedrms, sleeps 5, £70-£135, Jan-Dec, bus 1 ml, rail 14 mls, airport 15 mls

Mrs C Taylor, Delvine Gardens, Spittalfield, by Murthly, Perthshire, PH1 4LD
☎ *Caputh (073871) 259*
Detached stone estate cottages each with garden area. Quiet setting near River Tay. Riding/fishing.

ST ABBS Berwickshire Map Ref. 2G5

1 cottage, 1 bungalow, 1 pub rm, 3 bedrms, sleeps 6-8, min let weekend, £80-£130, Jan-Dec, bus 2 mls, rail 12 mls, airport 48 mls

Mrs B Barbour, Lumsdaine Farm, St Abbs, Coldingham, Eyemouth, Berwickshire, TD14 5UA
☎ *Coldingham (08907) 71218*

ST ANDREWS Fife Map Ref. 2E3

Craigtoun Meadows Holiday Park 34 caravans, sleeps 2-6, from £65, Mar-Oct, bus nearby, rail 4 mls, airport 10 mls

Craigtoun Meadows Holiday Park, No 9 Mount Melville, St Andrews, Fife, KY16 8PQ
☎ *St Andrews (0334) 75959*

Prices shown are for guidance only. Please send SAE with each enquiry.

COMMENDED
♛ ♛ ♛ ♛

4 flats, 1 pub rm, 2-3 bedrms, sleeps 4-6, min let weekend, £100-£190, mid Jun-Oct, bus 400 yds, rail 6 mls, airport 10 mls

♿ 🚻 E ⛟ 👜 🅿 ▤ 🍴 💾 ◎ 🖵 📞 🖵 📠 ⚥ 🛋 ☉ ❄ ∥ 🥾 🏛 🦆 ⛰   ⚟ ⚞ 🐚 ⚲ 🎿
♪ ∪ ⚓ ⚟ ⛷ ⚲ 🏸 ✗ 🧺 🔲

Mrs S D Room, Woodriffe, 44 Buchanan Gardens, St Andrews, Fife, KY16 9LX
☎ *St Andrews (0334) 72253*
Town centre flats in traditional building above shops. Convenient for local amenities.

---

1 flat, 1 cottage, 1 pub rm, 2-3 bedrms, sleeps 6-7, £145-£190, Apr-Oct, bus ¼ ml, rail 4 mls

♿ 🚻 E ⛟ 👜 🅿 ▤ 🍴 💾 ◎ 🖵 📞 🖵 📠 🍴 ☉ ❄ 🐓 🅿 ∥ 🥾 🏛 †   ♪ ∪ ⚓ ⚟ ⛷ ⚲ ✗
🧺

Mrs A R Hippisley, Rockview, The Scores, St Andrews, Fife, KY16 9AR
☎ *St Andrews (0334) 75844*

Fife Park & Albany Park 80 houses, 6 bedrms, sleeps 6, £95-£160, Jun-Sep, bus nearby, rail 6 mls

♿ 🚻 E 🍴 👜 🅿 ◎ 🖵 📞 🖵 📠 ☉ ❄ 🅿 🥾 ⛰ 🌐   🐚 ⚲ 🎿 ♪ ∪ ⚓ ⚟ ⛷ ✗ 🧺

Bursar of Residences, Uni. of St Andrews, College Gate, St Andrews, Fife, KY16 9AJ
☎ *St Andrews (0334) 76161 ext 547*

Stravithie Country Estate
STRAVITHIE · ST ANDREWS
Telephone: 033-488-251

A beautiful estate of 30 acres, gardens and unspoiled wooded grounds, 3 miles from St Andrews. The stone-built houses and cottages are of immense character. Colour TV. Sleeping 2-8.
Facilities within the grounds include horse riding, laundry, telephone, free fishing, table tennis, badminton, putting, golf practice, parking and nature trails.

Prices from £115-£270

For brochure and bookings:
Mr & Mrs J. Chalmers

Stravithie Country Estate 7 houses, 8 flats, 1 pub rm, 1-4 bedrms, sleeps 2-7, min let 2 nights, £120-£260, Apr-Oct, bus nearby, rail 7 mls, airport 14 mls

♿ 🚻 E ⛟ 👜 🅿 ▤ 🍴 💾 ◎ 🖵 📞 🖵 📠 ⚥ 🍴 ☉ ❄ 🐓 🅿 ∥ 🥾 🏛 🦆 ⛰ 🔴 🌐   ♪
∪ ⚓ ⚟ ⛷ ⚲ 🏸 ✗ 🧺 🔲 (riding lessons, table tennis, badminton)

Mr & Mrs Chalmers, Stravithie House, Stravithie, by St Andrews, Fife
☎ *Boarhills (033488) 251*

---

1 house, 9 flats, 1-2 pub rms, 1-5 bedrms, sleeps 3-8, min let weekend, £65-£195, Jun-Oct, bus 300 yds, rail 4 mls, airport 15 mls

♿ 🚻 E ⛟ 👜 🅿 ▤ 🍴 💾 ◎ 🖵 📞 🖵 📠 🍴 ❄ 🐓 🥾 🏛 †   ⚲ ♪ ∪ ⚓ ⚟ ⛷ ⚲ ✗ 🧺

Mrs K M J Mcmanus, 6 Norwood Crescent, Dundee, Angus
☎ *Dundee (0382) 68009*

VAT is shown at 15%: changes in this rate may affect prices.

1 cottage, 1 bungalow, 1-2 pub rms, 2 bedrms, sleeps 4, £60-£100, Jun-Sep, bus 1 ml, rail 9 mls

Mrs J Macniven, South Lambieletham, St Andrews, Fife, KY16 8NP
☎ *St Andrews (0334) 72923*

---

1 house, 2 pub rms, 4 bedrms, sleeps 7, max £140, Jun-Oct, bus ½ ml, rail 5 mls

Mrs Jessie Reid, 2 Beistane Cottage, Dunino, St Andrews, Fife
☎ *Boarhills (033488) 336(eve)*

---

1 flat, 1 pub rm, 1 bedrm, sleeps 2-3, £85-£90, Apr-Oct, bus nearby, rail 3 mls, airport 60 mls

Dr & Mrs D P Tunstall, 4 West Acres, St Andrews, Fife, KY16 9UD
☎ *St Andrews (0334) 73507*

---

7 houses, 6 flats, 6 cottages, 1 bungalow, 1-3 pub rms, 2-7 bedrms, sleeps 3-11, £70-£295, Mar-Oct, bus nearby, rail 5 mls

Mrs S L Underwood, Inchdairnie Holiday Properties Ltd, Denhead, by St Andrews, Fife, KY16 8PB
☎ *Strathkinness (033485) 342*

---

1 flat, 2 pub rms, 2 bedrms, sleeps 6, min let weekend, £60-£140, Jun-Sep, bus ¼ ml, rail 8 mls, airport 50 mls

Mrs M Wilkinson, Rannoch School, Rannoch, Perthshire, PH17 2QQ
☎ *Kinloch Rannoch (08822) 237*

---

1 cottage, 1 pub rm, 3 bedrms, sleeps 8, £115-£180, Apr-Oct, bus ¼ ml

WAP Fyfe, Acre Management Ltd, Acre Valley, Torrance, Glasgow, G64 4DJ
☎ *Balmore (0360) 20223*

---

1 house, 1 pub rm, 2 bedrms, sleeps 6, £100-£125, Jul-Sep, bus ½ ml, rail 8 mls, airport 14 mls

Valerie N Jamieson, Panmure Manse, 8A Albert St, Monifieth, Dundee, Angus
☎ *Dundee (0382) 532772*

---

1 flat, 1 pub rm, 1 bedrm, sleeps 4, min let weekend, £80-£100, Jan-Dec, bus nearby, rail 5 mls, airport 10 mls

Mrs M Reid, 28 City Road, St Andrews, Fife
☎ *St Andrews (0334) 73714(after 6pm)*

| up to COMMENDED 👑👑👑👑 | 3 houses, 6 cottages, 1-2 pub rms, 2-3 bedrms, sleeps 4-6, min let weekend, £60-£250, Jan-Dec, bus 2 mls, rail 5 mls, airport 50 mls |

🕭 � E ➡ 🕯 🛢 🖳 🖵 ◎ ∅ 🖵 ☎ 🖵 ⌹ ∥ 🗜 ⊙ ✳ 🐓 🅿 ∥ ⛾ 🎞 🛏 ⛰ ⌇ 🐟 ⌘ 🏌 🧿 ⚠ 🛫 ▸ ✐ ✗ 🎒 🏂 Ⓣ

Mrs A Wedderburn, Mountquhanie, Cupar, Fife, KY15 4QJ
☎ *Gauldry (082624) 252*
Smart town houses; comfortable country cottages with log fires; spacious flats in elegant mansion.

| AWAITING INSPECTION | 2 houses, 1 cottage, 1-2 pub rms, 3 bedrms, sleeps 5-10, £150-£220, Apr-Oct, bus nearby, rail 5 mls |

🕭 races E ➡ 🕯 🛢 🖳 🖵 ∅ 🖵 ☎ 🖵 ⌹ ∥ 🗜 ⊙ ✳ 🅿 ∥ ⛾ 🎞 ⛰ ⌇ 🐟 ⌘ 🏌 🧿 ⚠ ▸ ✐ ⚴ ✗ 🎒

Mrs A Rose, Gamekeepers Cottage, Newholm, Dunsyre, Lanarkshire
☎ *Dolphinton (09688) 2277*

---

1 flat, 2 cottages, 1 pub rm, 1-3 bedrms, sleeps 2-6, £75-£125, Jun-Sep

🕭 races E ➡ 🛢 🖳 🖵 ◎ 🖵 ☎ 🖵 ⊙ ✳ 🐓 🅿 ⛾ 🎞 † ⌇ ⌇ 🐟 ⌘ 🏌 🧿 ⚠ ⚴ ▸ ✐ 🏂

D A G Reid FRICS, 2 Bonnygate, Cupar, Fife
☎ *Cupar (0334) 54949*

---

1 house, 1 pub rm, 3 bedrms, sleeps 5, £100-£130, Jun-Sep, bus 600 yds, rail 5 mls

🕭 races E ➡ 🛢 🖳 🖵 ◎ 🖵 ☎ 🖵 ⌹ 🗜 ⛾ † ⌇ ⌘ 🧿 ▸ ✗ 🎒 Ⓣ

Mrs Gardiner, 14 Cumlodden Avenue, Edinburgh, EH12 6DR
☎ *031 337 3867*

10 houses, 16 flats, 2 cottages, 2 bungalows, 1-3 pub rms, 1-6 bedrms, sleeps 2-10, min let weekend (low season), £100-£250, Jun-Sep, bus nearby, rail 6 mls, airport 12 mls

🕭 races E ➡ 🕯 🛢 🖳 🖵 ◎ ∅ 🖵 ☎ 🖵 🗜 ⊙ ✳ 🐓 🅿 ∥ ⛾ 🎞 🛏 †

Eve Brown Property Management, 23A Argyll Street, St Andrews, Fife
☎ *St Andrews (0334) 73254*

---

1 cottage, 1 pub rm, 3 bedrms, sleeps 5, min let weekend, from £95, Jan-Dec, bus nearby, rail 9 mls, airport 20 mls

🕭 races C ➡ 🛢 🖳 🖵 ◎ 🖵 🖵 🗜 ☎ ⊙ ✳ 🐓 🅿 ⛾ 🎞 † ⌇ ⌘ 🧿 ⚠ ▸ 🏂 Ⓣ

Mrs S Paterson, Carloonan, Mawcarse, Milnathort, Kinross-shire
☎ *Kinross (0577) 62816*

VAT is shown at 15%: changes in this rate may affect prices.

1 flat, 1 pub rm, 2 bedrms, sleeps 6, £100-£160, Jun-Sep, bus 400 yds, rail 5 mls

♿ ⚕ E ➡ ⌂ ⌀ ▥ ♨ ◉ ⌨ ▢ ◙ ⌇ ▱ ☉ ❄ ✝ P ☍ ▦ † ⚲ ♪ ◡ ◬ ⚲ ▸ ✖ 🥾

Mrs Pumford, 16 Hepburn Gardens, St Andrews, Fife, KY16 9DD
☎ *St Andrews (0334) 74673*

---

by ST ANDREWS Fife Map Ref. 2E3

4 cottages, 1 pub rm, 3-4 bedrms, sleeps 5-7, £90-£155, mid Jun-Oct, bus nearby, rail 9 mls

♿ ⚕ E ➡ ⌀ ♨ ◉ ⌨ ⌇ ▱ ☉ ❄ ✝ P ☍ ▦ ➡ ⚞ ◕ ✪ ⚲ ♪ ◬ ⚲ ▸ ⚡ ✖ 🥾 🔭

Mrs A Baxter, Gilston House, Leven, Fife, KY8 5QP
☎ *Upper Largo (033336) 245*

Former Victorian stable block of Gilston House on private estate. Extensive grounds. Putting green.

Great Value Holidays!

CAMBO, Nr. ST ANDREWS, FIFE KY16 8QD
Telephone: (0333) 50313

Even if you never visit the enchanting fishing villages or historic houses or the abundant beaches and golf courses or the other many and varied attractions in this area, there is plenty for everyone just on this picturesque lowland estate—indoor and outdoor play areas, pet's corner, shop/restaurant, woodland walks, golden sands, tennis, fives, lawn games, etc.

AWAITING INSPECTION

Cambo House Holiday Flats 3 flats, 2 cottages, 1-2 pub rms, 2-4 bedrms, sleeps 6-8, min let weekend, £55-£145, Jun-Sep, bus ¾ ml, rail 13 mls

⚕ E ➡ ⌀ ♨ ◉ ⌀ ⌨ ▢ ◙ ▱ ❄ ✝ P ☍ ▦ † ⚞ ◕ ✪ ⚲ ♪ ◬ ⚲ ▸ Ⓡ ✖ 🥾 ♟ 🔭 (visitor centre)

Peter Erskine, Cambo House, Kingsbarns, by St Andrews, Fife, KY16 8QD
☎ *Crail (0333) 50313*

Clayton Caravan Park 5 caravans, sleeps 8, min let 2-3 nights, £70-£165, Mar-Oct, bus nearby, rail 2 mls, airport 11 mls

♿ ⚕ E ⌂ ⌀ ⌁ ⌨ ⌇ ▢ ◙ ⌇ ▱ ☉ ✝ P ☍ ▦ † ⚞ ◕ ✪ ♪ ◡ ◬ ▸ ✖ 🥾 Ⓣ

Clayton Caravan Park, by St Andrews, Fife, KY16 9YE
☎ *Balmullo (0334) 870242/870630*

---

9 chalet/log cabins, 1 pub rm, 2 bedrms, sleeps 4-5, min let 2 nights (low season), £90-£260, Jan-Dec, bus ½ ml, rail 2 mls

♿ ⚕ E ➡ ⌀ ▥ ♨ ◉ ⌨ ⌇ ▢ ◙ ⌇ ▱ ☉ ❄ P ⁄⁄ ☍ ▦ ➡ ⚞ ✪ ♞ ⚲ ⚓ ♪ ◡ ◬ ⚲ ▸ ⚡ ✖ 🥾 Ⓣ (windsurfing)

Kincaple Golf & Holiday Lodges, Kincaple, by St Andrews, Fife, KY16 9SH
☎ *Strathkinness (033485) 217*

AWAITING INSPECTION

1 bungalow, 1 pub rm, 3 bedrms, sleeps 6, £100, Jun-Sep, bus 440 yds, rail 4 mls

♿ ⚕ E ➡ ⌂ ⌀ ◉ ⌨ ⌇ ▢ ◙ ▱ ❄ P ☍ ▦ † ♪ ◡ ◬ ⚲ ▸ ✖ 🥾

Mrs P J McCash, Redclyffe, Peel Street, Cardross, Dunbartonshire, G82 5JX
☎ *Cardross (0389) 841364*

HIGHLY COMMENDED

Dron Court 10 houses, 1-2 pub rms, 1-4 bedrms, sleeps 2-8, £95-£345, Jan-Dec, bus nearby, rail 3 mls, eating out fac's within 2 mls, shops within 2 mls, commission to travel agents

♿ ⚕ E ➡ ⌀ ▥ ♨ ◉ ⌨ ⌇ ▢ ◙ ⌇ ▱ ☉ ❄ ✝ P ▦ ◬ ☍ ⚞ ⚲ ⚲ ♪ ◡ ▸ 18

Mrs M Harper, Dron Court, South Dron, by St Andrews, Fife
☎ *Balmullo (0334) 870835*

Converted farmhouse and building in courtyard setting. Clubhouse facility, barbecues, discos, etc.

Prices shown are for guidance only. Please send SAE with each enquiry.

ST BOSWELLS Roxburghshire Map Ref. 2E7

up to
COMMENDED
👑👑👑👑

2 flats, 1 cottage, 1 pub rm, 2-4 bedrms, sleeps 4-8, min let weekend, £30-£140, Jan-Dec, bus ½ ml, rail 40 mls, airport 37 mls

Mrs R Dale, The Holmes, St Boswells, Roxburghshire
☎ St Boswells (0835) 22356
Country house, built in 1895. 150 acres of attractive grounds, with many interesting walks.

ST CYRUS Kincardineshire Map Ref. 4G12

The Neuk Caravan Site 7 caravans, sleeps 6, min let 1 night, £50-£80, Apr-Oct, bus nearby, rail 5 mls, airport 40 mls

The Neuk Caravan Site, Lochside Road, St Cyrus, Montrose, Kincardineshire, DD10 0BD
☎ St Cyrus (067485) 389

ST FILLANS Perthshire Map Ref. 2A2

2 flats, 2 pub rms, 1 bedrm, sleeps 2, £90, Apr-Oct, bus nearby, rail 40 mls, airport 50 mls

Mr A Ferguson, Neish Villa, St Fillans, Perthshire, PH6 2NF
☎ St Fillans (076485) 238

COMMENDED
👑👑👑👑

1 house, 2 pub rms, 3 bedrms, sleeps 6, from £250, Jan-Dec, rail 24 mls

Bell-Ingram, Durn, Isla Road, Perth, PH2 7HF
☎ Perth (0738) 21121
Attractive country house of character in secluded grounds of estate. Fishing and stalking available.

HIGHLY COMMENDED
👑👑👑

Riverside Log Cabins 6 chalet/log cabins, 3 bedrms, sleeps 6, min let 3 nights, £85-£255, mid Mar-Jan, bus nearby, rail 26 mls

A Mathers, Riverside Log Cabins, St Fillans, Perthshire, PH6 2JZ
☎ St Fillans (076485) 310
Attractive riverside setting on banks of the River Earn. Ideally situated for walking and touring.

1 cottage, 3 pub rms, 3 bedrms, sleeps 5-6, £100-£120, Jan-Dec, bus nearby, rail 29 mls

Mr Bassett, Cairnies, Glenalmond, Perth, Perthshire, PH1 3RY
☎ Glenalmond (073888) 235

1 flat, 1 pub rm, 1 bedrm, sleeps 4, £45-£60, Apr-Oct, bus nearby, rail 21 mls

Mrs MacInnes, Holly, St Fillans, Perthshire, PH6 2NF
☎ St Fillans (076485) 242

ST MARGARET'S HOPE Orkney Map Ref. 5B12

2 caravans, sleeps 4-6, £30-£50, Jan-Dec, bus nearby, ferry 7 mls, airport 13 mls

Mr & Mrs Brown, Thorshaven, St Margaret's Hope, Orkney
☎ St Margaret's Hope (085683) 263

VAT is shown at 15%: changes in this rate may affect prices.

ST MICHAELS, by Leuchars Fife Map Ref. 2D2

6 cottages, 1 pub rm, 2-4 bedrms, sleeps 4-8, £80-£205, Apr-Oct, bus 1 ½ mls, rail 3 ½ mls, airport 10 mls

Mr Foster, Craigie Farm, St Michaels, by Leuchars, Fife
☎ *Leuchars (033483) 218*

STAFFIN Isle of Skye, Inverness-shire Map Ref. 3D8

1 croft, 1 pub rm, 2 bedrms, sleeps 4, £60-£80, Apr-Oct, bus nearby, ferry 10 mls, airport 40 mls

Mrs Annie Macleod, Lag-Uaine, Staffin, Isle of Skye, Inverness-shire
☎ *Staffin (047062) 213*

---

2 caravans, sleeps 6, £20-£35, Apr-Oct, bus nearby, rail 50 mls, ferry 7 mls, airport 45 mls

Mr John Mackenzie, Lynton, Staffin, Isle of Skye, Inverness-shire, IV51 9JS
☎ *Staffin (047062) 204*

---

1 cottage, 1 pub rm, 3 bedrms, sleeps 4-6, min let weekend, from £60, Jan-Dec, bus ½ ml, rail 60 mls, ferry 7 mls, airport 50 mls

Mrs A M Gilles, 2 Sartle, Staffin, Isle of Skye, Inverness-shire, IV51 9LB
☎ *Staffin (047062) 202*

Staffin Caravan & Camp Site 3 caravans, sleeps 4-6, min let 2 nights, £40-£60, Easter-Oct, bus nearby, rail nearby, ferry 10 mls, airport 40 mls

Mr Alasdair Macleod, Staffin Caravan and Camping Site, Staffin, Isle of Skye, Inverness-shire
☎ *Staffin (047062) 213*

by STAFFIN Isle of Skye, Inverness-shire Map Ref. 3D8

COMMENDED

1 house, 1 pub rm, 2 bedrms, sleeps 4-5, £65-£95, Apr-Oct, bus ¾ ml, rail 48 mls, ferry 48 mls, airport 40 mls

Mrs MacLeod, Quiraing, Badicaul, Kyle of Lochalsh, Ross-shire
☎ *Kyle (0599) 4677*
Detached unit on shores of Loch Meatt, overlooking Hills of Gairloch. Staffin Bay 2 miles (3km).

STANLEY Perthshire Map Ref. 2C2

2 houses, 2 cottages, 1-2 pub rms, 2-5 bedrms, sleeps 4-11, £75-£200, Apr-Oct

Finlayson Hughes, Bank House, 82 Atholl Road, Pitlochry, Perthshire, PH16 5BL
☎ *Pitlochry (0796) 2512*

STENNESS Orkney Map Ref. 5B11

1 bungalow, 2 pub rms, 2 bedrms, sleeps 6, £70-£135, Apr-Oct, bus nearby, ferry 4 mls, airport 14 mls

Mrs A H Francis, 13 Allan Road, Killearn, Glasgow, G63 9QF
☎ *Killearn (0360) 50476*

1 house, 1 pub rm, 4 bedrms, sleeps 8, min let 2 weeks (high season), £85-£115, Mar-Jan, bus 2 mls, ferry 5 mls, airport 12 mls

🏛 ♿ E 🏠 ◎ ☐ ☐ ☐ ☐ ♣ ❄ P ⌛ ▥ † ♪ ⚡ ✕ 🛒 ⛷

Mrs V Pirie, Orakirk, Orphir, Orkney, KW17 2RE
☎ *Orphir (085681) 328*

Outbrecks Holiday Cottages 3 cottages, 1 pub rm, 2 bedrms, sleeps 6, £60-£110, Jan-Dec, bus ½ ml, ferry 3 mls, airport 14 mls

🏛 ♿ E 🏠 ◎ ▦ ☐ ◎ ☐ ☐ ☐ ✎ ♣ ❄ ☂ P ⌛ ⚑ ⊕ ♪ ⚓ ⚡ ↟ ✕ 🛒

Mrs Laidlaw, Outbrecks, Stenness, Orkney
☎ *Stromness (0856) 850860(eve/wknd)/850664*

STIRLING Map Ref. 2A4

1 house, 2 pub rms, 3 bedrms, sleeps 5, £80-£110, Jan-Dec, bus 700 yds, rail 600 yds

🏛 ♿ E ➰ ◎ ▦ ☐ ◎ ☐ ☐ ♣ ☺ P † ♪ ∪ ⚓ ✕ 🛒

Mrs S Mackenzie, 48 Barnton Street, Stirling, FK8 1NA
☎ *Stirling (0786) 61031*

University of Stirling
STIRLING FK9 4LA. Tel: (0786) 73171

The University's easily accessible, beautifully developed Campus, located by the centre point of Scotland, with good road and rail access from England and to the Highlands, Edinburgh and Glasgow, encourages the individual tourist and family to stay, to see and to enjoy a holiday.

Amenities include a small golf course, trout fishing, a shopping precinct and theatre/cinema. Self-cater, individual bed and breakfast and group stay bookings are all welcome in high summer.

up to
COMMENDED
♛

Airthrey Estate 10 chalet/log cabins, 115 flats, 1 pub rm, 2-9 bedrms, sleeps 2-9, min let 4 nights, £145-£230, Jun-Sep, bus nearby, rail 1 ½ mls, airport 25 mls

🏛 ♿ E ➰ ◎ ▦ ☐ ◎ ☐ ✎ ♣ ☺ ❄ P ⌛ † ● ⊕ 🎣 ⛳ ⚲ 🎿 ♪ ∪ ⚓ ↟ ✓
Ⓡ ✕ 🛒 🍴 ♫ Ⓣ

University of Stirling, Vacation Letting Off, Administration Bldg, Stirling, FK9 4LA
☎ *Stirling (0786) 73171 Telex 777759 STUNIVG*
In landscaped grounds with lake and trees. Choice of restaurant, shops, theatre on site. Conferences.

Allan Park Holiday Flats 2 flats, 1 pub rm, 2 bedrms, sleeps 3-4, £120-£170, Jan-Dec, bus nearby, rail nearby, airport 30 mls

🏛 ♿ E ➰ ◎ ☐ ◎ ☐ ☐ ♣ ☺ ❄ ⌛ 🎣 ⛳ ⚲ 🎿 ♪ ∪ ⚓ ↟ ⚱ ⚡ ✕ 🛒 Ⓣ

Mrs A Hay, 1 Lennox Avenue, Stirling
☎ *Stirling (0786) 74042*

VAT is shown at 15%: changes in this rate may affect prices.

281

Cornton Caravan & Camping Park 6 caravans, sleeps 6, min let 1 night, £74-£118, Jan-Dec, bus 300 yds, rail 1 ml, airport 30 mls

♿ ⌨ E 🏠 🖊 🎱 ⌀ 📺 ☏ 🖥 📷 ⚡ 🧺 ☉ 🐎 P 🐕 🛏 ⬛ 🏔 🎣 🛶 🔍 🎿 ⛵ ∪ ⛰ ▸ ✗ 🏂 (curling, skating in winter)

Mrs Peebles & Mrs Thom, Cornton Caravan & Camping Park, Stirling
☎ *Stirling (0786) 74503/62481/75504/71180*

---

1 flat, 2 pub rms, 2 bedrms, sleeps 4-5, min let weekend, £100-£150, Apr-Oct, bus ¼ ml, rail ¼ ml

♿ ⌨ E ✈ 🏠 🖥 🎱 ⌀ 📺 ☏ 🖥 📷 ⚡ 🧺 ✳ 🐎 P ⫽ 🛏 † 🎣 🛶 🔍 🎿 ⛵ ∪ ⛰ ▸ ✗ 🏂

Mrs A Macaulay, 11 Victoria Square, Stirling
☎ *Stirling (0786) 75545*

---

1 flat, 2 pub rms, 2 bedrms, sleeps 4, £50-£90, Jan-Dec, bus nearby, rail nearby

♿ ⌨ E ✈ 🏠 🖥 🎱 ⌀ 📺 ☏ 🖥 📷 🧺 ☉ P † 🎣 🛶 🔍 🎿 ⛵ ∪ ⛰ ▸ ⚓ ✗ 🏂 T

McAree Bros Ltd, 55 King Street, Stirling
☎ *Stirling (0786) 73967*

by STIRLING Map Ref. 2A4

2 cottages, 1 pub rm, 1 bedrm, sleeps 4-5, min let weekend, £75-£100, Jun-Sep, bus 1 ml, rail 4 mls

♿ ⌨ E ✈ 🏠 🎱 ⊚ 📺 ☏ 🧺 ✳ 🐎 P 🛏 ⬛ 🏔 🎣 🛶 ∪ ▸ ✗ 🏂 🔧

2 caravans, sleeps 8, min let weekend, £65-£80, Apr-Oct, bus 1 ml, rail 4 mls

♿ 🛏 E 🏠 🎱 🖥 ⊚ ⌀ 📺 ☏ 🐎 P † 🏔 🎣 🛶 ∪ ▸ ✗ 🏂 🔧

Mrs G A Graham, West Drip Farm, by Stirling, FK9 4UJ
☎ *Stirling (0786) 72523*

STOER Sutherland Map Ref. 3F4

3 chalet/log cabins, 1 pub rm, 2 bedrms, sleeps 4-6, £65-£110, Apr-Oct, bus 7 mls, rail 50 mls

♿ ⌨ E ✈ 🎱 ⊚ 📺 ☉ 🐎 P 🛏 ⬛ 🏔 🛶 ⛰ ⚓ 🏂 🔧

1 caravan, sleeps 4-6, £50-£65, May-Sep, bus 7 mls, rail 50 mls

♿ 🛏 ⌀ 🐎 P † 🏔 🛶 ⛰ ⚓ 🏂 🔧

Mrs G MacLeod, 171, Stoer, Stoer, Sutherland, IV27 4JE
☎ *Stoer (05715) 224*

---

1 house, 2 pub rms, 3 bedrms, sleeps 11, min let weekend, £80-£95, Jan-Dec

♿ ⌨ E ✈ 🎱 ⊚ 📺 ☏ 📷 🧺 ✳ 🐎 P ⬛ † 🛶 ⚓ 🔧 (hillwalking)

Mr & Mrs D A MacDonald, Bayhead, Finsbay, Isle of Harris, Western Isles, PA85 3JD
☎ *Leverburgh (085982) 282/(0859) 2339*

STOW, by Galashiels Selkirkshire Map Ref. 2E6

1 cottage, 1 pub rm, 2 bedrms, sleeps 4, min let weekend, £75-£95, Apr-Oct, bus nearby, rail 25 mls, airport 25 mls

♿ ⌨ E ✈ 🏠 🖥 🎱 ⊚ 📺 ☏ ☉ ✳ 🐎 P 🛏 † 🏔 🛶 ∪ ▸ ⫽ ✗ 🏂 T

Mrs J Jarvie, Windylaws Farm, Eddleston, Peebles-shire
☎ *Eddleston (07213) 223*

---

1 flat, 1 pub rm, 1 bedrm, sleeps 2-3, £55-£65, May-Oct, bus nearby

♿ ⌨ E ✈ 🏠 🖥 🎱 ⊚ 📺 ☏ 📷 ⚡ 🧺 ✳ 🛏 ⬛ † ✗ 🏂 T

Mrs P Jack, 1 Cotland Place, Stow, Midlothian
☎ *Stow (05783) 317*

Prices shown are for guidance only. Please send SAE with each enquiry.

STRACHAN, by Banchory Kincardineshire Map Ref. 4F11

1 cottage, 1 pub rm, 2 bedrms, sleeps 4, £80-£100, Jan-Dec

    ♿ ⓦ E ⇥ ⌀ ▦ ◉ ⬛ ✦ ⚓ ✳ ⛺ 🅿 †   ≷ ⛵ ⚲ ⏏ ⚓ ⛴ ↱ ⚃ ⚒

Mr E F Stewart, 6 Ben Close, Kidlington, Oxford
☎ *Kidlington (08675) 71938*

---

by STRAITON Ayrshire Map Ref. 1H8

Blairquhan Estate
Holiday Cottages
STRAITON · MAYBOLE

Six early 19th-century cottages and flats improved to high standards and comfort. Fishing available (included in tenancy) and the freedom of the beautiful 2,000-acre Estate in this charming part of Scotland. Houses sleep 4-8.

From £65-£131 (October-May). High Season (June-September £132-£199).

JAMES HUNTER BLAIR
BLAIRQUHAN ESTATE OFFICE
STRAITON, MAYBOLE
AYRSHIRE KA19 7LZ
Telephone: (065 57) 239

> AWAITING
> INSPECTION

3 houses, 1 flat, 2 cottages, 1 pub rm, 1-3 bedrms, sleeps 5-8, min let weekend (low season), £65-£199, Jan-Dec, bus 4 mls, rail 7 mls, airport 14 mls

♿ ⓦ E ⇥ ⌀ ◉ ⬛ ⚓ ⊙ ⛺ 🅿 ⛵ ▦   ⚃ △ ✗ ⚒

Mrs J Hay, Blairquhan Estate Office, Maybole, Ayrshire, KA19 7LZ
☎ *Straiton (06557) 239*

STRANRAER Wigtownshire Map Ref. 1F10

8 caravans, sleeps 6-8, min let weekend, £50-£125, Mar-Oct, bus nearby, rail 4 mls, airport 80 mls

♿ ⓦ E ⌂ ⌀ ⬛ ⦿ ⬛ ☎ ⬛ ◉ ✦ ⚓ ⊙ ⛺ 🅿 ⛵ ▦ ⛰ ⛵ ❀   ≷ ⚃ ∪ △ ⏏ ↱ ⚓
⚃ ✗ ⚒

Wig Bay Holiday Park, Loch Ryan, Stranraer, Wigtownshire, DG9 0PS
☎ *Kirkcolm (0776) 853233*

Intermessan Croft Caravan Park 5 caravans, sleeps 4-6, min let 1 night, £75-£100, Jan-Dec, bus nearby, ferry 1 ½ mls

♿ ⓦ E ⌂ ⌀ ☎ ⦿ ⚓ ⊙ ⛺ 🅿 ⛰ ❀   ⚲ ⚓ ⚃ ∪ △ ⏏ ↱ ✗ ⚒
Innermessan Croft Caravan Park, Stranraer, Wigtownshire, DG9 8QP
☎ *Stranraer (0776) 3346*

---

by STRANRAER Wigtownshire Map Ref. 1F10

Drumlochart Caravan Park 15 caravans, sleeps 6, min let weekend, £50-£140, Mar-Oct, bus 1 ½ mls, rail 5 mls, airport 58 mls

♿ ⓦ E ⌂ ⌀ ⬛ ⌀ ⬛ ☎ ⬛ ◉ ✦ ⚓ ⊙ ⛺ 🅿 ⛵ ▦ ⛰ ❀ ❀   ≷ ⚓ ⚃ ∪ △ ⏏ ↱ ⚓
⚃ ⚒ Ⓣ

Mr P R Manning, Drumlochart Caravan Park, Lochnaw, Stranraer, Wigtownshire, DG9 0RN
☎ *Leswalt (077687) 232*

STRATHCONON Ross-shire Map Ref. 3H8

COMMENDED
♛♛♛

5 chalet/log cabins, 1 pub rm, 1-2 bedrms, sleeps 5-7, min let long weekend (low season), from £68, mid Mar-Oct, bus nearby, rail 15 mls, airport 37 mls

Mr & Mrs S W Tough, East Lodge Hotel, Strathconon, by Muir-of-Ord, Ross-shire, IV6 7QQ

☎ *Strathconon (09977) 222*

'A' frame units set among trees on north bank of River Meig, above beautiful Strathconan Valley.

STRATHDON Aberdeenshire Map Ref. 4E10

up to
COMMENDED
♛♛♛

1 house, 2 cottages, 2 pub rms, 2-4 bedrms, sleeps 8, min let weekend (low season), £75-£130, Mar-Oct, bus 500 yds, rail 20 mls, airport 45 mls

Mrs E Ogg, Buchaam Holiday Properties, Buchaam Farm, Strathdon, Aberdeenshire, AB3 8TN

☎ *Strathdon (09752) 238*

Modernised farm units in rural setting. Fishing stretch on River Don and Deskry.

---

1 bungalow, 1 pub rm, 2 bedrms, sleeps 4-6, £70-£100, Apr-Oct, bus nearby, rail 45 mls, airport 40 mls

Mrs P Marsh, Bellabeg House, Strathdon, Aberdeenshire, AB3 8UL

☎ *Strathdon (09752) 229*

STRATHMIGLO Fife Map Ref. 2C3

1 flat, 1 pub rm, 3 bedrms, sleeps 6, £100-£200, Jan-Dec, bus nearby, rail 6 mls, airport 32 mls

Bruce MacManaway, West Bank, Strathmiglo, Fife

☎ *Strathmiglo (03376) 233*

STRATHPEFFER Ross-shire Map Ref. 4A8

1 caravan, sleeps 6, min let 1 night, £45-£50, Apr-Sep, bus 2 mls, rail 5 mls

Mrs G Aird, Redbank, Achterneed, Strathpeffer, Ross-shire, IV14 9AE

☎ *Strathpeffer (0997) 21312*

COMMENDED
♛♛♛

Cnocmor Lodge 3 chalet/log cabins, 1 pub rm, 3 bedrms, sleeps 5-6, £80-£200, Apr-Oct, bus 400 yds, rail 5 mls, airport 25 mls

Mr Brebner, Cnocmor Lodge, Strathpeffer, Ross-shire, IV14 9BN

☎ *Strathpeffer (0997) 21618*

Scandanavian units in young forest near village. Ideal for outdoor interests; birds, hill walks etc.

---

1 cottage, 1 pub rm, 2 bedrms, sleeps 4-6, £150-£175, Apr-Oct, bus 500 yds, rail 6 mls, airport 23 mls

Mrs J Cameron, White Lodge, Strathpeffer, Ross-shire

☎ *Strathpeffer (0997) 21730*

2 chalet/log cabins, 1 pub rm, 3 bedrms, sleeps 6, £84-£210, Apr-Oct

Mr H G Whittick, 414A Perth Road, Dundee, DD2 1JQ
☎ *Dundee (0382) 67746/(0997) 21740(summer)*

STRATHTAY Perthshire Map Ref. 2B1

1 flat, 4 cottages, 1-2 pub rms, 1-2 bedrms, sleeps 2-5, £75-£160, Apr-Oct

Finlayson Hughes, Bank House, 82 Atholl Road, Pitlochry, Perthshire, PH16 5BL
☎ *Pitlochry (0796) 2512*

---

1 cottage, 1 pub rm, 2 bedrms, sleeps 4, £70-£90, Mar-Oct, bus nearby, rail 9 mls

Mrs A S McGillivray, The Cottage, Ben Darroch, Strathtay, Perthshire, PH9 0PG
☎ *Strathtay (08874) 202*

---

2 cottages, 2 pub rms, 2 bedrms, sleeps 4-5, £80-£150, Jan-Dec, bus nearby, rail 9 mls

Mrs Laing, Auchanross, Strathtay, Perthshire
☎ *Strathtay (08874) 374*

---

up to
COMMENDED

2 cottages, 1-3 pub rms, 3-4 bedrms, sleeps 6-7, min let weekend, £86-£144, Jan-Dec, bus 300 yds, rail 9 mls

Holiday Lets, Blagdon Estate Office, Seaton Burn, Newcastle-upon-Tyne, NE13 6DE
☎ *Stannington (067089) 621*
Converted stone built dairy on private estate. Quiet location with excellent views of countryside.

---

1 cottage, 1 pub rm, 2 bedrms, sleeps 4-5, min let weekend, £90-£130, Jan-Dec, bus nearby, rail 10 mls

(bowling green)

Mrs E Liddle, Glenburn House, Grandtully, Aberfeldy, Perthshire
☎ *Strathtay (08874) 330*

STRATHYRE Perthshire Map Ref. 1H3

COMMENDED

Strathyre Forest Cabins 17 chalet/log cabins, 1 pub rm, 2 bedrms, sleeps 5, min let 3 nights, from £67, Dec-Oct, bus 1 ml, rail 19 mls, airport 40 mls

Forestry Commission, Forest Holidays, Dept SC1, 231 Corstorphine Rd, Edinburgh, EH12 7AT
☎ *031 334 0303/2576*
On shore of Loch Lubnaig close to Mountains of Strathyre. Local walking, fishing, sailing etc.

COMMENDED

2 chalet/log cabins, 1 pub rm, 2 bedrms, sleeps 6, min let weekend, £70-£190, Jan-Dec, bus 1 ¾ mls, rail 26 mls, airport 50 mls

Mrs M Mylne & Miss E Haydock, Stroneslaney, Strathyre, Perthshire, FK18 8NF
☎ *Strathyre (08774) 676*
Peaceful riverside setting. Ideal for walking or touring holiday.

VAT is shown at 15%: changes in this rate may affect prices.

285

1 chalet/log cabin, 1 pub rm, 2 bedrms, sleeps 4-6, min let weekend, £60-£160, Mar-Nov, bus nearby

Mrs Heather Dewar, Inverasdale, Paterson Street, Galashiels, Selkirkshire
☎ *Galashiels (0896) 3445*

COMMENDED

1 cottage, 1 bungalow, 1 pub rm, 2-3 bedrms, sleeps 2-8, min let 3 nights, £90-£300, Jan-Dec, bus 2 mls, rail 26 mls, airport 46 mls

Ian & Barbara Winter, Laggan Estate, Strathyre, Perthshire
☎ *Strathyre (08774) 236*
On private estate in Trossachs National Park; rich in history and wildlife. Meals service. Sports.

STRICHEN Aberdeenshire Map Ref. 4H8

1 caravan, sleeps 8, min let weekend, £40-£75, Apr-Oct, bus 3 mls, rail 40 mls, airport 40 mls

Mrs M Banks, Kersiehill Farm, Strichen, by Fraserburgh, Aberdeenshire
☎ *Memsie (03464) 372*

STROMNESS Orkney Map Ref. 5A11

2 cottages, 1 pub rm, 2-3 bedrms, sleeps 6-10, £50-£70, Jan-Dec, bus ½ ml, ferry 1 ¼ mls, airport 17 mls

Mrs E Reid, Howe Farm, Stromness, Orkney
☎ *Stromness (0856) 850302*

---

2 chalet/log cabins, 1 house, 1 pub rm, 2 bedrms, sleeps 6-7, £50-£90, Apr-Oct, bus 1 ½ mls, ferry 1 ½ mls, airport 16 mls

Mrs J Chalmers, Braehead Farm, Cairston Road, Stromness, Orkney
☎ *Stromness (0856) 850410*

---

1 caravan, sleeps 4, from £40, Jan-Dec, bus nearby, ferry ½ ml, airport 19 mls

Mrs V Sclater, Rothiesholm, Cairston Road, Stromness, Orkney, KW16 3JU
☎ *Stromness (0856) 850034*

---

1 caravan, sleeps 4-6, min let 3 nights, from £40, Jan-Dec, bus ½ ml, ferry 1 ml, airport 18 mls

D & I Sinclair, Milldam, Stromness, Orkney, KW16 3HT
☎ *Stromness (0856) 850432*

---

1 house, 3 pub rms, 5 bedrms, sleeps 10, £160-£230, Apr-Oct, bus ½ ml, rail 20 mls, ferry ½ ml, airport 22 mls

Mrs Traill Thomson, 116 Union Grove, Aberdeen, AB1 6SB
☎ *Aberdeen (0224) 587278*

1 cottage, 1 pub rm, 2 bedrms, sleeps 4, min let weekend, £30-£60, Jan-Dec, bus 1 ½ mls, ferry 1 ½ mls, airport 20 mls

Mainland, Springlands, Stromness, Orkney
☎ *Stromness (0856) 850452*

STRONTIAN Argyll Map Ref. 1E1

Seaview Grazings 14 chalet/log cabins, 1 pub rm, 2-3 bedrms, sleeps 4-6, min let weekend (low season), £120-£300, Jan-Dec, bus ¼ ml, rail 22 mls

Seaview Grazings (Strontian) Ltd, Strontian, Acharacle, Argyll, PH36 4HZ
☎ *Fort William (0397) 2496*
Scandanavian units overlooking Loch Sunart and mountains. Village nearby. Boating and fishing. **(See colour ad. 20 p. xxxvi)**

1 house, 1 pub rm, 2 bedrms, sleeps 4, from £100, Apr-Oct

Bell-Ingram, Durn, Isla Road, Perth, PH2 7HF
☎ *Perth (0738) 21121*

STRUAN Isle of Skye, Inverness-shire Map Ref. 3C9

2 caravans, sleeps 6, min let 1 night, £45-£50, Jan-Dec, bus 2 mls, rail 48 mls, ferry 45 mls, airport 38 mls

Mrs Morrison, 6 Ullinish, Struan, Isle of Skye, Inverness-shire
☎ *Struan (047072) 271*

1 house, 1 pub rm, 3 bedrms, sleeps 6, £110-£175, Apr-Oct, bus nearby, rail 40 mls, ferry 40 mls, airport 30 mls

Mr Charles Beaton, Totearder, Struan, Isle of Skye, Inverness-shire
☎ *Struan (047072) 229*

1 caravan, sleeps 6, min let weekend, £40-£60, Jan-Dec, bus nearby, rail 36 mls, ferry 36 mls, airport 34 mls

Mrs K A MacDonald, Oronsay, Struan, Isle of Skye, Inverness-shire
☎ *Struan (047072) 213*

1 caravan, sleeps 4, £35-£40, Mar-Oct, bus 1 ½ mls

Miss M A MacLeod, 4 Ullinish, Struan, Isle of Skye, Inverness-shire
☎ *Struan (047072) 202*

STRUY, by Beauly Inverness-shire Map Ref. 3H9

Culligran Cottages 4 chalet/log cabins, 1 cottage, 1-2 pub rms, 2-3 bedrms, sleeps 5-7, £69-£209, Apr-Oct, bus 11 mls, rail 13 mls, airport 27 mls
(bicycles for hire)

Frank & Juliet Spencer-Nairn, Culligran Cottages, Glen Strathfarrar, Struy, by Beauly, Inverness-shire, IV4 7JX
☎ *Struy (046376) 285*
In nature reserve with deer and sheep farm; guided tours. Practice golf course, cycle hire, fishing.

SULLOM Shetland Map Ref. 5F3

1 caravan, sleeps 4, min let weekend, £20-£30, Jan-Dec, bus nearby

Mrs N Peterson, Northerhouse, Sullom, Shetland
☎ *Brae (080622) 239*

SWINTON Berwickshire Map Ref. 2F6

1 cottage, 1 pub rm, 3 bedrms, sleeps 6-8, £100-£120, Jan-Dec, bus ½ ml, rail 15 mls, airport 60 mls

Mrs O Brewis, Little Swinton, Coldstream, Berwickshire, TD12 4HH
☎ *Swinton (089086) 280*

SYMBISTER Whalsay, Shetland Map Ref. 5G3

1 chalet/log cabin, 1 pub rm, 2 bedrms, sleeps 6, min let 1 night, £50-£80, Jan-Dec, ferry nearby, airport 5 mls

Mrs J Irvine, West Green, Symbister, Whalsay, Shetland
☎ *Symbister (08066) 284*

SYMINGTON Ayrshire Map Ref. 1H7

1 cottage, 1 pub rm, 1 bedrm, sleeps 2, £90-£160, Apr-Oct, bus nearby, rail 4 mls, airport 4 mls

(bowling)

Scottish Country Cottages, Suite 2d, Churchill Way, Bishopbriggs, Glasgow, G64 2RH
☎ *041 772 5920*

TAIN Ross-shire Map Ref. 4B7

Meikle Ferry Caravan & Camping Park 10 caravans, sleeps 4-8, min let 1 night, £80-£135, Jan-Dec, bus nearby, rail 2 mls

Mr Calum Beaton, Meikle Ferry Caravan Park, by Tain, Ross-shire, IV19 1JX
☎ *Tain (0862) 2292*

TALMINE Sutherland Map Ref. 4A3

1 house, 2 pub rms, 3 bedrms, sleeps 6, £80-£110, Jan-Dec, bus nearby, rail 42 mls, airport 75 mls

Mrs Mackay, Post Office, Talmine, Sutherland, IV27 4YP
☎ *Talmine (084756) 200*

TANKERNESS Orkney Map Ref. 5C11

2 houses, 1 pub rm, 1-4 bedrms, sleeps 2-12, min let weekend, £70-£200, Jan-Dec, bus 1 ml, ferry 20 mls, airport 2 mls

Mr J Malloch, Bolgatanga, Hillside Road, Stromness, Orkney, KW16 3AH
☎ *Stromness (0856) 850296/850332(office)*

Prices shown are for guidance only. Please send SAE with each enquiry.

TARBERT Argyll Map Ref. 1E5

1 flat, 2 cottages, 1-2 pub rms. 1-2 bedrms, sleeps 4-8, min let 2 nights, £110-£295, Jan-Dec, bus nearby, rail 50 mls, ferry 4 mls, airport 38 mls

(cycles for hire)

Mr Scott, Barmore Farm, Tarbert, Argyll
☎ *Tarbert (08802) 222*

---

1 cottage, 2 pub rms, 4 bedrms, sleeps 7, £100-£120, Jan-Dec, bus nearby

Ms Mayo, 51 Onslow Gardens, London, N10
☎ *01 444 3833/(0256) 882379*

---

1 Apartment, 1 pub rm, 1 bedrm, sleeps 2, min let 2 nights, £70-£90, Jan-Dec, bus nearby

Mrs Sandy Ferguson, 24 Willoughby Drive, Anniesland, Glasgow
☎ *041 959 6740*

by TARBERT Argyll Map Ref. 1E5

1 house, 5 cottages, 1 bungalow, 2-3 pub rms, 2-5 bedrms, sleeps 5-10, min let weekend, £70-£420, Jan-Dec, bus 7 mls

Mrs K Kerr, Dunmore Home Farm, Dunmore, by Tarbert, Loch Fyne, Argyll
☎ *Tarbert (08802) 642*
Selection of units. Some housed in converted steading with courtyard, others scattered over estate.

TARBOLTON Ayrshire Map Ref. 1H7

Middlemuir Caravan Park 5 caravans, sleeps 6-8, min let weekend (low season), £66-£150, Jan-Dec, bus ¼ ml, rail 6 mls, airport 4 mls

Middlemuir Caravan Park, Tarbolton, Ayrshire
☎ *Tarbolton (0292) 541647*

TARLAND Aberdeenshire Map Ref. 4E10

1 cottage, 1 pub rm, 3 bedrms, sleeps 5, £90-£110, Apr-Oct, bus 6 mls, rail 35 mls, airport 35 mls

Tillypronie Estate Office, St Nicholas House, 68 Station Road, Banchory, Kincardineshire
☎ *Banchory (03302) 4817*

---

1 house, 1 pub rm, 3 bedrms, sleeps 6, £70, Apr-Oct, bus 4 mls, rail 30 mls, airport 30 mls

Mr W Clark, Coldhome, Tarland, Aberdeenshire, AB3 4XQ
☎ *Tarland (033981) 320/508*

TAYINLOAN Argyll Map Ref. 1D6

1 caravan, sleeps 8, £60-£80, May-Sep

Mrs M MacDonald, Beachmenach, Tayinloan, Tarbert, Argyll
☎ *Tayinloan (05834) 225*

VAT is shown at 15%: changes in this rate may affect prices.

1 house, 2 cottages, 2-4 pub rms, 2-5 bedrms, sleeps 4-12, min let weekend, £70-£400, Apr-Oct, bus ¼ ml

♿ �🅦 E ➡ 🏠 🖊 📺 🛏 🅟 ◎ 🍽 🗄 🔲 ✂ 🔌 ☉ ❋ 🐴 🅿 ⛴ 🏢 ᐟ ᐟ 🐟 ⚓ △ ⚔ ↑ ✗ 🔔 🔥

12 caravans, sleeps 6-10, min let 1 night, £75-£170, Apr-Oct, bus ½ ml

♿ �🅦 🏠 📺 🖊 🛏 🔲 🗄 ✂ 🔌 ☉ 🐴 🅿 ⛴ 🏢 🔺 🌐 ᐟ ⚓ △ ⚔ ↑ ✗ 🔔 [D]

Point Sands Caravans, Point Sands, Tayinloan, Argyll, PA29 6XG

☎ *Tayinloan (05834) 263/275*

---

by TAYINLOAN Argyll Map Ref. 1D6

2 caravans, sleeps 4, max £30, Apr-Sep

♿ �🅦 🛏 🔌 🐴 † 🔺

Mrs M Henderson, Ballochroy, Tayinloan, by Tarbert, Argyll

☎ *Clachan (08804) 232*

TAYNUILT Argyll Map Ref. 1F2

COMMENDED
🏆 🏆 🏆

4 chalet/log cabins, 1 pub rm, 2 bedrms, sleeps 6, min let weekend, from £90, Jan-Dec, bus 1 ml, rail 1 ml

♿ �🅦 E 🏠 🖊 📺 🛏 🅟 ◎ 🗄 🔲 ✂ 🔌 ☉ ❋ 🐴 🅿 ⛴ 🏢 🔺 ᐟ ∪ △ ✗ 🔔 [T]

Olsen, Airdeny Chalets, Airdeny, Taynuilt, Argyll, PA35 1HY

☎ *Taynuilt (08662) 648*

Wooded units in peaceful rural setting, but close to village shops and Oban town.

---

1 house, 2 pub rms, 3 bedrms, sleeps 6, £60-£175, Jan-Dec, bus ½ ml, rail 1 ml, airport 75 mls

♿ �🅦 E ➡ 🖊 📺 ◎ 🗄 🔲 🔌 ☉ ❋ 🐴 🅟 ⛴ 🏢 † ᐟ ∪ △ ⚔ ✗ 🔔 🔥

Lady Gray, Airds Bay House, Taynuilt, Argyll, PA35 1JR

☎ *Taynuilt (08662) 232*

Crunachy Caravan Park 3 caravans, sleeps 4-6, min let 3 nights, from £50, Mar-Oct, bus nearby, rail 2 mls

♿ ⛖ 🅦 🏠 🖊 📺 ◎ 🌐 🔦 🗄 🔲 🔌 ☉ 🐴 🅟 ⛴ 🏢 ᛜ ᐟ ∪ △ ⚔ ✗ 🔔 [T]

Mr A Douglas, Crunachy Caravan Site, Bridge of Awe, Taynuilt, Argyll, PA35 1HT

☎ *Taynuilt (08662) 612*

---

2 cottages, 1-2 pub rms, 1-2 bedrms, sleeps 2-4, from £50, Jan-Dec, bus 400 yds, rail 500 yds, airport 3 mls

♿ ⛖ E ➡ 🖊 📺 ◎ 🗄 🔌 ☉ ❋ 🅟 ✗ 🔔

Mrs E Major, Fir Cottage, Ightham, Kent, TN15 9AR

☎ *Borough Green (0732) 883167*

AWAITING INSPECTION

1 chalet/log cabin, 9 flats, 1-2 pub rms, 1-3 bedrms, sleeps 1-8, min let 3 nights (low season), £75-£250, Jan-Dec, bus 1 ml, rail 1 ml, airport 8 mls

♿ ⛖ E ➡ 🏠 🖊 📺 🛏 ◎ 🔦 🗄 🔌 ☉ ❋ 🅟 ⛴ 🏢 † ᐟ ∪ △ ⚔ ↑ ✗ 🔔 [T]

Mr H M & Miss S J Grant, Lonan House, Taynuilt, Argyll, PA35 1HY

☎ *Taynuilt (08662) 253/219(guests)*

---

2 flats, 1 pub rm, 2 bedrms, sleeps 4, £50-£125, Mar-Oct, bus nearby, rail nearby, airport 7 mls

♿ ⛖ E ➡ 🖊 🛏 ◎ 🗄 🔲 🔌 ☉ 🐴 🅟 ᛜ ᐟ ∪ △ ⚔ ✗ 🔔

Mrs R Cameron, Nant Bank, Taynuilt, Argyll, PA35 1JH

☎ *Taynuilt (08662) 697*

Prices shown are for guidance only. Please send SAE with each enquiry.

1 flat, 1 pub rm, 2 bedrms, sleeps 5, £70-£130, Apr-Oct, bus 1 ml, rail 2 mls

Mrs S B H Thomson, Clach-ma-Nessaig, Taynuilt, Argyll
☎ Taynuilt (08662) 663

COMMENDED
♛♛♛

1 house, 3 flats, 6 cottages, 1-2 pub rms, 1-4 bedrms, sleeps 2-7, min let 1 night (low season), £85-£280, Jan-Dec, bus ¾ ml, rail ½ ml

Bonawe House Holiday Cottages, 18 Maxwell Place, Stirling, FK8 1JU
☎ Stirling (0786) 62519
Converted 18C country house set amidst parkland. About 1 ml(2 km) from shops.

2 flats, 2 pub rms, 2-3 bedrms, sleeps 2-7, £45-£150, Jan-Dec, bus 2 mls, rail 2 mls, airport 80 mls

Mrs R Campbell-Preston, Inverawe Fisheries, Taynuilt, Argyll
☎ Taynuilt (08662) 262

1 cottage, 1 pub rm, 2 bedrms, sleeps 4, £80-£150, Jan-Dec, bus 300 yds, rail 2 mls, airport 80 mls

Mrs Campbell-Gray, Fanans, by Taynuilt, Argyll, PA35 1HR
☎ Taynuilt (08662) 393

TAYPORT Fife Map Ref. 2D2

Tayport Caravan Park 2 caravans, sleeps 6-8, min let 3 nights, £65-£155, Apr-Oct, bus ¼ ml

Largo Leisure Parks Ltd, Rankeilour House, Cupar, Fife, KY15 5RG
☎ Letham (033781) 233

TAYVALLICH Argyll Map Ref. 1D4

2 caravans, sleeps 6-8, min let weekends (low season), £70-£90, Apr-Oct, bus 12 mls

Mr J Pease, Auchentanavil, Tayvallich, Argyll
☎ Tayvallich (05467) 241

1 house, 4 pub rms, 8 bedrms, sleeps 14, £200-£350, Apr-Oct, bus 5 mls, rail 40 mls, airport 80 mls

Scottish Highland Holiday Homes, Wester Altourie, Abriachan, Inverness, IV3 6LB
☎ Dochgarroch (046386) 247

TEANGUE, Sleat Isle of Skye, Inverness-shire Map Ref. 3E10

♛♛♛

2 bungalows, 1 pub rm, 2 bedrms, sleeps 4, £60-£140, Jan-Dec, bus nearby, rail 18 mls, ferry 5/18 mls, airport 15 mls

Mr & Mrs G Abernethy, Toravaig House Hotel, Knock Bay, Sleat, Isle of Skye, Inverness-shire, IV44 8RJ
☎ Isle Ornsay (04713) 231

---

1 house, 1 pub rm, 2 bedrms, sleeps 4-6, £70-£90, Apr-Oct

♿ ⓦ E 🛏 🏠 🖥 ◎ 🗄 🗑 ⚡ 🧺 ☉ 🐎 🅿 ⛵ 🎵 ∪ ⛰ ⚓ ✈ ⚓ ✕ 🧰 🔥 Ⓣ

Mr N Robertson, Innes Mara, 2 Teangue, Sleat, Isle of Skye, Inverness-shire
☎ *Isle Ornsay (04713) 209/313*

TEVIOTHEAD Roxburghshire Map Ref. 2D8

1 cottage, 1 pub rm, 3 bedrms, sleeps 6, £60-£170, Jan-Dec, bus 4 mls, rail 35 mls, airport 40 mls

♿ ⓦ E 🛏 🍴 🖥 🖥 ◎ ◎ 🗄 🗑 🧺 ☉ ❄ 🐎 🅿 🧺 ⛵ 🏠 † 🎵 ∪ ✈ 🧰 Ⓣ

Mr Salvesen, Spylaw, Kelso, Roxburghshire, TD5 8DY
☎ *Kelso (0573) 24798*

THORNHILL Perthshire Map Ref. 2A4

Mains Farm Camp Site 2 caravans, sleeps 6, min let long weekend, £45-£70, Apr-Oct, bus nearby, rail 9 mls, airport 35 mls

♿ E 🍴 🗄 ☉ 🐎 🅿 † 🏠 🎣 🎿 🎵 ∪ ⛰ ✈ ✕ 🧰 🔥

Mr George Steedman, Mains Farm, Thornhill, Perthshire, FK8 3QB
☎ *Thornhill (078685) 605*

---

by THORNHILL Dumfriesshire Map Ref. 2B8

2 cottages, 1-2 pub rms, 2-3 bedrms, sleeps 4-6, £95-£155, Jan-Dec

♿ ⓦ E 🛏 🍴 🖥 🖥 ◎ 🗄 📞 🗑 ☉ ❄ 🐎 🅿 ⛵ 🏠 🎵 ✈ ✕ 🧰

Mrs P Kennedy, Holmhill, Thornhill, Dumfriesshire, DG3 4AB
☎ *Thornhill (Dumf) (0848) 30504*

THURSO Caithness Map Ref. 4C3

Thurso Municipal Site 8 caravans, sleeps 4-8, min let 1 night, £45-£95, May-Sep, bus ¾ ml, rail ¼ ml

♿ ⓦ 🏠 🍴 🧺 🐎 🅿 † 🏠 🔍 ✕ 🧰

Mr J Campbell, 15 Shore Street, Thurso, Caithness
☎ *Thurso (0847) 63524*

TIGHNABRUAICH Argyll Map Ref. 1F5

1 house, 1 pub rm, 3 bedrms, sleeps 6, £60-£160, Jan-Dec, bus 1 ml, rail 30 mls, airport 50 mls

♿ ⓦ E 🛏 🍴 🖥 🖥 ◎ 🗄 🗑 ⚡ 🧺 ❄ 🐎 🅿 ⛵ 🏠 † 🎵 ∪ ⛰ ⚓ ✕ 🧰

Mrs J Thomson, Ravenswood, Tighnabruaich, Argyll, PA21 2EE
☎ *Tighnabruaich (0700) 811207*
Modern detached storey unit. Open plan kitchen/lounge. Elevated site overlooks Kyles of Bute.

1 part house, 1 pub rm, 2 bedrms, sleeps 4, £50-£90, Apr-Oct

♿ ⓦ E 🛏 🍴 ◎ 🗄 🗑 ⚡ 🧺 ☉ ❄ 🅿 ⛵ † 🔍 🎵 ⛰ ⚓ ✕ 🧰

Mrs Avril Gordon, 4 Grant Avenue, Edinburgh, EH13 0DS
☎ *031 441 3373*

TIRORAN Isle of Mull, Argyll Map Ref. 1C2

1 cottage, 1 bungalow, 1 pub rm, 1-2 bedrms, sleeps 2-6, £75-£150, Mar-Oct, bus 5 mls

♿ ⓦ E 🛏 🍴 🧺 ◎ 🗑 ⚡ 🧺 ☉ ❄ 🐎 🅿 ⛵ 🏠 🔍 🎵 ∪ ⛰ Ⓡ

Wing Commander & Mrs R S Blockey, Tiroran House, Tiroran, Isle of Mull, Argyll
☎ *Tiroran (06815) 232*
Beautiful quiet location overlooking loch. In grounds of Tiroran House Hotel.

Prices shown are for guidance only. Please send SAE with each enquiry.

TOBERMORY Isle of Mull, Argyll Map Ref. 1C1

GLENGORM CASTLE
by Tobermory, Isle of Mull

Very comfortable flats in Castle and four cottages on beautiful 5,000-acre estate. Spectacular setting overlooking Atlantic Ocean. Free bank fishing on three well-stocked lochs—boats available. Bird-rich area; lovely wild flowers; red deer; golf; boat trips to Staffa, etc.

Brochure available · Telephone 0668-2321

---

up to
COMMENDED

2 flats, 5 cottages, 1-2 pub rms, 2-4 bedrms, sleeps 4-8, £100-£190, Mar-Nov, bus 4 mls, ferry 25 mls

J R E Nelson, Glengorm Castle, by Tobermory, Isle of Mull, Argyll
☎ Tobermory (0688) 2321
On 7000 acre farming estate, 4 miles/ 6km from village. Fishing, beaches, walks etc. Farm shop.

---

2 bungalows, 1 pub rm, 3-4 bedrms, sleeps 6-8, min let weekend, £50-£150, Jan-Dec, bus ½ ml, ferry 20 mls

Anderson & Sims, 59 Church Road, Epsom, Surrey
☎ Epsom (03727) 28525

COMMENDED

Heanish 10 chalet/log cabins, 1 pub rm, 2 bedrms, sleeps 6, £65-£210, Jan-Dec, bus ½ ml, rail 30 mls, ferry 22 mls, airport 100 mls

Normand Enterprises, Heanish, Tobermory, Isle of Mull, Argyll, PA75 6PP
☎ Tobermory (0688) 2097
Semi detached units connected by double carport. Near sea, shops, golf course, tennis. Owner on site.

---

5 chalet/log cabins, 2 flats, 1 cottage, 4 bothies, 1 pub rm, 1-3 bedrms, sleeps 14, min let 1 night, £25-£250, Jan-Dec, bus 400 yds, ferry 600 yds

(wildlife safaris)

2 caravans, sleeps 2-4, min let 1 night, £25-£85, Jan-Dec, bus 400 yds, ferry 600 yds

(wildlife safaris)

David and Hilarie Burnett, Ach-na-Craoibh, Tobermory, Isle of Mull, Argyll, PA75 6PS
☎ Tobermory (0688) 2301

---

1 chalet/log cabin, 1 pub rm, 4 bedrms, sleeps 8, £100-£120, Apr-Oct, bus ½ ml

Mrs T Brooke, 20 Manor Road, Glasgow, G12
☎ 041 954 8719

---

1 bunk house, 1 pub rm, 3 bedrms, sleeps 12, min let 1 night, £4 per person/night, Jan-Dec, bus nearby, ferry nearby

Mrs King, The Haven, Back Brae Restaurant, Tobermory, Isle of Mull, Argyll
☎ Tobermory (0688) 2422

VAT is shown at 15%: changes in this rate may affect prices.

293

| AWAITING INSPECTION | 1 flat, 1 pub rm, 3 bedrms, sleeps 5, £80-£160, Mar-Nov, bus 500 yds, rail 30 mls, ferry 21 mls |

♿♿E ♿ ♿ ♿ ♿ ♿ ♿ ♿ ♿ ♿ ♿ ♿ ♿ ♿ ♿ † ♿ ♿ ♿ ♿ ♿ ♿ ♿ ♿

Mrs J E Smithson, 33 Buchanan Avenue, Walsall, West Midlands, WS4 2ER
☎ *Walsall (0922) 22502*

TOMATIN Inverness-shire Map Ref. 4B9

1 cottage, 1 pub rm, 2 bedrms, sleeps 4-6, from £65, Apr-Nov, bus 1 ml, rail 8 mls, airport 20 mls

♿♿E ♿ ♿ ♿ ♿ ♿ ♿ ♿ ♿ ♿ ♿ ♿ ♿ ♿ † ♿ ♿ ♿ ♿ ♿ ♿ ♿ ♿ ♿ ♿ ♿ ♿

Mrs J A Glynne-Percy, Tomatin House, Tomatin, Inverness-shire, IV13 7XX
☎ *Tomatin (08082) 210*

| APPROVED ♛♛ | 2 cottages, 1-2 pub rms, 2-3 bedrms, sleeps 4-5, £58-£81, Jun-Oct, bus 2 mls, rail 15 mls, airport 20 mls |

♿♿E ♿ ♿ ♿ ♿ ♿ ♿ ♿ ♿ ♿ ♿ ♿ ♿ † ♿ ♿ ♿

Mrs P H MacKintosh-Grant, Balvraid Lodge, Tomatin, Inverness-shire, IV13 7XY
☎ *Tomatin (08082) 204*
Converted farm cottages amidst magnificent scenery in quiet location. Walking, wildlife etc.

TOMICH Inverness-shire Map Ref. 4A9

1 cottage, 2 pub rms, 2 bedrms, sleeps 4, £70-£95, Apr-Oct, bus 3 mls, rail 30 mls, airport 36 mls

♿♿E ♿ ♿ ♿ ♿ ♿ ♿ ♿ ♿ ♿ ♿ ♿ ♿ ♿ ♿ ♿ † ♿ ♿ ♿ ♿

Mrs M A Murray, The Old Brewery, Tomich, by Beauly, Inverness-shire, IV4 7LY
☎ *Cannich (04565) 280*

Guisachan Farm Chalets 2 chalet/log cabins, 1 cottage, 1 pub rm, 2-3 bedrms, sleeps 4-8, min let weekend (low season), £100-£220, Mar-Oct, bus nearby, rail 32 mls, airport 38 mls

♿♿E ♿

Mrs S J Fraser, Guisachan Farm, Tomich, by Beauly, Inverness-shire, IV4 7LY
☎ *Cannich (04565) 332*

TOMINTOUL Banffshire Map Ref. 4D10

1 cottage, 1 pub rm, 2 bedrms, sleeps 4, £120-£140, May-Sep

♿♿E ♿ ♿ ♿ ♿ ♿ ♿ ♿ ♿ ♿ ♿ ♿ ♿ ♿ † ♿ ♿ ♿ ♿ ♿ ♿

Mrs M Winton, Balmenach Distillery, Granton-on-Spey, Moray, PH26 3PF
☎ *Granton-on-Spey (0479) 2569*

---

by TOMINTOUL Banffshire Map Ref. 4D10

1 house, 2 pub rms, 5 bedrms, sleeps 10, min let weekend, £70-£120, Jan-Dec, bus 4 mls, rail 30 mls

♿E ♿ ♿ ♿ ♿ ♿ ♿ ♿ ♿ ♿ ♿ † ♿ ♿ ♿ ♿ ♿ ♿

Mrs Grant, Badnafrave, Tomintoul, Ballindalloch, Banffshire, AB3 9ES
☎ *Tomintoul (08074) 268*

---

1 caravan, sleeps 4-6, max £50, Jun-Oct, rail 30 mls

♿♿E ♿ ♿ ♿ ♿ ♿ ♿ ♿ ♿ † ♿ ♿ ♿ ♿ [T]

Mrs McArthur, Mains of Inverourie, Tomintoul, Ballindalloch, Banffshire, AB3 9HP
☎ *Glenlivet (08073) 398*

Prices shown are for guidance only. Please send SAE with each enquiry.

2 cottages, 1-2 pub rms, 3-4 bedrms, sleeps 6-7, £95-£170, Apr-Oct

Mr A N Donaldson, The Bower, Kilbarchan, Renfrewshire, PA10 2PD
☎ *Lochwinnoch (0505) 842555*

TONGUE Sutherland Map Ref. 4A3

1 cottage, 1 pub rm, 2 bedrms, sleeps 3-4, £63-£89, Mar-Oct

Sutherland Estates Office, Duke Street, Golspie, Sutherland, KW10 6RR
☎ *Golspie (04083) 3268*

1 house, 2 pub rms, 2 bedrms, sleeps 5-7, £85-£100, Apr-Oct

Mrs A Mackay, Larch Villa, St John's Road, Annan, Dumfriesshire, DG12 6AW
☎ *Annan (04612) 2911*

2 caravans, sleeps 6, min let 1 night, from £40, Jan-Dec, bus nearby, rail 44 mls

Macdonald, 117 Rhitongue, Tongue, by Lairg, Sutherland, IV27 4XW
☎ *Tongue (084755) 297*

TORNESS, by Dores Inverness-shire Map Ref. 4A9

1 cottage, 2 pub rms, 2 bedrms, sleeps 5, £45-£90, Apr-Oct, bus ½ ml, rail 14 mls

Mrs J H Macpherson, Abersky, Torness, Inverness-shire, IV1 2UD
☎ *Dores (046375) 252*

TORRIDON Ross-shire Map Ref. 3F8

2 houses, 1-3 pub rms, 2-3 bedrms, sleeps 4-7, from £75, Jan-Dec, bus nearby

1 caravan, sleeps 5, min let weekend, from £65, Apr-Oct, bus nearby

Annat Lodge, Torridon, Achnasheen, Ross-shire, IV22 2EW
☎ *Torridon (044587) 200*

1 bungalow, 2 pub rms, 3 bedrms, sleeps 5, £95-£160, Jan-Dec, bus nearby, rail 25 mls, airport 70 mls

Revd A M Roff & Mrs C E Roff, The Rectory, Allendale, Hexham, Northumberland
☎ *Allendale (043483) 336*

TOWARD Argyll Map Ref. 1F5

1 flat, 1 pub rm, 1 bedrm, sleeps 4, £35-£95, Jan-Dec, ferry 6 ½ mls

Mrs M Elliott, Tossa, Toward Point, by Dunoon, Argyll
☎ *Toward (036987) 327/365(home)*

TRESTA Shetland Map Ref. 5F4

1 flat, 1 pub rm, 2 bedrms, sleeps 4, min let 1 night, £30-£60, Jan-Dec, bus nearby

J Abernethy, Bayview, Tresta, Bixter, Shetland
☎ *Bixter (059581) 398*

TROON Ayrshire Map Ref. 1G7

1 flat, 2 pub rms, 1 bedrm, sleeps 4, min let weekend, £40-£90, Jan-Dec, bus nearby, rail nearby, airport 2 mls

  🚶 📶 E 🏠 ⬛ 🛋 ⌀ 🗄 ⬛ ⊙ 🐴 🅿 †   ⚲ ⤵ ∪ △ ⚓ ↗ ✗ 🧺

Mrs Mclean, The Borgie, 34 Greenlees Road, Cambuslang, Glasgow
☎ *041 641 1903*

---

1 flat, 1 pub rm, 1 bedrm, sleeps 5, from £75, Jan-Dec, bus nearby, rail ½ ml, airport 4 mls

  🚶 📶 E 🏠 ⬛ ⬛ 🛋 ◎ 🗄 ⬛ ⚡ ⬛ ⊙ ❄ 🅿 🐎 ▥ ➡ †   ⚲ ⤵ ∪ △ ⚓ ↗ ✗ 🧺

K & G Franklin, 13 Titchfield Road, Troon, Ayrshire, KA10 6AN
☎ *Troon (0292) 314228*

TUMMEL BRIDGE Perthshire Map Ref. 2A1

Tummel Valley Holiday Park 15 chalet/log cabins, 1 pub rm, 2 bedrms, sleeps 4-6, min let weekend, £115-£325, Mar-Oct, rail 12 mls

  🚶 📶 E ➡ ⬛ ⬛ 🛋 ◎ 🗄 ⬛ ⚡ ⬛ ⊙ 🅿 🐎 ▥ ⛰ ⚓ ✪   🎣 ⤵ ↗ Ⓡ 🧺 ♥ ♫ Ⓣ

75 caravans, sleeps 4-7, min let weekend, £69-£200, Apr-Oct, rail 12 mls

  🚶 📶 E 🏠 ⬛ 🛋 ⌀ 🗄 📞 ⬛ ◎ ⚡ ⬛ ⊙ 🐴 🅿 🐎 ▥ ⛰ ⚓ ✪   🎣 ⤵ ↗ Ⓣ Ⓓ

Hoseasons Holidays, Sunway House, Lowestoft, Suffolk, NR32 3LT
☎ *Lowestoft (0502) 62292*

Holiday park amidst wood and river. Shop, bar, restaurant on site. Live night entertainment in season.

---

1 house, 2 pub rms, 2 bedrms, sleeps 6, £90-£160, Apr-Oct, bus 300 yds, rail 12 mls

  🚶 📶 E 🏠 ⬛ ⬛ 🛋 ◎ 🗄 ⬛ ⬛ ⊙ ❄ 🐴 🅿 🐎 ▥ † ⛰   ⤵ △ ✗ 🧺

1 caravan, sleeps 6, £60-£75, May-Sep, bus 300 yds, rail 12 mls

  🚶 📶 E 🏠 ⬛ 🛋 ⌀ 🗄 ❄ 🐴 🅿 🐎 ▥ † ⛰   ⤵ △ ✗ 🧺

Mrs Pumford, 16 Hepburn Gardens, St Andrews, Fife
☎ *St Andrews (0334) 74673*

Modern purpose built house in own secluded wood. Easy access to village.

---

1 flat, 1 pub rm, 1 bedrm, sleeps 2, min let weekend, £100-£120, Jan-Dec, bus nearby

  🚶 📶 E ➡ ⬛ ⬛ 🛋 ◎ 🗄 ⬛ ⚡ ⬛ ⊙ 🐴 🅿 🐎 ▥ ➡ †   ⤵ △ ✗ 🧺 Ⓣ

Mrs S McKenzie, Bohally, Tummel Bridge, Perthshire
☎ *Tummel Bridge (08824) 253*

TURNBERRY Ayrshire Map Ref. 1G8

AWAITING INSPECTION

2 cottages, 1 pub rm, 2 bedrms, sleeps 6, £70-£135, Apr-Oct, bus nearby, rail 4 mls, airport 20 mls

  🚶 📶 E ➡ ⌀ ◎ 🗄 ⬛ ❄ 🐴 🅿 🐎 ▥   🎣 ⚲ ⤵ ∪ △ ↗ 🧺 🔭

Miss Crawford, Fairlight, Turnberry, Ayrshire
☎ *Turnberry (0655) 31331*

TURRIFF Aberdeenshire Map Ref. 4F8

1 house, 2 pub rms, 3 bedrms, sleeps 6-8, min let weekend, £45-£90, Apr-Oct, bus 8 mls, rail 28 mls, airport 41 mls

  🚶 📶 E ➡ ⌀ ◎ 🗄 ⬛ ⬛ ❄ 🐴 🅿 🐎 ▥ ➡ † ⛰   ⤵ ∪ △ ⚓ ↗ ✗ 🧺 🔭

Mrs Birnie, Cotwells, Fisherie, Turriff, Aberdeenshire, AB5 7SW
☎ *King Edward (08885) 253*

11 cottages, 1 pub rm, 3-4 bedrms, sleeps 6-8, min let weekend, £50-£180, Jan-Dec, bus 3 mls, rail 35 mls, airport 35 mls

Charles Barron Esq, East Side Lodge, Forglen Estate, Turriff, Aberdeenshire
☎ *Turriff (0888) 62918(eve)*

TWATT, Bixter Shetland Map Ref. 5F4

Kirkhouse Chalets 2 chalet/log cabins, 1 pub rm, 2 bedrms, sleeps 4, min let weekend, £58-£115, Jan-Dec, bus ¼ ml, ferry 20 mls, airport 15 mls

Mr P Tulloch, Kirkhouse Chalets, Kirkhouse, Bixter, Shetland
☎ *Bixter (059581) 320/404*

TWYNHOLM Kirkcudbrightshire Map Ref. 2A10

1 flat, 1 pub rm, 1 bedrm, sleeps 5, from £58, Apr-Sep, bus ½ ml, rail 27 mls, airport 75 mls

Mrs Jean W Clark, Valleyfield Farm, Kirkcudbright, DG6 4NH
☎ *Twynholm (05576) 213*

TYNDRUM Perthshire Map Ref. 1G2

Pine Trees Caravan Park 4 caravans, sleeps 4-8, £91-£99, Jan-Oct, bus ¼ ml, rail 500 yds, airport 50 mls

Mr & Mrs L Music, Pine Trees Caravan Park, Tyndrum, Perthshire, FK20 8RY
☎ *Tyndrum (08384) 243*

---

1 cottage, 1 pub rm, 2 bedrms, sleeps 4-5, from £70, Mar-Oct, bus nearby, rail ½ ml, airport 57 mls

Mrs M Brodie, The Bungalow, Tyndrum, Perthshire, FK20 8SA
☎ *Tyndrum (08384) 275*

---

1 bungalow, 1 pub rm, 2 bedrms, sleeps 4-6, £80-£180, Apr-Oct, bus nearby, rail 1 ml

Mrs G G Browning, 19 Kew Terrace, Glasgow, G12 0TE
☎ *041 334 6205*

Pine Trees Caravan Park 1 caravan, sleeps 6, £91-£99, Jan-Oct, bus 500 yds, rail 500 yds, airport 50 mls

(Climbing)
Mr Alan Fraser, 60 Causewayhead Road, Stirling
☎ *Stirling (0786) 72070*

by UDNY Aberdeenshire Map Ref. 4G9

1 house, 2 flats, 1 pub rm, 2-3 bedrms, sleeps 4-6, £253-£460, Jan-Dec, bus ¼ ml, rail 10 mls, airport 10 mls

Udny & Dudwick Estate Office, The Stables, Udny Castle, Udny Green, Ellon, Aberdeenshire
☎ *Udny (06513) 2428/Newburgh (03586) 297*

VAT is shown at 15%: changes in this rate may affect prices.

UIG Isle of Lewis, Western Isles Map Ref. 3B5

1 house, 2 pub rms, 5 bedrms, sleeps 1-8, max £100, Jan-Dec, bus nearby, ferry 31 mls, airport 33 mls

Mrs MacLeod, 6 Westfield Terrace, Aberdeen
☎ *Aberdeen (0224) 641614*
Set in splendid isolation overlooking Uig Bay, on the west coast of Lewis.

UIG Isle of Skye, Inverness-shire Map Ref. 3D8

1 caravan, sleeps 4, £70, Apr-Oct, bus nearby, ferry nearby

Mrs A Devy, Braeholm, Pier Road, Uig, Isle of Skye, Inverness-shire
☎ *Uig (047042) 396*

UIGINISH, by Dunvegan Isle of Skye, Inverness-shire Map Ref. 3C9

1 self catering hotel, 2 pub rms, 9-10 bedrms, sleeps 23, min let 1 night, £42-£56 (per person), Apr-Nov, bus 3 mls, rail 57 mls, ferry 56 mls, airport 50 mls

B & J Miller, Uiginish Lodge Self Catering Hotel, Uiginish, by Dunvegan, Isle of Skye, Inverness-shire
☎ *Dunvegan (047022) 445*

ULLAPOOL Ross-shire Map Ref. 3G6

Leckmelm Holiday Cottages
ULLAPOOL · ROSS-SHIRE *Telephone: 0854 2471*

The Leckmelm Holiday Cottages and Chalets are situated on the 7,000-acre Leckmelm estate, 3½ miles from Ullapool. The cottages and chalets are in rural surroundings of fields, woods and heather hills with magnificent views of Loch Broom, The Summer Isles and The Atlantic beyond. Sleeping 2-5, all are well equipped and extremely comfortable.

6 chalet/log cabins, 1 bungalow, 1 pub rm, 1-3 bedrms, sleeps 2-5, min let 3 nights, £60-£195, Jan-Dec, bus 3½ mls, rail 30 mls, airport 60 mls

Leckmelm Holiday Cottages, Lochbroom, Ullapool, Ross-shire
☎ *Ullapool (0854) 2471*
Compact timber units grouped on hillside above road overlooking Loch Broom.

Ardmair Point Caravan Site 1 chalet/log cabin, 1 pub rm, 2 bedrms, sleeps 2-6, min let 3 nights, £100-£175, Jan-Dec, bus nearby, rail 35 mls, airport 60 mls

2 caravans, sleeps 6, £70-£125, Mar-Oct, bus nearby, rail 30 mls, airport 60 mls

Peter J Fraser, Proprietor, Ardmair Point Caravan Site & Boat Centre, Ullapool, Ross-shire, IV26 2TN
☎ *Ullapool (0854) 2054*
Well designed and constructed of timber. Lochside site gives superb views of coast and hills.

Prices shown are for guidance only. Please send SAE with each enquiry.

1 cottage, 2 pub rms, 2 bedrms, sleeps 4-5, £70-£85, May-Oct, bus ¼ ml, rail 32 mls, airport 65 mls

  🖢 ᴡᴄ E ⛟ ⌀ ◎ ⬜ ❄ 🐴 🅿 ☕ † 🎣 ∪ ⚶ ⚡ ✕ 🥾

G B N Creswick, Egford House, Frome, Somerset, BA11 3JP
☎ *Frome (0373) 62794*

---

1 caravan, sleeps 4, max £50, Apr-Oct

  🖢 ᴡᴄ E ⌀ ⊘ 🐴 🅿 † ⌂ 🔥

Mrs K Stewart, 58 Rhue, Ullapool, Ross-shire, IV26 2TJ
☎ *Ullapool (0854) 2435*

---

1 cottage, 1 pub rm, 2 bedrms, sleeps 4, from £75, Apr-Oct, bus 1 ½ mls, rail 32 mls, airport 85 mls

  🖢 ᴡᴄ E ⛟ ⌀ ◎ ⬜ ⬛ ❄ 🅿 † ⚲ 🎣 ∪ ⚡ ✕ 🥾

Mrs Margaret MacLeod, Toscaig, Morefield, Ullapool, Ross-shire, IV26 2TH
☎ *Ullapool (0854) 2089*

---

1 house, 2 pub rms, 4 bedrms, sleeps 10, £120-£150, Jan-Dec, bus 500 yds

  🖢 ᴡᴄ E ⛟ ⌐ ⌀ ⬛ ◎ ⬜ ▣ ⬛ ❄ 🅿 ▦ † 🎣 ∪ ⚶ ⚡ ✕ 🥾

Mrs Joan C M MacNab, 13 Upper Bourtree Dr, Burnside, Rutherglen, Glasgow, G73 4EJ
☎ *041 634 1681*

---

1 cottage, 1 pub rm, 2 bedrms, sleeps 6, £65-£85, Apr-Oct, bus nearby, rail 50 mls, airport 50 mls

  🖢 ᴡᴄ E ⛟ ⌀ ⬛ ◎ ⬜ ⬜ ⬛ ⊙ ❄ 🅿 † 🎣 ∪ ⚶ ⚡ ✕ 🥾

Mr G MacDonald, Rosedale, Muir-of-Ord, Ross-shire
☎ *Muir-of-Ord (0463) 870281*

---

1 bungalow, 2 pub rms, 4 bedrms, sleeps 8, £100-£220, Apr-Dec, bus ¼ ml, rail 32 mls, airport 70 mls

  🖢 ᴡᴄ E ⛟ ⌀ ⬛ ◎ ⬜ ☎ ◙ ⊘ ⬛ 🐴 🅿 ☕ ▦ † ⌂ ⚲ 🎣 ∪ ⚶ ⚡ ✕ 🥾

Lady Troughton, Woolleys, Hambleden, Henley-on-Thames, Oxon
☎ *Henley-on-Thames (0491) 571244*

---

1 chalet/log cabin, 1 pub rm, 3 bedrms, sleeps 6, £90-£160, Jan-Dec, bus 1 ml, rail 30 mls, airport 60 mls

  🖢 ᴡᴄ E ⌐ ⌀ ⬛ ⬛ ◎ ⬜ ⬜ ⬛ ⊙ ❄ 🐴 🅿 ☕ ▦ ⛟ † 🛥 ⚲ 🎣 ∪ ⚶ ⚡ ✕ 🥾
🔥

Mrs M MacLennan, 17 Braes, Ullapool, Ross-shire
☎ *Ullapool (0854) 2272*

---

5 chalet/log cabins, 1 pub rm, 3 bedrms, sleeps 6, £50-£155, Apr-Oct, bus nearby, rail 30 mls, airport 70 mls

  🖢 ᴡᴄ E ⛟ ⌀ ⬛ ⬛ ◎ ⬜ ⬜ 🐴 🅿 ☕ ⬛ ⚲ 🎣 ∪ ⚶ ⚡ ⚡ 🥾 Ⓣ

5 caravans, sleeps 6, min let nightly (by arrangement), £50-£125, Apr-Oct, bus nearby, rail 32 mls, ferry 3 mls, airport 70 mls

  🖢 ᴡᴄ E ⌐ ⌀ ⬛ ⊘ ◎ ☎ ⬜ 🐴 🅿 ⚲ 🎣 ∪ ⚶ ⚡ ⁄ ⚡ 🥾 Ⓣ

Mrs Peukert, Far Isles Restaurant, North Road, Ullapool, Ross-shire
☎ *Ullapool (0854) 2385*

by ULLAPOOL Ross-shire Map Ref. 3G6

COMMENDED

1 bungalow, 1 pub rm, 2 bedrms, sleeps 6, £70-£110, Apr-Oct, bus 3 mls, rail 34 mls, airport 66 mls

Miss C M MacLeod, 13 Mansfield Estate, Tain, Ross-shire, IV19 1JN
☎ Tain (0862) 2178(after 6pm, no Sun enq)
Modern, detached unit in crofting community. 3 miles (5km) from Ullapool. Views of loch and isles.

URGHA Isle of Harris, Western Isles Map Ref. 3C6

1 bungalow, 1 pub rm, 3 bedrms, sleeps 6, £60-£80, May-Oct, rail nearby, ferry 1 ml, airport 40 mls

Donald MacKinnon, 5 Urgha, by Tarbert, Isle of Harris, Western Isles
☎ Harris (0859) 2114

WALKERBURN Peeblesshire Map Ref. 2D6

1 flat, 1 pub rm, 1 bedrm, sleeps 2-4, £45-£50, Feb-Nov, bus nearby, rail 32 mls, airport 32 mls

Mrs M G Black, 12 Iona Street, Edinburgh
☎ 031 554 8085

WATERFOOT, by Carradale Argyll Map Ref. 1E7

1 cottage, 1 bedrm, sleeps 4-7, £100-£110, Apr-Oct

Mrs E Campbell, Riverbank, Waterfoot, by Carradale, Argyll
☎ Carradale (05833) 651

WATERNISH Isle of Skye, Inverness-shire Map Ref. 3C8

1 cottage, 1 pub rm, 2 bedrms, sleeps 5, £60-£70, Apr-Oct, bus 5 mls

Mrs Maclean, The Rowans, Portree Road, Dunvegan, Isle of Skye, Inverness-shire
☎ Dunvegan (047022) 235

WATTEN Caithness Map Ref. 4D3

Oldhall Caravan Site 6 caravans, sleeps 6, min let 1 night, from £45, Apr-Oct, bus nearby

G Calder, Oldhall, Watten, by Wick, Caithness, KW1 5XL
☎ Watten (095582) 215

1 cottage, 1 pub rm, 3 bedrms, sleeps 9, £65-£80, Jan-Dec, bus ½ ml, rail 7 mls, airport 7 mls

Mrs B Oliphant, Bylbster, Watten, Caithness
☎ Watten (095582) 244

by WATTEN Caithness Map Ref. 4D3

1 cottage, 1 pub rm, 2 bedrms, sleeps 4-6, £35-£55, Apr-Oct, bus 3-4 mls, rail 4 mls, ferry 10 mls, airport 10 mls

Mrs E Allan, Gavinstown Lodge, Watten, by Wick, Caithness, KW1 5UP
☎ *Gillock (095586) 239*

WEMYSS BAY Renfrewshire Map Ref. 1G5

Wemyss Bay Holiday Park 40 caravans, sleeps 2, min let 2 nights (low season), £57-£230, Apr-Oct, bus 500 yds, rail 500 yds

Bourne Leisure Group Ltd, 51-55 Bridge Street, Hemel Hempstead, Herts, HP1 1EQ
☎ *Hemel Hempstead (0442) 48661*

WEST CALDER West Lothian Map Ref. 2C5

2 houses, 1 cottage, 1-5 pub rms, 3-8 bedrms, sleeps 4-16, min let weekend, £50-£300, Jan-Dec, bus 2 mls, rail 2 mls, airport 15 mls

(snooker, croquet, putting)

Mr & Mrs Spurway, Harburn House, West Calder, West Lothian
☎ *Livingston (0506) 410742*

WEST LINTON Peeblesshire Map Ref. 2C6

1 cottage, 1 pub rm, 2 bedrms, sleeps 4, £95-£155, Jan-Dec, bus 400 yds, rail 18 mls, airport 24 mls

Mrs C M Kilpatrick, Slipperfield House, West Linton, Peeblesshire, EH46 7AA
☎ *West Linton (0968) 60401*

---

1 bungalow, 1 pub rm, 3 bedrms, sleeps 6, from £80, Apr-Oct, bus 6 mls, rail 20 mls, airport 22 mls

Mrs Black, Drochil Castle, West Linton, Peeblesshire
☎ *Drochil Castle (0721) 52249*

WESTING Unst, Shetland Map Ref. 5G1

1 cottage, 1 pub rm, 2 bedrms, sleeps 4, £65-£90, Jan-Dec

Mrs M Ourossoff, The Old Rectory, Hasfield, Gloucester, GL19 4LG
☎ *Tirley (045278) 713*
Delightful comfortable cottage in idyllic beach setting and set in magnificent isolation.

WESTRAY Orkney Map Ref. 5B9

1 cottage, 1 pub rm, 2 bedrms, sleeps 4-5, min let 1 night, £40-£55, Jan-Dec, ferry ¼ ml, airport 2 mls

1 caravan, sleeps 6, min let 1 night, £35-£45, Jan-Dec, ferry ¼ ml, airport 2 mls

Mrs Groat, Sand-O-Gill, Westray, Orkney, KW17 2DN
☎ *Westray (08577) 374*

VAT is shown at 15%: changes in this rate may affect prices.

3 caravans, sleeps 2-5, min let 1 night, £40, Jan-Dec, ferry ½ ml, airport 3 mls

♿ ♿ E 🖣 ♿ ♿ ⚛ ♿ ♿ ♿ ♿ ♿ 🐴 P ♿ ♿ ♿ † ⌂   ♿ △ ♿ ✗ ♿ T (bird watching)

Mrs M Seatter, Mount Pleasant, Westray, Orkney, KW17 2DH
☎ *Westray (08577) 229*

WHITEBRIDGE Inverness-shire Map Ref. 4A10

Highland Lodges
WHITEBRIDGE · INVERNESS
Telephone: 0424 53207 (Reversed Charges Accepted)
The Lodges are situated on the banks of the River Fechlin and each Lodge has its own individual view of the Highlands, through their picture windows. Fully centrally heated. Your own Car Parking space and no hidden extras for electricity or dogs.
Your welcome will be in true Highland fashion.
Sleeps up to 5   AA Recommended   ♿ ♿ Commended

COMMENDED

Highland Lodges 9 chalet/log cabins, 2 pub rms, 2 bedrms, sleeps 4-6, £95-£247, Mar-Oct, bus nearby, rail 25 mls, airport 25 mls

♿ ♿ E ♿ ♿ ♿ ♿ ♿ ♿ ♿ ☉ ❄ 🐴 P ♿ ♿   ♿ U △ ♿ ♿ ✗ ♿ T

Highland Lodges,The House of Brandon-Bravo Ltd, Beauport Park, The Ridge, Hastings, Sussex, TN37 7PP
☎ *Hastings (0424) 53207*
Units of various style each with verandah and picture window. Scenic views, trout fishing:river/loch

---

1 bungalow, 1 pub rm, 3 bedrms, sleeps 6, £103-£170, Apr-Oct, bus 2 mls, rail 28 mls

♿ ♿ E ♿ ♿ ♿ ♿ ♿ ♿ ♿ ♿ ❄ 🐴 P ♿ † ⌂   ♿ U ✗ ♿

Blakes Holidays, Wroxham, Norwich, NR12 8DH
☎ *Wroxham (06053) 2917*

---

1 house, 1 cottage, 1-3 pub rms, 3-8 bedrms, sleeps 5-12, £80-£600, Jan-Dec, bus ½ ml, rail 25 mls, airport 30 mls

♿ ♿ E ♿ 🖣 ♿ ♿ ♿ ☏ ♿ ♿ ⚛ ♿ ♿ ☉ ❄ 🐴 P ♿ ♿ ♿ ♿ † ♿   ♿ U △ ♿ ♿ ♿ ✗ ♿ ♿ T

Mr & Mrs Lamb, Dell Farm, Whitebridge, Inverness-shire
☎ *Gorthleck (04563) 662*

WHITEHILLS Banffshire Map Ref. 4F7

Whitehills Caravan Park 4 caravans, sleeps 6, min let 1 night, £60-£135, Apr-Oct, bus ½ ml, rail 25 mls, airport 46 mls

♿ ♿ E 🖣 ♿ ♿ ♿ ♿ ♿ ♿ 🐴 P ⌂ ♿ ♿   ♿ △ ♿ ✗ ♿ T

Mrs Moore, Whitehills Caravan Park, Whitehills, by Banff, Banffshire
☎ *Macduff (0261) 32764/(02617) 474*

WHITEHILLS, by Banff Banffshire Map Ref. 4F7

1 cottage, 1 pub rm, 2 bedrms, sleeps 4, £95-£105, Apr-Oct, bus 1 ml, rail 16 mls, airport 50 mls

♿ ♿ E ♿ ♿ ♿ ♿ ♿ ♿ ⚛ ♿ 🐴 P ♿ ♿ ♿ ♿ †   ♿ ♿ ♿ ♿ ♿ ♿ U △ ♿ ♿ ♿ ✗ ♿ T

Mrs W Keith, Blackpotts Cottages, Whitehills, by Banff, Banffshire, AB4 2JN
☎ *Whitehills (02617) 396*

WHITENESS West Mainland, Shetland Map Ref. 5F4

APPROVED

4 chalet/log cabins, 1 pub rm, 2 bedrms, sleeps 6, min let 3 nights, £56-£140, Jan-Dec, bus nearby, ferry 9 mls, airport 2 mls

Mrs A S Morrison, Whiteness Chalets, Wormadale, Whiteness, Shetland, ZE2 9LJ
☎ *Gott (059584) 292*
Two storey A frame units quietly situated above scenic Whiteness Voe.

WHITHORN Wigtownshire Map Ref. 1H11

1 bungalow, 2 pub rms, 2 bedrms, sleeps 6, £60-£95, Apr-Oct, bus 1 ml, rail 35 mls

Mrs M Forsyth, Mid Bishopton Farm, Whithorn, Wigtownshire, DG8 8DE
☎ *Whithorn (09885) 315*

WHITING BAY Isle of Arran Map Ref. 1F7

Silverhill Chalets 4 chalet/log cabins, 1 pub rm, 2 bedrms, sleeps 6, min let weekend, £80-£150, Apr-Oct, bus 300 yds, ferry 8 mls

Mr R Fisher, Silverhill Chalets, Ardmhor Cottage, Whiting Bay, Isle of Arran
☎ *Whiting Bay (07707) 394*

up to
COMMENDED

3 houses, 1 cottage, 1-2 pub rms, 1-3 bedrms, sleeps 4-9, min let weekend (low season), £70-£195, Jan-Dec, bus nearby, ferry 8 mls

Mr T G Langmuir, Largiemeanoch, Whiting Bay, Isle of Arran
☎ *Whiting Bay (07707) 563*
Attractive stone villa and outbuildings with large garden on edge of village. Good holiday base.

1 flat, 1 pub rm, 3 bedrms, sleeps 4-6, min let weekend, £70-£100, Apr-Oct, bus nearby, ferry 8 mls

Mrs E McNeish, St Amand, Shore Road, Whiting Bay, Isle of Arran
☎ *Whiting Bay (07707) 229*

COMMENDED

Heatherhill Chalets 6 chalet/log cabins, 1 pub rm, 3 bedrms, sleeps 6, from £70, Jan-Oct, bus nearby, ferry 8 mls

Mrs S B Briggs, Heatherhill, Middle Rd, Whiting Bay, Isle of Arran
☎ *Whiting Bay (07707) 355*
Log cabins in elevated position, on small, quiet site overlooking bay. Good walking area.

1 flat, 1 pub rm, 2 bedrms, sleeps 6, min let weekend, £100-£130, Jan-Dec, bus nearby, ferry 8 mls

3 caravans, sleeps 6-8, min let 1 night, £80-£110, Jan-Dec, bus nearby, ferry 8 mls

Mrs A Hughes, Sandbraes, Whiting Bay, Isle of Arran
☎ *Whiting Bay (07707) 214*

VAT is shown at 15%: changes in this rate may affect prices.

303

Cooper Angus Park 41 caravans, sleeps 4-6, min let 2 nights, £86-£207, Apr-Oct, bus nearby, ferry 8 mls

[symbols]

Mr J Meehan, Viewgrand Ltd, Cooper Angus Park, Whiting Bay, Isle of Arran, KA27 8QP
☎ *Whiting Bay (07707) 381*

---

1 cottage, 1 pub rm, 2 bedrms, sleeps 4, min let weekend, £50-£100, Jan-Dec, bus ½ ml, ferry 6 ½ mls

[symbols]

Mrs Sangster, Craiglea, Kings Cross, Whiting Bay, Isle of Arran
☎ *Whiting Bay (07707) 442*

---

1 house, 2 pub rms, 4 bedrms, sleeps 10, £60-£180, Apr-Dec, bus nearby, ferry 6 mls

[symbols]

Mrs M Mackenzie, The Knowe Farm, Kings Cross, by Brodick, Isle of Arran, KA27 8RB
☎ *Whiting Bay (07707) 220*

---

1 caravan, sleeps 6, min let weekend, £80-£135, Apr-Oct, bus 300 yds, ferry 8 mls

[symbols]

Mrs U Milliken, Dal-na-Mara, Whiting Bay, Isle of Arran
☎ *Whiting Bay (07707) 368*

WICK Caithness Map Ref. 4E3

1 cottage, 1 pub rm, 3 bedrms, sleeps 7, £50-£80, Jan-Dec, bus nearby, rail 2 mls, airport 2 ½ mls

[symbols]

Mrs C G Budge, Barns of Hempriggs, Wick, Caithness
☎ *Wick (0955) 3475*

---

1 flat, 1 bedrm, sleeps 5, min let weekend, £70-£100, Jan-Dec, bus ¼ ml, rail ¼ ml, airport 1½ mls

[symbols]

Mrs Coghill, Dunelm, 7 Sinclair Terrace, Wick, Caithness
☎ *Wick (0955) 2120*

Prices shown are for guidance only. Please send SAE with each enquiry.

by WICK Caithness Map Ref. 4E3

BARROCK HOUSE
LYTH, Nr. WICK, CAITHNESS

BARROCK HOUSE offers self-contained, self-catering furnished accommodation for recreational visits, and is also available as a location for seminars, conferences, retreats and holidays-with-a-purpose. Units of accommodation can be booked either individually or in combination according to the needs of your group or party.

Please contact John Sinclair on 01-242 4240, or write to Barrock Estate Ltd., Lyth, by Wick, Caithness, Scotland, allowing time for mail to be forwarded when necessary.

1 chalet/log cabin, 2 houses, 2 flats, 1 cottage, 1-4 pub rms, 1-6 bedrms, sleeps 2-10, £32-£480, Apr-Nov, bus $\frac{1}{4}$ ml, rail 10 mls, airport 10 mls

Sir John Sinclair, 16 Great Ormond Street, London, WCIN 3RB
☎ *01 242 4240 (for info re bookings)*

---

1 cottage, 1 pub rm, 2 bedrms, sleeps 4-5, £75-£110, Apr-Oct

Finlayson Hughes, Bank House, 82 Atholl Road, Pitlochry, Perthshire, PH16 5BL
☎ *Pitlochry (0796) 2512*

---

by WIGTOWN Map Ref. 1H10

1 cottage, 1 pub rm, 3 bedrms, sleeps 5, £60-£120, Apr-Oct, bus 2 $\frac{1}{2}$ mls, rail 26 mls, airport 90 mls

Mrs B J Orr-Ewing, Torhousemuir, Wigtown, DG8 9DJ
☎ *Wigtown (09884) 2336*

WIGTOWN AREA Map Ref. 1H10

2 chalet/log cabins, 8 houses, 2 bungalows, 1-2 pub rms, 2-4 bedrms, sleeps 4-8, from £70, Apr-Oct

G M Thomson & Company, 27 King Street, Castle Douglas, Kirkcudbrightshire, DG7 1AB
☎ *Castle Douglas (0556) 2701*

WORMIT Fife Map Ref. 2D2

Peacehill Farm Cottages 2 cottages, 1 pub rm, 2 bedrms, sleeps 4, £85-£95, Jul-Oct, bus $\frac{1}{4}$ ml, rail 5 mls, airport 5 mls

Mrs P D Forster, Peacehill Farm, Wormit, Fife, DD6 8PJ
☎ *Newport-on-Tay (0382) 541783*

YARROW Selkirkshire Map Ref. 2D7

1 cottage, 1 pub rm, 3 bedrms, sleeps 4-6, min let weekend (low season), £45-£110, Jan-Dec, bus $\frac{1}{4}$ ml, rail 43 mls, airport 43 mls

Mrs Thompson, Whitehope Farm, Yarrow, Selkirk, TD7 5LA
☎ *Yarrow (0750) 82221*
Detached pebble-dashed cottage in field overlooking River Tweed. Fishing available.

VAT is shown at 15%: changes in this rate may affect prices.

YETHOLM Roxburghshire Map Ref. 2F7

1 cottage, 1 pub rm, 2 bedrms, sleeps 7, min let weekend, £60-£100, Jan-Dec, bus nearby, rail 22 mls, airport 55 mls

Mrs A Beveridge, Sunnyside House, Yetholm, Kelso, Roxburghshire, TD5 8RA
☎ *Yetholm (057382) 529*

Stone built semi detached unit on edge of small village. Small paved patio, car parking area.

1 cottage, 1 pub rm, 2 bedrms, sleeps 4-5, min let weekend, £50-£95, Jan-Dec, bus 5 mls, rail 20 mls, airport 50 mls

Mrs A Freeland-Cook, Cliftoncote Farm, Yetholm, Kelso, Roxburghshire
☎ *Yetholm (057382) 241*

Semi-detached unit on working farm. Superb views over surrounding countryside and Cheviots beyond.

by YETHOLM Roxburghshire Map Ref. 2F7

1 cottage, 1 pub rm, 2 bedrms, sleeps 4, £65-£105, May-Oct, bus ½ ml, rail 20 mls, airport 50 mls

Mrs L S Hurst, Lochside, Kelso, Roxburghshire, TD5 8PD
☎ *Yetholm (057382) 349*

Prices shown are for guidance only. Please send SAE with each enquiry.

HOLIDAY CARAVAN PARKS

322 British Holiday Parks Grading Scheme
328 Thistle Commendation Scheme

ALFORD Aberdeenshire Map Ref. 4F10

Haughton House 2 caravans, sleeps 6, min let 2 nights, £75-£80, Apr-Oct, bus 1 ml, rail 7 mls, airport 25 mls

D (putting green, narrow gauge railway)

The Warden, Haughton Caravan Park, Montgarrie Road, Alford, Aberdeenshire, AB3 8NA
☎ *Alford (0336) 2107*

APPLECROSS Ross-shire Map Ref. 3E9

Applecross Campsite 7 caravans, sleeps 4-8, min let 1 night, £47-£170, Apr-Oct, rail 20 mls

Mr Goldthorpe, Applecross Campsite, Applecross, Ross-shire
☎ *Applecross (05204) 284(reception)*

ARDLUI Dunbartonshire Map Ref. 1G3

Ardlui Caravan Park 5 caravans, sleeps 6-8, min let 2 nights, £120-£180, mid Mar-Oct, bus nearby, rail nearby, airport 36 mls

Ardlui Caravan Park, Ardlui, Loch Lomond, Dunbartonshire, G83 7EB
☎ *Inveruglas (03014) 243*

AVIEMORE Inverness-shire Map Ref. 4C10

Campgrounds of Scotland 15 caravans, sleeps 6, min let 1 night, £115-£240, Dec-Oct, bus nearby, rail 1 ½ mls, airport 30 mls

Campgrounds of Scotland, Coylumbridge, Aviemore, Inverness-shire
☎ *Aviemore (0479) 810120*

AYR Map Ref. 1G7

Sundrum Castle Holiday Park 103 caravans, sleeps 4-7, min let 2 nights, £69-£195, Apr-Sep, bus ½ ml, rail 4 mls

Hoseasons Holiday Ltd, Sunway House, Lowestoft, Suffolk, NR32 3LT
☎ *Lowestoft (0502) 62292/(0292) 261464*

BALLINTUIM Perthshire Map Ref. 2C1

Ballintuim Hotel & Caravan Park 8 caravans, sleeps 6, min let 2 nights (low season), £60-£150, Jan-Dec, bus nearby, rail 15 mls

Mr P Chisholm, Ballintuim Hotel & Caravan Park, Ballintuim, Bridge of Cally, Perthshire, PH10 7NH
☎ *Bridge of Cally (025086) 276*

Prices shown are for guidance only. Please send SAE with each enquiry.

BALLOCH Dunbartonshire Map Ref. 1H4

210

Tullichewan Caravan Park 6 caravans, sleeps 6-8, min let 2 nights, £90-£220, Jan-Dec, bus 500 yds, rail ¼ ml, airport 15 mls

(boardsailing, hillwalking)

Tullichewan Caravan Park, Old Luss Road, Balloch, Dunbartonshire, G83 8QP
☎ *Alexandria (0389) 59475*

BANCHORY Kincardineshire Map Ref. 4F11

103

ppp

Silver Ladies Caravan Park 7 caravans, sleeps 4-6, min let 3 nights, £70-£160, Apr-Oct, bus 2 mls, rail 15 mls, airport 15 mls

J G & I Anderson, Silver Ladies Caravan Park, Strachan, Banchory, Kincardineshire, AB3 3NL
☎ *Banchory (03302) 2800*

51

ppp

Feughside Caravan Park 2 caravans, sleeps 6, min let weekend, £80-£130, Apr-Oct, bus nearby, rail 18 mls, airport 25 mls

Mrs S Hay, Feughside Caravan Site, Strachan, Banchory, Kincardineshire, AB3 3NT
☎ *Feughside (033045) 669*

BEAULY Inverness-shire Map Ref. 4A8

81

ppp

Lovat Bridge Caravan Site 6 caravans, sleeps 4-8, min let weekend, £80-£160, Mar-Oct, bus nearby, rail 3 mls, airport 14 mls

Lovat Bridge Caravan Site, Beauly, Inverness-shire, IV4 7AY
☎ *Beauly (0463) 782374*

BIRNAM, by Dunkeld Perthshire Map Ref. 2B1

284

ppp

Erigmore House Caravan Park 30 caravans, sleeps 6-8, min let weekend, £65-£220, Mar-Nov, bus nearby, rail 400 yds, airport 40 mls

Erigmore House Caravan Park, Birnam, Dunkeld, Perthshire, PH8 9XX
☎ *Dunkeld (03502) 236*

BLAIR ATHOLL Perthshire Map Ref. 4C12

145

ppp

River Tilt Caravan Park 10 caravans, sleeps 2-8, min let 2 nights, £100-£200, Jan-Dec, bus nearby, rail 1 ml

(barbecue, bowling)

River Tilt Caravan Park, Bridge of Tilt, Blair Atholl, Perthshire, PH18 5TE
☎ *Blair Atholl (079681) 467*

VAT is shown at 15%: changes in this rate may affect prices.

309

BLAIR ATHOLL, *continued*

Blair Castle Caravan Park 25 caravans, sleeps 6-8, min let 3 nights, £85-£160, Apr-Oct, bus 500 yds, rail 500 yds

Blair Castle Caravan Park, Blair Atholl, Perthshire
☎ *Blair Atholl (079681) 263*

BLAIRGOWRIE Perthshire Map Ref. 2C1

Blairgowrie Caravan Park 6 caravans, sleeps 6, min let 1 night, £75-£150, Jan-Dec, bus 300 yds, rail 14 mls, airport 55 mls

Mr C Wood, Blairgowrie Caravan Park, Hatton Rd, Rattray, Blairgowrie, Perthshire
☎ *Blairgowrie (0250) 2941*

BOAT OF GARTEN Inverness-shire Map Ref. 4C10

20 caravans, sleeps 6, min let 1 night, £115-£240, Dec-Oct, bus nearby, rail 5 mls, airport 30 mls

Campgrounds of Scotland, Boat of Garten, Inverness-shire
☎ *Boat of Garten (047983) 652*

CARRADALE Argyll Map Ref. 1E7

Carradale Bay Caravan Site 3 caravans, sleeps 4-5, min let 2 nights, £65-£99, Apr-Sep, bus ¼ ml

Mrs Hurst, Wallis Hunter Extras, The Steading, Carradale, Argyll
☎ *Carradale (05833) 683*

CRAIL Fife Map Ref. 2E3

Sauchope Links Caravan Park 5 caravans, sleeps 6-8, min let 3 nights, £80-£196, Apr-Oct, bus 1 ml

Largo Leisure Parks Ltd, Rankeilour House, Cupar, Fife, KY15 5RG
☎ *Letham (033781) 233*

by CREETOWN Wigtownshire Map Ref. 1H10

Cassencarie Holiday Park 8 caravans, sleeps 6-8, min let 2 nights, £60-£180, Easter-Sep, bus 800 yds, rail 32 mls, ferry 32 mls

Cassencarie Holiday Park (TBG), Creetown, Wigtownshire
☎ *Creetown (067182) 264*

CRIEFF Perthshire Map Ref. 2B2

✓ ✓ ✓

🏕 **96** 🚐

ppp

Crieff Holiday Village 30 caravans, sleeps 4-8, min let 1 night, from £60, Jan-Dec, bus 300 yds, rail 9 mls, airport 18 mls

♿ 🚾 🅿 E 📞 🍴 🏪 🚿 🛒 🔌 🔥 🏧 ☀ ⛺ 🅿 🔥 🎱 † 🏔 🔍   🐟 🎣 🏹 ⚓ ⛵

▲ ▶ ⚡ ✗ 🦆

Crieff Holiday Village, Turret Bank, Crieff, Perthshire, PH7 4JN

☎ *Crieff (0764) 3513*

✓ ✓ ✓

🏕 **32** 🚐

Mill House Caravan Site 1 caravan, sleeps 4, £60-£75, Jan-Nov, bus nearby, rail 6 mls, airport 40-50 mls

♿ 🚾 E 🏪 🔌 🏪 ⚓ ☀ 🅿 †   ⚓ ⛵ ▶ ✗ 🦆

Mr Kelly, Mill House Caravan Site, South Bridgend, Crieff, Perthshire, PH7 4DH

☎ *Crieff (0764) 4700*

Recently modernised on ground floor of 18C house. Access through caravan park to banks of River Earn.

CROCKETFORD Kirkcudbrightshire Map Ref. 2B10

✓ ✓ ✓ ✓ ✓

🏕 **65** 🚐

ppp

12 caravans, sleeps 6-8, min let 2 nights, £68-£195, Mar-Oct, bus nearby, rail 9 mls

♿ 🚾 🅿 E 📞 🍴 🏪 🚿 🛒 🔌 🔥 🔥 🏧 ☀ ⛺ 🅿 🔥 🎱 🏔 🔍 🎡   🐟 🎣 ⚓ ⛵ ▲

⚡ ▶ ✗ 🦆 T

Mr & Mrs McDonald, Brandedleys, Crocketford, by Dumfries, Kirkcudbrightshire, DG2 8RG

☎ *Crocketford (055669) 250*

DAVIOT (EAST) Inverness-shire Map Ref. 4B9

✓ ✓ ✓ ✓

🏕 **98** 🚐

ppp

10 caravans, sleeps 2-8, min let weekend/3 nights, £40-£160, Dec-Oct, bus nearby, rail 7 mls, airport 12 mls

♿ 🚾 E 📞 🏪 🔌 🔥 🛒 🔌 🔥 🔥 ⚓ ☀ ⛺ 🅿 🔥 🎱 🏔 🔍   T

Mr & Mrs C Ponty, Auchnahillin Caravan Park, Daviot (East), Inverness-shire, IV1 2XQ

☎ *Daviot (046385) 223*

DUNOON Argyll Map Ref. 1G5

✓

🚐 **32** 🚐

Stratheck International Caravan Park 6 caravans, sleeps 6, min let weekend, £69-£140, Apr-Oct, bus ½ ml, rail 8 mls, ferry 6 mls, airport 30 mls

♿ 🚾 E 📞 🏪 🔌 🔥 🛒 🔌 🔥 🔥 ⚓ ☀ ⛺ 🅿 🔥 🎱 🏔 🔍 🎡   ⚓ ⛵ ▲ ⚡ ▶ ✗

🦆

Stratheck International Caravan Park, Loch Eck, Dunoon, Argyll, PA23 8SG

☎ *Kilmun (036984) 472*

by DUNOON Argyll Map Ref. 1G5

✓ ✓ ✓ ✓

🏕 **100** 🚐

ppp

Cowal Caravan Park 14 caravans, sleeps 6, min let 2 nights, £48-£108, Jan-Dec, bus nearby, rail 2 mls, ferry nearby, airport 20 mls

♿ 🚾 E 📞 🏪 🔌 🔥 🛒 🔌 🔥 ⚓ ☀ ☀ 🅿 †   🐟 🚲 🎣 🏹 ⚓ ⛵ ▲ ⚡ ▶ ⛷ 🏇 ⚡ ✗

🦆 T

Mr & Mrs A B Garner, Cowal Caravan Park, Hunters Quay, Dunoon, Argyll, PA23 8JY

☎ *Dunoon (0369) 4259*

---

by DUNOON *continued*

72

ppp

Loch Eck Caravan Park 4 caravans, sleeps 4-6, min let weekend, £60-£120, Apr-Oct, bus nearby, rail 10 mls, ferry 9 mls, airport 30 mls

⬚⬚⬚⬚⬚⬚⬚⬚⬚⬚⬚⬚⬚⬚⬚⬚⬚⬚⬚⬚⬚⬚⬚⬚⬚ ⬚⬚⬚⬚⬚⬚⬚⬚ ✓⬚⬚✗ (boat launching)

Mr & Mrs T J Forster, Loch Eck Caravan Park, Loch Eck, by Dunoon, Argyll
☎ *Kilmun (036984) 447*

EMBO Sutherland Map Ref. 4B6

▲ 290 🚐

Grannie's Heilan' Hame 62 caravans, sleeps 6-8, min let weekend, £60-£200, Apr-Oct, bus nearby, rail 15 mls, airport 55 mls

⬚⬚⬚⬚⬚⬚⬚⬚⬚⬚⬚⬚⬚⬚⬚⬚⬚⬚⬚⬚⬚⬚⬚⬚⬚⬚⬚⬚ ⬚⬚⬚✓✗⬚⬚ T

Grannies Heilan Hame & Co, Embo, Dornoch, Sutherland, IV25 3QD
☎ *Dornoch (0862) 810260*

EVANTON Ross-shire Map Ref. 4A7

▲ 65

ppp

Black Rock Caravan Site 2 caravans, sleeps 6-8, from £100, Apr-Oct, bus nearby, rail 2 mls, airport 20 mls

⬚⬚⬚⬚⬚⬚⬚⬚⬚⬚⬚⬚⬚⬚⬚⬚⬚⬚⬚⬚⬚⬚⬚⬚⬚ ✗⬚ T

Mr Donald, Black Rock Caravan Site, c/o Spar Shop, Evanton, Ross-shire
☎ *Evanton (0349) 830213*

EYEMOUTH Berwickshire Map Ref. 2G5

350 🚐

Northburn Caravan Park 200 caravans, sleeps 4-8, min let 2 nights, from £65, mid Mar-Oct, bus nearby, rail 8 mls, airport 50 mls

⬚⬚⬚⬚⬚⬚⬚⬚⬚⬚⬚⬚⬚⬚⬚⬚⬚⬚⬚⬚⬚⬚⬚⬚⬚⬚⬚ ⬚⬚⬚✗⬚ (air compressor/scuba diving)

James Wood & Son, Northburn Caravan Park, Eyemouth, Berwickshire
☎ *Eyemouth (08907) 50808/51050/50426*

---

30 caravans, sleeps 2-6, min let 2 nights, £85-£195, Apr-Sep, bus 2 mls, rail 2 ½ mls

⬚⬚⬚⬚⬚⬚⬚⬚⬚⬚⬚⬚⬚⬚⬚⬚⬚⬚⬚⬚⬚⬚⬚⬚⬚✓✗⬚ T

190

ppp

Glen Nevis Holiday Caravans, Glen Nevis Holiday Cottages, Glen Nevis, Fort William, Inverness-shire, PH33 6SX
☎ *Fort William (0397) 2191*

Traditional units in landscaped park close to mighty Ben Nevis. Shop on site and restaurant nearby.

by FORT WILLIAM Inverness-shire Map Ref. 3G12

▲ 410 🚐

ppp

Linnhe Caravan Park Ltd 77 caravans, sleeps 6, min let 2 nights, £90-£200, Apr-Sep, bus 1 ml, rail 1 ½ mls

⬚⬚⬚⬚⬚⬚⬚⬚⬚⬚⬚⬚⬚⬚⬚⬚⬚⬚⬚⬚⬚⬚⬚⬚⬚ ⬚ T (barbecue area, dinghy park)

Linnhe Caravan Park Ltd, Corpach, by Fort William, Inverness-shire
☎ *Corpach (03977) 376*

GAIRLOCH Ross-shire Map Ref. 3F7

192

ppp

Sands Holiday Centre 4 caravans, sleeps 6, £100-£170, Apr-Oct, bus 4 mls, rail 33 mls, airport 80 mls

P J & W Cameron, Gairloch Sands Holiday Centre, Gairloch, Ross-shire, IV21 2DL
☎ Gairloch (0445) 2152

GLENCOE Argyll Map Ref. 1F1

60

(cycles for hire)

Invercoe Caravan Site 5 caravans, sleeps 8, £64-£126, Easter-Oct, bus nearby, rail 14 mls, airport 88 mls

M Brown, Invercoe Caravan Site, Glencoe, Argyll
☎ Ballachulish (08552) 210

GLENDARUEL Argyll Map Ref. 1F4

55

ppp

Glendaruel Caravan Park 4 caravans, sleeps 6, min let 2 nights, £75-£150, Apr-Oct, bus ½ ml, ferry 18 mls

Mrs Q Craig, Glendaruel Caravan Park, Glendaruel, Argyll
☎ Glendaruel (036982) 267

by HADDINGTON East Lothian Map Ref. 2E5

50

ppp

Monksmuir Caravan Park 5 caravans, sleeps 4-6, min let 1 night, £50-£180, Apr-Oct, bus nearby, rail 8 mls

Mr & Mrs Inglis, Monksmuir Caravan Park, by Haddington, East Lothian, EH41 3SB
☎ East Linton (0620) 860340

INVERARAY Argyll Map Ref. 1F3

221

Argyll Caravan Park 11 caravans, sleeps 6-8, min let 1 night, £75-£140, Apr-Oct, bus nearby, rail 15 mls/24 mls, airport 65 mls

Argyll Caravan Park, Inveraray, Argyll, PA32 8XT
☎ Inveraray (0499) 2285

INVERBEG, by Luss Dunbartonshire Map Ref. 1G4

75

Inverbeg Caravan Park 15 caravans, sleeps 6-8, min let weekend, £80-£135, Apr-Oct, bus nearby, rail 12 mls, airport 33 mls

Inverbeg Caravan Park, Inverbeg, Luss, by Alexandria, Dunbartonshire, G83 8PD
☎ Luss (043686) 267

VAT is shown at 15%: changes in this rate may affect prices.

INVERMORISTON Inverness-shire Map Ref. 4A10

4 caravans, sleeps 6, min let 2 nights (low season), £50-£175, Mar-Oct, bus nearby, rail 28 mls, airport 38 mls

Loch Ness Caravan & Camping Park, Invermoriston, Inverness-shire, IV3 6YE
☎ *Glenmoriston (0320) 51207*

INVERNESS Map Ref. 4B8

Torvean Caravan Park 10 caravans, sleeps 6, min let long weekend, from £75, Mar-Oct, bus nearby, rail 2 mls, airport 9 mls

G N R Sutherland, Caravan Sales, Glenurquhart Road, Inverness, IV3 6JL
☎ *Inverness (0463) 220582*

INVERUGLAS Dunbartonshire Map Ref. 1G3

Loch Lomond Holiday Park 6 caravans, sleeps 6, min let weekend, £90-£140, Apr-Oct, bus nearby, rail 4 mls, airport 30 mls

Halley Caravans Ltd, Glasgow Road, Milngavie, Glasgow, G62 6JP
☎ *041 956 1126/Inveruglas (03014) 224*

JEDBURGH Roxburghshire Map Ref. 2E7

Jedwater Caravan Park 5 caravans, sleeps 6, min let 1 night, from £50, Apr-Oct, bus nearby

Jedwater Caravan Park, Jedburgh, Roxburghshire
☎ *Camptown (08354) 219*

KENMORE Perthshire Map Ref. 2A1

3 caravans, sleeps 6, min let long weekend, £60-£140, Apr-Oct, bus 20 mls, rail 6 mls

(hillwalking)

Diana & Duncan Menzies, Mains of Taymouth, Kenmore, Aberfeldy, Perthshire, PH15 2HN
☎ *Kenmore (08873) 226*
Stone units set around courtyard on home farm for Taymouth Castle. Walking, golfing, sailing locally.

KILNINVER, by Oban Argyll Map Ref. 1E3

Lagganmore Caravans 1 caravan, sleeps 6, min let 3 nights, £84-£139, Mar-Nov, bus ½ ml, rail 10 ½ mls

Mrs P S Sandilands, Lagganmore, Oban, Argyll
☎ *Kilninver (08526) 200*

KINGHORN Fife Map Ref. 2D4

Pettycur Bay Caravan Park 50 caravans, sleeps 4-6, min let 2 nights, £55-£180, Mar-Oct, bus nearby, rail ½ ml, airport 15 mls

Pettycur Bay Caravan Park, Kinghorn, Fife, KY3 9YE
☎ *Kinghorn (0592) 890321*

KINTORE Aberdeenshire Map Ref. 4G10

Hillhead Caravan Park 4 caravans, sleeps 6-8, min let 1 night, £58-£95, Easter-Oct, bus 1 ml, rail 3 mls, ferry 13 mls, airport 10 mls

D (bowls)

Mr L Gray, Hillhead Caravan Park, Kintore, Aberdeenshire, AB5 0YX
☎ *Kintore (0467) 32809*

KIPPFORD Kirkcudbrightshire Map Ref. 2B10

20 caravans, sleeps 6, min let weekend, £60-£180, Mar-Oct, bus nearby, rail 17 mls, ferry 70 mls, airport 60 mls

D (caravans suitable for wheelchairs)

P R Aston, Kippford Caravan Park, by Dalbeattie, Kirkcudbrightshire
☎ *Kippford (055662) 636*

KIRKCUDBRIGHT Map Ref. 2A11

25 caravans, sleeps 4-8, min let 2 nights, £60-£175, Apr-Oct, bus 2 mls, rail 35 mls

T D (windsurfing, parascending, jet skiing)

Brighouse Bay Holiday Park, Borgue, Kirkcudbrightshire, DG6 4TS
☎ *Borgue (05577) 267*

11 caravans, sleeps 6-8, min let 2 nights, £72-£180, Mar-Oct, bus nearby, rail 32 mls

T (mini golf, bicycle hire, sunbed)

Seaward Caravan Park, Dhoon Bay, Kirkcudbright
☎ *Borgue (05577) 267(off)/(0557) 31079*

LOCHGILPHEAD Argyll Map Ref. 1E4

Lochgilphead Caravan Park 10 caravans, sleeps 6, min let 2 nights, from £60, Apr-Oct, bus nearby, rail 37 mls

(sports centre)

Mr MacDonald, Lochgilphead Caravan Park, Lochgilphead, Argyll
☎ *Lochgilphead (0546) 2003*

LOCHGILPHEAD AREA Argyll Map Ref. 1E4

20 caravans, sleeps 6, min let 2 nights, £82-£170, Mar-Oct

Castle Sween (Holidays) Ltd, Ellary, Lochgilphead, Argyll, PA31 8PA
☎ *Ormsary (08803) 232*

LUNDIN LINKS Fife Map Ref. 2D3

Largo House Caravan Park 2 caravans, sleeps 6-8, min let 3 nights, £75-£155, Mar-Oct, bus ½ ml

Largo Leisure Parks Ltd, Rankeilour House, Cupar, Fife, KY15 5RG
☎ *Letham (033781) 233*

---

by MACDUFF Banffshire Map Ref. 4F7

Wester Bonnyton Farm Site 15 caravans, sleeps 4-8, min let 1 night, £40-£130, Apr-Oct, bus nearby, rail 17 mls, airport 40 mls

Mrs M Rothnie, Wester Bonnyton, Gamrie, Banff, Banffshire, AB4 3EP
☎ *Macduff (0261) 32470*

NAIRN Map Ref. 4C8

Lochloy Holiday Park 50 caravans, sleeps 2-6, min let weekend, £72-£228, mid Mar-Oct, bus ¼ ml, rail 1 ½ mls, airport 10 mls

Lochloy Holiday Park, East Beach, Nairn, IV12 4PH
☎ *Nairn (0667) 53764*

NEWTON STEWART Wigtownshire Map Ref. 1H10

9 caravans, sleeps 4-6, min let 1 night, £55-£110, Mar-Oct, bus nearby, rail 9 mls

Mrs Gaunt, Merrick Caravan Park, Bargrennan, by Newton Stewart, Wigtownshire, DG8 6RN
☎ *Bargrennan (067184) 280*

---

by NEWTON STEWART Wigtownshire Map Ref. 1H10

Three Lochs Caravan Park 16 caravans, sleeps 6, min let weekend, £85-£115, Apr-Oct, bus 7 mls, rail 19 mls, airport 80 mls

Mr Alan Brown, Three Lochs Caravan Park, Kirkcowan, Newton Stewart, Wigtownshire
☎ *Kirkcowan (067183) 304*

Prices shown are for guidance only. Please send SAE with each enquiry.

OBAN Argyll Map Ref. 1E2

145

Gallanachmore Farm Caravan Site 15 caravans, sleeps 6-8, £70-£100, Apr-Oct, bus 2 mls, rail 2 mls, ferry 2 mls

Brian & Sylvia Thompson, Gallanachmore Farm, Gallanach Road, Oban, Argyll
☎ Oban (0631) 62425/63502

PARTON Kirkcudbrightshire Map Ref. 2A10

56

ppp

15 caravans, sleeps 6, min let weekend (low season), from £105, end Mar-early Nov, bus nearby, rail 20 mls, airport 60 mls

Mrs Penny Bryson, Boreland, Parton, Castle Douglas, Kirkcudbrightshire, DG7 3NE
☎ Parton (06447) 282

PEEBLES Map Ref. 2C6

120

ppp

Crossburn Caravan Park 6 caravans, sleeps 6, min let 2 nights, £84-£126, Apr-Oct, bus nearby, rail 23 mls, airport 30 mls

Earnville Caravans, Crossburn Caravan Park, Edinburgh Road, Peebles, EH45 8ED
☎ Peebles (0721) 20501

129

ppp

Rosetta 7 caravans, sleeps 6, min let 1 night (exc Jul/Aug), £85-£110, Apr-Oct, bus ½ ml, rail 30 mls, airport 35 mls

Rosetta Caravan Park, Rosetta Road, Peebles, EH45 8PG
☎ Peebles (0721) 20770

PORT SETON East Lothian Map Ref. 2D5

693

Seton Sands Caravan Park 23 caravans, sleeps 2-8, min let 2 nights, £57-£230, Apr-Oct, bus nearby, rail 2 mls, airport 15 mls

Bourne Leisure Group Ltd, 51-55 Bridge Street, Hemel Hempstead, Herts, HP1 1EQ
☎ Hemel Hempstead (0442) 48661

PORTPATRICK Wigtownshire Map Ref. 1F11

100

3 caravans, sleeps 6-8, min let weekend, £75-£140, Apr-Sep, bus ¼ ml, rail 8 mls, airport 60 mls

(bowling)

Galloway Point Holiday Park, Portree House, Portpatrick, Wigtownshire, DG9 9AA
☎ Portpatrick (077681) 561

VAT is shown at 15%: changes in this rate may affect prices.

317

PORTPATRICK, *continued*

Castle Bay Caravan Park 10 caravans, sleeps 4-6, min let weekend, £75-£130, Mar-Oct, bus ¾ ml, rail 8 mls, airport 60 mls

Castle Bay Caravan Park, Portpatrick, Wigtownshire
☎ *Portpatrick (077681) 462*

ROSNEATH, by Helensburgh Dunbartonshire Map Ref. 1G4

Rosneath Castle Caravan Park 8 caravans, sleeps 8, from £100, Apr-Oct, bus ½ ml, rail 7 ½ mls, airport 30 mls

Rosneath Castle Caravan Park, Rosneath, by Helensburgh, Dunbartonshire
☎ *Clynder (0436) 831208*

---

by SALEN Argyll Map Ref. 1D1

Resipole Caravan Park 3 caravans, sleeps 6, min let 3 nights, £100-£140, Mar-Nov, bus nearby, rail 30 mls

Mrs Sinclair, Resipole Farm, Salen, by Acharacle, Argyll, PH36 4HX
☎ *Salen (096785) 235*

SCONE Perthshire Map Ref. 2C2

Scone Palace Camping Site 20 caravans, sleeps 4-8, min let 2 nights, £70-£180, Apr-Oct, bus ½ ml, rail 3 mls, airport 20 mls

Scone Palace Holiday Caravans, Estates Office, Scone Palace, Scone, Perthshire, PH2 6BD
☎ *Scone (0738) 52308*

SKELMORLIE Ayrshire Map Ref. 1G5

9 caravans, sleeps 6, min let 2 nights, from £75, Mar-Oct, bus ½ ml, rail 2 mls, airport 30 mls

Mrs M Stirrat, Mains Caravan Site, Skelmorlie, Ayrshire, PA17 5EW
☎ *Wemyss Bay (0475) 520794*

SOUTH CUAN Isle of Luing, Argyll Map Ref. 1E3

Sunnybrae Caravan Site 5 caravans, sleeps 6, min let 1 night, £50-£80, Mar-Oct, bus nearby, rail 16 mls, ferry nearby, airport 23 mls

Sunnybrae Caravan Site, South Cuan, Luing, by Oban, Argyll, PA34 4TU
☎ *Luing (08524) 274*

Prices shown are for guidance only. Please send SAE with each enquiry.

SOUTHERNESS Dumfriesshire Map Ref. 2B10

Southerness Holiday Village 30 caravans, sleeps 6, min let weekend, £46-£165, Mar-Oct, bus nearby, rail 17 mls

Southerness Holiday Village, The Estate Office, Southerness, by Dumfries, DG2 8AZ
☎ *Kirkbean (038788) 256/278/281*

ST ANDREWS Fife Map Ref. 2E3

Craigtoun Meadows Holiday Park 34 caravans, sleeps 2-6, from £65, Mar-Oct, bus nearby, rail 4 mls, airport 10 mls

Craigtoun Meadows Holiday Park, No 9 Mount Melville, St Andrews, Fife, KY16 8PQ
☎ *St Andrews (0334) 75959*

by ST ANDREWS Fife Map Ref. 2E3

Clayton Caravan Park 5 caravans, sleeps 8, min let 2-3 nights, £70-£165, Mar-Oct, bus nearby, rail 2 mls, airport 11 mls

Clayton Caravan Park, by St Andrews, Fife, KY16 9YE
☎ *Balmullo (0334) 870242/870630*

by STRANRAER Wigtownshire Map Ref. 1F10

Drumlochart Caravan Park 15 caravans, sleeps 6, min let weekend, £50-£140, Mar-Oct, bus 1 ½ mls, rail 5 mls, airport 58 mls

Mr P R Manning, Drumlochart Caravan Park, Lochnaw, Stranraer, Wigtownshire, DG9 0RN
☎ *Leswalt (077687) 232*

TAYINLOAN Argyll Map Ref. 1D6

12 caravans, sleeps 6-10, min let 1 night, £75-£170, Apr-Oct, bus ½ ml

Point Sands Caravans, Point Sands, Tayinloan, Argyll, PA29 6XG
☎ *Tayinloan (05834) 263/275*

TAYNUILT Argyll Map Ref. 1F2

Crunachy Caravan Park 3 caravans, sleeps 4-6, min let 3 nights, from £50, Mar-Oct, bus nearby, rail 2 mls

Mr A Douglas, Crunachy Caravan Site, Bridge of Awe, Taynuilt, Argyll, PA35 1HT
☎ *Taynuilt (08662) 612*

VAT is shown at 15%: changes in this rate may affect prices.

TUMMEL BRIDGE Perthshire Map Ref. 2A1

Tummel Valley Holiday Park 75 caravans, sleeps 4-7, min let weekend, £69-£200, Apr-Oct, rail 12 mls

Hoseasons Holidays, Sunway House, Lowestoft, Suffolk, NR32 3LT
☎ *Lowerstoft (0502) 62292*

Holiday park amidst wood and river. Shop, bar, restaurant on site. Live night entertainment in season.

WEMYSS BAY Renfrewshire Map Ref. 1G5

Wemyss Bay Holiday Park 40 caravans, sleeps 2, min let 2 nights (low season), £57-£230, Apr-Oct, bus 500 yds, rail 500 yds

Bourne Leisure Group Ltd, 51-55 Bridge Street, Hemel Hempstead, Herts, HP1 1EQ
☎ *Hemel Hempstead (0442) 48661*

WHITING BAY Isle of Arran Map Ref. 1F7

Cooper Angus Park 41 caravans, sleeps 4-6, min let 2 nights, £86-£207, Apr-Oct, bus nearby, ferry 8 mls

Mr J Meehan, Viewgrand Ltd, Cooper Angus Park, Whiting Bay, Isle of Arran, KA27 8QP
☎ *Whiting Bay (07707) 381*

Glasgow
Garden Festival '88

The Glasgow Garden Festival in 1988
guarantees to provide something for
everyone. In addition to six themed parks,
a varied and colourful programme of
open air concerts, live displays and
conferences will be staged from
April-September.

THE BRITISH HOLIDAY PARKS GRADING SCHEME

ABOUT THE SCHEME

The voluntary scheme for the grading of caravan and camping parks has now been adopted by the Scottish, English and Welsh Tourist Boards for operation throughout Britain. This follows the initiative taken in Scotland by the National Federation of Site Operators and the National Caravan Council and uses the Scottish Classification and Grading Scheme as its basis.

Each participating park has been visited by an independent inspector to ensure the highest standards of facilities, and to enable the visitor to select a holiday park with confidence. All aspects of the park have been assessed for their *quality*, and particular emphasis has been placed on the standard of *cleanliness* throughout.

The *range* of facilities on the parks is shown by the symbols in each line entry.

WHAT THE SYMBOLS TELL YOU

The type of park—whether touring and/or for holiday caravans—is shown by the 'caravan' symbols. Where a park has pitches for both touring and holiday caravans, both symbols are used. If pitches are also provided for tents and/or motor caravans, this is also indicated, as is the availability of holiday caravans for hire on the park, which meet Tourist Board Minimum Standards.

The number shown is the total number of pitches on the park and is, therefore, an indication of its overall size.

Other symbols indicate parks considered to be 'particularly peaceful'—these are usually parks in rural areas, away from main roads, railways or airports, and normally without bars, restaurants, etc.—and parks adjudged to be in areas of 'outstanding scenic beauty'.

THE BRITISH HOLIDAY PARKS GRADING SCHEME

THE QUALITY OF FACILITIES

The quality of facilities provided by the park is indicated by 1-5 'ticks', as follows:

5 ticks—parks providing comfort and service, maintained, decorated, furnished and equipped with facilities to an *excellent* standard throughout

4 ticks—parks providing comfort and service, maintained, decorated, furnished and equipped with facilities to a *very good* standard throughout

3 ticks—parks providing comfort and service, maintained, decorated, furnished and equipped with facilities to a *good* standard throughout

2 ticks—parks providing facilities maintained, decorated, furnished and equipped to a *fair* standard throughout

1 tick —parks providing facilities, decorated, furnished and equipped to *acceptable* standards throughout.

SYMBOLS USED IN THE BRITISH HOLIDAY PARKS GRADING SCHEME

✓|✓|✓|✓|✓ Grading category 1-5 ticks

🚐 Touring park

🚐 Holiday caravan park

🚐 Holiday caravan park with caravans for hire

160 Total number of pitches in park

⛺ Tents welcome

🚐 Motor caravans welcome

ppp Particularly peaceful park

⚓ Park in area of outstanding scenic beauty

LE SYSTEME DE CLASSIFICATION DES TERRAINS DE VACANCES BRITANNIQUES

LE SYSTEME DE CLASSIFICATION

Ce système classification volontaire des terrains de caravaning et de camping vient d'être adopté par les offices du tourisme écossais, anglais et gallois et il est valable dans l'ensemble de la Grande-Bretagne. L'instigation en a été donnée en Ecosse par la "National Federation of Site Operators" (Fédération nationale des responsables de terrains), et le "National Caravan Council" (Conseil national du caravaning) se base sur le système écossais de classification générale et qualitative.

Tous les terrains qui sont classés selon ce système ont été examinés par un inspecteur indépendant de manière à garantir qu'ils sont bien aménagés; les vacanciers peuvent donc choisir en confiance le terrain de camping ou de caravaning qui leur conviendra le mieux. Nous avons également évalué la *qualité* de tous les aspects du terrain et nous sommes particulièrement intéressés à leur *propreté* générale.

La *catégorie* des équipements dont sont munis les terrains est indiquée par des symboles figurant en face de chaque rubrique.

CE QUE LES SYMBOLES VOUS APPRENNENT

Le type de terrain—destiné aux caravanes de tourisme ou sédentaires—est indiqué par les différents idéogrammes représentant des caravanes. Si un terrain dispose à la fois d'emplacements pour les caravanes de passage et pour les séjours en caravane, les deux symboles seront utilisés. S'il y a des emplacements pour les tentes et/ou les camping-cars, cela sera également indiqué; de même la liste vous indiquera si vous pouvez louer des caravanes sur place (elles seront alors conformes au normes de l'Office du tourisme).

Le chiffre représente le nombre total d'emplacements du terrain et vous donne donc une idée de sa surface totale.

D'autres symboles désignent des terrains "particulièrement tranquilles" (qui sont généralement des terrains situés dans des régions rurales, loin des grandes routes, des voies de chemin de fer et des aéroports, et presque toujours sans bars ni restaurants) et les terrains situés dans des emplacements "particulièrement pittoresques".

LE SYSTEMS DE CLASSIFICATION DES TERRAINS DE VACANCES BRITANNIQUES

LE QUALITÉ DES ÉQUIPEMENTS

La qualité de l'aménagement est indiquée par un système de 1 à 5 "coches", qui ont la valeur suivante:

5 coches— terrains où vous trouverez confort et service, dont toutes les parties sont entretenues, peintes, décorées, meublées et aménagées d'équipements d'un *excellent* niveau

4 coches— terrains où vous trouverez confort et service, dont toutes les parties sont entretenues, peintes, décorées, meublées et aménagées d'équipements d'un *très bon* niveau

3 coches— terrains où vous trouverez confort et service, dont toutes les parties sont entretenues, peintes, décorées, meublées et aménagées d'équipements d'un *bon* niveau

2 coches— terrains dont toutes les parties sont entretenues, peintes, décorées, meublées et aménagées d'équipements d'un *assez bon* niveau

1 coche —terrains dont toutes les parties sont entretenues, peintes, décorées, meublées et aménagées d'équipements d'un niveau *satisfaisant.*

SYMBOLS UTILISÉS POUR LE SYSTÈME DE CLASSIFICATION DES TERRAINS DE VACANCES BRITANNIQUES

√|√|√|√|√ Classification (1 à 5 coches

Terrain pour caravanes de tourisme

Terrain pour caravanes sédentaires

Terrain pour séjours en caravane avec caravanes à louer

160 Nombre total d'emplacements sur le terrain

Tentes bienvenues

Camping-cars bienvenus

ppp Terrain particulièrement tranquille

Terrain situé dans un endroit particulièrement pittoresque

DAS BRITISCHE BEWERTUNGSSYSTEM FÜR CAMPINGPLÄTZE

DAS BEWERTUNGSSYSTEM

Das freiwillige Bewertungssystem für Campingplätze wurde jetzt von der schottischen, englischen und walisischen Fremdenverkehrsbehörde übernommen und gilt in ganz Großbritannien. Die Initiative dazu kam von der "National Federation of Site Operators" und dem "National Caravan Council" in Schottland und das schottische Klassifizierungs—und Bewertungssystem dient dabei als Grundlage.

Jeder daran angeschlossene Campingplatz wurde von einem unabhängigen Experten geprüft, um sicherzustellen, daß die Einrichtungen höchsten Ansprüchen gerecht werden, und daß der Besucher unbesorgt einen Campingplatz aussuchen kann. Alle Bereiche des Campingplatzes wurden nach ihrer *Qualität* beurteilt; dabei wurde immer besonders auf *Sauberkeit* geachtet.

Die Symbole neben jeder Eintragung geben Ihnen darüber Auskunft, um welche *Art* von Campingplatz es sich jeweils handelt.

WAS DIE EINZELNEN SYMBOLE BEDEUTEN

Die beiden Symbole für "Wohnwagen" zeigen Ihnen, ob ein Campingplatz für Wohnanhänger und/oder für fest stehende Wohnwagen eingerichtet ist. Wenn ein Campingplatz sowohl für Wohnanhänger als auch für fest stehende Wohnwagen Plätz hat, werden beide Symbole verwendet. Es wird ebenfalls angegeben, ob es Plätze für Zelte und/oder Wohnmobile gibt, und ob auf dem Campingplatz fest stehende Wohnwagen, die auf jeden Fall dem Mindeststandard der Fremdenverkehrsbehörde entsprechen, gemietet werden können. Die angegebene Zahl entspricht der Gesamtzahl der Plätze auf einem Campingplatz und gibt Ihnen einen Hinweis auf die Größe der Anlage.

Weiter Symbole kennzeichnen Campingplätze, die in "außergewöhnlich schöner Landschaft" gelegen sind und Campingplätze, die als "besonders ruhig" eingestuft werden—sie liegen dann gewöhnlich in ländlichen Gegenden, weit weg von den Hauptstraßen, Gleisen oder Flughäfen, und haben normalerweise keine Bars, Restaurants etc.

DAS BRITISCHE BEWERTUNGSSYSTEM FÜR CAMPINGPLÄTZE

DIE QUALITÄT DER EINRICHTUNGEN

Die Qualität der vom Campingplatz zur Verfügung gestellten Einrichtungen wird durch 1-5 "Häkchen" wie folgt angegeben:

5 Häkchen—Campingplätze, die Komfort und Service bieten, wobei die Instandhaltung, Ausstattung und Möblierung der Einrichtungen insgesamt als *hervorragend* bezeichnet werden können.

4 Häkchen—Campingplätze, die Komfort und Service bieten, wobei die Instandhaltung, Ausstattung und Möblierung der Einrichtungen insgesamt als *sehr gut* bezeichnet werden können.

3 Häkchen—Campingplätze, die Komfort und Service bieten, wobei die Instandhaltung, Ausstattung und Möblierung der Einrichtungen insgesamt als *gut* bezeichnet werden können.

2 Häkchen—Campingplätze mit Einrichtungen, deren Instandhaltung, Ausstattung und Möblierung insgesamt als *zufriedenstellend* bezeichnet werden können.

1 Häkchen—Campingplätze mit Einrichtungen, deren Instandhaltung, Ausstattung und Möblierung insgesamt als akzeptabel bezeichnet werden können.

DIE IN DEM BRITISCHEN BEWERTUNGSSYSTEM FÜR CAMPINGPLÄTZE VERWENDETEN SYMBOLE

✓ ✓ ✓ ✓ ✓	Bewertungskategorie: 1-5 Häkchen
🚐	Campingplatz für Wohnanhänger
🚙	Campingplatz für fest stehende Wohnwagen
🚐	Campingplatz für fest stehende Wohnwagen, auf dem Wohnwagen gemietet werden können
160	Gesamtzahl der Stellplätze
⚊	Zelte sind hier willkommen
🚍	Wohnmobile sind hier willkommen
ppp	besonders rhiger Campingplatz
⚓	in außergewöhnlich schöner Landschaft gelegener Campingplatz

THISTLE COMMENDATION SCHEME

The Thistle Commendation Scheme gives recognition to those Holiday Caravan Parks in Scotland which provide first class caravans for hire to the tourist, combined with very good facilities and attractive environment.

All parks have been inspected and only awarded the commendation after detailed scrutiny by the Commendation Panel.

Look out for the Thistle Commendation Plaques displayed by all commended parks, and by each caravan which meets the required standard.

LIST OF COMMENDED PARKS

Aviemore, Inverness-shire
CAMPGROUNDS OF SCOTLAND

Ayr
SUNDRUM CASTLE HOLIDAY PARK

Ballintium, Perthshire
BALLINTUIM HOTEL CARAVAN PARK

Balloch Dunbartonshire
TULLICHEWAN CARAVAN PARK

Banchory, Kincardineshire
SILVER LADIES CARAVAN PARK

Blair Atholl, Perthshire
BLAIR CASTLE CARAVAN PARK

Blair Atholl, Perthshire
RIVER TILT CARAVAN PARK

Boat of Garten, Inverness-shire
CAMPGROUNDS OF SCOTLAND

Brodie, by Forres, Moray
OLD MILL CARAVAN PARK

Crail, Fife
SAUCHOPE LINKS CARAVAN PARK

Crocketford, Kirkcudbrightshire
BRANDEDLEYS

Daviot (East), Inverness-shire
AUCHNAHILLIN CARAVAN & CAMPING PARK

Dunkeld, Perthshire
ERIGMORE HOUSE CARAVAN PARK

Dunoon, Argyll
STRATHECK INTERNATIONAL CARAVAN PARK

Embo, Sutherland
GRANNIES HEILAN' HAME

Edinburgh
MORTONHALL CARAVAN PARK

Fort William, Inverness-shire
GLEN NEVIS CARAVAN & CAMPING PARK

Fort William, Inverness-shire
LINNHE CARAVAN PARK

Gairloch, Ross-shire
SANDS HOLIDAY CENTRE

Glendaruel, Argyll
GLENDARUEL CARAVAN PARK

Inveraray, Argyll
ARGYLL CARAVAN PARK

Inverness
TORVEAN CARAVAN PARK

Kinghorn, Fife
PETTYCUR BAY CARAVAN PARK

Kippford, Kirkcudbrightshire
KIPPFORD CARAVAN PARK

Kirkcudbright
BRIGHOUSE BAY HOLIDAY PARK

Kirkcudbright
SEAWARD CARAVAN PARK

THISTLE COMMENDATION SCHEME

Lochgilphead, Argyll
CASTLE SWEEN CARAVAN PARK

Nairn
LOCHLOY CARAVAN PARK

Newton Stewart, Wigtownshire
THREE LOCHS CARAVAN PARK

Parton, Kirkcudbrightshire
LOCH KEN HOLIDAY CENTRE

Peebles
CROSSBURN CARAVAN PARK

Peebles
ROSETTA CARAVAN PARK

Port Seton, East Lothian
SETON SANDS HOLIDAY CENTRE

Scone, Perthshire
SCONE PALACE CAMPING SITE

St Andrews, Fife
CLAYTON CARAVAN PARK

St Andrews, Fife
CRAIGTOUN MEADOWS HOLIDAY
PARK

Tayinloan, Argyll
POINT SANDS CARAVAN PARK

Tummel Bridge, Perthshire
TUMMEL VALLEY HOLIDAY PARK

Wemyss Bay, Renfrewshire
WEMYSS BAY CARAVAN PARK

Whiting Bay, Isle of Arran
COOPER ANGUS PARK

LOGEZ A l'ENSEIGNE DE L'HOSPITALITE ECOSSAISE

En Ecosse, nous pouvons désormais vous garantir le confort de centaines de logements prêts à vous accueillir.

Plus besoin de vous demander quel hôtel, quelle pension, quel "bed and breakfast" ou quel appartement de vacances vous conviendra le mieux.

Nous venons d'introduire un nouveau système de classification; facile à comprendre, il vous permettra de trouver en un coup d'oeil *exactement* ce que vous cherchez.

En quoi consiste cette *classification*?
La classification générale, qui va de "agréé" (en anglais "listed") à "cinq couronnes" est fondée sur le degré de confort de l'établissement. Ainsi par exemple la classification "agréé" garantit dans les hôtels, pensions et "bed and breakfast" que votre lit est d'une taille convenable (supérieure à un minimum réglementaire), qu'il y a de l'eau chaude et froide en temps voulu, que le petit déjeuner est compris dans le prix de la chambre et qu'elle est bien chauffée (selon la saison).

Dans les appartements de vacances, une couronne représente une unité dont la surface est supérieure à un minimum réglementaire: les vacanciers y disposeront d'au moins une chambre à coucher avec un grand lit ou des lits jumeaux, ils pourront y faire la cuisine et manger confortablement; il y aura également un réfrigérateur.

Bien entendu, plus de couronnes signifient plus de confort. Dans un établissement doté de cinq couronnes, vous trouverez de nombreux éléments supplémentaires destinés à rendre votre séjour encore plus confortable. Deux examples: dans les hôtels à cinq couronnes, *toutes* les chambres ont des salles de bain particulières; et les apartements de vacances à cinq couronnes sont équipés de tout le confort moderne, y compris un lave-vaisselle.

Toutes ces classifications ont été vérifiées par notre équipe d'experts indépendants.

LOGEZ A l'ENSEIGNE DE L'HOSPITALITE ECOSSAISE

Qu'est-ce que la *classification qualitative*?
La première classification ne porte que sur la nature de l'aménagement des logements, tandis que la *classification qualitative* a pour objet leur *qualité*. Les mentions "homologué", "recommandé" et "chaudement recommandé" (en anglais "approved", "commended" et "highly commended") sont fondées sur une évaluation indépendante de toute une série d'éléments, allant de l'apparence du bâtiment et du jardin à la qualité de l'ameublement, des installations et des revêtements de sol. La propreté est une condition indispensable; et nos experts savent également combien compte un accueil chaleureux et souriant.

Tout comme la classification générale, la classification qualitative est effectuée par une équipe d'experts de l'Office du tourisme écossais.
Vous trouverez des logement d'excellente qualité un peu partout en Ecosse, indépendamment des équipements disponibles: par exemple un "bed and breakfast agréé", avec un équipement minimum, mais d'excellente qualité, pourrait se voir décerner la mention "chaudement recommandé" alors qu'un appartement de vacances à cinq couronnes recevra la classification "homologué" si l'on estime moyenne la qualité de ses nombreux équipements.

Alors, comment ce nouveau système vous aide-t-il à préparer vos vacances?
C'est tout simple: il vous offre la garantie du confort fourni et de la qualité de l'accueil. Nous avons inspecté un grand nombre des établissements figurant dans cette brochure et cela est indiqué la liste à la rubrique correspondante. En choisissant un logement qui a fait l'objet d'une classification, ou même des deux classifications, vous avez la garantie qu'il a été examiné par des experts indépendants.
Ce système peut également vous aider si vous faites le tour d'une région et si vous réservez une chambre différente tous les jours. Tous les logements qui ont été examinés sont munis, près de l'entrée, d'un signe ovale bleu qui indique la mention obtenue dans la classification générale et qualitative. Et si vous vous adressez à un bureau de tourisme ("Tourist Information Centre"), vous y obtiendrez une liste des établissements de la région qui sont classés selon ce système. Cette liste contiendra d'ailleurs les établissements qui n'avaient pas encore été examinés au moment où la présente brochure était mise sous presse.
Quel que soit le genre de logement que vous cherchez, ce nouveau système de classification vous aidera à le trouver.
Veuillez noter que lorsque des logements de vacances comprennent plusieurs unités dont la classification générale et qualitative n'est pas uniforme, ils seront accompagnés ci-dessous de l'indication "jusqu'a" (en anglais "up to") et de la mention la plus élevée qu'ils aient obtenue. Il vous faudra vérifier au moment d'effectuer votre réservation la classification exacte de l'unité que vous allez réserver.
Le système de classification générale et qualitative pour les terrains de caravaning est différent. Vous trouverez des données plus précises à ce sujet à la page 324.

ÜBERNACHTEN SIE DORT, WO SIE DAS ZEICHEN FÜR ECHT SCHOTTISCHE GASTLICHKEIT SEHEN

Wir haben dafür gesorgt, daß Sie in Schottland in Hunderten von Hotels, Gästehäusern und Pensionen willkommen geheißen werden.

Jetzt brauchen Sie sich nicht mehr den Kopf darüber zu zerbrechen, welches Hotel, Gästehaus, welche Frühstückspension ("B & B = bed and breakfast) oder welche Unterkunft für Selbstversorger für Sie am geeignetsten ist.

Wir haben ein neues, leicht zu verstehendes Klassifizierungsund Bewertungssystem eingeführt; so können Sie nun auf einen Blick *genau* das finden, was Sie suchen.

Was bedeutet *Klassifizierung*?

Die Klassifizierungen, die von "Listed" (— keine Krone) bis zu fünf Kronen reichen, werden nach dem Angebot der zur Verfügung stehenden Einrichtungen vergeben. In Hotels, Gästehäusern und Frühstückspensionen garantiert Ihnen die Klassifizierung "Listed", daß z.B. Ihr Bett einer Mindestgröße entspricht, daß es zu angemessenen Zeiten warmes und kaltes Wasser gibt, daß ein Frühstück serviert wird, und daß je nach Jahreszeit geheizt wird.

Bei einer Unterkunft für Selbstversorger bedeutet eine Krone, daß die Wohneinheit einer Mindestgröße entspricht und mit mindestens einem Schlafzimmer mit zwei Einzelbetten oder einem Doppelbett und mit einer der Anzahl der Bewohner entsprechenden Eß- und Kochgelegenheit sowie mit einem Kühlschrank ausgestattet ist.

Mehr Kronen bedeutet natürlich mehr Komfort. Ein Haus mit fünf Kronen bietet Ihnen viele zusätzliche Einrichtungen für einen komfortablen Urlaub. Um nur zwei zu nennen: In einem Hotel mit fünf Kronen haben *alle* Zimmer ein angeschlossenes Badezimmer; Wohneinheiten für Selbstversorger mit fünf Kronen sind mit arbeitserleichternden Haushaltseinrichtungen, einschließlich einer Geschirrspülmaschine, ausgestattet.

Alle Klassifizierungen sind von einem vollausgebildeten Team unabhängiger Experten überprüft worden.

ÜBERNACHTEN SIE DORT, WO SIE DAS ZEICHEN FÜR ECHT SCHOTTISCHE GASTLICHKEIT SEHEN

Wie sieht es mit der *Bewertung* aus?
Die Klassifizierung bezieht sich also auf die Einrichtungen, während sich die *Bewertung* ausschließlich mit der *Qualität* dieser Einrichtungen befaßt. Die drei Bewertungen: "Approved" (befriedigend), "Commended" (empfehlenswert) und "Highly Commended" (sehr empfehlenswert) basieren auf eine unabhängige Beurteilung einer Vielzahl von Kriterien, die alles umfassen: vom Aussehen der Gebäude und der Gepflegtheit der Gärten bis hin zur Qualität der Einrichtung, der Installationen und der Fußbodenbeläge. Sauberkeit wird immer vorausgesetzt, und unsere Experten wissen natürlich auch, wie wichtig ein freundliches Lächeln ist.

Die Bewertung wird, wie die Klassifizierung, von dem Expertenteam der schottischen Fremdenverkehrsbehörde durchgeführt.
Sie können bei jeder Art von Unterkunft in Schottland ausgezeichnete Qualität finden, unabhängig davon, welche Einrichtungen angeboten werden: so würde z.B. eine Frühstückspension ohne Krone ("Listed") mit einem Minimum an Einrichtungen, die aber von ausgezeichneter Qualität wären, die Bewertung "Highly Commended" (sehr empfehlenswert) erhalten., während eine Wohneinheit mit fünf Kronen mit "Approved" (befriedigend) bewertet würde, wenn die Qualität ihrer zahlreichen Einrichtungen als durchschnittlich eingeschätzt würde.

Wie hilft Ihnen also dieses neue System bei der Planung Ihres Urlaubs?
Ganz einfach, es garantiert Ihnen sowohl die Einrichtungen als auch deren Qualität. Die von Experten geprüften Häuser wurden in dieser Broschüre gekennzeichnet. Wenn Sie also eine Unterkunft auswählen, die klassifiziert oder klassifiziert *und* bewertet wurde, dann können Sie sicher sein, daß das entsprechende Angebot unabhängig überprüft wurde.
Wenn Sie umherreisen und erst an Ort und Stelle eine Unterkunft buchen, kann Ihnen das neue System ebenfalls helfen. Am Eingang aller bereits geprüften Häuser finden Sie ein unverkennbares blaues, ovales Zeichen, das die Klassifizierung und Bewertung angibt. Und wenn Sie zu einem Fremdenverkehrsbüro gehen, können Sie nach einer Liste der dortigen diesem System angeschlossenen Hotels, Gästehäuser etc. fragen. Auf dieser Liste sind dann auch die Hotels etc. aufgeführt, die zu dem Zeitpunkt, als diese Broschüre in Druck ging, noch nicht geprüft worden waren.
Ganz gleich welche Art von Unterkunft Sie suchen, Sie können sicher sein, daß das neue Klassifizierungs- und Bewertungssystem Ihnen helfen wird, die geeignete Unterkunft zu finden.
Bitte beachten Sie, daß in dieser Broschüre bei der Unterkunft für Selbstversorger immer die höchste Bewertung mit "Up To" (bis zu) angegeben wird, wenn Wohneinheiten mit verschiedenen Klassifizierungen und Bewertungen angeboten werden. Bevor Sie buchen, sollten Sie noch nachfragen, welche Klassifizierung und Bewertung eine bestimmte Wohneinheit erhalten hat.
Für Campingplätze für Wohnwagen gibt es ein gesondertes Klassifizierungs- und Bewertungssystem. Einzelheiten dazu finden Sie auf Seite 326.

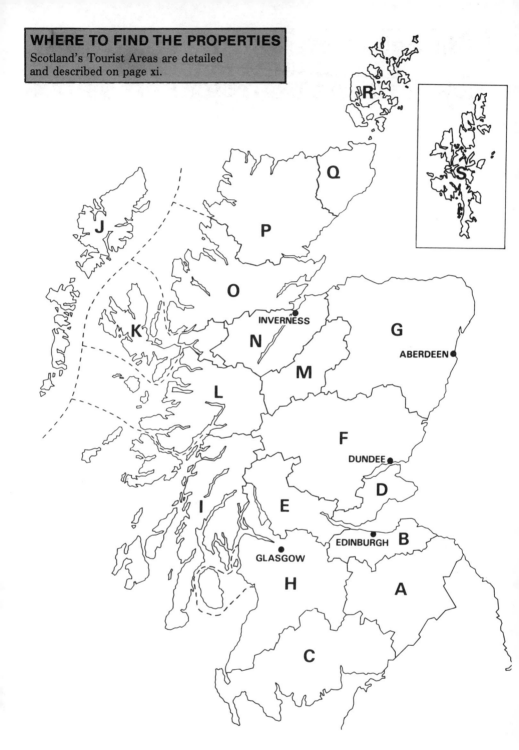

WHERE TO FIND THE PROPERTIES
Scotland's Tourist Areas are detailed
and described on page xi.

R

S

Q

J

P

O

INVERNESS

G

K

N

ABERDEEN

M

L

F

DUNDEE

D

I

E

EDINBURGH

B

GLASGOW

A

H

C

AGENCIES AND GROUP PROPERTY OWNERS

Listed below are the names and addresses of agencies/group property owners which have a selection of properties to let at a number of different locations. For further details of the properties and prices all you need do is telephone or write to the agency concerned indicating the time of year when the accommodation is required and also any preferred locations. Prices are based on weekly terms per unit. Low and high season periods may vary from agency to agency but usually the months of June to September make up the high season.

The Alphabetical Code after each entry refers to the Map on page 334. This covers the areas of Scotland in which properties are located.

SELF CATERING AGENTS' CODE OF CONDUCT

In addition to fulfilling their statutory obligations, the Agents or Group Property owners listed in this section have undertaken to observe the following Code of Conduct.

1. To deal promptly and courteously with all enquiries, reservations and correspondence from clients.
2. To describe fairly to all clients and prospective clients the amenities and facilities at each letting property whether by advertisement, brochure, word of mouth or any other means and where practicable to allow clients to view the accommodation if requested before booking.
3. To inspect every property prior to acceptance and to ensure that the facilities provided there are consistent with the details provided to visitors.
4. Where any property does not conform to Tourist Board Standards to inform the client to this effect, and of the particulars thereof.
5. To make clear to clients exactly what is included in all prices quoted and what additional charges will be incurred (e.g. meter for electricity/gas), and to return promptly any refundable deposit or balance thereof.
6. To give each client details of payments due and a receipt.

7. To ensure that satisfactory arrangements are made for cleaning between each let and that maintenance arrangements, including provisions for dealing with emergencies have been made for each property; also to ensure that the inventory is checked and items replaced as necessary between lets.
8. To be responsible for taking up any complaint with the proprietor on behalf of the complainant, and where the complaint is found justified to be responsible for making or securing reasonable restitution.

LATE BOOKING SERVICES

Many of these agencies operate late booking services for their properties, so that you can make a firm booking for your holiday at short notice.

Amaro Cottage Holidays
22 High Street
Alton
Hants GU34 1BN
Tel: Alton (0420) 88867
Tlx: 858963
3 flats, 10 cottages, 8 chalets.
Price range £68-£230 low season, £120-£380 high season.
Open Jan-Dec. Min let 3 nights.
See Map: C, E, F, N, L, O

Bell-Ingram
Durn, Isla Road
Perth PH2 7HF
Tel: Perth (0738) 21121
Tlx: 76538
15 houses, 16 cottages.
Price range £45-£375 low season, £60-£400 high season.
Open Apr-Oct, Jan-Dec (some properties).
Min let 1 week.
See Map: E, F, G, I, L, O, P.

Blakes Holidays Ltd.
Wroxham
Norwich
Norfolk NR12 8DH
Tel: Wroxham (06053) 2917
Tlx: 97114
200 properties of various types.
Price range £71-£449 low season, £126-£788 high season.
Open Jan-Dec (some properties).
Min let 3 nights.
Commission paid to travel agents by negotiation.
See Map: All areas.

AGENCIES AND GROUP PROPERTY OWNERS

Cabin Holidays Ltd
Bull Plain
Hertford
Herts SG14 1DY
Tel: Hertford (0992) 59933
Tlx: 817460
170 chalets, 3 flats.
Price range £80-£140 low season, £220-£290 high season.
Open Jan-Dec. Min let weekend.
See Map: A, C, D, E, F, G, I, K, L.

Country Cottages in Scotland
Dept 5685
Claypit Lane
Fakenham
Norfolk NR21 8AS
Tel: Fakenham (0382) 4011 (brochures, quote ref 5685);
51155 (bookings)
Tlx: ENGCOT 817252
120 cottages, farmhouses, wooden lodges and self-contained
parts of country houses.
Price range £75-£213 low season, £129-£486 high season.
Open Mar-Nov, Jan-Dec (some properties).
Min let 3 nights (Nov-Mar).
Commission paid to travel agents by arrangement.
See Map: A, C, D, E, F, I, L, M, N, O, Q.

Dundas Property Agency
61/63 Broughton Street
Edinburgh EH1 3RJ
Tel: 031-556 8363
30 flats.
Price range £100-£400 low season, £120-£440 high season.
Open Jun-Sept. Min let 1 week.
See Map: B.

Finlayson Hughes
Bank House
82 Atholl Road
Pitlochry
Perthshire PH16 5BL
Tel: Pitlochry (0769) 2512
30 houses, 2 flats, 23 cottages, 5 bungalows.
Price range from £70 low season, from £300 high season.
Open Jan-Dec, Apr-Oct (some properties).
Min let 1 week.
See Map: F, M, N, O, P, Q.

Highland Hideaways (Alexander Dawson)
5/7 Stafford Street
Oban
Argyll PA34 5NJ
Tel: Oban (0631) 62056/6390.
10 houses, 10 flats, 10 cottages, 10 bungalows.
Price range £50-£150 low season, £110-£350 high season.
Open Apr-Oct. Min let weekend (low season).
See Map: I.

Hosedsons Holidays
H45 Sunway House
Lowestoft
Suffolk NR32 3LT
Tel: Lowestoft (0502) 62292
Tlx: 975189
400 lodges/chalets, 200 caravans.
Price range from around £50 low season, from around £100
high season.
Open Jan-Dec (some properties), short breaks available low
season.
Commission paid to travel agents.
See Map: A, B, C, D, E, F, H, I, L, M, N, O, P.

Mackay's Agency
30 Frederick Street
Edinburgh EH2 2JR
Tel: 031-225 3539
Tlx: 72498 MACKAY
Over 2,000 properties of various types.
Price range £40-£100 low season, £80-£250 high season.
Open Mar-Oct, Jan-Dec (some properties).
Min let 2-3 nights low season.
Commission paid to travel agents.
See Map: All areas.

Scottish Country Cottages
Suite 2d, Churchill way
Bishopbriggs
Glasgow G64 2RH
Tel: 041-772 5920
Tlx: INSCOTG 777205
5 houses, 15 cottages.
Price range £125-£165 low season, £160-£220 high season.
Open Jan-Dec. Min let 1 week.
Commission paid to travel agents.
See Map: A, C, E, F, G, H, O.

Scottish Highland Holiday Homes
Wester Altowie
Abriachan, Inverness
Inverness-shire IV3 6LB
Tel: Dochganoch (046386) 247
80 various types of properties, e.g. lodges, mansions,
cottages.
Price range £65-£120 low season, £200-£450 high season.
Open May-Sept. Min let 1 week.
See Map: K, L, M, N, O, P, Q, R.

Summer Cottages
1 West Walks
Dorchester
Dorset DT1 1RE
Tel: Dorchester (0305) 66877/67545
Tlx: 418288 SUMCOT
45 properties of various types.
Price range £63-£260 low season, £119-£343 high season.
Open Jan-Dec. Min let 1 week (summer), 1 day (winter).
See Map: Most areas.

G. M. Thomson & Co
27 King Street
Castle Douglas
Kirkcudbrightshire DG7 1AB
Tel: Castle Douglas (0556) 2701/2973
170 properties of various types.
Price range £60-£270 low season, £95-£500 high season.
Open Mar-Oct. Min let 1 week.
See Map: C.

West Highland Estates Office
33 High Street
Fort William
Inverness-shire PH33 6DJ
Tel: Fort William (0397) 2433
12 cottages, 1 lodge.
Price range from £69 to £287.50 low season, £80.50 to £345
high season.
Open Apr-Oct. Min let 1 week.
See Map: L.

FURTHER INFORMATION FOR DISABLED VISITORS

We are pleased to announce that from 1987, establishments in the accommodation guides displaying one of the three wheelchair access symbols, are now inspected under the Scottish Tourist Board's Classification and Grading Scheme. The three symbols indicate:

&. Access for wheelchair users without assistance

Adequate parking or letting down area for visitor in wheelchair.

Clear, safe approach and entrance in wheelchair.

Access to reception and social area in wheelchair.

Public toilets fully suitable for all disabled use.

At least one bedroom on ground floor, or accessible by lift, with appropriate dimensions and facilities with suitable private bathroom for unattended visitor in wheelchair.

&. A Access for wheelchair users with assistance

Parking, letting down and approach and entrance possible for the visitor in wheelchair with attendant help.

Access by permanent or portable ramps, or by lift, to reception and social areas.

Public toilets suitable for wheelchair use with attendant help.

At least one bedroom with appropriate dimensions and bathroom facilities, accessible by wheelchair user, or other disabled person, with attendant help.

&. P Access for ambulant disabled (other than wheelchair users)

Parking, letting down, approach and entrance with safe steps or ramps, not too steep and preferably with hand rails.

Access to reception and social areas all accessible on same level, by lift or safe steps.

Public toilets suitable for walking, disabled visitor.

At least one bedroom suitable for visitor with walking disability with bathroom and toilet facility nearby.

Please use your discretion and telephone the establishments in advance if you require further information.

Self Catering
in Luxury Cabins

Ten of Scotland's very best self-catering cabin developments all
bookable through us. You can stay at two or three without extra
charges.

Special prices for motorail, insurance, etc.

For our free colour brochure detailing the best in Scottish Cabins please
write or telephone

Cabin Holidays
Dept. H.B., Bull Plain, Hertford, Herts SG14 1DY
Tel: (0992) 553535

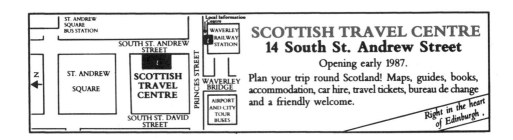

Hoseasons – Britains best choice in Holiday-Homes.

For the finest and widest selection of self-catering Holiday-Homes throughout Scotland you'll find Hoseasons just can't be beaten.

Prices start from as little as £15 per person per week.

Countless activities. Just the peace and quiet of beautiful scenery. Or plenty to do for both young and old alike. Heated swimming pools. Night clubs and a host of sports and relaxation activities.

Clip the coupon or use our fast Dial-a-Brochure service, for your free brochure today.

ASSOCIATION OF SCOTLAND'S SELF-CATERERS

The Association of Scotland's Self-Caters seeks to promote the best in self-catering accommodation. All members' properties have been inspected to ensure high standards at all times. So before booking your holiday, look for this logo beside the entry — it is your guide to satisfaction.

HOLIDAY SCOTLAND 1987

The most exciting collection of easy-to book top value holidays in Scotland!

Get a free brochure now from your travel agent.

CRAIGENDARROCH LUXURY SELF-CATERING LODGES
ON ROYAL DEESIDE

OUTSTANDING NATURAL BEAUTY

The ultimate year-round holiday resort. Breathtaking scenery: a surprisingly mild climate, and the opportunity to experience all country pursuits; not to mention hang-gliding and skiing.

Just down river from that ultimate holiday retreat, Balmoral, is Craigendarroch the finest holiday development in Europe and crowning glory of Royal Deeside.

THE ULTIMATE IN LUXURY

Self-catering luxury lodges, to sleep from 4 to 8 people, have every conceivable modern convenience, including the latest and most sophisticated Hi-Fi, TV and video systems – and in many cases, saunas and whirlpools.

Most balconies have commanding views of the River Dee and the mountain of Lochnagar, which moved Prince Charles to write the fable 'The Old Man of Lochnagar.'

THE GREAT INDOORS

Self-catering holiday-makers, during their stay, have full use of the Craigendarroch Country Club with its swimming pool, whirlpool, squash courts, snooker and hair and beauty area, plus bar and restaurant.

Or you can dine in fine old baronial style in the magnificent Oaks restaurant in the Craigendarroch Hotel. (Both the Hotel and Country Club are on site.)

Telephone Chris Gordon on Ballater **(0338) 55558** for more details.

347

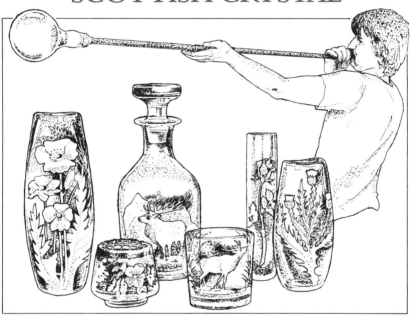

FREE·FACTORY·TOUR·

An Invitation
to see the art of Glassmaking
SCOTTISH CRYSTAL

Factory open seven days a week. Self-conducted tours showing the manufacture of crystal. Video on glassmaking and decoration.
Factory seconds shop open 9am–5pm Monday–Saturday, 11am–5pm Sundays, (extended hours during June – September)
Picnic Area. Children's Playground.
Muthill Road, Crieff, Perthshire,

Telephone Crieff (0764) 4004
for further information.

STUART STRATHEARN

349

CLASSIFICATION AND GRADING OF ACCOMMODATION IN SCOTLAND

NEW FOR 1987

As you travel around Scotland this year, you will see signs that look like this. These denote the classification and grade of a particular establishment which has been checked out by our trained team of inspectors (see pages vi and vii for details). We hope this new scheme will be of benefit to you when booking accommodation and would welcome your views on it.

Q. Do you have any comments on the classification or grade of any establishment you stayed at?

A.

Thank you for your help.

Please return to:

Department of Verification and Grading
Scottish Tourist Board
23 Ravelston Terrace
Edinburgh EH4 3EU

BOOKS TO HELP YOU

SCOTLAND: WHERE TO STAY HOTELS AND GUEST HOUSES 1987 — £4.40 inc p&p

2,000 places to stay in Scotland, ranging from luxury hotels to budget priced guest houses. Details of prices and facilities available. Location maps included. Completely revised each year. Now entries classified and graded. All full colour.

SCOTLAND: WHERE TO STAY BED AND BREAKFAST 1987 — £2.80 inc p&p

Over 2,000 bed and breakfast establishments throughout Scotland offering inexpensive accommodation. The perfect way to enjoy a budget trip—and to meet the Scottish people in their own homes. Location maps included. Completely revised each year. Now entries classified and graded.

SCOTLAND: SELF CATERING ACCOMMODATION 1987 — £4.50 inc p&p

Over 2,000 cottages, apartments, caravans and chalets—many in scenic areas—which can be rented. Details of prices and facilities available. Location maps included. Completely revised each year. Now entries classified and graded.

SCOTLAND: CAMPING AND CARAVAN PARKS 1987 — £2.50 inc p&p

Nearly 400 parks detailed with prices, facilities available and other useful information. Location maps included. Completely revised each year. Entries now graded.

ENJOY SCOTLAND PACK — £5.70 inc p&p

A handy plastic wallet which contains the Scottish Tourist Board's **Touring Map of Scotland** (5 miles to inch) showing historic sites, gardens, museums, walks, beaches, etc together with **Scotland: 1001 Things to See**, which describes and locates these places with details of opening times and admission charges. Map completely revised this year.

SCOTLAND TOURING MAP — £2.70 inc p&p

As above, available separately. Completely revised this year.

SCOTLAND: 1001 THINGS TO SEE — £3.10 inc p&p

As above, available separately.

SCOTLAND: WALKS AND TRAILS — £1.90 inc p&p

A selection of walks over a wide variety of terrain, most of which do not require specialist equipment and are suitable for children.

SCOTLAND: HILLWALKING — £2.10 inc p&p

Detailed descriptions of over 60 more difficult walks and scrambles on hills in different parts of Scotland. Written by an expert.

POSTERS

A series of colourful posters is available, illustrating a wide range of Scotland's attractions for visitors. All posters are available on high quality paper, and the entire range is available with a plastic coating. This makes the posters much harder wearing—no more tears of folds—and gives them an attractive glossy sheen. They represent excellent value for money as a souvenir of Scotland.

Paper posters cost £2.50 inc p&p
Plastic coated cost £3.60 inc p&p

PLEASE ALLOW 21 DAYS FOR DELIVERY

ALL PRICES INCLUDE POSTAGE & PACKAGE
ORDER FORM OVER PAGE

351

PUBLICATIONS ORDER FORM

Please mark the publications you would like, cut out the complete page and send it with your cheque, postal order (made payable to the Scottish Tourist Board) or credit card details to: **The Scottish Tourist Board, PO Box 15, Edinburgh EH1 1UY.**
For free information/general enquiries only phone: 031-332 2433.

Scotland: Where to Stay Hotels and Guest Houses	£4.40	☐
Scotland: Where to Stay Bed and Breakfast	£2.80	☐
Scotland: Self-Catering Accommodation	£4.50	☐
Scotland: Camping and Caravan Parks	£2.50	☐
Enjoy Scotland Pack	£5.70	☐
Scotland: Touring Map	£2.70	☐
Scotland: 1001 Things to See	£3.10	☐
Scotland: Walks and Trails	£1.90	☐
Scotland: Hillwalking	£2.10	☐

	Plastic Coated £3.60	Paper £2.50
Posters		
Piper (24" × 34")	☐	☐
Edinburgh Castle (24" × 34")	☐	☐
Land o' Burns (27" × 40")	☐	☐
Isle of Skye (27" × 40")	☐	☐
Souvenir Wall Map of Scotland (24" × 37")	☐	☐
Highland Cattle (24" × 34")	☐	☐
Curling (24" × 34")	☐	☐
Scottish Post Boxes (24" × 34")	☐	☐
Five Sisters of Kintail (27" × 40")	☐	☐
Loch Eilt (24" × 34")	☐	☐

BLOCK CAPITALS PLEASE:

NAME (Mr/Mrs/Miss/Ms) _____

ADDRESS _____

_____

POST CODE _____ TELEPHONE NO. _____

SIGNATURE _____ DATE _____

TOTAL REMITTANCE ENCLOSED £ _____

PLEASE CHARGE MY *VISA/ACCESS ACCOUNT (*delete as appropriate)

| Card No. | | | | | | | | | | | | | | | Expiry Date | | | | |

To order BY PHONE ring 0 800 833 993 quoting the items you require and your credit card details.

Please tick for FREE BROCHURES:

Spring ☐   Summer ☐   Autumn ☐   Winter ☐   Ski Holidays ☐

Printed in Scotland by Scotprint Ltd., Musselburgh